# The Peoples of the
# British Isles

# Related books of interest

**The Peoples of the British Isles:**
**A New History From Prehistoric Times to 1688, Fourth Edition**
Stanford E. Lehmberg and Samantha A. Meigs

**The Peoples of the British Isles:**
**A New History From 1688 to the Present, Fourth Edition**
Thomas William Heyck and Meredith Veldman

**The Peoples of the British Isles:**
**A New History From 1870 to the Present, Fourth Edition**
Thomas William Heyck and Meredith Veldman

**The New Nature of History: Knowledge, Evidence, Language**
Arthur Marwick

# The Peoples of the
# British Isles

*A New History* **Fourth Edition**

*From 1688 to 1914*

**Thomas William Heyck**
*Northwestern University*

**Meredith Veldman**
*Louisiana State University*

LYCEUM
BOOKS, INC.
Chicago, Illinois

© Lyceum Books, Inc., 2014

Published by

LYCEUM BOOKS, INC.
5758 S. Blackstone Ave.
Chicago, Illinois 60637
773+643-1903 (Fax)
773+643-1902 (Phone)
lyceum@lyceumbooks.com
http://www.lyceumbooks.com

18 17 16     2 3 4 5

ISBN: 978-1-935871-57-6

Library of Congress Cataloging-in-Publication Data

Meigs, Samantha A., 1958–
   The peoples of the British Isles : a new history / Samantha Meigs, Stanford E. Lehmberg. — Fourth edition.
      volumes cm
   Stanford E. Lehmberg's name appears first on the third edition.
   Authors of volumes 2-3 are Thomas William Heyck and Meredith Veldman.
   Includes bibliographical references and index.
   Contents: v. 1. From prehistoric times to 1688 — v. 2. From 1688 to 1914 — v. 3. From 1870 to the present.
   ISBN 978-1-935871-56-9 (v. 1 : alk. paper) — ISBN 978-1-935871-57-6 (v. 2 : alk. paper) — ISBN 978-1-935871-58-3 (v. 3 : alk. paper) — ISBN 978-1-935871-59-0 (v. 2 and v. 3 : alk. paper)
   1. Great Britain—History. 2. Ethnology—Great Britain. 3. Ireland—History. 4. Ethnology—Ireland. I. Lehmberg, Stanford E. II. Heyck, Thomas William, 1938– III. Veldman, Meredith. IV. Title.
   DA30.L44  2014
   941—dc23
                                                                                 2014017285

*For Hunter and Shannon, literally*
*For Bill*

# Contents

# List of Illustrations

# List of Maps

# Preface

The purpose of this book is to tell the story (or rather, stories) of the peoples of the British Isles in the first two centuries of the modern period. It is a great story, full of drama and relevance to the peoples of the former Empire and the United States. The book is meant to be different from the conventional English history textbooks in two ways. First, it covers *British and Irish*—not just English—history. Second, it takes as its central focus the lives of all the peoples of the British Isles, not just those of the political elite. Because England has long been the largest and most powerful country in the British Isles, English history will receive the most coverage. Indeed, one of the main themes of British history in the modern period—that is, since the end of the seventeenth century—has been the expansion of English power and influence within the British Isles. But Wales, Scotland, and Ireland have in the last fifty years or so become the subjects of vital, growing, and fascinating historiographies that demand the attention of students of British history. The histories of the peoples of what came to be called the Celtic fringe often had much in common with the history of the English, but at times they diverged sharply. To study comparatively the development of the different societies in the British Isles often throws new light on seemingly well-known events. Moreover, the Welsh, Scots, and Irish were often problems for the English, but the English were problems for them as well. To treat the Celtic peoples as mere intrusions into the English story yields not only a deformed historical account of Wales, Scotland, and Ireland, but also an incomplete history of the British Isles as a whole.

Cultural, economic, and social history form the backbone of this account. The book thus follows the most exciting trends in recent historiography. When dealing with national politics, the book offers two things: (1) an account of the origin and development of the British state; and (2) an analysis of the structure, functions, and impact of the political system as it evolved rather than as a detailed narrative. It places international, parliamentary, and party politics in the context of the whole way of life of the peoples of the British Isles. The focus, then, throughout is on the lives of real people—how they made a living, how they organized their society and institutions, how they related to each other individually and in groups, and how they understood themselves and their world. What was it like to be a farm laborer in the English Midlands in the 1730s or a Highland clansman in the 1760s? How did a handloom weaver experience the advent of steam-powered textile mills? How did middle-class men and women understand class and gender? What were the consequences of famine in Irish society? This book will attend to these kinds of questions.

Each of the historical eras spanned by the years 1688 to 1914 has its own character, its own special mix of economic arrangements, social structure, political style, and cultural expressions. The four parts of the book are meant to mark out for analysis these historical eras—the age of the landed oligarchy, the age of revolutions, the rise of Victorian society, and the decline of Victorian Britain. The flow of historical events is continuous, and certain themes tie the historical eras together. One is the expansion of English influence within the British Isles and the formation under English leadership of the multinational British state. Related to that is the development of separate national identities in the Celtic countries. A second theme is the rise of Great Britain to great power status and the concomitant expansion of the British Empire. This expansion was to a large degree propelled by the remarkable economic growth of the late eighteenth and nineteenth centuries. Britain's emergence as the first industrial nation in the world thus constitutes our third theme. Fourth, we focus on changing social structure and social relations—the origins and development of class society from the social hierarchy of preindustrial Britain. Finally, the theme of the evolving structure of the state and the political system involves the expansion of the role of the state in the British economy and society, even in an era of strong ideological mistrust of political intervention and regulation.

If this book succeeds, it will be by helping students understand the peoples of the British Isles in the early twenty-first century—why they are the way they are. It should also help American students understand themselves and their own society a little better, for the British are enough like the Americans to make comparisons numerous and enough different to make contrasts revealing.

## A NOTE ON TERMINOLOGY

Because Britain is a multinational state that does not now include all of the peoples of the British Isles, one should be very careful about using labels such as "English" and "British." But this is an area in which it is difficult to be perfectly consistent and to avoid irritating nationalist sensibilities. Geographically speaking, "Britain" correctly denotes the whole island composed of England, Wales, and Scotland, but not Ireland. However, Britain has also been used by people around the world to refer to the United Kingdom, which came to existence only in 1707 and which included Ireland from 1801 to 1921, but which today includes only Northern Ireland as well as England, Wales, and Scotland. For much of the nineteenth century, Britain meant not only the United Kingdom, but also the British Empire. At the same time, many people both within the British Isles and around the world said "England" when they meant "Britain," and by force of habit many people still do. Today, Britain technically means the United Kingdom of Great Britain and Northern Ireland, but it would make no sense to apply that usage to any historical period before 1921.

We have done our best to refer to the English, Welsh, Scots, and Irish as the circumstances require, to be careful when speaking of Britain, and to be accurate in distinguishing the political entity of England from that of Great Britain.

## ACKNOWLEDGMENTS

We would like to thank a number of people for the help they have provided in the writing of this book. First and foremost are all the scholars of modern British and Irish history on whose work this volume depends. They are too numerous to name here, and even the "Suggested Reading" after each chapter gives only a partial indication of our debts to them, but we hope that all will understand how much we appreciate their contributions even where we have given our own twist.

We both wish to acknowledge our undergraduate students—at Northwestern University and at LSU—who played a larger role in this book than they will ever know. We thank the scholars who have read and commented on all or parts of the book: Stewart J. Brown, James Cronin, Stanford Lehmberg, and Standish Meacham. Thanks also go to the reviewers—Nancy Fix Anderson, Loyola University, New Orleans; George L. Bernstein, Tulane University, New Orleans; Jodi Campbell, Texas Christian University, Fort Worth; Anna Clark, University of North Carolina, Charlotte; Guy Ortolano, New York University; Kimberly K. Estep, Auburn University; Kevin James, University of Guelph, Guelph, Ontario; Walter R. Johnson, Northwestern Oklahoma State University, Alva; Neil Rabitoy, California State University, Los Angeles; Karl Von den Steinen, California State University, Sacramento; and Amy Whipple, Xavier University, Cincinnati—for their helpful comments.

David Follmer has been supportive at several stages of the work. Bill would like particularly to thank Larry McCaffrey of Loyola University, Emmet Larkin of the University of Chicago, and his colleagues and friends at Northwestern: Lacey Baldwin Smith, Tim Breen, and Harold Perkin, as well as his energetic and resourceful research assistants: Kevin Mahler, Jill Marquis, Helen Harnett, and Suzette Lemrow. Meredith thanks Brian Levack and Victor Stater, who advised her on 1688; Joe Skillen and Natasha Bingham, who helped her figure out Ireland; and most of all Bill Heyck, who shaped her understanding of not only British history but so much else. Greatest thanks of all go to our spouses, Denis Heyck and Randy Nichols, who willingly helped in countless ways.

# Part I

# The Age of the Landed Oligarchy

# 1688–1763

*Historic counties of Great Britain and Ireland.* The counties served as both administrative structures and sources of regional identity. This map remained unchanged
until 1972.

# Chapter 1

# The Lands and Peoples of the British Isles at the End of the Seventeenth Century

In the more than three centuries since 1688, life has changed almost totally for the peoples of the British Isles. Most people at the end of the seventeenth century were engaged in agriculture; at the beginning of the twenty-first, most are involved in industry or allied services. In the seventeenth century, most people lived in rural villages; in the twenty-first, most live in dense metropolitan areas. In the late seventeenth century, society was characterized by face-to-face relationships; today, social relations tend to be more impersonal and bureaucratic. Most women before 1700 lived in subordination to men; relations between men and women are now more equal. Life expectancy in the seventeenth century was perhaps thirty-five years; today it stands at more than seventy. The number of people living in the British Isles has increased more than fivefold. The scope as well as the pace of individual experiences has increased at a dizzying rate. In those three centuries Britain solidified as a nation, grew to great power status, and now has receded to a more normal position as an average European state. In short, since 1688 the British and Irish peoples have experienced as much change as any on earth, and more than most.

One of the most striking ways in which the British Isles of the late seventeenth century differed from that of the 2000s was the degree to which geography and climate dominated people's lives and contributed to sharp regional differences—differences not only in local customs, but also in economy, politics, and culture. The British Isles are not spacious, containing approximately 121,000 square miles (slightly more than half the size of France). They include a remarkable variety of regional topographies, everything from rolling hills to craggy peaks, from watery bogs to storm-beaten rocky islands. The suddenness of changes in landscape can make Britain seem a large country to the traveler. This fact was accentuated in the late seventeenth century by poor roads and slow means of travel. In 1700, it took more than two days to travel from London to Bath, four and one-half days from London to Manchester, and eleven days from London to Edinburgh. In bad weather, many roads became impassable and travel by sea impossible. Even in good conditions, communications were slow and undependable; hence, there was little central government control.

In 1700, Great Britain as a political entity did not exist. Wales had been administratively absorbed by England in the sixteenth century, but Scotland and Ireland retained much of their ancient independent status. In 1603, an accident of inheritance made James VI of Scotland also James I of England, but this union of crowns did not unite the two countries. Scotland had its own Parliament, legal system (based on Roman law rather than common law), and established church (Presbyterian rather than Anglican). Across the Irish Sea, Ireland, too, resisted English control. True, in 1541 the Irish Parliament designated the English monarch Henry VIII king of Ireland, but it was not until the beginning of the nineteenth century that the English took the final step in eradicating Irish autonomy—only to find that autonomy successfully reasserted 120 years later.

In the late seventeenth century, then, there was no British state, nor was there a single national or religious community. Many people, isolated and illiterate, probably identified with nothing larger than a county, a region, a village, or a clan; insofar as they felt any national allegiance, it was as an Englishman, a Welshman, a Scot, or an Irishman. The English amounted to slightly more than one-half of the 9 to 9.5 million people in the British Isles toward the end of the seventeenth century, and their culture as well as power tended to spread outward into Wales, Scotland, and Ireland. Generally speaking, the closer any part of the British Isles was to England, more specifically London, the more strongly it felt English influence.

But the peoples of the British Isles were (and are) a mixture of a variety of ethnic groups, and various regional and local cultures were still much in evidence. Cornish was still spoken in the southwestern corner of England, and Welsh was spoken in Herefordshire. In Wales, Scotland, and Ireland, the Celtic heritage remained prominent. The vast majority of the people in Wales and Ireland spoke no English, nor did many clansmen in the Scottish Highlands. English common law was alien to these Celtic areas, though in Wales it had prevailed officially for a century. The Church of England was the official or *established* church, not only in England, but also in Wales and

Ireland. Yet in Wales, the religious loyalties of many Welsh men and women rested with non-Anglican Protestantism, whereas in Ireland the overwhelming majority of the people were Roman Catholics. In Scotland, the church preferred by a majority of people was Presbyterian, and this *kirk* was much more strongly influenced by Calvinism than by the Church of England. In sum, by neither political tradition, language, cultural heritage, nor religious affiliation was there yet a British nation.

## ENGLAND

England is the largest and most geographically blessed of the countries in the British Isles. It encompasses 50,851 square miles, with nearly 2,000 miles of coastline. No point is more than 75 miles from the sea, and rivers and river mouths deeply etch most of England. Naturally, the proximity of the sea has had a great impact on English history and culture. For a long time, the seas provided relatively easy avenues of invasion for peoples from the Continent, and this remained a threat through the eighteenth century. But the sea also made the English enthusiastic sailors, turning their attention to fishing, to overseas trade, and eventually to oceanic empire. Out of their seafaring tradition the English developed the resources in ships and skilled men by which they converted their position as an offshore island of Europe into a great source of security. But in the late seventeenth century, the threat from the sea still seemed as great as the safety it offered.

Rolling hills and valleys characterize most of English topography. The land is highest in the North and West and gradually drops away to green undulating plains in the Midlands, South, and East. The Pennine chain of low mountains, running southward from Northumberland and Yorkshire to the Midland plain, dominate the North of England. Too rough for tillage, this hill country supported mostly hill pasturage and eventually iron and coal mining. The Midland plain is extremely fertile rolling land, long the heart of rural England. To the south and east of the Midland plain, from the English Channel on the south to the eastern part of Yorkshire, extends a wide belt of rich agricultural land, very productive of grain, vegetables, and cattle. In the Southwest lies a high plateau covering much of Devon and Cornwall. This corner of England has a dramatic, picturesque coast with excellent natural harbors; inland it includes desolate, boggy moors—Exmoor, Bodmin Moor, and Dartmoor—on which even today a traveler can scarcely imagine that he or she is still on a densely populated island.

*Topography of the British Isles.* The 121,000 square miles of the British Isles vary greatly in topography, which helped shape not only distinctive national cultures—English, Welsh, Scottish, and Irish—but also unique regional cultures.

Like the topography, England's weather does not run to extremes. The English climate is moderate and well suited for farming. The prevailing wind is from the southwest, which means that the warm waters of the Gulf Stream tend to pull average temperatures upward. Consequently, although England lies as far north as Labrador, its coldest month has a mean temperature of 40°F (and its warmest 62°F). Rainfall is plentiful everywhere in England, though heaviest in the western hills, where it averages thirty-five inches per year. Because of the moderate climate and the fertile soils, agriculture spread through most of England. The once dense forests, characterized by oak, ash, and elm, had largely been cut by the last half of the seventeenth century, especially in the South and East. As early as Queen Elizabeth's reign, the English were concerned about a shortage of timber for fuel and shipbuilding—perhaps the earliest indication that the English population would put great pressure on natural resources.

The English population stood at about five million at the end of the seventeenth century. The Midlands and Southeast were relatively densely populated compared to the Uplands of the North and Northwest and the moors of the Southwest. Throughout England the population was distributed in *nucleated villages* (clusters of houses, surrounded by cultivated fields or pasture lands) in the valleys and river bottoms. About three-fifths of all English men and women lived in villages of three hundred to four hundred people, and given the poor roads and lack of economic impetus, few moved far. There were about eight hundred country market towns, but together they housed less than 15 percent of the population. Apart from London, only Bristol and Norwich had more than twenty thousand people.

London was the great exception to the rule of rural life in the seventeenth century. Its population was 550,000 in 1700, about 11 percent of the population of England, and it was growing rapidly, having doubled in size since 1600. The largest European city west of Constantinople, London was the center of national politics, the location of the high courts, the greatest port in England by far, the radiating nucleus of foreign trade, and the home of a growing financial interest. Into London poured thousands of unemployed from the provinces; as a result, the city teemed with street people of all sorts—vagrants, venders, cutpurses, confidence men, prostitutes, gamblers, and beggars. Although the focal point of fashion, London was also regarded as an unhealthy influence on the nation, partly because it drained away wealth and population and partly because it housed the makings of a mob that might intimidate the government.

*London in the late seventeenth century: a view from the River Thames at London Bridge. This engraving, completed in 1675, shows London as rebuilt after the Great Fire of 1666. Note the magnificent dome of the new St. Paul's Cathedral, designed by Sir Christopher Wren.*

Important as it was, London was not England. The great majority of English men and women of the late seventeenth century spent their lives in the villages and fields of the countryside. To be sure, the elite of the social order—the families of the two hundred temporal and spiritual lords, plus those of the richest of the non-noble landowners—liked to spend several months a year enjoying the London *season*. Yet even these wealthiest of families lived for most of the year in their great country houses. Maintenance of social order, which was crucial to people who had lived through the turmoil of civil war in the 1640s and 1650s, required that the elite display their superiority in person, exact deference from their inferiors, and carry out local administration and justice. Moreover, many of the local squires were too poor and socially inept to venture into London.

The aristocracy (titled nobility) and gentry (large landowners)—a total of approximately fifteen thousand families—stood at the top of the social hierarchy, which ranged downward through yeomen, tenant farmers, village tradesmen and craftsmen, farm laborers, cottagers, and paupers. Backwoods squires—coarse-mannered, rough-and-ready in dispensing justice, patriotic, independent, and suspicious of London monied interests—regarded themselves as the heart of the nation. After the restoration of the Stuart line in 1660, the gentry reigned like little kings in the countryside. There were no police and no standing army, and the gentry controlled the militia. As justices of the peace (JPs), the gentry took responsibility for law and order at the local level; as justices of the Quarter Sessions, teams of JPs ruled the counties. They were not paid for this work. As Sir William Petty said, "The honour of being trusted and the pleasure of being feared hath been thought a competent reward."

The populace over whom the aristocracy and gentry ruled was divided into a number of social orders. Some (perhaps 30 percent of the population) were small farmers, both owners and tenants, and their families; others (another 10 to 12 percent) were professionals, merchants, tradesmen, shopkeepers, and craftsmen (and craftswomen) and their families. Most of the rest—*the laboring poor*—led precarious lives of relentless work. The majority were farm laborers (men, women, and children) who worked the land for the farmers and landowners. The landowners took care to win for themselves absolute rights of private property during the seventeenth century, but they gave no such rights to tenants and laborers, who remained completely dependent on them. The only restraints recognized by the big landlords were the documented rights of small owners, the goodwill arising from immemorial custom, and the stubborn insistence by the poor on their traditional rights. The customs of *paternalism*, by which those in the top ranks of society accepted responsibility to care for those in the bottom ranks (in exchange for the lower orders' deference and obedience), constituted the best hope for the poor.

Compared to the rest of the British Isles, England in the late 1600s was a prosperous nation, but standards of living varied wildly. The wealthiest aristocrats and gentry enjoyed upward of several thousand pounds sterling (£) a year, but most laborers earned £20 a year or less. Agricultural techniques had been very slowly improving, however, and by the late seventeenth century the English people were beginning to leave behind the subsistence crises that from time immemorial had periodically afflicted the population. Nevertheless, bad weather could still cause a poor harvest, high bread prices, and widespread hunger. In addition, wages were kept low because the privileged thought that the pinch of poverty alone made the common people work. The bulk of the population lived at the margin of real hardship.

Agriculture was the main source of wealth as well as the principal occupation. The medieval system of agriculture had long been in decline in England. Under that system, lords of manors had held their land from their feudal superiors in return for military service and had farmed the land with both free and unfree labor. In early modern England, however, estate owners leased parcels of land to tenant farmers, all of whom were legally free. The tenants and their wives worked the land with the assistance of hired farm laborers, both male and female. Moreover, early modern English agriculture was commercially oriented. Most crops were produced for the market rather than for subsistence, although very little English farming was yet specialized, except in a few areas such as the environs of London, where market gardening for the ever expanding London population prospered.

England already had a bustling manufacturing sector, much of it centered on wool. England had long been known for wool production, but in the seventeenth century, the government prohibited the exportation of unfinished woolen fabric in order to encourage the various English industries involved in producing finished woolens. Between 1660 and 1700 the value of finished woolen cloth exported probably doubled. Woolens were produced everywhere, but principally in the West Country between Exeter and Bristol, in East Anglia, and in Yorkshire. Most woolen products were manufactured through the *domestic* or *putting-out* system—that is, the wool was put out by a merchant to craftsmen in their cottages and carried through the various stages of hand production: carding, spinning, weaving, fulling, and dying. Most of the laborers were farmers and their families who supplemented their agricultural income by producing the woolens. Hence, even this key industry remained highly seasonal and deeply attached to country life.

Woolens were not the only source of England's industrial strength. In fact, although wool production increased in the last decades of the century, its share of industrial exports fell. Assisted by the aggressive English foreign and colonial policy, and by the immigration into England of skilled French Huguenot craftsmen, a number of industries rose in the last part of the century, including paper, glass, cheap housewares, and textiles such as silk and linen. Brewing and soap making became major enterprises, as did tin, copper, lead, and coal mining. The organization of industry remained largely unchanged, with most production still carried out in households by nuclear families and apprentices and laborers. Even so, England was moving beyond the usual European level in manufacturing and far beyond most of the rest of the British Isles.

The commercial expansion of England was even more impressive. As Professor Charles Wilson wrote, "England was becoming a world entrepôt [trading center], serving not only Europe, but the extra-European world, and was herself served by a growing fleet of merchant shipping, a growing equipment of docks, shipyards, wharves and warehouses, a growing community of merchants and tradesmen." Again assisted by the government's aggressive trade policy, and building on the fact that England was the largest free-trade area in Europe, England's foreign trade expanded in both volume and variety. Exports went up by about 50 percent between 1660 and 1700 and imports by more than 30 percent. Most important in this remarkable expansion of trade were reexports: English merchants imported raw materials and food (such as sugar, cotton, and tobacco), as well as slaves from colonial areas, and reexported them all over the world. Every transaction brought profits to Englishmen and encouraged the development of comparatively sophisticated financial institutions. Merchants, shipowners, and shipbuilders needed to borrow, and their needs brought into existence a new set of middlemen between lenders and borrowers, principally in London. Scriveners and goldsmiths, with whom lenders could deposit their money, as well as lending merchants, thus began to act in some ways like bankers, or *protobankers*. By the 1670s, a highly unpopular but very important group of men in the city of London was carrying out the essentials of banking: taking deposits, discounting bills of credit, and issuing notes. This commercial revolution was producing a *monied interest*, a sign of the unique (except for the Netherlands) commercialization of the English economy.

The merchants and financiers of England were often *Dissenters*, non-Anglican Protestants who played an important role in the shifting the religious composition of the country. Religion was crucial to the English people in the seventeenth century; it was capable of arousing strong emotions and radical political action. Most people still believed that questions of church polity and doctrine were matters of eternal life and death. Moreover, most members of the landed elite (the aristocracy and gentry) thought that, without an established, unified religion, the nation would splinter and the social order would crumble. "Religion it is that keeps the subject in obedience," said English statesman Sir John Eliot.

The experience of the Civil War years only confirmed this truth in the minds of the landowners. The triumph of the Puritan forces under Oliver Cromwell and the execution of King Charles I in 1649 had ushered in a time of political and religious experiment. The great iceberg of English society had turned over for a decade. With the Restoration of Charles II in 1660, the iceberg had been righted and the common people resubmerged. Landowners wanted to make sure the great overturning could never happen again.

They believed that an established Church of England on the *episcopal model* (that is, with bishops ruling dioceses) was a main instrument of social as well as religious order.

The English had long adhered to the tradition that church and state are two parts of one organism. Thus, even though many varieties of Christianity grew up after the Reformation, most believed in a uniform established church, to which all the English people should belong. By the 1660s the form of that church had been in dispute for more than a century. Queen Elizabeth's settlement of the church issue had taken the form of a compromise between the Anglo-Catholicism of her father, Henry VIII, and the more extreme Protestantism advocated by Continental reformers. Thus, in Elizabeth's time, the Church of England recognized the monarch as its supreme governor; maintained not only the traditional episcopal structure, but also much of the old Roman Catholic liturgy; and adhered to a modified sacramental doctrine: the Church was regarded as the true institution established by Jesus Christ to be the necessary intermediary between God and the individual.

Such views had come under attack by the Puritans of the late sixteenth and seventeenth centuries. A force for reform within the Church of England, Puritanism emphasized individual judgment based on reading the Christian scriptures firsthand and so downplayed the role of the Church as a divinely established intermediary. Puritans not only preferred a simple liturgy and greater strictness in the conduct of life, but they also rejected the hierarchical principles embodied in the episcopal structure of the Church. Puritan beliefs shaped both English Presbyterianism and the Independent (Congregationalist) movement of the seventeenth century: Presbyterians demanded that councils (or *presbyteries*) of ministers and lay elders take the place of bishops, whereas Independents sought to place ultimate church power in the individual congregations. During the Civil War, Puritanism was, for a time, triumphant: Parliament abolished the episcopacy and installed a Presbyterian church structure. In 1660, however, the Church of England in its episcopal form was restored as firmly as the Stuart monarchy. For most of the ruling elite, Puritanism meant social upheaval, religious turmoil, and radical politics.

One thing the various brands of Protestants agreed on was their opposition—perhaps *fear* and *loathing* are more accurate words—to Roman Catholics. Although the Anglican church was not far removed from Catholicism in doctrine or church structure, it had long been strongly anti-Catholic. The Puritans were even more militantly anti-Catholic, and for many years they had demanded strict enforcement of the laws against the remaining English Catholics (known as *recusants*), of whom there were very few, mainly some landed families in the North and Northwest.

When Charles II was invited in 1660 to return to England, he promised "liberty to tender consciences," but Parliament was in no mood to encourage religious pluralism. Both Roman Catholics and Puritans faced legal penalties. The Act of Uniformity of 1662 required all clergymen to use the Anglican *Book of Common Prayer* and to subscribe to the Thirty-Nine Articles, the defining creed of Anglicanism. The Act also reestablished the authority of the bishops and removed from their *livings* (clerical positions) all clergymen who would not submit. About two thousand clergymen (of nine thousand total) were thus ejected from the Church of England; they constituted the formal foundation of English *Nonconformity* (or Dissent): non-Anglican Protestantism. At the same time, a series of parliamentary acts (collectively known as the Clarendon Code) suppressed any unauthorized religious meetings, required municipal officials to take communion in the Anglican church, and limited the civil rights of Nonconformist clergy. The Clarendon Code was not strictly enforced, but it did succeed in dividing Protestantism in England.

Puritans offered surprisingly little resistance to the reimposition of Anglicanism in the 1660s. Perhaps they had been demoralized and discredited by their association with sedition, or perhaps Puritanism's emotional power was being eroded by the growing atmosphere of rationalism and scientific revolution. In any case, Puritanism survived in many English families, both within the Church of England and without, and stood ready to catch fire again in the evangelical movement of the eighteenth century as well as to express its unbending anti-Catholicism at the slightest whiff of *popery* in England.

## WALES

Unlike England, Wales is almost entirely mountainous. Nearly all of its area (7,467 square miles, about one-sixth the size of England) is covered by a series of mountains extending roughly from north to south and dominating the whole of the interior. The mountains are highest in the north and south, the central section being a high, broken plateau. Even the narrow coastal plains to the south and west are hilly. The mountainous interior is deeply cut by a number of rivers that fan down and out from the central ridges toward the Lowland areas. The rivers that rush down steep slopes into broader valleys are especially numerous in South Wales, where great deposits of iron and coal were eventually found.

The Welsh people settled in the valleys of their rugged country. The difficulty of the terrain kept the population sparse: there were not more than four hundred thousand Welsh people at the end of the seventeenth century. The deep valleys with their steep slopes had long made invasion difficult and enabled the Welsh to preserve much of their ancient Celtic culture. The isolation of individual settlements and the vestiges of Celtic tribalism exaggerated the importance of certain great families, whose aggressive assertion of family rights and pride earned for Wales in the minds of Englishmen a reputation for turbulence. An English member of Parliament in the seventeenth century declared that the Welsh are "an ydolatrous nation and worshippers of divells . . . thrust out into the mountains where they lived long like thiefs and robbers and are to this day the most base, peasantly, perfidious peoples of the world."

Of course, the English themselves had much to do with turbulence in Wales. Land-hungry Norman barons based in England had conquered Wales, often by a process of allying themselves with locally powerful Welsh families. Two subsequent major wars of independence by the Welsh—most notably that of Owen Glendower in the early fifteenth century—encouraged a strong sense of Welsh separateness from Anglo-Norman England. But Welsh attachment to England was strengthened and order spread in the countryside by the fact that Henry Tudor (Henry VII of England) was partly of Welsh blood. By the famous Acts of Union of 1536 and 1542, Henry VIII's eminent civil servant Thomas Cromwell redefined the Welsh border, extended the English system of shires and common law to Wales, and incorporated Welsh representatives into the English Parliament at Westminster.

The Acts of Union did not integrate the Welsh and English cultures, but they did begin the long process of separating the Welsh ruling order from the mass of the people. In Wales, the aristocracy did not amount to much, and the country was in the hands of the gentry families, most of them Welsh in origin. During the sixteenth and seventeenth centuries, many of the men in these gentry families were attracted by the economic and political opportunities in London; many became pensioners of the English Crown; some married English heiresses. As a result, the Welsh gentry became steadily more anglicized in language, tastes, and style of life. By the latter 1600s, many gentry were losing their ability to speak Welsh, which, however, remained the language of the overwhelming majority of the common people.

Under these conditions, both geographic and cultural, Welsh agriculture in the seventeenth century was comparatively backward. On the whole, the soil was poor, and the topography encouraged isolated farms rather than village settlements. Many estates were in the hands of either anglicized Welsh gentry living in England or absentee English landlords. Roads were extremely bad, maintained if at all by forced labor commanded by the local vestry (parish ruling council). Local loyalties remained very strong, as each community was virtually self-supporting. Modern farming techniques spread very slowly; even the scythe was uncommon outside the richest wheat-growing valleys. Arable land was scattered in the valleys and river bottoms throughout the Highland interior, but it was always combined with pasturage. Even in the more easily farmed vales of the South and East, only about one-third of the land was arable, the rest being meadows for hay. Hence, Welsh agriculture was predominantly pastoral, with sheep and cattle being the most important products. By the late seventeenth century, Welsh drovers herded cattle along eight or nine main roads eastward into the Midlands and South of England.

The conditions of agriculture kept standards of living in Wales very low for the great bulk of the population, lower than those of all but the poorest English men and women. With incomes almost totally dependent on farming, the laboring poor teetered on the edge of starvation, eating at the best of times milk and bread but almost no meat. They lived in squalid huts with mud floors and rush-thatched roofs, heated by peat fires. Most were illiterate. Their lives revolved around the seasons and offered little leisure except at Christmas season and on saints' days. Communal activities such as harvesting and threshing provided occasions for singing and dancing, nearly the only bright spots in otherwise drab lives. Wandering bards (poets and harpers) still spun fantasies of the heroic past, but bardic culture was in decline.

As is usual in such premodern societies, religion was the main consolation of life. The Welsh accepted the Reformation of Henry VIII without much trouble. As in England, Welsh monasteries were dissolved, churches plundered, and clerical land sold. The gentry benefited; the poor were indifferent. What mattered most to the Welsh was that Queen Elizabeth appointed Welshmen to vacant Welsh bishoprics and had the Bible and Prayer Book translated into Welsh. These steps were important, both because they helped preserve Welsh as a living language and because they kept Wales attached to Protestantism. No religious divide appeared between Wales and England such as would poison Anglo-Irish relations.

*Within* Wales, however, an important religious (as well as linguistic and social) divide developed. During the Civil War, Wales remained largely Anglican and Royalist, but the reign of Parliament saw Puritanism make headway in Welsh parishes. The Restoration of 1660 sought to sweep away Welsh Puritanism, but it failed. The restored Church of England in Wales stood unreformed. Welsh bishops regarded their appointments as stepping-stones to the richer dioceses of England and furthermore had to spend a good part of each year attending the House of Lords in London. The resulting lack of oversight, in conjunction with a shortage of trained clergymen and the overly large size of Welsh dioceses and parishes, allowed Nonconformity to thrive. Rising mainly from the lesser gentry—substantial *freeholders* (farmers who owned rather than leased their land), tenants, and townsmen—

*Horeb Chapel, Cwm Teigl, Llan Ffestiniog. Numerous chapels such as this one in North Wales dot the Welsh countryside and testify to the importance of Nonconformity in shaping Welsh identity and culture.*

Welsh Nonconformists were strongly attached to the Welsh language and opposed to Anglicanism, the religion of the anglicized gentry and magistrates. Eventually, this division would produce a severe tension in Welsh society.

## SCOTLAND

Nowhere in the British Isles has geography had a more striking effect than in Scotland. The nearly thirty-two thousand square miles of Scotland (about three-fifths the size of England) break into three distinct physical regions: (1) the Highlands; (2) the central plain; and (3) the Southern Uplands, just north of the English border. By long tradition, the latter two regions are referred to as the Lowlands. Here is found the most fertile land, especially in a broad crescent extending from the central plain around to the eastern and northern coastal areas. But even the fertile crescent is fairly hilly, with much moorland and boggy fields. In the seventeenth century, no natural or man-made borders broke the vista into compact patches. The Lowlands were relatively treeless, a succession of windy moors, fields, and pastures.

The Highlands—about two-thirds of the total land area of Scotland—are much less hospitable than the Lowlands, though Highland scenery is often dramatic and beautiful. The Highlands are defined by the famous Highland Line, a geological fault that runs from southwest to northeast, from the Firth of Clyde to Stonehaven. Behind the Highland Line—that is, to its north and west—the mountains of the Highlands spring up abruptly in a succession of parallel ridges to the west coast. Off the coast are more than 750 rugged, stony islands; in the far northeast rise the islands of Orkney and Shetland. The Highlands and islands have a rugged terrain. Ben Nevis, at 4,500 feet the highest mountain in the British Isles, is in the Scottish Highlands. Deep valleys, called straths and glens, cut through the mountain ridges; travel between the valleys is often difficult. The mountains affect all of Scottish weather because they receive heavy rainfall (sixty inches a year in the west) while protecting eastern Scotland, which is comparatively dry. The Highlands therefore are considerably wetter and colder than the Lowlands—a tough terrain for a tough people.

The isolated straths and glens of the Highlands served as a haven for ancient cultures: Scandinavian in Orkney, Shetland, and Caithness (the northernmost county) and Celtic in the mainland. Celtic peoples once dominated all of Scotland, but were pushed into the Highlands by Anglo-Saxon invasions from the Southeast. In the seventeenth century, Norn, a variety of old Norse, was still spoken in the northern isles, and Scots, a derivative of Anglo-Saxon, in the Midland valleys. Most Highlanders spoke only Gaelic. English was the language of the Southern Uplands, gradually spreading north and west.

The population of Scotland in the late seventeenth century stood at about one million, and was distributed very differently from today. About half lived in the Highlands and half in the Lowlands, with most of the latter in the central plain. Scotland generally was much more sparsely settled than England. There were about 275 towns (*burghs*), but most were tiny, with 100 people or fewer. Only Edinburgh (with thirty thousand inhabitants) and Glasgow, Aberdeen, and Dundee (with about ten thousand each) were burghs of significant size. More than 80 percent of all Scots lived in the countryside, usually in hamlets (or *farmtouns*), consisting of a farm large enough to support a plow team. The arable land was too dispersed to support English-style nucleated villages. In the Highlands and Lowlands alike, people clustered on the slopes of strath and glen near the scattered arable land. Most of these country people were peasants, either tenant farmers, subtenants called *crofters* and *cottars*, or farm laborers and servants. The upper social orders alone owned land—the nobility, the substantial non-noble landowners (the *lairds*), and the petty landlords (the *bonnet lairds*).

Law and custom alike retained much more of the feudal system in Scotland than in England. The most unusual feature of Scottish society in the seventeenth century was the Highland clans. The clans originated in the Middle Ages when feudal social and eco-nomic relations were grafted onto the old Celtic tribal system. Kinship—real or mythical—was the key to the clans. Every member of a clan, from chieftain to shepherd, was thought to be related by common ancestry to the clan chief; hence, a bond of kin loyalty underlay the connection between landlord and tenant. Traditionally, clan bards celebrated the heroism of the tribal ancestors and kept the folkloric genealogy of the clan. Because the primary function of the clan was military, the clan chief had the right to call to battle all the men of his clan. In fact, most clansmen held land by a form of tenure called *ward-holding* that obliged the tenant to military service as well as rent.

The clans were quite warlike. Succession to clan leadership was by *primogeniture* (the right of the firstborn son), but the new chief was supposed to prove his bravery and honor by leading raids on other clans or on the long-suffering Lowlanders. Further, a crime against a clansman was to be punished not by the national government, but by retaliation on the part of the victim's clan. Therefore, the Highlands were the scene of almost constant feuding—raiding and counterraiding as the debts of blood feuds were collected. The fighting often centered around the theft of cattle because the wealth of a clansman was measured in cattle, the main product of Highland agriculture. The feuding often escalated to near civil war as a result of shifting alliances among the clans, and especially because of a long struggle between the Campbells and the Macdonalds for leadership of Highland culture.

This state of society in the Highlands and its contrast with Lowland society must be understood if Scottish politics in the late seventeenth and early eighteenth centuries is to be unraveled. Much of the bloodshed that characterized those years was a matter of one clan taking revenge on another. In particular, the expansion of the power of the Campbells in the Southwest was crucial because it set the Campbells at loggerheads with the MacLeans and the Macdonalds. Moreover, the Lowlanders and the Scottish government for many decades sought to end what they saw as lawlessness in the Highlands, as well as frequent eruptions of Highlanders into the Lowlands. The sight of a Highland clan on a raid, dressed in their belted plaids and armed with broadswords, shields, and dirks, was enough to turn any peaceful man's bowels to water—and to call forth repressive edicts known as *Letters of Fire and Sword* from the government. By the late seventeenth century, the clans were under severe pressure and believed that their way of life was at stake.

The standard of living in the Highlands was noticeably lower than in the Lowlands, but it was precarious everywhere. Scottish agriculture was devoted to raising barley, oats, and cattle. Most Scots ate little other than oatmeal, plus some milk, cheese, and butter. They ate oatmeal mixed with milk as porridge, mixed with water as gruel, or baked as oatbread and bannocks. If the oat crop failed—as it did in the mid-1670s and later 1690s—peasants starved. They usually wore coarse linen shirts and the blanket-like plaids (the kilt was not worn until the eighteenth century), both woven by the family at home. The nobility lived in substantial homes, more like castles than country manors, but the peasantry lived in miserable huts. The usual peasant cottage had stone and turf walls, a turf-thatched roof, a mud floor, no glass in the windows, and no chimney. Most were heated by peat fires. Farm animals lived in the cottage with the family, though usually confined by a partition to one end of the single room. The most valuable parts of the cottage in that treeless country were the roof beams, which a family took with them, if allowed, when forced to move.

The Scottish economy suffered from both the harsh natural environment and the political instability of the country. In the central plain, grain growing was fairly successful, though the techniques were almost wholly traditional. The Highland clans grew as much grain as the land allowed, but almost always needed to import it from the Lowlands. They paid for their grain imports with exports of cattle. Scottish trade was recovering from the terrible years of war, disease, and confiscation of the 1640s and 1650s, but it could not match the volume or sophistication of the English mercantile sector. The Scots traded agricultural products (hides, skins, fish, and wool) to northern Europe and France in return for timber, iron, and manufactured articles. The most important development in Scottish trade was an increase in the regular export of black cattle (the ancestor of the Angus breed) to England. The London market reached all the way to the Highlands and made cattle droving southward a major enterprise. Close to twenty thousand head of cattle a year passed through Carlisle in the 1660s. Eventually, this trade would be a crucial link between England and Scotland, sufficient even to overcome centuries of hostility.

The Highland-Lowland division of Scotland had as great an effect on religion as on social structure and standards of living. Broadly speaking, the Highlands in the seventeenth century were too remote for the people to be deeply attached to any branch of religion, whereas the Lowlands were profoundly committed to Protestant Christianity. In the Highlands, a few clans—most notably the Macdonalds—remained Roman Catholic, whereas most of the others were loosely Episcopalian (that is, they believed in a Protestant church ruled by bishops). In the Lowlands, however, Calvinist Presbyterianism prevailed.

The intensity of Lowland Presbyterianism is worthy of note. The Reformation in Scotland had not been led by the Crown as in England, but rather by a broad alliance drawn from the nobility, gentry, and burghers (town dwellers). These reformers believed that the Roman Catholic Church had long neglected the spiritual welfare of the Scottish people. To revitalize Scottish Christianity and to battle clerical corruption, they adopted a *presbyterian* system of church government that allowed the laity to share power: elected kirk sessions (church councils) at the parish level and presbyteries (representative bodies) instead of bishops at the diocesan level. An attempt by Charles I (king of both England and Scotland from 1625 to 1649) to force the Scottish church to adopt the Anglican prayer book and to crush Presbyterianism radicalized the Scottish reformers and led to armed rebellion against the king. It also put the Scottish church in the hands of the

*Covenanters*—militant Puritans who brooked no compromise with bishops and who espoused a stern moral code.

The Covenanters took their name from a Scottish Reformation tradition that drew on the ancient Hebrew ideal of a covenant between God and his chosen people. In 1557, reformers signed the first formal Covenant, by which they promised to resist the "Congregation of Satan" (the Roman Catholic Church), but it was the National Covenant of 1638 that became the foundational document of the Covenanters. Declaring themselves bound to act "as beseemeth Christians who have renewed their Covenant with God," the men who signed this document asserted their opposition to Charles I's political and religious aims and their commitment to Presbyterian doctrine and polity.

The Covenanting tradition remained a vital part of Scottish life in the Lowlands. There, the reformers largely succeeded in establishing schools as well as kirk sessions in every locality. Presbyterianism penetrated deep into the social structure, and literacy spread much more widely than in any other part of the British Isles. Hence, when Charles II was restored to the Scottish as well as the English throne in 1660, his determination to bring the episcopacy back to Scotland was decidedly unpopular in the Lowlands. Approximately three hundred Scottish clergymen refused to accept the bishops and were ejected from the Church of Scotland. Many of these were extreme Covenanters, as were many of the common people. The government tried in the 1660s and 1670s to quell the Covenanters by force. Violence flared, notably in a Covenanter rising in the Southwest of Scotland in 1679, which the government put down with the assistance of Highland troops. At the Battle of Bothwell Brig, the Highlanders seized the occasion to pay back with savage ferocity the grudge they bore from earlier Covenanter persecution. Radical Covenanting factions continued to erupt in sporadic rebellions throughout the early 1680s, and the Covenanter tradition remained a potent force in Presbyterianism and an important dimension in the clash of cultures between Lowlanders and Highlanders.

## IRELAND

Everywhere in the British Isles of the seventeenth century, land and religion were vital to the lives of the people, but nowhere were they of such significance, nor was their intertwining so explosive and tragic, as in Ireland. The peculiar way that issues of land ownership and religious affiliation became tightly bonded would make for extraordinary political violence and economic backwardness in Ireland, as well as for strained constitutional relations with England for more than two hundred years.

It seems doubly tragic that Ireland should suffer so because the Emerald Isle by nature should be a bountiful country. Ireland is the westernmost of the British Isles, situated about thirteen miles from Lowland Scotland and seventy miles from England. It consists of thirty-two thousand square miles; hence, it is slightly larger than Scotland and about three-fifths the size of England. Unlike Scotland and Wales, Ireland has no central spine of mountains. The central region of Ireland is a broad, gently rolling plain, surrounded by low mountains. These mountains are clustered, and routes between them offer easy access to the central plain. No part of Ireland is wholly cut off from the rest, although the mountainous areas of the North and West are remote as well as barren. Further, the northeastern province, Ulster, is fairly clearly defined by a chain of mountains and lakes. The Celtic culture held on longest in the North and West. Indeed, Ulster was the last of the four provinces (the others being Leinster, Munster, and Connacht) to fall to English conquest.

For the most part, the soil of Ireland is good and the climate equable. As the westernmost European offshore island, Ireland is the most subject to the influence of the Atlantic. The weather is consistently cool and damp and does not go to extremes in any direction. Ireland is neither as warm and dry as southeastern England nor as cold and wet as Wales and the Scottish Highlands. A typical day is cloudy and rainy: rain falls 250 days a year in the West and 180 days in the East. A fairly warm drizzle causes the Irish to say, "It's a fine soft day, thanks be to God." The island is green all year long, with lush pastures, meadows, and fields, but the wet climate makes for numerous bogs, heaths, lakes, and streams. Peat bogs even today cover one-seventh of Ireland.

The population of Ireland in the 1680s was about two million. It had increased significantly since mid-century, for the population was recovering from the destructive wars of English conquest in the late sixteenth century and the civil wars of the 1640s and early 1650s. The population was almost entirely rural. As in Scotland and Wales, Celtic culture had never held towns to be of great importance, and even in the late seventeenth century, there were few Irish towns of any size. Dublin, the capital and center of trade, had a population of sixty thousand in 1675. Only a few other port and trading towns had more than five thousand inhabitants—most notably, Cork, Limerick, Waterford, and Galway.

By the 1700s, the Irish population was deeply divided over religion. About 75 or 80 percent of the people in Ireland were Roman Catholic; the rest were Anglican or Presbyterian. In Leinster, Munster, and Connacht, the Protestants were a thin veneer laid over a vast block of rough Catholic wood—95 percent of the population was Catholic in these three provinces. Not so in Ulster, where Protestants amounted to about half of the population, with most concentrated in the northeast. Everywhere, most Catholics were native Irish (a category which by this time included the descendants of the Norman knights who had invaded and seized much of Ireland in the twelfth century), whereas most Protestants were of English or Scottish descent. To aggravate matters, most landowners by the late seventeenth century were Protestants, and most tenants and farm laborers were Catholics.

This startling and dangerous socio-religious alignment developed during the sixteenth and early seventeenth centuries as a result of both the Protestant Reformation and the English monarchy's efforts to centralize and expand its control over Ireland. When Henry VIII began his reign in 1509, the English Crown effectively controlled only a small portion of Ireland, *the Pale* around the city of Dublin. Henry's efforts to solidify and extend English governmental control beyond the Pale aroused fierce opposition from Irish landowners. The Reformation strengthened the forces of Irish resistance. Unlike in England, Wales, and Scotland, the Reformation did not *take* in Ireland. The Irish did not object to Henry VIII's substituting himself for the pope as head of the Church of England, but they rebelled when his more enthusiastic Protestant successors tried to impose significant doctrinal reforms on Ireland.

English *plantation policy* further aggravated Anglo-Irish relations. In 1556, Henry VIII's Roman Catholic daughter, Queen Mary I, sought to extend English control over Ireland by confiscating the land of Irish rebels and redistributing it to English colonists, thus *planting* loyal Englishmen in Ireland. After Mary's Protestant sister, Elizabeth I, took the throne, this policy took on religious dimensions, with the planting of Protestant English landowners in Munster. It was, however, Elizabeth's Stuart successor, James I of England and VI of Scotland, who implemented the plantation policy most broadly. In 1610, the last two Irish chieftains able to mount large-scale resistance to English conquest fled Ireland for France. This infamous Flight of the Earls provided the opportunity for James to effect the plantation of Ulster on a large scale. Between 1610 and 1625, Ulster was planted by Scottish and English adventurers who were willing to undertake colonization. Their plantations were more successful than earlier attempts because they

*The Provinces of Ireland.* Connacht and the westernmost reaches of Munster contained the poorest of Ireland's population, whereas Ulster was home to the largest percentage of Protestants. Leinster included the capital of Dublin, the center of British political power in Ireland.

brought colonists at all levels of society—tradesmen, artisans, and tenants as well as landowners. Most of these colonists were in fact Scottish Presbyterians, who from that day to this have given Ulster much of its uniquely hard-working but rather dour character.

Additional transfers of land were yet to come in the seventeenth century. In 1641, the Catholic aristocracy and gentry—of both Celtic (or Gaelic) and Norman descent—still owned about 58 percent of all Irish land. But the Civil War, which was more confused and bloody in Ireland than anywhere else in the British Isles, resulted in the confiscation of more Catholic land. In 1641, Irish Catholics precipitated a furious rebellion in Ulster with an outburst of pent-up frustration against Protestant colonists. As many as four thousand Protestants were killed, but initial reports in England put the number of deaths at two hundred thousand. This alleged massacre eventually brought down on Ireland the wrath of Oliver Cromwell and his New Model Army, which crushed the Catholic rebels and opened the way for a massive transfer of land ownership. In order to repay English entrepreneurs who had financed the expedition, to reward the soldiers of his army, and to plant in Ireland Protestant veterans who might bring order to the countryside, Cromwell expropriated large numbers of Catholic landowners—essentially, all who could not prove their "constant good affection to the commonwealth of England," during the Civil War. Thousands were forced into the rocky and barren land west of the River Shannon in Connacht; others were packed off into servitude in the West Indies. The percentage of Irish land owned by Catholics fell to just 8 percent.

The expropriated Irish Catholic landlords never accepted their fate. Those who could pursued every legal and political means to recover their estates. Some became tenants and laborers—understandably sullen and uncooperative—of the Anglo-Protestants. Others became bandits who roamed the countryside, half rebels and half thieves—men called *Tories*, who assuaged their family pride by stealing from the colonists. All of the dispossessed hoped that a restoration of the Stuarts to the throne would bring return of their lands.

When Charles II was restored in 1660, the moment of vindication for the expropriated Catholics seemed at hand. But their dreams were not to be realized. Charles II did not entirely reverse the Cromwellian settlement of Ireland. He did arrange a compromise that returned one-third of the Cromwellian estates to Irish landlords, Catholic or not, who had not been guilty of rebellion against the Crown. Nevertheless, nearly 80 percent of the land remained in the hands of English and Scottish Protestants, with

*Monea Castle in County Fermanagh, Ireland. This fortified house, built in the early seventeenth century, attests to Irish concerns about security.*

most of the Gaelic-speaking Irish Catholics reduced to tenants and farm laborers.

Under these circumstances, it is remarkable how well the Irish economy performed in the late seventeenth century. The wars had been devastating, the transfer of land ownership disruptive, and the social and religious divisions debilitating. Yet the Irish economy made a significant if gradual recovery in the second half of the century. Ulster in particular prospered, for the plantation policy established new towns, revived old ones, and invigorated farming. The new landlords everywhere in Ireland felt unrestricted by custom, and by hard work and a commercial outlook they increased the output of the hard-pressed agricultural sector. The domestic production of woolens and linen, iron smelting, and the cutting of barrel staves were the most important industries. The latter two, however, tended to disappear locally when the deposits of iron ore and the stands of trees were exhausted. Cattle constituted the main export, and Irish cattle exporters did so well after the 1650s that English cattle breeders brought pressure on Parliament at Westminster to stop the importation of Irish cattle into England.

By the 1680s, Ireland was probably marginally more productive than Scotland. Nevertheless, Ireland remained a backward country, even by pre-modern standards. The landlords could live in comfort, but as their castle-like fortified houses showed, they were never free from the fear of raids by Tories or of a general uprising by the Catholic populace, whose Gaelic tongue they could not understand. Living in isolation, the landlords developed a fortress mentality. Many of them were upstarts—ex-soldiers and men on the make. Hence, the squires and squireens of back-country Ireland were known in England as an exceptionally rough lot—hard-drinking, hard-riding, heavy-gambling swaggerers.

The bulk of the population lived on the brink of starvation and in the midst of unrelenting hardship. Most lived on milk, oatcakes, and potatoes—the last a South American import that became common in Ireland by the 1650s. Potatoes and grains alike are vulnerable to wet weather; thus, when the summer growing season was cold and wet, the Irish people had nothing to fall back on. During good weather and bad, most Irish men and women lived out their lives in miserable huts, usually of wattle and mud, sometimes of whitewashed stone, but rarely with floors, chimneys, or even the most primitive furniture. They toiled in their landlords' fields, cut their own peat for fuel, and grew potatoes on small plots with only the simplest tools.

For comfort, the majority of Irishmen turned to traditional folkways. One was simple hospitality: sitting around a peat fire in a dark cabin gossiping and telling stories of superstition and the heroes of legend. Sometimes they could welcome one of Ireland's wandering poets, the vestiges of the bardic tradition in which great Celtic families had retained poets and harpers to celebrate clan genealogy and glory. Another folkway was Catholicism, brought to them by hard-pressed priests, most of whom were on the run (for it was the Catholic clergy who suffered most from persecution in Ireland during the Restoration period). Finally, the Irish peasantry enjoyed occasions, such as weddings and wakes, when they could come together with singing, eating, and drinking. The peasants had no education and no books. For news they depended on traveling peddlers. All of these were highly oral activities, which under the circumstances encouraged the telling, retelling, and embroidering of Celtic myths; the manufacture of martyrs; and the fantasizing about the day when the "army of the Gael" would again rise to restore the land to the Irish people. For them, Restoration had not occurred in 1660; it lay in the future.

## Suggested Reading

Beckett, J. C. *The Making of Ireland, 1603–1922*. Boston: Faber & Faber, 1987.

Bingham, Caroline. *Beyond the Highland Line: Highland History and Culture*. London: Constable, 1991.

Burgess, Glenn. *The New British History: Founding a Modern State, 1603–1715*. London: I. B. Tauris, 1999.

Canny, Nicholas. *Making Ireland British, 1580–1650*. Oxford: Oxford University Press, 2001.

Cullen, L. M. *An Economic History of Ireland Since 1660*. London: Batsford, 1972.

Davies, John. *A History of Wales*. London: Penguin, 2007.

Davies, Norman. *The British Isles: A History*. New York: Oxford University Press, 1999.

De Paor, Liam. *The Peoples of Ireland, from Prehistory to Modern Times*. Notre Dame, IN: University of Notre Dame Press, 1986.

Devine, T. M. *The Scottish Nation: A History, 1700–2000*. New York: Viking, 1999.

Dodgshon, R. A., and R. A. Butlin, eds. *An Historical Geography of England and Wales*. New York: Academic Press, 1978.

Evans, E. Estyn. *Irish Folk Ways*. London: Routledge & Kegan Paul, 1957.

Foster, R. F. *Modern Ireland, 1600–1972*. New York: Allen Lane, 1988.

Grant, I. F. *Highland Folk Ways*. London: Routledge & Kegan Paul, 1957.

Hill, James Michael. *Celtic Warfare, 1595–1763*. Edinburgh: John Donald, 1986.

Jenkins, Geraint. *A Concise History of Wales*. Cambridge: Cambridge University Press, 2007.

———. *The Foundations of Modern Wales: Wales, 1642–1780*. New York: Oxford University Press, 1988.

Kearney, Hugh. *The British Isles: A History of Four Nations*. Cambridge: Cambridge University Press, 1989.

Mitchison, Rosalind. *The History of Scotland*. London: Routledge, 2002.

Ohlmeyer, Jane H., ed. *Political Thought in Seventeenth-Century Ireland: Kingdom or Colony*. Cambridge: Cambridge University Press, 2000.

O'Siochru, Micheal. *God's Executioner: Oliver Cromwell and the Conquest of Ireland*, London: Faber & Faber, 2008.

Royle, Trevor. *Civil War: The Wars of the Three Kingdoms 1638–1660*. London: Abacus, 2004.

Tompson, Richard S. *The Atlantic Archipelago*. Lewiston, NY: E. Mellen Press, 1986.

Wilson, Charles. *England's Apprenticeship, 1603–1763*, 2nd ed. London: Longman, 1984.

Withers, Charles. *Gaelic Scotland: The Transformation of a Cultural Region*. London: Routledge, Chapman, & Hall, 1988.

Wrightson, Keith. *English Society, 1580–1680*. New Brunswick, NJ: Rutgers University Press, 1982.

# Chapter 2

## The Revolution of 1688 and the Revolution Settlement

The tumultuous events of 1688–90 marked a decisive moment in British history, the culmination of a half-century of political upheaval, religious crisis, and constitutional experimentation, and in many ways the beginning of the modern period. In the standard interpretation, the Revolution of 1688 laid the groundwork for the remarkable constitutional stability of Britain for the next three centuries by asserting the supremacy of Parliament, the liberties of the individual, the security of property, and the rule of law against the arbitrary power of the Crown—and all without massive bloodletting, in England at least. Not surprisingly, the English have long thought of the developments of 1688 and after as the Glorious Revolution. This view, however, ignores not only the very different way that the revolution played out in Scotland and Ireland, but also the precariousness of what became known as the Revolution Settlement. It took another twenty-five years for the English to resolve many of the constitutional issues between Crown and Parliament that had been contested since early in the seventeenth century—and even longer for the Settlement to *take* in Scotland and Ireland (and one could argue that in many parts of Ireland, it never did).

Many of these crucial changes in politics and constitution derived from the international conflict in which the peoples of the British Isles found themselves in the late seventeenth century. The Revolution of 1688 was not an exclusively *English* event: it not only affected all of the British Isles, but it also formed part of the wider story of European power politics, particularly the rivalry between France and the Dutch Republic. Thus, the political turmoil of 1688 necessarily involved England in two major European wars, during which the English asserted their influence on a new scale. These processes—the successful rebellion of 1688, the constitutional settlement, and the expansion of English power—were three sides of the same triangle.

## From the Restoration through the Revolution Settlement

| | |
|---|---|
| 1660 | The Restoration; Charles II succeeds to the English and Scottish thrones |
| 1673 | Parliament passes the Test Act |
| 1678 | The Popish Plot |
| 1679–81 | The Exclusion Crisis |
| 1685 | Accession of James II (of England, Wales, and Ireland)/ VII (of Scotland) |
| 1688 | The Glorious Revolution; invasion of William of Orange; overthrow of James II in England |
| 1689 | Battle of the Boyne; final flight of James from the British Isles; Battle of Dunkeld; defeat of Jacobite forces in Scotland; beginning of the War of the League of Augsburg |
| 1691 | Treaty of Limerick; defeat of Jacobite forces in Ireland |
| 1692 | Massacre of Glencoe |
| 1694 | Creation of the Bank of England |
| 1701 | Beginning of the War of Spanish Succession |
| 1702 | Accession of Queen Anne |
| 1707 | Union of England and Scotland |
| 1713 | Treaty of Utrecht |
| 1714 | Hanoverian succession; accession of George I |

## THE REIGN OF CHARLES II, 1660–1685

To understand the events of 1688 and after, we must begin with the Restoration and the reigns of two brothers, Charles II and James II. On May 8, 1660, Charles Stuart returned from exile and was proclaimed king of England, Scotland, and Ireland. This Restoration of the monarchy ended eleven years of rule by Parliament and its army, dominated throughout by Oliver Cromwell. Despite the joyous celebration that greeted Charles's return from exile, many of the constitutional issues that had torn England apart since the early years of the century remained unresolved. Charles II survived partly by virtue of his personal qualities and partly by exploiting the fear of civil war. The "Merry Monarch" was a splendid politician, determined not to "go on his travels" again and therefore prepared to give way before a crisis on most issues. He was also a man of few principles and a master of dissimulation. Although indolent, Charles possessed grace and wit. Because of the widespread relief at being out from under the bony thumb of Puritanism, the *political nation* (those with a say in political affairs) was more than ready to forgive, and even to appreciate, his many mistresses, his lusty appetites, and his hearty enjoyment of sport with his rakish young friends. Ever the pragmatist and shrewd tactician, Charles held dear only one principle: legitimate succession to the throne.

Not even religious belief was vitally important to him. Charles was the cousin of Louis XIV and had spent much of his exile in France; consequently, many Englishmen suspected that he was a Catholic. But Charles remained a regular communicant in the Anglican church, converting to Catholicism only on his deathbed. In public policy, he preferred toleration; hence, the Clarendon Code, with its penal laws directed against Protestant dissenters, did not originate with him. In 1672, Charles suspended the penal laws by his Declaration of Indulgence, an act of the royal prerogative (independent royal authority). But when Parliament pressured him to cancel the Declaration of Indulgence, he bent to its wish, and the next year, when Parliament passed the Test Act (1673), requiring all Crown officeholders to take the sacraments in the Anglican church, swear the oath of supremacy, and deny the Catholic doctrine of transubstantiation, Charles signed it. Throughout his reign, Charles took care never to appear as an enemy of Protestantism, nor to alienate the Anglican establishment and its supporters.

In another potentially dangerous matter—royal finances—Charles again avoided ultimate confrontation with the English Parliament and the country even though he never thought he had enough money. His first Parliament granted him for life far greater revenues than his predecessors had ever enjoyed, but Charles was supposed to "live of his own"—that is, conduct the ordinary affairs of government on these revenues—and expected to return to Parliament to seek money for extraordinary expenses, such as he incurred in two wars against the Dutch Republic (1665–67 and 1672–74). By keeping Charles on a short leash, Parliament meant to retain some control over his conduct of affairs. In fact, however, the short leash made Charles partly dependent on Louis XIV, monarch of the richest and most powerful nation in Europe, and put Crown and Parliament on a collision course.

The issue over which Charles clashed with Parliament most fiercely was the proposed exclusion from the throne of his heir, his brother James, duke of York. Much to Charles's annoyance, James had converted to Catholicism in 1668. James tended thereafter to display the zeal characteristic of converts. Where Charles was clever and flexible, James was far more rigid. From the early 1670s, the desire grew among many Protestants to keep James from succeeding to his inheritance, and then reached a fever pitch in 1678 with the so-called Popish Plot. This unsavory episode originated with Titus Oates, a former Anglican clergyman who had been convicted of perjury and accused of sodomy. Oates converted to Catholicism, but even so, he insisted he had uncovered a Jesuit plot to assassinate Charles II and replace him with James. The plot was a fantasy, but more than twenty innocent men were executed in the resulting panic.

The bogus Popish Plot helped spark the most serious struggle between Charles and his Parliament: the Exclusion Crisis. In 1679, the House of Commons passed a bill that would have excluded James from the succession. Many members of Parliament (MPs) hoped to substitute Charles's illegitimate son, the duke of Monmouth. A handsome young man of considerable physical prowess and charm, Monmouth was also a Protestant. Charles doted on this favorite child, but he would not allow him to supplant James. To defend the legitimacy of the succession, Charles deployed one of the strongest weapons still in the monarch's political arsenal: he dissolved Parliament. In 1680, a new House of Commons passed a second Exclusion Bill, and the exclusion of James remained such a threat that Charles dissolved Parliament twice more in 1681. It did not meet again in his lifetime.

The Exclusion Crisis of 1679–81 brought about the formation of political parties in England that were restricted to the tiny political nation consisting of the aristocracy and gentry, plus perhaps 250,000 voters. Those who proposed to exclude James became known as the *Whigs*, a derisive label first applied to the ultra-Protestant Covenanter rebels of Scotland. Although certainly not republicans or democrats, the Whigs opposed royal absolutism, advocated limited monarchy, and defended individual liberties, which in that day meant not only personal freedom, but also the untrammeled right to exploit private property. They tended to favor the growing commercial sector and to view trade rather than land as the life blood of the English economy. The Whigs were also fierce defenders of Protestantism, which they equated with the rule of law and free Parliaments. To them, Roman Catholicism meant *popery*, and popery necessarily led to absolutism, particularly because James, in their eyes, had so alienated the Protestant people of England that he inevitably must try to rule absolutely.

The *Tories*—their label taken from Irish rebels—were devoted to divine right monarchy, though not necessarily to rule by royal prerogative. They were concerned with maintaining order in the state, which implied protection of the divinely established social hierarchy with the king at the top. They felt especially strongly about maintaining the power of society's "natural" rulers—the aristocracy and gentry—in local matters. The Tories saw themselves as defenders of societal harmony and the Whigs as proponents of demagogy, faction, and rebellion. They believed that an established church was essential to social unity and so, unlike the Whigs, they rejected toleration of Dissent. In short, the Tories took the Crown and the Anglican church as the twin pillars of social order and peace.

Charles resisted depending on either party, for while in exile he had learned to trust no man or set of advisers. As one official wrote, "He lived with his ministers as he did with his mistresses; he used them, but he was not in love with them." The parties as yet had no means of forcing the king to accept a particular group of advisers for any length of time. Nor could the Crown control Parliament, even with the liberal application of government bribery. The inability of Charles to command the Commons during the Exclusion Crisis proved that, from the king's point of view, a more certain means of control was mandatory.

Cushioned by Louis XIV's financial support, Charles chose to do without Parliament altogether until he could assure himself of a majority of members of Parliament. From 1681 until his death in 1685, Charles used his prerogative powers to revise the composition of the voting constituencies of the boroughs (that is, towns chartered by the Crown) in order to make them politically favorable. Similarly, he tried to win control over the militia and local government by purging Whigs from the ranks of the lords lieutenant (the chief political officers or royal representatives in the counties), sheriffs, and justices of the peace. This royalist intervention in local power politics alarmed not only Whigs but also Tories who treasured their autonomy. Nevertheless, the extraordinary Tory fear of a recurrence of civil war prevented a confrontation between the king and a united class of landowners. The Tories hastened to support the monarchy. Charles was also fortunate in dying in 1685: he had failed to bring about toleration of Catholics, but he had throttled his opponents and then died at the peak of the Tory reaction.

## WHIGS AND TORIES REBEL, 1685–1688

His brother James was to be far less fortunate. Given the opposition to him during the Exclusion Crisis, James succeeded his brother with surprising ease in 1685. The Parliament he summoned immediately after his accession was almost uniformly Tory and eager to please him, a result of Charles's careful remolding of parliamentary constituencies. Parliament granted James for life almost twice as much in annual revenues as Charles II had enjoyed.

Moreover, when James faced armed rebellion in the early months of his reign, he received the backing not only of Parliament but also of the aristocracy and gentry, both Whig and Tory. Three months after James took the throne, the earl of Argyll, head of the troublesome Campbell clan, returned from exile with the intention of overthrowing him. The Scottish government moved preemptively against the Argyll clan, however, and swiftly quelled the threat.

One month later, James faced a more serious rebellion. In June 1685, Charles's bastard son, the duke of Monmouth, landed in Dorset with a small force. Monmouth claimed that James had usurped the throne and now threatened the Protestant religion and the rights of Englishmen. Such a claim appealed to the remnants of Puritanism and radicalism found among the artisans and small farmers of the West Country. In a final manifestation of support for the "good old cause," about six thousand men joined Monmouth. But the crucial Whig and Tory gentry did not, nor did radicals in the rest of England. The king's army defeated Monmouth's ragtag and pathetic rebels at Sedgemoor in July. Fierce reprisals against the rebels followed. Monmouth was executed and Judge George Jeffreys carried out a savage judicial repression of those who had followed the duke into battle. "Good God!" Jeffreys exclaimed, "That we should live in such an age, when men call God to protect them in a rebellion." More than three hundred men (and a few women) were hanged, their corpses left dangling until they rotted, in the Bloody Assizes. Thousands were deported to the colonies. The landed elite were inclined to think that the rebels got what they deserved.

The failure of Monmouth's rebellion indicated the political nation's willingness to cooperate with James, yet the new king quickly squandered this good will. He and his Parliament were soon at odds. James was an apprehensive and suspicious man. He believed himself to be divinely anointed, yet this elevated idea of his status as a king gave him no sense of security. He feared what he knew of the English—their inclination toward faction and obstreperous opposition, not to mention regicide. He regarded concession and compromise as signs of weakness and independent opinion as a badge of disloyalty. In his anxiety, James assumed any opposition was a harbinger of rebellion. Never in English history was there such a clear case of a self-fulfilling prophecy.

Even James's religious policies bore the marks of his apprehensiveness. In his own time, James was thought of as a king who would destroy the Church of England and return the nation to Roman Catholicism. He was indeed an ardent Catholic who insisted on attending mass in public, tended to trust only Catholic advisers, viewed Protestants as heretics, and opened diplomatic relations with Rome. But although James frequently spoke of *establishing* the Catholic church in England, he was not misguided enough to think he could make Catholicism the state church in his own lifetime. He was keenly aware that, at the time of his accession, the heirs to the throne—his daughters (by his first wife), Mary and Anne—were both Protestants. Apparently James reasoned that, to protect Catholicism in England, he would have to move swiftly to establish it on a more secure basis—that is, free from the penalties of the penal laws. He imagined that, once Catholicism was free from the penal code, converts would multiply. Thus, despite the obvious difficulties, James was determined to execute his Catholic policy. As he admitted, if he had just kept his religion a private matter, he would have had a successful reign, "but, having been called by Almighty God to rule these kingdoms, he would think of nothing but the propagation of the Catholic religion . . . for which he had been and always would be willing to sacrifice everything, regardless of any mere temporal situation."

James pursued his *Catholicizing* aims aggressively. He encouraged Catholic priests to return to England, allowed them to proselytize by education and propaganda, exchanged representatives with the Vatican, accepted a vicar apostolic (bishop) from Rome, and even took two Jesuits into his intimate circle. In 1686, he began the tactic of *closeting* members of Parliament—meeting with them individually and pressuring them to repeal the Test Act and the penal laws against Catholics. James also issued numerous dispensations from the Test Act to enable Catholics to take office. All of these acts deeply disturbed English Protestants, who believed that the king was undermining the laws, the constitution, and the Church of England.

James's actions also roused opposition on a second front—defense of parliamentary liberties. The MPs feared that James's Catholic policy formed part of a wider project of remaking English government along the lines of absolutist France. Their fears were not ungrounded. James said more than once that "he had rather reign one month as the King of France, than twenty years as his brother the King of England had."[1]

Once his accession was ensured, James moved rapidly to centralize his power and to establish a modern state bureaucracy that could implement his bidding more efficiently and effectively, and most crucially, to establish a standing army. Inheriting a weak military force of just nine thousand troops, he expanded the number of men at arms to forty thousand. James's

---

[1]Pincus, *1688: The First Modern Revolution*, 162.

*Playing card: A Jesuit Preaching against our Bible. This playing card, one of a set made in 1688 or 1689, depicts Jesuit missionaries in England during James II's reign. The card set illustrates the hostility incurred by the king's Catholicizing policies.*

solution to the question of how to house this suddenly enlarged force illustrates the growing reach of the Stuart state: his government counted and mapped the available beds in every English inn and tavern and then threatened to revoke the trade licenses of any uncooperative innkeeper. In towns and villages throughout England, the army was now a physical presence. Moreover, in violation of the Test Act, James appointed Catholics as military officers. His growing military power and his defiance of parliament convinced the political nation—Tories included—that their liberties and their power were under threat.

Moreover, James's policies destroyed any chance he had of maintaining an alliance with the Church of England, which had been a bulwark of royal legitimacy and had adopted a posture of passive obedience to the king's will. James aggravated his relations with the Church by reestablishing in new form the old prerogative Court of High Commission, by which he disciplined recalcitrant clergymen. He also sought to break the Anglican monopoly over higher education by opening Oxford and Cambridge to Catholics. When, however, he attempted to Catholicize Oxford's Magdalen College, the fellows (all of whom were Anglican clergymen) resisted. James then removed the fellows from their posts, which struck English Protestants not only as a blow to Protestantism, but also as a threat to the rights of private property.

By the spring of 1687, the growing divide between James and the Church of England convinced the king that his best hope of support lay with the Protestant Dissenters rather than with the Anglicans. Thus, in April he issued a Declaration of Indulgence, suspending by royal edict the Test Act and penal laws against Catholics and Dissenters alike. His strategy put the Dissenters in a quandary. They resented the political restrictions and at times outright religious persecution that they had endured since the Restoration. But although the Dissenters welcomed toleration, they did not trust its author, James. As the descendants of the Puritans, they had long been more hostile to Roman Catholicism than had Anglicans. Many Dissenters agreed with the marquis of Halifax, who described any alliance of Dissent with the king as "bringing together the two most contrary things that are in the world." They concluded that the threat James posed to English civil liberty trumped any religious freedom that he might offer and increasingly opted for allying with Anglicans against the king.

James, however, pressed on doggedly with his plan of establishing toleration in order to secure Catholic freedom and his crown. Like Charles II, he embarked on a purge of the boroughs, the lord lieutenancies, the magistracy, and Parliament—but now the purged individuals were Tories. Between 1687 and 1688, a remarkable 75 percent of local government officials lost their places. Then, in April 1688, James reissued the Declaration of Indulgence, and in May ordered the Church of England to have it read aloud in all its parish churches. This demand was too much even for the most passive Anglicans, for it required them to participate in propagating what they regarded as religious error. Seven Anglican bishops, including the archbishop of Canterbury, petitioned James on the grounds that his prerogative powers gave him no right to force the clergy to read the Declaration. Surprised and outraged by the petition, James had the seven tried for seditious libel. He, however, failed to win a verdict of guilty. Dissenters and Anglicans alike rallied round the bishops, and London crowds cheered them when they were acquitted.

Thus, in only three years James had succeeded in alienating Whigs and Tories, Anglicans and Dissenters. The announcement of a surprising pregnancy only increased this alienation. One of the reasons that Protestants had accepted James was that his heirs were Protestant. James was fifty-one when he acceded to the throne, and his second wife, the Catholic Mary of

Modena, was thought to be infertile. But in November 1687, she announced to a skeptical England that she was with child. On June 10, 1688, Mary gave birth to a son, which meant that James's Catholic goals would be continued. Frantic Protestant propaganda suggested that the baby was not the queen's child, but had been smuggled into the royal bedchamber in a warming pan.

By mid-1868, Richard Hampden observed that "the whole nation is alienated from the government in their inclination." A radical opponent of James, Hampden was perhaps not the most trustworthy observer, yet even James's supporters noted how popular sentiment had turned against the king. One soldier stationed in Wales noted "how prone all were to mutter about breach of laws, and invading of religion," and cautioned that "many who said Well Well thought very evil."[2] Hence, the atmosphere in the early summer of 1688 was full of hysteria and intrigue. On the evening of June 30, just twenty days after the baby's birth and the same day the bishops were acquitted, seven men—six English nobles and one bishop, three of them Tories and four Whigs—wrote William of Orange, the Protestant stadholder (governor of the provinces of the Dutch Republic and, ironically, James's nephew and son-in-law). They asked William to come to England with an army to assist them in resolving their problems with James. The "Invitation of the Seven" assured William that "nineteen parts of twenty of the people" backed their actions.

## WILLIAM III AND THE REVOLUTION IN ENGLAND

William, in fact, had already made up his mind to intervene in England. His agents were in frequent contact with English political leaders, and he had been carefully watching English affairs for years. A cautious, shrewd opportunist, William sought to take advantage of the English opposition to James in order to fulfill the great goal of his life: to block the expansion of Louis XIV's France.

The hawk-nosed, thin, and chronically ill William of Orange was a silent and moody man who would become an unpopular king of England. He was not a brilliant politician or soldier, but he had a dogged tenacity that served him well. He believed God had assigned him a monumental task: to defeat the Catholic France of the Sun King. His design on England was simply to commit England against France, or at least to keep it neutral. A grandson of Charles I and husband of Mary, eldest daughter and heiress presumptive to

---

[2]Pincus, *1688: The First Modern Revolution*, 226.

James II, William harbored no desire to diminish the power of the English Crown. From his point of view, the ideal would be for England to escape civil war with the monarchy intact for Mary to inherit, meanwhile allying with the Dutch against France. Alas, James was destroying any chance for the ideal to become real.

The decisive event for William was the birth of an heir to James and Mary of Modena—which William was all too ready to consider as a fraud perpetrated by the Jesuits. In April 1688, he decided to invade England, if, as the Whig Gilbert Burnet wrote, "invited by some men of the best interest to . . . come and rescue the nation and the religion." His agents in England told him that most of the Whig and Tory aristocracy and gentry had become disaffected from James and that the royal army would not fight. An invasion in sufficient strength would succeed.

William's fleet of 275 ships, carrying an army of 15,000 men, sailed on October 30, taking advantage of an unusual wind blowing from the east. This "Protestant wind," coupled with indecision in the English navy, stranded James's fleet in the mouth of the Thames. William's army landed unopposed near Exeter, his banner proclaiming "The Protestant Religion and the Liberties of England." The manifesto William circulated cleverly stated the purposes of his invasion: it rehearsed the long list of complaints about James's attack on the Church, the parliamentary boroughs, and the privileges of the county elite; it asserted the rights of Parliament as against James's unlawful use of the prerogative; and it promised election of a free Parliament and investigation of the birth of the new baby prince.

While the Whigs threw their support to William, it was uncertain whether the Tory landlords would remain loyal to James and legitimacy. James hastily reversed his recent policies in order to appeal to the Tories, reinstating, for example, the fellows of Magdalen College. But the Tories no longer trusted James, who in early 1688 had horrified English Protestants by importing three thousand Catholic troops from Ireland. James forced the Tories to choose between the Church and their local power on the one hand and the principle of monarchical legitimacy on the other. They chose the Church and their local power.

If the people had rallied to James, William perhaps would have been thrown back into the sea. But they did not. As William began his slow, deliberate march from Exeter to London, ordinary people, as well as members of the aristocracy and gentry, joined his cause. In York, for example, a force of three thousand Williamite supporters—described by an observer as "a diabolical rabble"—seized the city, while in the manufacturing city of

Manchester, men of the "ordinary sort" had to be turned away from the Williamite ranks because "the Prince of Orange had foot enough, it was horse he wanted."[3] James could not depend even on his army. Although it was far larger than William's, it was weakened by a stream of desertions, the most important of which was that by John Churchill, the greatest soldier in England.

As his army retreated toward London without fighting, James lost his nerve—and then his crown. On December 8, he sent the queen and the baby prince to France and fled himself two days later. He did not abdicate, but he apparently sought to bring all government to a halt because he disbanded the royal army and threw the Great Seal into the Thames River. England hovered on the brink of chaos as mobs targeted tax collectors and others who symbolized James's absolutist ambitions and as anti-Catholic riots erupted in London. Nearly all the aristocracy and gentry now looked to William to keep public order. William could not have hoped for a better chain of events, which was spoiled only by some Kentish fishermen who captured James and returned him to London. William had no intention of making a martyr of James; hence, he arranged for James to escape again, this time successfully.

With the administration of the nation already effectively in his hands, William summoned a Convention Parliament in January 1689 to settle affairs. This Convention Parliament faced a complicated question: Who was now the monarch and by what right? All agreed that William should run the country, but not necessarily as king. The Whigs argued, as they had done in the Exclusion Crisis, that the monarchy existed for the utility of its subjects. If the king broke the original *social contract* by which civil society had been initially formed, then the people, through their representatives, had the right to depose him and select a new monarch. This view received its clearest statement by John Locke in his *Two Treatises of Government*, which he wrote during the Exclusion Crisis but published first in 1689. The Whigs, therefore, did not hesitate to interrupt the strict line of succession and to have Parliament act as the source of the royal title. Under Whig influence, the House of Commons resolved that James had broken the original contract and by fleeing the country had abdicated the throne.

The Tories, however, remained reluctant to abandon their adherence to the legitimate succession. They abhorred the notion of an elected monar-

---

[3]Pincus, *1688: The First Modern Revolution*, 238–239.

chy, to which they believed Whig logic inexorably led. Few had resisted William's invasion but none was happy about taking arms against the king, which contradicted their deep-seated patriarchal view of social and political order. In short, the Tories were confused. As one gentleman wrote, "How these risings and associations can be justified, I see not; but yet it is very apparent had not the Prince come and these persons thus appeared, our religion had been rooted out." Hence, the Tories, who had considerable power in the House of Lords, insisted that the throne was not and never could be vacant, and preferred to make William and Mary regents for James.

William settled the argument in characteristically abrupt fashion. He refused to act as regent for James or to serve as mere consort to Mary. Mary, ever the submissive wife, agreed. In the face of William's firm stand, the Lords gave way. William and Mary received the crown jointly. William now had a firm grip on the reins of English policy, following an invasion that few resisted and a settlement of the throne that defied logic.

Many historians argue that this change of rulers was no revolution but rather a rebellion instigated by one section of the English ruling order, the Whigs, and more or less reluctantly accepted by another, the Tories. The real revolution, in this interpretation, came in events subsequent to the change of rulers—the alteration of the English constitution known as *the Revolution Settlement*. Along with the crown, Parliament presented William and Mary with the Declaration of Rights (enacted in 1689 as the Bill of Rights). This famous act prevented the monarchy from continuing certain of James's objectionable practices. It declared illegal the royal power of dispensing with and suspending laws, abolished all prerogative courts, forbade taxation without parliamentary approval, prohibited the raising of an army without parliamentary consent, asserted that parliamentary elections should be free, and mandated that the monarch could neither be a Catholic nor marry one. In the long run, the Bill of Rights helped establish the rule of law, free speech for Parliament, and the power of the landed elite.

In addition to the Bill of Rights, the Revolution Settlement included four significant constitutional changes. First, the Mutiny Act (1689) was passed for a year only; thereafter, the monarch could maintain discipline in the military services only if Parliament met annually and renewed the Mutiny Act. Second, a new coronation oath required the monarch to govern England according to the laws agreed to by Parliament. Third, William voluntarily pledged that judges would serve on good behavior rather than at the king's pleasure. And finally, in 1694, Parliament provided for frequent elections by passing the Triennial Act. All of these measures represented a significant expansion of parliamentary power and judicial independence vis à vis the Crown

Of even greater consequence was the financial settlement that evolved during William's lifetime. Parliament refused to grant William revenues for life, thereby forcing him to consult Parliament frequently for funds. The financial restriction became all the more important because, as we will see below, William was at war with the French from 1689 almost to his death in 1702. The revenues required were enormous, and only Parliament could grant them. William's need to seek funding regularly from Parliament gave MPs the opportunity to inquire about how the funds were spent, a powerful means of oversight on executive activities. The king still functioned as first minister, but with the power of the purse in hand, Parliament (especially the House of Commons) had won a much more powerful role in the workings of the constitution.

The Parliament of 1689 also settled the religious issue, and in a way that was to last for nearly 150 years. Given the alliance between Anglicans and Dissenters that had emerged in 1688, some kind of religious freedom for Dissenters was inevitable. The toleration that Dissenters won in 1689 was, however, narrow. It simply exempted from the penalties of the Clarendon Code all who would swear allegiance to the Crown and deny Catholic doctrines of the mass. Henceforward, Dissenters—but not Catholics or Jews— could worship freely in their own chapels (provided the doors were unlocked), but they remained second-class citizens. They were still excluded from Oxford and Cambridge, they had to pay tithes to the Church of England, they could not hold national or municipal office, and they could not sit in Parliament without taking communion according to Anglican rites. Dissent had won civil *relief* rather than civil *rights*.

The final step in the Revolution Settlement came in 1701 with the Act of Settlement. The Bill of Rights had declared that Mary's sister, Anne, would succeed after William and Mary both died. Anne was a strong Anglican, and it was expected that her eldest son would succeed her, thus keeping the crown on a Protestant brow. But though the unfortunate Anne had seventeen pregnancies between 1683 and 1700, none of her children survived childhood. Parliament felt compelled to pass the succession to the Electress Sophia of Hanover, the nearest Protestant relation. The Act of Settlement did this, along with insisting that all English monarchs be Anglicans. In this way, Parliament clearly affirmed its authority over the succession and limited the power of the Crown.

## THE REVOLUTION IN IRELAND, 1688–1691

In England, William's army faced little resistance. The situation, however, was far different in Ireland, where the events of 1688 brought about large-scale warfare that was of great significance in the European-wide struggle between William's Grand Alliance and France, as well as in the century-long struggle between native Catholics and Protestants planted in Ireland to secure the island for the English monarchy. James II made his stand in Ireland; as a result, for the Irish, the Glorious Revolution was far from glorious and very bloody indeed.

During the reign of Charles II, two issues—land and religion—dominated Irish public affairs and ensured ongoing instability. The Restoration disappointed most expropriated Irish Catholic landowners; with only a small percentage restored to their estates, the vast majority sought ceaselessly to reclaim their land. Protestants from England and Scotland, who now controlled 80 percent of Irish landholdings and dominated the Irish Parliament (on the rare occasions when it met), lived in fear that the Catholics might recover their land. At the same time, the Restoration religious settlement, which reimposed the Episcopal Church of Ireland, disappointed not only Catholics but also Protestant Nonconformists. Ulster Presbyterians had supported the Restoration in hopes of having Presbyterianism established throughout Ireland, but it brought instead the condemnation of the Covenant (see chapter 1) as treasonous. Charles's rule was maintained only by the firmness and moderation of his viceroy, the duke of Ormond, head of one of Ireland's oldest and most loyal Protestant families.

When James succeeded Charles, he was determined to pursue an aggressive Catholicizing policy in Ireland. Implementing this policy fell to the Irish Catholic Richard Talbot. A swaggering adventurer and incorrigible liar, Talbot was a member of James's household and one of the principal agents of the Catholic ex-landowners. Raised to the peerage in 1685 as the earl of Tyrconnell, Talbot became lord lieutenant of Ireland in 1687, much to the delight of Catholics and the horror of Protestants. As one Englishman wrote, "Lord Tyrconnell has gone to succeed the lord lieutenant in Ireland, to the astonishment of all sober men, and to the evident ruin of the protestants in that kingdom." Tyrconnell increased the size of the Irish army with Catholic recruits, staffed it with Catholic officers, and placed Catholics in key local political positions.

When William invaded England, Tyrconnell held Ireland for James. But the Ulster Protestants quickly raised troops for William; seized control of several walled towns, including Derry (always called Londonderry by Protestants); and proclaimed William and Mary king and queen. Civil war in Ireland began, characterized by the pitiless brutality that religious conflict often inspires. In March 1689, James himself arrived in Ireland from France. James intended not to make Ireland independent but with French assistance to defeat the Irish Protestants and then lead a Catholic army against England. He laid siege to Derry, which held out in the face of overwhelming strength and terrible hardship. "This garrison hath lived upon cats, dogs and horse flesh this three days; above 5000 of our men are dead already for want of meat and those that survive are so weak that they can scarce creep to the walls, where many of them die every night at their post," reported Derry's governors as the siege wore on.[4] The suffering continued until William's ships lifted the siege of Derry at the end of July—one of the great moments in Ulster Protestant historical memory.

The actions of a new Irish Parliament (the Patriot Parliament), which sat in the early summer of 1689, accentuated the desperate urgency with which the Irish Protestants fought in this war. Overwhelmingly Catholic, the Patriot Parliament expressed the land hunger and the anti-English resentments of the native Irish elite—sentiments that the thoroughly English James disliked but could not resist. It asserted the exclusive right of Irish Parliaments to legislate for Ireland, enacted religious toleration, and repealed the Cromwellian and Restoration land settlements. It also ordered the seizure of the estates of nearly twenty-five hundred Protestants. Together, these acts would have meant the end of Protestant domination of Ireland.

Instead, William and his army strengthened that Protestant domination. William landed in June 1690 with a large and experienced force made up of Dutch, French Huguenot, Danish, English, and Anglo- (and Scots-) Irish troops. On July 12, William's army met and defeated James's army of French regulars and ill-trained Irish peasants on the River Boyne, north of Dublin. Still commemorated by the Protestants of Northern Ireland in patriotic parades, the Battle of the Boyne was the decisive battle in modern Irish history and one of the most important in the larger struggle between William and Louis XIV. James fled to France again, this time for good. Wounded in battle, William returned to England, though the war in Ireland lasted another year. The Williamite troops defeated the French and Irish in an awful bloodletting at Aughrim and then penned them up in the town of

---

[4]Pincus, *1688: The First Modern Revolution*, 270.

Limerick. Despite the inspired leadership of Patrick Sarsfield, the Irish rebels were forced to surrender in October 1691.

The Treaty of Limerick (1691), which ended the war in Ireland, gave honorable terms to the Irish, but was soon tragically undone. The treaty allowed Irish troops to take service in France if they wished; about eleven thousand did so. It also secured a degree of toleration for Catholics in Ireland, plus protection of property for James's supporters (called Jacobites after *Jacobus*, the Latin for James) who chose to remain in Ireland. William and Mary ratified the Treaty, but the Irish Parliament—once again completely dominated by Protestants—refused to accept its civil articles.

This Parliament, bent on revenge, ignored the provisions for toleration and passed instead a series of laws against Catholics, a *penal code* that was extended in the early eighteenth century (although only sporadically enforced). Aimed at crushing the Catholic gentry, the penal laws prohibited Catholics from buying land or acquiring land from a Protestant by inheritance or marriage. On the death of a Catholic landowner, his land would be divided equally among his sons unless the eldest converted to the Protestant (Anglican) Church of Ireland, in which case he got it all. Catholics could not send their children abroad for education or open schools in Ireland. Catholics could not enter the professions or (after 1727) vote. Catholic bishops were banished, and Catholic priests were required to register and take an oath against the Stuarts.

The penal laws came on top of yet another confiscation of Irish Catholic land—this time the estates of about 270 rebels. By 1700, only one-seventh of all Irish land remained in the hands of Catholics, and the penal code would further reduce that proportion. The Protestant landlords were known thereafter as *the Protestant Ascendancy*, an apt term for this utterly dominant elite.

## SCOTLAND: FROM REVOLUTION TO UNION

James VII had advantages in Scotland that (as James II) he did not have in England. First, the tradition of the Scottish Crown was more autocratic than the English and the power of the Scottish Parliament correspondingly weaker. Second, as a Scottish dynasty, the Stuarts touched the patriotism of all Scotsmen, who displayed their support by giving James an enthusiastic welcome when he first visited Scotland in 1679. Finally, as the nominal head of clan Stewart (*Stuart* is an Anglicized version of the clan name), James had a unique claim on the loyalty of the Highlanders. Nevertheless, the turbulence of the Highlands and the gravity of Scottish religious disputes caused difficulties for James, no less than for any other monarch.

The biggest problem for the Scottish government in the 1670s and 1680s was that the established Church of Scotland was Episcopalian, whereas the religion of the most forceful section of the Lowland Scots was Presbyterian. Fortified by their Covenanting tradition, Presbyterians could not abide prelacy (that is, episcopacy or government by bishops). The Episcopal Church of Scotland thus depended wholly on royal authority and military might. Nevertheless, when James succeeded to the throne of Scotland, the government seemed to be consolidating its power, and James's prospects looked good.

James, however, weakened any advantages he enjoyed in Scotland when he asked the Scottish Parliament to repeal the penal laws against Catholics, but not (at first) those against Presbyterians. Parliament refused, and in 1687 James used his prerogative powers to extend toleration to Catholics. When in June 1688 he also granted indulgence to Presbyterians, it was too late. To make matters worse, James began rearranging parliamentary boroughs in the same way that he had done in England. Still, Scotland remained quiet when William landed in England. James even moved his Scottish troops south to help fend off William—a major mistake, for there went the ultimate source of royal power in Scotland.

James's flight to France in the face of William's invasion left the Royalist party in Scotland in disarray. Many a canny Scottish politician, not wishing to be left out in the cold, hurried to London to make his peace with William. Jacobite power in Scotland was still potentially as great as that of the Williamites, but when William called a Scottish Convention Parliament, the confusion of the Royalists allowed the Whigs and Presbyterians to dominate it. The convention declared that James had *forefaulted* his crown, invited William and Mary to rule jointly, and abolished Episcopalianism in favor of an established Presbyterian church—one shaped by its militants at that.

Seeing this remarkable flow of power to their Whig and Presbyterian opponents, the Scottish Jacobites abandoned Parliament and took up arms against William. Led by John Graham, viscount Dundee, some of the Highland clans rallied to the Stuart cause, partly because of their sense of loyalty to their sworn king, but more significantly because of their hostility to the Campbells (including the new earl of Argyll), who were prominent Whigs. In July 1689, Dundee's Highland host of perhaps three thousand men swept down the slopes of the Pass of Killiecrankie and overwhelmed a royal army. But Dundee himself was killed, and no one else was able to thwart the natural tendency of clansmen to drift back to their glens after a fight. James sent little assistance, though the Highland leaders declared, "We will all dy with our swords in our hands before we fail in our loyaltie and sworn allegiance." At the little town of Dunkeld, the remaining Highlanders were broken by a disciplined force of Covenanters. The clansmen retired to their remote lairs, beaten for the moment, but not reconciled to William's regime.

To subdue the Highlands, William's government took two steps. First, it built a fort in the heart of the Highlands, Fort William. Second, it sought to bribe the clan chiefs into loyalty. The key figure behind this scheme was the unscrupulous Sir John Dalrymple, the master of Stair, who loathed the Highland clans. Stair coupled bribes with a requirement that clan chiefs complete an oath of allegiance to William by January 1, 1692—in the hopes that, if some chief missed the strict deadline, he could punish that clan as an example to all the others. Ideally, the clan so punished would be the Macdonalds of Glencoe, widely thought to be Catholic.

Stair's hopes were realized. MacIan, chief of the Glencoe Macdonalds, came in five days late after slogging through a blizzard. Stair, probably with William's knowledge, then sought to annihilate the Glencoe Macdonalds by a dishonorable plan. A company of troops (Campbells, of course) were sent to Glencoe, where they claimed traditional Highland hospitality. After spending almost two weeks in the homes of the Macdonalds, the troops in February 1692 rose before dawn and slaughtered all of the clan they could lay their hands on—men, women, and children. About forty Macdonalds were butchered, but most escaped, much to the anger of the master of Stair.

In the short run, the massacre of Glencoe helped quell the clans. In the longer run, however, it alienated them from William's government. Beneath their temporarily lawful behavior, many of the clans continued to harbor strong Jacobite feelings. The Revolution Settlement in Scotland remained precarious.

A three-part economic crisis in the 1690s further imperiled the Revolution Settlement. First, William's long-running war against France hindered Scottish commerce. Scottish merchants found themselves cut off from their Continental trading partners while England imposed tariffs on Scottish imports. Second, by the mid-1690s a series of poor harvests brought famine in their wake. "God helpe the poor people, for I never did sie or hear such outcryes for want of meall," wrote one Scot in 1696. As thousands died, discontent with the political status quo increased. Famine relief efforts were hampered by the third factor in the economic crisis: the *Darien fiasco* that swallowed up to one-quarter of Scotland's liquid capital and severely restricted the ability (or will) of wealthier Scots to assist the starving. In 1695 the Scottish Parliament sanctioned a colonizing effort in Darien (modern Panama). Across Scottish society, hopeful investors, ranging from small merchants and local lawyers on up to the very wealthiest of the landed elite, as well as many town councils, sank money into the scheme. William, however, opposed the Darien colony because of his desire to placate the Spanish (who also had claims on the region and with whom he was fighting against France). William refused to allow English forces in North America to assist the Darien colonists, and the colony collapsed in just over a year, at the cost of hundreds of lives and hundreds of thousands of pounds.

Scotland's plunge into economic crisis in the 1690s convinced many among the Scottish elite that the existing relations between England and Scotland could not continue. Many thought Scotland must be completely independent; others, however, believed the only remedy to Scotland's economic woes lay in a parliamentary union. "This nation," one argued, "being poor, and without force to protect its commerce, cannot reap great advantage by it, till it partake of the trade and protection of some powerful neighbour nation."

At the same time, William's difficulties in dealing with two Parliaments were leading him to conclude that he was in an impossible constitutional situation. The Scottish Parliament frequently disagreed with his English ministers. Committed to a long war against France, William and his ministers wanted Scotland simply to supply money and troops; instead, Scotland supplied trouble. Most ominously, in 1696 the Scottish Parliament asserted the right to choose a monarch independently from England should there be no Protestant heir to William. By the time William died in 1702, he had become convinced that the monarchy's relationship with two Parliaments could not continue. On his deathbed he advised his ministers to unite the Parliaments of England and Scotland.

Five years later, in 1707, the Act of Union did just that, as a result of both economic and constitutional issues. Frustrated by English restrictions on Scottish commerce, the Scottish Parliament in 1704 once again declared that it would select its own successor to Queen Anne if Scotland were not granted free trade in England's empire. England, however, was too large and too wealthy to be bullied by Scotland. In 1705, the English Parliament declared that, unless Scotland agreed to negotiate a union and accept the Hanover succession, key Scottish imports—including black cattle, linen, and coal—would be banned, and Scots would be treated as aliens in England (which would limit their rights to any English property they held). These measures struck at Scottish merchants and aristocrats alike. Cut off from English consumers, Scotland's economy faced devastation. Negotiations for a union began. A liberal application of patronage and some outright bribery ensured the passage of the resulting Treaty of Union. The Scottish Parliament voted itself out of existence and the British state into life.

A marriage of convenience rather than affection, the Union united the English and Scottish kingdoms as *Great Britain*. Scotland gave up its separate parliament; instead, sixteen nobles in the House of Lords and forty-five MPs in the House of Commons sat in the *British* Parliament at Westminster. In exchange, the Scots received free trade throughout England and within England's empire, as well as the *Equivalent*, a monetary payment to compensate investors for their losses in the Darien scheme and to encourage Scottish economic development. Scotland's and England's religious establishments and legal systems remained separate, and the Scottish and English peoples retained their separate national identities. As we will see in chapter 5, the Act of Union did not reconcile all Scots to the Revolution Settlement. In both 1715 and 1745, Scottish rebels took up arms in support of the Jacobite cause. Yet a sense of *Britishness* would grow among the peoples of Scotland, Wales, and England over the course of the next century.

## FOREIGN WARS

The events of 1688 and after in Scotland, Ireland, and England played out against the backdrop of a European-wide conflagration between the forces led by William III and the armies of Louis XIV. The war that began for England in 1689 was to last even past William's death in 1702; in fact, it continued (except for a brief respite) until 1713. By the end of this protracted and exhausting struggle, England (by then properly known as Britain) had emerged as a great power in Europe.

In 1688, the League of Augsburg—the Dutch Republic, Spain, Sweden, Savoy, the Holy Roman Empire, and some smaller German states—had gone to war against Louis's vainglorious aggression in 1688; French support for James brought the English into it. Thus, for the English the war was primarily a matter of defending William III and deposing James II, but economic motives also came into play: the expansion of French commercial

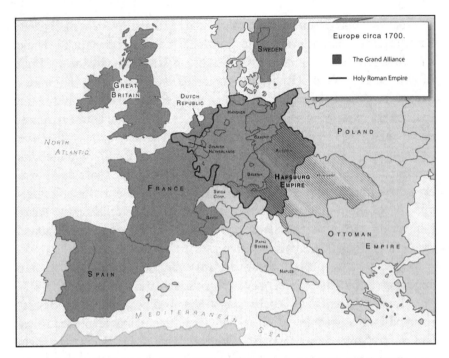

*Europe during the Williamite Wars.* William of Orange died in 1702, but the Williamite Wars continued until 1713. The wars helped establish Britain as one of the great powers of Europe.

strength threatened English trading prospects. William himself was mainly concerned with defending Dutch interests and above all with keeping France out of the Spanish Netherlands (roughly, modern Belgium). "Dutch William" used English resources to subsidize his allies, buy mercenaries, and supplement the Dutch navy with the English. Though he was not a great general, he was an able diplomat. With English cash he kept his Grand Alliance together and put pressure on the French, which helped him to achieve his objectives.

The war soon became one of attrition. After the Dutch and English navies defeated the French fleet at La Hogue (1692), the British Isles were safe from a French invasion. The war, however, continued for another weary five years. The Peace of Ryswick of 1697 resulted in important gains for William and for England: Louis recognized William as king of England, allowed the Dutch to garrison forts in the Spanish Netherlands, and ceded Newfoundland and the Hudson Bay territories to England.

Just four years later, however, the conflict between France and its opponents resumed with the War of the Spanish Succession, touched off by the childlessness of Charles II of Spain. This complex struggle taught the English to think for the first time in terms of supporting a balance of power in Europe. For Louis, to install his dynasty on the Spanish throne would be the culmination of his quest for glory, as well as confirmation of French dominance in Europe. For the Dutch, such an augmentation of French power would spell the end of Dutch independence. For the English, French success would threaten anew to restore the Catholic Stuarts, to do grave damage to English commerce with the Continent, and to end their own hopes of feasting on the Spanish Empire. For all these various reasons, the opponents of France formed another Grand Alliance and went to war when Louis claimed the Spanish throne for his grandson in 1701.

William died in 1702, and his successor, Anne, could not personally lead her armies into battle. Overall direction of the allied war effort thus fell to John Churchill, duke of Marlborough, the greatest soldier in Europe. Immensely charming and good-looking, Marlborough was none too fastidious in furthering his own career by exploiting Queen Anne's fondness for him and his wife Sarah, duchess of Marlborough. For nearly ten years, Marlborough was the effective ruler of England. A supreme strategist and diplomat as well as a great battlefield commander, he succeeded in keeping the Grand Alliance together while leading its armies in another war of attrition against France. Between 1702 and 1709, he directed the allied army to

*Blenheim Palace. Built between 1705 and 1720, this monumental country house (one of the largest in England) was a reward to the Duke of Marlborough for his military victories against France. It became the country seat of the Churchill family; in 1874, Winston Churchill was born in one of its many rooms.*

an unprecedented series of victories in set-piece battles: Blenheim (1704), Ramillies (1706), Oudenarde (1708), and Malplaquet (1709). He was rewarded with the highest honors England could bestow, including his famous house, Blenheim Palace.

Marlborough failed, however, to take advantage of the allies' strong position to settle with France in 1708, and as the war dragged on, Tory opposition grew stronger. To the backwoods Tory gentry, Marlborough's unreasonable demands on the French were unnecessarily prolonging a bloody and expensive war. In 1710, a general election put a Tory peace ministry in office; a year later, Marlborough was dismissed. The Tories succeeded in negotiating the Treaty of Utrecht in 1713, leaving Britain's allies to settle with France as best they could. One such ally, Prince George, elector of Hanover and Queen Anne's heir presumptive, was furious that the British left Hanover and the rest of the Grand Alliance in the lurch. The Whigs, too, condemned the treaty for selling out the war effort.

Nevertheless, the Treaty of Utrecht won real gains for Great Britain. The British recognized Louis's grandson as king of Spain, but on condition that the crowns of France and Spain never be joined. The Spanish Netherlands were divorced from Spain and garrisoned by the Dutch. Further, the British

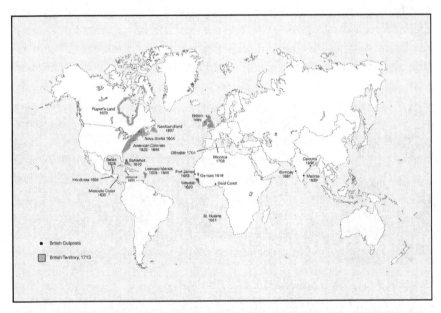

*The British Empire in 1713.* As a result of the Treaty of Utrecht at the end of the Williamite Wars, Britain established its claim to Newfoundland, Nova Scotia, St. Kitts, Gibraltar, and Minorca. More important, however, is what the map does not show: the British won the right to trade in the Spanish Empire, a lucrative prize indeed.

acquired or were confirmed in important colonial holdings: Newfoundland, Nova Scotia, St. Kitts, Gibraltar, and Minorca. Finally, they won the *Asiento*, the right to trade in the Spanish Empire and the symbol of England's displacement of France as the chief predator in the Spanish Empire.

## THE FINANCIAL REVOLUTION

These military and commercial gains were closely intertwined with a set of fiscal innovations so striking that historians call these developments the Financial Revolution. As we noted above, an important part of the Revolution Settlement was parliamentary control of the purse. To pay for the tremendous costs of the wars, William and Anne had to turn to Parliament, which in these years became a unique instrument of financial power. Through Parliament, William and Anne were able, by consent of the social and political elite, to gain access to England's wealth through new taxes. William, for example, levied taxes at a level undreamed of by his predecessors—an annual average more than twice the revenues of James II. The land tax was the key, raising almost one-half of total revenues, a sure sign of the landowners' willingness to pay for their revolution.

Taxes, however, paid for only two-thirds of the cost of war and constituted only one element of the Financial Revolution. To pay for the remaining third of the war's costs, Parliament authorized William to borrow money and, even more importantly, by voting for taxes to pay the interest on the loans, created the concept of the *national debt*. To manage this new and rapidly growing national debt and to help mobilize credit for the government, Parliament formed the Bank of England in 1694. The centerpiece of the Financial Revolution, the bank served a crucial public function in financing the war—and the remarkable century of British imperial and economic expansion that followed. One way that the bank injected credit into the economy was by issuing reliable paper bank notes. Paper money became part and parcel of daily life, and paper credit in the form not only of bank notes but also stock certificates and bonds became an important tool for creating a modern economy. In addition to the Bank of England, the East India Company (1709) and the South Sea Company (1711) were chartered in part to finance the national debt. Financiers and bankers—the "monied men," most of them Whigs—emerged as powerful political interests, who made great profits from this new financial environment. The entire *monied interest* had a stake in continuing the wars and was hated by the Tories (who paid the bulk of the land tax). There can be no doubt, however, that this greedy financial clique played an important role in making England a great power.

## THE HANOVERIAN SUCCESSION, 1714

By the time the Treaty of Utrecht ended war with France in 1713, the English had defended their successful rebellion of 1688, forced a political union on Scotland, developed strong public financial institutions, and become a great power in Europe. Yet nearly a quarter of a century after the revolution, the Revolution Settlement still seemed shaky. Prince George of Hanover, Anne's heir, was distinctly unpopular with the Tories, who in the waning years of Anne's reign began to flirt with the idea of restoring the Stuart dynasty to the throne. To many, James II's son, James Edward, seemed preferable to a German Lutheran. Called "The Old Pretender," James Edward had grown up in France, supported by Louis XIV, who recognized him as King James III of England when his father died in 1701.

Tory Jacobitism had been growing since Anne's accession. Jacobite sentiments fed not only on Tory resentment at the prolonged war, but also on belief in hereditary divine right and the authority of the Established Church. Many Tories still regarded the Stuart dynasty as ordained by God to rule England. They dismissed William's reign as a one-time aberration and believed that the Stuart dynasty—Mary, Anne, and now The Old Pretender—constituted the only legitimate occupants of the throne. Such Tories also tended to dislike what they regarded as the subordination of the Anglican Church to the state and to view the Revolution Settlement's religious toleration as a threat to right religion. They were particularly outraged by *occasional conformity*, a practice that allowed Dissenters to hold municipal and state offices, in violation of the Clarendon Code and the Test Act, provided that they took communion once a year in the established Church. The Tories succeeded in abolishing occasional conformity in 1711, but they recognized that George's Whiggish respect for toleration meant that, if he became king, the practice would resume. Such a prospect horrified these staunch advocates of establishment.

As a result, a number of Tories began conspiring to deny the throne to George and to restore it to James; how many were involved and how far they went are not clear. Robert Harley (earl of Oxford) and Henry St. John (viscount Bolingbroke), the leaders of the Tory ministry that signed the Peace of Utrecht, certainly flirted with Jacobitism. They tried to persuade The Old

Pretender to convert to Anglicanism, which would have solved their central problem, but James did not regard the English throne as worth the price of renouncing his religion. Hence, when Anne died on August 1, 1714, and the Privy Council proclaimed George I king, his accession met no resistance. The installation of the Hanoverian line saved the Revolution Settlement, and England entered a period of remarkable stability, commercial prosperity, and imperial expansion.

## Suggested Reading

Barnett, Corelli, *Marlborough*. London: Eyre Methuen, 1974.

Brown, Keith. *Kingdom or Province? Scotland and the Regal Union, 1603–1715*. New York: St. Martin's Press, 1992.

Childs, John. *The Army, James II, and the Glorious Revolution*. Manchester, UK: Manchester University Press, 1980.

Clark, J. C. D. *English Society, 1688–1832*, 2nd ed. Cambridge: Cambridge University Press, 2000.

Claydon, Tony. *William III and the Godly Revolution*. Cambridge: Cambridge University Press, 2004.

Coward, Barry. *The Stuart Age: England, 1603–1714*, 3rd ed. New York: Pearson, 2003.

DeKrey, Gary. *Restoration and Revolution in Britain: Political Culture in the Era of Charles II and the Glorious Revolution*. London: Palgrave, 2007.

Gray, Tony. *No Surrender! The Siege of Londonderry, 1689*. London: Macdonald and Janes, 1975.

Harris, Tim. *Revolution: The Great Crisis of the British Monarchy: 1685–1720*. London: Allen Lane, 2006.

Holmes, Geoffrey. *The Making of a Great Power: Later Stuart and Early Georgian Britain, 1660–1722*. New York: Longman, 1993.

Hopkins, Paul. *Glencoe and the End of the Highland War*. London: John Donald, 1986.

Jenkins, Geraint H. *The Foundations of Modern Wales, 1642–1780*. New York: Oxford University Press, 1987.

Jones, D. W. *War and Economy in the Age of William and Marlborough*. Oxford: Blackwell, 1988.

Kishlansky, Mark. *A Monarchy Transformed: Britain, 1603–1714*. London: Penguin, 1997.

Levack, Brian. *The Formation of the British State: England, Scotland, and the Union, 1603–1707*. Oxford: Clarendon Press, 1987.

MacInnes, Allan I. *Clanship, Commerce, and the House of Stuart, 1603–1788*. East Linton, UK: Tuckwell Press, 1994.

———. *Union and Empire: The Making of the United Kingdom in 1707*. Cambridge: Cambridge University Press, 2007.

McBride, Ian. *The Siege of Derry in Ulster Protestant Mythology*. Dublin: Four Courts Press, 1997.

Miller, John. *The Glorious Revolution*. London: Longman, 1983.

Moody, T. W., and F. X. Martin, eds. *A New History of Ireland.* Vol. III, *Early Modern Ireland 1534–1691.* Oxford: Oxford University Press, 2009.

O'Gorman, Frank. *The Long Eighteenth Century: British Political and Social History, 1688–1832.* London: Arnold, 1997.

Ohlmeyer, Jane E., ed. *Political Thought in Seventeenth-Century Ireland: Kingdom or Colony.* Cambridge: Cambridge University Press, 2000.

Ormrod, David. *The Rise of Commercial Empires: England and the Netherlands in the Age of Mercantilism, 1650–1770.* Cambridge: Cambridge University Press, 2003.

Pincus, Steven. *1688: The First Modern Revolution.* New Haven, CT: Yale University Press, 2009.

Pocock, J. G. A., ed. *Three British Revolutions: 1641, 1688, 1776.* Princeton, NJ: Princeton University Press, 1980.

Schwoerer, Lois G. *The Declaration of Rights, 1689.* Baltimore: Johns Hopkins University Press, 1981.

Somerset, Anne. *Queen Anne: The Politics of Passion.* London: HarperBooks, 2012.

Sowerby, Scott. *Making Toleration: The Repealers and the Glorious Revolution.* Cambridge, MA: Harvard University Press, 2013.

Speck, W. A. *James II.* London: Longman, 2002.

Speck, W. A. *Reluctant Revolutionaries.* New York: Oxford University Press, 1988.

Stasavage, David. *Public Debt and the Birth of the Democratic State: France and Great Britain, 1688–1789.* Cambridge: Cambridge University Press, 2003.

Szechi, Daniel. *The Jacobites: Britain and Europe, 1688–1788.* Manchester, UK: Manchester University Press, 1994.

Troost, Wout. *William III, the Stad-holder King: A Political Biography*, trans. J. C. Grayson. London: Ashgate, 2005.

Wennerlind, Carl. *Casualties of Credit: The English Financial Revolution, 1620–1720.* Cambridge, MA: Harvard University Press, 2011.

Whatley, Christopher. *The Scots and the Union.* Edinburgh: Edinburgh University Press, 2006.

# Chapter 3

# Society and Economy in Eighteenth-Century England

The rebellion of 1688 and the subsequent Revolution Settlement set the stage for the golden age of the English landlords. Having secured the rule of law (which they wrote and enforced), the rights of property (which they defined and enjoyed), and the power of Parliament (which they monopolized and wielded), the English landed magnates surveyed Britain from a pinnacle of wealth and power. The society over which they ruled seemed one of stability and cohesiveness, whether viewed in terms of the culture, the social order, or the economy. The landed elite's serene domination of the nation resembled Caesar Augustus's rule of the early Roman Empire; hence, eighteenth-century England has long been labeled the *Augustan Age.*

In fact, however, the eighteenth century was a time of contrast and paradox—between the majestic stability of the social hierarchy and the unseemly scramble of people for higher rungs on the social ladder, between the warmth of paternalist social relations and the naked lust for power, between the breathtaking wealth of a few and the heartbreaking poverty of the many, between the rituals of deference given by inferiors to superiors and the startling frequency of riots, and above all between the security of custom on the one hand and the opportunities offered by commercialism on the other. The problem for the historian of eighteenth-century England is not to find "the truth that lies in between" these contrasts, but to see how all of them can have been true at once.

## THE SOCIAL STRUCTURE: AN OPEN HIERARCHY

The key feature of eighteenth-century English society was that it was arranged as a *status hierarchy*, not as a class society. In the sense that a historian or sociologist can assign the people he or she is studying to predetermined pigeonholes called *classes*, then all societies are and have been class societies. But in the historically more important sense of how people actually related to each other and identified themselves in their social order, then eighteenth-century English men and women ordered themselves in a status hierarchy, in terms of vertical rather than horizontal relationships. In other words, individuals formulated their self-identity not through any sense of solidarity with those who shared their economic interests, but rather through their connections with those who stood above and below them in the social order. Each person was thought to have been assigned at birth a position in the natural—indeed, divinely established—social hierarchy. Hence, the social structure was like a ladder, or rather a number of parallel ladders, each rung constituting a status gradation with its own generally accepted duties and privileges. If a person moved up or down the ladder, it was off one rung and onto another; the ladder itself remaining unchanged. Dr. Samuel Johnson, the great wit and man of letters, remarked that the English people were set in their hierarchical places "by the fixed, invariable rules of distinction of rank, which create no jealousy, since they are held to be accidental." Thus, when the English talked about social position, they spoke in terms of degrees, order, and ranks—gradations of social status, not of economic class.

"Mankind," Dr. Johnson observed, "are happier in a state of inequality and subordination." Such was the view unanimously held by those at the top of the hierarchy and ceaselessly preached to those below them. This is not

Mr and Mrs Andrews, *by Thomas Gainsborough (1748). This painting reflects the comfortable self-assurance of the English country gentry in the eighteenth century.*

surprising because the distance in wealth and prestige from top to bottom was enormous. On the highest rung of the hierarchy stood the titled nobility, consisting of fewer than two hundred families. All the nobles were great landlords who dominated their counties in near-majestic splendor. They lived in palatial country homes, often gigantic edifices of close to one hundred rooms, and enjoyed on average £8,000 a year. A few, like the duke of Bedford and the duke of Devonshire, raked in more than £30,000 a year from rentals alone, the equivalent of many millions of dollars today. Just below the nobility came the ranks of the big landlords—baronets, knights, esquires, and gentlemen—more than fifteen thousand families, each enjoying upward of £1,000 a year and each living in a stately country house. Together, these landlords and their families—the nobility and the gentry— amounted to less than 3 percent of the population, but they enjoyed 15 percent of the national income. All also enjoyed the vitally important title of *gentleman*—a position of honor, to be fought for if necessary, that was assigned to the lucky few born into "good" families and displayed by badges of status such as genteel education, graceful deportment, and conspicuous consumption. Gentle status was defined as the ability to live well without working for a living, or, as the novelist Daniel Defoe put it, gentlemen were "such who live on estates, and without the mechanism of employment."

In the countryside, below the gentlemen (and ladies) came those who actually worked the land: freeholders, tenant farmers, and farm laborers. *Freeholders* were owner-occupiers, distinguished from the gentry in that they managed their farms themselves. Freeholders still claimed the traditional label of *yeomen*, but this was a dwindling order. Most farms were worked by tenants, some well-off, others struggling, all leasing land from the landlords for cash. Their access to a tenancy and the terms of their leases were normally set by custom, though some landlords simply rented to the highest bidder. Together, the freeholders and farmers of England numbered about 350,000 families, most earning between £40 and £150 a year. They employed large numbers of farm laborers and domestic servants, who were themselves ranked in distinct hierarchies: butlers, footmen, and hallboys; housekeepers, cooks, chambermaids, and scullery girls; husbandmen, gardeners, stable boys, and milkmaids.

Some of the farm laborers and domestics were hired on a yearly basis and *lived in* the farmer's household. Most worked on a daily or seasonal hiring, having offered their labor for sale at a local market. The latter were the *cottagers*, who rented a cottage and a scrap of land on which to grow vegetables, who usually had customary rights to the use of village commons and waste lands, and who with their wives undertook some craft such as weaving, glove making, or straw plaiting in slack times. In good years, cottagers and their families could scrape together a meager living; in bad years, they had to look to the parish for assistance. The leading statistician of the day made no distinction between cottagers and paupers, four hundred thousand families with an average of only £6 or £7 a year. In rural England, the laborers ranked above only those with no claim on the society at all—vagrants, beggars, thieves, and the like.

The rural laborers formed part of the *laboring poor*, the base of the social hierarchy that comprised almost a quarter of the population. The other segment of the laboring poor lived in the towns. The urban laboring poor, like those in the countryside, were often in need of assistance from the Poor Law (local governmental assistance dating from the Elizabethan era) or private charity; they included vagrants, beggars, criminals, soldiers, sailors, and unskilled male and female workers.

Above the urban laboring poor came the wide range of *the middling sort*, who constituted a dynamic and growing element in English society, amounting to about 15 percent of the English and Welsh population in the early 1700s. The middling sort did not fit neatly into the traditional social hierarchy. At the lower end of the middling scale stood artisans, shopkeepers, tradesmen, and their families, earning perhaps £50 a year. Artisans had their own hierarchies—apprentices, journeymen, and masters—most of whom were male, though women sometimes did become apprentices and learn the trades. Some master artisans owned their own shops and employed apprentices and journeymen. The *London Tradesman* in 1747 listed more than 350 different crafts and trades, not only butchers, bakers, and candlestick makers, but also jewelers, goldsmiths, shipwrights, carpenters, shoemakers, saddlers, harness makers, tailors, lace makers, weavers, cutlers, printers, chain makers, spurriers, gunsmiths, hatters, clockmakers, and all the rest of a world of manufacturing now largely gone.

Above the artisans and shopkeepers in income and standard of living were the merchants and professional people. Rich businessmen could earn anything from hundreds to thousands of pounds a year. Professional men (women could not enter any of the professions until the late nineteenth century) earned a wide range of incomes and improved their status throughout the century. There were only five recognized professions: law, the Church, medicine, the army, and the navy (officer ranks, of course). At the beginning of the century, professional men were regarded, like tradesmen and merchants, as overly ambitious and therefore not genteel. By the end of the century, however, they had gained considerable respectability and were even thought of as satellites of the landed orders.

Eighteenth-century society, then, was a finely graded hierarchy in which status distinctions were carefully defined, observed, and protected. Yet England was not a caste society. Although there was little movement at the top level, the *titled aristocracy*, none of the rungs on the social ladder was legally closed to outsiders. Landowners enjoyed privileges, but the privileges defined by the law were surprisingly few: the titled nobility sat in the House of Lords and were entitled to trial by their peers; otherwise, nobility and gentry were subject to the same body of law as everyone else and theoretically opened their ranks to newcomers.

These concessions composed the social price that the landowners paid for the preeminence they won in 1688. In eighteenth-century England, property determined status, and property could be purchased. In medieval society, property followed status, but this rule had now been reversed. It was possible for a person to acquire a fortune, buy property, and move up to the appropriate rung on the social ladder. At the same time, it was possible for a family to squander its fortune and its estates and thus to find itself reduced in status. Rich businessmen tried to marry daughters of the gentry to acquire status; younger sons of landed families often had to marry mercantile wealth or to find positions in the professions. In sum, there were opportunities for social mobility, up and down, in eighteenth-century England.

There was also an often unseemly scramble as people jostled for positions in the social hierarchy. Barons sought to become earls, squires to become knights, farmers to become squires, merchants to become gentlemen, and shopkeepers to become merchants. Money was the key, and Englishmen impressed foreigners with their love of money. The most significant aspect of the upward scramble was for wealthy merchants and financiers to buy estates and so cross the all-important line into gentle status. The society was full of men who had achieved privileged status, such as Sir George Dashwood, a London brewer; Sir Josiah Child, a banker; and Sir George Wombwell, a merchant of the East India Company. The most famous example was Thomas ("Diamond") Pitt, the son of an Anglican clergyman who became a sea captain, an *interloper* in the trade of the East India Company (interlopers violated a trading company's monopoly on commercial transactions), and finally a merchant and governor in the Company itself. A poacher turned gamekeeper. Pitt made so much money in the Indian trade that he was eventually able to buy more than ten estates in England and set himself up as a member of Parliament. (He also brought home from India a diamond of 410 carats, which he later sold for £135,000.) Such businessmen usually lacked the social graces to be fully accepted by landed society, but one or two generations later the family passed as the genuine article. As Defoe put it, "After a generation or two, the tradesmen's children, or at least their grandchildren, come to be as good gentlemen, statesmen, parliament men . . . bishops and noblemen as those of the highest and most ancient families."

The upward and downward flow of people did not destroy the status hierarchy, but rather preserved it. Each person and family assumed the style, the duties, and the privileges of their new position as they moved up the rungs. Limited social mobility thus provided a safety valve for the economic dynamism of the country. It marked off England as very different from Wales, Ireland, and even Scotland, where the social hierarchies were comparatively frozen. In England, as long as everyone recognized and accepted the hierarchy itself and behaved according to the prescribed forms and standards at each level, then the structure itself was stable.

## SOCIAL RELATIONS: PROPERTY, PATRONAGE, AND DEFERENCE

Property was one of the pillars of eighteenth-century society because it provided a person or family with the means of survival, because it formed the basis of power, and most of all because it determined social status. "The great and chief end . . . of men uniting into commonwealths, and putting themselves under government," John Locke had written, "is the preservation of their property." The central features of social relationships were closely related to property: *patronage* and *deference*. Property enabled a person to disburse patronage—gifts, jobs, appointments, contracts, favors—and the ability to act as a patron was the crucial measure of property and status. To be a great man or lady was to be able to dispense patronage to clients, called in that day one's *friends* or *interest*. From the recipient's point of view, to have a niche in life—a means of survival and advancement—required being within the circle of some patron's friends. According to essayist Joseph Addison, "To an honest mind the best perquisites of place are the advantages it gives a man of doing good"; by "doing good" he meant being helpful to one's friends.

In eighteenth-century England patronage played the role that merit and achievement play in modern democratic societies. Almost all government offices, clerical (that is, church) appointments, tenancies on landed estates, jobs for laborers, apprenticeships for boys, commissions for artists and architects, assignments for writers, military and naval posts, and the vast array of positions in domestic service were distributed by patronage. No one took entrance or civil service exams or had to show certificates of qualification. Furthermore, few looked on patronage as corruption, for it was simply the way that the political, economic, and social systems worked. Nor did English men and women believe that seeking help from a patron was degrading or that receiving such help was unfair. As Sir Robert Walpole, great landowner and politician, declared, "nothing was more reasonable, or more just" than the use of a man's position "to serve his friends and relations."

In return for their patronage, patrons demanded deference, which included postures of gratitude, loyalty, service, and obedience. If a man felt entitled to claim assistance from his superior, he also felt it right to defer to that patron's opinions and wishes. Laborers were expected to move aside and pull their forelocks when the landlord or members of his family rode by, tenant farmers to vote the way the landowner wished, sons and daughters to defer to their parents, artists to render their patrons (or even their patrons' prize animals) beautiful in portraits, and clergymen to preach on the lines preferred by their patrons. Deference was not regarded as servile, but as honorable. As one late seventeenth-century guide for husbandmen put it, "A just fear and respect he must have for his landlord, or the gentleman his neighbour, because God hath placed them above him, and he hath learnt [in the Fifth Commandment] that by the father he ought to honour is meant all his superiors."

There were plenty of occasions, as we will see, when deference broke down in the eighteenth century, for people, even the common folk, also had a strong sense of traditional rights and privileges, and sometimes this sense of rights clashed with that of obligations. Nevertheless, patronage and deference, more than force, held the society together. Face-to-face relationships up and down the social hierarchy connected people to each other. These personal relationships were not, however, necessarily loving or friendly. The patron could be unfair or abusive, and the connection between patron and client was always unequal. Exploitation, then, was an inevitable feature of such an inegalitarian society.

The face-to-face relationships could exist only because the "scale of life," as Professor Harold Perkin called it, was small. As late as 1760, 75 to 80 percent of the 6.5 million people in England lived in villages or small towns. It remained true that few people outside the elite ever traveled beyond the parish or the nearest market town. Few people ever saw more than several hundred others gathered at one time—church services, markets, fairs, and traditional celebrations at the manor house being the main occasions. Each of these moments reinforced the local community. In rural England, everyone knew everyone else. Even the units of production were small. The greatest noble households may have numbered a hundred servants and laborers, but most farm households were much smaller. Even in the towns, most work was done in households by the master or journeyman, his wife and family, and his apprentices and laborers. A large shop consisted of fifteen to twenty people. Peter Laslett wrote: "Time was when the whole of life went forward in the family, in a circle of loved, familiar faces, known and fondled objects all to human size."[1] This observation perhaps sentimentalizes the small scale of life, but it highlights the very different quality of human relationships in preindustrial England from those in the modern world.

## LAND, MARRIAGE, PATRIARCHY, AND THE FAMILY

Landed property was the foundation of the social hierarchy. Land produced much of the nation's wealth and gave employment to most of the laboring force. Land was the source of prestige and therefore the key to status. To own an estate placed a man at the top of the social ladder and gave him political power. But the size of estates grew throughout the century, and the number of estates was small; hence, land was expensive and increasingly so during the eighteenth century. Two features of the society followed from these facts: (1) there was severe competition among the wealthy to buy (or to add to) estates and (2) the object of all landowners was to keep their estates intact.

The landowners used several devices for these purposes. The first was the principle of *primogeniture*, or inheritance of the property by the eldest son. Younger sons and daughters might be given a lump sum of money or an annuity, but the estate as a whole passed to the eldest son, or in the absence of a son, to the designated heir. Landowners did everything possible to avoid and prevent sale of an estate or parts of it. Primogeniture was largely a matter of custom and operated in law only when a property owner died without a will, which no competent landowner would ever allow to happen. Hence, the most important device for ensuring the passage of an estate intact was the *strict settlement*. These settlements, wills carefully drawn up and defended by the law, provided that each inheritor got the land under

---

[1]Laslett, *The World We Have Lost*, 21.

severe restriction: he must not alienate (sell) any of it; it was thus *entailed*. By the principle of entailment, therefore, strict settlements turned the owner of an estate into a sort of life tenant. A squire might settle his land on his son, but on legal condition that the son in turn pass the estate to the grandson. And the son, by powerful social custom, resettled the estate on his son by making the same sort of will, and so on down the generations.

This desire to keep estates intact had heavy consequences for other sons in the family and for all daughters. Because only the eldest son would inherit, different means of support had to be found for all the other offspring. Here is where patronage came into play. With proper connections, younger sons could be sent into *the professions*—the law, Church, army, navy, or medicine. Entry into business was much less favored because work of a self-interested sort was thought to be tainted by trade and therefore to some degree dishonorable and thus ungentlemanly. But no landlord opposed money itself; the typical landlord would be delighted if his sons married wealthy heiresses, regardless of the source of their fortunes. Marriage to a rich banker's or merchant's daughter might provide a financial base for a second or third son to launch an effort to buy an estate. The flow downward of non-inheriting sons into the professions and upward of mercantile daughters into landed society helped bond landed and commercial wealth.

Daughters were a major problem for landowning families. Women could own landed property—and a significant number (mainly widows) did—but the custom in landed families was to keep the estates in men's hands. Thus, to find and secure suitable marriages for their daughters was a matter of ceaseless calculating and campaigning for the landowner and his wife. To make her attractive on the marriage market, a landowner customarily bestowed a dowry on his daughter at the time of her marriage. These dowries might amount to thousands of pounds, and everyone thought it perfectly proper if the prospective groom (or rather his family) bargained to get the dowry increased. Thus, having a bevy of daughters was a serious drain on a family's resources and was regarded by most landlords as at best a mixed blessing.

These circumstances made marriage arrangements within the landowning orders a matter of delicate negotiations and bargaining between families, not unlike diplomatic negotiations between countries. Family fortunes and the status of the lineage were at stake, so parents played a major role in choosing partners for their children. The precise weight assumed by parental opinion varied from family to family, depending on the particular

Marriage à-la-Mode, *by William Hogarth (1743). Here the great satirical English painter depicts mercenary negotiations held by the heads of two wealthy families and their lawyers while the prospective bride and groom wait, unconsulted, at the side.*

mix of personalities involved. Moreover, the balance between parental choice and the young person's preference was shifting during the century, as individualism, reason, and eventually romantic sensibility grew in cultural importance. As the decades passed, young people expected to play a bigger role in their own matchmaking and the parents a lesser role. In the seventeenth century, the parents largely arranged the marriages; in the eighteenth century, their role slowly moved toward one of exercising a veto over their children's choices.

Nowhere are these familial tensions better illustrated than in Henry Fielding's great comic novel, *Tom Jones.* In it, the dashing, handsome Tom and the lovely, maidenly Sophia Western love each other. Alas, Tom is illegitimate and thus an unsuitable match for Sophia, whose aunt expresses to her the traditional view:

> So far, madam, from your being concerned alone [in your marriage], your concern is the least, or surely the least important. It is the honor of your family which is concerned in this alliance; you are only the instrument. . . . The alliance between the families is the principal matter.

But Mr. Allworthy, Tom's excellent guardian, has a more modern view: young people should marry if they love one another, provided that their families are consulted and have the right of refusal. This is also Sophia's position and clearly that of Fielding: Sophia vows never to marry without her father's consent, but she also refuses to marry *his* choice (in this case, the sniveling Mr. Blifil) because she does not love him.

Such issues reached to the heart of marriage and family life themselves. What was the nature of the relationship between husband and wife, or between parents and children, in eighteenth-century England? The surviving evidence sheds most light on the families of the landowners and the well-to-do people of the middling sorts. English law was clear: upon marriage, the wife lost legal personhood. As the famous legal philosopher Sir William Blackstone put it, "In marriage husband and wife are one person and that person is the husband." The wife did not own property or sign contracts; she could not sue or be sued; she could not serve on juries. In the gentry and aristocracy, a woman was supposed to be under the care (and the control) of a man all her life: first her father, then her husband.

But here, too, actual behavior was changing. Family life, like the social structure itself, had long been authoritarian and patriarchal. In the seventeenth century, Puritanism had accentuated patriarchal control in the family and had intensified the parental desire to subordinate the will of the children to their own, as well as to close the nuclear family to the claims of the lineage as a whole. That peculiar Puritan intensity tended to diminish during the eighteenth century. The reasonableness and tolerance advocated in late seventeenth- and early eighteenth-century thought mitigated some of the harsh intensity of the Puritan-style family and led to more companionable relations between husbands and wives, as well as to more affectionate concern by parents for their children. For this reason, toys and children's books emphasizing fun and pleasure became important consumer items for the first time in the eighteenth century. Of course, not all English families were warm and affectionate. Among the wealthiest landed families, the great fortunes still allowed parents to neglect their children. In the eighteenth century, the English custom emerged of sending the children away to school as early as possible. For example, Robert Walpole, who was later to become prime minister, was sent away at age six to boarding schools and later to Cambridge; he returned only at age twenty-two, rarely having spent more than a few weeks at home.

At the other end of the social scale, poverty ensured that parental attitudes toward children varied widely, with the harsh struggle for survival sometimes sapping family affections. Young men and women among the lowest levels of the laboring poor could marry without fearing that their parents would punish them through disinheritance (because there was no property to be inherited), but they also found all too often that they could not feed all the children they produced. Although marriage among the laboring poor did not entail the diplomatic negotiations characteristic of the rich, it was nevertheless a calculated decision. Within the ranks of the laboring poor, marriage was preeminently a practical matter. Most work in eighteenth-century England went on in households, and the family functioned as an economic unit. "Dogged determination," as one historian has called it, often characterized the relationship of husband and wife. Divorce, legally possible only by private act of Parliament, was available only to the ruling elite, but the practice of *wife sale*, a ritualized form of ending a marriage in which a man took his wife to a fair and sold her by prearrangement, sometimes occurred in rural areas. Desertion was appallingly common.

The decision of a couple to marry depended on their ability to set up a household and make a living. The number of opportunities to do so was growing slowly, but the society was relatively stingy in the niches it made available. Young men had to finish apprenticeships or wait for a cottage or tenancy to open up; young women often had to spend time in domestic service or as a farm girl. Thus, the average age at marriage was relatively high—about twenty-seven years for men and twenty-five for women—and marriages lasted for a comparatively short time. On average, each couple had five children, but only three survived to age twenty. Large families were rare, and extended families (with more than one generation of adults living together under the same roof) were even more unusual.

Life was difficult and brief, and death and pain were constant presences. No census was taken until 1801, but surviving records make it clear that life expectancy was short, perhaps thirty-five years. Medical care that helped rather than harmed its recipients was practically nonexistent. Neither villages nor cities had any sewerage system except open gutters; refuse was dumped into the streets to rot and pollute water supplies. The stench was staggering and the health hazards grim. Diseases such as smallpox, typhus, and influenza repeatedly swept through the population. The poor had no defenses against the cold and damp of winter. One physician watched the poor in his district die from an epidemic in 1727: "Nor did any other method which art could afford relieve them; insomuch that many of the little country towns and villages were almost stripped of their poor people." Women frequently died while giving birth, and infant mortality was especially high:

about one-fifth of all babies died before they were one year old. Children in both rural and urban households were put to work very early, perhaps at six or seven years, scaring crows and picking rocks from the fields or helping with carding and spinning. Boys and girls between eleven and fourteen years old received training by formal and informal apprenticeship in the work that would occupy them the rest of their lives.

## THE COMMERCIAL REVOLUTION

At the start of the eighteenth century, agriculture remained the largest industry in England: the income of landlords and tenants alone composed half of the national income, and farming directly or indirectly employed more than half of the English people. Commerce, however, composed the real growth sector of the English economy. Dr. Johnson observed: "There never was from earliest ages a time in which trade so much engaged the attention of mankind, or commercial gain was sought with such general emulation." This was an age of *commercial capitalism*, for capitalist practices (investment of money in commercial enterprises for the purpose of increasing profits) had emerged in the 1600s, a century before industrialization began. The middling sort provided a substantial number of men with the commercial skills to direct the expansion of trade and take the necessary risks. As the historian Roy Porter wrote, "England teemed with practical men of enterprise, weather-eye open, from tycoons to humble master craftsmen."[2]

The state did not plan or direct the economy; individual initiative rather than government fiat established the mercantile houses, banks, shipping firms, turnpike trusts, woolens companies, and countless shops that sprung up across the country. The state did, however, play an active role in English commercial expansion: it responded to the needs of powerful commercial interests by protecting domestic manufacturing with tariffs and other regulations, promoting and securing foreign trade (by war if necessary), chartering exclusive commercial and financial companies, and avoiding both the heavy taxation and the internal tariffs that would have dampened trade.

Commercial expansion both generated and was generated by domestic consumption and foreign trade. England enjoyed what has been called a *consumer revolution* during the eighteenth century. Landlords, tenant farmers, and people of the middling sort all indulged their desire for luxury,

---

[2]Porter, *English Society in the Eighteenth Century*, 95.

fashion, and convenience by consuming goods of all kinds. Shops providing consumer goods sprang up in even the small cities and towns. Not only did the landlords build, reconstruct, and redecorate their great houses with marvelous furniture and objects of art, but also professional and other middling sorts with less ostentatious wealth enjoyed consumer products such as textiles, tablecloths, china services, pottery, cutlery, ceramics, prints, books, and newspapers to a degree that was entirely new in any European society. Refinement of manners usually accompanied the goods. Some aristocrats became anxious about the consumer pretensions of their social inferiors, and many traditional moralists denounced society's growing taste for luxury. But the desire for consumer goods could not be quashed, for the intent of the landlords to impress each other and overawe those below them in the hierarchy only inspired the desire among the less wealthy to emulate them.

Foreign trade continued to grow in all its branches—exports, imports, and reexports. The new trades, such as the importing and reexporting of tobacco, sugar, linens, calicoes, and slaves, grew steadily relative to the old staple export, finished woolens. The basic pattern of English trade was shifting, for although the proportion of English imports from northern Europe still stood at over 30 percent in 1750, the English gradually imported less from Europe and more from the East Indies, the West Indies, and North America. Similarly, exports and reexports to Europe (especially to Spain and Portugal) remained of great importance, but shipping to North America and the East Indies won a larger share. Overall, English overseas trade doubled between 1700 and 1760, accelerating from a growth rate of about 1 percent a year in 1700 to 2 percent a year in 1760—a remarkable performance for a preindustrial society. This foreign trade, as well as the coastal trade in coal and foodstuffs, made shipping a formidable business. In the 1740s, for instance, more than two hundred ships (most of them English) worked the tobacco trade alone. Because of the Navigation Acts, more than 80 percent of all ships calling at British ports were British owned; British shipping tonnage more than doubled between 1700 and 1770.

London continued to be the largest port by far and to grow in size—to more than seven hundred thousand people in 1760, probably a quarter of whom worked in the port trades. London's insatiable consumer demand drew in goods from most of the British Isles: cattle from Wales and Scotland; fruits and vegetables from the Thames Valley and the West Country; grains from the Midlands and East Anglia; coal from Newcastle; and iron from Sussex, the western Midlands, and eastern Wales. Yet London's *share* of England's expanding trade declined as provincial wealth grew. The new trades also stimulated the expansion of other cities, Liverpool, Bristol, and Glasgow in particular. Liverpool, the center of the slave trade, grew from about five thousand people in 1700 to thirty thousand in 1750. London, then, should be seen as the hub of an internal market that incorporated most of the regions of England, as well as parts of Ireland, Wales, and Scotland. London's financial institutions grew in size and number, as ambitious entrepreneurs scrambled to service and profit from England's soaring national debt. A craze for joint-stock companies and speculation in their stock soared until 1720, when the South Sea Company's inflated stock collapsed. Thereafter, laws severely restricted joint-stock company foundation, but the commercial sector found its own ways of raising capital and facilitating transactions, as private merchants and attorneys in growing numbers performed banking functions. In addition, the formation of private turnpike trusts began to improve England's notoriously poor roads by financing their construction and maintenance through tolls. Water transport—slower but cheaper than road haulage—improved as well, again by private efforts that added to the mileage of navigable rivers and began in the 1750s to construct a system of canals.

To get a sense of commercial development in the first half of the century, one can look at the example of Abraham Dent, who ran a general store in the small town of Kirkby-Stephen in Westmorland. In the 1750s and 1760s, Dent sold a remarkable variety of items to customers from the town and nearby villages: tea, sugar, wine, beer, cider, barley, soap, candles, tobacco, lemons, vinegar, silk, cottons, woolens, needles, pins, books, magazines, paper, ink, and a great many other goods as well. His supplies came from a surprisingly wide area, including Halifax, Leeds, and Manchester in the North; Newcastle in the Northeast; Coventry in the Midlands; and Norwich and London in the East. He financed his operation in a sophisticated way: by handling bills of exchange (versions of our modern-day checks) and by extending credit to his customers and receiving it from his suppliers. He bought stockings knitted locally for retail to his customers and soon was having thousands made on order. Increasingly, then, he became a small capitalist, ordering goods made to sell to large-scale buyers, usually wholesalers in London. Almost inevitably, as he dealt in more complex financial transactions, Dent became a banker. Not all shopkeepers were as successful as Abraham Dent, but his case illustrates the integration of the market economy and the growing connections between commerce and industry.

## MANUFACTURING BEFORE THE INDUSTRIAL REVOLUTION

As commerce flourished and the average Englishman's love of cash and profits intensified, entrepreneurs looked for more efficient ways to produce the goods that English consumers wanted. The eighteenth century was the heyday of the *domestic* or *putting-out* system. By this system, manufacturing remained decentralized, located in the cottages of hundreds of villages and small towns. It was not yet mechanized, as it would become during industrialization, but it was highly commercialized. An individual capitalist, often a merchant like Abraham Dent, bought raw materials and supplied them to the village craftspersons or to farm families, paying each a piece rate (a set amount per piece) for his or her work in finishing the product; then the capitalist collected and sold the product himself. Such was the mode of production in woolens, the metal trades, nailmaking, watchmaking, leather goods, and many others. Throughout the English countryside, many farm families supplemented their incomes by doing one of the steps in the production process. Other families found that poor soil in their locality or the increasing demand for textiles or other manufactured goods drew them, and their whole villages, into full-time manufacturing. In these areas, such as the Northwest or the Pennines, the laborers left their work to help in the fields only at harvest time. This system was of great advantage to the capitalist, whose investment was limited to raw materials. Further, when demand declined, the supplier reduced production simply by laying off workers; none of his own machines or tools stood idle. Finally, the system left problems of labor relations and work discipline to the laborers themselves.

The domestic system provided no golden age for its laborers, however. True, the nailers, weavers, and other craftsmen and craftswomen worked in their own cottages, alongside their families, and usually on machines they had purchased themselves. In many instances, there was a strong pride in independence that was later to be remembered with powerful longing. Many, however, went into debt to buy their looms or other tools and in effect had nothing to sell but their labor. The domestic workers were able to control the rhythm of labor themselves—typically slow early in the week and rapid toward the end—but they worked very long hours and were subject to abrupt layoffs as the market demanded. Many habitually were indebted to the master; in other words, although the domestic worker may have been an independent artisan, he (or she) had to struggle to maintain that independence. Most domestic workers depended as heavily on the merchant capitalist as the tenant or farm laborer depended on the landlord.

In much domestic industry, women worked alongside their husbands, whether in preparing the raw materials or in polishing or waxing the finished products. Artisanal households were different: although male craftsmen such as shoemakers and carpenters needed their wives to produce income, they liked to keep their shops separate from the homes and to keep women out of them. Theirs was a culture of male solidarity born during their years of preparing as apprentices and journeymen and maintained by male bonding in alehouses and in craft guilds. In such families, wives generally were relegated to traditionally female occupations such as needlework, laundry work, and street selling.

Work, however, was unrelenting for all because the family economy required each member to contribute. Employment was seasonal and casual for most people, pay for women amounted to only about half that for men, and life was too precarious to enable any but the very lucky to accrue savings. Thus, a slump in demand, a poor harvest, or the death of a husband usually threw families onto the meager mercy of the Poor Law. A product of paternalism, the Poor Law dated to 1662. By this statute, every pauper in England had a right to economic assistance from his or her parish of birth or residence. Funded by *ratepayers* (those who paid the local property tax), this assistance could come either through admission to a poorhouse or in the form of *outdoor relief* (money, food, or clothing given to a person outside a workhouse). About 20 percent of the population was in receipt of poor relief at any one time, the great majority of them women and children.

## THE CHANGING AGRICULTURAL ORDER

The bustling aggressiveness of England's towns and commercial economy may at first seem to contrast sharply with the stately calm of English agriculture. Yet in the countryside, too, commercialism was rapidly transforming not only the techniques of production but also the relationships between people. Like a fast-running stream carving its way down a hillside, so commercialism eroded the seemingly timeless features of the English countryside.

English agriculture had been changing at least since the sixteenth century as estates were integrated into the market economy. Landlords enjoyed luxurious consumption and the requisite making of money just as much as the merchant or banker, and they increasingly saw agricultural innovation as the way to earn the money necessary for the Augustan style of life. Highly responsive to the needs of landlords, Parliament after 1688 put no obstacles in the path of increased farm profits. It clarified the rights of private property, paid a bounty for the export of grain until 1750, and most important of all, facilitated the process of *enclosure*.

At its core, enclosure constituted a massive reorganization of landholding and an overwhelming attack against the traditional agricultural order. Four features characterized this traditional order: (1) the three-field or open-field system, (2) cooperative management, (3) common rights, and (4) relatively low yields. Traditional estates normally included a manor house and one or more villages, surrounded by several kinds of fields, including the home farm, near the manor house, farmed directly by the landlord's steward; the large unfenced (open) fields divided into strips; and the common land (the *commons* or *wastes*). Each of the large fields was allowed to lie fallow every third year so that it could restore itself naturally; therefore, an estate typically had one-third of the fields in wheat, one-third in barley, and one-third in natural grasses. Small owners and tenant farmers held strips in each—the number depending on the size of the ownership or tenancy—and with hired laborers went out daily from the village to work their strips. Because not all small owners and tenants could afford an expensive plow team, plowing usually had to be cooperative, as did certain seasonal activities such as haymaking and harvesting. Moreover, by custom, tenants and cottagers had certain rights to the common land: to pick up fallen branches or to cut peat for fuel, to turn a few pigs and geese onto the common to forage, to graze cows and sheep, or to dig clay for making bricks. Such rights often shifted the balance from starvation to survival for cottagers and their families. The traditional system as a whole, however, was inefficient. Not only did millions of acres lie fallow each year, but also tenants and laborers had to slog long distances from strip to strip. One Buckinghamshire farmer, for example, held two and a half acres, which were divided into twenty-four strips scattered among different fields.

Beginning in some areas as early as the sixteenth century, profit-oriented and efficiency-minded landlords sought to dismantle this traditional agricultural order through enclosure—consolidating and fencing open fields and common land, as well as bringing wastes (woods, bogs, fens, and the like) under cultivation or pasturage. Parishes with only a small number of owners could often agree to end open-field farming, but where there was opposition to enclosing the land, the proponents of enclosure had to resort to private acts of Parliament. All it took, however, was for the owners of a substantial majority of the acreage in the parish—often

The Warrener, *by George Morland. In this drawing we have a glimpse of the rural laboring poor—in this case a rabbit hunter and his family.*

a small minority of the owners concerned—to petition Parliament for an enclosure act. Parliament routinely passed these acts, usually with no real opportunity for opposition. An enclosure act nullified all existing leases and customary arrangements in the parish and named several commissioners (usually agents of the big owners) to survey the land and to divide it up as compact farms among proprietors with *documented* claims. Proprietors were then required to erect fences or hedges around their new properties.

Enclosure thus created the emblematic and aesthetically pleasing English rural landscape with its neat, compact farms demarcated by well-tended hedges and stone fences. Its social impact was far more ambivalent. Large landowners benefited greatly. Enclosed farms were more efficient than open-field property. Rents went up by about 13 percent overall; thus, expensive as it was, enclosure probably brought big proprietors a return of 20 percent or more on their investment. It liberated the agricultural entrepreneur from the restrictions of tradition and contributed to the aggregate increase of agricultural output and income during the eighteenth century.

Not everyone, however, shared in the profits. Small owners generally had a much harder time than did the large landowners. Although a few of the more aggressive small owners seized the opportunity to farm more efficiently, most had to mortgage their land to pay their share of enclosure costs, and many ended up selling out to their rich neighbors. Many thousands of small owner-occupiers, as well as small tenant farmers, were reduced to day laborer status.

Many cottagers, moreover, could not document their claims to use common land; they had only a customary right and so they received nothing. Not only did they find that enclosure prevented them from tilling particular plots of land that they and their ancestors had worked from time immemorial, but also they lost the communal arrangements of the open-field system and the cherished use rights to common and waste land. The abolition of the commons destroyed one of the main sources of independence for the small holder or cottager. As one observer said in 1780, "Strip the small farms of the benefit of the commons, and they are all at one stroke leveled to the ground." A clergyman in Berkshire said that by enclosure "an amazing number of people have been reduced from a comfortable state of partial independence to the precarious condition of mere hirelings."

Enclosure accelerated the tendency in English agriculture toward concentration of ownership into a relatively few hands, with the actual work of farming being done by substantial tenants who hired landless laborers on a wage basis. Put more abstractly, enclosure stands as the symbol of the gains and losses that occurred as the *cash nexus*—the depersonalized connection between boss and worker—elevated cash and contract over custom and personal relations. In traditional English society, everyone except the very poorest had a place in the hierarchical social order, with privileges and duties attached. Face-to-face relations meant that most people lived their lives amid known, although certainly not always loved, faces. Paternalism was often abused, but its claims were not easily ignored, and it ensured that members of the elite felt a personal responsibility for those within their circle of clients and dependents. Custom was stultifying for the ambitious man, as it was for many women, but it taught rich and poor, landlord and tenant, farmer and laborer, journeyman and apprentice what their rights and responsibilities were.

During the eighteenth century, however, commercial attitudes slowly altered all these features of an earlier way of life. The commercialization of

English life was not uniform in its effects in every place or in every set of relationships, nor was the transition complete by the end of the century. Nevertheless, the desire for profit and for maximizing the return from every parcel of property unceasingly worked to shift the basis of relationships from customary arrangements to contractual bargains. For some, this shift meant liberation; for others, it was misery. But whether liberating or immiserating, the shift from an old to a new kind of society, from one based on custom to one based on contract, stands out as the main trend in the social history of eighteenth-century England.

## Suggested Reading

Ashton, T. S. *An Economic History of England: The Eighteenth Century*. London: Methuen, 1966.

Beckett, J. V. *The Aristocracy in England, 1600–1914*. Oxford: Blackwell, 1986.

Berg, Maxine. *The Age of Manufactures: Industry, Innovation and Work in Britain 1700–1820*. Totowa, NJ: Barnes & Noble, 1985.

Brewer, John, Neil McKendrick, and J. H. Plumb. *The Birth of a Consumer Society: The Commercialization of Eighteenth-Century England*. Bloomington: Indiana University Press, 1982.

Cannon, John. *Aristocratic Century: The Peerage of Eighteenth-Century England*. Cambridge: Cambridge University Press, 1984.

Cockayne, Emily. *Hubbub: Filth, Noise, and Stench in England*. New Haven, CT: Yale University Press, 2007.

Earle, Peter. *The Making of the English Middle Class: Business, Society, and Family Life in London, 1660–1730*. Berkeley: University of California Press, 1989.

Fletcher, Anthony. *Gender, Sex, and Subordination in England 1500–1800*. New Haven, CT: Yale University Press, 1996.

Hay, Douglas, and Nicholas Rogers. *Eighteenth-Century English Society*. New York: Oxford University Press, 1997.

Hill, Bridget. *Women, Work, and Sexual Politics in Eighteenth-Century England*. Montreal: McGill-Queen's University Press, 1994.

Hoskins, W. G. *The Midland Peasant*. London: Macmillan, 1957.

Hunt, Margaret R. *The Middling Sort: Commerce, Gender, and the Family in England, 1680–1780*. Berkeley: University of California Press, 1996.

Langford, Paul. *A Polite and Commercial People: England, 1727–1783*. New York: Oxford University Press, 1989.

Laslett, Peter. *The World We Have Lost*. New York: Scribner's, 1965.

Laurence, Anne. *Women in England, 1500–1760*. New York: St. Martin's Press, 1994.

Malcolmson, Robert W. *Life and Labour in England, 1700–1780*. New York: St. Martin's Press, 1981.

Mingay, G. E. *English Landed Society in the Eighteenth Century*. London: Routledge & Kegan Paul, 1963.

————. *The Gentry*. London: Longman, 1976.

Neeson, J. M. *Commoners: Common Right, Enclosure and Social Change in England, 1700–1820*. Cambridge: Cambridge University Press, 1996.

Olsten, Kirsten. *Daily Life in Eighteenth-Century England*. London: The Greenwood Press, 1999.

Perkin, Harold. *Origins of Modern English Society, 1780–1880*. Toronto: University of Toronto Press, 1969.

Porter, Roy. *English Society in the Eighteenth Century*. London: Allen Lane, 1983.

Rule, John. *Albion's People: English Society, 1714–1815*. New York: Longman, 1992.

Sharpe, J. A. *Early Modern England: A Social History 1550–1760*. Baltimore: Edward Arnold, 1987.

Shoemaker, Robert B. *Gender in English Society, 1650–1850: The Emergence of the Separate Spheres?* London: Longman: 1998.

————. *The London Mob: Violence and Disorder in Eighteenth-Century England*. London: Continuum, 2004.

Smail, John. *The Origins of Middle-Class Culture: Halifax, Yorkshire, 1660–1780*. Ithaca, NY: Cornell University Press, 1994.

Snell, K. D. M. *Annals of the Labouring Poor: Social Change and Agrarian England, 1660–1900*. New York: Cambridge University Press, 1985.

Speck, W. A. *Stability and Strife: England, 1714–1760*. London: Edward Arnold, 1977.

Stone, Lawrence. *The Family, Sex and Marriage in England, 1500–1800*. London: Weidenfeld & Nicolson, 1977.

————. *Uncertain Unions and Broken Lives: Marriage and Divorce in England, 1660–1857*. New York: Oxford University Press, 1995.

Sweet, Rosemary, and Penelope Lane, eds. *Women and Urban Life in Eighteenth-Century England: On the Town*. London: Ashgate, 2003.

Tadmor, Naomi. *Family and Friends in Eighteenth Century England: Household, Kinship, and Patronage*. Cambridge: Cambridge University Press, 2001.

Thompson, E. P. *Customs in Common: Studies in Traditional Popular Culture*. New York: Norton, 1991.

Vickery, Amanda. *The Gentleman's Daughter: Women's Lives in Georgian England*. New Haven, CT: Yale University Press, 1998.

Wahrman, Dror. *The Making of the Modern Self: Identity and Culture in Eighteenth-Century England*. New Haven, CT: Yale University Press, 2006.

# Chapter 4

# Political Structure and Politics in Augustan England

In the eighteenth century, England's propertied elite modeled itself on imperial Rome: just as Caesar Augustus had ended a period of civil war and brought peace and expansion to the Roman Empire, so English landowners believed themselves to have ended a century of constitutional and religious strife and sponsored an era of stability and expansion. Strong contrasts, however, characterized the politics of the so-called Augustan Age. Political violence and intense party competition marked the first twenty years of the century, in contrast to the political peace and stability of the middle four decades. Political theory also contrasted with political practice. The ideal of a *mixed constitution* of king, Lords, and Commons—resting on the consent of the governed—diverged from the reality of rule by a narrow oligarchy. By the 1730s, England had become almost a one-party state, its apparent calm resting not so much on the support of a majority of the people as on the economic and social power of the Whig property owners. Moreover, although the English praised individual liberty and cheap government, the eighteenth-century state grew expansive and powerful. Finally, there was a profound contrast between the sedate world of parliamentary maneuvering and the raucous and riotous world of popular politics. These contrasts give a sense of the rich and complex flavor of eighteenth-century English politics.

## ACHIEVING POLITICAL STABILITY, 1700–1720

The twenty-five or thirty years after 1688 were an unstable and dangerous period in British politics. As Professor J. H. Plumb wrote, "Governments teetered on the edge of chaos, and party strife was as violent as anything

England had known since the Civil War."[1] Opposing ideologies as well as personal and family disputes drove Whigs and Tories to clash at both the national and local levels. Hence, the *rage of party* afflicted the first decades of the eighteenth century. General elections were frequent, and the number of constituencies contested in each election was high. Yet by 1750, general elections had become few and far between and electoral contests rare. By then the Tories had been reduced to a small group in permanent opposition, and the Whigs dominated Parliament and alone formed governments. What brought about such a transformation? Institutional changes, the resolution of divisive issues, and certain long-term social trends all contributed to the emergence of this oligarchy and the growth of this peculiar kind of stability.

The growing cost of elections shaped the institutional developments. Although very small by modern standards, the electorate of England and Wales was growing to unprecedented size, with perhaps three hundred thousand voters in 1700. Voters regarded their franchise as a possession from which they were entitled to benefit. Thus, rival candidates in a constituency had to ply the electors with copious servings of food and beer, as well as to patronize local tradesmen. The price of entertainment went up throughout the century: the Grosvenors, for instance, spent £8,500 on food and drink for the electors of Chester in 1784. Candidates also had to pay the fees of election officials and make donations to local charities—town halls, churches, almshouses, and so on. In some boroughs, bribery was a major expense. Voters in Weobly, for example, got £20 apiece from the candidate of their choice. Moreover, because patronage greased the wheels of the social system, candidates were expected to find offices for their supporters.

Soaring expenses led to a widespread desire among the ruling elite to hold down the growth of the electorate, to reduce the number of contested seats, and to cut the frequency of general elections. Many men opted not to stand for Parliament or simply were not wealthy enough to do so. In numerous boroughs, aldermen raised the admission expenses of becoming a freeman of the borough. By 1715, the electorate was distinctly narrower than twenty years before. In addition, Parliament in 1716 passed the Septennial Act, which required general elections only every seven years instead of every three. Consequently, whereas twelve general elections occurred between 1689 and 1715, there were only thirteen between 1715 and 1800.

---

[1] J. H. Plumb, *The Growth of Political Stability in England. 1675–1725* (Harmondsworth, Middlesex: Penguin Books, 1969), 74.

The Polling, *by William Hogarth. In this painting, Hogarth gives a clear picture of the somewhat chaotic and public quality of voting in the eighteenth century, complete with bribery and influence.*

Another institutional change contributing to stability was the concentration of government patronage. As the number of men who could afford a candidacy dwindled, patronage became increasingly centralized in the hands of the government, as opposed to the court. Largely because of the demands of war and the need to conduct complex foreign relations thereafter, the machinery of the British state grew. The number of government offices increased, particularly in the Treasury and the military services. Tax-collecting posts multiplied especially quickly: in 1714, nearly four hundred men collected salt taxes alone. The government doled out all such jobs as patronage. Robert Walpole, Whig prime minister between 1721 and 1742, used thousands of government appointments to build and maintain a massive structure of government support—and one that perpetuated an oligarchy of the wealthiest families.

Such institutional changes, however, would not have sufficed to reduce political conflict if the political nation had been violently divided on the issues. Before 1715, Whigs and Tories, as we have seen, differed radically on a number of crucial issues such as the legitimacy of and the succession to the Crown, Britain's military role on the Continent, trade policies, and the proper place of the Church of England. The Tories of the early eighteenth century took as their slogan "Peace and the Church in danger," and the Whigs countered with "Trade and the Protestant succession." The intensity of these issues dimmed over time, however. The succession of George I and the Hanoverian line proceeded fairly smoothly. Religious fervor gave way to reasonableness, and property owners lost interest in theological controversy. Under Whig rule, Nonconformists suffered no additional harassment, but neither did they win repeal of the Test Acts: the compromise of occasional conformity (see chapter 2) was restored in 1718 and remained in place. Likewise, war and its attendant taxation disappeared temporarily from the political agenda. The great Whig leader Walpole pursued a pacific foreign policy, with a view to reducing the land tax; indeed, his slogan for all policy was *"quieta non movere"* (freely translated as let sleeping dogs lie).

The Whig and Tory parties continued to exist through the 1760s, but until the last decade of the century, Whigs alone enjoyed the perquisites of power. The Tories' association with the Jacobite cause contributed to their decline in political importance. The Jacobite threat broke out with drama and danger in 1715, when some Highland chiefs raised the Stuart banner in Scotland (see chapter 6). In the eyes of many Englishmen (and Lowland Scots), these Jacobites sought not only to upset the Revolution Settlement, but also to restore tyranny and Catholicism to Britain. Most Tories remained loyal to the new Hanoverian regime: as one Jacobite put it, the English Tories "are never right hearty for the cause, till they are mellow as they call it, over a bottle or two." Still, enough Tories retained their sentimental attachment to the Stuarts to allow Walpole to exploit the issue by accusing all Tories of harboring Jacobite sympathies.

Increasingly, the Whigs became the "Court party," enjoying the ear of the monarch and speaking for the aristocracy, the financiers, and the most aggressive commercial captains. It is hard to determine what the Whigs after 1715 stood for, besides the Glorious Revolution itself, the privileges of the landowning elite, the expansion of trade, and the exploitation of state patronage. The Tories more and more adopted an opposition mentality. Along with some "Country" Whigs, the Tories opposed the corruption attendant on the Whig oligarchy's wallowing in the spoils of politics. They contended that Walpole's corrupt use of patronage subjugated the House of Commons to the executive and so upset the constitutional balance among king, Lords, and Commons established in 1688. Yet most of the Tories and

Country Whigs did not oppose the principle of patronage, but only what they regarded as the abuse of it. On the whole, the interests of all property owners, Whig and Tory alike, in eighteenth-century England were similar enough to dull the edge of political divisions. In the end, the prosperity, security, and self-interest of the propertied elite—and above all, of the landowners—brought political stability to England.

## LOCAL GOVERNMENT AND THE LAW IN THE AGE OF OLIGARCHY

The landed oligarchy's power was firmly based in local government. Landlords in the counties and propertied men of commerce in the towns ruled without much control from either the central government above them or usually from the populace below them. These men, after all, had won their struggle with the Crown about who would rule in the localities. The power they exercised was of great importance, partly because it was bound up with the structure of social authority and partly because, other than paying taxes, most people had direct contact with government and law *only* on the local level unless they were taken into the armed services. Unlike those in an absolutist state, the functions of the national government in Britain were severely limited: maintenance of law and order; conduct of foreign affairs in war and peace; protection of the rights of property; and a minimum of economic control, the most important aspect of which was taxation. At the local level, the nation ruled itself, in the sense that the "natural leaders" of society, acting as local officials, ruled the country—enforcing the laws, repairing the roads, caring for the poor, regulating fairs and markets, maintaining churches, and the like.

The institutions of local government composed a patchwork quilt sewn from swatches of historical accident, many of them reaching back to medieval times. But the presence of local autonomy, the variety of local governing institutions, and the rowdiness of the age did not mean that England was an ungoverned or frontier society. The social homogeneity of local officials created a coherent and effective system. All local officials were men of property, not elected but self-perpetuating by means of co-optation. Men in positions of local power selected others for county and parish offices. This social solidarity was buttressed by the face-to-face relations of rural and small-town England (see chapter 3). Except in the big cities—and above all in London, where anonymity was a fact of life—and some remote districts, men of property controlled everything.

The basic unit of local government was the parish. In each of England's approximately ten thousand parishes, unpaid amateurs, selected by the substantial property owners of the parish, carried out the work of local government, ranging from collecting the church rates (local taxes to maintain the church's buildings), maintaining the roads, acting as the local policemen (there being no national or even county police force), apprehending criminals, and relieving paupers.

The work of these parish officers was supervised by the justices of the peace (JPs), who were by far the key figures in eighteenth-century English local government. Appointed by the county's lord lieutenant (usually the greatest nobleman of the county), the JP was a member of the gentry whose estate was worth at least £100 per year. To serve as JP was a heavy and expensive responsibility, but also one of great social prestige. These unpaid officials held broad executive and judicial powers. A single JP exercised summary justice over petty criminals: the power to arrest, try, and punish drunks, game poachers, gamblers, and any other threat to the social order. In Quarter Sessions, a county's JPs together tried all criminal cases below capital crimes and administered the growing burden of laws put on their shoulders by Parliament—laws governing wages and prices (more and more ignored), roads, bridges, jails, and licensing of tradesmen, to name only a few. Britain, then, unlike many Continental countries, was ruled not by royal agents sent from the capital to the provinces, but by volunteers from the landed orders, whose social and economic roots lay in the districts they governed.

The boroughs were as oligarchical as the counties. In most of them, the ruling corporation consisted of a mayor, a dozen aldermen, and two or three dozen councilmen. In a few boroughs, these officials were elected by the *freemen* (men who possessed a certain level of property); such elections were hotly disputed. In most boroughs, however, the aldermen and councilors selected themselves by co-optation—that is, they chose their own members. In any case, power increasingly flowed to the relatively small number of ex officio JPs, who had the same powers as their rural brethren.

In the eighteenth century, the rule of law was already England's pride and joy, and it remains so to this day. Nevertheless, the oligarchy managed to make the law work for itself. The penal code became increasingly severe over time and, most strikingly, laws protecting property became more obtrusive. Picking pockets of more than one shilling and shoplifting items worth five shillings both became capital crimes, as did destroying turnpike gates, forgery, or theft from a master by a servant. In 1689, there were fifty capital crimes on the books; in 1800, there were more than two hundred—and most people were hanged for theft, not murder. Frequent executions, staged as public events, reinforced the oligarchy's power.

One example, eloquently described by the historian E. P. Thompson, illustrates these legal developments. In about 1720, in the Windsor Forest area on the border of Hampshire and Berkshire, new landlords were eager to exploit the economic opportunities of the Forest more efficiently. Unfortunately, their lust for money clashed with the customary *use rights* of the forest's common people. These small owners, tenants, and laborers could eke out a living only if they supplemented their earnings from farm or craft by taking a deer occasionally, fishing in the streams, collecting *lops and tops* of felled timber, and cutting turf for fuel. Such traditional rights, however, did not square with the landlords' newly established absolute rights of private property. The landlords naturally had the power of both Parliament and king at their disposal, but the Forest people had resources of their own—secrecy, stealth, intimidation, and violence. A ferocious conflict erupted between the rangers and gamekeepers, enthusiastic to carry out the landlords' will, and the Forest commoners, desperate to maintain their traditional means of survival. The landlords turned to the law: the Waltham Black Act, passed in 1723, added about fifty items to the already long list of capital crimes on the books, including such offenses as deer poaching, going about the forest at night with face blacked for disguise, and breaking the dams of landlords' fish ponds. Although exceptionally dramatic—after all, there was only one Waltham Black Act during the eighteenth century—the fight in Windsor Forest revealed the iron fist that lay beneath the lacy gloves of the oligarchy. As the novelist Oliver Goldsmith put it, "Laws grind the poor, and rich men rule the law."

## THE STRUCTURE OF NATIONAL POLITICS, 1715–1760

The purposes of national politics, if limited in range, were of great importance to the propertied elite. Britain was at war with scarcely an interruption between 1689 and 1713; war began again in 1739, and as we will see, went on continually thereafter. The logistical requirements of this so-called Second Hundred Years War raised taxes, increased the national debt, and swelled the state bureaucracy, especially in the revenue departments. The landed oligarchy needed to control this burgeoning state apparatus and limit the negative influence of war-related taxes. Above all, these privileged and propertied few recognized the vital importance of winning through political influence a share of the succulent outpouring of state patronage: government contracts, military and naval commissions, posts in the civil service or tax-collecting agencies, clerical appointments, sinecures in the court, and many other juicy morsels.

These purposes of politics shaped the way the constitution worked. Theoretically, England had a mixed constitution of king, Lords, and Commons, in which each element checked and balanced the others—the monarchical element checked the aristocratic and democratic, and so on. The king remained the nation's chief executive officer, shorn of many of his former prerogatives, but retaining the right to appoint and dismiss his ministers. No one could serve in the government for long without the confidence of the king. But if those ministers were to carry on the king's government, they had to have the confidence of Parliament as well. Inevitably, eighteenth-century kings often had to struggle to sustain their favorites in office at times when they lacked the support of the House of Commons. Given the power of the Commons after 1688, this was a struggle that in the long run the kings could not win.

The difficulties of the Crown were aggravated by the unfortunate personalities of the first two Hanoverian kings. George I and II both were block-headed German princes (George I spoke very little English), not incompetent, but stubborn, unimaginative, and unattractive. George I (1714–27) was shy and indolent; George II (1727–60) was opinionated but could be bullied. Neither was capable of forging parliamentary alliances; hence, both were dependent on their parliamentary leaders. Moreover, the two royals detested each other. As Horace Walpole dryly observed, "It ran a little in the blood of the family to hate the eldest son." Partly for this reason, George I absented himself from group meetings of his ministers, where he would have had to meet his son, and so inadvertently helped the cabinet system of government to evolve.

"Ministers are the Kings in this country," George II complained; yet in fact, Georgian ministers stood in a constitutionally precarious position. The principle of the collective responsibility of the cabinet to the House of Commons did not yet exist; instead, ministers were responsible as individuals to the Crown. The evolution of the cabinet system was sporadic and unplanned. In the late seventeenth century, a *cabinet council* replaced the privy council as the effective organ of the king's advisers, simply because the privy council had become too large. In the first half of the eighteenth century, the cabinet council, too, proved cumbersome and so monarchs tended to turn to a smaller, secret cabinet. This effective cabinet, consisting of the five or six key ministers, slowly assumed a corporate identity, meeting in the king's private closet (or *cabinet*). The Hanoverians retained the right to meet with ministers individually, however, and only reluctantly gave up the right of consulting political advisors who were *not* "in the cabinet." The cabinet did not function consistently as a corporate entity until after the end of the eighteenth century.

What drove the kings to deal with a cabinet collectively was their continuing need to have as ministers men who could command a majority in Parliament and, above all, in the House of Commons. Much under the sway of royal influence, the House of Lords rarely presented problems, but the House of Commons was different. The well-disciplined parties of modern times did not yet exist. Hence, ministers did not ride to power readily as the pre-chosen spokesmen of a majority party in the Commons, nor did they, once in office, dictate votes to an organized, obedient party. The House of Commons had 558 members, of whom about 100 were active politicians (all Whigs) seeking ministerial office, plus about 100 to 150 *placemen*, who depended on the court and government for their livelihood, and about 250 *Independents*. The ministers of the day could count on the votes of the placemen, but to make up a majority they had to win the support of sufficient numbers of the active politicians and Independents as well.

Patronage was the means to this end. Not all MPs were vulnerable to political patronage: Tories and Country Whigs loudly opposed its use to build government majorities. But many could be bought by offices and favors—if not for themselves, then for relatives, friends, and other clients. Including military officers, the number of officeholders usually stood at between one-third and one-half of all MPs. Opponents among the active politicians were especially susceptible to influence. Indeed, the normal pattern of parliamentary politics was for some person outside the cabinet to make such a nuisance of himself by his opposition that the ministers of the day would have to find a place for him in the government. This was known as *storming the closet*, a game played to perfection by the two leading politicians of the period, Sir Robert Walpole and William Pitt the Elder.

Outside the House of Commons, members of the landed elite used patronage to win elections for their favorites and even to buy seats in the House of Commons. The power of patronage depended on the curiously variegated nature of the constituencies and the small size of the electorate in many of them. The major categories of constituencies were the *counties* and the *boroughs*. In the fifty-two English and Welsh counties, all males possessing freeholds worth at least forty shillings (£2) a year could vote.

Differences in local and regional landed values meant that county electorates varied from several hundred to over ten thousand. In most cases, aristocratic or leading gentry families dominated county elections.

The borough franchise was even more irregular. In some boroughs, owners of particular houses voted; in others, just the members of the corporation voted. In still others, all ratepayers (males who paid the local tax) voted. In a few boroughs, all male householders held the franchise. As a result, several boroughs had upward of four thousand voters, but more than half had fewer than five hundred; Old Sarum, a parliamentary borough in southwestern England, had three or four. The government could control small boroughs where there were military installations, shipyards, or large concentrations of civilian officials. Wealthy patrons who had the voters "in their pockets" (hence, the term *pocket borough*) controlled many of the other small boroughs.

The essence of the parliamentary game, consequently, was for the king to appoint as ministers men who could win a working majority in the House of Commons by force of personality and by judicious use of *influence* (patronage), and for ambitious members of the opposition to force the government to buy them off. Electoral promises and party platforms—developments of the future—were not factors, though voters usually did demand that their MPs meet their expectations of proper paternalist behavior. Except for some backwoods opposition radicals, MPs all regarded themselves as independent representatives, not as delegates from their constituencies. Men went into politics not to legislate platforms, but to exercise their judgment on issues as they arose, to protect their interests, to win their share of the spoils, and to act out the political dimension of social authority.

## WALPOLE AND THE ROBINOCRACY

Sir Robert Walpole (1676–1745) was the consummate master of the oligarchical system. The son of a Norfolk squire and himself the image of the blunt, coarse country gentleman, Walpole was the most brilliant political operator of the century. Short, fat, and red-faced, he exuded rustic power. He liked to munch Norfolk apples during parliamentary debate and to claim that his gamekeeper's letters took precedence over official dispatches. But he was no backwoods bumpkin. An efficient administrator, a tireless manipulator of patronage, a formidable debater, and a master of national finance, Walpole was most of all a genius in understanding ordinary human motives. He could deftly detect and exploit the weaknesses of royalty and country MPs alike.

Sir Robert Walpole as Ranger of Richmond Park, *by John Wootton. Walpole liked to present himself as the rugged English country squire.*

Walpole rose to power from a sound basis. As a loyal Whig member of Parliament (MP) from 1700 to 1721, he served in a number of administrative posts that gave him an unmatched understanding of government operations and finance. He won the friendship and influence of the prince of Wales (heir to the throne). His great opportunity came in 1720, with the bursting of the "South Sea bubble." The South Sea Company had taken over a part of the national debt, on the basis of which it raised huge sums through inflated stock. The company bribed a number of politicians in order to win privileges, and when thousands of investors were ruined by the collapse of its stock, they angrily demanded that *someone* be punished. Walpole had escaped corruption when many national political leaders had discredited themselves; furthermore, he stepped forward with practical measures to restore public credit. Most important, he screened ministers from attack, limited the political damage, and won the gratitude of George I. In 1721 he was made first lord of the Treasury (the top ministerial post) and within a year had made himself in effect prime minister—the first in English history.

Walpole ruled from 1721 to 1742, his domination of court and Parliament earning the epithet of "the Robinocracy" (*Robin* being a nickname for Robert). With the assistance of his brother-in-law, Lord Townshend, an expert in European affairs, Walpole took control of every aspect of government policy. He systematically rooted out opponents from government departments, the royal household, the army, the navy, and the Church and replaced them with his own supporters, many of them relatives and friends. With painstaking attention to patronage, he molded a dependable majority in the Lords and the Commons alike. The Tory newspaper the *Craftsman* called Walpole's House of Commons a monster "who had above 500 mouths . . . fed on gold and silver." The ease with which Walpole was able to get the king's business done, not to mention his adroit handling of the royal mistresses, made George I dependent on him. When George I died in 1727, many politicians thought that Walpole was finished, but they reckoned without his shrewd human insight. Walpole recognized that the new king depended more on his queen, Caroline of Anspach, than on his mistresses, and Walpole got on famously with Caroline. Walpole influenced George II through her; as he put it, he "took the right sow by the ear."

The king's support enabled Walpole to survive the first crisis of his regime—a furor over an excise tax scheme in 1733. Walpole's policy in general was non-activist: peace, trade, and tax reduction. By his excise plan, which would have extended the existing system of excise taxes (taxes levied on the consumption of certain goods) to wine and tobacco, Walpole hoped to reduce or even end land taxes. Much to his surprise, the proposal caused a great public outcry, for the opposition was able to play on popular resentments of tax collectors as agents of governmental control who threatened every Englishman's liberty. Walpole was forced to withdraw his plan, but because he retained the king's confidence, he remained in office.

Walpole's grip on power slowly loosened, however, after Queen Caroline died in 1737. As a result, he was unable to withstand the opposition during the second crisis of his regime. This arose over his ineffective conduct of war with Spain. For years, the eagerness of English merchants to milk the Spanish Empire and the efforts of the Spanish coast guard in the West Indies to stop them had soured relations between England and Spain. Walpole preferred negotiations to war, but patriotic English merchants and squires thought he was too meek in asserting English interests. In 1739, he reluctantly agreed to their demands: "It is your war," he told the duke of Newcastle, "and I wish you joy of it." As we will see in chapter 7, the conflict with Spain soon merged with a general conflict on the Continent called the War of Austrian Succession, which was to last through 1748. Because he opposed Britain's involvement, Walpole conducted the war effort ineffectually. His support in the Commons dwindled, as Independents withdrew their support and as holders of place and pensions sensed that a new source of patronage would soon hold office. When he lost control of the committee that decided disputed elections, he saw that the game was up. Despite the king's support, Walpole resigned in 1742.

## THE GREAT COMMONER: WILLIAM PITT THE ELDER

Walpole may have fallen in 1742, but his system did not. The government that succeeded Walpole was headed by Henry Pelham, an unprepossessing but efficient House of Commons manager, and his brother, the duke of Newcastle, an eccentric, incredibly wealthy, anxiety-ridden master of patronage. Together, the Pelhams used Walpole's system to hold in harness a fractious ministry until 1754, when Henry Pelham died. In 1746, they even succeeded in neatly buying off their most troublesome critic, a young man of sweeping vision and rhetorical power named William Pitt (1708–78), by appointing him as paymaster general of the forces. Pitt, however, could not be silenced for good. A man of insatiable ambition, Pitt had inherited the uncontrollable temper of his grandfather, "Diamond" Pitt. His moods swung violently from depression and lethargy to demonic energy. In his manic phases, Pitt had the self-assurance and the broad designs of a global statesman. He was also the most brilliant orator of the century, capable of making his listeners believe that they—and England—were walking with destiny. Hailed as "the Great Commoner," Pitt was not a good political operator, but his grandiose theatricality and inspirational rhetoric gave him power of a different sort—the emotional support of independent MPs and makers of public opinion.

As we will see in chapter 7, Pitt inspired the English to seize world power status. He couched the ruthless pursuit of English commercial interests around the world in terms of the highest principles. He began his political career in 1735 as a member of the opposition, passionately believing that Walpole was corrupting English politics at home and betraying English interests abroad. His first speeches were so threatening that Walpole had him dismissed from his army commission: "We must muzzle this terrible cornet of the horse." But Pitt was not to be muzzled. In 1739, he spoke for war with Spain: "When trade is at stake, you must defend it or perish. . . . You throw out general terrors of war. Spain knows the consequences of war in America, but she sees England dare not make it."

William Pitt, First Earl of Chatham, *by Richard Brompton (1772). Here Pitt the Elder, who had become a great national hero as a result of his imperial leadership, is shown in noble's robes.*

Pitt *would* dare make it, for he pictured England's destiny to be one of commercial empire. Denied office in 1742 and then harnessed by office in 1746, Pitt was relatively quiet when new fighting with the French began in 1755. But his imperial vision and the lure of higher office finally led Pitt into opposition, and his debating power opened the way to the prime ministership. As the duke of Newcastle told the king, no one could rule without Pitt: "No one will have a majority at present, against Mr. Pitt. No man, Sir, will in the present conjecture set his face against Mr. Pitt in the House of Commons."

We will examine in chapter 7 the objectives and the course of the war of 1756–63. The point here is to understand how Pitt operated within the political system. He stormed the closet in grand style by making himself the voice of outraged patriotism among both commercial interests and independent country gentlemen. His argument that England should contain France on the Continent while defeating them overseas spoke to their prejudices. Eventually Pitt forced his way into office on his own terms. He was a poor parliamentary manipulator, however, and so needed the duke of Newcastle to manage the patronage. Newcastle had the votes of the *Old Corps* of Walpolean Whigs, and Pitt supplied the support of independent country squires—a potent combination that expressed the unity of the ruling oligarchy.

Yet the significance of the king as a factor in the equation showed itself in 1760, when George III succeeded to the throne. George III hated Pitt and dreamed of reigning *above party*. Even the Great Commoner could not retain office without the king's confidence; hence, Pitt resigned and went into opposition. The oligarchical system, which depended on the monarch's compliance, spun into disarray.

## POPULAR POLITICS

The excise crisis of 1733 and the surge of patriotism in 1755–57 show that, despite the power of patronage, public opinion had a part to play in the political drama. Parliamentary politicians sometimes tried to drum up popular opinion for their own purposes by patronizing journalists, manipulating the press, or stirring up crowd demonstrations. They found, however, that public opinion was a dangerous weapon, not easily controlled. Both voters and nonvoters typically played active roles in the often lively and boisterous politics of the constituencies. Thus, outside the politics of the elite, outside the maneuverings of Parliament and the great country houses, there existed an alternative structure of politics.

Much of this alternative political world depended on written matter. Literacy in Georgian England was limited to perhaps 50 percent of the adult population (significantly more men than women), and even that figure includes many whose reading ability was elementary. Literacy was, however, significantly higher in urban centers, especially in London, where it may have reached 80 percent. This urban reading public supported an energetic, growing, and highly politicized newspaper, magazine, and pamphlet press. Moreover, improvements in communications such as the turnpike roads and the postal service made widespread distribution of publications possible. By 1760, there were at least twelve newspapers in London and thirty-five in provincial towns. These newspapers, and the accompanying flood of pamphlets and broadsides, were intensively read and debated, most notably in the coffeehouses that enlivened public life in all the cities. In 1740 there were 550 coffeehouses in London and at least one in each of the larger market towns. Politicians tried to channel this obstreperous press toward their own views and to control it by means of the Stamp Tax, but without much effect. Public opinion as seen in the newspaper and pamphlet press remained staunchly patriotic and oppositional, except for papers such as *Lloyd's Evening Post*, which were controlled by the government.

An even more active role in popular politics was played by crowds. We have seen that demonstrations in London and elsewhere helped force Walpole to withdraw the excise in 1733; similarly, they caused repeal of an act allowing for the naturalization of Jews in 1753. But their targets extended far beyond national issues. Riots occurred over a wide variety of issues: the game laws (which prevented anyone but landlords from hunting), turnpike tolls, efforts by customs officers to stop smugglers, conditions of labor, denial of traditional rights to common land, and high food prices. Benjamin Franklin wrote in 1769: "I have seen, within a year, riots in the country, about coin; riots about elections; riots about workhouses; riots of colliers, riots of weavers, riots of coal-heavers. . . ."

The ruling elite wanted deference and subordination from the public, but insubordination and riot were often what they got. London was the worst afflicted, but the forest regions were also notorious for riotous behavior; riots could break out in any village or town where squire and parson either lacked authority or transgressed the popular sense of just rule. These riots were not blind, aimless protests; still less were they the simple brimming over of energy in a lawless society. Riots in preindustrial England had clear, limited objectives and conformed to a popular consensus about moral principles and acceptable social practice—to a sense of a traditional *moral economy*. Rioters were essentially traditionalists, not revolutionaries, for they ordinarily sought to get the natural leaders of the community—the squire and the JP—to enforce the law and to restore customary practices and standards.

The food riot was the most common form of crowd action. It is easy to see why: a rise in food prices in any locality confronted many families with hunger and destitution. Thus, in 1756–57, there were more than one hundred food riots in thirty counties. The pattern in each of these was the same: rioters intervened in the local market system by intimidation or violence to restore what they regarded as a just price. They got JPs to enforce a just price for wheat or to prevent the export of foodstuffs from the region, they forced bakers to reduce the price of bread, or they evicted middlemen from the market. In 1757, for instance, [laborers in a small town in Yorkshire] forcibly rung the Corn [wheat] Bell, and their Ringleader proclaimed the Price of Corn . . . ; which done, they seized the Sacks of the Farmers, and insisted upon having the Corn at the Price by them set, some of them paying, and others taking it without paying any Thing. Others of the Rioters set the price on Oatmeal, Potatoes, etc.

The outcome of this riot was typical in that the rioters succeeded. The magistrates could, of course, call in the army to put down any riot, but they did not like to do so. The gentleman JPs did not want to show their weakness by calling in outside forces, for that would have destroyed the aura of their social authority. The rioters normally were appealing to the local officials' sense of paternalist duties, which was in everyone's interest to maintain. Thus, the governing authority at the local level was exercised by the established landed rulers, but was ultimately subject to the consent of the populace. Ordinary people deferred to and obeyed the propertied, but often only on condition that they ruled through traditional moral wisdom.

Ordinary people also ruled themselves, through the rituals of rough music or *skimmingtons*. These traditional expressions of popular opinion took different forms in different areas, but all consisted of stylized means of regulating behavior that was regarded as immoral or unnatural. A journeyman who took less than the trade's customary price could be ducked in a river or ridden out of town on a rail. A man who beat his wife, a man who was bullied by his wife, or a woman who beat her husband could be hanged in effigy. A parish officer could be subjected to an elaborate, stylized drama on his doorstep. Usually these popular rituals, whose form was handed down by local custom, included a procession in which the offender was caricatured and ridiculed to the accompaniment of raucous music on cow bells, tin pots, warming pans, and the like.

Only rarely did rough music lead to physical violence. Its object was to express public disapproval in a way calculated to humiliate the offender. Rough music signified to all that the offender had stepped outside the moral boundaries of the community. By this public rebuke and the ostracism that followed, rough music sometimes drove its culprit to flight or even suicide. Like popular riots, rough music could not operate on behalf of a legislative platform or form the base of a sustained political movement. It worked where the established local authorities either could not or would not function in the customary way, as in popular marital issues. It was a form of law that came from within the community and lasted as long as the understanding of law was customary rather than contractual, as long as popular culture was oral rather than literate. In some localities rough music lasted well into the nineteenth century.

## THE GROWTH OF THE BRITISH STATE

The realities of this informal and customary world of popular local politics contrasted sharply with the great game of parliamentary politics played by the masters of the grand country houses. Until the last decade of the century, however, popular politics did not seriously threaten the landowners' regime, nor did the oligarchy establish overly repressive rule—not in England and Wales, at least. Compared to the heavy-handed and in some cases militarized states on the Continent, the English landowners in the eighteenth century provided comparatively light government for the English, if not the Scottish and Irish people. The landed oligarchy was narrow and self-interested, but it made England a bastion of law, liberty, and localism.

Paradoxically, however, the size and power of the British state grew during the eighteenth century. The reason for its growth was the almost constant state of war. Britain was involved in major wars from 1689 to 1713, 1739 to 1748, 1755 to 1763, 1775 to 1784, and 1792 to 1815. Thus, governments did not take on much in the way of social legislation, but they nevertheless expanded the state's machinery in order to supply the logistical support for the army and navy and to subsidize allied military forces. It was typical for Britain to have more than 120,000 men under arms during wartime. To raise and supply such forces cost huge sums of money. Governmental expenditures more than tripled between 1689 and 1763, and almost three-quarters of these expenditures went to support the army and the navy. To pay the bills, the British state increased taxes by about 300 percent over the same period and raised the national debt by about 800 percent. The British state in the eighteenth century had its biggest impact on the ordinary subject by recruitment of soldiers and sailors and by taxation. Except for a few examples, all having to do with Jacobitism, battles were not fought on the soil of the British Isles, but everyone paid taxes. The excise tax became the principal form of national revenue, and because it was a tax on the sale of certain products, it affected the price of consumer goods and the cost of living.

To collect the taxes and manage the swollen expenditures, the British had to increase the number of state officials. The number of employees in the central administrative departments went up by almost 700 percent to nearly 1,000 men in the first half of the eighteenth century. In addition, the number of officials in the revenue bureaucracy tripled (to about 7,500 employees) during the same period; those in the excise office quadrupled. Tax collectors ranged throughout the country. Although all of these offices were filled by patronage, the level of professional competence and honesty was fairly high. Patronage, in fact, worked to ensure that the new tax bureaucracy did not become alienated from the traditional ruling elite: landowners wanted to put their friends and relatives in the jobs, not to destroy the bureaucracy. At the same time, the acute sense of liberty and property that had been affirmed in 1688 and in the Revolution Settlement made the political public alert to potential abuses by the state. British political rhetoric thus was filled with the vocabulary of law and liberty. Most real government occurred at the local level, but politics became intensely focused on the central government. This was one of the clearest examples of the contrasts so characteristic of eighteenth-century British politics and government.

## Suggested Reading

Ayling, Stanley. *The Elder Pitt*. London: Collins, 1976.

Black, Jeremy. *Walpole in Power*. Stroud: Sutton, 2001.

Bradley, James E. *Religion, Revolution, and English Radicalism: Nonconformity in Eighteenth-Century English Politics and Society*. New York: Cambridge University Press, 1991.

Brewer, John. *Party Ideology and Popular Politics at the Accession of George III*. Cambridge: Cambridge University Press, 1976.

———. *The Sinews of Power: War, Money, and the English State, 1688–1783*. New York: Knopf, 1989.

Brown, Peter Douglas. *William Pitt, Earl of Chatham: The Great Commoner*. London: Allen & Unwin, 1978.

Colley, Linda. *Britons: Forging the Nation. 1707–1837*. New Haven, CT: Yale University Press, 1992.

———. *In Defiance of Oligarchy: The Tory Party, 1720–1760*. Cambridge: Cambridge University Press, 1982.

Dickinson, H. T. *The Politics of the People in Eighteenth-Century Britain*. New York: St. Martin's Press, 1995.

Emsley, Clive. *Crime and Society in England, 1750–1900*, 3rd ed. New York: Longman/Pearson, 2005.

Harris, Bob. *Politics and the Nation: Britain in the Mid-Eighteenth Century*. New York: Oxford University Press, 2002.

Hill, Brian. *The Early Parties and Politics in Britain, 1688–1832*. New York: St. Martin's Press, 1996.

Jenkins, Philip. *The Making of a Ruling Class: The Glamorgan Gentry, 1640–1790*. Cambridge: Cambridge University Press, 1983.

Kramnick, Isaac. *Bolingbroke and His Circle*. Cambridge, MA: Harvard University Press, 1968.

Langford, Paul. *A Polite and Commercial People: England 1727–1783*. Oxford: Oxford University Press, 1994.

O'Gorman, Frank. *The Long Eighteenth Century: British Social and Political History, 1688–1832.* London: Arnold, 1997.

———. *Voters, Patrons, and Parties: The Unreformed Electoral System of Hanoverian England, 1734–1832.* Oxford: Clarendon Press, 1989.

Pearce, Edward. *The Great Man. Sir Robert Walpole: Scoundrel, Genius and Britain's First Prime Minister.* London: Jonathan Cape, 2007.

Plumb, J. H. *The Growth of Political Stability in England, 1675–1725.* London: Macmillan, 1967.

Rogers, Nicholas. *Crowds, Culture, and Politics in Georgian Britain.* Oxford: Oxford University Press, 1998.

———. *Whigs and Cities: Popular Politics in the Age of Walpole and Pitt.* Oxford: Clarendon Press, 1990.

Rude, George. *The Crowd in History: A Study of Popular Disturbances in France and England, 1730–1848.* London: Lawrence & Wishart, 1964.

Speck, W. A. *Stability and Strife: England, 1714–1760.* London: Edward Arnold, 1977.

Thompson, E. P. *Customs in Common: Studies in Traditional Popular Culture.* New York: Norton, 1991.

———. *Whigs and Hunters: The Origin of the Black Act.* New York: Pantheon Books, 1975.

Williams, E. N. *The Eighteenth-Century Constitution.* Cambridge: Cambridge University Press, 1965.

Wilson, Kathleen. *The Sense of the People: Politics, Culture and Imperialism in England, 1715–1785.* Cambridge: Cambridge University Press, 1998.

# Chapter 5

# Religion, Rationality, and Recreation: Culture in Eighteenth-Century England

In English culture, just as in English politics, the eighteenth century was the Augustan Age. Keenly aware of the similarities between their own time and Augustan Rome, the landlords naturally took Rome as their model, adopting its standards and styles of thought in literature and the arts. The justly famous *English phlegm*—an approach to life reflecting calm deportment and a stiff upper lip—was an invention of the eighteenth century, much under the influence of Roman stoicism. Important also was the notion of "politeness," a cultural style combining civility, decorum, and propriety that proved particularly attractive to the better-off middling sort with whom the gentry often socialized. Stately and dignified houses, superbly serene and well-crafted paintings, and realistic but cheerful literature all reflected a highly civilized life. The English Enlightenment, which flourished in the second half of the century, reinforced this culture of order, symmetry, and stability. In England, the Enlightenment stress on *reason* often translated into an emphasis on *reasonableness* and *restraint*.

Augustan high culture set the respectable ranks apart from those they regarded as the vulgar populace. Indeed, popular culture displayed little of the Augustan serenity and nothing of its classical values. Whereas eighteenth-century high culture reflected the elite's desire to display a consensus that would legitimate and solidify the social hierarchy, the culture of the people, in contrast, was sometimes rebellious, often brutal, and always reflective of popular belief in traditional, custom-oriented standards and values.

The apparent cultural chasm between the privileged and the populace was, however, only that: apparent. Like gentlemen bedecked in silks and lace who, in common with their servants, often went unwashed for weeks (daily full body bathing remained highly unusual in this era), the rationality and politeness of high society flourished alongside a delight in bawdiness found at all social levels. Even more importantly, the emergence of a vibrant, science-minded, commercial culture spread Enlightened values far beyond the ranks of the wealthy and privileged. This commercial culture served as the rails of the eighteenth-century English social ladder, linking its many rungs.

## THE ENLIGHTENMENT IN ENGLAND

On the Continent, the ideas of the Enlightenment challenged much of the established political and religious order. In England, however, the philosophy and theology of the Augustan Age reflected the landed property owners' view of the world. For this reason, the power and security of the English landowners made the English version of the Enlightenment more moderate and less corrosive. True, in England, as elsewhere, the principal themes of Enlightened thought were *nature* and *reason*; educated English men and women generally agreed that God had designed both the natural and the social orders and had endowed humanity with the faculty of reason as a perfectly adequate means of understanding them. Because nature moves according to a divine plan and because the deity is benevolent, then whatever *is* is right. In this sense, the Augustan view of the world was essentially conservative. Similarly, the divine plan was thought to entail a static *great chain of being*, a graded hierarchy of all living things from lowest to highest in which all beings had their proper place. Within that great chain stood the human social hierarchy, with the aristocracy and gentry near the top: English gentlemen enjoyed a cosmic status just below the angels. The word *natural* tended to mean whatever was comfortable to gentlemen.

Reason held the key to decoding natural laws. Reason has often connoted a purely rational or speculative quality of thought, the special capacity that allows humanity to transcend worldly limitations. But in eighteenth-century England, reason referred to more humble powers—the logical, calculating faculty and the *reasonableness* of cool common sense and restraint. Men and women in the propertied elite disliked extremism, or what they called "enthusiasm." Bishop Joseph Butler, for instance, said that enthusiasm is "a horrid thing, a very horrid thing." Englishmen had learned from their experience of civil war and revolution in the seventeenth century that extremism in politics and religion leads to conflict, war, and social turmoil. Just as they sought stability in the political structure, so they would have moderation preached in philosophy and theology. Alexander Pope, the greatest of the Augustan poets, wrote:

> For forms of Government let fools contest;
> Whate'er is best administered is best;
> For Modes of Faith, let graceless zealots fight;
> His can't be wrong whose life is in the right.

## THE EMPIRICIST TRADITION

The themes of nature and reason received their clearest treatment by the empiricist philosophers of the late seventeenth and eighteenth centuries. They established the *empirical tradition*, perhaps the greatest British contribution to philosophy. British empiricism centered on the assumption that scientific observation and the accumulation of facts lead to true knowledge. In the development of this tradition, the work of Isaac Newton (1642–1727) played a pivotal role. The towering figure of the late seventeenth-century Scientific Revolution, Newton built on the earlier achievements of Galileo, Copernicus, and Kepler to set out universal laws of astronomy, mechanics, and physics. Newtonian science revealed God's creation to be an exquisite but comprehensible machine. In *Principia Mathematica* (1687), Newton combined experimental science with sophisticated mathematics to reveal that the law of gravity explains even the movements of the planets.

Newton's achievement, widely popularized, gave tremendous impetus to belief in the scientific method—careful observation, rigorous inference, and meticulous experimentation—as the avenue to true knowledge. Reason in the form of science seemed to banish mystery and open all the secrets of the world and the heavens. Pope wrote:

> Nature and Nature's laws lay hid in night:
> God said, *Let Newton* be!' and all was light!

For the next two centuries, many a scientist and intellectual sought to become the Newton of his or her own field by reducing scientifically gathered data to one or a few elegant laws.

Great as Newton's influence on philosophy was, however, that of John Locke was perhaps even greater. Locke (1632–1704) clearly articulated the three themes of central importance to eighteenth-century English thought: (1) empiricism, (2) civil government, and (3) religious toleration. In Locke's thought, and in that of most of the later empiricists, these three themes were tightly bound. They shared the notion, crucial to individual liberty, that there are natural limits to the proper claims of human thought and endeavor.

A friend of Newton and other late seventeenth-century English scientists, Locke served the Whig earl of Shaftesbury in the 1670s and 1680s. Locke was forced to flee to the Dutch Republic with his patron in 1683, returning to England only after the Revolution of 1688. He soon became known as the leading philosopher of the Whig cause. The basis of his philosophy of political moderation and religious toleration lay in his empiricist epistemology—his philosophy of how knowledge originates. Like so many other Englishmen of the time, Locke wanted to find absolutely certain answers to any number of fundamental questions. He came to think, however, that the human understanding was not capable of absolute certainty in most realms of thought because all knowledge derives from experience, the basis of which is sense perception. By reason, we are able to combine simple sensory data into complex ideas, and we are able to reflect on our own mental operations. But because all knowledge originates in sensations, we are not able to go beyond experience except in a few limited areas. Hence the boundaries of *certain* knowledge are very narrow, whereas the boundaries of *probable* knowledge are quite wide.

Locke and his followers found it unreasonable to persecute others on the basis of probable knowledge. Consequently, he disliked absolutism in politics and enthusiasm in religion. In his second *Treatise of Civil Government* (1690), Locke set out a theory of limited government. He argued that men in the state of nature are essentially reasonable and obey the basic natural law of society—that "no one ought to harm another in his life, liberty or possessions." This was the English property owners' social ideal. Unfortunately, not everyone obeys natural law, so in order to protect their property, people form a civil society by agreeing to a *social compact*. They give up certain of their powers to a government, but they do not relinquish their natural right of liberty and independence, nor do they surrender their sovereignty. A government therefore rules only by consent of the governed, and absolutism is incompatible with natural law and the social compact.

Obviously, Locke was justifying the outlook of his Whig patrons—individualism, rights of property, and constitutional monarchy. He did the same with his ideas on religion. Locke believed that the existence of God is demonstrable and that divine revelation of truths is possible. But he also contended that reason is the proper test of revelation and that people should beware of religious extremism. Consequently, he argued for toleration (except for Catholics, Muslims, and atheists). A church, he wrote, is a purely voluntary body and should have no compulsive authority; nor should the state try to enforce a particular religious view. A person's religious opinions necessarily are a matter for his or her own reasoning; furthermore, the alliance of church and state normally leads to oppression.

The empiricist tradition did not remain stagnant in the positions that Newton and Locke set out. For example, the most able empirical philosopher of the next generation, George Berkeley (1685–1753), used empiricist reasoning to refute the assumed materialism (that is, that matter exists) underlying Locke's philosophy. One generation further along, the Scotsman David Hume (1711–76), perhaps the most acute thinker among the British empiricists, used reason to defeat reason and to arrive at a position of skepticism concerning the nature and existence of material objects and causal relations among them. Berkeley sought to prove the existence of God, whereas Hume hovered on the edge of atheism. But on the whole, eighteenth-century empiricists supported the assumptions and conclusions of Newton and Locke—that nature is orderly and operates by laws accessible to reason; that reason is largely a matter of manipulating the data of the senses and of restraining the passions; that reason, though limited, is perfectly adequate for human purposes; that civil society exists for the convenience of the individuals who make it up; and that as a practical matter, the members of society who count are restricted to the propertied stratum.

## NATURE, GOD, AND MORALITY

Hume's religious skepticism was unusual in eighteenth-century England. The more typical Augustan view was that reason and Christian revelation were entirely compatible; indeed, this religiosity was the most clear-cut difference between the Enlightenment in England and that in France. Locke, who remained a Christian, believed that the very order of nature reveals the existence of God. "The works of Nature," he said, "everywhere evidence a Deity."

Locke's view expressed the essence of a central position of Augustan thinkers—namely, *natural theology*. Most eighteenth-century English men and women believed that Nature was, like the Bible, a "book" of divine revelation: the study of nature, via reason and science, shows its providential design—that is, that God governs the world and human development. Reason supports revelation, and revelation reason. The world, including its human inhabitants, is no ruin reflecting the fall of Adam; rather, it is the product of divine wisdom and benevolence. Every thing and every person, then, has its proper place——in the words of theologian William Law, "each man walking in Godly wise in his state of wealth and poverty." Even poverty and ignorance have their appropriate roles to play. Poverty is beneficial because it calls forth the charity of the rich. Ignorance, said the Reverend Soames Jenyns, "is the opiate of the poor, a cordial administered by the gracious hand of providence."

For some Augustan thinkers, however, the orderly whirl of the universal machine removed the need for providential action. *Deists* such as John Toland and Viscount Bolingbroke believed that reason and nature teach that God exists, but not a personal, intervening, or active God. The deity, they contended, created the universe according to natural law and then let it operate on its own. Insofar as Christianity teaches a morality consistent with reason, then Christianity is useful, but insofar as it rests its claims to authority on miracle stories (for which there can be no scientific evidence), then Christianity is merely a superstition.

Many of these ideas structured one of the most important books published in eighteenth-century England: Edward Gibbon's *Decline and Fall of the Roman Empire.* In his insistence on looking to evidence rather than tradition for historical truth, Gibbon (1737–94) was very much a man of the Enlightenment. He treated early Christianity as one among many eastern religions; looked to historical rather than supernatural explanations for its expansion; and, most controversially, identified that expansion as a key factor in eroding the martial values of Roman civilization. Gibbon's depiction of early Christians as intolerant zealots may have been a little extreme for eighteenth-century Englishmen, but his argument reflected the prevailing skepticism and rationality of Enlightened culture. "My book," he recalled, "was on every table, and on almost every toilette; the historian was crowned by the taste or fashion of the day."

Deism remained the religion of a relatively small number of people and never had the influence in England that it had elsewhere; nevertheless, it struck orthodox theologians as the great danger of the day and thus called forth one of the most influential books of the eighteenth (and nineteenth) century—Joseph Butler's *Analogy of Religion.* Bishop Butler wanted to show that acceptance of Christianity is perfectly reasonable. Everyone agrees, he argued, that scientific truths are only probable and leave many questions unexplained, yet devotees of reason such as the deists unhesitatingly accept scientific findings as natural laws. By the same token, Butler wrote, we should have no qualms in believing religious truths, which, if ultimately mysterious, are also probable.

Butler also contended that it is probable that our behavior in this world determines our happiness in the next. This formulation of a system of ethics based on *reason* characterized much of eighteenth-century English thought. Because the educated elite were shifting their attention from speculation about the supernatural to more mundane concerns, moral philosophy was of great interest to them. They wanted to know how to lead virtuous lives (as long as virtue did not disturb their pursuit of happiness) and they liked to think their ethical code was based on reason. The interests of the property owners made *utilitarian* ethics popular. Utilitarianism holds that behavior should be based on a calculation of pleasures and pains. Although the pleasures and pains Butler had in mind would come in heaven or hell, other eighteenth-century utilitarians were more worldly: if we pursue our individual pleasure and avoid pain on this earth, we will in fact be pursuing virtue and avoiding vice. This was Locke's view, and a very convenient one it was for the Whig oligarchy.

Not all moralists, however, subscribed to the *reason* school of ethics, whether in its utilitarian or its less extreme forms. Some moral philosophers contended instead that people have an *innate moral sense*. To know how to act, all one has to do is look within the conscience. Yet whether moralists were of the moral sense or the reason school, all agreed that in the refined and reasonable English gentleman would be found the proper standard of behavior. Lord Shaftesbury, the son of Locke's patron, put it this way: "The Taste of Beauty, and the Relish of what is decent, just, and amiable, perfects the Character of the Gentleman and the Philosopher."

Such a morality, of course, led easily to complacency, for it tended to confuse superficial attributes with genuine morals, and those failings in turn sometimes encouraged dissimulation and cynicism. These qualities were perfectly displayed by the career diplomat and politician Lord Chesterfield in his justly famous *Letters to His Son* (1774). In these charming epistles of advice, Chesterfield tried to sculpt his son into the epitome of the courtly gentleman—reserved while seeming frank, mannered while seeming natural. The essence of his message was the *utility* of moral virtue and social graces, to the point that they became almost identical. "Pleasure is now, and ought to be, your business," Chesterfield advised. To get ahead in the gentlemanly world, one should bring pleasure to others by an artful cultivation of speech, deportment, fashion, and flattery. By this cultivation of refinement, Augustan empiricism and worldliness were put to good use: "Every man is to be had one way or another, and everywoman almost any way."

## RELIGION AND THE CHURCH IN ENGLAND

The twin forces of the Enlightenment and the dominance of the landed elite shaped the institutions of religion in eighteenth-century England. The Church of England stood in a position of unparalleled power. Even though the Toleration Act allowed Dissenters to worship in their own congregations and the practice of occasional conformity allowed them to take public office, the Church of England enjoyed the benefits of establishment, and Anglicans monopolized national and local government. Scarred by the anti-Puritan reaction of the late seventeenth century, Dissenters were content for the time to protect the toleration they had been granted and to work quietly for full political rights. Their numbers dwindled to about 250,000 by 1760. Roman Catholics remained a tiny and passive element in England, growing slightly after 1780 because of Irish immigration, but still numbering only about 80,000 in 1760. Almost everyone else was at least nominally an Anglican.

Both the hierarchical social structure and the preeminence of reason in English thought and culture shaped the eighteenth-century Church of England. Because the preference of propertied folk was for balance and moderation and for matters of this world, the fires of religion burned low. Confident in their understanding of divine providence, the Anglican landed elite believed firmly in the importance of the church for upholding the social, political, and moral order, but tended to equate more emotional forms of religiosity with fanaticism. (John Wesley was to react strongly against this religious restraint, but because the impact of his teachings came late in the century, it will be discussed in chapter 12.)

Anglicanism's dominance and the elite's disavowal of emotional religion did not mean that religious issues were unimportant. Religious debates, in fact, continued to characterize party political life and to roil Anglican affairs. Those who came to be known as *High Churchmen* resented the subordination of the Church to the state. They thought that the toleration of Dissenters should cease, for they believed that the Church of England as a divine institution ought to be recognized by the state as the only means of salvation. High Churchmen got Tory support, but as Toryism declined in political influence, the High Church position lost out in the corridors of power to the *Low Church*. The Low Church view was *Erastian*—that is, Low Churchmen believed that the church is properly subject to the dictates of the state because it is essentially a voluntary association of believers, not a uniquely divine institution. The Low Church view prevailed among the Anglican bishops partly because of the general cultural trend toward moderation and toleration and partly because the Crown and the Whigs favored the Low Church position. Hence, the triumph of Whiggery threw the weight of patronage behind Low Churchmen.

The Church's hierarchy was thus deeply enmeshed in Whig politics. As members of the House of Lords, the twenty-six bishops were crucial to Whig control of the upper chamber. Walpole and his successors made sure that no one except politically sound men were appointed to the episcopal bench, and they made it clear to every bishop or lower church appointee what political behavior was expected. Any clergyman hoping for promotion had to be loyal to the government. Ambitious clergymen spent their careers jostling for places and maneuvering for political favors. When the holder of a desirable church office died, likely contenders scrambled for the spot. It was not unusual to see anxious candidates waiting in an anteroom, while inside a bishop breathed his last. Sometimes a candidate could not wait. One Thomas Newton wrote the duke of Newcastle, "I think it my duty to acquaint yr. grace that the Archbishop of York lies a-dying, and, as all here think, cannot possibly live beyond tomorrow morning, if so long; upon this occasion of two vacancies, I beg, I hope, I trust your Grace's kindness and goodness will be shown to one who has long solicited your favour."

Once appointed, such people often focused their sights on the next juicy plum dangling above. Bishop Hoadly, the most outspoken Low Churchman and a favorite of the Whigs, was made bishop of Bangor in 1715 and was promoted to Hereford in 1721, having gone only once to Bangor. In 1723, he was promoted from Hereford, never having traveled there at all. He occupied himself with politics and was finally raised to the wealthy See of Winchester in 1734. Some bishops attended to their duties in the House of Lords, at least, but at other times conducted themselves like wealthy landowners.

Such behavior was bound to affect the performance of the ordinary clergy of the parishes. They typically behaved as what they were, members of the gentry, for the clergy became a respectable and undemanding livelihood for younger sons of the landed orders. An increasing number served alongside the squires as JPs. Critics noted that the country clergy often seemed more concerned to keep up in the swirl of society and politics in the great country houses of the oligarchy than to tend to their parishes. The

Anglican clergy justifiably won the reputation of eating well, hunting foxes, and drinking port. One foreign observer noted:

> . . . it is pleasant to see how fat and fair these parsons are. They are charged with being somewhat lazy, and their usual plumpness makes it suspected that there's some truth in it. It is common to see them in coffee houses, and even in taverns, with pipes in their mouths.

Of course, there was many a kindly and caring parson, a brother to the squire and father to the laborers in the parish. Certainly, the parsons helped maintain the wholeness, if not always the holiness, of society. But the economics of clerical arrangements often made performance of their duties difficult. Most parish priests were paid by endowments (*livings*) established years before by individual landlords, whose descendants still held the right of appointment. In many cases, inflation had made the salary criminally low—£15 or £20 a year. Further, many parsons, once appointed to a living, had no intention of going there. Such a rector would hire a curate to do his duties. Of course, because the holder of the living paid the curate out of his own stipend, he would keep the pay as low as possible. Whereas the rector of Warton parish enjoyed £700 a year, one of his curates got only £5. Other clergymen, in order to make ends meet or simply to maximize their incomes, took more than one parish. As a consequence, plural holdings and nonresidence were grave problems. As late as 1809, 7,358 clergy out of 11,194 were nonresident. Moreover, as towns grew, ancient parish divisions no longer coincided with the real distribution of the population. Few new churches were built, so some large towns—Manchester, for example, with a population of twenty thousand—had only one church. Many clergymen were badly overworked and underpaid; others, blessed by the scramble for preferment, were overpaid and underworked.

Many of the backwoods parsons were rabid Tories, even Jacobites, and therefore High Churchmen. Most others, however, held a position in between the individualism of Puritanism and the authoritative centralism of Catholicism. This position, called *latitudinarianism*, held that human reason was sufficient to deal with most issues; for the rest, revelation was necessary—revelation as interpreted by the one true church, the Church of England. In any case, most clergymen in their teachings shied away from theological principles and concerned themselves with everyday ethics and morals. Their message inevitably reflected the outlook of their patrician patrons, tempered by reasonableness and benevolence: charity for the rich and obedience for the poor. The point of the established church, after all, was to give liturgical expression to the existing social order.

## COMMERCIALIZATION AND CULTURE: THE WRITTEN WORD

The existing social order, however, was undergoing enormous change during the eighteenth century. England was the most rapidly urbanizing region in Europe: urban growth in England accounted for 50 percent of all European urbanization between 1700 and 1750, and for a colossal 70 percent between 1750 and 1800. Provincial towns grew at an even faster rate than London, with the expansion of aristocratic leisure spots such as Brighton and Bath and important manufacturing centers such as Manchester and Sheffield. As early as 1750, more English men and women worked in manufacturing, commerce, and services than in agriculture. These commercial and industrial populations constituted a new reading public and challenged the landed elite's long domination of English cultural production. Eighteenth-century literature thus provided powerful testimony to the contrasts and contradictions of Augustan England—elegant order versus unrestrained exuberance, rational discourse versus bawdy satire, classical regulation versus commercial experimentation, the power of the landed elite versus the expanding influence of the middling sort.

In poetry we can see the power of the landed elite. Poetry continued to find its support in patronage, but poets now turned to the aristocracy rather than the Crown for patrons. Poetry accounted for a remarkable 47 percent of all titles published in the eighteenth century and provides a literary parallel to the emphasis of the Enlightenment on natural law. Just as the physical universe ran according to laws discernible to the rational observer, so each poetic genre was thought to have its appropriate kind of diction, meter, and versification, as discovered by classical authors. Thus, poetry of the Augustan Age, at least until the beginnings of Romanticism toward the end of the century, emphasized correctness of feeling and expression. Augustan readers and writers believed that poetry must conform to nature, in the sense of the permanent, universal attributes of human nature, and that classical poets expressed these eternal qualities best. As Pope wrote:

Those RULES of old discovr'd, not devis'd
Are Nature still, but Nature Methodized;
Nature, like Liberty, is but restrain'd
By the same Laws which first herself ordained.

Although poets such as Pope wrote for their aristocratic patrons, prose writers turned increasingly to the new reading public—larger, of middling social status, commercialized, and consisting of women as well as men. Thus, the demands of the marketplace rather than classical rules governed the production of prose. One sign of this change appeared in the first pages of prose publications: prefaces for the general reader replaced the traditional dedication to an aristocratic patron. The members of the new reading public wanted two things: first, entertainment for their leisure hours, and second, information and guidance about every aspect of life and thought. Many of them had just climbed up the next rung of the status ladder; ambitious and insecure, they looked to literature to teach them how to behave. Hence, a popular press flourished, producing books of sermons, dictionaries, encyclopedias, histories, and periodicals such as *The Spectator* and the *Gentleman's Magazine*. By mid-century, the leading periodicals sold perhaps ten thousand copies per issue—not a huge number by twenty-first-century standards, but unprecedented for the time.

Such periodicals featured superbly clear prose and clever satire, the two literary tools most suitable for social instruction and for moderate social criticism—and the literary tools most characteristic of Enlightenment writing. Many periodical writers, such as Joseph Addison, editor of *The Spectator*, sought through their works to encourage the free exchange of ideas that they believed to be essential for human advancement. Addison explained that the purpose of *The Spectator* was to lift "Philosophy out of Closets and Libraries, Schools and Colleges, to dwell in Clubs and Assemblies, at Tea-Tables and in Coffee-Houses." By stimulating "polite conversation" (that is, reasoned discussion), periodical writers and book authors aimed to contribute to the "wearing out of Ignorance, Passion, and Prejudice."

Women joined fully in this new ideal of rational exchange. Periodicals such as *The Ladies' Mercury* testified to the growing presence of women in the new public space that Enlightenment thinkers regarded as essential for the free trade of ideas. Writers such as Hester Chapone (1727–1801) wrote *conduct books* in which they not only advised their female readers on proper etiquette, but much more importantly, insisted on the right and responsibility of women to educate their minds and to join in Enlightened conversation. Chapone was part of the famous *bluestocking circle* of female intellectuals that centered on the lavish home of the one of the wealthiest women of the era, Elizabeth Montagu (1718–1800). A writer herself, Montagu used her money and position to foster the careers of many leading eighteenth-century essayists, novelists, and artists. At her well-known *salon*, the brightest men and women of eighteenth-century society gathered for witty conversation and intellectual exchange.

The most important response to the new reading public was the novel, which was for all practical purposes invented in the eighteenth century.

With its emphasis on realism, its focus on the individual, its freedom from classical rules, and its capacity to combine entertainment, instruction, and moral guidance, the novel was the perfect format for the age. Published in 1719, Daniel Defoe's *Robinson Crusoe* is often regarded as the first genuine novel. Despite its rollicking story line—the fictional Crusoe endures two shipwrecks; fights off mutineers, pirates, cannibals, and wolves; and constructs his own little European kingdom on the island on which he is marooned for many years—it offered readers a hero with whom they could identify, a man endowed with no special powers other than his own natural wit and rational faculties, as well as his developing religious faith. To many readers, it was the supreme Enlightenment tale, the triumph of human rationality over nature and savagery, as well as an assertion of the supremacy of Western technology and trade. Others embraced it as primarily a Protestant parable, in which a shipwrecked soul reads the Bible and finds salvation. In any case, it went through four editions in its first year of publication and remained hugely popular throughout the eighteenth century.

A generation after Defoe, writers turned to less exotic settings to offer novels that dissected English society and laid bare its inner workings. At the age of fifty-one, printer and publisher Samuel Richardson (1689–1761) decided to try writing his own book. *Pamela, or Virtue Rewarded*, proved to be a sensation and catapulted Richardson into high society. *Pamela*-themed playing cards, waxworks, paintings, and prints testified to the novel's popularity. At first glance, the heroine of *Pamela*, an innocent fifteen-year-old maidservant, seems a sharp contrast to the adventurous Crusoe. Yet, like Crusoe, Pamela triumphs over great adversity. Her young master attempts to seduce her, kidnaps her, and even tries to rape her, yet she remains virtuous and in the end is rewarded with marriage into the gentry and the admiration of her new peers. Although Pamela's triumph purifies and thus strengthens the social order, the novel defined virtue not by birth but by behavior, a message profoundly appealing to the expanding middling sort of eighteenth-century England.

Richardson's colleague Henry Fielding (1707–54) offered a similar lesson in his riotous satire *Tom Jones* (1749). On his path to virtue (and marriage to the beautiful Sophia), the high-spirited Tom indulges in a variety of sexual escapades, but he proves himself to be fundamentally honest and good-hearted. The novel concludes with a clear affirmation of Enlightened England's faith in reasoned discourse and human improvement: "Whatever in the nature of Jones had a tendency to vice, has been corrected by continual conversation with this good man [his uncle, Squire Allworthy], and by his union with the lovely and virtuous Sophia. He hath also, by reflection on his past follies, acquired a discretion and prudence very uncommon in one of his lively parts."

Women played a central role in defining and expanding the boundaries of the early novel. For example, in *The Female Quixote* (1752), Charlotte Lennox (1729–1804) used the misadventures of her heroine Arabella to draw the lines between traditional romance, with its excited emotions, exotic settings, and over-the-top plots, and the new realistic novel. As Lennox's young, female, and English version of the famous Don Quixote searches for a chivalrous knight in eighteenth-century London and Bath, her failures and successes provide a delightful commentary on both the society she encounters and the limits of romantic dreaming.

*The Female Quixote* can be seen as an early form of the *novel of manners*, a genre that took on its developed form later in the century. An intricate exploration of the social mores and ethical values of a particular class of people in a particular place and time, the novel of manners highlights the tensions between individual ambitions and wider social expectations and regulations. It is no surprise that this genre first flourished in eighteenth-century England, with its emphasis on proper behavior and its tendency to confuse manners with morality and etiquette with ethics. Nor is it a surprise that women, often the ultimate arbiters of proper behavior, helped define the genre. Frances or Fanny Burney (1752–1840) had great success with her novels of manners, most particularly *Evelina*, published in 1778. Brought up in the simple household of the worthy Reverend Villars, Burney's heroine is completely unprepared for the complexities and intrigues of English high society. As Evelina stumbles from one hilarious embarrassment to the next, her journey helps the reader map out the tortuous terrain of England's social hierarchy.

The novel of manners reached its culmination in the works of one of the greatest of all English novelists, Jane Austen (1775–1817). Austen stands at the turning point between the eighteenth and nineteenth centuries: although her six novels were first published between 1811 and 1818 (the last two posthumously), she wrote the early drafts of a number of them in the 1790s. Like Burney, Austen focused her novels on the gentry; in witty comedies of manners such as *Pride and Prejudice* (1813) and *Emma* (1815), she punctured the pretensions of the landed elite without, however, challenging that elite's position. Duty and deference, patronage and place, order and authority all regulate Austen's characters. At the same time, however, her strong and sassy heroines laid claim to their roles as rational individuals, making reasoned choices to improve their lives.

## COMMERCIALIZATION AND CULTURE: THE VISUAL ARTS

Like most aspects of eighteenth-century society, the visual arts reflected both the continuing power of traditional patronage and the new dominance of more market-oriented arrangements. The values and wishes of their patrician consumers heavily shaped architecture and painting, which thus tended to express symbolically the hierarchical social order and the sensibility of the ruling elite. At the same time, however, the growing wealth of England generated a booming market in art objects—paintings, sculpture, furnishings, and the like. This market, associated as it was with the consumer revolution, went a long way toward commodifying high culture and adapting it to a new commercial age.

The main achievement of late seventeenth-century architecture was in ecclesiastical building; here, the Church played its traditional role as an important patron of the arts. Sir Christopher Wren (1652–1725), the friend and colleague in the Royal Society of Newton and Locke, helped recast the skyline of London after the Great Fire of London (1666). Wren's fifty-five city churches—plus St. Paul's Cathedral—embodied his main themes of compromise, moderation, and harmony. He managed to merge the Italian Catholic baroque style (with its ornate decoration, classical forms, and sensual rhythms of concave and convex lines) with the Dutch Calvinist preaching hall (with its plain rectangular shape and severe decoration). In the work of his successors, such as James Gibbs (1682–1754), who designed St. Martins-in-the-Fields, the compromise shifted more to classical style, combining a single steeple (a Gothic element) with a rectangular hall fronted by classical columns and a hexastyle (triangular) portico. These serene churches expressed perfectly the Anglican compromise between Catholicism and Calvinism and appealed immediately to reason as well. The style spread widely in Protestant Britain and to America also, where it became the standard form of Protestant architecture.

In the eighteenth century, however, the great architectural monuments were the homes of the landed elite. According to one French traveler, "The multitude of gentlemen's houses, scattered over the country, is a feature quite peculiar to the English landscape; the thing is unknown in France." English patricians thought it important to live most of the year on their estates so as to play the social and governmental roles they had claimed for

*St. Martin's-in-the-Field, designed by Sir James Gibbs (early eighteenth century). This beautiful church, a favorite with tourists, is perhaps the best example of neo-classical church architecture in England.*

themselves. Those who could afford it moved to London for the spring *season* and rotated through spas such as Tunbridge Wells and Bath. But their country houses composed the focal points of high culture, set as they were in pleasing parks and filled with rich furnishings and fine paintings. The gentleman's country "seat" was the principal means by which he showed his taste and refinement and served as the base of operations for his beloved hunting sports. Thus, the great country houses were the setting for endless entertaining, for local estate and governmental business, for partisan political talk, and not least for sheer enjoyment of the fat of the land. Lord Hervey recalled of his visits to Houghton, Walpole's estate in Norfolk: "We used to sit down to dinner a snug little party of about thirty odd, up to the chin in beef, venison, geese, turkeys, etc.; and generally over the chin in claret, strong beer, and punch."

The design of the great country houses reflected these functions. Magnificent and elegant on the interior, they displayed the wealth and taste of the owner to others of the same social stratum; stately and grave on the

*Mereworth Castle, Kent, designed by Colen Campbell (1723). Mereworth Castle is a fine example of the Palladian house. Notice the perfect symmetry.*

exterior, these striking buildings overawed the common folk. *Symmetry* was the pervasive theme. In the late seventeenth and early eighteenth centuries, the taste for the Baroque produced symmetrical but monumentally heavy piles, of which the great representative was (and is) the duke of Marlborough's Blenheim Palace. But as the eighteenth century advanced, the Whig preference for the appearance of moderation made the country houses less formal. The surrounding parks, designed by landscape architects such as Capability Brown, shifted away from geometrical formality toward the *natural*—nature tamed by reasonableness. The houses themselves retained the symmetry of baroque, but now stressed simplicity and proportion.

The new style was called *Palladian*, after the sixteenth-century architect Andrea Palladio, who was thought to have derived perfect formulas from Roman buildings. The typical Palladian house, exemplified by Mereworth Castle, began with a main rectangular block of several stories flanked on either side by precisely matched wings, fronted by rows of classical windows, and topped by a hexastyle portico over the main entrance. Inside, the design separated the business rooms and servants' areas *below stairs* from the elegant halls, drawing rooms, and chambers of the family *above stairs*.

Perhaps it is almost inevitable that portraiture was the characteristic mode of English painting. The patricians were, after all, deeply interested in the individual—and above all, in themselves. Moreover, the production of portraits remained thoroughly ensconced in the traditional patron-client relationship; commissioning portraits was yet another way for members of the landed elite to demonstrate their social power. Yet portraits under their influence became less heroic and grandiose than in the seventeenth century, for the landlords intended to have themselves depicted at ease in the world they had won. Leading Augustan portrait painters, such as Sir Joshua Reynolds (1723–92) and Thomas Gainsborough (1727–88), often painted their subjects at home in their country houses, lords of all they surveyed. Reynolds, the son of an Anglican priest, grew up on the edge of the gentry. but climbed to the top of London society through the patronage of important peers, including the duke of Cumberland, George II's third son. Reynolds traveled and trained on the Continent, and became famous for his theory of the *grand style*—painting by the classical rules established by the old masters, concern for the general and ideal, and strict proportion—even at the expense of taking liberties with the actual features of the subject. Gainsborough came from the lower rungs of the social ladder; the son of a weaver, he was first apprenticed to an engraver, but by moving to Bath, the favorite elite holiday spot, and turning to portrait painting, he was soon able to attract wealthy patrons. Less formalized than Reynolds, he too portrayed his ladies and gentlemen in such a way as to express an ideal of ease, dignity, and grace.

Few people below the ranks of the landed elite could afford formal portraits; nonetheless, in the prosperous English towns and cities, and above all in London, well-to-do commercial people—men and women alike—joined the landed elite in pursuing and purchasing paintings, sculpture, tapestries, drapes, furniture, and decorative items. The members of this cultural elite were intent on equipping their grand country homes and town houses to impress each other, and on distinguishing themselves by their refined taste—their politeness—from the common folk, particularly those individuals of the middling sort who dared aspire for gentle status. The demand for Old Masters resulted in the importation from the continent of some fifty thousand paintings between 1720 and 1770, and ten times that many etchings and engravings. The establishment of galleries and auction houses in London, as well as the founding of the Royal Academy in 1768, helped to define and control high standards of taste. As an unintended consequence of

Mrs. Siddons as the Tragic Muse, *by Sir Joshua Reynolds (1784). Reynolds painted in the grand style, striving for classical proportions and the ennoblement of his subjects through their pose or costume.*

this process of commodification, the very notion of the fine arts as a distinct (and superior) realm of human activity came into being.

The harmonious symmetry, exquisite furnishings, and elegant portraits of the great country houses thus speak to a culture of restraint and refinement. Other forms of visual art, however, reveal a very different picture. The rapid commercialization of English society meant an expanding market for engravings and woodcuts that could be cheaply reproduced in large quantities. These prints strip away the decorum of polite society and expose a culture as dedicated to excess and debauchery as to rational conversation and intellectual improvement. Brash and bawdy, these prints remind us that, as the historian J. H. Plumb has written, "an exceedingly frank acknowledgement, one might almost say a relish, of man's animal functions was as much a part of the age as the elegant furniture or delicate china."[1]

From this context arose one of the eighteenth-century England's maverick geniuses—William Hogarth (1697–1764), widely acknowledged as the father of satirical caricature and the grandfather of the political cartoon. Hogarth came out of the ranks of the London middling sort, but he

---

[1]Gatrell, *City of Laughter: Sex and Satire in Eighteenth-Century London,* 4.

A Row at a Cock and Hen Club *by Richard Newton (1798). Men in the middle ranks and above joined private clubs where they ate, drank, and as this print shows, engaged in other, more rowdy, activities.*

experienced the rough edges of life: his father had to enter debtor's prison after the school he ran foundered. Standing on the outside of the landed elite, Hogarth had a keen eye for the hypocrisy and corruption of the day. He hated what he called *phiz-mongering*—idealized portraiture to please the rich—and sought to give a broad view of social life in the mode of dramatic narrative paintings. Each of these is as delightfully satirical, instructive, and morally didactic as a Fielding novel—and like a Fielding novel, Hogarth's work appealed especially to the expanding middling sort, who delighted in his wit. In numerous paintings and engravings, Hogarth revealed the greed, vanity, and turmoil that surged beneath the veneer of Augustan high culture.

## POPULAR CULTURE, COMMON CULTURES

The finely graded hierarchies of eighteenth-century society and the vast gap between rich and poor meant that the laboring poor and the wealthier orders often seemed to inhabit separate worlds. The fine arts, of course, did not enter much into the lives of laborers, although it must not be assumed that their work demanded no knowledge or cultural framework. A husbandman, for instance, had to know about the soil, the weather, and the crops; about feeding and caring for animals; about plowing, cultivating, draining, hedging, thatching, brickmaking, and woodworking; and about spinning or weaving for the slack season. A woman had to know about dairying, brewing, and gardening and about spinning, sewing, and lace making. Even more impressive were the skills, often carefully guarded "mysteries," of particular crafts. A wheelwright, for instance, had to know which wood was best for spokes (oak), hubs (willow or elm), and felloes (ash). He had to cut and season the wood properly, and then saw and plane it with great precision so that the wheel was perfectly round and the spokes chamfered out at the right degree. All such knowledge was passed on during years of hands-on experience and through oral and traditional culture.

Schooling and literacy had comparatively little to do with how common people made a living, nor did they contribute a great deal to the common folk's understanding of themselves and their world. In rural districts, probably less than half the men and a quarter of the women possessed even a rudimentary ability to read and write. Schools available to the laboring people consisted of some charity schools; a growing number of Sunday schools (which taught the basics of reading and arithmetic); and a larger number of tiny, ephemeral schools run by individuals on a private-enterprise basis. The teachers in this last category often hung out their teaching shingle simply because they could find no other way to make a living. (In contrast, in Scotland the kirk established schools in many localities.) Probably a majority of the English laboring poor who could read learned from their parents or taught themselves. Only in the cities (and especially in London) among the skilled craftsmen and shopkeepers did literacy penetrate very far.

Although traveling peddlers brought information about politics and public events from outside the parish, people were very parochial and intensely suspicious of strangers. This localism obviously was under attack from the expanding network of trade and consumer goods, but it remained of real importance well into the nineteenth century. What ordinary villagers knew about themselves and their world came from an amalgam of custom, oral traditions, and religion. Nursery rhymes, legends, folk tales, popular songs, and other oral traditions all taught traditional wisdom. Weekly sermons in the parish church provided a conceptual framework as well as moral guidance—at least in those parishes where clergymen did not neglect their pastoral responsibilities.

In any case, common folk tended to attribute their own meanings to Christian rituals. Baptism, for example, was sometimes thought to make a child physically strong. Puritanism, inherited from the seventeenth century, did continue to hold sway in some households, particularly among town craftsmen who remembered the ideal of the freeborn Englishman and who cherished two books—the Bible and John Bunyan's *The Pilgrim's Progress*, the seventeenth-century Puritan allegory of a Christian's progress through temptation and despair. In the countryside, however, popular consciousness largely depended on beliefs passed on through oral culture. Superstition and magic gave the laboring poor, especially in the countryside, some sense of control over their environment. Thus, they continued to believe in ghosts and witchcraft and resorted to magical folk medicine for healing the sick and to village wise men for foretelling the future or finding lost articles.

The poor found relief from the harsh realities of life in a wide variety of recreations, many of which have now disappeared. There were routine enjoyments such as telling stories over domestic work, singing in the fields or at the loom, or behaving playfully on trips to the market. The more public recreations often took a more ritualized form and sprang from the traditional calendar of holidays—a combination of Christian holy days and significant moments in the agricultural year. Almost every parish held annual festivals, or *wakes*. For instance, in Claybrook at the parish wake, it was observed, "The cousins assemble from all quarters, fill the church on Sunday, and celebrate the Monday with feasting, with music, and with dancing." Annual fairs for hiring laborers or for selling horses, cattle, leather goods, and the like gave opportunities for mixing business with pleasure. Christmas, Easter, and Whitsuntide were the occasions for holidays and festivities, as were plow and harvest times. Many such festivals mixed the secular and the sacred calendars; all of them gave the populace a chance to play games, eat heartily, get drunk, and flirt with the opposite sex—in short, to escape the rules of everyday life.

Many of the popular recreations were purely of and for the laboring people. Varieties of soccer, for example, pitted the men of one village against those of another. Drinking and games of quoits and bowling in the omnipresent public houses were strictly for the populace. Yet many of the popular recreations were approved, and even sponsored, by the gentry. Some recreations were exclusively for the gentry—most notably fox hunting, whereby the rich displayed their finery, horsemanship, boldness, and power. Other recreations allowed for social mixing, like horse racing, staged by the rich (and indeed becoming a fetish among them, which it remains), but also attracting large numbers of ordinary spectators, as did cock fights and boxing.

Further, the gentry customarily entertained the local folk at important moments in the great family's life—the birth, coming of age, and marriage of a son. On such occasions, the landowners incorporated the laboring poor into rustic celebrations of the continuity of the lineage. Similarly, the gentry typically treated the common people to food and drink at harvest home and parish feast days. Tradition and the need to preserve the loyalty of the laborers dictated the squire's generosity. As Sir Joseph Banks noted ruefully in 1783: "This is the day of our fair when according to immemorial custom I am to feed and make drunk everyone who wishes to come which cost me in beef and ale near 20 pounds." In a more bloodthirsty line, gentlemen usually provided the unfortunate animal for bull baiting, which was a popular activity, not least because it normally ended with the slaughter of the bull for the poor to eat. Like the squires' typical willingness to negotiate with food rioters, their cooperation with popular recreations helped preserve the coherence of the local community and the deference on which their rule stood.

Vauxhall Gardens *by Thomas Rowlandson (1784). At pleasure gardens such as Vauxhall, eighteenth-century English men and women could choose to see and be seen—or to disappear down the dark pathways for illicit meetings. Rowlandson placed many well-known figures in this painting, including on the right the prince of Wales whispering to his lover, actress Perdita Robinson.*

In the cities, too, rich and poor intermingled in a common culture. Laborers, for example, jostled alongside their social betters at the windows of the print sellers to view the latest scandalous pictures. Concert hall and opera house tickets were well beyond the reach of ordinary folk, but at theaters, laborers in the cheap seats and the wealthy in the boxes enjoyed booing and cheering the same performances. Because the house was not darkened for the performance, watching and commenting on fellow audience members was as much a part of the show as what happened on stage. Pleasure gardens also provided a venue for the mixing of social ranks and the enjoyment of a common culture. Featuring concerts, art exhibitions, acrobatic performances, and fireworks displays, as well as elaborately landscaped gardens dotted with pathways and secluded enclosures, pleasure gardens such as the famed Vauxhall attracted enormous crowds drawn from all ranks of society. With its blend of the refined and the raucous, the pleasure garden in many ways epitomized eighteenth-century English culture in all its contrasts and contradictions.

### Suggested Reading

Barker-Benfield, G. J. *The Culture of Sensibility: Sex and Society in Eighteenth-Century Britain*. Chicago: University of Chicago Press, 1992.

Black, Jeremy, ed. *Culture and Society in Britain, 1660–1800*. Manchester, UK: Manchester University Press, 1997.

Borsay, Peter. *The English Urban Renaissance: Culture and Society in the Provincial Town, 1660–1770*. New York: Oxford University Press, 1989.

Brewer, John. *The Pleasures of the Imagination: English Culture in the Eighteenth Century*. New York: Farrar, Straus and Giroux, 1997.

Chamberlain, Jeffrey. *Accommodating High Churchmen: The Clergy of Sussex, 1700–1741*. Urbana: University of Illinois Press, 1997.

Christie, Christopher. *The British Country House in the Eighteenth Century*. Manchester, UK: Manchester University Press, 1999.

Colley, Linda. *Britons: Forging the Nation. 1707–1837*. New Haven, CT: Yale University Press, 1992.

Cowan, Brian. *The Social Life of Coffee: The Emergence of the British Coffeehouse*. New Haven, CT: Yale University Press, 2005.

Cragg, G. R. *Reason and Authority in the Eighteenth Century*. Cambridge: Cambridge University Press, 1964.

Friedman, Terry. *The Eighteenth-Century Church in Britain*. New Haven, CT: Yale University Press, 2011.

Gatrell, Victor. *City of Laughter: Sex and Satire in Eighteenth-Century London*. London: Atlantic, 2006.

Gibson, William. *The Church of England, 1688–1832: Unity and Accord*. London: Routledge, 2001.

Girouard, Mark. *Life in the English Country House*. New Haven, CT: Yale University Press, 1978.

Harris, R. W. *Reason and Nature in the Eighteenth Century*. London: Blandford, 1968.

Harris, Tim, ed. *Popular Culture in England, c. 1500–1850*. New York: St. Martin's Press, 1995.

Hartley, Dorothy. *Made in England*. London: Eyre Methuen, 1939.

Jacob, W. M. *Lay People and Religion in the Early Eighteenth Century*. Cambridge: Cambridge University Press, 1996.

Malcolmson, Robert W. *Popular Recreations in English Society, 1700–1850*. Cambridge: Cambridge University Press, 1973.

Myers, Sylvia Harcstark. *The Bluestocking Circle: Women. Friendship, and the Life of the Mind in Eighteenth-Century England*. New York: Oxford University Press, 1990.

Newman, Gerald. *The Rise of English Nationalism, 1740–1830*. New York: St. Martin's Press, 1987.

Rivers, Isabel, ed. *Books and Their Readers in Eighteenth-Century England: New Essays*. Leicester, UK: Leicester University Press, 2002.

Rupp, Gordon. *Religion in England, 1688–1791*. Oxford: Clarendon Press, 1986.

Sack, J. J. *From Jacobite to Conservative: Reaction and Orthodoxy in Britain, c. 1760–1832*. Cambridge: Cambridge University Press, 1993.

Snape, M. F. *The Church of England in Industrialising Society. The Lancashire Parish of Whalley in the Eighteenth Century*. Woodbridge, UK: Boydell, 2003.

Spaeth, Donald. *The Church in an Age of Danger: Parsons and Parishioners, 1660–1740*. Cambridge: Cambridge University Press, 2000.

Thomas, Keith. *Man and the Natural World*. New York: Pantheon Press, 1983.

Vincent, David. *Literacy and Popular Culture: England, 1750–1914*. New York: Cambridge University Press, 1989.

Virgin, Peter. *The Church in an Age of Negligence*. Cambridge: James Clarke, 1989.

Walsh, John, Colin Haydon, and Stephen Taylor, eds. *The Church of England, c. 1689–c. 1833: From Toleration to Tractarianism*. Cambridge: Cambridge University Press, 1993.

Watt, Ian. *The Rise of the Novel*. London: Chatto & Windus, 1957.

White, Jerry. *London in the Eighteenth Century: A Great and Monstrous Thing*. London: Bodley Head, 2012.

Willey, Basil. *The Eighteenth Century Background*. New York: Columbia University Press, 1940.

# Chapter 6

# Scotland in the Eighteenth Century

Scotland's transformation in the eighteenth century was even more rapid and dramatic than England's, and even more strongly driven by the tension between custom and contract. In the Highlands, in particular, a traditional society based on personal ties and paternalist loyalties battled against a new social order engineered by market forces and characterized by a faith in human rationality. Economic and political instability marked the first half of the century, erupting into armed rebellion as Jacobite forces sought to undo not only the Union but also the Revolution Settlement. The Jacobites were defeated, however, and so too was the culture that had most strongly nourished Scottish Jacobitism. By the end of the eighteenth century, the Highland culture, the most coherent and complete stronghold of Gaelic life and of the traditional customary order in the British Isles, was nearly eradicated as the economy and the society of the Highlands was made over in the English image. Ironically, the triumph of contract and its Whig proponents in Scotland coincided with a wonderful flowering of Enlightened high culture in the cities of the Lowlands during the latter half of the century. As in England, then, the eighteenth century in Scotland was a period of sharp contrasts.

## THE JACOBITE REBELLION OF 1715

We saw in chapter 3 that the Act of Union of 1707 abolished the Scottish Parliament and created the new state of Great Britain. The predicted economic benefits of union eventually came true, but not in the short run. Scottish goods proved to be of a quality that was too low to compete well in the vast market the Scots had joined. The trade in cattle flourished, but most others languished. The Scottish representatives in Parliament could offer little help because they were too few to be effective and were soon co-opted by patronage into the Whig political system. The English-dominated Parliament proceeded to administer a series of blows that further alienated Scottish opinion. In 1712, it restored the right of lay patrons (usually large landowners) to appoint ministers to parish livings in the Church of Scotland, an extension of patronage that violated the very principle of Presbyterianism. Scottish fears that the Union would "bind up our hands from asserting our religiouse and civil libertys, and meanteaning a work of Reformation" seemed well-founded. The next year, Parliament attempted to extend the English malt tax to Scotland, which would have raised the price of beer and whiskey. Scots regarded this tax as the last straw, and the Scottish members of Parliament (MPs) in London actually moved for dissolution of the Union—to no avail, of course.

All of this discontent in Scotland fed the fires of Jacobitism. Scottish Jacobitism amounted to more than ceremonial toasts to "the king over the water." The Treaty of Union, intensely unpopular in its own right, made the Jacobites the heirs of Scottish patriotism because the Union had been closely tied to recognition of the Hanoverian succession. Moreover, Jacobitism had particularly strong roots in the Catholic and Episcopal populations, especially in the Highland clans. The clans had never taken to Presbyterianism, and the Highland tradition of loyalty to one's chief made the Jacobite principle of hereditary right to the monarchy ring true. For all these reasons, Jacobitism was a more formidable force in Scotland than in England, and by 1714 Scotland stood on the verge of a major rebellion.

Yet the chances of such a rebellion succeeding were limited by Jacobite weaknesses, the same that hobbled the movement throughout its history. First, there was the obstinacy and political clumsiness of the Stuart line. James II had died and had been succeeded in exile by his son, James Edward ("The Old Pretender"), a melancholy and reserved man incapable of inspirational leadership. Second, the Stuarts in exile were completely dependent on the French, whose support for the Jacobite cause waxed and waned as French interests dictated. Third, there was a fundamental confusion in Jacobitism: the desire for Scottish independence clashed with loyalty to the Stuarts, who considered themselves to be kings of England and Ireland as well as Scotland, and who wanted to maintain the union of the crowns.

Despite these weaknesses, a major Jacobite rebellion erupted after Queen Anne died and was succeeded by George I. Influenced by Whig slander, George snubbed one of his secretaries of state, the Scotsman John Erskine, earl of Mar, who had in fact helped to bring about the Union. Mar fled to Scotland and raised the standard of James Edward as King James VIII of Scotland (James III to English Jacobites) in August 1715. Partly on the basis of false claims of French support, Mar rapidly assembled a force of about twelve thousand men, mainly Episcopalians from the Northeast of Scotland plus elements of many Highland clans. Not all of the Highland clans came out, however, for the decision as to whether to rebel or support the Hanoverians often depended on the clan chief's position in local feuds and local politics. The Campbells, for instance, supported the Whig regime, as did some great northern clans such as the Sutherlands and the Mackays.

The ordinary clan member, who was the foot soldier of the Highland host, had nothing to do with the decision of his clan to join the fray. The decision was strictly a matter for the clan chief and his immediate family. In the Highland clans, the chief leased land at a low rent to his principal lieutenants, called *tacksmen*, who were often kinsmen of the chief. In return for their land, the tacksmen pledged military service to the chief and in turn subleased their land in small portions to the clansmen who served as the clan troops. Bound by the closest ties of blood, land tenure, and military duty, the tacksmen of a clan had to respond unquestioningly to the call of the chief to go to war, as did the ordinary subtenant soldiers. In relatively short bursts, this clan army would fight with great élan, mobility, and offensive striking power, but it was not suited to long campaigns or defensive warfare.

Mar failed to understand either the opportunities or the limits offered by the Highland army. The Hanoverian forces in Scotland were very weak; had he moved quickly, Mar might well have consolidated Scotland for James Edward and then moved to gather Jacobite forces in England. Certainly the Jacobite army needed quick successes in order to prove to waverers that joining the rebellion was the politically astute thing to do. But Mar, an indecisive commander, failed to take Edinburgh. Finally, the duke of Argyll (head of the Campbells) and his small British army drew Mar into battle at Sheriffmuir in November. Sheriffmuir made a significant difference in Scottish national history. The bloody battle was a draw, but Argyll's troops held the field. Mar's Highlanders began to drift back to their mountain glens.

At this point James Edward arrived from France. He had been given no help by the French government, which was in a cautious mood after the

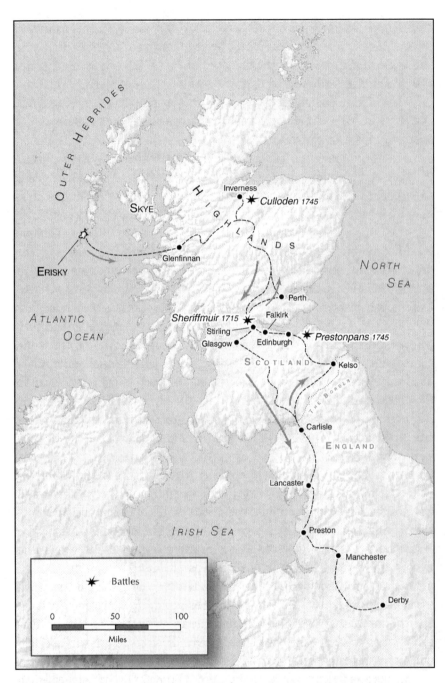

*Jacobite Rebellions.* The Battle of Sherrifmuir ended before James Edward, the Old Pretender, landed on Scottish soil. Thirty years later, his son endured longer and fought harder, but in the end fared no better. The map traces the route of the Young Pretender's march into England and his lengthy retreat.

death of Louis XIV earlier in 1715. James Edward was a brave man, but his perpetual gloominess hindered his cause. On his arrival in December, he announced to his officers: "For me, it is no new thing to be unfortunate, since my whole life from my cradle has been a constant series of misfortunes"—hardly a speech to inspire wavering men. The dwindling of Mar's army continued. Argyll received reinforcements, and in February 1716, James Edward and Mar left for France. Thus ended what was probably the Scots' best chance of restoring their independence by force.

## THE '45

The Stuarts did not stop trying to promote their cause after 1715. Forever involved in intrigue in European courts against the Hanoverian regime, they even managed in 1719 to get Spanish support for an armed expedition to Britain. In this case, as in so many others, the winds blew against the Jacobites, and a storm destroyed much of the Spanish fleet off Corunna. Only a few hundred Spanish troops reached Scotland, and they were soon defeated and their meager clan allies scattered.

The rebellion of 1715 and the abortive invasion of 1719 were of great help to the Whigs in establishing their preeminence *in England*: they could claim that the Tories were unsafe because of their Jacobite associations and that Whig rule was the only alternative to popery and foreign invasion. *In Scotland*, however, Whig efforts to integrate the Highlands with the already anglicized Lowlands and to incorporate both in the British state proceeded fitfully during these years. In the wake of the 1715 rebellion, the Whig government suppressed the titles of about nineteen leading Jacobites and seized a few estates, yet most of the clan chiefs were able to avoid serious punishment. The Jacobite clans simply ignored the Disarming Act of 1716, which prohibited them from possessing a broadsword, gun, or "other warlike weapon."

Yet anglicization did begin to chip away at the structures of Highland society. The construction of a system of roads proved effective in breaking the isolation of the Highlands and strengthening state control. Under General George Wade, the British army in the 1720s built approximately 260 miles of roadway, penetrating the central Highlands and connecting the British outposts on the Great Glen, Fort William and Fort Augustus, to Inverness. Wade instituted a system of policing the main Highland routes against Jacobites by recruiting Whig clansmen into independent army units (later organized as the famous Black Watch Regiment).

At the same time, a semiofficial educational movement undertaken by the Lowland gentry increased the pressure on traditional Highland society. The Scottish Society for the Propagation of Christian Knowledge (SSPCK) was founded in 1709 after the model of the English SPCK to establish Presbyterian schools that would teach "religion and virtue" to Highlanders, who were perceived by many Lowland Scots (and many English) as savages. The SSPCK founders believed that the barbarism of Highland culture stemmed from three mutually supportive factors: Catholicism, the Gaelic language, and Jacobitism. By inculcating Highland children with Calvinist religious doctrines and teaching them the English language, the SSPCK sought to weaken Jacobitism and hasten the integration of the Highlanders into the mainstream of Anglo-Scottish life. The (Presbyterian) Church of Scotland, which had experienced great difficulty in penetrating the Gaelic-speaking areas, supported the SSPCK, and Parliament granted it £20,000 from the revenue raised by the forfeited estates of rebel clansmen. By 1758, the SSPCK had established 176 schools, most of them in the Highlands. Through the SSPCK, one Presbyterian minister proclaimed, "Christianity is increased, Heathenish Customs are abandoned, the number of Papists is diminished, disaffection to the Government is lessened, and the English language is so diffused, that in the remotest glens it is spoken by the young people."[1] His confidence may have been misplaced: illiteracy rates in the Highland remained among the highest in Europe. Nevertheless, the isolation of Highland culture was dwindling. At the same time, the Highland aristocracy and gentry, who increasingly had to live in both the Gaelic and the anglicized worlds, slowly began to accept the manners and speech of "polite"—that is, English—culture.

The Jacobite revolt of 1745, then, was not the outburst of a vigorous Gaelic society, but the last stand of traditional Highland culture against the forces causing its decline: commercialism, anglicization, and governmental pressure from England and Lowland Scotland. The prosperity and stability of Walpole's long premiership had made the 1720s and 1730s relatively peaceful in Scotland. But when Britain went to war with Spain in 1739, and France soon after, the opportunity again rose for a Jacobite rebellion in Britain, this time with French help. Charles Edward, son of The Old Pretender and one of the few charismatic figures produced by the Stuarts, saw his opportunity and seized it.

---

[1]Allen, *Scotland in the Eighteenth Century*, 120.

Charles Edward, "The Young Pretender," or Bonnie Prince Charlie as the Scots called him, was then in his early twenties, none too intelligent, but tall, good-looking, graceful, and chivalrous. Born and reared in the Jacobite court in Rome, he was energetic and ambitious. Early in 1744, Charles went to France in order to persuade the French government to assist the Jacobite enterprise. The French, as usual, were interested in using the Stuarts solely to advance their own interests. As it happened, the French in 1744 were planning an invasion of England, but a storm destroyed the invasion fleet. The French abandoned their invasion plans, turned their attention to the Continent, and left Charles on his own. In 1745, with little help from the French, Charles had two ships fitted out for an expedition to Scotland. Unfortunately for Charles, the British navy intercepted and drove off the larger of the two ships, which carried most of Charles's troops. The prince, however, persevered and landed in the Outer Hebrides, leading a grand total of seven men.

For some time, Charles had been in contact with the Jacobite clans, but the absence of French troops discouraged most of them from joining him. Only by an emotional appeal to the Highlanders' sense of personal loyalty was Charles initially able to win any support at all, and that predictably came from the Macdonalds and the Camerons. He boldly set out for the central Highlands and Edinburgh with no more than one thousand men. Luckily for him, the British had stripped Scotland of almost all of its forces, including the new Black Watch regiment. Moreover, the few troops remaining, inexperienced and untrained, were commanded by Sir John Cope, an incompetent officer who threw away what advantages he had by embarking on a long and pointless march to Inverness. Gathering support as he went, Charles moved directly to Edinburgh, which opened its gate to the Jacobites without a fight. Cope shipped his men back to Edinburgh, but arrived too late. Shortly afterward, Charles's forces attacked Cope's army at Prestonpans and routed it with a furious Highland charge.

These astonishing events meant that Charles now held all of Scotland except Glasgow and the Southwest. Yet Charles's army never numbered more than about five thousand Highlanders, and he had no means of actually administering the country. Moreover, the bonnie prince was not content to win Scottish independence; he held true to the Stuart aim of reclaiming *both* crowns. Hence, with his small and restless Highland army, Charles invaded England. In a dramatic march he moved through Carlisle and Manchester as far south as Derby, only 130 miles from London. The British

The Battle of Culloden, *by D. Morier (April 1746). This painting shows the desperation of the struggle when the Highland charge met the British lines. The Jacobite clans suffered total defeat.*

government panicked, and George II prepared to return to Hanover. In fact, however, Charles's advance had not brought out any significant *English* Jacobite support. After a heated argument with his commanders, Charles was prevailed upon to retreat to Scotland.

The long retreat was disastrous for the Jacobite army. The Highlanders' morale dwindled, and desertions increased. Behind them came a large, well-supplied, and methodical army led by William, duke of Cumberland, George II's enormously fat but capable son. The two forces met at Culloden, on a boggy field ill-suited to the impetuous Highlanders' mode of combat. The miserably cold and starving Highlanders endured a fearful pounding by the British artillery before they could stand no more and charged. This time the British troops knew what to expect from a Highland attack. The result was a complete defeat for the Jacobite army and the slaughter of the High-landers. Led from the field, Charles said only, "Let every man seek his own safety the best way he can." On the run across the Highlands for five months, Charles took shelter with loyal clansmen. His adventures gave rise to many a romantic legend, but the Jacobite movement was shattered. Charles returned to France in September 1746 and spent the rest of his life in futile attempts to revive the Jacobite cause. He died in Rome in 1788; by then the British had ceased to worry about Jacobitism and the no longer very bonny prince.

## THE DESTRUCTION OF THE CLANS AND THE TRANSFORMATION OF THE HIGHLANDS

The Battle of Culloden itself was a severe blow to the Highland clans, but British policies after Culloden did even more lasting damage. The duke of Cumberland pursued the remnants of the clan army with ruthless persistence. This pursuit, which earned Cumberland the nickname "Butcher Billy," was a matter of official policy, a concerted effort to reduce the power of the Highlanders so that they could never again sponsor a Jacobite rebellion. Lord Chesterfield, the elegant exponent of worldly manners and lord lieutenant of Ireland, in fact urged a policy of genocide on Cumberland— capture the chiefs, massacre the peasantry, and eradicate the clans. Cumberland and his successors did not go that far, but their activities were thorough enough. British troops deliberately ravaged clan estates all through 1746, burning crops, destroying cottages, driving off cattle, and smashing tools. Any rebel captured with weapons was shot outright. Most ordinary clan soldiers who surrendered were transported to the colonies as indentured workers. About 120 Scottish Jacobite officers were executed.

These brutal acts were only the opening efforts at destroying the Highland way of life. The British forts in the Highlands were strengthened, Wade's system of military roads vastly expanded, and military patrols extended and increased. Law and order came to the Highlands with an iron hand. In 1746 Parliament passed another Disarming Act, forbidding the Highlanders to carry or possess arms or to wear Highland dress (that is, the tartan and plaid). The act even banned the bagpipe as a warlike instrument. The British state seized a substantial number of estates belonging to clan chiefs, and this time (unlike in 1715) allowed no legalistic evasion of forfeiture. Most important, the claims of the chiefs over their tenants that had made the clans such potent military units were broken. The abolition of military tenures and the clan chiefs' judicial powers ensured that the landlord-tenant relationship in the Highlands came to resemble that prevailing in England. Now the chief was no longer prosecutor, judge, and jury in his territory, and Scottish gentry and tenantry had access to courts established by the central government. Legal administration in Scotland was brought into line with English policies, though Scottish law itself remained separate.

The English (and many Lowland Scots) had long regarded the Highlanders as primitives, prone to rebellion and lawlessness. To tame these supposed barbarians, the British government sought to inculcate Highland culture with English-style efficiency and industriousness. Military discipline provided one avenue. Recruited for new regiments in the British army, thousands of Highland clansmen—themselves the targets of English imperialism—played a vital role in the expansion of the Empire. The British state also attempted to use the forfeited Jacobite estates as models of improved farming along a corridor of land thirty to forty miles wide from Stirling to Inverness. All rents here were to be used for "civilising the Inhabitants upon the said Estates and other Parts of the Highlands and Islands of Scotland, thus promoting amongst them the Protestant religion, good Government, Industry and Manufactures, and the Principles of Duty and Loyalty to his Majesty, his Heirs and Successors." Gradually, however, the government lost interest in the scheme as fear of Jacobitism died out, and by 1784 the estates had returned to private hands.

It was the landlords of the Scottish Highlands, not the British state, who largely completed the destruction of the clans. In increasing numbers since the beginning of the eighteenth century, Highland chiefs sent their sons to be educated in the Lowlands so that they could acquire the polish (and the language) of the polite world. Inevitably, some of the values of that world rubbed off on them. After Culloden, these semi-anglicized chiefs faced a choice of trying to sustain the traditional Highland culture against overwhelming odds or converting themselves into landlords along English (or Lowland) lines. During the century after 1750, most clan chiefs opted for the latter route, sometimes reluctantly, often intermittently, but inexorably nonetheless. By this slow trend—as much a nineteenth as an eighteenth-century development—the clan chiefs transformed themselves into English-style great landlords and in the process severed the close personal and patriarchal bonds that had knitted the clans together.

The landlords called this transformation *improvement*, a resonant term that captures perfectly the optimism in human endeavor and scientific rationality that characterized eighteenth-century Enlightened thought. Highland landlords sought not only to increase their own profits, but also to replace what they regarded as inefficient, unproductive, and irrational agricultural practices with progressive, scientific techniques. They consolidated the holdings on their estates (as was being done in England and in the Lowlands through enclosure), eliminated the tacksmen as intermediary tenants, and leased the parcels of land directly to the highest bidder, often someone from outside the community. Some landlords saw the tacksmen, subtenants, and cottagers who stood in their way merely as obstacles to be removed. Others, however, were genuinely horrified by the poverty and vulnerability to recurrent famine that characterized Highland society. By establishing a more sustainable economy, they believed they would improve the lives of the ordinary people who resided on their lands—as well, of course, as their own incomes.

No matter what the motivation of the landlords, the fact remains that what came to be called the *Highland Clearances* constituted the destruction of an entire way of life—in some cases, achieved with astonishing rapidity. Sheep figure largely in the story of the Clearances. As wool prices climbed steadily in the second half of the eighteenth century, "improving" landlords discovered that sheep meant profit. To make room for sheep, they ordered the removal of entire communities to coastal regions. There, the improvers proclaimed, displaced tenants would shrug off their traditional way of life and evolve into modern, productive wage laborers in the linen, fishing, and kelp-burning (alkali) industries.

Few of the dispossessed regarded the Clearances as improvement. Suddenly evicted from land that they had long regarded as their communal inheritance, they now had to learn entirely new skills to survive in a harsh new environment. The infertile and overcrowded coastal regions proved unable to sustain the new populations, and all the optimistic plans to develop the Highlands as a manufacturing region crumbled. In the nineteenth century, an increasing number of landlords abandoned resettlement programs and instead simply forced their tenants off their lands.

Thus the improvement policies drove tens of thousands of Highlanders to emigrate—to the Lowlands, to England, and to North America and Australia. In the late 1760s and early 1770s, for example, about twenty thousand Scotsmen, most of them Highlanders, left for America. In the early phases of the Clearances, tacksmen often organized the substantial tenant families on the estate to emigrate with them, leaving the poorest peasants to stay on. By the later decades, emigrants were often extremely poor. In many cases, landlords arranged the emigration—at times forcibly.

Ordinary Highlanders did not simply acquiesce in this eradication of their traditional way of life. Villagers petitioned against eviction, sought legal and political redress, refused to vacate their homes, and at times turned violent, taunting eviction officers, pelting them with mud and stones, and assaulting them. Women led these charges—in part because they played such an essential role in the household economy and in part because both sides assumed that men would be less likely to hurt women. (In a number of cases, however, constables did not hesitate to bludgeon women with their batons.) Frequently, Highlanders turned against the creatures that seemed to be the fundamental cause of their woes: the sheep. Sheep maiming and killing were commonplace, and in 1792—the Year of the Sheep—tenants across the northern Highlands rose up in spontaneous mass rebellion that focused on driving all sheep out of the region. The sheep, however, stayed. The rebels did not.

The Highland Clearances took place over the course of more than a century and, as historian T. M. Devine has shown, "gradual and relentless displacement, rather than mass eviction, was the norm."[2] Nevertheless, the wholesale removal of entire communities so traumatized Highland culture that such mass evictions came to symbolize the Clearances as a whole. Moreover, as is always the case in popular memory, the most notorious and dramatic cases (by definition, the atypical) are those that are recalled the most frequently. Thus the early nineteenth-century Sutherland clearances have most deeply etched themselves in folk memory. A great "improver," the Countess of Sutherland sought to remake her vast but debt-ridden estate in the northern Highlands into a showpiece of the benefits of Enlightenment rationality and capitalist economics. As her estate manager put it, "it will be a blessing to a great proportion of [the people] to be taught a new and improved application of their industry and labour."[3] To make room for sheep, the countess's agents expelled about ten thousand people and burned many of the cottages to prevent tenants from reoccupying their farms. In at least one instance, they set fire to a house with the occupant still inside; in many more cases, they forced elderly and sick people out into the cold. One Sutherlander recalled "the cries of the women and children, the roaring of the affrighted cattle, hunted at the same time by the yelling dogs of the shepherds amid the smoke and fire."[4]

The Highland Clearances offer a particularly concentrated version of the way in which industrial capitalism wore away traditional, customary, agrarian practices and relationships. Episodic clearances continued through the 1850s, but the signs were already clear for Dr. Johnson to read when he visited the Highlands in the 1770s:

---

[2]Devine, *Clanship to Crofter's War*, 37.
[3]Richards, *The Highland Clearances*,126
[4]Donald Macleod, *Gloomy Memories in the Highlands* (Glascow: Sinclair, 1892).

There was perhaps never any change of national manners so quick, so great, and so general, as that which has operated in the Highlands by the last conquest and subsequent laws. We came hither too late to see what we expected—a people of peculiar appearance and a system of antiquated life. The clans retain little now of their original character: their ferocity of temper is softened, their military ardour is extinguished, their dignity of independence is depressed, their contempt of government subdued, and their reverence for their chiefs abated. Of what they had before the late conquest of their country there remains only their language and their poverty.

## DEVELOPMENTS IN LOWLAND SCOTLAND

In sharp contrast to the turbulence and tragedy that marked the history of the Highlands in the eighteenth century, Lowland Scotland embarked on a period of prosperity and stability. Although the period immediately following the Union did not bring the predicted economic benefits, by the 1740s, the Scottish economy began to show signs of progress. In widening circles of the Lowlands, agricultural improvers were introducing new crops, new farming techniques, and new financial management. Perhaps more important, the urban commercial economy of the Lowlands developed relatively rapidly. Linen and woolen manufacturing, hit hard by competition from more modernized and productive English firms in the early eighteenth century, rebounded. Fishing, too, became an important export industry, with sales of herring, salmon, and cod all generating significant revenue.

Scotland's commercial expansion was most pronounced in Edinburgh and Glasgow, which, however, developed in very different ways. Edinburgh, the largest city in Britain except London and Bristol, was no longer the capital of an independent country, but it became the administrative and legal center of "North Britain." Professional people dominated the town, and lawyers were by far the most influential and prosperous professional group. Glasgow, in contrast, was a commercial center, and by 1801, the largest city in Scotland. Its traders and merchants aggressively took advantage of the new market of England and its empire opened to them by the Union. Linen manufacturing, sugar refining, and shipping all became important Glasgow trades. The tobacco trade with North America became the most important of all: already by the 1730s Glasgow's merchants had claimed a large share of this vital trade. By 1771, the Scots were importing forty-seven million pounds of tobacco a year, most of it into Glasgow, and the Scots had won 52 percent of all British trade in tobacco. Wealthy "tobacco lords" inspired much of Glasgow's bustling import/export trade and injected a great amount of liquid capital into the Scottish economy.

The commercialization of the Scottish economy did not mean that Scotland's landed elite lost its economic, social, or political preeminence. The eighteenth century was, in Scotland as much as in England, a golden age for the landed order. At the highest levels, the Scottish aristocracy merged into the British ruling class; like their English counterparts, Scottish nobility built graceful country homes on their estates, maintained townhomes in London, and used the London *season* as a marriage market for their offspring.

Scottish lairds and bonnet lairds, however, were more likely to converge on Edinburgh or Glasgow for a smaller scale Scottish version of the season, where they intermingled and intermarried with the upper levels of Scotland's flourishing middle orders. Glasgow's tobacco lords were only the most visible of the merchant captains who made spectacular fortunes from the opportunities offered by imperial trade. Military service, too, offered social mobility to ambitious young men from professional as well as landed families. By the 1790s, Scotsmen accounted for more than one-quarter of all officers in Britain's line infantry battalions. Moreover, as we will see below, scholars, printers, scientists, writers, and artists also prospered in this period, in conjunction with Scotland's prominent position in the European Enlightenment. Lower down the social scale, urban prosperity meant widening chances and choices for all sorts of tradesmen and women—shoemakers and shopkeepers, hatters and hoteliers, butchers and bakers, tailors and tinkers, and on and on. As in England, the growing prosperity fostered greater sex segregation, with more women in the professional and propertied levels of society withdrawing from economic production into the domestic sphere.

Yet Scottish women possessed, at least in legal terms, some distinct advantages over their sisters to the south. The English principle of *coverture*, whereby a woman lost legal personhood upon marriage, did not apply in Scottish law; Scottish women, therefore could make contracts, sue and be sued, and bequeath property. Moreover, under Scottish law, a woman's *paraphernalia*—her clothing and jewelry—remained her personal property even after marriage; this right offered Scottish wives a degree of financial protection not yet available in England. When a Scottish marriage broke down, moreover, divorce did not require an act of Parliament as it did in England, and Scottish women could sue for divorce on the same grounds—adultery or desertion—as men. Patriarchy remained fundamental to Scottish marriage and family relations, but both the Scottish legal concept of marriage as a divine contract and the deeply embedded Presbyterian fear of tyranny fostered the ideal (although certainly not always the reality) that a man had a religious duty to care for and love his wife.

Religion continued to play a central role, not only in Scottish law, but also in Scottish life. Religious debates and doctrinal disputes remained fierce, although the age of religious warfare had thankfully ended. As we have already noted, the Patronage Act of 1712 stabbed at the very heart of Presbyterianism by granting the right to place ministers in parish appointments not to the kirk session but to lay patrons, such as large landowners and the Crown itself. Not surprisingly, clergymen tended to promote the interests of the patrons to whom they owed their livings. As a result, ministers in the established Church of Scotland more and more resembled their Anglican counterparts in England: gentlemen-scholars whose primary interest was in upholding the political and social order. The spreading practice of *laird's lofts*—specially reserved pew sections for the landed elite—reflected this tendency to see the church as a bastion of rather than a challenge to the ways of the world.

Yet not all Presbyterian clerics submitted to the new realities of lay patronage. In the Secessions of 1733 and 1761, Presbyterian ministers led their people out of the established church and into the ranks of Dissent. By the end of the century, the numbers of dissenting Presbyterians rivaled those in the established church in many villages. Although the issue of patronage remained central, doctrinal divisions also emerged, with Dissenting Presbyterians more inclined to preserve Calvinist rigor and a strict morality and to reject the Enlightenment stress on science rather than divine revelation as the source of absolute truth.

## THE SCOTTISH ENLIGHTENMENT

Considering its small population (approximately 1,200,000 in 1750) and its record of rebellion and war, eighteenth-century Scotland hardly seems to be a country capable of giving rise to a renaissance in high culture. Yet that is precisely what happened. In the second half of the century, Scotland produced a galaxy of intellectuals and artists to equal any in the European world. Social philosophers such as Francis Hutcheson, Adam Ferguson, David Hume, and Adam Smith; scientists such as Joseph Black; architects such as William and Robert Adam; and painters such as Allan Ramsay and Henry Raeburn established Scotland as a center of the European Enlightenment. The French Enlightenment thinker Voltaire proclaimed, "It is from Scotland that we receive rules of taste in all the arts." Or as Scottish philosopher David Hume put it, "Really it is admirable how many Men of Genius this Country produces at present."[5]

How can we explain this remarkable cultural efflorescence in a small nation that in the seventeenth century was seen as economically backward and in the early eighteenth century lost its separate political identity? What was the connection of the cultural renaissance to the union with England and the destruction of the clans? Such questions are not easy to answer and to a degree at least must remain a matter of speculation. Nevertheless, it seems reasonable to say that this particular cultural flowering was the result not of any nationalistic reaction *against* the union or of a nostalgic defense of Highland values, but of a solid *joining* of the Lowlands to the wider English economy and culture. Enlightened thought in Scotland, as elsewhere, was urbane, cosmopolitan, and secular. It drew on old cultural connections between Scotland and Continental Europe. One of the preconditions that had to exist before the Enlightenment could take root anywhere was an end to isolation and the forging of links to the wider cultural world. The union helped to create this for Scotland. Similarly, Enlightened ideas could flourish only in conditions of political stability. Here, too, the union with England was important because English power ended the incessant strife between Highlands and Lowlands and installed Lowland values and styles of life in a preeminent position.

Other important preconditions include (1) sufficient economic prosperity, (2) adequate institutional support, and (3) an absence of intellectual or religious restrictions. Each of these conditions came to exist in the urban centers of Lowland Scotland by the middle decades of the eighteenth century. We have seen that, by the 1740s, Scotland possessed both the commercial vibrancy and the urban culture to sustain its Enlightenment. In Edinburgh, especially, the interconnected professional and landed elites generated a lively intellectual life of legal philosophizing, political talk, and social thought. They were also largely responsible for the building of New Town, the elegantly classical district that made Edinburgh the "Athens of the North," one of the great monuments of eighteenth-century taste. Laid out on a grid, with standard roof lines, paved roads, a sewer system, and wide sidewalks to allow room for leisured strolls conducive to polite conversation, Edinburgh's New Town embodied Enlightenment values.

---

[5]Allen, *Scotland in the Eighteenth Century*, 126.

Institutional support for the Scottish Enlightenment came from Scotland's reformed universities. Because of the kirk's tradition of establishing a school in every parish, Lowland Scotland had a higher literacy rate than England, and boys from the commercial and professional ranks regularly attended one of the four universities: Edinburgh, Glasgow, St. Andrews, and Aberdeen. In the eighteenth century, the Scottish universities grew in size and (unlike Oxford and Cambridge, which remained shackled to classics and mathematics) expanded the range of subjects taught to include law, medicine, rhetoric, and the natural sciences. In addition, the mode of teaching changed, and the Scottish universities became famous for teachers who lectured in English (rather than Latin) in their specialized subjects. The leader in this teaching reform was Francis Hutcheson, professor of moral philosophy at Glasgow from 1729, through whose classes many of the leaders of the Scottish Enlightenment passed.

Finally, developments in the Church of Scotland were crucial to the country's intellectual life. If the kirk had remained the oppressive, puritanical institution of the seventeenth century, then the secular, tolerant thought that was central to the Enlightenment would have been stifled. But slowly from the 1690s on, the theological temperature of the kirk went down. For instance, the last execution for blasphemy in Scotland occurred in 1696 and the last for witchcraft in 1727; the laws against witchcraft were repealed in 1736. By the 1750s, the Moderate party—tolerant, reasonable, and respectable—came to preeminence in the kirk and the universities. On the key Scottish religious issue of the century, the question of lay patronage, the Moderate party sided with the state: patronage ensured the appointments of reasonable men like themselves. Many Moderates abandoned the Calvinism of traditional Scottish Protestantism for a more pragmatic, this-worldly religion that stressed the possibilities of human progress rather than the need for divine redemption.

The concerns of the Moderate *literati* of the Church of Scotland reflected the main themes of Scottish Enlightened thought. Scottish Calvinists had always been preoccupied with individual moral reformation and with the associated social discipline; now, in the more sociable spirit of the eighteenth century, leading Scottish thinkers turned to the issue of the moral improvement of human beings in society. Like Locke and the English moralists, these Scots assumed that human beings are naturally social beings and therefore that moral progress is to be understood in the context of social institutions—legal, political, and religious. They were among the first social scientists. Furthermore, the Scottish thinkers all believed that

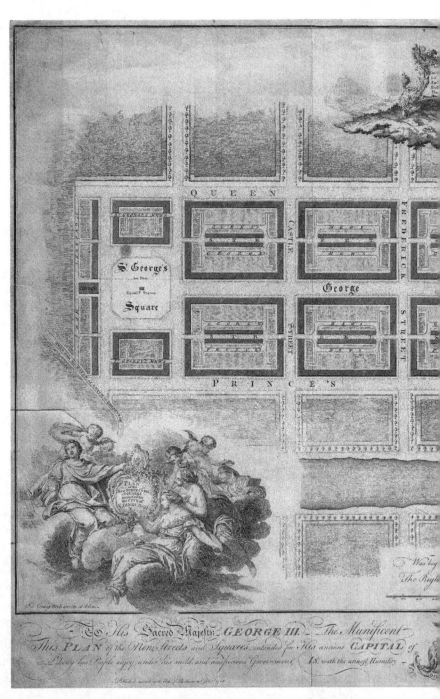

*Edinburgh New Town. This early nineteenth-century map shows Edinburgh's New Town, an embodiment of Enlightenment rationality and order. The straight,*

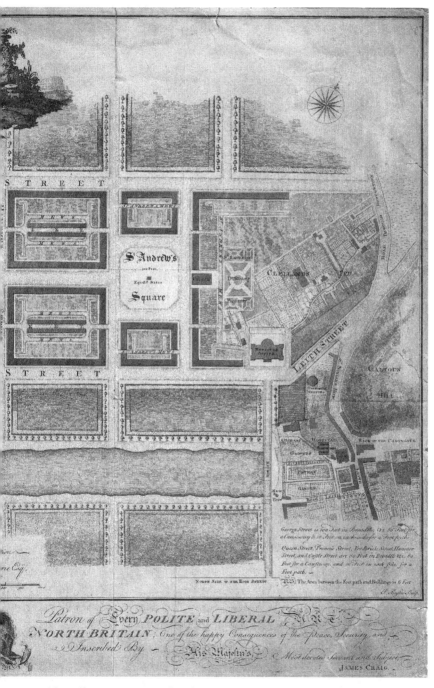

*wide walkways encouraged "polite" conversation and the numerous parks offered a vision of nature tamed and transformed for human benefit.*

Scotland was emerging from an age of barbarism into an age of civilization; thus, they focused on the *history* of various societies by which they could measure Scotland's progress. Like all Enlightened thinkers, they assumed that human nature is everywhere the same and that the purpose of moral philosophy and history is to discover the universal laws of human behavior. Therefore, philosophical history—history as the record of the fundamental laws of nature—was their characteristic mode of thinking.

Next to David Hume, whose work has already been examined in connection with British empiricism (see chapter 5), the greatest thinker in the Scottish Enlightenment was Adam Smith. Smith's work is best understood in the context of *preindustrial* Enlightened thought. Later, his work was taken to be the bible of industrialism, which it emphatically was not, for Smith had little or no experience with factories and steam power; his world was that of Lowland Scottish commerce. Born in 1723 in the small port of Kirkaldy, Smith was the son of a lawyer and customs official. He attended Glasgow University, where he learned much from the lectures of Francis Hutcheson. Later, he studied at Oxford, which he found to be mostly asleep. He read widely in Enlightenment thought and was especially impressed by the works of Locke, Newton, Hutcheson, and Hume. In 1751, he succeeded Hutcheson at Glasgow University, where he taught natural theology, ethics, jurisprudence, and political economy.

Smith hoped to do for the whole field of moral philosophy what Newton had done for natural science: to construct a new understanding of the entire moral and social universe. In his first important work, *The Theory of Moral Sentiments* (1759), Smith gave a systematic, "scientific" treatment of human nature based on two key assumptions: first, that people are motivated by "self-love"—that is, they pursue pleasure and avoid pain—and second, that people are by nature social animals and have a natural faculty of sympathetic behavior. What truly brings pleasure, Smith reasoned, is the approval of others: "It is not wealth that men desire, but the consideration and good opinion that wait upon riches." By exercising the power of sympathetic imagination, individuals know what others approve. A person therefore behaves as if there is an "impartial spectator," or conscience, watching every move. Through the operation of this fundamental quality of human nature, Smith contended, our pursuit of self-interest leads to socially benevolent behavior as if by an "invisible hand."

This was the moral foundation of Smith's *Inquiry into the Nature and Causes of the Wealth of Nations* (1776), one of the most influential works in modern Western history. In it, Smith set out a theory of self-regulating economics, but his moral theory always stood in the background. *The Wealth of Nations* reflects the Scottish interest in how societies progress. Its basic framework, therefore, is philosophical history. Smith believed that nations go through four stages of development: hunting, pastoral, agricultural, and commercial. In each age, the mode of production shapes the political and social institutions. The division of labor characterizes the commercial stage: according to the principle of self-interest, each person (and each nation) takes up what he or she (or it) does best. In this way, production is maximized provided that nothing (such as the state) interferes with the natural operation of the market and the division of labor. Smith thus argued for the *utility* of natural liberty because any intervention by the state in the economy by definition deflects people from natural behavior and maximum production.

Smith's economic theories challenged the prevailing economic orthodoxy: *mercantilism*. Although most fully developed and implemented in France, mercantilism shaped economic policy throughout eighteenth-century Europe. Mercantilists argued that the power of the state depends on national wealth, and that the wealth of a nation depends primarily on its holdings in precious metals such as gold and silver. To maximize these holdings, then, the state must regulate and protect the nation's commerce—through tariffs on imports, the establishment of trade monopolies and overseas colonies, the use of naval and military power to protect trading interests, and a host of other economic activities. Smith's belief in the utility of natural liberty led him to reject the economically active state demanded by mercantilism and instead to advocate laissez-faire domestic policies and free trade between nations. Yet Smith was never the proponent of dog-eat-dog competition, and he expressed concern that the routinization of work resulting from the division of labor would dull the wits and imagination of the laborer. He imagined that the invisible hand of benevolence would work to keep the self-regulating economic system he advocated from being vicious and exploitive. In this way, Smith expressed the confidence and reasonableness of Lowland Scotland as it claimed the benefits of joining the prosperous and expansive English society.

Smith's faith in economic exchange was also part of the wider Enlightenment belief in the virtues of intellectual exchange. Just as the free trade of goods would lead to greater prosperity and thus material progress, so the free trade of ideas would guarantee intellectual progress. Through conversation, whether in coffeehouses or on Edinburgh sidewalks or in the pages of the many eighteenth-century periodicals, Enlightenment thinkers throughout Britain sought to nurture a rational approach to living and learning that would, they believed, lead to social betterment.

A great achievement by *Scottish* intellectuals fostered in specifically *Scottish* institutions, the Scottish Enlightenment nevertheless contributed to the formation of a *British* nation. As we saw, the Union of 1707 created a British *state*, but not an integrated British people. The English in the eighteenth century aggressively eradicated that part of Scottish culture they regarded as dangerous to Britain, but they showed no interest in building an emotional bond between Englishmen and Scots or in blending the two peoples. Still, the long, slow process of integration into Britain did begin for the Scots in the eighteenth century. The incorporation of clansmen into the British army was one major integrative force, as was the participation of Scotsmen in the administration of foreign and imperial affairs, an arena in which Britain did function as a single unit. At the same time, the market economy tied the Scots tightly to English commerce and industry, while the long series of wars against the French inspired a sense of British rather than more narrowly English or Scottish patriotism. In addition, there was the common Protestantism that most Scots shared with the English.

Finally, and not least importantly, the Scottish Enlightenment brought Scottish thinkers and writers into intimate relationship with the mainstream of English intellectual life. Enlightened Scottish thinkers such as Hume and Smith, along with the books they wrote, moved easily among Edinburgh, Glasgow, and London. Empirical ideas, which were cosmopolitan rather than provincial, became the common property of minds on both sides of the River Tweed. Significantly, the *Encyclopedia Britannica*, a splendid embodiment of Enlightenment faith in fact gathering and the exchange of information, began in 1768, not in London, but in Edinburgh. A sphere of intellectual discourse grew up during the 1700s that was genuinely British and that helped Scottish men and women develop parallel identities, Scottish and British.

### Suggested Reading

Abrams, Lynn, Eleanor Gordon, Deborah Simonton, and Eileen Yeo, eds. *Gender in Scottish History Since 1700*. Edinburgh: Edinburgh University Press, 2006.

Allan, David. *Scotland in the Eighteenth Century: Union and Enlightenment*. New York: Longman, 2002.

Barclay, Katie. *Love, Intimacy and Power: Marriage and Patriarchy in Scotland, 1650–1850*. Manchester, UK: Manchester University Press, 2011.

Black, Jeremy. *Culloden and the '45*. New York: St. Martin's Press, 1990.

Broadie, Alexander. *The Scottish Enlightenment*. Edinburgh: Birlinn, 2001.

Brown, Keith. *Noble Society in Scotland: Wealth, Family and Culture From Reformation to Revolution*. Edinburgh: Edinburgh University Press, 2000.

Camic, Charles. *Experience and Enlightenment: Socialization for Cultural Change in Eighteenth Century Scotland*. Chicago: University of Chicago Press, 1983.

Chapman, Malcolm. *The Gaelic Vision in Scottish Culture*. London: Croom Helm, 1978.

Chitnis, Anand C. *The Scottish Enlightenment: A Social History*. London: Croom Helm, 1976.

Clyde, Robert. *From Rebel to Hero: The Image of the Highlander, 1745–1830*. East Lothian, UK: Tuckwell Press, 1995.

Daiches, David. *Charles Edward Stuart: The Life and Times of Bonnie Prince Charlie*. London: Thames & Hudson, 1973.

Devine, T. M. *Clanship to Crofters' War: The Social Transformation of the Scottish Highlands*. Manchester, UK: Manchester University Press, 1994.

———. *The Scottish Nation: A History, 1700–2000*. New York: Viking, 1999.

Dwyer, John. *Virtuous Discourse: Sensibility and Community in Late Eighteenth-Century Scotland*. Edinburgh: John Donald, 1987.

Hill, James Michael. *Celtic Warfare, 1595–1763*. Edinburgh: John Donald, 1986.

Houston, R. A. *Social Change in the Age of Enlightenment, Edinburgh, 1660–1760*. Oxford: Clarendon Press, 1994.

Leneman, Leah. *Alienated Affections: The Scottish Experience of Divorce and Separation*. Edinburgh: Edinburgh University Press, 1998.

Leneman, Leah, and Rosalind Mitchison. *Sexuality and Social Control: Scotland, 1660–1780*. Oxford: Basil Blackwell, 1989.

Lenman, Bruce. *An Economic History of Modern Scotland, 1660–1976*. Hamden, CT: Archon Books, 1977.

———. *Integration, Enlightenment, and Industrialization: Scotland, 1746–1832*. Toronto: University of Toronto Press, 1981.

———. *The Jacobite Risings in Britain, 1689–1746*. London: Eyre Methuen, 1980.

Lynch, Michael. *Scotland. A New History*. London: Pimlico, 1999.

MacInnes, Allan I. *Clanship, Commerce, and the House of Stuart, 1603–1788*. East Linton, UK: Tuckwell Press, 1994.

McLynn, Frank, *The Jacobites*. London: Routledge & Kegan Paul, 1985.

Mitchison, Rosalind. *Lordship to Patronage: Scotland, 1603–1745*. London: Edward Arnold, 1983.

Pittock, Murray G. H. *Inventing and Resisting Britain: Cultural Identities in Britain and Ireland, 1685–1789*. New York: St. Martin's Press, 1997.

———. *Jacobitism*. New York: St. Martin's Press, 1998.

———. *The Invention of Scotland: The Stuart Myth and the Scottish Identity, 1638 to the Present*. New York: Routledge, Chapman & Hall, 1991.

Raphael, D. D. *Adam Smith*. New York: Oxford University Press, 1985.

Richards, Eric. *Debating the Highland Clearances*. Edinburgh: Edinburgh University Press, 2007.

———. *The Highland Clearances: People, Landlords and Rural Turmoil*. Edinburgh: Birlinn, 2000.

Roberts, John L. *The Jacobite Wars: Scotland and the Military Campaigns of 1715 and 1745*. Edinburgh: Polygon, 2002.

Rochschild, Emma. *Economic Sentiments: Adam Smith, Condorcet, and the Enlightenment*. Cambridge, MA: Harvard University Press, 2001.

Sher, Richard B. *Church and University in the Scottish Enlightenment*. Princeton, NJ: Princeton University Press, 1985.

Speck, W. A. *The Butcher: The Duke of Cumberland and the Suppression of the '45*. Oxford: Blackwell, 1981.

Todd, Margot. *The Culture of Protestantism in Early Modern Scotland*. New Haven, CT: Yale University Press, 2002.

Whatley, Christopher, *Scottish Society, 1707–1830: Beyond Jacobitism, Towards Industrialization*. Manchester, UK: Manchester University Press, 2000.

Youngson, A. J. *After the Forty-Five: The Economic Impact on the Highlands*. Edinburgh: Edinburgh University Press, 1973.

# Chapter 7

# The Expansion of British Power and Empire, 1715–1763

By the end of the War of Spanish Succession (1713), Britain had become a major European power. Between 1715 and 1763, Britain became a genuine world power as well, not only ranking among the half-dozen strongest European states, but also holding an empire larger and richer than any other in the Western world. Thus, in the first half of the eighteenth century, Britain began to assume a global role that it held until the mid-twentieth century. The expansion of British power was to have a great impact on the lives of ordinary Britons—Scots, Welsh, Irish, and English—and of millions of other peoples around the world as well. By any accounting it was a remarkable achievement for such a relatively small group of islands off the shore of Europe.

How did British power in the eighteenth century expand so rapidly? No one could have predicted it in 1550 or even 1650. World-power status was not the goal of any deliberate, unified British plan, except in the sense that Britain, like all European states of the eighteenth century, sought incessantly to aggrandize itself at the expense of others. Britain's position of power on the Continent and overseas came as the by-product of a century-long struggle with France (only half over by 1763) and the expansion of British trade. These two mutually reinforcing factors were rooted in the general economic prosperity and political security of eighteenth-century Britain.

## THE EUROPEAN STATE SYSTEM

The British ascended to world power in the context of an extremely competitive system of European states. Spain's great century of wealth and power had come to an end, and a long war with French absolutism had exhausted the Dutch Republic. France, with more than 20 million people and a peacetime army of 150,000, remained the leading state in Europe, but it no longer dominated as it had before 1715. The Hapsburg Monarchy (also called Austria-Hungary) and Russia were enormous empires, but economically underdeveloped. In the first half of the eighteenth century, then, Britain and Prussia were the two up-and-coming states in Europe.

Prussia had a population of only 2.25 million (less than Ireland), no naturally defensible borders, and meager resources, yet the ruling Hohenzollern family had made this northern German state into a great power by building an army of enormous size (80,000 men in 1750) and by enforcing exemplary training. Almost the entire Prussian state apparatus was devoted to raising and maintaining the army. In contrast, Britain operated under the handicap of the landowners' fear of a standing army. Nevertheless, the British navy, an effective tax-collecting machinery, and the taxable wealth of the country (including now Wales, Scotland, and Ireland) made Britain a power to contend with. The British navy had shown its supremacy in the wars against Louis XIV, and British governments thereafter maintained it fairly consistently. Parliament's ability to tax the whole of the British Isles made it possible for Britain not only to maintain the navy (which supported the bountifully taxable overseas trade), but also to subsidize the armies of Continental allies. Britain could fight for itself on the seas and pay others to fight for it on land.

Different as they were, European states in the eighteenth century conducted their diplomacy and warfare with broadly similar objectives. In all of them, governments took foreign policy as their primary concern, and the people who made foreign policy were a tiny elite consisting of the monarch and his or her aristocratic advisers. This was true even of Britain, although Parliament and public opinion could on occasion make themselves felt in foreign affairs. The mind-set of all the European governing elites held that the *increase of state power* was what counted in foreign affairs. The age of religious wars had largely passed, and the age of ideological wars had not yet arrived. What mattered to eighteenth-century policymakers was adding to state power by increases in territory, population, and trade, all of which enabled a state to support a larger army and win yet more resources. Hence, the state system of eighteenth-century Europe was a Machiavellian world of rapacious power and violence with no end beyond power itself.

The economic theory of *mercantilism* both explained and motivated this mentality of incessant competition and war. It constituted an elegant circular theory worthy of the rationalistic age in which it was born: quite simply, trade engenders wealth, wealth supports armies and navies. armies and navies increase state power, and state power expands trade. European statesmen saw commerce as a means of increasing the strength of the state, merchants saw state power as a means of increasing commerce, and both saw warfare as a handy means to both political and commercial ends.

Eighteenth-century wars tended to be limited conflicts. The goal, after all, was not to obliterate an opposing political or social system. (England's wars in Ireland and Scotland, where the existence of the regime itself was at stake, were significant exceptions.) The object of commanders was to conduct campaigns of limited engagements, bloody and terrible to the troops involved, but meant to gain finite advantages that could be useful at the bargaining table. Pieces of territory, trading stations, fortifications, and colonies were all power resources that made up the coinage of the state system, its warfare, and its treaties.

Military technology also restrained the scale of military conflict. In this era, infantry troops carrying flintlock muskets became the dominant force on the battlefield. Especially when used with the newly invented ring bayonet (which turned a musket into a pike), muskets could defeat cavalry troops and were regarded as more important than the artillery, long disdained by aristocratic officers. But muskets were inaccurate and slow to load and fire (three rounds per minute at best); hence, they were most effective when used by massed troops to deliver murderous volleys at close range. Such tactics required elaborate maneuvering and iron discipline on the part of the infantry, both acquired only after lengthy training according to rigid drill. As a result, the best armies were *professional* armies rather than feudal levies or militia because professionals trained full time. Professional armies, however, became so precious that kings and generals hesitated to commit them to a protracted war.

## BRITISH INTERESTS AND POWER

In order to see how British interests operated within the European state system, it is important to understand how British policymakers perceived these interests. First, British statesmen (almost all of them English) assumed that what was good for England was good for the rest of the British Isles; hence, they pursued *English* interests with the resources of all of Britain and Ireland—which in turn meant that the very unity of the new state of Great Britain was *the* fundamental English interest. Second, the Whig oligarchs believed that the Hanoverian—that is, Protestant—

succession was crucial to British unity, independence, liberty, and prosperity. As we saw in chapter 6, however, both the state and the Protestant succession came under the pressure of Jacobite risings supported by foreign powers. Jacobitism, therefore, had vital implications for British foreign affairs, among them continual suspicion and hostility toward the Catholic powers Spain and France and alliance in one form or another with the Protestant Dutch Republic.

Third, because George I and II were not only kings of Britain but also electors of Hanover, they insisted on viewing the independence and integrity of their little German state as a British interest. This matter was never popular among the British, for it involved them in expensive entanglements that seemed secondary to purely British concerns. Hanover was rightly thought of as a hostage to French or Hapsburg or Prussian power. As Lord Chesterfield wrote in 1742, "Hanover robs us of the Benefit of being an Island, and is actually a pledge for our good Behaviour on the Continent." Finally, because the British government was keenly aware that its global power derived in large part from overseas commerce rather than military might, trade bulked even larger in the aggregate of British interests than in other European countries. British officials felt particularly sensitive about maintaining access to the Dutch ports, through which British goods entered the Continent, and about sustaining trade in the Baltic, from which Britain imported naval stores, spars, and masts.

Two additional aims, both resulting from an unconscious process of elevating means into ends, also factored into British policymaking. One was the pursuit of a balance of power in Europe. This strategy, which was to be long honored in British policy, first emerged during the wars against Louis XIV, as William III and Marlborough constructed alliances to counter French might. The notion was that Britain should not seek permanent alliances, but should throw its weight into the balance of nations in order to check any one power (usually France) that seemed to be achieving dominance over Europe. By the 1720s and 1730s, many English statesmen regarded this policy as an end in itself.

The second, and somewhat contradictory concern, was simply to oppose France at every turn. By 1713, Britain had been at war with France for twenty-five years, and most Englishmen habitually assumed that this rivalry was somehow natural and that Britain should always range itself against France. Thus, in the eighteenth century, Britons began to equate the French national character with popery, poverty, wooden shoes, unmanly groveling

*F. W. Fairholt,* John Bull smoking, with cornucopia, roast beef, ale, and his dog. *A nineteenth-century image of John Bull as the epitome of British prosperity and strength.*

before aristocracy, and frog eating. British patriotism, expressed in stirring songs such as "God Save the King," "Rule Britannia," and "Hearts of Oak," all of which date from the decades before 1760, came to mean all the things the French allegedly lacked: honesty, independence, forthrightness, endurance, John Bull (the sturdy cartoon symbol of England), and the roast beef of Old England.

In pursuit of these interests, Britain could deploy impressive and durable strengths: the army, navy, trade and finance, and colonies. Britain's position as an island enabled it to get maximum effect from a professional army large enough only to drain French resources away from its own navy. Younger sons of aristocratic families provided the officers; the dregs of society, recruited by patriotism, poverty, or alcohol, supplied the enlisted ranks. The heaviest expenditures went to the navy, which was the best-led and largest in Europe (normally more than one hundred ships) and backed by a very large merchant marine. Parliament, as we have seen, served as an excellent taxing machine, and British financial institutions were second only to those of the Dutch in mobilizing private wealth for official purposes. The colonies, like the merchant marine, could be a liability as well as an asset because they had to be protected. Yet in the colonies the British found bold and determined people who were willing and able to provide some, at least, of the material resources to fight Britain's battles—and more important, to advance their own interests and so indirectly contribute to the growth of British power.

## THE COLONIES

The British Empire in the first half of the eighteenth century included colonies stretching from the Mediterranean and the Atlantic to North America and the West Indies, and even to Africa and Asia. Some of the colonies were simply military stations or trading posts, whereas others were full-scale settlements with substantial British populations. All told, in 1750 perhaps fifteen million people outside the British Isles lived under the British flag. The empire they peopled had grown up in an unplanned and sporadic process dating back to the sixteenth century and largely the product of mercantilist assumptions. The three main areas of the British Empire were India, the West Indies, and North America.

India would one day be the most fabulous jewel in the imperial crown, but in the early eighteenth century British rule had scarcely penetrated the Indian subcontinent. The British did not *colonize* India at all, in the sense of establishing permanent settlements as home to a significant number of Britons. The British Empire in India was the result of private (though officially sanctioned) commercial initiative. A group of English merchants had formed the East India Company and received a royal charter in 1600 that granted it a monopoly on all English trade in the East Indies (in exchange for hefty contributions to the Crown). The East India Company established trading posts (called factories, but having nothing whatsoever to do with manufacturing) at Surat and subsequently Bombay, Madras, and Calcutta, where the company merchants bought pepper and cotton fabrics for export and resale in England. The Company also traded for coffee in Arabia and tea in China, and by the late seventeenth century, its merchants were doing a big business selling opium in both China and England.

The East India Company found in India the Moghul Empire at its height. The Moghuls were Muslims who ruled the northern two-thirds of India and who in the 1600s were seeking to expand into the South. The Company established normal relations with the Moghuls and negotiated for trading rights. But the Moghul Empire had a feudal structure, and its emperors could not exercise consistent rule over all their vassals; therefore, the Company had to deal with a large number of local rulers and fend off Dutch and Portuguese rivals as well. Company traders, never known for their timidity or moderation, did not hesitate to use force to exploit the weakness of the Moghul Empire, and by the eighteenth century the Company was behaving like a middle-rank Indian vassal, though it as yet *ruled* very little territory. In the early 1700s, the Moghul Empire began to break up, and its power began to slip away to important princes, including those of the Hindu Maratha Confederacy of central India. In this fluid situation, one of irresistible opportunity as well as political complexity, the East India Company eagerly scuffled for juicier trading concessions, but from the 1730s it faced increased competition from a new rival—the French East India Company.

The West Indian colonies also began as private initiatives in the early seventeenth century. Bermuda and the Bahamas were settled by an enterprise that had separated from a group of adventurers called the Virginia Company. Smaller chartered companies colonized other islands such as St. Kitts, Barbados, Jamaica, and Antigua. It did not bother these entrepreneurs that the islands they settled were claimed by Spain, but they did have to seize and defend their "plantations" in a long series of clashes not easily distinguishable from piracy. Eventually, treaties between England and Spain sanctioned English control of colonies in the West Indies.

Unlike India, but like North America, the West Indian islands attracted large numbers of British settlers. The British regarded them as "empty" and there for the taking. Further, the adventurers who went to the West Indies seeking their fortunes found that they could grow tobacco there and sell it for handsome profit in England. Tobacco plantations required labor, so the West Indian landowners began to import from England and Ireland indentured servants, who for the cost of their passage, food, and clothing, worked for a period of time (four to seven years) before achieving independence and moving on to their own land. By the 1640s there were twenty-five thousand English and Scots in the West Indies.

The tobacco trade, however, peaked in the mid-1600s, and West Indian plantation owners switched to growing sugar cane instead. An immensely profitable crop, sugar made the West Indies the most valuable part of the British Empire in the early eighteenth century. Sugar was harder to grow than tobacco, however, and required a larger and tougher work force. The planters found the solution to their labor problem by importing black slaves from Africa. The slave population in the West Indies grew rapidly, forcing many smaller white landowners to sell out and move to North America. By the 1660s, there were more black slaves than white settlers in the British West Indies.

The growth of slavery in the West Indies (and the simultaneous importation of slaves into some North American colonies) transformed the Atlantic economy. Chartered companies—the Company of Royal Adventurers and its successor, the Royal African Company—established fortified trading posts in West Africa where they traded English manufactured goods such as guns and rum for slaves, who were crammed onto ships for the infamous Middle Passage across the Atlantic. Thousands of Africans died on the crowded slave ships; the survivors were then traded in the West Indies and southern American colonies for raw materials such as sugar, tobacco, and cotton. This *triangular trade* became enormously profitable for merchants in Glasgow, Bristol, and Liverpool. In the early 1750s, for instance, fifty-three slave ships a year left Liverpool on this triangular route.

In North America, the pattern of colonization was much more varied than in the West Indies, in terms of both who went and why. A number of North American colonies were founded by Englishmen seeking to practice without interference their own brands of Christianity. Puritans and other Nonconformists settled Massachusetts, Rhode Island, and Connecticut, whereas Roman Catholics founded Maryland and Quakers Pennsylvania. Other colonies were founded for straightforward purposes of commerce and profit. The company of Londoners who colonized Virginia simply wanted to make money any way they could. Tobacco plantations based on slave labor soon proved the answer. Later, English forces seized New Netherland from the Dutch and divided it into sections (New York, New Jersey, and Delaware) for great proprietors. Similarly, Charles II granted North and South Carolina as money-making opportunities to court favorites. Charles also chartered the Hudson Bay Company to allow certain English merchants a monopoly of the fur trade west of Hudson Bay in what is now Canada. Newfoundland, too, was settled under a commercial charter to exploit its rich fishing grounds and formally ceded to Britain in 1713. The last North American colony, Georgia, was established in 1732 by a philanthropic trust as a refuge for Englishmen released from debtors' prison.

The British colonies in North America differed from each other in religion, economic activity, and political structure, but they did have some features in common. One was that the colonies—or at least the thirteen strung out along the Atlantic coast—all had some degree of representative self-government. The English government, after all, had always allowed people to undertake colonizing enterprises on the condition that it cost the state nothing; thus, colonies were expected to take charge of their own local rule and protection. It would have been impossible for the English to exert direct rule across three thousand miles of ocean. Hence, by the 1700s, a standard form of government had grown up in the colonies based on a combination of normal company organization and the model provided by the English constitution. Most had a royal governor, an appointed advisory council, and elected assembly. The assemblies had the right, or rather the responsibility, of legislating and raising taxes to pay the governor and support other local government activities.

A second common feature of the colonies was the rapid growth of their populations. Like their counterparts in the West Indies, the British colonists in North America re-garded the land they found as empty and open to their settlement. It seems likely that over the previous century a wave of killing diseases had come up from Mexico, a product of the indigenous people's disastrous encounter with an entirely new microbiology brought in the respiratory and digestive systems of Spanish and Portuguese explorers. Mass death had slashed the Native American population even before the British arrived; hence, the Native Americans populated the land thinly and presented the British colonists with no civilization of visible splendor such as the British merchants found in India. In any case, the diseases brought by the English themselves ravaged the Native Americans, killing over 90 percent of some eastern tribes. Thus, what appeared to be open land beckoned to many people of middling ranks in the British Isles, some of whom were willing to risk the hazardous voyage, frontier hardships, and often a period of indentured servitude for a chance to better their lot.

Some English emigrants wanted a religious environment more suitable to their liking. Most hoped eventually to set up as small farmers or even as gentlemen. Relatively few of the very top and bottom rank of the English social hierarchy came—few aristocrats on the one hand or landless vagrants or beggars on the other. Highland Scottish clansmen led by their tacksmen came in large numbers after the Battle of Culloden. Scotch-Irish Presbyterians, unhappy in Anglican-dominated Ulster, came in droves—perhaps 250,000 came between 1700 and 1775. By 1700, the white population (overwhelmingly British) stood at 250,000 in the thirteen colonies; by 1750 it had grown to almost a million, and there were 250,000 African slaves as well. In 1750, then, there were more Britons in North America than in Wales and almost as many as in Scotland.

These prosperous, enterprising, aggressive people were excellent trading partners for British trade and therefore pivotal to the increase in British power. Even though the British Empire in North America was never as centralized as the French in Canada or the Spanish in Central and South America, British trade with the American colonists was extremely lucrative. The Navigation Acts of the 1660s still provided that all ships trading in the colonies be either British or American and that certain *enumerated* products exported from the colonies had to go first to a British port. Among these were tobacco, sugar, indigo, rice, molasses, and naval stores—either extremely valuable goods not produced in Britain or items vital to the British navy. Further, most goods shipped from anywhere to America had to come through a British port. The Navigation Acts were never rigorously enforced, but they did help channel colonial trade to Britain's advantage. Even as the North American population grew, more than half of its exports went directly to Britain. By 1760, 15 percent of all British trade was with the North American colonies.

## THE WAR OF JENKINS' EAR—KING GEORGE'S WAR (1739–1748)

Colonists could also, however, reshape British foreign affairs to their own advantage. British colonists in the West Indies were determined to exploit trade opportunities in the Spanish-American Empire in the teeth of efforts by the Spanish coast guard to stop them. Local clashes went on in the Caribbean throughout the 1720s and 1730s. In 1738, one Captain Jenkins displayed to an outraged House of Commons the ear (pickled in a jar) that he had lost to a Spanish cutlass. Although the incident had happened seven years before and despite Prime Minister Robert Walpole's own preference for peace and low taxes (see chapter 4), British and West Indian merchants, plus a number of political opportunists in Parliament, insisted on war. No doubt this colonial war (known in America as King George's War) would have involved France soon because French commercial efforts in India, the West Indies, and North America alike were beginning to rival British interests. In any event, in 1740 a general European conflict that erupted over the succession to the Hapsburg monarchy enveloped the Anglo-Spanish war and made France Britain's chief enemy.

The combination of military war on the Continent and naval war overseas revived a dispute in Britain over what the best strategy was—to fight France directly by armies on land (the *Continental* strategy) or to take advantage of Britain's naval strength to strike overseas (the *maritime* or *blue-water* strategy). The concern of George II over Hanover and the commitment of the leading British policymakers to the European balance of power swung the debate in this instance toward the Continental approach. Britain sent an army of twelve thousand to Europe, hired thousands of German mercenaries, and subsidized both the Austrian and the Hanoverian armies. The British also pursued an aggressive naval policy, bottling up the French fleet in Brest, attacking numerous points in the West Indies, and preying on French merchant shipping.

The longer the war on the Continent dragged on, the more expensive and unpopular it became, especially among the English country gentry, whose patriotism always burned hot until taxes went up. The rising political star William Pitt (see chapter 4) expressed the general unhappiness with the Continental war: "The confidence of the people is abused by making unnecessary alliances; then they are pillaged to provide the subsidies. It is now apparent that this great, this powerful, this formidable Kingdom is considered only as a province of a despicable electorate [Hanover]." By 1747, both Britain and France were weary of war and ready for peace, as the resulting treaty (Aix-la-Chapelle) demonstrated: it merely restored the *status quo ante bellum* (the situation before the war). Neither side had gained anything of significance.

## THE FRENCH AND INDIAN WAR—THE SEVEN YEARS' WAR (1756–1763)

The Treaty of Aix-la-Chapelle said nothing about the West Indian issues over which Britain had gone to war. This curious fact suggests that the treaty marked not a genuine settlement but a truce as far as Britain was concerned. The rivalry for empire between Britain and France intensified after 1748, particularly in North America. British colonists along the Atlantic seaboard wanted to push into the interior to claim land for commercial purposes. Two Virginia land companies, for example, sought to claim large tracts in the Ohio Valley. British colonial expansion, however, ran into French opposition. Though there were only about seventy-five thousand French settlers in North America, they had established forts and trading posts along the St. Lawrence, through the Great Lakes, and down the Mississippi. Now the French sought to extend their lucrative fur trade with

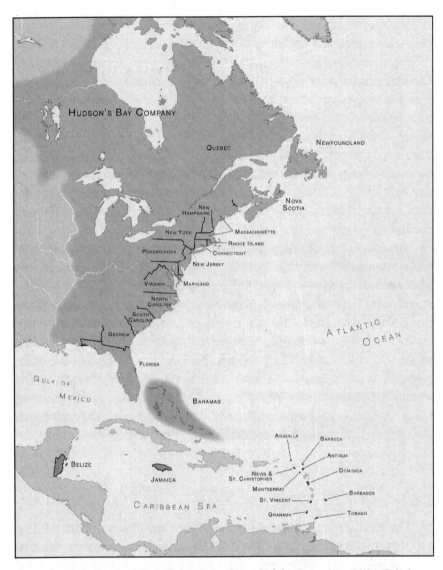

*Britain's North American Empire, 1763.* At the end of the Seven Years' War, Britain controlled Canada and the rest of North America east of the Mississippi. It also expanded its control in India and the Caribbean and so emerged as the most powerful commercial, colonial, and naval country in the world.

the Indians by seizing control of the Ohio Valley. Skirmishes between British and French colonists resulted.

In 1754, the French and their Indian allies defeated several militia companies from Virginia led by George Washington. In a fateful and unprecedented decision, the British government dispatched regular army troops under General Braddock to aid the Virginians and directed the navy to prevent France from reinforcing its Canadian garrison. The British navy began capturing French merchant vessels, but the French ambushed Braddock's little army in July 1755. The British now felt they could not turn back; in May 1756 they declared war.

These events in America sent the British and French scrambling for allies in Europe. Britain traditionally supported Austria as a counterweight to France, but this time the British government thought that an alliance with Prussia would best protect Hanover and check the French; meanwhile, the Austrians settled into an alliance with France and Russia. The Anglo-French colonial war that broke out in 1755 thus expanded into a general European struggle. In fact, because this Seven Years' War was fought simultaneously in Europe, Asia, and the Americas, it was the first world war.

Initially the war went disastrously for the British, and parliamentary and public opinion alike demanded that Pitt, who had caught the imagination of the country with his imperial vision and blue-water strategy (fighting mainly on the oceans), be given control of the government. Horace Walpole wrote, "The nation is in a ferment. Instructions from counties, boroughs, especially the City of London, in the style of 1642 . . . all these tell Pitt he may command such numbers without doors [outside—in other words, in public opinion] as may make majorities within the House tremble." George II loathed Pitt, but in 1757, the king was forced to give way. Pitt came to power on a wave of supreme confidence: "I know that I can save this country and that no one else can."

Once in office, Pitt concentrated all his prodigious energy on the war effort. Recognizing that the nature of the war demanded simultaneous success on the Continent and in the colonies—otherwise, the winnings in one theater would have to be traded to compensate for losses in the other—Pitt gave up his extreme maritime strategy. Britain increased its own army to more than fifty thousand men, subsidized Prussia with £670,000 a year for four years, and paid for large numbers of German mercenaries as well. Largely because of the military genius of the Prussian king, Frederick the Great, the allied armies fought the French and Austrians to a standstill. Pitt in fact claimed that Canada was won for Britain in Germany.

Pitt did not neglect the war at sea and overseas, for he was able to see the war effort as a whole. The British navy imposed a close blockade on the French coast, turned the Mediterranean into a "British lake," and fended off French invasion of England by crushing the French fleet at Quiberon Bay in 1759. Combined army and navy forces plundered French islands in the West

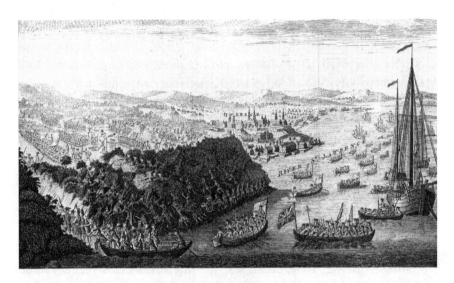

The British Victory at Quebec (1759). *This illustration from the* London Magazine *shows the British troops (Scottish Highlanders) under General Wolfe making their way up a hidden path to the Plains of Abraham above Quebec, where they defeated French forces under General Montcalm. Though Wolfe was mortally wounded, the battle was a key to British supremacy in North America.*

Indies. In North America, Pitt directed a three-pronged offensive against New France: one force proceeded up the St. Lawrence to Quebec, a second moved north along Lake Champlain to attack Montreal, and a third marched west to take Fort Niagara and Fort Frontenac on Lake Ontario. All three campaigns were successful. By 1760, the British controlled all of North America east of the Mississippi.

Pitt refused to commit regular British forces to the struggle in India. He did increase the size of the British navy in the Indian Ocean to equal that of the French; otherwise, he left the East India Company on its own. John Company, as it was called, proved equal to the task. The Company and its French rival, struggling for influence in south-central and south-eastern India, put up rival Indian candidates for rule in the Carnatic (the area inland from Madras) in 1749. The British won, thanks to the heroic efforts of a small Anglo-Indian army led by a twenty-five-year-old clerk named Robert Clive, a man who was like Pitt in many ways—depressive but gifted, ambitious, and energetic. Pitt rightly called him a "heaven-born general."

In the 1750s the British and French East India Companies began to clash in an even wealthier region, Bengal, with its great trading city,

Calcutta. In 1756 the *nawab* (prince) of Bengal, Siraj-ud-Daula, marched on the fat British post in Calcutta with a massive army. The nawab's troops plundered Calcutta and imprisoned the British survivors in a miserable cell later called the Black Hole of Calcutta. About one hundred people died. The Company sent Clive with a force of three thousand men to relieve Calcutta. Siraj-ud-Daula withdrew, but Clive elected to join an Indian conspiracy against him. In June 1757, Clive led his small force of about one thousand Europeans and two thousand Indian sepoys against Siraj-ud-Daula's sixty thousand at the Battle of Plassey. Well-disciplined in the European style of drill, Clive's minuscule army won.

Although only fifty French artillery men had fought for Siraj-ad-Daula at Plassey, this victory marked a decisive shift of power on the subcontinent from the French to the British. Bengal fell to the Company, which now installed its own puppet as nawab. Indian politicians and bankers showered money on Clive, who returned to England with £234,000 in cash plus rentals worth £27,000 a year. Given the possibilities for riches in India, it was not actually so much. "By God," Clive later testified, "I stand amazed at my own moderation."

Politics in India thus proved even more profitable to the Company than trade; consequently, the Company made politics its business. Company officials in Bengal made prodigious sums by replacing one nawab after another: each time they threw out a native governor, hopeful political and commercial Bengalis came forward with magnificent bribes and gifts. In 1760–61, the Company succeeded in driving the French out of southern India, and by 1763 the East India Company, without ever really meaning to, had become a major political power in India.

## THE PRIZES OF VICTORY

Given the impressive string of British victories on sea and land in all major theaters of the Seven Years' War, one would think that Pitt could have remained prime minister as long as he wished and that the British would proceed to crush France once and for all. Neither was to be the case. Pitt wanted to extend the war in a preemptive strike on the Spanish Empire. His grandiose plans, however, alarmed the more cautious members of the cabinet and, by 1760, the French were already making overtures for peace. Meanwhile, when George II died in 1760, Pitt lost a major pillar of support. In October 1761, he resigned. Ironically, Spain entered the war anyway, and in 1762 the British took Havana and Manila.

The Seven Years' War ended the next year with the Peace of Paris. In the House of Commons, an ill and shaky Pitt denounced the treaty as a surrender of the fruits of victory, but in fact the British did very well. They won back Minorca from France and retained Grenada, Domenica, St. Vincent, and Tobago in the West Indies; Canada, Cape Breton Island, Florida, and all of North America east of the Mississippi River; Senegal in Africa; and the East India Company's winnings in Bengal. Britain thus emerged as the most powerful commercial, colonial, and naval country on earth—a startling development from the small, bitterly divided state of the mid-seventeenth century.

Were these prizes worth the cost of seven years (nine, counting the skirmishes of 1754–55) of war? No one asked the ordinary British and colonial soldiers and sailors who shed their blood in battles around the globe. By custom, the soldiers in a victorious army were allowed to loot the enemy dead and wounded on the battlefield, and sailors were given a share in the spoils of captured *prize* ships, but the surviving evidence does not say whether they regarded these rewards and the simple pleasures of triumph as sufficient recompense for years of weary marching, harsh discipline, and privation, as well as moments of sheer terror and suffering. No doubt colonial North American soldiers, particularly those in the militia, found the removal of danger from the French and Indian forces on the northern and western frontiers very satisfying. Britons of the ruling elite and the mercantile classes not only benefitted from colonial investments, but also took pride in Britain's imperial identity.

For the common farmer or laborer of the British Isles, however, the war in the short run made little difference. To be sure, excise taxes and land taxes were high (four shillings to the pound for landowners); thus, consumer prices went up and some landlords may have raised their rents as a result. As we saw in chapter 3, the state apparatus grew because of the need to collect taxes and supply the army and navy. Otherwise, for the vast majority of Britons, the most important facts for the short term were that no battles were fought on British soil and that agricultural life went on as usual.

In the long run, however, the Seven Years' War, like all those since 1689, contributed to British economic development. Some economic historians have argued that Britain's entry into industrialization would have occurred sooner had these wars not happened. Britons of the day did not think so. To be sure, many enlightened philosophers like Adam Smith believed that trade and wealth grew best in the soil of peace. But most Britons, landowners and commercial men alike, thought that success in war had increased national prosperity. They were probably right, especially in the case of the Seven Years' War. The war interfered very little with trade, and it stimulated many industries associated with shipbuilding, weapons manufacturing, and military supply. It also assured British control over many of the possessions that made Britain a great maritime and colonial power and that fueled the commercial sector of the economy. Perhaps that was reward enough.

## Suggested Reading

Anderson, Fred. *Crucible of War: The Seven Years' War and the Fate of Empire in British North America, 1754–1766*. London: Faber, 2000.

Bayly, C. A. *Imperial Meridian: The British Empire and the World, 1780–1830*. New York: Longman, 1989.

Bence-Jones, Mark. *Clive of India*. London: Constable, 1974.

Black, Jeremy. *British Foreign Policy in the Age of Walpole*. Edinburgh: John Donald, 1985.

———. *Eighteenth-Century Britain, 1688–1783*. New York: Palgrave, 2001.

———. *The British Seaborne Empire*. New Haven, CT: Yale University Press, 2004.

Brewer, John. *The Sinews of Power: War, Money, and the English State, 1688–1783*. New York: Knopf, 1989.

Cain, P. J., and A. G. Hopkins. *British Imperialism: Innovation and Expansion*. London: Longman, 1993.

Dalley, Jan. *The Black Hole: Money, Myth and Indian Empire*. New York: Viking, 2006.

Daunton, Martin, and Rick Halpern, eds. *Empire and Others: British Encounters With Indigenous Peoples*. Philadelphia: University of Pennsylvania Press, 1999.

Davis, David Brion. *Inhuman Bondage: The Rise and Fall of Slavery in the New World*. Oxford: Oxford University Press, 2006.

Fischer, David Hackett. *Albion's Seed*. New York: Oxford University Press, 1982.

Gauci, Perry. *The Politics of Trade: The Overseas Merchant in State and Society, 1660–1720*. New York: Oxford University Press, 2001.

Greene, Jack P., and J. R. Pole, eds. *Colonial British America*. Baltimore: Johns Hopkins University Press, 1984.

Howard, Michael. *War in European History*. New York: Oxford University Press, 1976.

Kennedy, Paul M. *The Rise and Fall of British Naval Mastery*. London: Allen Lane, 1976.

Lloyd, Trevor. *Empire: A History of the British Empire*. London: Bloomsbury, 2006.

Marshall, P. J., ed. *The Oxford History of the British Empire: The Eighteenth Century*. New York: Oxford University Press, 1998.

Mason, Philip. *A Matter of Honour: An Account of the Indian Army: Its Officers and Men*. London: Cape, 1974.

McKay, Derek, and H. M. Scott. *The Rise of the Great Powers, 1648–1815*. New York: Longman, 1983.

Moon, Penderel. *The British Conquest and Dominion of India*. London: Gerald Duckworth, 1989.

Peckham, Howard. *The Colonial Wars, 1689–1762*. Chicago: University of Chicago Press, 1969.

Scott, David. *Leviathan: The Rise of Britain as a World Power*. London: HarperPress, 2013.

Stern, Philip J. *The Company-State: Corporate Sovereignty and the Early Modern Foundations of the British Empire in India*. Oxford: Oxford University Press, 2011.

Wilson, Kathleen. *The Island Race: Englishness, Empire and Gender in the Eighteenth Century*. London: Routledge, 2003.

———. *The Sense of the People: Politics, Culture and Imperialism in England, 1715–1785*. New York: Oxford University Press, 1995.

Woloch, Isser. *Eighteenth-Century Europe: Tradition and Progress, 1715–1789*. New York: Norton, 1982.

# Part II

# The Age of Revolutions

# 1763–1815

# Chapter 8

# The Crisis of Empire, 1763–1783

No sooner had the British attained the heights of imperial power than they were beset by a series of major revolutions—colonial, economic, social, and political. Thus, the fifty years after 1763 constituted an age of crisis, a time when British industry was transformed, the society restructured, and the nation locked in a colossal struggle against the French Revolution. Even the religious temper and intellectual outlook of Britain were radically altered. It is a tribute to the stability and strength of eighteenth-century foundations—not least the landowners' regime—that Britain was able to weather these shocks without completely collapsing.

The first of these great crises came in the imperial realm. The British lost the American colonies they had fought with such determination to win. In the long discussions leading to the Treaty of Paris (1763), British policy makers chose to keep all of North America at the expense of advancing British interests in the West Indies. They consciously ranked the American colonies at the very top of their imperial plans. Yet it was precisely these colonies—the *most English* of all British possessions—that broke away. How this happened and how it might have been avoided are questions that have intrigued students of history ever since. In retrospect, two things seem certain: first, the Americans insisted almost to the end that all they wanted were the rights of Englishmen, and second, the British contributed mightily to the outcome, less by asserting despotic authority than by political insensitivity, a failure of imagination, and military blundering.

## GEORGE III AND THE POLITICIANS

The failure to retain the American colonies was, therefore, a *political* failure for which both the British political system itself and the politicians who ran it shared the blame. At the center of the system after 1763 was the king, George III, who played a bigger political role than either of his

George III in Coronation Robes, *by Allan Ramsay. The famous Scottish portraitist painted George III in his most elegant ceremonial costume, making the king appear rather grander than he actually was.*

Hanoverian predecessors. For many years, both patriotic American historians and their liberal British colleagues believed that George III drove the American colonies out of the Empire by trying to make himself a despot—in other words that he attempted to arrogate all power unto himself and thus to undo the events of 1688 and the Revolution Settlement. More recent and exhaustive research, however, supports a more ironic interpretation of George III and his behavior. Far from being a tyrant, George III was a thoroughgoing Whig in his constitutional views. What he insisted on was the sovereignty of Parliament within a balanced constitution, and his obstinacy on that score constituted his contribution to the rupture with the American colonies.

George III was one of the most pathetic figures in modern British history. He was not up to the massive crises that Britain faced during his long reign (1760–1820), and from 1788 on he periodically suffered from severe mental imbalance caused by the disease porphyria. He spent the last ten years of his life in a state of pitiable madness, often confined in a straitjacket. He was not insane at the time of the American crisis, however. Born in 1738, George III was only twenty-two when he succeeded his grandfather to the throne, and he was emotionally and intellectually immature. His father, Frederick, the prince of Wales, loathed King George II, and the feeling was mutual. Frederick and his advisers believed that wily politicians had duped George II and reduced him to puppet status. Although Frederick died in 1751, he passed on these semi-conspiratorial views to his son George. The young prince grew up in a lonely and stifling atmosphere. He was of average intelligence, but was diffident, shy, lethargic, and awkward.

The dominant figure in George's early life was the earl of Bute, a Scottish nobleman who was George's tutor and his mother's adviser. Bute clearly became a beloved father figure for the young prince of Wales. Bute was learned in a bookish way, elegant, polished, and ambitious. That he won the task of teaching George how to be king proved unfortunate because beneath Bute's arrogant exterior there lay only cleverness but no wisdom. George became completely dependent on Bute, and Bute reinforced the view that George II was caught in the web of the politicians. The prince of Wales grew up determined to rise above the corruption that typified Augustan politics, to free the Crown of political entanglements, and to exemplify virtue and morality. He would rule *above party*. There was in these intentions a good deal of priggish self-righteousness but no tyrannical leaning. "The pride," he wrote in a youthful essay, "the glory of Britain and the direct end of its constitution, is political liberty." In short, George accepted fully the Glorious Revolution and the supremacy of Parliament.

When George III became king in 1760, he felt he desperately needed Bute beside him. He hated the cabinet of the moment, including Prime Minister Pitt, whom he suspected of having betrayed his beloved father, the late Frederick. George made it clear that Bute spoke for him and that Bute would stand first among his ministers: "Whoever speaks against My Lord Bute speaks against me." As we have seen, Pitt resigned in 1761, and Bute became first lord of the Treasury (prime minister), though he had no claim to high office other than being the king's favorite.

Disgruntled Whig politicos interpreted the king's support for Bute as evidence that the king and Bute were subverting the constitution by restoring the royal prerogative. Such rhetoric had long been the resort of oppositional politicians of the Tory and Country Whig types. As we will see, the rhetoric found acceptance in America. Now three other factors seemed to give substance to the rhetoric. One was that Bute was not tough or smart enough for the job of prime minister; although he soon resigned the office, he wanted to retain his personal influence with the king and thus to exercise power without responsibility. Many people believed—falsely—that Bute's influence depended on illicit relations with George III's mother.

A second factor was that George III, under Bute's tutelage, did wish to rise above party—indeed, to put an end to party divisions, which he called *factions*. Hence, George in effect adopted old-fashioned Country party ideology and accepted Tories back into the pale of court and office. This meant that George was adopting Whig *theory* but not Whig *practice*, which were two very different things. The Whigs who had run the political machine since Walpole's day claimed that George was in fact restoring Tory/Stuart ideas from before 1688.

Whig propaganda against George and the supposed backstairs illegitimate power of Bute became intense. Various proposals to limit the power of the Crown—to eliminate placemen from the House of Commons, for instance, or to abolish sinecures (jobs without real work attached) in the gift of the Crown—gained fairly widespread approval. The best example of Whig criticism of George III was Edmund Burke's *Thoughts on the Cause of the Present Discontents* (1770). Burke, an émigré Irish intellectual, was the client of a Whig magnate, the marquess of Rockingham. He argued that, in trying to rule without party, the king was substituting personal rule and royal influence for the proper supremacy of the House of Commons. To Burke, parties were not mere factions seeking office, but bodies of men "united for promoting by their joint endeavours the national interest upon some particular principle in which they are all agreed." This noble idea became the classic definition of political parties in the nineteenth century, but it was not an accurate description in the eighteenth century. It was only a sublime rationalization of Whig self-interest and quest for office and power. In fact, George III had better claims to constitutionality than did Burke and the Rockingham Whigs. Yet in this case, as in most politics, what people believed was more important than the facts.

## JOHN WILKES AND POPULAR POLITICS

The third factor leading people to suspect George III of working to establish royal tyranny was one that had great impact on colonial American political consciousness—the affair of John Wilkes. More than any other individual of eighteenth-century Britain, Wilkes challenged the assumption

John Wilkes, *by William Hogarth (1763). The great caricaturist portrayed Wilkes, the popular political gadfly, in his most devilish aspect.*

that the populace should be excluded from the legitimate political system. He was a very unlikely radical hero. The son of a rich London brewer, Wilkes was a debauched spendthrift who got by on his audaciousness, wit, and charm. Though he was startlingly ugly, he could, as he said, talk away his looks in half an hour. He was ambitious to cut a figure in the world of the governing elite. By spending thousands of pounds in the ways customary to Augustan politics, Wilkes got himself elected to Parliament, but soon gambled and drank away the rest of his (and his wife's) fortune. To make ends meet, he became a journalist, dependent on the patronage of the Whig grandee, Lord Temple. Then his political troubles and triumphs began.

Wilkes's paper, the *North Briton*, was a flashy, aggressive critic of Bute's government and that of his successor, George Grenville. In issue number 45, Wilkes launched a fierce attack on the king's speech of 1763 (the policy statement of the government on the day that opened the annual session of Parliament) and the terms of the Treaty of Paris. Wilkes not only described the king's ministers as "tools of despotism and corruption," but he also seemed to call the king a liar. The prime minister of the moment, George Grenville, thought that this was seditious libel and issued a general warrant for the arrest of "the authors, printers, and publishers" of the *North Briton*. Wilkes was arrested, but he fought the charges on grounds that general warrants (which specified no names and therefore could be used to arrest any troublemaker) were illegal. Moreover, he deliberately identified himself with the ordinary citizen by claiming that his arrest threatened the liberty "of all the middling and inferior sort of people who stand most in need of protection."

Wilkes won his case and became a popular champion of civil liberties as well. But the Wilkes affair had only just begun. In a triumphant mood, he republished Number 45. This enraged the House of Commons, which now expelled him. Wounded in a duel and intimidated by government pressure, Wilkes fled to Paris, but he was prosecuted and outlawed in absentia for having published an indecent satire called *Essay on Woman*. In 1768, however, Wilkes, dogged by his creditors in France, returned to England and stood for Parliament in Middlesex. This constituency in North London was one of the few with a broad electorate. Wilkes's candidacy was popular with the artisans and shopkeepers (as well as with the mobs of nonvoters) of London and of the provincial cities as well. He was elected, but denied his seat by the House of Commons and then imprisoned on the old charge of seditious libel. Well-to-do merchants and workmen alike rallied to his cause, and while in prison he was reelected by the Middlesex voters twice more, only to be expelled by the House of Commons. Finally, after a third reelection, the Commons simply declared the election of the government-supported candidate, who actually had lost miserably to Wilkes.

By then the radical Wilkesite movement was well under way. Everywhere the slogans "Wilkes and Liberty" or simply "45" were chalked on walls or paraded on banners. Provincial newspapers speaking for the middling and lower ranks still excluded from the vote brimmed over with stories about Wilkes and defenses of his cause. Affluent business and professional men, and even some country gentlemen, in 1769 founded the Society of Supporters of the Bill of Rights. Initially it was chartered to pay Wilkes's debts, but it later advocated a program of reform including both civil liberties and political change. For the first time in England there was a nationwide popular political movement. It was anti-aristocratic and civil libertarian in sentiment, for Wilkes had challenged general warrants and asserted freedom of the press. But the Wilkesite movement also advocated parliamentary reform: the right of a constituency to send to Parliament anyone they pleased, the removal of government officeholders from the House of Commons, more frequent elections, and more equal representation in the sense of disqualifying *rotten boroughs* (areas that had lost most or even all of their population yet still had a member of Parliament) in order to give representation to the large cities. Implicit in all these ideas was a new and different concept of parliamentary membership—that is, that an MP ought to *represent* (consciously speak for) his constituents. The enormity of this claim was clear to the elite. As one MP complained, "Such is the levelling principle that has gone forth, that the people imagine that they themselves should be judges over us."

Wilkes in 1774 was again elected to Parliament and allowed to take his seat. This helped defuse the radical bomb. Wilkes did not prove to be a vigorous reform MP and referred to himself as "an exhausted volcano," although he did insist on the right of newspapers to publish accounts of parliamentary proceedings. George III had once called him "that devil Wilkes," but now was surprised to find him a gentleman. However, the effect of the Wilkes affair on British politics had been profound, partly because it was a transitional movement between the riotous popular politics of eighteenth-century England and the more focused and better organized mass politics of nineteenth-century Britain, and not least because many American politicians followed the case closely and became enthusiastic Wilkesites.

## BRITONS INTO AMERICANS

The sympathy of British colonists in North America for Wilkes was but one of many pieces of evidence indicating that they were, in ways mostly unnoticed, becoming a people less British and more American. The conscious identity of the colonists clearly remained British until July 1776, but the Wilkesite seeds fell onto the soil of a political culture that already was subtly different from the dominant culture in Britain. The slow growth of a new national identity for America was so complex, and the emotional and mental roots of most colonists so firmly planted in Britain, that the discovery of their differentness in the heat of events after 1763 came as a disagreeable surprise to people on both sides of the Atlantic. Unless this growth is understood, the violence of American reaction to post-1763 imperial policies and the rapid growth of the independence movement must remain a mystery.

The growth of American identity was not a steady linear development. Broadly speaking, the earliest English settlers in America retained close personal and economic ties to England. Then, in the course of the seventeenth century, as a result of coping with wilderness conditions in isolation from the mother country, colonial cultures in North America began to grow apart from Britain. With the taming of the coastal (or tidewater) areas and the original river valley settlements, however, came an economic and social stability and a relative ease of intercourse with England that tended to anglicize the colonies. The ideas of the Enlightenment, which spread to North America, incorporated colonial high culture into the British world. The great evangelical religious revival of the early eighteenth century, called the Great Awakening in the colonies, did the same for popular religion. Perhaps more important, the tremendous sale of English consumer goods in America anglicized colonial material culture. As one historian, T. H. Breen, has put it, "Staffordshire china replaced crude earthenware; imported cloth replaced homespun." In these ways, the colonies were never so English as in the third quarter of the eighteenth century.

Nevertheless, there were some important differences between the colonists in North America and the English at home. For one thing, by the 1760s there were substantial numbers of people in America who were not English by origin or descent. By 1775, probably 20 percent of the 2.5 million people in the colonies were of African origin or descent. Another 10 percent were Scotch-Irish immigrants from Ulster, and another 9 percent were Germans. There were also thousands of Scots, Dutch, French Huguenots, Swedes, and other national groups.

Moreover, it is important to remember that many of the original English colonists were religious refugees who had deliberately rejected England. The Pilgrims, for instance, had sought to found a utopia of pure, simple piety separate from the corrupting power and wealth of England. The Puritans had rejected the English state in order to establish perfect Calvinist communities that would stand as cities of righteousness for all the world to follow. Neither ideal was sustainable over the long haul, but the sense implicit in both, that the colonization of America was the fulfillment of God's plan, sounded chords that would resonate in the emerging American identity.

There were differences, mostly unremarked, between English and American social structures as well. As has been noted in chapter 7, the English social hierarchy was not completely replicated in the colonies because the very top and bottom ranks did not cross the ocean. To be sure, colonial elites did form during the 1700s, and most of their members aped English ways. Their efforts to make themselves into English-style aristocrats and gentry were not very successful, however. The colonial aristocracy was based on money alone, and most of the families had made their fortunes so recently that the hard work showed. They lacked the polish and time-honored traditions that served as the emblems of social distinction in England. Further, the deference that English landed families enjoyed and that colonial elites desired simply was not forthcoming from the ordinary colonist. The ready availability of land and the rigors of the frontier life bred a sense of independence that fitted poorly into a hierarchical social structure. Even in the southern colonies, where the planters liked to think of themselves as landed gentry, the resemblance to English gentlemen was strained: the planters, after all, were slave owners and hard-pressed agricultural businessmen who treated their slaves more like industrial workers than tenant farmers or farm laborers protected to a degree by custom and paternalism.

Some recognition of such differences began to be articulated during the colonial wars, when colonial troops came into contact with the British army. Especially during the Seven Years' War (called the French and Indian War in the colonies), feelings of dissimilarity between themselves and the British became widespread among American militiamen. More than twenty thousand colonists served during the war, many of them in operations with regular British army units. Neither side liked what it saw. The British thought the colonials were ill-disciplined, unreliable, and incapable of executing a sustained campaign. The Americans found the British officers to be impenetrably arrogant and inflexible and the troops to be servile and brutalized.

The differences between British and American governmental institutions went largely unrecognized because most colonists believed that colonial political arrangements duplicated in miniature the British constitution. Yet there were differences. The colonial governors had more formal powers than did the king at home—they could, for example, dismiss judges at will and dissolve or delay sessions of the colonial assemblies—but much less informal power in the shape of patronage and influence. More important, the assemblies in the American colonies more directly represented their constituents than did the House of Commons. The colonies had no rotten or pocket boroughs. In New England, town meetings customarily instructed their representatives about the policies they should pursue. Because landownership was so widespread in America, the ordinary forty-shilling freehold franchise gave the vote to 50 to 75 percent of the adult male population. The sense of independence characteristic of colonial British American society was thus reflected in colonial politics.

Finally, there developed in the thirteen colonies a distinctive political ideology. The colonial self-image of simplicity and uncorrupted innocence inclined the Americans to accept Lockean political theory in pure form. Hence the *opposition* or *Country* philosophy, the stance of a minority in Britain, became the dominant ideology in America. The colonists believed in natural, unalienable rights; in the concept of an original social contract; in government by consent of the governed; and in the necessity of a balance in the constitution to protect liberty. Like British Country oppositional publicists such as John Trenchard (d. 1723), Thomas Gordon (d. 1750), and Viscount Bolingbroke (d. 1751), Americans thought that a virtuous citizenry was necessary to maintain the constitutional balance. In the 1740s and 1750s, some colonial visitors to Britain began to believe that political corruption was ruining the ideal British constitution and thereby threatening liberty. John Dickinson of Pennsylvania wrote of the English election of 1754: "Bribery is so common that it is thought there is not a borough where it is not practiced. . . . It is grown a vice here to be virtuous." It was this prevailing Country ideology that led British Americans to understand imperial events after 1763 as a conspiracy to subvert the British constitution and destroy their liberty.

## TIGHTENING THE EMPIRE

It would be a mistake, however, to say that the slow development of a colonial self-identity led inevitably to independence and war. The imperial crisis that began in 1763 and ended in 1776 should have been manageable if the British had shown some imagination and flexibility. An arrangement giving the colonies *some* kind of home rule—provincial autonomy under Parliament and/or the Crown—was a distinct possibility even after the colonials had taken up arms. How different the history of the modern world would have been if some such solution had been found! But the course of events after 1763 led the British government to think that the very foundation of the Empire and the sovereignty of Parliament were being challenged and the colonials to think that their cherished British liberties were being denied. Once locked into these positions, the two sides could find no compromise.

After the Peace of 1763, the British quite reasonably and naturally took up the problem of how to manage their vastly expanded empire. During the first half of the eighteenth century, British policy toward the North American colonies had been one of *benign neglect*. Now, however, the king and his ministers believed that a degree of rationalization was in order so that the expense of maintaining the colonies would not cancel their positive value to Britain.

The policies that resulted from this concern bore the imprint of George Grenville, who had succeeded the egregious Bute as the king's chief minister. Grenville was an able man in a plodding sort of way. George III heartily disliked him: "That gentleman's opinions are seldom formed from any other motives than such as may be expected to originate in the mind of a clerk in a counting house." Like most British politicians, Grenville knew little about American attitudes and traditions. He began tightening the lines of imperial rule by ordering customs officials to enforce the various laws regulating colonial trade. Next, by the Proclamation of 1763, Grenville set the western limit of British settlement at the Appalachian mountains, beyond which the mother country would not defend American settlers. By this act, he hoped to keep down the cost of the Empire, for he knew that colonial expansion into the vast territory between the Appalachians and the Mississippi would cause endless trouble with the Indians. Defense of the region would require many thousands of regular army troops and expenditures far beyond what the British taxpayer would tolerate.

The British government thought that taxes at home had already stretched public support to the limit. The Seven Years' War had increased the national debt to nearly £140 million. Grenville did not seek to have the Americans pay any of the annual debt charge, but he did think it reasonable for them to help pay for their own defense, namely for the ten thousand redcoats now left in America. He might simply have imposed a quota on each colony and let them raise the money as they pleased, but such a requisition system had not worked during the war. Thus, Grenville chose to treat the colonies as a single unit and tax them directly. By the Sugar Act of 1764, Parliament reduced the duty on foreign molasses imported into the colonies, with the view of actually collecting the smaller duty. By the Stamp Act of 1765, the government imposed fees on legal papers, newspapers, customs documents, diplomas, advertisements, and the like.

Grenville's policies were logical, but they ignored colonial opinion. The colonists erupted in protest to the point that war almost broke out in 1765–66. The land-hungry colonists were unhappy about the Proclamation Line, and they complained loudly that the Sugar Act took away their property (that is, money) without their consent. They were even angrier about the Stamp Act. Newspapers lashed out in editorials and letters of protest; riots flared all along the Atlantic seaboard. Crowds harassed stamp officials and attacked their homes and offices. In most towns, colonials formed groups called the Sons of Liberty to defy the tax. Merchants organized a boycott of British goods.

In their protests, the Americans did not bother with the details of the Stamp Act, but went directly to the fundamental issue of constitutional rights. This is what made their defiance of the law so alarming to the British and inspired the official British response to be so inflexible. Against the colonial cries of "no taxation without representation," the British argued that the colonies *were* represented in Parliament, not directly but *virtually*. Just as the people of Manchester or Birmingham, who sent no members to Parliament, were yet represented there, so were the people of America because each MP, as one writer put it, "sits in the House not as a Representative of his own Constituents, but as one of that august Assembly by which all the Commons of Great Britain are represented." Moreover, when the colonists rejected the will of Parliament, they denied the most crucial element of the British constitution—the sovereignty of Parliament. Without that principle, British liberties would collapse.

The colonists readily agreed that British *rights* reached across the Atlantic to the New World, but they denied that British *jurisdiction* did. From their beginnings, the Americans contended, the colonies had borne the responsibility and right of legislating for themselves. Parliament might regulate imperial trade for the benefit of the Empire, but to *tax* the colonists denied the principles of 1688 and laid the basis for the destruction of colonial liberty. They dismissed as ridiculous the claims that the colonies enjoyed any kind of representation in Parliament. American traditions of voting and representation were straightforward and direct: all freeholders voted for representatives in the colonial assemblies, which were thereby empowered to tax. But they were not represented in Parliament in any sense, nor did they ask to be. The Americans preferred their own assemblies, which would be more responsive to their needs than a Parliament three thousand miles away in London and in which the few American MPs would be as ineffective as the Scottish representatives after 1707.

Grenville possibly would have backed up the Stamp Act by force, but in 1766 he fell from office after a personal dispute with George III. Into power came a ministry of "old"—that is, mainstream—Whigs led by the marquess of Rockingham. They sought to embarrass Grenville and placate commercial interests in Britain who were hurt by the American boycott by repealing the Stamp Act—but they then undid much of the good will thus generated by passing a Declaratory Act, which insisted that Parliament did in fact have the authority of legislating for the colonies. Even Pitt, who had supported the American protests against the Stamp Act, agreed with the Declaratory Act. Such was the limit to which even sympathetic British politicians would go: all Britons agreed that the principle of parliamentary sovereignty over every part of the Empire must be defended.

Despite its accomplishments, the Rockingham ministry lacked the confidence of both king and Commons, and it inevitably fell from office later in 1766. The stage was set for one of the great *what if* moments in British history. The politically adept Pitt—whom we now must call Chatham, as he had been elevated to the peerage as earl of Chatham—could conceivably have constructed a lasting accommodation with the colonies. But Chatham's mental stability gave out in 1767, and the lead was taken by his chancellor of the exchequer, Charles Townshend, who proceeded to reverse Chatham's policy of reconciliation with America. Townshend, a brilliant but politically obtuse man, wrongly believed that the colonies would not object to external taxation. Thus, he sought to relieve Britain's financial troubles and to free the colonial governors from their dependence on their assemblies at the same time by laying duties on the importation into the colonies of glass, lead, paints, paper, and tea. The revenue would be used to pay the salaries of the governors and other colonial officials.

Townshend's grievous mistake in judgment roused colonial opposition that was as fierce and effective as the earlier opposition against the Stamp Act. The Americans revived their arguments about fundamental rights and renewed the boycott of British goods. Worse, the British officials sent to America to collect the Townshend duties behaved little better than rapacious racketeers. Confrontation between bureaucrats and protesters became very intense. Townshend died later in 1767, and because an insignificant amount of revenue was actually collected, Parliament backed away. In 1770, the Townshend duties were repealed, except one on tea, which was retained as a symbol of British authority.

The repeal of the Townshend duties did little to dissipate the mistrust between Parliament and the colonials. The British government sent troops to Boston to help enforce the Townshend duties, and the colonists interpreted this action as another step in the campaign to deprive them of their liberty. The Wilkesite affair, which the colonists watched closely, confirmed their suspicions. At home, incidents between the army and the citizens of Boston resulted, the worst being the so-called Boston Massacre of 1770, when five colonials were killed. In 1772, after further clashes between American merchants and British revenue collectors, the colonies began to set up

*Committees of Correspondence* to coordinate their opposition. In 1773, Parliament made the matter worse by its attempt to help the financially troubled East India Company. The Company was granted the right to sell tea in America at a cut rate and without dealing through colonial merchants. People in all the colonies resisted what they saw as a British conspiracy to establish a monopoly, and in Boston protesters dumped the tea into the harbor. Parliament responded with a number of laws punishing Boston, which only roused the solidarity of other colonies with their Massachusetts neighbor.

By this point, a growing body of Americans was reacting to every move Parliament made in an almost paranoid fear of British tyranny. Thomas Jefferson, for instance, claimed that the British imperial reforms amounted to "a deliberate, systematical plan of reducing us to slavery." In June 1774, with a ghastly sense of timing, Parliament aggravated these suspicions by passing the Quebec Act. This set up a civil government with only an appointed council, gave special recognition to Roman Catholicism, and extended the boundary of the former French province into the Ohio Valley. The Americans saw the Quebec Act as an obvious attempt to frustrate American expansion to the West, to sponsor the spread of popery, and to establish nonrepresentative colonial institutions to boot. Coupled with the *Coercive Acts* on Boston, the Quebec Act stood as tyranny exposed. Representatives of twelve colonies gathered in Philadelphia to discuss collective efforts to defend colonial rights. Independence was still too extreme a measure for them, but probably a majority agreed with Jefferson that Parliament had no sovereignty over the colonies even though the colonies and Britain were united under the Crown. Hence, this Continental Congress rejected the idea of a united colonial government exercising *home rule*, but subordinate in imperial affairs to Parliament. Perhaps something like *dominion status* (colonial authority under the Crown, but not under Parliament) was still possible, but the British (including George III) were incapable of imagining such a solution. In their view, as Thomas Hutchinson, the governor of Massachusetts, said in 1772, "No line can be drawn between the supreme authority of parliament and the total independence of the colonies."

## THE WAR FOR COLONIAL INDEPENDENCE

Given the determination of the king and his ministers to force the colonies to submit to the will of Parliament and given the resolve of many Americans to resist, violence was inevitable. In 1775, General Thomas Gage, commander of the British forces in North America, decided to carry out a preemptive strike by seizing the powder and shot that the local militia was storing in Concord. On the way, his troops were fired on by Massachusetts minutemen at Lexington and then suffered severe losses on the return march to Boston.

The outbreak of fighting radically altered the situation. When the Second Continental Congress gathered in May 1775, it had to conduct a revolution that already had started. Still, the Congress petitioned George III, asking that he redress their grievances and treat the colonial assemblies as coequal with Parliament. George III, determined to protect the supremacy of Parliament, rejected this "olive branch" petition and declared the colonies to be in rebellion. Colonial opinion now swung sharply against him. In January 1776, colonial animus against the king was articulated and spread by Tom Paine's *Common Sense*, one of the most effective political tracts in the history of the English-speaking world. Paine, who had only emigrated to America from England in 1774, argued with telling simplicity and cogency that the colonies ought to break with Britain completely, and that meant breaking with the king as well as with Parliament. The American faith in monarchy, he wrote, was entirely unjustified, for the Crown itself stood as a principal source of arbitrary government. The law ought to be king in America, not the "royal brute of Britain." Paine's tract was crucial in turning the Americans into republicans.

Finally, in July 1776, the Continental Congress adopted the Declaration of Independence, ironically one of the greatest documents of the British Enlightenment. It was a thoroughly Lockean piece of reasoning—a statement of natural rights philosophy that explained why the Americans believed that their consent to be governed had been violated and why they therefore dissolved the original contract of civil government with Britain. It explored, in short, a contradiction in standard Whig philosophy between the sovereignty of Parliament (which Britain chose) and the consent of the governed (which America chose).

George III, his ministers, and a majority in Parliament all resolved to end the rebellion by force. Given this intention, the British should have waged the war with full commitment, energy, and ruthlessness while holding out a constitutional compromise to woo colonial moderates. But they never understood either the extent of colonial opposition or the kind of war they faced. Moreover, they underestimated the staggering difficulty of coordinating and supplying military operations in hostile territory an ocean away. The British government thought that its basic role was to assist the loyal colonists (whose numbers it overestimated) to overcome the disloyal ones. In fact, though the British army (with German mercenaries) won many battles, colonial opposition sprang up again as soon as the army left a given locality. Thus, the British never committed the number of troops necessary, and worse, they eventually lost their accustomed mastery of the seas.

British tactics were adequate had they been executed with sufficient vigor and resources. At the outset, the British aimed sensibly enough at cutting New England off from the rest of the colonies. General William Howe's forces took New York in 1776, and in the following year, General Burgoyne moved south from Canada along the Hudson toward Albany. Howe should have pushed north from New York to link up with him, but he allowed himself to be diverted by Washington's Continental army and the prospect of capturing Philadelphia. Burgoyne found his army isolated and outnumbered near Saratoga, New York, where he surrendered.

The defeat at Saratoga proved doubly disastrous because it gave the French sufficient confidence in the Americans to ally with them and ended the continuing hope among some Britons that the colonies could ultimately be salvaged. Since 1763, the French had been anxious to restore their own prestige and reduce British power. The American war for independence gave the French a splendid opportunity. From 1778, therefore, the British faced a renewal of world war, struggling with France in the East Indies and in the West Indies, as well as in America. Fearing a French invasion of the British Isles, the British government committed a large number of ships to the English Channel. It also shifted army and navy units from America to the West Indies. Moreover, in 1779, Spain joined the conflict against Britain, and in 1780 Britain had to declare war on the Dutch in order to protect the Baltic trade. These developments drained British resources away from the war in America.

Nevertheless, in 1780, the British effort in America fared better, as the army captured Georgia and South Carolina. Had the British commander in the South, Earl Cornwallis, been able to launch an effective attack northward, he might have separated the southern colonies from the rest and then put down the rebellion in the mid-Atlantic region. But colonial guerrilla warfare harassed the British and Loyalist detachments in the South, and Cornwallis soon found himself in Virginia without adequate support and besieged by Washington. In 1781, a French fleet in the Chesapeake cut Cornwallis off from relief or retreat by sea, and Cornwallis surrendered.

By then the failure of the British government to conduct the war effectively had stimulated much opposition at home inside and outside Parliament. The chief minister, Lord North, had been in office since 1770 and was

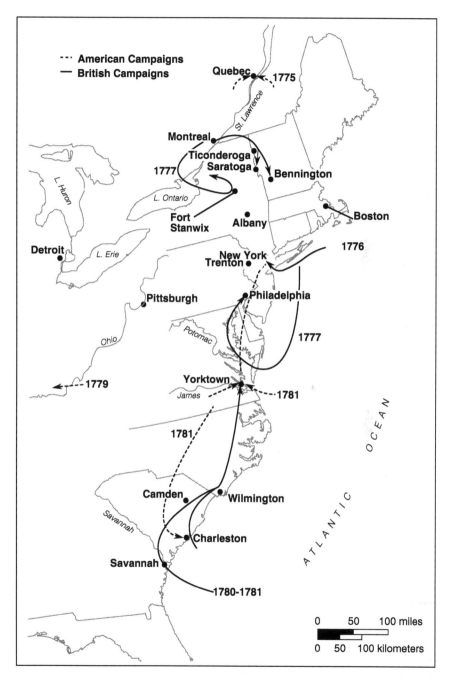

*Military campaigns against the American colonists during the American Revolution.*
The British captured Georgia and North Carolina, but were unable to capitalize on
these victories. Penned between George Washington's troops and a French fleet,
General Cornwallis surrendered at Yorktown.

the first politician since Bute whom George III trusted. The two thought alike, and North was intelligent, witty, and an able public financier. Yet North was not a strong war minister, for he was indolent and lethargic. He was unable to weld the cabinet into a single unit, and even the two ministers in charge of the army and the navy pulled in different directions. North knew his own weaknesses and frequently begged George III to let him resign. But George III himself was facing the war with stubborn, if dull-witted, courage, and he insisted that North stay on. George's political activism only aggravated the sense among the opposition that he was imposing personal rule on the nation. Independent country gentlemen joined commercial men who were unhappy about the disturbance of trade to form a radical movement devoted to ending financial waste and war profiteering and to "restoring" the balance in the constitution. At the same time, certain Whig factions—the Rockingham and Chathamite interests—took up the related issues of peace and parliamentary reform. Finally, in 1782, a sufficient number of independent MPs joined the opposition to force North to resign and the king to accept a cabinet committed to peace.

## THE AFTERMATH

The Treaty of Versailles (1783) that ended the war granted the American colonies independence and ceded to them all the land between the Appalachians and the Mississippi. This was a grievous loss to Britain—perhaps one-fifth of all the people in the Empire and a territory that was bound to grow in prosperity and trade. Otherwise, the British did fairly well in the treaty making. France was the biggest loser in the war. The British navy had reasserted its preeminence in the West Indies; consequently, the French won only a few West Indian islands, plus Dakar and Senegal in West Africa. Spain got Florida and Minorca, but Britain kept Gibraltar, Canada, and the Newfoundland fisheries. Most importantly, the British kept the trans-Appalachian west out of French hands. Moreover, though few expected it in 1783, British trade with America rebounded with amazing speed. By 1790, for instance, British exports to America exceeded prewar levels.

Nevertheless, from the British point of view, it obviously would have been better to keep the American colonies in the Empire. Could they have done this after 1763? Certainly the American colonies were growing and maturing so rapidly that some degree of autonomy would have been necessary by the early nineteenth century. Further, the removal of the French threat to the colonies by 1763 reduced the need for British protection. However, timely and intelligent constitutional concessions might well have attracted moderate colonial opinion and strengthened the Loyalists, who composed between a fourth and a third of the colonial population. Three factors seem to have prevented such conciliatory proposals: (1) the near-universal assumption of Britain that colonies existed to serve the home country, (2) the complete agreement of Britons on the principle of parliamentary sovereignty, and (3) the inadequacy of the political system. It is important to remember that the British political structure actually functioned to promote the political interests, narrowly conceived, of the members of various elite factions and not to formulate policies directed to the welfare of the country. Hence, it was no accident that the domestic cry for reform and the constitutional claim of the colonists coincided.

As for the war, it was possible for the British to win militarily, but impossible to impose direct parliamentary rule on the colonies or even to return to pre-1763 conditions. To win the war would have required the British government to recognize that this was no conventional European campaign wherein holding the battlefield at the end of the day meant victory, and it would have required a huge commitment of money and men—perhaps even in Europe—to draw off the French. Neither requirement ever came close to being met. But blame should not rest too heavily on the shoulders of George III and his hapless ministers: not even the great powers of the twentieth century had much success in fighting against movements for national liberation.

## Suggested Reading

Bailyn, Bernard. *The Ideological Origins of the American Revolution*. Cambridge, MA: Belknap Press, 1967.

Bayly, C. A. *Imperial Meridian: The British Empire and the World, 1780–1830*. New York: Longman, 1989.

Bradley, James, *Popular Politics and the American Revolution in England*. Macon, GA: Mercer University Press, 1986.

Breen, T. H. *The Marketplace of Revolution: How Consumer Politics Shaped American Independence*. New York: Oxford University Press, 2004.

Breen, T. H., and Timothy Hall. *Colonial America in an Atlantic World*. New York: Longman, 2003.

Brewer, John. *Party Ideology and Popular Politics at the Accession of George III*. Cambridge: Cambridge University Press, 1976.

Brooke, John. *King George III*. London: Constable, 1972.

Cain, P. J., and A. G. Hopkins. *British Imperialism: Innovation and Expansion*. London: Longman, 1993.

Cash, Arthur H. *John Wilkes: The Scandalous Father of Civil Liberty*. New Haven, CN: Yale University Press, 2006.

Christie, Ian. *Crisis of Empire: Great Britain and the American Colonies, 1754–1783*. New York: W. W. Norton, 1966.

———. *Wars and Revolutions: Britain, 1760–1815*. London: Edward Arnold, 1982.

———. *Wilkes, Wyvill, and Reform*. London: Macmillan, 1962.

Clark, Anna. *Scandal: The Sexual Politics of the British Constitution*. Princeton, NJ: Princeton University Press, 2004.

Conway, Stephen. *The British Isles and the War of American Independence*. Oxford: Oxford University Press, 2000.

Dickinson, H. T., ed. *Britain and the American Revolution*. London: Longman, 1998.

Guttridge, George H. *English Whiggism and the American Revolution*. New York: AMS Press, 1979.

Langford, Paul. *A Polite and Commercial People: England, 1727–1783*. Oxford: Clarendon Press, 1989.

Mackesy, Piers. *The War for America, 1775–1783*. Cambridge, MA: Harvard University Press, 1964.

Maier, Pauline. *From Resistance to Revolution: Colonial Radicals and the Development of American Opposition to Great Britain, 1765–1776*. New York: Knopf, 1972.

Morgan, Edmund S. *The Birth of the Republic, 1763–1789*. Chicago: University of Chicago Press, 1977.

Morgan, Edmund S., and Helen M. Morgan. *The Stamp Act Crisis*. New York: Collier Books, 1971.

O'Gorman, Frank. *The Long Eighteenth Century: British Political and Social History, 1688–1832*. London: Arnold, 1997.

Perry, Keith. *British Politics and the American Revolution*. New York: St. Martin's Press, 1990.

Pocock, J. G. A., ed. *Three British Revolutions: 1641, 1688, 1766*. Princeton, NJ: Princeton University Press, 1980.

Rudé, George. *Wilkes and Liberty*. Oxford: Clarendon Press, 1962.

Wills, Garry. *Inventing America: Jefferson's Declaration of Independence*. Garden City, NY: Doubleday, 1978.

# Chapter 9

# The Rise of the Protestant
# Nation in Ireland

America was not the only source of colonial troubles in Britain in the eighteenth century. Just across St. George's Channel in Ireland, a political movement threatened to lead the Emerald Isle along the trail toward independence blazed by the Americans. In fact, the spirit of independence in America reinforced that in Ireland, and vice versa. The Irish Patriot movement, however, was not the product of the nation as a whole, but of the Anglo-Protestant population—that exceptionally narrow landowning elite that had been planted in Ireland as an English garrison. Hence, this movement had only tenuous links to the mass of the Irish people, Celtic and Catholic as they were. In America, the white population formed a social order heavily weighted toward the middling sorts—small farmers and merchants. In Ireland, there existed two separate cultures, the one standing uneasily on the back of the other. Indeed, the rise of the so-called *Protestant nation* in Ireland depended on the absolute ascendancy of the Anglo-Protestant landlords over the impoverished native Irish. That relationship of ascendancy and subordination first allowed and then limited the development of the Protestant nation.

## THE PROTESTANT LANDLORDS AND THEIR CULTURE

The victory of William III's army in 1689–91 left the Protestant Ascendancy firmly in control of Ireland. Although they numbered no more than about 250,000 people (approximately 10 percent of the total Irish population) in 1700, Anglo-Protestants owned 85 percent of the land. The Catholic aristocracy and gentry had for the most part been reduced to the status of tenant farmers, some living sullenly on the edge of estates they had once owned. The Irish Parliament, once more in the hands of Anglican landlords, ensured Protestant power by passing the penal laws (see chapter 2), which, among other things, prevented Catholics from acquiring land and made it difficult for the remaining Catholic owners to hold onto their estates. By 1739, one writer could say with some accuracy that "there are not twenty Papists in Ireland who possess each £1,000 a year in land."

The Anglican landowners sought to exclude even the Nonconformists of Ulster from their monopoly of power and privilege. In the early 1700s, the Irish Parliament passed a Test Act similar to that in England, excluding Dissenters from public office. The Nonconformists of Ulster, most of them Presbyterians of Scottish origin, amounted to perhaps 9 percent of the total Irish population but held a majority in the northern province. Though few were landlords, they were a hard-working and prosperous people who despised the episcopal system of the established Church of Ireland. Consequently, Anglican landlords viewed them with suspicion. This treatment drove many of the Scotch-Irish to immigrate to North America between 1700 and 1775.

The Church of Ireland itself showed little interest in proselytizing either Ulster Nonconformists or Irish Catholics. Afflicted by the same diseases of political patronage, plural holdings, and nonresidence of clergy that handicapped the Church of England, the Church of Ireland contented itself with maintaining its position of established privilege, including the requirement that everyone, regardless of religion, had to pay the tithe to the Church of Ireland. The bishops were usually English appointees, and few took any interest in their duties. One bishop remarked that "a true Irish bishop had nothing more to do than eat, drink, grow fat, rich and die." Here and there humane Anglican priests brought a note of English-style civilization to their remote Irish parishes, but most had little contact with the mass of the population. The Anglican parsons were mostly English educated and spoke only English, whereas many ordinary Irish people were illiterate and spoke only Gaelic, a language that most Anglican clergymen and gentry alike regarded as barbaric.

The relationship of the Irish Catholic priest to his flock was totally different. The penal laws did not prohibit the practice of Catholic services, but they banned Catholic bishops and *regular clergy* (that is, members of religious orders) from Ireland, and they prevented priests from coming into Ireland from abroad. Most Irish Catholic clergymen were recruited, therefore, from the impoverished people whom they served. Few were well educated, and many spoke only Gaelic. But their roots in the Irish population and their own poverty made for close relations with their parishioners. Many received payment in kind. As one priest said, "The people give the fruit of their labours liberally to me and I give them my time, my care and my entire soul. . . . Between us there is a ceaseless exchange of feelings of affection." Because of these relations of trust, and because of the absence of a native Catholic gentry, the Catholic clergy in Ireland inherited the leadership of the populace.

That leadership did not contribute to any Catholic revolutionary movement, except at the very end of the century. For most of the eighteenth century, the ascendancy of the Anglo-Protestant landlords was unquestioned. Jacobitism caused no ripples in Ireland in either 1715 or 1745. Agrarian crime, which always expressed an element of religious and political resentment, was never entirely absent, but it stood at a low level through the first half of the century. Neither the Catholic clergy nor the gentry was in a position to provide leadership of a popular political movement, and a Catholic merchant class developed only slowly. Thus, the Protestant landlords for the time being could push to the recesses of their consciousness the natural insecurity that arose from their isolation amid the sea of native Irish.

In the eighteenth century, therefore, the Anglo-Protestant gentry lived in what was for them a time of comparative security and ease. Many of them, however, never felt comfortable in Ireland and spent most of their time in England. Some of the newcomers, whose families had obtained their land only toward the end of the seventeenth century, failed to win acceptance at the top of their local social hierarchy. Others naturally gravitated to the center of their culture—London. These absentee landlords, who often were the butt of English scorn for their Irish brogue and backwoods manners, had a damaging effect on the Irish economy and society. They drained capital away from the country, and they deprived the agricultural sector of much-needed leadership. They also failed to establish the face-to-face relations that might have bridged the enormous gap between rulers and ruled.

Yet the resident landlords were sometimes not much better. The rate of imprudent, lavish, and riotous living was unusually high among the Irish gentry. They prided themselves so much on their swashbuckling independence that dueling was an important aspect of Irish life. The wastrel Irish landlord with no interests other than field sports and hard drink became an English stereotype. One critic, for example, wrote in the 1770s that the Irish gentry "enjoy their possessions so thoroughly, and in a manner so truly Irish, that they generally become beggars in a few years' time, by dint of hospitality and inadvertence." Even in an age when, as we have seen, many of the English and Scottish landlords were rejecting customary relationships for contractual profits, the lack of a sense of paternal responsibility among the Anglo-Protestant landed elite was striking.

Although the landlords ultimately depended on English power and thought of themselves as part of English culture, they could be quite aggressive in defense of their political interests as Irishmen. This was the inevitable result of the fact that the British tended to treat them as colonials. Various Irish MPs and publicists claimed that the Irish Parliament was the coequal of the British Parliament, but the facts spoke otherwise. Clearly subordinate to both the British Crown and the British Parliament, the Irish Parliament was more like an American colonial assembly than like the pre-1707 Scottish Parliament. The lord lieutenant, a British official, was the chief executive in Ireland. Because he was responsible to the British government, the Irish Parliament could not turn him out, no matter how unpopular his administration. The lord lieutenant's principal task was to ensure that the Irish Parliament regularly passed bills of supply to pay for the administration of Ireland, including approximately twelve thousand troops of the British army kept in Ireland.

In 1719, by a declaratory act called the Sixth of George I, the British Parliament asserted unequivocally its right to legislate for Ireland, yet even before the passage of this act, the British Parliament at Westminster had legislated directly for Ireland. In 1699, for example, the English Parliament responded to complaints of English woolen manufacturers by passing an act prohibiting the export of Irish woolens to any country except England, where they were already subject to prohibitory duties. As a result, the fledgling Irish woolen industry died.

The Irish Parliament was even more unrepresentative than was the British, as well as limited in its powers. No Catholic could sit in Parliament, and after 1727, no Catholic could vote. The exclusively Anglican electorate was very small, and parliamentary constituencies were even more subject to influence and bribery than in England. The Irish Parliament technically could initiate no legislation. During the seventeenth century, however, Parliament had developed some power of initiative through the practice of passing *heads of bills*, which were statements of intention to legislate. Either the lord lieutenant or the king could reject or alter such a bill, and if a bill were so altered, the Irish Parliament could only accept it or reject it in the new form. In Ireland, then, the Patriot movement had to be directed toward making Parliament effective within its own sphere.

## ECONOMY, LAND, AND POTATOES

The overriding fact of eighteenth-century Irish social history was chronic poverty. Ireland's economic development did not reach the level attained in England or Lowland Scotland, though it was to improve sharply in the last few decades of the century. The market system for the exchange of goods was inadequate and would continue to be so until well past the middle of the nineteenth century. Both coins and paper money were scarce, especially in the western regions, and barter was still used in all parts of the island. Agriculture remained relatively backward. Peasants' squalid cabins, hardly more than mud huts, littered the countryside, and beggars crowded the towns. As Jonathan Swift, Anglican dean of St. Patrick's Cathedral in Dublin, wrote in 1726: "The whole country, except the Scottish plantation in the north, is a source of misery and desolation, hardly to be matched this side of Lapland."

The fundamental cause of the problem was that many Irishmen had no economic resort except the land. There was not enough commercial or economic development to absorb excess rural population or to give peasants some alternative to farming. The lack of commercial growth itself had multiple causes. Ireland had little in the way of mineral resources, and absentee landlords tended to divert capital to England. The infrastructure of educational, banking, and transportation facilities was totally inadequate. The great mass of the population had not adopted a consumer orientation, and the landed elite showed little of the English or Lowland Scots' commercial instincts. In sum, the backwardness of the Irish economy itself created an inertia that resisted expansion.

British policy also contributed to Ireland's poverty. The export of cattle to England had been cut off in the 1660s, and the export trade in woolens was ruined in 1699. By various acts of the British Parliament in the 1700s, Britain damaged promising growth in brewing and glassmaking. Thus, only two economic activities other than farming developed to any extent before the 1770s: linen manufacturing and the provision trade. Irish linens did not compete with any major British industry and so were encouraged to grow, especially in Ulster, where French Huguenot settlers brought their skill and capital. The provisioning of ships with beef, butter, hides, and the like was a product of the agricultural sector that could thrive on the expanding colonial trade; hence, the provision trade contributed to the prosperity of southern Irish coastal towns such as Cork.

Much of the Irish population, over 90 percent of whom lived in rural areas, thus depended almost exclusively on agriculture for a living. Yet Irish agriculture, even by the standards of the traditional segment of English farming, was very backward. The English observer Arthur Young figured in the 1770s that Irish farming in some respects lagged two hundred years behind England's agriculture. Tools were relatively primitive—the clumsy wooden plow, the spade, and the sickle were the peasant's main implements. *Drawing by the tail* rather than by harness still was the means by which peasants used horses to pull plows and harrows. Landlords rarely undertook improvements on their estates and usually allowed leases for short periods only. If a tenant made an improvement on his holding, he was likely to find his rent raised accordingly. Living in almost complete ignorance of scientific farming methods and without capital or security of tenure, the peasants themselves rarely made improvements to their land. Yet the landlords were always able to find tenants to bid up the rent and often let holdings by a kind of auction to the highest bidder—a system known as *rackrent*. As Lord Chesterfield, a man of no great humanitarian sympathies, wrote, "The poor people of Ireland are used worse than negroes" (that is, slaves).

Only in Ulster were these conditions avoided. There, by the so-called Ulster custom, the tenant was recognized to have some salable interest in his holding. This custom generally took two forms. First, the tenant's occupancy itself could be sold. Thus, if a tenant wished to sell his occupancy to another, he could; or if the landowner wished to evict a tenant, he felt obliged to buy the tenant's right to occupancy. Second, a tenant was entitled, at the time of eviction or the sale of his right to occupancy, to collect the full value of any improvements that he had made. If a tenant built a fence or drained a bog, then the value of that improvement was his. Ulster custom gave the tenant some sense of security and encouraged improvements. Not surprisingly, rents were paid more regularly in Ulster, and farming was more efficient than in the rest of the country.

All over Ireland, unlike in England, tenancies tended to become increasingly subdivided; hence, the land was let in ever smaller parcels. In England, the landlords believed that it was in their own interest to honor the customary size of holdings or even to increase them. But in Ireland, where landlords normally were interested *only* in rental income, they leased their land to *middlemen*, who then sublet to the tenants. The middlemen—easily the most hated group in Ireland—wanted only immediate profit and so promoted subdivision of holdings. By custom, the tenant provided for each of his sons by separating pieces of his holding until there was very little left.

The novelist Maria Edgeworth, whose father owned an estate in Longford, wrote:

> Farms, originally sufficient for the comfortable maintenance of a man, his wife and family had, in many cases, been subdivided from generation to generation; the father giving a bit of land to each son to settle him. . . . It was an absolute impossibility that the land should ever be improved, if let in these miserable *lots.*

Pressure on the land in Ireland was heightened by population growth. From 2.5 million in 1700, the Irish population rose to 3 million in 1750 and 4.6 million in 1790. It grew fastest in the poorest areas, the South and West. We will see in the next chapter that this population growth was not unique to Ireland, and in that chapter we will look more closely at the causes of population growth.

Suffice it to say here that one factor was an increase in the supply of food, and in Ireland, the nature of the plentiful food supply was simple: the potato, which had been introduced into the British Isles in the sixteenth century, dominated the Irish peasants' diet. The average tenant grew grain for rent and potatoes for food. Easily cultivated and requiring only the simplest tools, the potato was relatively high in nutritional value: one acre devoted to growing potatoes could support eight people. By the latter 1700s, Irish families consumed on average about 280 pounds of potatoes a week—about 10 pounds a day for each adult! In the infertile western regions, many families ate little else. Coupled with buttermilk, some oatmeal, fish (in the coastal areas), and occasionally a little meat, the potato provided an excellent, if monotonous, diet. Travelers in Ireland often remarked on the healthy, strapping appearance of the Irish peasants, as well as their grinding poverty.

Unfortunately, the potato crop sometimes failed, and localized famine was the result. In the years 1727–30, there were four bad seasons in a row, with much consequent suffering. One observer wrote of the old and ill "dying and rotting by cold and famine and filth and vermin." In 1740–41, conditions were even worse, and a report was made of "roads spread with dead and dying bodies" and of "corpses being eaten in the fields by dogs for want of people to bury them."

Even in good years, however, the material conditions of life for the Irish peasantry in many regions were extremely low. Regional variations were important: the absolute poverty of the unfortunate souls struggling to scrape a living from the rocky soil of Connaught or the western edges of Munster contrasted with the greater prosperity of regions around Dublin. Throughout Ireland, however, tenants and *cottiers*—agricultural laborers who held only a few acres and who depended on wages to pay the rent—often lived at the subsistence level. Possessions were sparse and housing primitive. One observer recorded in 1777 that, "upon the same floor, and frequently without any partition, are lodged the husband and wife, the multitudinous brood of children, all huddled together upon the straw or rushes, with the cow, the calf, the pig, and the horse, if they are rich enough to have one." Amid this riot of smells and noises and a total lack of sanitation or privacy, the Irish peasantry lived in illiteracy and superstition, subject to the whims of weather, disease, and landlords. Yet they were not without the pleasures of hospitality and sociability. Arthur Young has left this indelible picture of Irish peasant life:

> . . . mark the Irishman's potatoe bowl placed on the floor, the whole family on their hams around it, devouring a quantity almost incredible, the beggar seating himself to it has a hearty welcome, the pig taking his share as readily as the wife, the cocks, hens, turkies, geese, the cur, the cat, and perhaps the cow—and all partaking of the same dish. No man can often have been a witness of it without being convinced of the plenty, and I will add the cheerfulness that attends it.

Of course, this cheerfulness disappeared when the potato crop failed, and it masked the violence that bubbled just below the surface of Irish agrarian society. Yet rural violence in Ireland did not usually result from bad growing seasons. It broke out instead when the peasants had reason to feel that the landlords were abusing their power. For instance, in the early part of the century, a well-organized body of men in Connacht killed and mutilated cattle and sheep in protest against the expansion of pasturage. After 1759, when Britain removed its restrictions against the importation of Irish cattle and thus encouraged the spread of pastures, agrarian violence became more serious and widespread. Bands of men known as Whiteboys terrorized the countryside, tearing down fences and killing cattle. They also protested the collection of the tithe. Even in Ulster, Oakboys and Steelboys clashed with landlords over mandatory labor on the roads and over rent increases. Agrarian violence was made a capital crime, and the landlords ferociously combated it. Nevertheless, sporadic rural violence remained endemic, as much a part of popular culture as Celtic legends, harps, and leprechauns.

## RISE OF THE PROTESTANT NATION

In retrospect, it is clear that the enormous social and economic gap between the two cultures in Ireland—the Protestant Ascendancy and the native peasantry—created a dangerous fault in Irish society. In the eighteenth century, however, the landlords' disproportionate power allowed them a temporary sense of security within which the seeds of colonial patriotism could take root. British governments actually helped fertilize those seeds by frequently antagonizing the Protestant Ascendancy and unwittingly goading Anglo-Protestant landlords into considering themselves as Irish. In defense of its own interests, the Protestant Ascendancy developed a kind of settler-nationalist identity, which grew into a movement for political autonomy.

This idea originated late in the seventeenth century, when the English had moved to limit the Irish woolen industry. An Irish MP, William Molyneux, published in 1698 a pamphlet (*The Case of Ireland's Being Bound by Act of Parliament in England, Stated*) arguing that Ireland was as separate from England as was Scotland. In 1720, the brilliant essayist and satirist Jonathan Swift urged that Irishmen express their grievances with English policy by boycotting English-made clothes. In 1724 Swift voiced the anger of the Protestant landlords at the high-handed and casual way in which the British government had granted a patent to an Englishman to produce coin for Ireland. He asserted that the people of Ireland were connected to the people of England *only* by having a common sovereign. Moreover, as he was to argue in his savage essay, "A Modest Proposal," *all* the people of Ireland, Catholics as well as Protestants, would be better off if Ireland had more autonomy under the Protestant Ascendancy.

The Irish Protestant Patriot movement crystallized in the 1720s and thereafter kept alive the issue of constitutional relations between Ireland and Britain. The British, always concerned to rule Ireland in the interests of England, remained confident that the Protestant landlords in Ireland would be mindful of their ultimate dependence on British power. The lord lieutenant and his political managers, called *undertakers*, could normally put together a majority for English purposes in the Irish Parliament. The Patriots, however, expressed Irish interests at every turn, and like the Americans, habitually leapt from particular issues to constitutional questions. Separation from Britain was never one of their aims. They sought simply the right of the Irish Parliament alone to legislate for Ireland, whether the topic was taxation, surplus revenue, parliamentary elections, or the penal laws.

The Irish Patriots were well aware of the relevance of American issues to their aims. Because of emigration, many of the Protestants in Ireland had personal ties with America. Further, they recognized that the American protest against taxation without representation was identical to their own concerns. A Dublin newspaper argued: "By the same authority which the

Irish Volunteers Firing a Salute in Lisburn, 1782, *by John Carey. The Volunteers, an almost exclusively Protestant military organization, had become very well armed and trained by 1782. They represented the Irish patriotism of the Protestant Ascendancy.*

British parliament assumes to tax America, it may also and with equal justice presume to tax Ireland without the consent or concurrence of the Irish parliament." After the American Revolution began, Irish trade suffered, and the Patriots complained loudly about a British embargo on the provisions trade. Irish public opinion sympathized with the Americans. As one Irish Tory declared, "Here there are none but rebels."

Such discontent coalesced into a potent organization in 1778, when the French entered the war and the British government removed most of the regular army from Ireland to fight elsewhere in the Empire. Fearing a French invasion, the Protestant Ascendancy established volunteer army units to defend the country. These Volunteers were not under the control of the British armed forces or the lord lieutenant. Almost exclusively Protestant—the officers coming from the gentry, the rank and file from Protestant merchants and tenant farmers—the Volunteers represented, as one Patriot said, "the armed property of the nation." Not content with their defensive role, the Volunteers took up the Patriots' issues, and especially *free trade—*

that is, removal of British restrictions on Irish trade. They dressed in splendid uniforms made of Irish cloth and paraded menacingly in Dublin and elsewhere. As the sense of crisis grew, Britain's troubles in America proved to be Ireland's opportunity. The Irish Parliament, taking its lead from the Volunteers, demanded free trade and threatened to withhold Irish revenue from the British until its demands were met. The prime minister at the time, Lord North, was in no position to resist, and in 1780, the British Parliament granted free trade to Ireland.

The Patriot movement also accomplished some reform of the penal laws. The liberal spirit of the Enlightenment worked some effect even in Ireland, and as a result, the Irish Parliament during the 1770s passed a series of acts allowing Catholics to own and inherit property on nearly the same basis as Protestants. The Rockingham government that succeeded Lord North's in 1782 believed in accepting measures of reform to stave off social strife and included relief of Irish Catholic grievances in its liberal program. The last of the landholding provisions of the penal laws were abolished, and Catholics were given the right to serve as schoolmasters and teachers. Nevertheless, Catholics still suffered from certain restrictions: Catholics could not vote, Catholic universities were prohibited, and no Catholic could own a horse worth more than five pounds.

In this sense, *Catholic relief* for a time became identical with Irish nationalism, but as the views of the two key leaders of the Patriot movement show, it was an issue that had the potential of dividing the Protestant Ascendancy. The first great leader of the Patriots was Henry Flood (1732–91), a wealthy and well-connected landowner of impressive oratorical ability and one of the few members of the Ascendancy to take an interest in Gaelic literature and language. He was, however, unalterably opposed to granting Irish Catholics any *political* standing. In 1775, Flood accepted office in the Irish administration, and because the administration ruled Ireland in England's interests, he forfeited his standing among the Patriots. His successor as leader, Henry Grattan (1746–1820), remarked that Flood stood "with a metaphor in his mouth and a bribe in his pocket." Grattan was a young lawyer of small stature and awkward mannerisms, but an inspirational and poetic speaker. Unlike Flood, he favored greater toleration for Catholics because, he argued, until the penal laws were relaxed, the British could play the Protestants off against the Catholics: "The Irish Protestant could never be free till the Irish Catholic had ceased to be a slave." Despite such rhetoric, Grattan no more than Flood sought to end the Protestant Ascendancy; for both of them, an autonomous Ireland was still to be a Protestant nation.

After the crisis and triumph of 1778–80, the Patriots moved to consolidate their victories by establishing the sole right of the Irish Parliament to legislate for Ireland. In 1782, a Volunteer convention representing about forty thousand armed men passed a series of resolutions calling for the autonomy of the Irish Parliament in Irish affairs. Irish popular enthusiasm again reached a fever pitch. The new Rockingham ministry in London feared that Ireland might go the way of the American colonies. Therefore, in 1782, the British granted full legislative initiative to Ireland. Thus, the Protestant Ascendancy in Ireland not only won (in 1779–80) the same commercial benefits for which Scotland had abandoned its Parliament, but it also (in 1782) gained without fighting the status that most American patriots had sought as late as 1774. This was no small achievement, but it probably would never have occurred if Britain had not faced a general imperial crisis.

## GRATTAN'S PARLIAMENT

The period of legislative autonomy in Ireland was to last eighteen years. Because of Grattan's inspirational leadership in winning the rights of the Irish legislature, the period has become known as "the time of Grattan's Parliament." Indeed, Grattan was awarded £50,000 by the Irish Parliament in gratitude for his services. For all their importance, the constitutional arrangements won in 1782 did not grant full *responsible government* to Ireland. This limitation was to put a serious crimp in Irish national development. The constitution of 1782 gave the Irish Parliament sole authority to legislate for Ireland, but it left the Irish executive in British hands. The lord lieutenant remained the chief executive for Ireland, and he was not responsible to the Irish Parliament, but to the British cabinet and Parliament. The British government, which remembered the constitutional difficulties with the Scottish Parliament before 1707 and which had clashed disastrously with the American colonial assemblies after 1763, had no intention of encouraging the development of an independent Irish executive in Ireland. Curiously, the Irish Patriots seem never to have realized the importance of developing their own executive system responsible to the Dublin Parliament, though it is very probable that such a development would naturally have occurred if the period of legislative independence had lasted long enough. But it did not.

Still, the period of legislative autonomy was one of significant achievement for Ireland. The Irish Parliament received credit for the remarkable

*Parliament House, Dublin. Parliament House was one of the most imposing examples of the neo-Classical architecture of eighteenth-century Ireland and a symbol of the power of the Protestant Ascendancy.*

blossoming of high culture and economic prosperity. The trade concessions that the Patriots had won in 1779–80 paid off in the mid-1780s. Linen manufacturing tripled in volume, the woolen and brewing industries recovered, and Irish trade in general expanded. In 1784, the Irish Parliament enacted the Irish Corn Law (*corn* meaning grain), which offered a bounty to encourage the growing of wheat and caused the expansion of tillage at the expense of pasturage. Moreover, because the Dublin Parliament now really mattered, formerly absentee landlords were more inclined to stay at home. The proportion of rents paid to absentees went down.

Irish prosperity and self-confidence were reflected in the blossoming of Dublin, which took its place as a major capital city in the British Isles. Building in the classical style flourished, and Dublin became (and remains) a splendid monument to Augustan taste. The late eighteenth century saw the construction of a wonderful collection of public buildings in Dublin: the Royal Exchange (1768), the Custom House (1780s), and the Four Courts (1780s) joined Parliament House (1730s) as noble expressions of the Protestant nation's temperament and outlook—serene, confident, haughty, and masterful.

Although the monumental buildings of Dublin testify to the Ascendancy's power, the solid shops and houses of smaller towns throughout Ireland bear witness to an important change in Irish Catholic society: the emergence of Catholics in the middling ranks. The penal restrictions on

Catholic land ownership had tended to funnel enterprising Catholic men and women into commerce. These shopkeepers, pub owners, and small manufacturers benefited from the expansion of trade that characterized the era of Grattan's Parliament, as did the lawyers, doctors, and bankers who serviced them. Educated and ambitious, Catholics of the middling sort increasingly demanded a say in the political life of Ireland.

The majority of Irish Catholics, however, remained linked to the land. Unfortunately, the expansion of commerce that followed the winning of free trade and the founding of Grattan's Parliament did little for the peasantry. The Corn Law of 1784 was supposed to aid the tenants by encouraging tillage, but even it could not solve the fundamental problems of Irish agriculture, nor could it counter the growing pressure exerted on the land by the rapidly increasing population. By the 1780s, competition for tenancies had caused a revival of agrarian violence, especially in County Armagh in Ulster, where the rural terrorism took on a sectarian character. Protestant Peep o'Day Boys and Catholic Defenders fought each other as well as the landlords. Poverty, ignorance, and sectarian bitterness remained the chief features of rural Ireland.

The Irish Parliament itself (and the Patriot movement generally) became bitterly divided over two issues: parliamentary reform and Catholic emancipation. Parliamentary reform—abolition of rotten boroughs and extension of the franchise—had by the 1780s become as heated an issue in Ireland as in England. The Volunteers eagerly sought reform because their recruits increasingly came from Protestants in the middling ranks of society who as yet were denied the vote. But the rumbling of rebellion that accompanied the talk of reform frightened the landlords in the Irish Parliament. Parliament rejected reform and thereby broke with the Volunteers.

Granting political rights to Roman Catholics was an even more emotional issue. Like Flood, many members of the Ascendancy believed that, if the Catholics got the vote, they would destroy the liberties of Protestants. Others like Grattan thought that, if the Catholics were *not* brought into the constitution, they might turn to political extremism and eventually destroy Protestant liberties. Once the French Revolution began in 1789, and democratic ideas radiated from Paris throughout Europe, the need to placate the slowly growing middling ranks of Irish Catholics seemed more pressing. The British prime minister, William Pitt the Younger, thought so. Under his pressure, the Irish Parliament in 1793 granted the franchise to the as-yet small number of Catholics possessing the required property qualifications.

But Catholics still were not able to sit in Parliament or hold the highest offices under the Crown.

The French Revolution caused ominous reverberations in Ireland, just as it did in England and Scotland (see chapter 11). Its ideals of toleration, equality, and democracy won support among many Irishmen of middling rank, particularly among the Presbyterians of Ulster, who still were second-class citizens. Liberal and even republican principles were advocated publicly in Belfast and Dublin. At least among urban lawyers and journalists, a desire for an alliance between Protestants and Catholics became a potent force. In 1791, a young Anglican barrister from Dublin, Theobald Wolfe Tone, helped found the Society of United Irishmen, which aimed to bring about political reform and complete religious equality—in one sense, to form a genuine Irish nation, and in another to bring the French Revolution to Ireland. The United Irishmen wanted to enlist Catholics and Protestants alike, and they recruited effectively among the Protestant professional and mercantile ranks. The Irish executive, with the specter of a peasant rising always looming, was alarmed.

The atmosphere in Ireland became even more tense in 1793, when Britain went to war with revolutionary France. The extension of the franchise to propertied Catholics failed to pacify Tone and the United Irishmen. The British government believed that a French invasion and revolution in Ireland were immediate threats. In May 1794, the Irish executive tried to suppress the United Irishmen, but only forced them underground. Tone began plotting to convert peasant unrest into political revolution, and the United Irishmen began to make contact with both the (Catholic) Defenders and French revolutionaries.

At the same time, however, growing political tensions pushed religious hostilities to the surface. As the great geological fault running through Irish society began to shift and crack, the two cultures of Ireland became more polarized than ever. In 1795, rural sectarian violence between Protestant Peep o'Day Boys and Catholic Defenders escalated into large-scale riots. In response, Protestant landlords, many of them Anglicans, founded the Orange Society to defend Protestant Ascendancy. (The choice of *orange* reflected the powerful Protestant folk memory of William of Orange's military triumph in 1689.) Ireland was now caught up in a European struggle. The question was whether the consequent seismic shocks would thwart the further development of Ireland under the guidance of the Protestant nation or propel the development of a united, nonsectarian, democratic Ireland.

## Suggested Reading

Bartlett, Thomas. *The Fall and Rise of the Irish Nation: The Catholic Question, 1690–1830*. Savage, MD: Barnes & Noble, 1992.

Bartlett, Thomas, and D. W. Hayton, eds. *Penal Era and Golden Age: Essays in Irish History 1690–1800*. Ulster: Ulster Historical Foundation, 2004.

Beckett, J. C. *The Making of Modern Ireland, 1603–1923*. Boston: Faber & Faber, 1981.

Connell, K. H. *The Population of Ireland, 1750–1845*.Westport, CT: Greenwood Press, 1975.

Connolly, S. J. *Religion, Law, and Power: The Making of Protestant Ireland, 1660–1760*. New York: Oxford University Press, 1992.

Conway, Steven. *Britain, Ireland, and Continental Europe in the Eighteenth Century: Similarities, Connections, Identities*. Oxford: Oxford University Press, 2011.

———. *War, State, and Society in Mid-Eighteenth-Century Britain and Ireland*. Oxford: Oxford University Press, 2006.

Cullen, L. M. *An Economic History of Ireland Since1660*, 2nd ed. London: Batsford, 1987.

Dickson, David. *New Foundations: Ireland 1660–1800*, 2nd ed. Dublin: Irish Academic Press, 1999.

Fischer, David Hackett. *Albion's Seed: Four British Folkways in America*. Oxford: Oxford University Press, 1991.

Foster, Roy. *Modern Ireland 1600–1972*. New York: Penguin Press, 1988.

Hachey, Thomas, Joseph Hernon, and Lawrence J. McCaffrey. *The Irish Experience*. Englewood Cliffs, NJ: Prentice-Hall, 1988.

McBride, Iain. *Eighteenth Century Ireland: The Long Peace (New Gill History of Ireland)*. Dublin: Gill and Macmillan, 2009.

McDowell, R. B. *Ireland in the Age of Imperialism and Revolution, 1760–1801*. New York: Oxford University Press, 1979.

———. *Irish Public Opinion, 1750–1800*. London: Faber & Faber, 1994.

Moody, T. W., and W. E. Vaughan, eds. *A New History of Ireland: IV. Eighteenth-Century Ireland, 1691–1800*. Oxford: Clarendon Press, 1986.

O'Brien, Gerard. *Anglo-Irish Politics in the Age of Grattan and Pitt*. Dublin: Irish Academic Press, 1987.

Powell, Martyn J. *Britain and Ireland in the Eighteenth-Century Crisis of Empire*. Houndmills, UK: Palgrave Macmillan, 2003.

Smyth, Jim. *The Making of the United Kingdom, 1660–1800*. New York: Longman, 2001.

———. *The Men of No Property: Irish Radicals and Popular Politics in the Late-Eighteenth Century*. New York: St. Martin's Press, 1992.

Whelan, Kevin. *Tree of Liberty: Radicalism, Catholicism and Construction of Irish Identity 1760–1830*. Cork: Cork University Press, 1996.

York, Neil L. *Neither Kingdom nor Nation: The Irish Quest for Constitutional Rights, 1698–1800*. Washington, DC: Catholic University of America Press, 1994.

# Chapter 10

# The Triple Revolution, 1760–1815

The waves of the French Revolution, as we will see, were to pound the British Isles from the 1790s through 1815. As it happened, the British were already experiencing enormous economic and social change in the form of a *Triple Revolution*: agricultural, demographic, and industrial. This three-pronged revolution caused the greatest alteration of life in the British Isles since the prehistoric invention of agriculture. It destroyed the bulwarks of traditional society and transformed Britain into the first "modern" nation in the world. In a sense, British economic and social history from the late eighteenth century to the present has been the working out of the consequences of the Triple Revolution.

Such a massive change cannot be fitted into convenient chronological boxes, nor can it be easily analyzed. Each element in the Triple Revolution had origins that extended far back in time, and none had completed its course in 1815 or even in 1850. Yet each took off in the second half of the eighteenth century and had important results by 1815 or so. To be sure, the elements did not happen at the same time in all parts of the British Isles. But one or another element in the Triple Revolution, and often two or three together, eventually affected nearly every locality in the British Isles; hence, it is safe to say that, because of the Triple Revolution, Britain was a very different place in 1815 than it had been in 1750.

This process of economic and social change is often known simply as *the Industrial Revolution* because the rise of modern, factory-based industry was the most dramatic and visible force in the Triple Revolution. The Industrial Revolution has seized the attention of a great many historians and policymakers alike. It is important, however, to remember that the three prongs of economic and social change occurred simultaneously, roughly speaking, and that they were mutually interactive: each had a major influence on the others. For instance, without the Agricultural Revolution, there would have been no population explosion; without population growth, there would have been no Industrial Revolution; and without an Industrial Revolution, there would have been no permanent increase in the population. But such simple statements only lead to more difficult questions. Why did population growth *not* result in industrialization everywhere in the British Isles? To what extent were the social disorders of the new industrial cities the result of any one of the three forces? Such are the complex issues to which we now turn.

## THE AGRICULTURAL REVOLUTION

The Agricultural Revolution began in England and then spread to Wales and Lowland Scotland. We have seen that agricultural innovation in England began as early as the sixteenth century. All of the elements of the Agricultural Revolution—reorganization of land ownership and tenancies, new crops, new patterns of crop rotation, and systematic improvements of livestock breeds—had been introduced by the late seventeenth century. By the early eighteenth century, traditional English open-field agriculture prevailed mainly in the great Midlands grain belt; much of the rest of England already had either been "improved" or turned into pasturage. Hence, the Agricultural Revolution was a long process whereby progressive organization and techniques caught on in different areas at different times. By 1815, it is safe to say, most of the English open-field and the equivalent Scottish systems were gone, and even the Scottish Highlands were yielding to commercial pasturage. If this was not a revolution in the *pace* of change, it was a revolution in *results*. By 1800, the agricultural sector of England and Wales was producing at least 60 percent more than in 1700. Almost everywhere in the British Isles a rational, commercial outlook prevailed in agriculture.

Once underway, the spirit of agricultural improvement took on a momentum of its own. Adoption of new crops and new farming techniques became the fashion among British landlords. The Welsh gentry, and later, the Scottish aristocrats and lairds emulated the English improvers; thus, progressive farming served as an agent of anglicization. English landlords took an active interest in their estates and sponsored local and county fairs to promote new methods of cultivation, new crops, and improved breeds of livestock. They devoured farming journals. Some landowners such as Thomas Coke of Holkham in Norfolk worked diligently to spread the gospel of progressive agriculture to their friends and neighbors. Even George III caught on to this public-spirited fad, involving himself thoroughly in the farms at Windsor and welcoming the nickname of "Farmer George."

The fashionable interest in improved farming helped make English landlords into more efficient estate managers. The new techniques available for adoption steadily multiplied. For instance, Jethro Tull (1674–1741), a Berkshire squire, advocated the use of sanfoin grass (a good cattle crop that does not exhaust the soil), the seed drill (a tool that provides for greater yield from seed than the traditional broadcast sowing), and French vineyard cultivation (cultivation of fields after as well as before planting). Charles "Turnip" Townshend (1674–1738) promoted the planting of clover and turnips, which restore nutrients to the soil and provide winter feed for animals. Townshend also helped popularize the *Norfolk* (or four-field) *system*, in which wheat, barley or oats, grasses, and turnips were rotated, so that no field ever had to lie fallow. Robert Bakewell (1725–95) advocated a similar rational and experimental approach to animal breeding. A sheep, he said, was simply "a machine for turning grass into mutton." Such innovations paid off in increased output. By the 1790s, the average yield per acre of wheat had risen from ten to twenty-two bushels per acre, and much higher numbers of heavier livestock were reaching the markets.

The spread of progressive agricultural techniques was accompanied by the controversial practice of *enclosure* (see chapter 3). By 1700, about half of the land in England had already been removed from the open-field system, but in the eighteenth century enclosure acts were passed with increasing frequency: 189 enclosure acts between 1730 and 1760, 926 between 1760 and 179, and 1,394 between 1790 and 1820. Thus, as the historian John Brewer has noted, "A long-term process accelerated to its final climax."[1]

## THE POPULATION EXPLOSION

In 1700, one person in the British agricultural sector fed 1.7 people, but in 1800, one person in farming fed 2.5 people. Because the total number of people engaged in agriculture remained about the same, British farming by the latter date obviously was supporting a markedly increased population. Indeed, the British population grew rapidly after 1760; this growth was one of the great social facts of late eighteenth- and early nineteenth-century social history. As Table 10.1 shows, the British and Irish population grew by about 145 percent in 120 years.

---

[1]John Brewer, *Pleasures of the Imagination* (New York: Farrar, Straus & Giroux, 1997), 625.

**Table 10.1: British and Irish Population 1700–1820**

|          | 1700      | 1750       | 1800       | 1820       |
|----------|-----------|------------|------------|------------|
| England  | 5,000,000 | 6,000,000  | 8,400,000  | 11,340,000 |
| Wales    | 400,000   | 500,000    | 587,000    | 660,000    |
| Scotland | 1,000,000 | 1,256,000  | 1,608,000  | 2,100,000  |
| Ireland  | 2,500,000 | 3,000,000  | 5,000,000  | 7,800,000  |
| Total    | 9,900,000 | 10,750,000 | 15,595,000 | 21,900,000 |

*Source:* Chris Cook and John Stevenson, eds., *The Longman Handbook of Modern British History, 1714–1980* (London, Longman, 1983), pp. 96–97.

Except for Ireland, where there was a terrible setback in the years 1845–48, the population of the British Isles continued to increase throughout the nineteenth century. Thus, the population for the first time broke through the upper limits that had seemed to be set by nature.

The population grew at different rates in different geographical areas. In all parts of the British Isles, population growth was slight between 1700 and 1750, but very marked thereafter. Between 1750 and 1800, the rate of increase in Ireland was clearly greater than in England and two or three times greater than in Scotland. During the first half of the nineteenth century, the Irish population grew at a rate unequaled in British history—and it grew fastest in the poorest areas (Munster and Connacht). In contrast, in Scotland, the population growth was concentrated in the comparatively prosperous Lowlands. In England, the population growth was more evenly distributed, but occurred principally in the more prosperous regions—the South and Southeast, the Midlands, and the industrial North and Northwest.

Why did the population of the British Isles grow? Given the different rates of growth and the spotty nature of the statistical data (the first census did not come until 1801), the answers must remain speculative. It is helpful to remember that a number of obstacles traditionally operated to keep population numbers down. First, the great majority of people before 1700 lived at the subsistence level; therefore, a series of poor harvests could cause at least localized starvation and disease. Second, the state of medical knowledge was poor and offered no defenses against killer diseases such as the plague, typhus, smallpox, dysentery, and influenza. These periodically swept through the population and caused great peaks in the death rate. Third, the people themselves exerted some control over population growth by delaying marriage and limiting the number of children within marriage, effectively maintaining a rough equilibrium between the numbers of people and material resources. In pre-eighteenth-century Britain, neither the food supply nor the number of *slots* available to people—tenancies, cottages, apprenticeships and so on—was very expandable. Thus, in that comparatively static world, both the average age at marriage and the proportion of unmarried women were high.

In the late eighteenth century, in different ways in different places, these obstacles were partly broken down. Whether the resulting increase in the British population was due more to a decreased death rate or to an increased birth rate is hotly disputed by demographers. It seems reasonable to say that both were involved. In England, for instance, the death rate declined from 26 per thousand to 22 per thousand between 1750 and 1850, not because of improvements in either medical practice or public sanitation, but because certain killer diseases, most notably the plague, disappeared from the British Isles for reasons not yet understood. Perhaps it was that the plague-carrying fleas did not take to the brown rat, which seems to have replaced the black rat in the early 1700s. Perhaps there was a natural genetic weakening of the plague bacillus, or perhaps the European population had gradually developed antibodies against the disease. Whatever the reason, the last great outbreak of the plague in Britain occurred in 1667, and typhus also gradually disappeared.

Another factor reducing the death rate was improved nutrition. In Ireland and the Scottish Highlands the potato, and in England and Lowland Scotland general agricultural improvement enhanced the diet of ordinary people. The impact of the potato on nutrition and population growth in Ireland has already been discussed in chapter 9. The potato had much the same benefit in the western Highlands of Scotland and Wales and a lesser effect in England. In England and Lowland Scotland, agricultural progress provided a more diverse and regular diet. Further, because of the improvement of the transport and market systems there, food could be moved more easily from one region to another. Localized famine became less likely because one area could support another. The improvement in nutrition made for a healthier population, one more resistant to disease.

Meanwhile, the birth rate also was increasing in all parts of the British Isles. There was, as far as demographers can tell, no *biological* change—no increase in human fecundity—that might explain the increased birth rate. Rather, more people married earlier, and because couples were together longer, they had more children. In Ireland, poverty was so pervasive that a peasant could not lift himself out of it by thrift or by delaying marriage. Why not marry young? According to one observer, "The only solace these miserable mortals have is in matrimony." Apparently, Irish couples did not practice either contraception or abortion, partly because of the teachings of the Catholic church and partly because they saw no reason to. Children contributed to the family economy and when they were older they could be provided for by subdivision of the parents' holding. For these reasons, every discouragement to early marriage and a large number of children failed to operate in Ireland.

A shift to earlier marriage also happened in England and Lowland Scotland, but for different reasons. Between about 1660 and 1760, the population grew slowly, but gradual agricultural improvement kept food prices low. This relatively favorable standard of living seems to have encouraged people to marry younger and to have more children. Likewise, commercial expansion and the growth of domestic manufacturing tended to multiply the number of slots available to young men and women. It slowly became easier for couples to set up households and begin to raise families. Similarly, certain other gradual economic and social changes encouraged comparatively early marriages. The custom of apprenticeship, which delayed marriage for young men, slowly faded in the face of commerce and capitalism. The acceleration of the Agricultural Revolution reduced the number of young people who *lived in* the household of the farmers and correspondingly increased the number who worked for wages. Both trends gave a greater degree of personal freedom to young people and thus contributed to early marriages. For all these reasons, the average age at marriage in England and Scotland declined from twenty-eight years (for men) to twenty-four between 1700 and 1800, and the birth rate rose from 33.8 per thousand to 37.5 per thousand. These trends produced a bulge in the demographic curve in the third quarter of the century. In the absence of traditional checks of famine, disease, and utter economic privation, the population represented by this bulge was able to reproduce, thus causing the demographic curve to soar during the early nineteenth century.

The social consequences of the population revolution can hardly be overestimated. For one thing, the age structure of the population was altered; thus. in England at least, the population on average was significantly more youthful in 1815 than in 1760. For another, this expanded and more youthful population contributed to the further erosion of traditional economic and social arrangements because its teeming numbers put irresistible pressure on customary rents and on traditional artisanal control over wages, standards of work, and entrance into trades and crafts. A third consequence was to help keep real wages (wages in terms of the cost of living) down. The economy was expanding in terms of commerce and output, but partly because of the rapid growth of the population—which tended to push prices up and wages down—real wages did not increase until after 1820.

Finally, the growth of the population caused severe overcrowding in both rural and urban areas. The total number of people living in the countryside (excluding Ireland) could grow only slightly; therefore, the surplus population settled in the towns and cities, swelling the urban areas and completely overwhelming urban governments and facilities. In 1750, England had only one town with a population of fifty thousand (London); in 1801, there were eight; in 1851, there were twenty-nine. By 1851, a majority of people in mainland Britain lived in urban areas. In the late eighteenth- and early nineteenth-century urban areas, housing was miserable, sanitary conditions shocking, and water supplies polluted and insufficient. Mortality rates in the cities actually went up and life expectancy went down. Urbanization in Britain was closely associated with industrialization; yet one should remember that, because agricultural arrangements (outside Ireland) did not allow for a big increase in the rural population, the historic population increase alone would have accounted for much of the misery of the new urban centers. Seen in this light, the Industrial Revolution was a godsend, for eventually it provided the means by which the burgeoning population could be supported and British cities could be made tolerable.

## THE INDUSTRIAL REVOLUTION

The Industrial Revolution in Britain is one of the most intensively researched and hotly disputed subjects in all historiography, and rightly so. It now seems clear that the industrialization process began earlier, was more uneven, and worked its effects over a longer period than historians once thought. Still, Britain industrialized before any other nation, and this head start was the principal reason for its preeminent position in the nineteenth century. By 1880—and earlier for most of the population—industrialization altered the way that the British led their lives. It was the process by which Britain broke through to levels of output and consumption unparalleled in human history. Hence, the questions debated by economic and social historians are of great consequence: What were the causes of industrialization in Britain? Why did the British industrialize first, and why in the eighteenth century? What was its impact on the quantity and quality of life?

Let us first define the term *Industrial Revolution*. It implies a vast expansion of the economy by means of the substitution of a factory system for domestic manufacturing: the factory system is based on machines that replace human muscle and multiply the productivity of each worker. *Industrial revolution* or *industrialization*, then, denotes not an *event* but a *process*, by which the economy as a whole is transformed and reaches a level of self-sustained growth. Such a revolution took root and flourished in Britain between about 1760 and 1830, though the seeds were sown well before and though it continued to throw out shoots and branches long past the mid-nineteenth century. In 1750, Britain remained a land of farms, pastures, and commercial towns; by 1830, congested industrial cities clustering around factories housing iron machines driven by steam power were common features of the landscape.

A few figures will give a sense of the magnitude of the change. Industrial and commercial output rose by 50 percent between 1700 and 1750, but increased by more than 160 percent between 1760 and 1800. Between 1750 and 1800, coal production doubled; between 1788 and 1830, iron production increased by more than 600 percent. Between 1760 and 1820, cotton production went up 6,000 percent. Production in all these areas continued to surge upward through the 1800s. Foreign trade also leapt ahead, almost tripling between 1750 and 1820. In domestic manufacturing, the average capital invested per worker was between two and three pounds. But in the cotton mills of 1820, it stood at between forty and fifty pounds per worker. According to one estimate, 750 operatives in a cotton mill produced as much yarn as 200,000 domestic spinners. One lace-making machine operated by two workers could produce as much as 10,000 hand weavers. In short, individual and national productivity in 1820 was far beyond what anyone in 1650 or 1700 might have dreamed. Britain was experiencing, as one observer said, "the accumulation of property beyond all credibility . . . and [it was] rapid in growth beyond what the most sanguine mind could have conceived."

Yet a note of caution is in order. Industrialization did not affect the whole economy at once. In effect, two different economies—the traditional and the modern—worked side by side during the decades after 1760. The modern economy—including coal mining, iron, engineering, cotton textiles, pottery, and transportation—got rapidly larger, whereas the traditional sector—agriculture, domestic industries, and most trades and crafts—shrank by comparison. Still, by 1820, the industrial sector did not encompass half the economy.

## KEY INDUSTRIES: IRON, COAL, AND COTTON

Iron, coal, and cotton were the key industries in the early decades of industrialization. Iron had been produced for many centuries before 1760, but a series of technical obstacles inhibited the iron industry's growth. Traditionally, iron smelters used charcoal as fuel to produce iron ore. The resulting pig iron was impure and brittle, and its impurities could be removed only by repeated hammering in the forge. These processes were slow and expensive. They also required proximity to rivers and forests because water wheels operated the big bellows of the blast furnaces and the huge mechanical forge hammers. In addition, the charcoal which heated the blast furnaces came from the slow burning of wood, and by the mid-eighteenth century, wood was scarce.

Technological breakthroughs opened the way to rapid expansion of iron production. Abraham Darby, a Quaker ironmaster from Coalbrookdale in Shropshire, succeeded in 1709 in substituting coke (from coal) for charcoal in the production of iron. The iron industry slowly adopted the new technique, and thereby put new demands on the transport system for the shipment of coal, stimulating the development of canals and iron barges. Then,

The Iron Bridge at Coalbrookdale, *as painted by William Williams. This was the world's first cast iron bridge, a wonderful example of the artistry of the early iron founders.*

in the early 1780s, Henry Cort developed processes for rolling and puddling molten pig iron that removed impurities much more quickly than forging. In the 1770s, John Wilkinson, an ironmaster in the Midlands, applied the steam engine to the blast process, liberating iron manufacturers from the need to be near a source of water power. The iron industry took off.

Technological developments also transformed coal production. Miners could not sink coal pits very deep because of drainage problems and because of the difficulty of lifting (*winding*) the coal from coal face to pithead. Moreover, the sheer bulk of coal made transportation difficult; thus, mining was confined either to locations near water transport or to production for a local market. These technical difficulties began to be overcome by the use of the steam engine early in the eighteenth century. Thomas Newcomen designed a commercially useful steam pump that, by mid-century, was widely used for winding; the Newcomen engine, however, was too inefficient to allow for big profits. In 1769, a laboratory technician at the University of Glasgow, James Watt, developed a much more efficient engine by adding a separate condensing cylinder. In 1775, Watt and a Birmingham manufacturer, Matthew Boulton, secured a patent and established a firm to produce Boulton and Watt steam engines. These engines revolutionized British coal mining, solving both the winding and pumping problems. Then, in the 1780s, Watt learned how to turn the reciprocal motion of his engine into rotary motion, thereby making it possible to apply the steam engine to many kinds of machinery, including textile spinning and weaving, and to pulling coal wagons on iron rails—that is, the earliest railways.

Cotton textiles proved to be the most rapidly growing and most typical industry in the British Industrial Revolution. To think of British industrialization is to think of cotton mills. England had long been noted for the manufacture of woolen cloth in the domestic system. Until the eighteenth

*Boulton and Watt Steam Engine, late eighteenth century. This kind of engine was perhaps the key machine of the early Industrial Revolution.*

century, cotton could offer little competition to wool because raw cotton, grown only in India and North Africa, was too expensive. In the 1770s, however, the southern American colonies began to produce cotton in tremendous quantities, and this cotton was readily available to British merchants. Further, a series of technological innovations made it easier and cheaper to spin and weave cotton fiber: for weaving, the flying shuttle (1733), and for spinning, the spinning jenny (1767), the water frame (1769), and the "mule" (1785).

By the latter 1780s, spinning cotton had been revolutionized. In huge spinning mills, machines turned out thousands of threads at once. Hand-loom weavers using the flying shuttle multiplied by the thousands to keep up with mechanized spinning. Whole villages turned to weaving cotton cloth in the domestic system. The demand for cheap cotton cloth at home and abroad was insatiable; hence, the early years of mechanization in the cotton industry were also a golden age for handloom weavers. Steam power was eventually applied to weaving as well as spinning, and this shifted weaving from a domestic to a factory industry. Because weavers were reluctant to give up their independence and go into factories, the spread of power looms was slow until 1815. Thereafter, it accelerated. By 1825, nearly 100,000 power looms were in use. By the 1850s, most hand weavers of cotton textiles were gone. Cotton production went forward in great clattering mills of two hundred to three hundred workers each, most of them located in the swollen, soot-blackened "cotton towns" of Cheshire, Lancashire, and the Clyde Valley of southwest Scotland—Manchester, Wigan, Bolton, Bury, Preston, Blackburn, Burnley, Glasgow, Paisley, and so on.

## GEOGRAPHICAL SPECIALIZATION

The concentration of cotton production in the English and Scottish cotton towns was typical of the geographical specialization that resulted from industrialization. After the woolen industry industrialized in the 1830s and 1840s, it became concentrated in the West Riding of Yorkshire, where coal was readily available; the older woolen-producing areas—East Anglia, Gloucestershire, Wiltshire, and Devon—faded in importance. The coal industry depended on the location of coal deposits, but it continued to be scattered in rural mining villages in the West Midlands (Shropshire and Staffordshire), Derbyshire, the West Riding of Yorkshire, South Wales, and Lowland Scotland. Iron production had been widely scattered before the advent of coke smelting; afterward, it settled in South Wales, Shropshire,

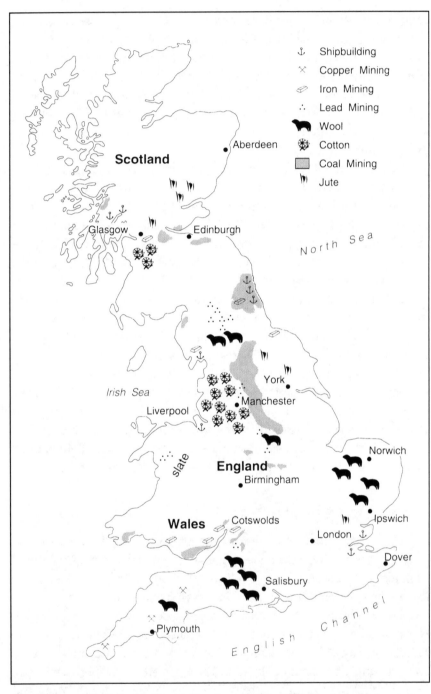

*The advance of the Industrial Revolution from 1760 to 1848. The Industrial Revolution in 1760.*

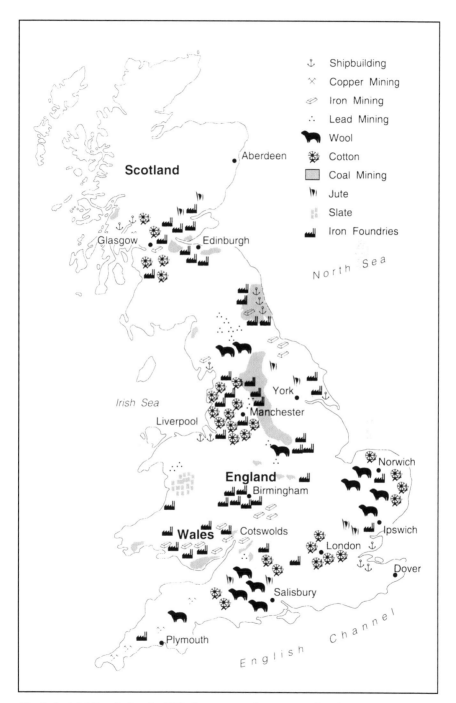

*The Industrial Revolution in 1848.* Cotton manufacturing and coal mining dominated the early Industrial Revolution. By the mid-nineteenth century, England's Midlands and North, the Scottish Lowlands, and southern Wales were heavily industrialized.

Staffordshire, Derbyshire, and Yorkshire. The South of England remained comparatively unindustrialized.

In Ireland, the only province to experience significant industrialization was Ulster. In the Belfast area, linen manufacturing had prospered during most of the 1700s. When Ireland won free trade in the 1780s, Irish merchants got direct access to North American cotton, and the cotton industry then won a foothold in Ulster. Ulster cotton manufacturers were quick to adopt the new technology: the first power-driven machinery in Ireland was used in 1784 in a cotton mill near Belfast. In the 1790s and early 1800s, cotton rivaled linen in Ulster. In the 1820s, however, certain governmental supports to the Irish cotton industry were removed. Without such assistance, Ulster cotton manufacturers could not compete with the English, and they rapidly faded out. The linen industry expanded again to take the cotton industry's place, once again locating in the Belfast region of eastern Ulster. The linen industry constituted the basis of Ulster's prosperity in the 1830s and 1840s. This industrial base distinguished the northern province sharply from the rest of Ireland, which remained largely unindustrialized.

Industrialization in Wales took yet a different form. It occurred slightly later than in England, the key years being 1790–1840. The principal Welsh industry in those decades was iron, as ironworks proliferated in the great South Wales coalfield. This remarkable area included parts of Monmouthshire, Glamorganshire, and Breconshire. Here entrepreneurs (many of them English) found rich iron and coal deposits together in the numerous river valleys that descend from the mountains eastward to the Severn Estuary. By 1839, South Wales was producing over 40 percent of the iron made in England and Wales. The burgeoning iron and coal industries drew in tens of thousands of Welsh peasants as workers, making the population density of the valley communities of South Wales in 1840 as great as anywhere in Britain. This concentration of Welsh-speaking workers played a great part in saving the Welsh language, but it created a volatile situation in which ironmasters and colliery owners spoke English and thought of themselves as part of English life, whereas the vast majority of workers spoke Welsh and remained part of traditional Welsh popular culture.

## CAUSES OF INDUSTRIALIZATION

What were the causes of the Industrial Revolution in Britain? Some historians think that the principal cause was technology: innovations in manufacturing drove the whole process. Others believe that the root cause was population growth: the expansion of the population provided cheap labor, which stimulated entrepreneurs to adopt the factory system. Still other historians have cited external trade, or internal trade, or the availability of capital. But the research of the last fifty years suggests that no one cause was both necessary and sufficient. The Industrial Revolution was a complex process with origins that lay deep in the history of the British economy and society. Therefore, it is useful to think in terms of the *preconditions* for industrialization—factors without which the age-old obstacles to industrial revolution would have remained insurmountable. Yet, even granted the existence of all the preconditions, the Industrial Revolution did not begin automatically, as if by spontaneous combustion. There had to be a significant number of people with the knowledge and the desire to take advantage of the preconditions—entrepreneurs with the right frame of mind to exploit the circumstances.

The preconditions for industrialization can be classified as economic, social, and cultural. In considering the economic preconditions, it is crucial to remember that England and Lowland Scotland had experienced significant economic expansion in the century before 1760. Much of mainland Britain by 1760 had a market economy of a maturity and vitality unmatched in any European nation except the Dutch Republic. A serviceable banking system included the Banks of England and Scotland. The English and Scots in 1707 had established a large free-trade area, with no internal obstacles such as customs duties or political borders to impede the flow of money and goods. By mid-century, the commercial sector of the economy was generating significant amounts of capital that could be mobilized, either through the emerging banking system or through networks of personal contacts. The amount of capital required to set up a small spinning mill or forge was not large—perhaps £500 to £1,000. Such amounts could be raised by an entrepreneur, an ironmaster, or a textile merchant, and then magnified by plowing the profits back into the industry.

Another economic precondition was an adequate level of technology in the appropriate areas—steam power, iron metallurgy, and mechanical devices for spinning and weaving. In fact, the basic technology was available significantly before the late eighteenth century. As we have seen, the innovations initially required were not very complicated and could be produced without a sophisticated scientific education. Very few of the early inventors were scientists: James Hargreaves, who invented the spinning jenny, was a carpenter; Edmund Cartwright, who developed the power loom, was a preacher; many others—including Abraham Darby, Henry Cort, and Josiah

Wedgwood—were businessmen who learned by doing. Nevertheless, scientific knowledge and thought in a general sense were necessary for technological innovation, and here again the British had an advantage. The Scientific Revolution of the seventeenth century, which provided the background knowledge, was a Europe-wide phenomenon. Because of the empirical tradition, however, British science tended to be more practical and less abstract than Continental science.

Final economic preconditions included access to raw materials and to potential markets for manufactured articles. Although better endowed with coal and iron than the Dutch Republic, Britain had a supply of natural resources that was not significantly better than that of other European countries. Britain did, however, have exclusive access to one essential raw material—the cotton grown in the southern United States. American independence did not hinder Britain's capacity to exploit this resource. As for potential markets, historians disagree as to whether the external market (including the British Empire) or the internal market was more important. Foreign trade unquestionably expanded more rapidly than production after 1760, and in the cotton industry exports accounted for about one-half of all goods produced. This is not to say that exports *caused* British industrialization, though colonial demand for British manufactured goods undoubtedly accelerated technological innovation. About two-thirds of the goods produced in the modern industrial sector were consumed at home. The growth of the population combined with a relatively high degree of commercialization to generate an extremely powerful domestic demand.

## SOCIAL PRECONDITIONS

The issue of domestic demand is related to the domain of *social* preconditions of industrialization. It is apparent that British (or, more specifically, English, Lowland Scots, and Ulster Irish) society was well suited to nourish revolution in industry. How so? The first factor was the population increase. The case of Ireland shows that population growth by itself could not cause industrialization. Rapid population growth can, in fact, inhibit industrialization by creating poverty, dampening demand, and discouraging the adoption of labor-saving devices. By good luck, the British population growth hit just the right level to stimulate domestic demand and provide a large surplus of cheap labor.

The population explosion was a Europe-wide phenomenon; therefore, British society (excluding most of Ireland) seems to have been uniquely equipped to take advantage of the opportunity when other nations could not. The relatively *open* nature of the British social hierarchy (see chapter 3) explains the difference. In Britain, property brought status, and property could be purchased. This inspired a love of money and a desire to buy the badges of status that went much deeper into the society in Britain than anywhere in Europe except the Dutch Republic. To some degree, the laboring poor had to be taught to desire consumer goods; capitalists such as Richard Arkwright systematically undertook to inculcate acquisitive instincts in their workers. On the whole, however, the desire of each person in Britain to emulate his or her social superiors, and thus advance his or her status, generated a powerful desire for riches. As Adam Smith said, what drove people to economic activity was in the last analysis "the consideration and good opinion that wait upon riches."

British society also shaped political arrangements in such a way as to encourage economic enterprise and expansion. The landlords, victorious in 1688, established the rule of law. Although they used the law for their own benefit, the rule of law itself supplied a regularity and predictability essential to commercial and industrial initiative. Further, the English landlords established absolute rights of private property because they needed to be able to buy and sell land and exploit their estates. For instance, among the landlords of Western Europe, only the British owned the minerals beneath the soil. This encouraged them, if not to lead the process of industrialization, then at least to cooperate with it, by making capital and mineral resources available (for a price) to entrepreneurs. Moreover, the landlords made sure to limit the state's interference with their liberties, including the liberty to make money. Thus, out of self-interest, the English landlords and their Scottish imitators created the political conditions suitable for industrialization: the rule of law, individual liberty, relatively low and highly predictable taxes, and a bare minimum of state control over internal economic activity. Finally, it is worth remembering that England, Wales, and after 1746, Scotland, were free from the destruction and turmoil of war fought at home. The comparative unity and security of Britain encouraged economic growth.

## CULTURAL PRECONDITIONS

None of these opportunities would have been exploited had there not existed a body of people with the appropriate values and outlook. By the 1700s, Britain had an unusual number of people, each acting on individual initiative, with the requisite qualities. The reason had to do in part with Protestantism. The Protestant "ethic" of worldly success within any calling, including commerce and industry; of rational application of means to ends; and of divine sanction for human exploitation of nature helped create an atmosphere favoring hard work in the pursuit of worldly success. Such an explanation can be pushed too far. Many Europeans before the Protestant Reformation had pursued riches. Moreover, from a worldwide perspective, Protestantism and Catholicism do not seem very different in their attitudes toward rationality and the manipulation of the natural environment.

Nevertheless, there was in the eighteenth and early nineteenth centuries a rough correlation between Protestantism and economic advancement. Furthermore, in Britain Dissenting Protestants, increasingly called *Nonconformists*, played a special role in promoting values that were essential to capitalism and economic innovation. They also took a prominent part in organizing the early industries. Nonconformists—Quakers, Baptists, Presbyterians, Congregationalists, and (later) Methodists—made up less than 10 percent of the population, but almost 50 percent of the most important industrial entrepreneurs. Their moral code encouraged hard work and self-denial. Moreover, their social position channeled them into business. Because they were not part of Anglican landed society, they were second-class citizens, usually relegated to the towns. Their psychological need for economic success was great, as was their practical need, because a Nonconformist could join the elite by making a fortune and buying enough land. Often, a switch to Anglicanism followed a man's purchase of an estate; meanwhile, Nonconformity had done its work.

To give one example, Jedediah Strutt (1726–97) was a major entrepreneur in the cotton industry. Strutt was a Unitarian, the son of a small farmer. He was apprenticed to a wheelwright in 1740, but after completing his apprenticeship, he returned to farming. However, because of his mechanical skill, Strutt was able to improve the standard stocking frame so that it could be used to knit ribbed stockings. He was not content to apply his innovation to the local cottage industry. Granted patents in 1758–59, Strutt set up a factory in Derby that became extremely lucrative. In 1768, he took into partnership the great inventor Richard Arkwright, who had developed the water frame for spinning cotton threads. Their firm rose to even greater levels of profit. When Strutt died, he left a huge fortune and a fine country estate. His grandson became the first Lord Belper. Strutt had provided his own highly appropriate epitaph: "Here lies JS—who, without Fortune, Family or friends rais'd to himself fortune, family & Name in the World."

The point is that men like Strutt could see the opportunities presented by the economic situation, and they had the skills and the motivation to take advantage of them. Britain in the 1700s was producing a substantial number of such people—managers of aristocratic estates, ambitious tradesmen, capitalists in the putting-out system of domestic manufacture, and opportunistic commercial captains. They proved to be willing to take the risks necessary not only to expand production, but also to expand it by wholly new means. Thus, the answer to the questions "Why Britain?" and "Why then?" is that both the preconditions for industrialization and a set of people capable of exploiting them came to exist in eighteenth-century Britain, but not elsewhere (at least to the same degree) and not before. Britain's advantages over wealthy nations such as France and commercialized nations such as the Dutch Republic were not great, but they were enough to give Britain a head start, and that head start was decisive in widening the differential.

## SOCIAL CONSEQUENCES OF THE TRIPLE REVOLUTION

The social consequences of the Triple Revolution were both complex and comprehensive. They did not happen overnight and were to reverberate throughout the whole length of the nineteenth century. Even by 1815, however, British society was being strikingly altered. Some of the effects have already been noted: the substitution of contract for custom in agriculture, the reduction of many small owners and tenants to the status of farm laborers, overcrowding in both rural and urban areas, the erosion by pressure of numbers of customary arrangements in trades and crafts, and the general forcing of real wages down. Now we will factor in the short-run consequences of industrialization and then consider the impact of the whole.

No one would deny that, because of industrialization, the great majority of Britons enjoyed a higher standard of living in 1880 than in 1750. They earned more, consumed more, and lived longer lives. But it is far from clear that industrialization had worked any such beneficial result by 1815. True, the gross national product (GNP—the total of goods and services produced by a nation) doubled in the period from 1760 to 1815 so that, even though the population increased, output per head also increased. Unfortunately, rents and prices also went up markedly, partly because of the war with France from 1793 to 1815. Thus, it would be only after 1815 that average real wages improved over the levels of the 1750s. Moreover, to estimate standards of living in terms of averages is misleading. For instance, there is good reason to believe that, during early industrialization, the distribution of income shifted away from wages and toward profits. In other words, the share of the national income enjoyed by the rich grew at the expense of the share going to the poor. The expansion of economic opportunities caused the middling sorts to proliferate. It would have been cold comfort to an artisan whose wages were falling because of competition with factories to know that statistically the per capita national income was going up or that commercial and industrial captains were prospering.

The increase or reduction of an individual's actual standard of living depended in large part on his or her occupation. Overcrowding in the countryside kept wages low and work irregular for most farm laborers. Factory workers were relatively well paid because most working men disliked factory work and had to be enticed into it by higher wages. Women and children, who dominated the early factory labor force, were paid less than men. Moreover, by 1815, only about 35 percent of the British labor force worked in industry, and the percentage actually working in factories was much smaller yet.

Craftsmen (and women) whose skills were in demand—printers, cabinet makers, cutlers, blacksmiths, engineers, and cotton spinners—benefited from industrial expansion. These, however, remained a small minority of the work force. Other craftsmen who had to compete with the machines or who could not protect their trades from the rising tide of population—wool combers, calico printers, wool shearers, and handloom weavers—suffered acutely from falling wages. The handloom weavers constituted the most tragic case. At their peak in the late 1700s, the weavers numbered about four hundred thousand men, earning an average of twenty-three shillings a week. By the 1830s, the weavers averaged five shillings a week, and their numbers had been cut in half. On balance, in the period from 1760 to 1815, probably more workers suffered in standard of living because of the Industrial Revolution than gained from it.

The Industrial Revolution affected more than material standards of life. The family, for example, was in some ways profoundly changed. It was not that industrialization altered the structure of the family from extended to nuclear; the basic pattern of the family in England, at least, had been nuclear from the earliest times for which there is evidence. Nor did industrialization initiate women's and children's labor. Among the laboring people, they had always worked. But industrialization tended to break up the old pattern of families working cooperatively in the home. For one thing, industrialization caused a *de-skilling* of many traditional occupations, as machines did the work formerly done by human beings, and, in particular, machines tended by women did the work formerly belonging to men. Many artisans under this pressure responded by reemphasizing the male exclusivity of the work—and, all too often, vented their frustration by beating their wives.

For another, as industrialization shifted manufacturing work from the home to the factory, it changed the nature of work for many women. In the preindustrial world, spinning at the wheel, for example, had always been women's work. But in the new mills that were devoted to cotton spinning by large spinning machines, men took over spinning, and women and children were relegated to auxiliary tasks such as piecing yarn and cleaning the machines. As women lost access to spinning, many took up weaving, formerly reserved to men, so that by 1800 perhaps half of all handloom weavers were women. And in the case of weaving, women retained employment when power looms were introduced and gathered into factories. In the early nineteenth-century weaving factories, men usually worked as *tenters* (power loom mechanics) whereas women operated the looms. But whatever the change in men's versus women's work, industrialization undermined the traditional family economy.

It can be argued that industrialization helped emancipate women by increasing their opportunities for work outside the patriarchal family, but the facts appear to argue otherwise. Certainly, factory owners recruited women and children whenever possible, both because their hands were smaller and more nimble than men's, and because they were more easily disciplined and could be paid less than men. In general, industrial capitalists avoided paying adult males if they could. In 1835, more than 60 percent of all cotton mill workers were women and children. Moreover, women slaved underground in some coal mines and on the surface of most lead mines. The contribution of female workers was crucial if their families were to survive. But the standard pattern was for girls to work in the factories until marriage, after which they were confined to household duties and to such domestic work as sewing or straw-plaiting to make ends meet. Only a quarter of all women working in factories in the early nineteenth century were married. At the same time, attitudes among the upper orders, especially in the middling sorts, were hardening about what constituted proper women's work. Women who worked for a living outside the home gradually came to be regarded as lacking virtue and morality because, it was increasingly assumed, a woman's proper place was in the home where she would be provided for by an adult male.

*Woman and child dragging a basket of coal in a mine. From the Report of the Royal Commission on the Employment of Children in the Mines, 1842.*

All of the workers—men, women, and children—in the early Industrial Revolution were subjected to severe discipline. The laboring poor were used to working at their own (or nature's) pace and rhythms. But in the new industries, the work force had to be *tamed*—that is, it had to be subjected to the pace of the machines, which represented too great an investment to stand idle. With the advent of the factory came a culture of time—clocks, steam whistles, and factory bells. Time became something that was to be *saved* and *spent*, not *passed*. Factory owners adopted a variety of insistent devices to discipline their preindustrial workers: educational exhortations and warnings, code books, clocks, fines, corporal punishment, and dismissals. Rule books of hundreds of precise orders were not unusual. Workers arose before dawn by the factory whistle; went to work by the whistle; ate breakfast, lunch, and dinner by the whistle; and at the end of a fifteen-hour day slogged home in the dark after the final whistle.

The Industrial Revolution—indeed the Triple Revolution as a whole—transformed social relations, the way that people related to each other in the work place and in society generally. As the sheer number of people grew, as they coagulated in the dense and harsh new urban environment, as contract replaced custom in the countryside, and as the factory replaced the household in the manufacturing sector, the face-to-face relations of the preindustrial world crumbled. The towns in which an increasing number of people lived and the institutions in which they worked became larger, more complex, and less manageable. Although some factory owners adopted paternalist policies in managing their workers, the way that employers and employees related to each other inexorably became more formal—more rule bound, contractually defined, and bureaucratic. Because landed proprietors and factory owners alike were driven by the pressure of competition and the fear of failure, social relations with the work force became harsher. The laboring poor on their part were driven to try to defend their customary rights and independence, as well as their standards of living, from the pressures applied by property owners and the marketplace.

Eventually, the worsening of social relations helped produce a new kind of social structure—namely, a class society. But because the formation of social classes in Britain occurred during the highly politicized atmosphere of war against revolutionary France, that process will be discussed in chapter 11. What must be emphasized at this point is that the Triple Revolution greatly intensified social conflict. In one locality after another, by efforts that were not at first coordinated or even understood in a national context, working men and women strove to protect their wages, working conditions, and preindustrial community. They petitioned Parliament, formed local *combinations* (unions), issued threatening letters and manifestoes, and went on strike. Employers reacted by refusing to hire workers unless they agreed not to join workers' combinations. They also resorted to Parliament to obtain laws that would control the laboring poor. By 1799 Parliament had passed more than forty laws against trade unions; in 1799–1800, it passed the Combination Laws, which prohibited any industrial combination whatsoever.

Two dramatic sets of events, the Luddite movement and the Swing Riots, illustrate the intensity of the social conflict resulting from the Triple Revolution. Luddism is the name given to machine-breaking activities that erupted in the Midlands, Lancashire, and the West Riding of Yorkshire in 1811–12 and again in 1814–16. Crowds of working men and women who believed that new machines were threatening their traditional crafts and livelihoods conducted secret operations to smash the machines and intimidate the factory owners. Often they issued proclamations signed by "Ned Ludd" or "General Ludd." Several factories were attacked by Luddites and defended by armed mill owners. Frustrated by the failure of their petitions to Parliament and by the authorities' suppression of their unions, the Luddites turned to machine-wrecking as a way of demanding restoration of the traditional *moral economy*, a return, in other words, to more customary

*A threatening letter from General Ludd to the foreman of a Nottingham jury, March 1812. The writer warns: "Remember the time is fast approaching when men of your stamp will be brought to Repentance."*

and reciprocal economic arrangements and the guarantee of a fair day's wage for a fair day's labor. Thus, they were heirs on a wider and more dangerous scale of the food rioters of the eighteenth century.

Much the same can be said of the Swing Rioters, who struck at threshing machines, burned hayricks, and issued threatening proclamations throughout the South, Southeast, and Midlands of England. Agrarian change had produced sporadic riots and machine breaking during the years before 1830. But "Captain Swing," as the rioters named their fictional leader, swept through the countryside like wildfire in 1830–31. Sometimes the agricultural laborers who rioted were seeking to abolish threshing machines (which deprived them of winter work) and sometimes simply to raise wages to a livable standard. The Swing Rioters were not seeking political or social revolution—though the property owners thought so—but wished to force the landowners to acknowledge once again their traditional paternal obligations. Like the Luddites, they were attempting to stop the erosion of traditional society, and like the Luddites, they failed.

The Luddites and the Swing Rioters can be seen as indices of the social effect of the Triple Revolution. By the early nineteenth century, the agricultural, demographic, and industrial revolutions were transforming life in Britain. Output and productivity were increasing by leaps and bounds so there existed the potential for an improved standard of living for a rapidly growing population. The Triple Revolution was also causing acute social conflict. Already threatened by an Irish uprising and engulfed by an economic and social revolution, Britain in the last years of the eighteenth century and the early years of the nineteenth century now found itself buffeted by revolutionary winds from France.

## Suggested Reading

Allen, Robert. *The British Industrial Revolution in Global Perspective*. Cambridge: Cambridge University Press, 2009.

Berg, Maxine. *The Age of Manufactures: Industry, Innovation and Work in Britain, 1700–1820*, 2nd ed. London: Routledge, 1994.

Chambers, J. D., and G. E. Mingay. *The Agricultural Revolution, 1750–1880*. London: Batsford, 1966.

Clark, Anna. *The Struggle for the Breeches: Gender and the Making of the British Working Class*. Berkeley: University of California Press, 1995.

Daunton, M. J. *Progress and Poverty: An Economic and Social History of Britain, 1700–1850*. New York: Oxford University Press, 1995.

Floud, Roderick, and Donald McCloskey. *Economic History of Britain Since 1700*. Vol. I, *1700–1860*, 2nd ed. New York: Cambridge University Press, 1994.

Honeyman, Katrina. *Women, Gender and Industrialisation in England, 1700–1870*. London: Palgrave Macmillan, 2000.

Hudson, Pat. *The Industrial Revolution*. London: Arnold, 1992.

Humphries, Jane. *Childhood and Child Labour in the British Industrial Revolution*. Cambridge: Cambridge University Press, 2011.

Jones, Eric L. *The European Miracle*. New York: Cambridge University Press, 1981.

McKeown, Thomas. *The Modern Rise of Population*. New York: Academic Press, 1976.

Mokyr, Joel. *The Enlightened Economy: Britain and the Industrial Revolution, 1700–1850*. New Haven, CT: Yale University Press, 2009.

Morgan, Kenneth. *Slavery, Atlantic Trade and the British Economy, 1660–1800*. New York: Cambridge University Press, 2000.

Perkin, Harold. *The Origins of Modern English Society, 1780–1880*. Toronto: University of Toronto Press, 1969.

Price, Richard. *British Society, 1680–1880*. Cambridge: Cambridge University Press, 1999.

Rule, John. *The Labouring Classes in Early Industrial England, 1750–1850*. London: Longman, 1986.

———. *The Vital Century: England's Developing Economy, 1714–1815*. London: Longman, 1992.

Sharpe, Pamela. *Adapting to Capitalism: Working Women in the English Economy, 1700–1850*. New York: St. Martin's Press, 1996.

Taylor, Barbara. *Eve and the New Jerusalem*. London: Virago, 1983.

Thompson, E. P. *The Making of the English Working Class*. London: Victor Gollancz, 1963.

Tranter, N. L. *Population and Society, 1750–1940*. London: Longman, 1985.

Valenze, Deborah. *The First Industrial Woman*. New York: Oxford University Press, 1995.

Voth, Hans-Joachim. *Time and Works in England, 1750–1830*. New York: Clarendon Press, 2000.

Williamson, Tom. *The Transformation of Rural England: Farming and the Landscape, 1700–1870*. Exeter, UK: University of Exeter Press, 2002.

Wrigley, E. A. *Energy and the English Industrial Revolution*. Cambridge: Cambridge University Press, 2010.

Wrigley, E. A., and R. S. Schofield. *The Population History of England, 1541–1871*. Cambridge, MA: Harvard University Press, 1981.

# Chapter 11

# The War Against the French Revolution, 1789–1815

The pressures on the British ruling elite generated by political developments in Ireland and by economic and social change in the United Kingdom were acutely intensified by the French Revolution. This violent transformation, which gripped all all of Europe for a quarter of a century, began in the summer of 1789 and seemed to surge with breathtaking speed from one event to the next: the calling of the Estates General; the formation of a National Assembly; the fall of the Bastille to a Parisian crowd; the rebellion of the peasantry; the issuance of the Declaration of the Rights of Man and of the Citizen; the articulation of a radical ideology—liberty, equality, and fraternity; the flight of King Louis XVI; war; the execution of the king; and the Reign of Terror. Almost immediately on its outbreak, the French Revolution began radiating its ideals of democracy and nationalism in waves that threatened to swamp all of the European states of the old regime.

The aristocratic regimes of Europe found their rule shaken by a dual conflict: by war with French armies abroad and by ideological struggle with radical movements at home. Armed conflict between revolutionary France and reactionary states began in April 1792, when France declared war on Austria and Prussia, and it was to go on ferociously if sporadically until Napoleon's final defeat in 1815. Britain stood apart from the war at first, but soon aligned itself with the reactionary powers and eventually became the principal and most consistent opponent of the French Revolution. At several times, the struggle of the British ruling elite with the revolution abroad and at home became desperate. Yet the oligarchy survived and was able to bring about the defeat of France. Three important questions arise from these facts: (1) Why did Britain, the most progressive state of Europe, throw its weight with the reactionary powers? (2) Given the dangerous state of affairs in the

British Isles, how was the British oligarchy able to survive the challenge? (3) What were the consequences of the war effort on British society?

## WILLIAM PITT THE YOUNGER AND NATIONAL REVIVAL

The answer in part to all three questions had to do with the extraordinary character and ability of William Pitt the Younger, prime minister from 1783 to 1801 and again from 1804 to 1806. The second son of the great earl of Chatham (William Pitt the Elder), Pitt inherited many of his father's talents and ideas. Like his father, he was a man easy to respect but hard to love. Born in 1759, Pitt the Younger was reared in an atmosphere of worship for Chatham's oratorical genius and statesmanship. Doted on by his parents, he was trained for distinction in public life and was convinced of his own surpassing ability and virtue. He was educated at home and at Cambridge and seems to have skipped adolescence. He emerged from the university with a mature understanding of the classics, mathematics, and modern literature, as well as a unique self-assurance. A boon companion to a small circle of friends, Pitt by age twenty-one displayed icy self-control in his public demeanor. He was an unnaturally mature statesman before most young men have found their way in life.

Prime Minister William Pitt the Younger addressing the House of Commons on the French Declaration of War, 1793, *by K. A. Hickel. Pitt was thirty-four at the time.*

Pitt was returned to Parliament in 1781 from Appleby, a pocket borough controlled exclusively by a wealthy patron. Despite his position as a client, Pitt rapidly won a reputation as an independent reformer. From his first speeches, he impressed the House of Commons with his mastery of detail, his clarity of mind, and his debating skill. By advocating parliamentary reform, by criticizing the war in America, and by attacking the corruption and incompetency of Lord North's government, Pitt earned a commanding position as a *patriot*—a man working above party for the national interest. In 1782, only eighteen months after first taking his seat, Pitt became chancellor of the exchequer.

Scarcely a year later, Pitt became prime minister at the age of twenty-four. The events leading to his elevation were among the most convoluted and controversial in modern British political history. As we saw in chapter 8, Lord North's unpopular government was replaced in 1782 by a ministry devoted to peace and headed by the marquess of Rockingham. The key figure in this new government was Charles James Fox, a brilliant orator, urbane leader of fashionable society, and outspoken defender of civil liberty. Fox believed in reducing the patronage of the Crown and in the right of Parliament's leaders to form their own cabinet, regardless of the king's views. These ideas clashed with the constitutional arrangements of the day (though they eventually became accepted political practice and thus part of the unwritten British constitution). When Rockingham died suddenly in July 1782, Fox tried to implement his novel constitutional claims, but George III rejected them and Fox resigned. The earl of Shelburne, a Whig in the Chatham (Pitt) camp, formed a government. Fox took his revenge by cynically forming an alliance with his former archenemy Lord North, and toppling Shelburne's government. This move forced George III to accept what he and all independent politicians, including Pitt, regarded as a corrupt ministry, the Fox-North coalition.

Eager to dismiss this ministry, the enraged monarch found his opportunity in 1783, when Fox introduced a bill to reform the government of British India. George III let it be known that he would consider as an enemy anyone who supported the bill. That was sufficient to kill it; the bill's rejection overturned the Fox-North coalition, and George III invited the young Pitt to form a new cabinet. Whig doggerel commented:

A sight to make surrounding nations stare;
A Kingdom entrusted to a school-boy's care.

Because the new ministry lacked majority support in the House of Commons, the Foxites declared it an expression of royal tyranny. Both Pitt and

George III, however, were content to have the government rely exclusively on the king's confidence, certain that the electorate supported them. They proved to be right. In 1784, Pitt called a general election. With the liberal application of funds from the Crown and from the East India Company, but also relying on his reputation as a patriot and reformer, Pitt swept to a big victory. In the process, he earned the abiding hostility of Fox, who regarded himself as the "tribune of the people" and a "martyr" for popular liberty. In truth, Pitt's victory revealed the political nation's unhappiness with the cynicism of the Fox-North coalition and its support for George III's view of the constitution.

In the next eight years Pitt rebuilt the governmental machinery that the war against the American colonies had overstrained. Having at last found a first minister in whom he trusted and who was also effective, George III supplied steady support. For his part, Pitt did not press issues likely to upset the king. He supported bills to abolish slavery and to reform Parliament, but when they were defeated, he let them go. At the same time, Pitt resolutely pursued governmental efficiency. He gradually improved the civil service by appointing competent professional administrators. He abolished sinecures (functionless state offices), rationalized administrative departments, substituted government salaries for private fees, and opened government financing and contracts to competitive bidding. All this earned Pitt the image of a cold-hearted bureaucrat, but it also enabled the British state to withstand the shocks of the war and social change to come.

Pitt also renovated government finances. The American war had driven the national debt to an unprecedented level, and the disruption of trade had cut into government revenues. Pitt had learned from Adam Smith's *Wealth of Nations* that free trade and reduction of governmental encumbrances would actually increase commerce and the state revenue from it. At one public dinner, he declared to Smith himself, "Nay, we will stand until you are seated, for we are all your scholars." Thus, he promoted British commerce and negotiated a mutual reduction of duties on trade between Britain and France. He made smuggling unprofitable by cutting import duties drastically—and then aggressively collected the remainder. He concocted a long list of new items to be taxed, including racehorses, carriages, servants, windows, and hair powder. He invented a national lottery, and he established a *sinking fund* to reduce the national debt—an appropriation of £1 million that was allowed to accumulate at compound interest, which was used to repay the debt. He also introduced a system of accounting in government finances. By 1792, Pitt's measures had restored public confidence, for they had increased governmental income by 50 percent and had decreased the national debt by £10 million. By the time the French Revolution began, the British state had revived from the dangerous ailments of the American war years.

## ORIGINS OF THE WAR WITH FRANCE

The outbreak of the French Revolution presented Pitt with a new set of challenges and eventually turned his tenure of office into a nightmare. At first, the British received the news of revolutionary events with complacency. Weren't the French simply trying to accomplish what the English had done in 1688? Fox said the fall of the Bastille was "much the greatest event that ever happened in the history of the world." Pitt himself declared that the convulsions in France would eventually calm down, and then France "will enjoy just the kind of liberty which I venerate." Young poets such as William Blake, William Wordsworth, and Samuel Taylor Coleridge greeted the French revolution as if it were the great news of human liberation. In Wordsworth's famous words,

Bliss was it in that dawn to be alive,
But to be young was very heaven!

Another poet, Robert Southey, declared that the Revolution meant "the regeneration of the human race."

This complacency, however, soon turned into ferocious controversy. Events in France not only rapidly assumed a visage frightening to the British oligarchy, but they also inspired radical reform movements at home. In Ireland, the principles of the French Revolution led to the formation of the United Irishmen. In England, the French Revolution reinvigorated and broadened the reform movement that had originated during the Wilkesite controversy of the 1760s and that had applied significant pressure to the government during the war against the American colonies.

Moreover, because of the rapid social and economic changes of the late eighteenth century—population growth, industrialization, urbanization, and social conflict—hopes for constitutional reform penetrated more deeply into British society than ever before. Thus, whereas organizations such as the Society of the Friends of the People (1792) were aristocratic, most other reform organizations grew from the middling and artisanal ranks. The Revolution Society, for instance, had been founded by urban Nonconformists to celebrate the centenary of 1688 and now called for repeal of the Test and Corporation Acts and affirmation of the sovereignty of the people. Similarly, the Society for Constitutional Information, originally established in 1771, and re-formed in 1780 to promote the ideals of popular sovereignty and peace with the American colonies, was revived in 1789 by business and professional people such as John Cartwright and John Horne Tooke and included a few artisans and craftsmen. Broadly speaking, the objective of all such societies was *moderate* parliamentary reform—abolition of rotten boroughs, redistribution of seats to provide for more fair and independent representation, and extension of the franchise.

More ominous, from the vantage point of the oligarchy, was that thousands of artisans and shopkeepers in London and the provincial towns began on their own to organize and demand *radical* constitutional change: universal manhood suffrage, annual elections, and constituencies of equal size. Of these groups the most important was the London Corresponding Society (LCS), formed in 1792 by shoemaker Thomas Hardy. Such societies did not mean to establish a republic, but they did associate themselves with the French Jacobins and criticized the principle of aristocracy. As was typical of British reformers, the radical artisans talked in terms of *"restoring"* lost liberty, but that restoration would have overturned oligarchical rule; it would mean, the LCS declared, "the press free, the laws simplified, judges unbiased, juries independent, needless places and pensions retrenched, immoderate salaries reduced, the public better served, taxes diminished and the necessaries of life more within the reach of the poor."

The inflow of revolutionary ideas caused a strenuous ideological dispute in Britain. In 1789, the dissenting minister Richard Price celebrated the French Revolution by comparing it to the Glorious Revolution of 1688. His sermon provoked Edmund Burke, the leading Whig intellectual, into writing a sustained attack on the French Revolution, *Reflections on the Revolution in France* (1790). This brilliant polemic became the chief statement of growing counterrevolutionary movement in Britain and has remained a powerful influence in British conservatism to the present day. Burke argued that the events of 1688 and 1789 had nothing in common. Whereas the English in 1688 had revered the past and therefore had taken care that their actions were consistent with tradition, the French in 1789 broke with their past and sought to create a new political order according to pure reason. History, Burke contended, is a safer guide in human affairs than reason, for the principles of societal arrangements are, "like every other experimental science, not to be taught *a priori*." Experience, as the English knew, teaches better than an abstract Rights of Man. The propensity of the French to follow abstract rights must lead to destruction of the monarchy, debasement of the currency, anarchy, and tyranny.

Events in France were to make Burke's argument seem more and more correct, but *Reflections* aroused great fury among British radicals. One of the earliest replies came from Mary Wollstonecraft, whose *Vindication of the Rights of Man* (1790) condemned Burke's inconsistency in supporting the American but not the French Revolution and insisted that all human institutions and customs, including marriage, must be subject to rational scrutiny. This work led to Wollstonecraft's far more famous publication, *The Vindication of the Rights of Woman* (1792), in which she argued for women's education and political rights as the only means of ensuring that all of human society reached its full potential.

The most sensational of the radical responses to Burke, however, came from Tom Paine, who had played such a crucial role in the American independence movement. In *The Rights of Man* (1791–92), Paine argued with unequaled clarity and simplicity for a complete break with the past: "It is the living, and not the dead, that are to be accommodated." Reason, not tradition, should form the basis of society and constitution. In truth, he said, the vaunted British constitution merely defends inequality and injustice. Reason says that all people have natural rights. The British constitution, however, denies natural rights in order to protect a hereditary monarchy and aristocracy, of which the former is useless and the latter degenerate. In contrast, a *representative democracy* (that is, a republic), Paine argued, would bring real benefits to all the people. It would eliminate corruption and waste and install a progressive income tax. These reforms would pay for material improvements such as family allowances, education grants, old age pensions, and funeral expenses. Such arguments made *The Rights of Man* the bible of popular radicalism in Britain; indeed, it helped thousands of people among the laboring poor to understand their common experiences and aspirations and so begin forming *a working class consciousness*. More concretely, Paine gave radicalism a positive program: destruction of the oligarchy, enactment of universal manhood suffrage, and the foundation of a welfare state.

The spread of radical societies and the popularity of Paine's tract increasingly worried George III and his government. Radicalism seemed to suggest that poor laborers might throw off their habits of deference and obedience. In May 1792, the king issued a "Proclamation Against Seditious Writings." At the same time, Pitt said that under the circumstances any further effort at parliamentary reform would cause anarchy and confusion. Nevertheless, Pitt remained more concerned about the traditional balance of power in Europe than about embarking on an ideological crusade against the French Revolution. Even when Austria and Prussia went to war against France in 1792, Pitt did nothing. But French encroachment on the Low Countries, through which the British had their commercial entrepôt to the Continent, dragged him toward war. Already in 1788, Pitt had arranged a triple alliance with the Dutch Republic and Prussia to defend the Low Countries. When in 1792, France defeated the Austrians, opened the river Scheldt to French commerce, and then annexed the Austrian Netherlands (roughly, modern Belgium), Pitt and his government decided to go to war with France.

## WAR WITH FRANCE, 1793–1798

Pitt little anticipated that the war begun in 1793 would continue almost without interruption until 1815. He thought that the Revolution had so weakened France that the war would not last long, and he viewed it as a chance to make up for British losses in the New World between 1775 and 1783. Indeed, he saw the war in terms made popular by his father: the British would pick up French colonial holdings around the world by use of their peerless navy, while buying mercenaries from the small German states and paying subsidies to larger allies such as Austria and Prussia to divert French energy and resources to the Continent. The British regular army in 1789 was, as usual, relatively small, and it remained under the thumb of the aristocracy, who, regardless of any lack of competency, purchased their commissions and raised their own regiments. About twelve thousand of the fifty thousand troops were stationed in Ireland, and eighteen thousand others were in the colonies overseas. But Pitt had done much to refurbish the navy, and it stood capable of fairly rapid expansion. Pitt and his chief strategists thought that, as long as the government could raise the funds to maintain the army, subsidize the Continental allies, and keep the navy afloat, Britain could not lose.

The problem was that Pitt's strategy was vulnerable on two points. First, Britain's main Continental allies—Austria, Prussia, and Russia—as yet understood no better than the British that they were fighting a new kind of opponent. Consequently, they paid too much attention to their individual territorial ambitions, especially in Poland, over which they competed greedily. The first coalition against France (1793–97) organized by the British was at best a loose collection of headstrong dynastic states, with no common strategy or integrated command.

The second weak point was that France was a new kind of nation conducting a new kind of war against traditional eighteenth-century states. France rapidly became a society mobilized for war—a *nation in arms*. The French revolutionary armies were not the comparatively small professional armies of the eighteenth century but the product of the *levée en masse* (conscription) and fervent patriotism. The officer corps, purged of its aristocratic element, became a force organized by merit and courage as opposed to birth and social position; the rank and file became a mass of men motivated by nationalism and democratic ideology. The French armies struck with shocking enthusiasm, and they aimed not at winning prizes to be traded later at the negotiating table, but at total defeat of the enemy. Further, the French were assisted by political radicals and ethnic nationalists within each of the conservative powers. The French Revolutionary War, therefore, was a struggle between a modern society and a number of traditional societies. The British landed oligarchy almost failed to meet this challenge, but in the end it was able to do so by harnessing the economic power of Britain's own modern sector—industry and commerce.

The war went badly for Britain during the first five years. The French threw the allied forces (including British expeditionary units) out of France and moved into the Rhineland and Northern Italy. Then in 1794–95, they conquered the Dutch Republic, dealing a severe blow to the British army in the process. The coalition began to break up. Spain and Prussia made their peace with France in 1795, and after defeat in Northern Italy at the hands of the brilliant young French general Napoleon Bonaparte, the Austrians followed suit in 1797. The coalition collapsed, and the British stood alone against the French. Pitt had focused on taking the French possessions in the West Indies, but that theater turned out to be a sinkhole for the British army and navy, which together lost nearly forty thousand men, mostly to yellow fever.

Only the navy had much to show for its efforts. In naval warfare, the British retained their traditional advantage over the French. A century of war at sea gave the British an impressive backlog of experience in tactics and commanders. To be sure, the British navy remained a traditional aristocratic institution, with the officer ranks a preserve for oligarchy and the enlisted men a mistreated and brutalized segment of the laboring population. Yet naval operations required much knowledge and skill of its officers. The necessity of promoting according to merit had asserted itself and made the

Royal Navy into a highly professional service. French revolutionary enthusiasm, so effective in the army, could not make up for the loss of professional skill that resulted from the purging of aristocrats from the French navy.

The British navy never lost a major engagement during the twenty-five years of the war, and the French suffered about ten times as many casualties as the British in naval battles. Throughout the war, the British navy showed enthusiasm and aggressiveness in battles and flexibility and opportunism in tactics. In the years from 1793 to 1797, the navy collected French colonies in the West Indies; a fleet under Admiral Richard Howe defeated the French off Brest (The Glorious First of June, 1794); and Admirals John Jervis and Horatio Nelson destroyed a large Spanish flotilla at Cape St. Vincent (and thus prevented them from joining the French). By 1797, then, the war was a standoff: French victories on land and British victories at sea. The British navy alone stood between Britain and the French army that was making preparations for invasion.

## THE WAR AT HOME

Meanwhile, the war at home was intensifying. British trade with France collapsed, and French privateers had some success in preying on British commercial shipping. An economic recession was the result. This was followed by a poor harvest in 1794, which caused serious food shortages, high prices, and food riots. Such economic disruptions were to occur sporadically throughout the war. Combined with high taxes and unpopular recruiting practices by the army and navy, economic troubles contributed to the growth of radicalism among the laboring ranks.

The extent of popular radicalism in the 1790s is very difficult to determine, for the evidence is shadowy at best. Clearly the radical movement was significant and was regarded as dangerous by the government. The LCS had perhaps five thousand members by 1795, and radical societies in other big cities sometimes enrolled half that many. They could rally very large crowds: the LCS, for instance, gathered at least one hundred thousand in central London on several occasions. These societies corresponded with each other and with the French Jacobins (the most militant revolutionaries), and the government heard rumors of nocturnal drillings on Yorkshire moors. In Scotland, most of the Lowland boroughs produced radical societies, and in 1792–93, delegates from eighty of them met in a convention in Edinburgh. The Scottish Convention and the massive demonstrations in London were the boldest radical activities of the early 1790s. On the whole, the radicals before 1797 stuck to petitioning and persuasion. Certainly they failed to mobilize the mass of the laboring poor; hence, they remained a minority of the population.

In the eyes of the government, however, the radical movement was a grave threat. Beginning in 1793, Pitt's government undertook to suppress the radicals by authoritarian, if legal, action. In Scotland, two radicals—a lawyer and a Unitarian preacher—were convicted and sentenced to transportation to Botany Bay in Australia for spreading *The Rights of Man* and an address from the United Irishmen. When the Scottish Convention reconvened in November and December of 1793, the authorities broke it up, arrested the leaders, and sentenced three more of them to transportation. In England, the government adopted an extensive system of spies and paid informants. With secret (and shaky) evidence, Pitt secured from Parliament suspension of habeas corpus in 1794. Shortly after, the government arrested twelve London reformers, including Hardy and Horne Tooke, and tried them for treason. Although the jury refused to convict them, the effect of this pressure on the radical societies was great. Many respectable reformers such as Hardy and Horne Tooke withdrew from politics. Then in 1795, following one of the largest demonstrations in London, Pitt got Parliament to pass the Two Acts, which prohibited meetings of more than fifty people and made speaking or writing against the Crown and constitution treasonable.

This repression occurred within the context of a very strong conservative reaction. Burke's *Reflections on the Revolution in France* was the first but far from the last work of conservative propaganda. Conservative writings such as *The Anti-Jacobin*, edited by George Canning, and the *Cheap Repository Tracts*, published by Hannah More, emphasized to rich and poor alike that British liberty depended on maintaining the existing constitution, the "natural" social hierarchy, and the rights of private property. They played very effectively on the nationalist sentiment that had developed during the century of war against France by portraying revolutionary ideas as corrosive of good old English forthrightness and purity. The government, too, deliberately concocted rituals celebrating loyalty to the Crown. The ideology of the inseparability of church and state was revived, and the Church and King mobs rioted against reformers such as Joseph Priestley, a Unitarian minister and chemist whose laboratory was sacked in 1791. In 1792, men of property founded the Association for the Preservation of Liberty and Property against Republicans and Levellers, with hundreds of branches in both rural and urban areas. A volunteer force drawn from the gentry and yeomanry was established in 1794; it enlisted over four hundred thousand men by 1804.

The upshot of this potent movement was to identify conservatism with nationalism and reform with disloyalty and to provide the emotional background for the formation of a new Tory party made up of Pittites and conservative Whigs.

## THE CRISIS OF 1797–1798

The repression of the years 1793–97 did not kill the radical movement, but drove it underground. Because many of the more cautious reformers dropped out, leadership of the movement fell into the hands of extremists, some of whom had revolutionary intentions. The LCS, for example, now turned into a revolutionary conspiracy. Such revolutionary organizations established close connections with the United Irishmen, who by 1796–97 were actively plotting to set up an independent republic in Ireland with French help. Agents of the United Irishmen formed United Irish societies among the Irish Catholic immigrants in London, Lancashire, and southwestern Scotland. More ominously, societies of United Englishmen and United Scotsmen were formed. They intended to establish independent republics in England and Scotland as well as in Ireland. The British state itself was to be dismembered.

How serious was the revolutionary movement? Again, the evidence is spotty and often tainted by official paranoia. Probably not every member of the widespread but small revolutionary cells was committed to violence. But the government received reports of drilling and arming among by people in a number of districts. And there is no question that some United Irish agents and English radicals did try to coordinate a revolutionary outbreak. Clearly, the conspirators could not have succeeded by themselves, but with French intervention and a simultaneous mass peasant revolt in Ireland, they might well have brought an end to the British oligarchy in 1798.

The French certainly hoped to invade and were prevented from doing so only by the British navy. In 1797, Napoleon was appointed commander in chief of France's army and began assembling a massive invasion force. Worse, in April 1797 the British Channel fleet at Spithead mutinied, and the North Sea fleet at the Nore followed suit in May. This was the most perilous moment in the history of Great Britain between 1707 and 1940. Undoubtedly, the low pay and miserable conditions of life at sea lay behind the mutinies, but radical ideology also contributed: over 10 percent of the sailors were Irish, many of them former Defenders or United Irishmen, and

The Death of Nelson *by Benjamin West (1806). West exhibited this painting at his studio to admiring crowds not many months after the Battle of Trafalgar. West took some liberties with the facts: after he fell wounded, Nelson was carried below decks, where he died.*

the LCS spread radical literature among the men. Rapid liberal concessions to the mutineers, however, settled the Spithead mutiny. In contrast, the Nore mutineers were put down by force; twenty-eight of the leaders were hanged and nearly a hundred were flogged. By October 1797, the French had missed their great chance. In that month, the Nore fleet was able to smash the Dutch navy at Camperdown. Napoleon gave up his plans to invade and turned to the conquest of Egypt instead. His army was cut off there by Nelson's crushing victory over a French fleet in the Battle of the Nile (Aboukir Bay) in 1798.

The timing of those events was extremely unlucky for the revolutionaries in Britain and Ireland because it deprived the United Irishmen of French assistance just as they rebelled. The United Irishmen had busily prepared for revolution throughout 1796. Irishman Wolfe Tone went to Paris to seek French assistance. In December 1797, a large French invasion force under General Lazare Hoche and accompanied by Wolfe Tone actually appeared in

Bantry Bay in southwestern Ireland. As usual, the weather was Protestant, and the force had to turn back; it was a near miss, however, and the United Irish continued to badger the French for help. Thousands of Irish peasants were mobilized and armed with pikes by the revolutionaries. All through 1797–98, the British executive in Ireland struggled to break up the rebellion before it started. The British general, Lake, relying on the ill-disciplined Irish militia and yeomanry, set out to disarm the populace by brute force. In their search for weapons, Lake's troops burned cottages and arrested, flogged, and tortured thousands of Catholics. Hideous wooden triangles on which men were tied for flogging blemished the landscape. Then, having penetrated the United Irish organization, the government arrested many of its leaders in March 1798. The remaining conspirators in desperation decided to go ahead with the rebellion even without French help. It began in May 1798.

The rebellion was supposed to break out simultaneously all over Ireland, but the only significant outbursts occurred in Wexford and Ulster. Small numbers and lack of coordination condemned the rebels to defeat. In Wexford, the insurrectionaries were almost exclusively Catholic. Badly armed and trained, the largely peasant forces attacked Protestants indiscriminately, taking revenge for centuries of oppression. The Wexford rebellion was beaten and the Protestant retribution was begun before the Ulster rebellion broke out in June. In Ulster, the rebels were mainly of Protestant origin and reflected the nonsectarian ideals of the French Revolution. They, too, were defeated by the end of June.

Only in August did French assistance arrive—too little, too late. The French had dithered and dissembled because they never trusted the United Irishmen's estimates of popular support. Thus, the French force that landed in Mayo in August 1798 amounted to only one thousand men. They fought gallantly for a month and then surrendered, while the small band of United Irish enthusiasts and illiterate Catholic peasants who had joined them was cut to pieces by British troops (including Scottish and Welsh regiments). Shortly after, the British navy intercepted a somewhat larger French expedition and captured it—among the captured troops was Wolfe Tone, who was tried and convicted of treason. He cheated the hangman by committing suicide with a razor.

The reprisals taken by British troops, especially by the Irish militia and yeomanry, were savage. But the British government, including Pitt and his lord lieutenant in Ireland, Lord Cornwallis, hoped to prevent further rebel-

*The Rising of 1798 in Ireland*. Irish nationalists hoped that the entire island would erupt in rebellion, but the Rising of 1798 was largely confined to eastern Leinster.

*Cartoon of the Irish Rebellion of 1798. The original caption read, "Irish Rebellion of 1798: Rebels execute their Protestant prisoners at Wexford, June 20, 1798. The rebel flag's MWS stands for 'Murder Without Sin.'" Copper engraving by George George.*

lion by more humane means—union between the British and Irish Parliaments plus Catholic emancipation (that is, allowing Catholics the same political rights as Protestants).

Unfortunately, George III opposed emancipation: "Mr. Pitt," he wrote, "has in my opinion saved Ireland, and now the new Lord Lieutenant must not lose the present moment of terror for frightening the supporters of the Castle into a Union with this country; and no further indulgences must be granted to the Roman Catholics." Pitt was not the man to press the king on a matter he felt strongly about, especially because in 1788 George III already had suffered one bout of debilitating illness from porphyria (thought at the time to be insanity). Thus, the bill of union that was presented to both the British and the Irish Parliaments included no measure of Catholic emancipation. The bill passed easily in Britain, but met strong opposition in Ireland, especially among Protestant Patriots who did not want to give up what they had won in 1782. In addition, many nervous Protestants believed that their religion would be more secure from Catholicism under the protection of their own legislators. Gradually, however, some members of the ruling elite became persuaded that their best defense in the long run lay in close connection with the British, and the government meanwhile used all the tools of eighteenth-century corruption to get its way. After furious debate in Ireland, the Irish Parliament in Dublin passed the Act of Union in 1800— and so abolished itself. Irish voters would not elect one hundred members to the British Parliament at Westminster. Pitt resigned in 1801 because of his failure to carry Catholic emancipation, but he did not press the issue further. The United Kingdom of Great Britain and Ireland thus came into being; it was to last until 1921, an unhappy and only partly consummated union that was, however, essential to resolve the crisis of 1797–98.

## WAR, 1798–1815

After 1798, the war became a long and drawn out slogging match. Pitt (who died in 1806) and his successors relied on the British navy to stave off a French invasion of the British Isles and to apply economic pressure on France, but not until 1813 could Britain and the allies defeat Napoleon on land. The war went through five main phases:

1. 1798–1802, when Britain organized a second coalition against France, only to see it hammered to pieces by Napoleon;
2. 1802–03, when by the Peace of Amiens the British and French agreed to a truce in the fighting;
3. 1803–12, when Napoleon won unparalleled domination over Europe, defeating a third coalition of aristocratic states but losing at the Battle of Trafalgar (1805) his last chance to invade Britain and then suffocating from a British naval blockade;
4. 1812–13, when Napoleon invaded Russia but was forced to retreat and then suffered a devastating defeat at the hands of the fourth coalition—the first alliance to involve all four anti-French powers: Britain (the organizer and paymaster), Prussia, Austria, and Russia; and
5. 1815, when Napoleon, having escaped from exile in Elba, rallied his army, only to be defeated once and for all at Waterloo.

During the entire period from 1798 to 1815, the British government sustained the war effort by tapping the tremendous economic resources of the nation. Here Pitt's administrative reforms of the 1780s and his wartime financial prowess proved decisive. The increasingly dynamic British economy—whether in cotton textiles, iron, coal mining, or agriculture—suffered repeated temporary dislocations, but each time it bounded back. Pitt used both borrowing and taxation to tap into this economic power. Annual governmental war loans tripled between 1794 and 1797; as the national debt soared, the annual interest charge alone rose to £30 million—more than the entire national budget of 1792! Recognizing the impossibility of financing the war wholly from loans, Pitt turned to heavy tax increases. Eventually, taxes covered about one-half of war expenditures. Customs and excises remained the principal source, but Pitt also invented the income tax in 1799. Although this tax was extremely unpopular, industrialists as well as landowners paid it. In this way, the propertied classes showed their willingness to support the oligarchical state against revolution and French domination.

Napoleon eventually recognized that, if he were to win, he had to weaken the British economy; consequently, by his Continental System (1806), he sought to exclude British trade from Europe. But this was a game two could play: the British in 1807 responded with their *Orders in Council*, which blockaded French ports and allowed neutrals to trade with France only if they first shipped their goods through Britain. This was Europe's first major economic war, a kind of struggle for which the British were very much better equipped than the French. Napoleon was unable to stop up all the spigots through which Europeans sought to quench their thirst for British and colonial goods—manufactured articles, textiles, tobacco, tea, sugar, and so on—and his attempt to do so alienated people throughout the Continent. British merchants and manufacturers became extremely unhappy with the Orders in Council, which disrupted their trade, but the French failure to cut off all trade to the Continent for any sustained period gave outlets to their pressure. When the British government (then led by Lord Liverpool) revoked the Orders in Council in 1812, Napoleon was only too glad to abandon the Continental System. "Undoubtedly," he wrote, "it is necessary to harm our foes, but above all we must live."

Napoleon invaded Portugal in 1807 to close off one of the biggest leaks in the Continental System. The British sent an expeditionary force under Arthur Wellesley (later the duke of Wellington) to stop the French in Portugal and to assist the Spanish who were rebelling against French rule. The consequent Peninsular War never absorbed more than 40,000 British troops, but it tied down 250,000 Frenchmen. Eventually, Wellington was able to go on the offensive and in 1813 to cross the Pyrenees into France.

The economic war also led Napoleon into the decisive and disastrous invasion of Russia in 1812. By then, Napoleon needed to coerce the Russians into cooperating with his exclusion of British trade. His gigantic army was successful at first, but after taking Moscow it had to withdraw in bitter cold and privation through land destroyed by the Russians themselves. The fourth coalition, again organized and paid for by the British and now including all four anti-French powers, defeated Napoleon and sent its army into Paris in 1814. The French emperor abdicated and retired to Elba.

Meanwhile, the Orders in Council caused war between Britain and the United States (1812–14). This conflict was a diversion that the British wanted to avoid, but their insistence on stopping and searching American ships for British seamen aggravated American touchiness about freedom of the seas. The French could give the Americans no assistance this time, but the British were unable to deploy enough manpower to defeat and occupy the United States. British troops burned Washington, DC, but by 1814, the war was a stalemate and both powers were ready for peace. The only outcome from the British point of view was the lesson that, to protect Canada in the future, the British must maintain good relations with the United States.

The final act of the great war between Britain and France was played in the summer of 1815. Napoleon slipped away from Elba, rallied the French army once more, and reclaimed power in France. The allied powers dispatched a huge army under the duke of Wellington to defeat him. The two forces crashed together at Waterloo, near Brussels in Belgium. The battle was, as Wellington said, "the nearest run thing that you ever saw in your life," but the combined British and Prussian armies won the day. Napoleon abdicated again and spent the remainder of his days in exile on the tiny British island of St. Helena.

Now we are ready to understand why the British went to war in 1793 and how the oligarchy was able to survive. Pitt and his successors were principally concerned about protecting British interests on the Continent, interests defined as the need to export goods to Europe and to prevent any one power from dominating all the others. Only toward the end did the British government insist on the expulsion of Napoleon, and that was simply because they regarded him as insatiably aggressive. In this way, the British government reflected the concerns of its modern as well as traditional propertied elements.

The regime was able to survive the stress for several reasons. First, Pitt had restored the effectiveness of the government between 1783 and 1793; indeed, he unwittingly had taken important steps toward creating a modern state. Second, he and his successors were able to use parliamentary taxing authority to harness the burgeoning British economy. Third, the British navy kept the French from invading the British Isles in force.

Fourth, resolute repressive action by the government—plus a large measure of luck—kept the French, the Irish, and the British revolutionaries from coordinating their efforts. Finally, in the ideological struggle at home, conservative nationalism proved to be marginally stronger than reformism and revolution.

## THE PRIZES AND COSTS OF WAR, 1793–1815

It is important to remember that mere survival of the state and security of limited interests on the Continent were all that Britain had fought for; otherwise, one would not think they gained much for their efforts. In the negotiations at Vienna that produced the postwar settlement, the British sought no territory in Europe and not a great deal elsewhere. They kept a few colonial prizes that turned out to be valuable later: Malta in the Mediterranean; Guiana, Tobago, and St. Lucia in the West Indies; the Cape of Good Hope in South Africa; and Mauritius in the Indian Ocean. But the British negotiator, Viscount Castlereagh, was a supreme realist and did obtain what Britain wanted most: security of British interests in Europe. France was not broken up, but its borders were reduced to pre-1792 lines, and the Bourbon monarchy was restored. The Dutch Republic and the Austrian Netherlands were merged into a stronger state, the United Netherlands, and given British cash to fortify against French intrusion. Further, Castlereagh obtained a balance of power: Britain, Austria, Prussia, and Russia signed an alliance against a recurrence of French might, and Prussia and Austria were made strong enough to block a Russian advance into Central Europe. Finally, Castlereagh persuaded all the powers to meet periodically to settle disputes by discussion.

For these benefits the British had paid dearly. The war had not been distinguished by technological innovations in weaponry; nevertheless, British manpower losses were bad enough—upward of 210,000 died in combat or from disease, or one in every eighty-five people in the British Isles, a more severe loss proportionately than in World War II. Further, the war cost the British about £1.5 billion in direct expenditures, plus untold sums in economic gains forgone because of the diversion of resources into war making. But here one has to be careful about cost accounting. First, the propertied few suffered much less than the unpropertied many from the economic burden because the massive loans floated by the government took the form of bonds purchased by the rich. These were redeemed after the war through taxation, and now once again in the form of customs and excises, which put

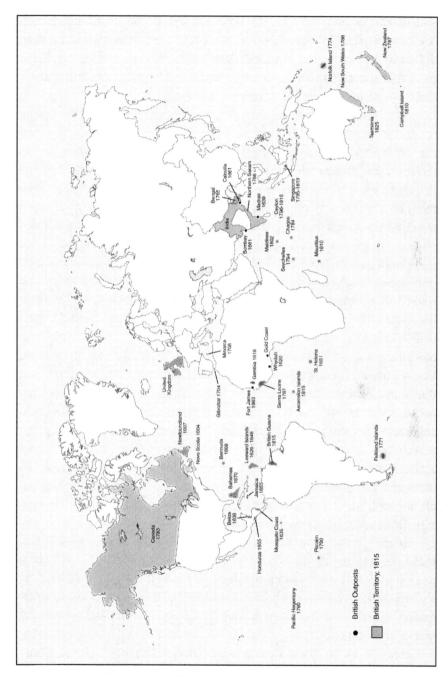

*The British Empire in 1815.* At the end of its wars with revolutionary and Napoleonic France, the British Empire did not look substantially larger than it had a century earlier (see map, p. 52). But Britain's foothold in South Africa would prove to be enormously important over the next century.

a disproportionate weight on the poor. Second, British economic growth continued during the war, though it was not as great as it would have been if Europe had remained at peace. Because the French economy suffered more than did the British, Britain emerged in 1815 very much farther ahead of its closest economic rival than it had been in 1793.

Great wars almost inevitably alter the societies of the participating states, including those of the victors. This was true of British society during the war from 1793 to 1815, even though the regime went to war in part to defend itself from revolutionary social change. It is safe to say that the British ruling elite—the landowners—came out of the war stronger and more secure than any other European aristocracy. This fact would have a great impact on nineteenth-century Britain. Not only did no successful revolution occur in Britain, but also land values and rentals increased.

The British landed orders felt sufficiently threatened by domestic agitation and external revolution that they thrust off many of their remaining traditional paternalist obligations. Most notably, they passed the Combination Acts of 1799 and 1800, prohibiting workers from negotiating collectively to regulate wages; they repealed in 1813–14 the old Tudor legislation regulating wages and entry into crafts; and in 1815 they passed the Corn Law, a duty on the importation of grain to keep prices high on the wheat grown in England. This *abdication of paternalism* was likely to have happened, war or no war, for as we have seen, it was well underway in the general transition from custom to contract. The resentment and anxiety the oligarchy felt in the face of popular radicalism during the war simply accelerated the process. In any case, the landowners' abdication of paternalism—and simultaneous insistence on political repression and social discipline—contributed powerfully to a great transformation of the social structure, from social hierarchy to social classes.

By 1815, Britain was well on the way to being a *class society*, that is, a society organized into three large, self-conscious, and hostile *layers* of people. Each of these horizontal groupings—the landed class, the middle class, and the working class—was becoming aware that its members shared interests and experiences that were different from the interests and experiences of the other classes.

The process of class formation was a matter of *consciousness*. Under pressure from below, the British landed oligarchy between 1793 and 1815 became conscious of the need to stand shoulder to shoulder and protect their power. The commercial and industrial ranks likewise experienced a growing consciousness of their own special interests. They regarded themselves as the people responsible for the commercial and industrial expansion of the nation; hence, they considered themselves to be the source of Britain's power and progress. Yet they felt they were denied social and political power equal to their economic accomplishments. Nonconformists, especially, felt aggrieved by their exclusion from Parliament and municipal office. People of the middling ranks continued during the war years to agitate for parliamentary reform and then objected when the government's suppression of radicalism fell on them as well as laborers. They complained loudly when the Orders in Council and the new Corn Law infringed their interests. Thus, in the course of organizing to promote their interests, the British middle class came on the stage of history—self-confident, aggressive, blunt, and feeling aggrieved.

It took laboring people much longer than the landed orders and the middle class to develop and disseminate widely a consciousness of themselves as a class. In some ways the process was not complete until the late nineteenth century, for obstacles such as illiteracy, poverty, and social dependency were too strong to be overcome easily. How far the working class was formed by 1815 and how much the experience of the war had to do with it are not easy to determine. Radicalism spread fairly widely through the British artisan ranks, but it remained a minority movement. Most of the laboring poor seem to have been loyalist and conservative, or simply ignorant and apathetic, rather than radical or revolutionary. Clearly, the massive social changes of the Triple Revolution had more to do with working-class formation than did democratic parties during the war with France. Nevertheless, the foundations, at least, of the British working-class consciousness were laid by 1815, and radicalism and repression played a part in the shared experience underlying class consciousness. Tom Paine's *Rights of Man*, for instance, became one of the most widely read books in working-class homes.

In the years between 1805 and 1815, artisanal radicalism slowly revived, and popular patriotism began to merge with the movement. The key figure here was William Cobbett, a farmer's son, journalist, and consummate political polemicist. Cobbett was an instinctive Tory, full of nostalgia for traditional rural England, and he criticized the government at first only for its ineffectiveness against the French. But in 1804–06, his criticism of government inefficiency made him the victim of official prosecution; afterward, he became for many years the leading radical critical of corruption, patronage, the overmighty oligarchy, and the unreformed Parliament.

Critics such as Cobbett by 1815 were helping the laboring people understand the relations between the abdication of paternalism, the corrupt self-interest of the landowners and London financiers, the abuse of civil rights, and the need for parliamentary reform. This line of thinking proved to be the main connection between the French Revolution and the emerging working-class consciousness in Britain.

### Suggested Reading

Ayling, Stanley. *Edmund Burke: His Life and Opinions*. London: Cassell, 1988.

Barrell, John. *Imagining the King's Death: Figurative Treason, Fantasies of Regicide, 1793–1796*. Oxford: Oxford University Press, 2000.

Christie, Ian. *Stress and Stability in Late-Eighteenth-Century Britain*. Oxford: Clarendon Press, 1984.

———. *Wars and Revolutions: Britain, 1760–1815*. Cambridge, MA: Harvard University Press, 1982.

Claeys, Gregory. *French Revolution Debate in Britain: The Origin of Modern Politics*. London: Palgrave Macmillan, 2007.

Curtin, Nancy J. *The United Irishmen: Popular Politics in Ulster and Dublin, 1791–1798*. New York: Clarendon Press, 1994.

Derry, J. W. *Politics in the Age of Fox, Pitt and Liverpool*. New York: St. Martin's Press, 1992.

Duffy, Michael. *The Younger Pitt*. New York: Longmans, 2000.

Ehrman, John. *The Younger Pitt*, 3 vols. London: Constable, 1969, 1983, 1996.

Elliott, Marianne. *Partners in Revolution: The United Irishmen and France*. New Haven, CT: Yale University Press, 1982.

———. *Wolfe Tone: Prophet of Irish Independence*. New Haven, CT: Yale University Press, 1989.

Emsley, Clive. *Britain and the French Revolution*. London: Longman, 2000.

———. *British Society and the French Wars, 1793–1815*. London: Macmillan, 1979.

Goodwin, Albert. *The Friends of Liberty: The English Democratic Movement in the Age of the French Revolution*. Cambridge, MA: Harvard University Press, 1979.

Macleod, Emma Vincent. *A War of Ideas: British Attitudes Towards the Wars Against Revolutionary France, 1792–1802*. Aldershot, UK: Ashgate, 1998.

McFarland, Elaine. *Ireland and Scotland in the Age of Revolution: Planting the Green Bough*. Edinburgh: Edinburgh University Press, 1994.

McKay, Derek, and H. M. Scott. *The Rise of the Great Powers, 1648–1815*. London: Longman, 1983.

Newman, Gerald. *The Rise of English Nationalism: A Cultural History, 1740–1830*. New York: St. Martin's Press, 1987.

Perkin, Harold. *The Origins of Modern English Society, 1780–1880*. Toronto: University of Toronto Press, 1969.

Philp, Mark, ed. *The French Revolution and British Popular Politics*. Cambridge: Cambridge University Press, 2004.

Powell, David. *Charles James Fox: Man of the People*. London: Croom Helm, 1989.

Royle, Edward. *Revolutionary Britannia? Reflections on the Threat of Revolution in Britain, 1789–1848*. Manchester, UK: Manchester University Press, 2000.

Taylor, Barbara. *Mary Wollstonecraft and the Feminist Imagination*. New York: Cambridge University Press, 2003.

Thompson, E. P. *The Making of the English Working Class*. London: Victor Gollancz, 1963.

Todd, Janet. *Mary Wollstonecraft: A Revolutionary Life*. London: Weidenfeld and Nicolson, 2000.

Wahrman, Dror. *Imagining the Middle Class: The Political Representation of Class in Britain, 1780–1840*. New York: Cambridge University Press, 1995.

Williams, Gwyn A. *Artisans and Sans-Culottes*. London: Arnold, 1968.

# Chapter 12

# Intellectual and Spiritual Revolutions, 1780–1815

The period from the 1780s to 1815 was one of revolutions in thought as well as in society and politics. Indeed, social and political change during these years of crisis set in motion major transformations in the ways that the British people understood themselves, their society, and their place in the universe. Not all of the lines of change went in the same direction, for the society was too complex to call forth only a single set of intellectual and spiritual responses. Thus, there emerged in this period two directly opposed strands of thought: one—broadly speaking, the utilitarian—characterized by extreme rationalism and cold calculation, and the other—the evangelical and romantic—marked by heightened emotions and otherworldliness. The tension between the two contributed as much as did social and political revolutions to the unique drama of the period. Both strands, however, were alike in that they broke with essential aspects of Augustan ideas and beliefs.

## UTILITARIANISM

The utilitarian strand of thought seems in some ways not to break with the main lines of eighteenth-century ideas but to extend them. As we saw in chapter 5, a form of utilitarianism was a common philosophy of early eighteenth-century moralists. The utilitarianism of the last decades of the century stood firmly in the British empiricist tradition. Yet the leading utilitarian of the late eighteenth and early nineteenth centuries, Jeremy Bentham, extended these earlier lines of thought so radically as to produce something entirely new: not a cheerful philosophy for the landed gentry, but a clanking ideology for the new industrial captains.

Jeremy Bentham (1748–1832) was one of the most influential British thinkers of the modern era, but a distinctly odd character. Like Adam Smith, whose economic ideas he came to adopt, Bentham was a simple and unworldly man, an empiricist with little actual experience of the world. His father, a Tory lawyer, was very anxious to climb the ladder of London society. But Jeremy, a weak, shy, painfully awkward youth, found success only in his studies. He became a man of books, almost totally intellectualized. He read Latin and Greek at age six, entered Oxford at thirteen, and took his MA at eighteen. Though he studied law, he was not fit for the rough and tumble of practice at the bar. He turned instead to the philosophical criticism of English law and from that to moral and social philosophy in general.

Bentham thought of himself as doing for moral philosophy what Newton had done for physics—reducing all data to one or a few principles. To him the greatest principle was utility. In general, utilitarianism is an ethical philosophy that judges behavior or social action according to its consequences. Bentham was a *hedonistic* utilitarian—that is, he believed any act is good or bad depending on whether it promotes happiness (or pleasure). To him, this principle was based on the very essence of human nature: that each person behaves so as to pursue pleasure and avoid pain. Unlike earlier utilitarians, Bentham separated this hedonistic principle from any concept of a divine plan and set it squarely in a materialistic philosophy. The divine played no part in the Benthamite universe, nor did elevated ideas of beauty and truth. Bentham had no sensitivity to beauty in art or poetry, and he carried empiricism to the extreme. He disparaged words such as *society, beauty, good*, or *social contract* as simply abstractions because they stood for no real objects in the world. Use of such words, Bentham believed, leads people to think that abstract objects do exist and thus to make mistakes in moral and legal philosophy. All we can know comes through the senses. Complex ideas of the imagination are nothing but the mechanical manipulation and combination of sensory experience. Indeed, human beings are little more than calculating machines that register sensations and sum up pleasures and pains.

Bentham's first book, published in 1776, was an attack on the orthodox legal thought of the day, best expressed by Sir William Blackstone, the century's most eminent legal philosopher. Blackstone believed that the existing system of English law was natural and reasonable, its basis being the idea of social contract. Bentham, however, regarded the law as an irrational tangle of historical precedent and accident, and dismissed the social contract as a fiction, a metaphysical mistake. What was needed, he insisted, was a radical simplification and codification of the laws according to the principle of utility. A law (past, present, or future) ought to be judged as to whether it increases or decreases the happiness of the society. Because society, Bentham said, is nothing but the aggregate of individuals who make it up, the happiness of all is just a matter of calculating the total of individual pleasures and pains.

Bentham laid out his system in exhaustive (and exhausting) detail in his *Introduction to the Principles of Morals and Legislation*, first published in 1789. The moral and legal thinking he advocated in it is remarkably mechanical and mathematical. Bentham even called his system of analyzing, measuring, and summing up pleasures and pains the *felicific calculus* (from the Latin *felicis* or happy). He made no qualitative distinctions between types of pleasures and pains: all are to be weighed according to the physical sensations they cause. "Prejudice apart," he insisted, "the [child's] game of push-pin is of equal value with the arts and sciences of music and poetry." Consequently, he argued that no motive in itself is either good or bad, nor, in fact, do *goodness* and *badness* exist as such. All actions, by individuals or the state, are good or bad only according to their consequences—that is, whether on balance the action brings more pleasure or more pain. Lawmaking and governing are simply matters of weighing and counting.

Bentham argued that the purpose of every government is to promote the greatest happiness of the greatest number of people. This principle would seem to provide the basis for interventionist policies by the government, and indeed, some Benthamite civil servants and social scientists in the nineteenth century definitely favored interventionist social engineering. But Bentham himself adopted Adam Smith's laissez-faire ideas, and so generally opposed state intervention in matters of economic policy. He regarded the self-regulating aspect of Smith's free market economic model as simple and seemingly scientific. Further, he agreed with Smith that the individual knows best what is good for himself or herself. Because all laws essentially restrict human behavior, they inevitably cause pain; consequently, they should be minimized. Bentham's utilitarian philosophy was, therefore, materialist, calculating, and individualistic.

It was not, however, necessarily democratic. In theory, every kind of government can pursue the greatest happiness of the greatest number. In his early years, Bentham was a Tory who opposed both the American and French Revolutions because of their talk of "natural rights"—to Bentham a clear case of philosophical fiction. After 1800, however, Bentham became a democrat—indeed, one of the leading theoreticians of radical parliamentary reform. He did so because he became disillusioned with the British oligarchy, which refused to accept particular schemes he proposed, notably an elaborate plan for prison reform. By 1810 he reasoned that the only way to make the interests of the rulers coincide with the interests of the ruled was

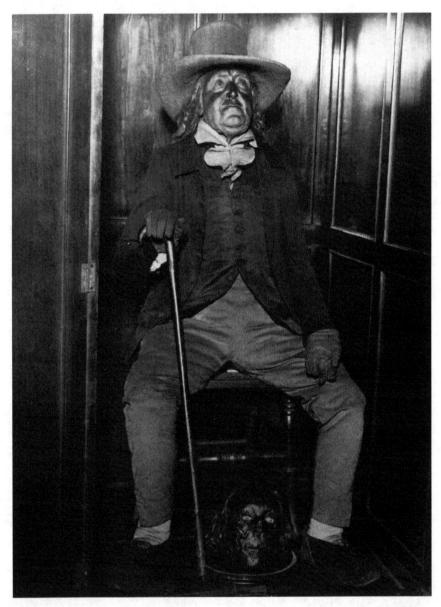

*The mummified body of Jeremy Bentham now resides in University College, London.*

to bring about a more democratic representative government. He and his disciples like James Mill thus combined the ideas of utilitarian legal codification and laissez-faire economics with parliamentary reform. By the time Bentham died in 1832, this package formed a potent program, the dominant political ideology of the new British middle class.

## PARSON MALTHUS

There was yet another aspect of the utilitarian package—the population principle of the Reverend Thomas Malthus. This was an odd element in utilitarianism, for the ideas of Bentham and Smith were basically optimistic and progressive, whereas those of Malthus were pessimistic and even reactionary. Nevertheless, many early nineteenth-century Britons believed that these ideas fit together. Malthus (1766–1834) was the son of an Enlightened English country gentleman, a friend of Hume and Rousseau, and a believer in the power of reason to improve humankind. In the late 1790s, father and son (who was by then a clergyman in the Church of England) engaged in a profound argument about the fate of humanity. Malthus's father contended that progress was possible and likely. But Malthus himself argued a fundamentally pessimistic position based on his deep concern about the long-term effects of the population explosion. Malthus committed his views to paper in *An Essay on the Principle of Population*, first published in 1798.

Parson Malthus reasoned with great logical force that the population of any country tends to outstrip the food supply. His explanation was that the population tends to increase geometrically—that is, 1, 2, 4, 8, 16, 32, and so on—whereas the food supply can increase only arithmetically—that is, 1, 2, 3, 4, 5, 6, and so on. As any farmer knew, food production could be expanded only by adding increments of land to the already cultivated land—increments of less fertile soil, to boot. But the population would double itself in each generation until it was more or less brutally checked. Malthus thought that the only checks on population increase are natural (vice and misery) and prudential (delay of marriage). Hence, Malthus argued against the paternalism of the Poor Law, which, he said, only spreads poverty and hunger while encouraging the poor to have more children. The Poor Laws, he wrote, "tend to create the poor they maintain."

Malthus was himself a humane and cheerful man. But his gloomy predictions, seemingly based on inexorable facts, appeared to make economics a dismal science. In fact, Malthus became England's first professional economist when he accepted a professorship of political economy at the East India College in 1805. Many utilitarians, who admired his mathematical reasoning and his sticking to hard facts, thought that Malthus was advising against any humanitarian social policy. Thus, his ideas strongly reinforced the laissez-faire weapons in the utilitarian arsenal. Moreover, he seemed to blame the poor for their own poverty, for it was their own imprudence that increased the number of mouths to feed. This, of course, was a comfortable doctrine for the wealthy, but was not exactly what Malthus meant. His own view was that land reform and a shift of resources to agriculture were necessary to mitigate the harsh facts of life.

## JOHN WESLEY AND THE EVANGELICAL REVIVAL

Parson Malthus's assumption that passion as well as reason determines human behavior forms a bridge to the second great stream of British thought in the age of revolutions. Both evangelicalism and romanticism were intensely emotional movements. The evangelical revival had an enormous impact on the tone and temper of British society. It raised the religious temperature of British Christianity at the same time that it chilled the bawdy and licentious behavior of preindustrial culture. Evangelicalism stood in vigorous opposition to conventional Augustan religion. Whereas eighteenth-century religion (both Anglican and Nonconformist) was dry, unemotional, and complacent, evangelicalism was emotional, highly moralistic, and intensely personal. Beginning in the 1730s, the evangelical spark glowed warmly until in the 1780s it burst into flames that swept through the British Isles. It spawned a dynamic new denomination, Methodism; transformed torpid Dissent into enthusiastic and aggressive Nonconformity; and reinvigorated a segment of the Church of England. By 1815, the evangelical revival had transformed the religious life of Britain.

The core of evangelicalism was Methodism, whose principal founder was John Wesley (1703–91), arguably the most important individual in British history between 1750 and 1850. His own quest for holiness set the pattern for Methodism and the wider evangelical revival that fanned out around it. Born in rural Lincolnshire to an Anglican clergyman and his strong-willed wife, John Wesley inherited from his ancestors the spark of Puritanism. He was the favorite son in a family of nineteen children, but because of his mother's domineering personality he had severe problems in feeling his own worth. At Oxford he shunned the drinking and wenching enjoyed by most other students, but his real turn to seriousness did not come until he was ordained shortly after graduation. As a young tutor and newly minted priest, Wesley joined a few undergraduates in forming a holy club devoted to regular study, prayer, fasting, and charitable work. The methodical activities of this little circle won for its members the derisive label of *Methodists* and became the model for later Methodist practice, but they did not bring Wesley the assurance of holiness he sought.

In the 1730s, Wesley's quest for holiness came to a crisis. He embarked on a missionary expedition to Georgia, hoping to convert the Indians and

John Wesley
Preaching in
Cornwall, *by Frank
Dadd. Here the
founder of Method-
ism preaches one
of his outdoor ser-
mons to people of
all social orders.*

to learn religious truth himself in the process. Alas, the expedition was a
disaster, and Wesley returned to London in 1738, more persuaded than ever
of his own unworthiness. But during his service in Georgia he had met
some Moravians (German pietists) who deeply impressed him with their
simple, calm religiosity, even in the face of the terrifying Atlantic storms.
They stressed personal salvation in their theology, and they pressed Wesley
on the issue. For a time, Wesley could answer their questioning only by saying he knew Christ had died to save people in general. But in May of 1738,
in the depths of depression, Wesley finally had a conversion experience and
found relief from his agony of self-doubt. One evening at a religious meeting, he reported, "I felt my heart strangely warmed. I felt I did trust in
Christ, Christ alone for salvation; and an assurance was given me that He
had taken away my sins, even mine, and saved me from the law of sin and
death."

Wesley spent the rest of his long life carrying the message of personal salvation to everyone who would listen. He never took a parish, but became an itinerant preacher. He preached in churches, homes, village halls, and open fields to high and low, regardless of social rank. He is thought to have traveled some 250,000 miles on horseback and to have preached more than 40,000 sermons. He and his disciples, including his brother Charles and the spellbinding orator George Whitefield (1714–70), were amazingly effective. Conventional bishops and parish clergymen condemned them and hostile mobs attacked them, yet Wesley and his team of preachers touched thousands of souls neglected by the Church of England. Their intensely emotional words, and above all their hymns, moved crowds of people to conversion, sometimes causing men and women to gesture uncontrollably, to writhe on the floor, and to groan loudly as they parted company with evil. Moreover, Wesley left behind him in each locality small societies of the converted called *classes*, devoted to Bible reading, regular prayer, and mutual confession of sin. Enfolded within these tightly organized, mutually supportive groups, individuals were able to sustain their initial religious enthusiasm. By 1780, there were over 80,000 Wesleyan Methodists in Britain, and in 1815 almost 220,000.

These figures, however, show only part of Wesley's influence, for the great revival he inspired affected many thousands of people never organized into Methodist classes as it swept through Nonconformity (and as we will see below, through one wing, at least, of the Church of England). Like the established church, English Dissent in the first half of the eighteenth century had adopted a restrained and rational religiosity that bore few traces of the Puritan crusading spirit or emotional power. Wesley's message of *vital religion* injected Nonconformity (and Scottish Presbyterianism) with evangelical energy. This evangelical transformation helps account for the remarkable rise in the number of Nonconformist worshippers and in Nonconformist social and cultural influence in nineteenth-century England and Wales, as well as the vitality of Scottish Presbyerianism.

## THE THEOLOGY AND APPEAL OF EVANGELICALISM

What was the theology of the evangelical revival? It was intensely personal and salvation oriented; it put relatively little emphasis on the church as an institution, but focused instead on the direct relationship between the individual and his or her God. Wesley and his followers began with a strong sense of original sin: the inherent degradation of human nature tends always to pull the individual into sin and therefore to separate him or her from God. Hence, Wesley stressed that people are worms, corrupt, diseased, and enslaved. But God is merciful and sends grace to everyone to save all from the "law of sin and death." In this regard, Wesley rejected the Calvinist doctrine of the elect. His message was that Christ died for *all* sinners. Whitefield and a number of other evangelicals split with Wesley on this point and formed the Calvinistic Methodist branch. But most evangelicals followed Wesley: saving grace is a gift to all, which an individual can do nothing to earn or deserve, but which he or she has the free will to accept or reject. Acceptance is made by an act of faith in personal salvation. Thus, the essence of evangelical theology was *salvation by grace through faith.*

Wesley, however, did not believe that a person could remain in that initial state of grace. By accepting grace, one is justified, or forgiven. But he or she would either move forward to *sanctification* (holiness) or backslide into sin. Wesley set great store by the journey of sanctification; consequently, Methodists emphasized the practice of good works such as prayer, reading the Scriptures, visiting the sick, and giving to charity. As a result, Methodists, and evangelicals in all the denominations, became known for their social action—and above all, as we will see, for their efforts to abolish slavery. Good works, Wesley said, are necessary for holiness. At the last day, each person will stand before the divine throne and receive judgment on the balance of good and evil done in his or her whole life. Everything we have is a gift from God; therefore, we are bound to use it well. Wesley urged his followers to give to the poor not a tenth or a half, "no, not three fourths, but all!"

Evangelical theology led believers to philanthropy, but it also tended to make them repressed personalities. Evangelicals spoke of joyful liberation, but often were humorless and censorious toward themselves and others. They regarded life as a struggle toward the final eternal accounting, inevitably a matter of gravity and earnestness. The stakes, after all, were paradise or hellfire. Every little act counted. God had given each person talents and abilities—and in many cases, property that it was sinful to waste. The stewardship of God's gifts required people to avoid frivolous behavior and to discourage it in others. As the *Methodist Magazine* said in 1807, "If dancing be a waste of time . . . if it be a species of trifling ill suited to a creature on trial for eternity . . . then is dancing a practice utterly opposed to the whole spirit and temper of Christianity." If dancing was wrong, still more so were many of the pastimes in traditional popular culture: gambling, drinking, brawling, cock fighting, bull baiting, and all the rest. Methodism proved to be a primary weapon in the destruction of the preindustrial popular way of life.

Serious and grave though it was, evangelicalism appealed to people at all levels of the social spectrum except the very highest and lowest. It had little effect on the aristocracy until the nineteenth century, and it failed to draw in the dregs of society. But in between, from the gentry down through the middling sorts to the shopkeepers, artisans, and industrial workers, Methodism and its evangelical offshoots made converts. Not all the gentry responded favorably to Methodism, for it plainly aimed to put a damper on their hard-drinking, hard-riding self-indulgence. Many of the ordinary clergymen of the Church of England took their cue from the *squirearchy* in resisting Methodism; moreover, they believed that Wesleyan preachers violated decorum and church discipline. In some parishes, squire and parson joined to condemn Methodists as Jacobites, Jacobins, or revolutionaries and to rouse the village roughs against them. One Wesleyan itinerant preacher was stoned to death, and many of the others, including Wesley himself, had to flee from crowds intent on bodily harm. But others among the gentry came to think of Methodism as a bulwark to the social order. They believed rightly that it taught paternalism to the upper ranks on the one hand and orderliness and deference to the laboring poor on the other. Members of the oligarchy found it especially attractive during the French Revolution. They believed that the terrors of the French Revolution were a divine punishment for atheism and infidelity. As one clergyman recalled in 1817: "England was alarmed by the judgements, of which . . . she was a close spectatress, and panted for an opportunity to take the lead in restoring man to his allegiance to his Heavenly Sovereign."

People in the middling ranks responded to the message of evangelical revival almost en masse. Whether they became Methodists or participated in the emotional renovation of one of the old Dissenting denominations, they took to evangelicalism enthusiastically. They found it expressed values of duty, work, and thrift so important to their lives as directors of commerce and industry. Wesley noticed that Methodism was helpful to people in the market economy and that Methodists often became successful and complacent. He warned his listeners to remember that the purpose of a Christian's labor is "to please God; to do, not his own will, but the will of Him that sent him into the world." Nevertheless, the economic usefulness of evangelicalism was too strong for people in the competitive world of trade to resist. Moreover, industrial entrepreneurs recognized that evangelicalism helped tame the preindustrial laboring poor and turn them into a regular, orderly industrial work force. Evangelicalism, then, served as a weapon for the early industrialists, but one that worked *on* them as well as *for* them.

The attractions of Methodism for the laboring poor were more complex. The social and political message of Methodism plainly was conservative and quietist. Wesley remained a Tory all his life, and he told his listeners among the common people to remember their places in the social hierarchy and to bear their sufferings in this world by concentrating on their rewards in the next. Why then did so many respond favorably? First, the Wesleyans actively reached out to them and offered spiritual solace in a time when life was hard and short and when customary conditions were breaking down. Second, Methodism, through its chapels, love feasts (quarterly dinners with prayers and singing), and classes, offered working people opportunities for community. This was vital because the course of economic and social change was rapidly eroding traditional supports of communal life. Third, whatever Wesley's hierarchical and conservative views, Methodism carried a message of equality and independence. There were even female preachers in early Methodism, something not acceptable in the Church of England.

Wesleyan preachers defied the wishes of the Anglican elite by preaching to all the people, even outside the parochial system. They gave ordinary people—miners, artisans, blacksmiths, and shopkeepers—a chance to express some independence by participating in revival meetings. Methodism also offered the laboring poor some means of maintaining their independence by teaching them to read in Sunday schools and by inculcating in them sober and industrious habits. Above all, Methodism taught that all people are equal before God; salvation is equally available to all, not just to the rich. By this message of equality and independence, Methodism was eventually to spawn generations of working-class leaders.

This spirit of equality and independence meant that popular Methodism was subject to repeated splintering. Wesley always regarded himself as a clergyman of the Anglican church, but in 1784, he was forced to begin ordaining priests in order to supply the revival in North America with clergymen. By this step, he took on the rights of a bishop and in effect separated himself and the Methodists from the Church of England. After his death, some groups of working-class Methodists broke away from his organization. In 1797, one Alexander Kilham led a number of northern working men and women out of the Methodist connection because of the orthodox Wesleyan opposition to radicalism.

In 1811, two artisan lay preachers founded yet another sect—the Primitive Methodists—because the Wesleyans turned against the revivalist camp meetings that were popular with working people. In the crises of the 1790s, still other laborers turned to various strange forms of millenarian

Christianity, such as that led by the mystic Joanna Southcott, a domestic servant from Devon who thought she would give birth to Shiloh, the new divine ruler of the earth. One way or another, all such sectaries hoped for the establishment in England of a New Jerusalem—a new society of purity and justice.

Some historians have argued that Methodism prevented revolution in England. The French liberal Elie Halévy, for instance, said in the early 1900s that social quietism spread by the Methodists was what kept the English from following the French example. To what extent is this Halévy thesis true? As we saw in chapter 11, revolutionary efforts in Britain failed for a number of different reasons, among them the determination and power of the oligarchy, the strength of the state, the ability of Parliament to tap Britain's burgeoning wealth, and the antirevolutionary influence of nationalist sentiment. Yet it seems certain that because Methodism—or, more accurately, the evangelical revival in general—taught people to be patient with their lot in life and to expect their rewards in another world, it did help defuse the revolutionary bomb in Britain. In the long run, Methodism helped the British working people to organize and lead themselves; in the short run, it channeled the enormous energy of popular discontent into safe outlets.

## METHODISM IN WALES

The Methodist revival was even more important to Wales than to England. Wesley visited Wales forty-six times, but because of what he called "the heavy curse of the confusion of tongues," native Welsh-speaking revivalists played a greater role than he in converting Wales. The Welsh revivalists began their crusade independent of Wesley. Their efforts were closely associated with the educational work of Griffith Jones. From the 1730s, Jones established a system of schools taught by itinerant masters, who made many thousands of ordinary Welsh children literate in Welsh. At about the same time, revivalism caught fire in southern Wales. The key figures were Howell Harris, a layman of prodigious energy and ego; Daniel Rowland, an Anglican preacher of hypnotic power; and William Williams (known as "Pantycelyn"), another Anglican priest, whose hymns became a vital part of Welsh culture. Around the turn of the nineteenth century, Thomas Charles led the expansion of Methodism into northern Wales.

Methodism grew rapidly in Wales between 1750 and 1775, and then from the 1780s its evangelical energy reinvigorated the old dissenting sects:

Baptists, Independents, and Presbyterians. The Welsh Methodists cooperated with Wesley, but they preferred Calvinist theology and so sided with Whitefield. Eventually, in 1811, the Welsh Methodists broke with the established church to form a new Welsh sect, Calvinistic Methodism. By then, the Calvinistic Methodists and other Dissenters amounted to almost 20 percent of the Welsh population, and Dissent continued to grow rapidly. In 1851, Dissenters outnumbered Anglicans in Wales by 5 to 1.

The new and old Dissenting denominations took the place of the fading Celtic bardic tradition to form the heart and soul of Welsh popular culture. Even before the evangelical revival, there had been a sharp divide between the increasingly anglicized gentry and their Welsh-speaking tenants and laborers. Because the evangelical revival was carried out in Welsh, it added a religious dimension to the great divide: now the gentry were Anglican and English-speaking, and the people were Dissenters and Welsh-speaking. When the Industrial Revolution took hold in South Wales (see chapter 10), it concentrated there a large number of Welsh-speaking Dissenters. There, the church-versus-chapel social division coincided with conflict between upper class and working class.

## THE EVANGELICALS IN THE CHURCH OF ENGLAND

The fires of evangelicalism also burned within the Church of England, where the men and women who were inspired by Wesley's message of vital religion were called the Evangelicals or Saints. These believers, largely from the higher social classes, saw evangelical theology as a means of combating lower class radicalism; above all, however, they wanted to abandon merely nominal Christianity and to make religion count in every way in their lives. They remained a numerical minority in the Anglican church, but their enthusiasm and their relentless determination to renovate society and reinvigorate the church gave them influence out of proportion to their numbers. From the 1780s on, the Evangelical insistence on a personal and emotional faith (as opposed to subtle dogma, ecclesiastical privileges, or latitudinarian complacency) made for a formidable Low Church position.

The most famous of the early Evangelicals was a small group of wealthy and well-connected philanthropic activists called the Clapham Sect—so named because they lived in the village of Clapham just south of London. The Clapham Sect included Henry Thornton, a banker who owned the estate of Clapham around which they clustered; John Venn, the inspirational vicar of Clapham; Zachary Macaulay, a businessman, former West

Indian slave overseer, and colonial governor; Hannah More, a one-time poet and playwright who became the leading popular publicist of evangelical social doctrines; and William Wilberforce, heir to a Yorkshire commercial fortune and a friend of Pitt the Younger. This little group founded a tradition of high-minded but practical public service that characterizes many British intellectual families even to the present day. They involved themselves in a wide variety of philanthropic enterprises: personal charity (Thornton gave away five-sixths of his income until he was married and one-third there-after); Sunday schools and elementary education for the poor; prison reform; Sabbatarianism (banning any nonreligious diversions on Sundays); and the *reformation of manners*—the suppression of what they regarded as immoral activities such as dueling, gambling, drunkenness, prostitution, blasphemy, and traditional blood sports. They also came out strongly against political radicalism after 1793. Hannah More, for instance, wrote a series of *Cheap Repository Tracts* preaching hard work and deference to laborers, the *Tracts* to be distributed to the poor by their betters.

## THE ANTISLAVERY MOVEMENT

The greatest of all the Evangelical crusades was against slavery and the slave trade. When this crusade began in the 1780s, slavery was part and parcel of British life, even though a judicial ruling in 1772 had in effect made slavery illegal within England. In the second half of the eighteenth century, British ships carried over 40 percent of all African slaves across the Atlantic. Sugar harvested by slaves sweetened the British diet, tobacco cut by slaves burned in British pipes, cotton picked by slaves fueled the great Northern textile factories, and the profits generated by slaves percolated through British banks and paid for many of the splendid buildings that still grace the great slave ship ports of Liverpool, Bristol, and London. Even the Church of England owned slave plantations in the West Indies.

In 1774 John Wesley became the first British religious leader to denounce slavery with his pamphlet *Thoughts upon Slavery*, but he did not organize an antislavery campaign. That initiative arose from the ranks of the Quakers, who in 1783 became the first Christian denomination in Britain to condemn slavery. Their efforts achieved little notice, however, until they joined forces with Anglican Evangelicals in 1787. With Quaker businessmen providing financial support and Anglican Evangelicals utilizing their greater social and political influence (as members of the established church), the

Am I Not a Man and a Brother *by Joseph Wedgwood (1787). One of the first political logos ever made, this seal was designed by pottery entrepreneur Joseph Wedgwood as a contribution to the abolitionist movement. It soon appeared on plates, buttons, and jewelry; by buying these items, women and men without the vote could participate in the political process.*

antislavery movement became a prominent political force in British society. Over the next few years, the campaign originated many of the tactics now common to political pressure groups: it devised the first political logo, a kneeling slave begging for help; it distributed the first modern political poster, a diagram showing the way slaves were packed into the hold of a typical slave ship; it generated paintings, hymns, and what would now be called protest songs; it mobilized women and men without the vote through popular petitions and rallies; and it organized a nationwide boycott of slave-grown sugar.

The leader of the Saints' antislavery campaign was William Wilberforce (1759–1833), who worked tirelessly against slavery in and out of Parliament for almost fifty years. Wilberforce converted to Evangelicalism as a young man; thereafter, he devoted himself to the eradication from British life of those practices he saw as sins or as conducive to sin. He organized the Proclamation Society (later the Society for the Suppression of Vice) in 1787. But if he was something of a killjoy, he also led the British parliamentary elite to see what should have been obvious—the cruelty and horror of slavery—and he persuaded them to reject the pleas of the powerful West Indian slavery interest. Parliament finally abolished the slave trade throughout the British Empire in 1807 and slavery itself in the British Empire in 1833.

## ROMANTICISM

The equivalent in high culture of evangelical emotionalism was the Romantic movement. Between 1780 and 1830, British writers, painters, and architects produced a body of work steeped in emotion and miraculous in quantity and quality. The romantics fashioned works that have provided for countless literate men and women an image of what it means to be British—a pastoral, nonindustrial, nostalgic vision. The romantic tradition pitted *nature* against *artifice*, the organism against the machine, the past against the present, and so provided the inspiration for continuing and profound critique of urban industrial life.

How is this wonderful flowering of culture to be explained? Despite their claims to be setting out eternal truths, the romantics were deeply engaged with their times, and it is in that engagement—sometimes enthusiastic, sometimes highly critical—that the explanation is to be found. First, there was political revolution. Almost all the British romantic poets at one time or another found the events of France to be exhilarating. The French Revolution seemed to be liberating humanity from ancient bonds and to be drawing all the social and political lines anew. As William Wordsworth wrote,

But Europe at that time was thrilled with joy,
France standing on the top of golden hours,
And human nature seeming born again.

Yet the British romantics were sensitive to a wide variety of political and social changes. Economic expansion, population explosion, and the destruction of traditional social relations all gave them a sense of rapid transformation. Static views of nature would no longer do; dynamic views would have to replace them. Thus, the romantics, whether radical or conservative, developed a strong sense of historical change and committed themselves to philosophies emphasizing the living, organic quality of nature. Likewise, the static formulas of classical art no longer seemed appropriate. As Wordsworth put it, the times demanded a new kind of art: a "multitude of causes, unknown to former times" were reducing the mind "to a state of almost savage torpor." Among these causes were great national events, the accumulation of men in cities, the uniformity of occupations, and a "craving for extraordinary incident," all of which required as an antidote poetry that is "the spontaneous overflow of powerful feelings."

Next, the new commercial and industrial society—and the utilitarian philosophy that went with it—seemed to convey a one-dimensional view of human life and to leave no room for the arts. The romantics reacted against this confinement by aggressively asserting the primacy of art and of a life devoted to it. They sharply pitted art against the pursuit of riches—"the God and Mammon of the world." This reaction contributed to the image of the romantic hero, with whom the poets and painters identified, the genius who defies conventional rules and asserts special power and insight into the world.

Closely related to economic change was a fourth cause of romanticism—the growth of commercial market for writing. As we saw in chapter 5, art was being commodified during the eighteenth century. As the economy expanded, the middle class grew and generated a demand for literature as well as for instruction and information. The market for fine arts took the place of aristocratic patronage. Many artists reacted against the dictates of this commercial market by insisting on the higher status of art and the independence of individual artistic genius. They claimed that the poet or painter has a special faculty—the imagination—that is superior to reason and offers special insights into nature or the cosmos. The imagination illuminates, or even creates, reality rather than simply mirroring it. It moves in the realm of the strange and finds magic in the commonplace.

## THE ENGLISH ROMANTIC POETS

The English romantic poets may be divided into two generations. The first generation included William Blake (1757–1827), William Wordsworth (1770–1850), and Samuel Taylor Coleridge (1772–1834). Blake was not only the first, but also most unusual of the first generation in that he was trained as an artisan. A master engraver, Blake expressed his prophetic vision in highly symbolic poems illustrated by his own magnificent engravings. He was a self-conscious visionary, "the Bard/who Present, Past, & Future sees." The vision revolved around an unorthodox but intense brand of Christianity, his often prophetic poems dealing with the creation, fall, and redemption of humanity. Blake saw the French Revolution as a violent force that foretold the final apocalypse, when humanity would overcome its fragmented and isolated existence. That fragmentation, he believed, was in part the result of industrialization, the advent of "dark Satanic Mills," which Blake defied:

I shall not cease from Mental Fight
Nor shall my sword sleep in my hand,
Till we have built Jerusalem
In England's green and pleasant land.

Wordsworth began his career in a similar enthusiasm for the French Revolution, but he turned eventually to deeply religious and conservative poetry. He became the most English of poets, often celebrating the calming quiet of the English countryside, and was made poet laureate in 1843. Wordsworth and Coleridge as young men published the poetic manifesto of English romanticism in *Lyrical Ballads* (1798). In the "Preface" to *Lyrical*

*Ballads*, Wordsworth announced a new style in poetry, throwing over Augustan decorum in favor of language "really used by men." This was considered radical at the time, but by 1798 Wordsworth had already become disillusioned by the French Revolution. He rejected extreme rationalism and resorted to "the wisdom of the heart." Thereafter, he taught the healing power of nature, especially in particular experiences of everyday life in which a person can enjoy sudden insight into the supernatural:

> There are in our existence spots of time
> Which with distinct pre-eminence retain
> A renovating virtue, whence . . . our minds
> Are nourished and invisibly repaired.

Coleridge was the ablest philosopher among the English romantic poets. As a young man, he was a radical empiricist in philosophy and religion and even dreamed of establishing a utopian community in America. But in the later 1790s, Coleridge turned away from radicalism to Anglicanism and from empiricism to German Idealist philosophy. As an Idealist, he articulated what is implicit in most romantic poetry: that there is a realm of spirit that suffuses and transcends material objects. That transcendent reality, he said, is not known by the senses but by intuition. The mind participates in creating reality in the process of perception; it makes visible the mind of God. In poetry, the mind repeats "the eternal act of creation in the infinite I AM." Thus, to Coleridge, the poetic imagination, not sensory perception, is the foundation of all knowledge.

The second generation of English romantic poets—Lord Byron (1788–1824), Percy Bysshe Shelley (1792–1822), and John Keats (1795–1821)—were deeply influenced by Wordsworth and Coleridge, but they remained more radical than these two elder statesmen of the movement. As one of the most famous and notorious figures of the day—a kind of pop star of the literary world—Byron was the classic romantic hero who rejected orthodox behavior in both his life and his poetry. His poetic protagonists were moody, disdainful, isolated characters offering ironic criticism of current civilization. Byron died in 1824 in Greece, having taken up the cause of Greek independence from Turkey.

Shelley was also an extreme political radical and social nonconformist who fought all his life against what he saw as tyranny and oppression. Over time, Shelley became one of the most learned and philosophically abstract of poets. He took as his goal the moral reform of humanity through the power of his art. His masterpiece, *Prometheus Unbound* (1819), concerns the hero of Greek myth who stole fire from the gods on behalf of humanity;

in it Shelley showed how tyranny and oppression are the products of morally unreformed humankind. To Shelley, poets should be acknowledged as the "author to others of the highest wisdom, pleasure, virtue and glory," for in modern times it is not knowledge and productive capacity that are needed, but the generous creative faculty—"the poetry of life"—which alone can free people from enslavement to the pursuit of material gain.

In his short life as a poet, Keats wanted to re-create sensuous beauty for its own sake and as a symbol for the life of the spirit. It was Keats who gave the most elevated statements of the romantic exhaltation of the aesthetic imagination: "What the imagination seizes as Beauty, must be truth"; "Beauty is truth, truth beauty—that is all/Ye know on earth, and all ye need to know."

Probably the most well-known text to come out of the second generation of English Romantics was not, however, a poem but a short novel: *Frankenstein* (1818). The daughter of Mary Wollstonecraft and the wife of Percy Shelley, Mary Shelley (1797–1851) was only twenty years old when she wrote the story of the idealistic scientist Victor Frankenstein who uses his scientific knowledge to create life, but then rejects that life as monstrous and pays in full for his actions. By setting himself above and against nature, Frankenstein violated the primary romantic credo of a life lived in harmony with natural and spiritual life forces. Frankenstein's monster stands as the creation of human intellect detached from the very qualities that make us most human, according to the romantics: soul, spirit, the quest for beauty.

## ROMANTICISM IN WALES AND SCOTLAND

The Augustan Age had been a time of integration of provincial cultures into the English cultural mainstream throughout the British Isles. Enlightened thinkers in the British Isles helped create an arena of public discourse common to Britain as a whole. But the Romantic movement, though it crossed national borders, gave rise to cultural nationalist reactions in Wales and Scotland. In both countries, the romantic interest in the strange, the picturesque, and the remote led to delving in the literary and historical past. As early as the 1750s, Welsh expatriates in London founded the Cymmrodorion Society to carry out antiquarian studies. A more radical group of London Welsh founded the Society of Gwyneddigion in the 1770s. It published Welsh literature in the Middle Ages, including an edition of the medieval Welsh poet Dafydd ap Gwilym. One of the collaborators in this effort was a stonemason-turned-scholar, Iolo Morganwg, who made a career for himself as the prototype of the Welsh bard while fabricating a number of "ancient" texts. The main result of romanticism in Wales was the revival of the *eisteddfod*—the traditional meeting of the bards and celebration of popular culture, all of which took place in Welsh. This was accompanied by a renewed affection for druidism, seen by the romantics as an authentic religion of nature. In Wales, then, the fifty years after 1780 were a period of revival for purely Welsh traditions in high culture as well as Methodism in popular culture.

In Scotland, there was similar interest in traditional literature and legends, including those of the Highlands. But the great days of Highland culture were over. The best Gaelic poets had flourished in the mid-eighteenth century, and the Ossian epic, the most famous Highland "medieval" manuscript, was a forgery. Neither of the two primary Scottish romantic writers—Robert Burns (1759–96) and Sir Walter Scott (1771–1832)—wrote in Gaelic. Burns composed some poems in elegant English, but he cast his most vivid and memorable work in the Lowland Scots tongue; for this he became the national poet of Scotland. Born the son of a poor tenant farmer in southwestern Scotland, Burns by sheer determination made himself into a well-read man. In his poetry he was able to combine the best of Lowland Scots folk ballads and lyrics with English poetic style. His short poems and songs—including "To a Louse," "Scots Wha Hae," "For A' That and A' That," and "Auld Lang Syne"—written in the language of ordinary people with marvelous zest and heartiness, deal with common events and emotions: love, hard drink, friendship, radicalism, and patriotism. Burns was greeted by the English romantics as the primitive plowman-poet. As Byron said of him, Burns was "tenderness and roughness—delicacy, coarseness—sentiment, sensuality—soaring and grovelling, dirt and deity—all mixed up in that one compound of inspired clay."

Sir Walter Scott was from the Lowland region near the English border, but he assimilated Highland as well as Lowland history and legend. In both his poetry and his fiction he created romantic historical pictures that won enormous popularity—and a great fortune that Scott spent in trying to live in the style of a feudal lord. His Waverley novels, including *Waverley* (1814), *Rob Roy* (1818), and *The Heart of Midlothian* (1818), provide dramatic historical portraits of Scottish life in the age of the Convenanters and Jacobites. More than anyone else, Scott revived English and Scottish interest in Highland clan culture—a safe thing to do because the clans by then had been tamed, and besides Scott preached accommodation with Britain, not defiance.

The Tory Scott drew sympathetic portraits of Jacobitism in his novels, but his message was essentially one of social and political harmony, and for that he was rewarded. In 1820 he was made a baronet, and in 1822 he acted as the manager of pageantry for King George IV's magnificent state visit to Scotland. By then the Hanoverian line thought it right to wear Highland kilts! During the war against the French Revolution, the British monarchy had been made the focus of patriotic ceremony, and now it served as a device for creating a *union of hearts* between the English and the Scots. As nostalgia for the Highlands became popular, English and Lowland Scottish textile firms did a big business in concocting the whole scheme of clan tartans that prevails in the popular mind even today. Scott, then, contributed mightily to Scottish national consciousness, but in the context of a somewhat bogus, commercialized, and domesticated vision of gallant Highland chiefs and their loyal clan warriors.

## BRITISH ROMANTIC ARCHITECTURE AND PAINTING

The romantic interest in the natural, the remote, the picturesque, and the exotic encouraged architects to call on a number of different historical traditions. The parks surrounding the homes of country gentlemen, with their newly constructed temples, "medieval" bridges, and Gothic ruins, showed this sensibility, for they were carefully designed to look natural and unplanned while including items meant to recall the wonders of the past. Many architects continued to draw on the classical tradition, ancient Greece especially being regarded as the epitome of noble simplicity. For example, John Nash (1752–1835) created imaginative and picturesque city villas in the classical style. Yet Nash also designed the Royal Pavilion in Brighton (1815–18) in a bizarre Indian style (cupcake domes, fantasy minarets, and lace doily interiors) inspired by the "stately pleasure dome" of Coleridge's poem "Kubla Kahn."

The tradition most favored by British romantic architects, however, was the Gothic. Augustan taste had held that the Gothic was barbarous, but the British of the Romantic period were drawn to its irregularity, its lack of symmetry, its religious aspirations, and its rustic quality. To the romantic sensibility, the medieval society that had produced the Gothic increasingly seemed attractive because it was "natural" and not reduced to the formulas of pure reason. Gothic architecture, whose monuments stood in varying states of decay all around the British Isles, thus represented not only the his-

*The Royal Pavilion, Brighton, designed by John Nash. The Royal Pavilion is an example of English Regency romanticism at its most fanciful.*

torically remote, but also the sublime and the mysterious. As early as the mid-1700s, Horace Walpole rebuilt his home, Strawberry Hill, in the Gothic style: plenty of turrets, towers, battlements, and pointed arches over the windows. Most of the Gothic buildings of the Romantic period were homes, from thatched-roof cottages to sprawling manors, of which the most imposing was Fonthill Abbey, built between 1796 and 1807 by James Wyatt for a millionaire (alas, its 276-foot tower collapsed in 1825). The Gothic came to be regarded as the English national style of building, in part no doubt because it recalled past times when the laboring poor stayed in their place.

British painters also reacted against the formalism and artificial qualities of Augustan art in order to express the new taste for the drama and strangeness of life. A painter as well as a poet, William Blake created an awesome mythological world in his visionary engravings and watercolors, whereas John Henry Fuseli (1741–1825), a Swiss émigré living in London, painted mysterious Gothic nightmares from the darkest regions of the mind. But the two greatest British romantic painters were both landscape artists: John Constable (1776–1837) and J. M. W. Turner (1775–1851). Constable seems to have been the Wordsworth of painting—a careful observer of the familiar localities of the English countryside. Constable's paintings have a calming effect, not because they are sedate, but because his landscapes are filled with divine benevolence. This he expressed with free techniques in oil that endowed the landscape with light, life, and movement. Turner, on the

The Hay-Wain, *by John Constable. Nature and the English countryside depicted by the best-known of the English romantic painters. In Constable's work, humanity and human commodities are absorbed into the wider natural (and supernatural) world.*

other hand, painted nature's violence in powerful canvases that Constable called "airy visions, painted with tinted steam." In his immensely powerful paintings of storms in mountain passes and on the sea, Turner showed nature at its most violent and even catastrophic, a living thing beyond the control of human reason.

### Suggested Reading

Abrams, M. H. *The Mirror and the Lamp.* New York: Oxford University Press, 1953.

Bebbington, D. W. *Evangelicalism in Modern Britain: A History from the 1730s to the 1980s.* Winchester, NH: Unwin Hyman, 1989.

Brown, Christopher. *Moral Capital: Foundations of British Abolitionism.* Chapel Hill: University of North Carolina Press, 2006.

Butler, Marilyn. *Romantics, Rebels, and Reactionaries: English Literature and Its Background, 1760–1830.* New York: Oxford University Press, 1982.

Carlson, J. A. *England's First Family of Writers: Mary Wollstonecraft, William Godwin, Mary Shelley.* Baltimore: Johns Hopkins University Press, 2007.

Dinwiddie, J. R. *Bentham.* Oxford: Oxford University Press, 1989.

Drescher, Seymour. *The Mighty Experiment: Free Labour Versus Slavery in British Emancipation.* New York: Oxford University Press, 2002.

Evans, E. D. *A History of Wales, 1660–1815.* Cardiff: University of Wales Press, 1976.

Furneaux, Robin. *William Wilberforce*. London: Hamilton, 1974.

Halévy, Elie. *The Growth of Philosophic Radicalism*. London: Faber, 1972.

Hempton, David. *Methodism and Politics in British Society, 1750–1850*. Stanford, CA: Stanford University Press, 1984.

———. *Methodism: Empire of the Spirit*. New Haven, CT: Yale University Press, 2005.

———. *The Religion of the People: Methodism and Popular Religion c. 1750–1900*. London: Routledge, 1996.

Hilton, Boyd. *The Age of Atonement: The Influence of Evangelicalism on Social and Economic Thought, 1785–1865*. New York: Oxford University Press, 1987.

Hobsbawm, E. J., and Terence Ranger, eds. *The Invention of Tradition*. New York: Cambridge University Press, 1985.

Hole, Robert. *Pulpits, Politics and Public Order in England, 1760–1832*. New York: Cambridge University Press, 1989.

Honour, Hugh. *Romanticism*. London: Allen Lane, 1979.

Kidson, Peter, Peter Murray, and Paul Thompson. *A History of English Architecture*, 2nd ed. New York: Penguin Press, 1979.

Kroeber, Karl. *British Romantic Art*. Berkeley: University of California Press, 1986.

Mack, Mary P. *Jeremy Bentham: An Odyssey of Ideas*. New York: Columbia University Press, 1963.

Mack, Phyllis. *Heart Religion in the British Enlightenment: Gender and Emotion in Early Methodism*. Cambridge: Cambridge University Press, 2008.

Midgley, Clare. *Women Against Slavery: The British Campaigns, 1780–1870*. London: Routledge, 1995.

Newman, Gerald. *The Rise of English Nationalism: A Cultural History, 1740–1830*. New York: St. Martin's Press, 1987.

Rosen, F. *Jeremy Bentham and Representative Democracy: A Study of the Constitutional Code*. New York: Oxford University Press, 1983.

Ryan, Robert M. *The Romantic Reformation: Religious Politics in English Literature, 1789–1824*. New York: Cambridge University Press, 1997.

Schlossberg, Herbert. *The Silent Revolution: Evangelicalism and the Making of Victorian England*. Columbus: Ohio State University Press, 2000.

Semmel, Bernard. *The Methodist Revolution*. New York: Basic Books, 1973.

Thomas, William. *The Philosophic Radicals*. Oxford: Clarendon Press, 1979.

Turley, David. *The Culture of English Anti-slavery, 1780–1860*. New York: Routledge, Chapman & Hall, 1991.

Wahrman, Dror. *The Making of the Modern Self*. New Haven, CT: Yale University Press, 2004.

Williams, Gwen A. *When Was Wales?* London: Black Raven Press, 1985.

Wordsworth, Jonathan, Michael Jaye, and Robert Woof. *William Wordsworth and the Age of English Romanticism*. New Brunswick, NJ: Rutgers University Press, 1987.

# Part III

## The Rise of Victorian Society

## 1815–1870

# Chapter 13

# The Emerging Class Society, 1815–1850

The British landed oligarchy survived the French Revolution with its status and its hold on the positions of power intact. Yet the incessant forces of the Triple Revolution—agricultural, demographic, and industrial—were too powerful to be confined to the old channels of a hierarchical society, particularly because the landowners set aside their paternalist role during the war against the French. In the half-century after 1815, industrialization accelerated and widened the British lead as the most powerful nation on earth, but it also drew into its vortex ever-widening circles of the traditional economy. Growing numbers of people swarmed into the urban areas. Remnants of the social hierarchy of preindustrial Britain crumbled away, and over time broad, self-conscious, and mutually antagonistic societal layers—landed class, middle class, and working class—formed and hardened. These trends generated severe social tensions and gave Britain in the first half of the nineteenth century an air of crisis; yet in the 1850s and 1860s the tensions eased and the sense of crisis passed. The result was one of the most remarkable civilizations in modern Western history—Victorian society (so named because of the monarch, Queen Victoria, who reigned but did not rule from 1837 to 1901).

The Victorians still have the reputation of being earnest, moralistic, complacent, and hypocritical. This reputation is partly the result of the very strong negative reaction against Victorianism that occurred in the early twentieth century, but it is also partly due to a failure to appreciate the gravity and novelty of the problems the Victorians faced and to an overly narrow focus on one element of Victorian society: the middle-class English male. It is important not to forget the other social classes of Victorian Britain, the people of what came to be called the "Celtic fringe" (Scotland, Wales, and Ireland), and women of all social orders and nationalities. But even if one looks at the English middle class alone, contradiction and complexity come into view. They were proud and even arrogant people, but they were also bedeviled by self-doubts and social concerns and divided by gender. They prided themselves on the evolution of parliamentary government, but they liked deferential behavior by the working class. They believed in individualism, but were profoundly conformist. They congratulated themselves on progress, but were deeply concerned that change was destroying their society. They were very religious, but increasingly obsessed with their own religious doubts. Such complexity presents many challenges to historians— above all how to explain the formation of a stable, coherent society out of economic and social change of an unprecedented scope and pace.

## BRITISH AND IRISH POPULATIONS, 1815–1850

As we have already noted, one of the most important social facts of early nineteenth-century Britain was the rapid growth of the population. As Table 13.1 shows, if we take the census of 1821 as the starting point, the British and Irish population grew 31 percent by 1851.

This population was increasingly *English*. It is worth remembering that the British nation of 1815—formally entitled the United Kingdom of Great Britain and Ireland was not very old. The union between England and Scotland had occurred only in 1707 and that with Ireland only in 1801. The English dominated this young nation. Throughout the nineteenth century and to a degree even until our own times, both the English and foreigners commonly called Britain "England." To an extent, the population figures justified this practice, for the proportion of the British people living in England increased from 54 percent in 1821 to 62 percent in 1851, a fact explained in part by the disastrous effect of the Irish famine and in part by the net inflow

| Table 13.1: British and Irish Population 1821–1851 (in millions) | | | | |
|---|---|---|---|---|
| | **1821** | **1831** | **1841** | **1851** |
| England | 11.3 | 13.1 | 15.0 | 16.9 |
| Wales | .7 | .8 | .9 | 1.0 |
| Scotland | 2.1 | 2.4 | 2.6 | 2.9 |
| Ireland | 6.8 | 7.8 | 8.2 | 6.6 |
| Total | 20.9 | 24.1 | 26.7 | 27.4 |

*Source:* Chris Cook and John Stevenson, *Longman Handbook of Modern British History, 1714–1980* (London, Longman, 1983), pp. 96–97.

of Irish and Scots into England. By 1851, for instance, there were approximately 600,000 people of Irish birth in England and more than 250,000 of Scottish birth.

Of more importance in the *Englishness* of the British was English cultural domination. Because England was the wealthiest and most powerful segment of Britain, its culture exerted steady pressure on the Celtic peoples. If an individual anywhere in the British Isles wanted to succeed in business or to cut a figure in fashion or politics, he or she had to be proficient in English. Likewise, English was the official language of government and law, and the British government tended to promote schooling in English in Celtic areas. Thus, an increasing majority of the British peoples spoke English and not one of the Celtic languages. In Scotland, the proportion of Gaelic speakers fell as the Highland Clearances took their toll, from about 20 percent in 1801 to 10 percent in 1861. In Ireland, about 50 percent of the people spoke Irish as their main language in 1801; by 1851, only about 23 percent of the Irish did so. In Wales, the overwhelming majority of people spoke Welsh in 1801, but as Welsh industrial areas were integrated into the English economy and English and Irish workers emigrated to Wales, the percentage of Welsh speakers declined. In 1891, only 54 percent of the Welsh people spoke Welsh.

Urbanization was the other great feature of British population growth in the first half of the nineteenth century. The flood of people into the cities and towns that began in the late eighteenth century continued in the nineteenth. By 1851, for the first time, 50 percent of the British population (not counting Ireland) lived in towns, and 34 percent lived in towns of over 20,000. By 1851, there were nine cities with more than 100,000 each: London, Liverpool, Manchester, Birmingham, Leeds, Glasgow, Bristol, Sheffield, and Bradford. With 2.4 million people, London was home for a larger portion of the British population (excluding Ireland) than ever—11.5 percent. Outside of London, the population tended to collect in the heavy industrial regions of the Midlands and the North of England, in the Scottish Lowlands (a wide belt from Edinburgh to Glasgow), and in South Wales.

Unplanned, unregulated, and horrifically unhealthy, these heaving cities epitomized the economic energy and social inequality of nineteenth-century Britain. In most cases, the working-class districts stood cheek-by-jowl with factories and warehouses. These districts almost invariably became squalid slums with high mortality rates. Such housing as was available was built by private construction contractors, responding to working-class demand in

Over London by Rail, *by Gustave Doré. The artist has shown the backs of working-class houses in early Victorian London.*

the free market. In their natural drive for profit, the contractors cut corners on space and construction, cramming as many houses into the smallest possible area. Typically, the houses were of the back-to-back variety: rows of small two-level houses that were one room deep and that backed up on each other so as to share a common rear wall. Often these rows of houses were laid out around dark, airless "courts," in which were located the common privy and water spigot. Bleak as such housing was, it was far better than the cramped tenements and foul cellars into which hundreds of thousands of the poorest city dwellers swarmed.

Manchester was the greatest of the industrial cities and the prototype of the early urban industrial environment—the "shock city of the Industrial Revolution." It grew from 95,000 to over 300,000 between 1801 and 1851. As the center of Britain's cotton industry, Manchester was busy, productive, and noisy, humming with thousands of spindles in great smoky mills. It was also crowded and largely without paving, sewerage, or water supply for its working-class denizens. Built at the junction of three rivers (the Irwell, the

Irk, and the Medlock, all of which had turned oily black from pollution), Manchester became a jungle of narrow, filthy, cramped streets and alleys. The great French political thinker Alexis de Tocqueville visited Manchester in 1835:

> From this foul drain the greatest stream of human industry flows out to fertilize the whole world. From this filthy sewer pure gold flows. Here humanity attains its most complete development and its most brutish; here civilization works its miracles, and civilized man is turned back almost into a savage.

The young German cotton manufacturer (and close friend of Karl Marx) Friedrich Engels was similarly shocked by what he saw in Manchester in the early 1840s: a labyrinthine collection of wretched industrial and working-class slums. The well-to-do had moved outward in order to spare themselves the horrors of the town, but in the inner city, the poor lived amid their own stench and filth. In many crowded districts, he wrote, "the inhabitants can only enter or leave the court by wading through puddles of stale urine and excrement." Everywhere he saw pollution and decay: "filth, ruination and uninhabitableness." In such appalling conditions lived a growing proportion of Britain's industrial population.

## THE BRITISH ECONOMY, 1815–1850

The British economy in the early Victorian years continued its startling growth, but it was afflicted with alternating short-term cycles of boom and slump. The gross national product (GNP, the annual total of all goods and services produced) went up by more than 300 percent in the forty years between 1810 and 1850. The annual growth rate of the economy averaged more than 2.5 percent—more than twice as fast as in the early 1700s. Agriculture did well, but industry drove the expansion. Capital invested in productive capacity tripled between 1800 and 1860. Exports streamed out of Britain's workshops, factories, and mines, increasing 400 percent between 1800 and 1850. By today's standards, Britain's industrial growth in the early nineteenth century may have been moderate, but by the standards of the day it was both astonishing and unique.

Even as late as 1850, Britain remained the only industrialized nation in the world; thus, it dominated world trade. In 1850, the British enjoyed nearly 25 percent of the world's commerce. In the mechanized production of cotton and woolen textiles, pottery, iron machinery, steam engines, firearms, cutlery, and pots and pans, the British simply faced no competition. This fact shaped Britain's overseas trade patterns. The British typically exchanged manufactured goods (cotton textiles above all) for primary products, that is, foodstuffs and raw materials. This exchange was all in Britain's favor because foreign buyers could obtain manufactured articles from them alone; hence, the British needed no elaborate marketing strategies or skills. In addition, the British increased their earnings from *invisible income*—the profits from overseas banking and investment and from trade itself: shipping, insurance, docks, warehouses, and brokerage.

These patterns shaped governmental policies toward trade. The nineteenth century was the era of free trade in British history. British industry and commerce did not need tariff protection; they needed conditions in which British goods had open access to foreign markets and in which foreigners could sell their products in Britain to earn the money with which to buy British industrial goods. Free trade was the obvious policy for Britain, and British industrial captains and their spokesmen, known as the Manchester School of economics, vigorously promoted free enterprise and free trade. Though the Corn Law of 1815 remained on the books until 1846, British governments of both parties otherwise moved steadily toward abolition of import duties and other restrictions on trade. William Huskisson, a Tory president of the Board of Trade, abolished a number of restrictive policies in 1822 and at the same time negotiated several reciprocal trade treaties by which Britain and foreign countries mutually reduced import duties. The trading monopolies of most of the old chartered companies such as the Royal African Company and the East India Company were ended. The Navigation Laws were repealed in 1849. In this context, the Corn Law of 1815 stood out as an anomalous and divisive issue through the early 1840s.

The undeniable success of British capitalism in expanding output was marred by periodic depressions. The state took little role in guiding or regulating economic growth; hence, businessmen acted not only in self-interest, but also without adequate information in their highly volatile economic environment. Industrial capitalism was as yet such a new phenomenon that speculation and fraud were as common as enterprise, and sudden failure was as frequent as success. Recessions or depressions followed boom periods with bewildering speed. Almost immediately after peace was attained in 1815, for example, demand rapidly deflated and a depression set in until 1821. From that year until 1836 the economy expanded feverishly, but overspeculation and overinvestment broke the fever, causing a severe depression—the worst in the nineteenth century—from 1836 to 1842. Thereafter, the economy began to recover, though times remained very hard through the mid-1840s.

Each of the downturns in the trade cycle threw people out of work. Statistics on unemployment in the period are very unreliable, but one can be certain that substantial numbers of people were unemployed or under-employed at all times and that the so-called reserve army of unemployed went up drastically in bad years. For instance, in Bolton (a cotton town), unemployment among mill workers reached 60 percent in 1842 and stood even higher among construction workers. In general, factory operatives probably enjoyed more regular employment than most others, including skilled craftspersons, few of whom escaped unemployment for part of each year. This vulnerability to the seemingly uncontrollable trade cycles was one of the gravest psychological pressures shouldered by early nineteenth-century urban workers.

Unemployment and underemployment were two of the reasons why, on the whole, material standards of living did not improve until the 1850s. Average output per capita and income per capita were increasing, and at the same time, the long-term trend of prices after 1815 was downward. Yet these promising trends did not improve standards of living for most working people before mid-century. A greater share of the national income went toward profits and rents and away from wages, and a somewhat higher proportion of the nation's wealth was put to investment rather than to consumption. Furthermore, as we have seen in chapter 10, some occupational groups such as the handloom weavers suffered dramatic reductions in their wages, both because of overcrowding in the trade and because of competition with machine manufacturing. For all these reasons, the material benefits of industrialization for most working people were long delayed. As the great social critic Thomas Carlyle put it, the economy seemed "enchanted." Britain was like Midas with the golden touch: there was work to be done, but people stood unemployed; there was wealth all around, but the poor suffered hunger and degradation.

The industries that led the initial burst of mechanization—cotton, coal, and iron—were joined from the 1820s by a new industry, the railways. Because railways used over three hundred tons of iron rails per mile, consumed vast quantities of coal, and employed thousands of unskilled as well as skilled workers in vast feats of civil engineering, their effects reverberated right through the economy. Beginning in 1825, a steam engine was used to pull wagons on iron rails for the twelve miles between Stockton and Darlington. The opportunities for cheap and fast transportation of goods and passengers became obvious to private entrepreneurs. In the next ten years a *railway mania* swept the country (except Ireland); Parliament

Excavation of the Olive Mount on the Liverpool to Manchester Railway, *by Thomas Valentine Roberts. This remarkable painting shows not only an early railway engine, but also the huge task of civil engineering required for railway construction.*

authorized private companies to build fifty-four new lines. The depression of 1836–37 slowed construction, but after 1845, railway building began again. By 1850, more than five hundred railway companies had come into existence and had completed the trunk of the British railway system: more than six thousand miles of track stretching from Penzance to Aberdeen. This second burst of railway building pulled Britain out of the "Hungry '40s."

The railways tied the regions of Britain more tightly together than any force, political or economic, ever had done (or would do, until the world wars and television). Businessmen expanded their markets into all corners of the country. Perishable goods such as milk, beer, and fish could be processed in one place and sold in cities hundreds of miles away. Travel for ordinary middle-class people became a reality, not least because an act of the 1844 Parliament required the railways to run at least one cheap train a day on every line. Commuting by rail was still a thing of the future, but day outings from the cities to the countryside became a common feature of life for bourgeois families as early as the 1840s. By 1850, nearly any place in Britain (excluding Ireland, where railways were constructed later) was reachable within a day from any other place. In 1854, for instance, travel time from London to Plymouth was only seven hours; to Manchester, five and one-half hours; and to Edinburgh, eleven hours. London newspapers put on the early morning trains were being read by late afternoon all over the country.

## THE LANDED CLASS: ARISTOCRACY AND GENTRY

The nation that was being knitted together by the bonds of iron rails was at the same time slowly dividing into social classes—broad layers of people who shared similar experiences, ways of life, and values and who understood themselves as having interests conflicting with those of other broad social groups. These classes, of course, did not exist as material objects, but as cultural constructions. They were none the less real for that. Class identity offered one way for individuals to find their place in the industrial society that was taking shape around them. The idea that the interests of workers clashed with those of their middle-class bosses provided, for many, an appealing way to make sense of their experiences. Older ways of articulating social identity did not disappear, however. Many political radicals, for example, perceived the middle and working classes in terms of solidarity rather than conflict: "the People," who stood against "the Privileged," the hereditary landed elite. Moreover, the social hierarchies and status ladders that, as we have seen, structured eighteenth-century society, remained intact, still useful ways of articulating social experience and organizing social relationships. As the nineteenth century progressed, however, *class* increasingly pushed these other social perceptions aside. The story of Britain in the nineteenth century is the story of the emergence of a class society.

At the top of this emerging class society stood the landed class. One might think that the aristocracy and gentry could not flourish in the new world of industries, towns, and class conflict, but in the short run they did. British landowners enjoyed high rental income in the first half of the nineteenth century, and they also benefited both from their investments in industry and from the vast increase in the price of real estate they owned in and around the big cities. Landowners frequently cooperated with developers to make large profits on new urban housing districts. The dukes of Bedford, Portland, and Westminster, for example, each received more than £50,000 a year (the equivalent of about $7.5 million today) from ground rents in London. As late as the 1880s, more than half of the wealthiest men in Britain got their money from land. Of course, not all the landowners were so wealthy. Nevertheless, the aristocracy—some three hundred families headed by dukes, marquesses, earls, viscounts, and barons—all owned more than ten thousand acres and enjoyed at least £10,000 a year. All had palatial country homes and large, elegantly decorated townhouses in London. Most owned hunting lodges as well.

The landed gentry, of which there were about three thousand families, owned between one thousand and ten thousand acres and earned £1,000 to £10,000 a year. Their fine homes dappled the countryside: handsome halls, often in the Gothic style, with upward of twenty rooms. Each was set in a fine park and maintained by a platoon of stewards, housekeepers, gamekeepers, cooks, gardeners, grooms, stable boys, chambermaids, and scullery girls, all arranged in a self-contained social hierarchy, all arranged in a self-contained social hierarchy.

Life in these country houses was extremely pleasant for the landed gentlemen and their families. Aristocrats and country gentlemen alike, as well as their wives and daughters, shunned work as demeaning to high status. Being a gentleman (or lady) meant inheriting the bloodlines of fine families, but it also meant inheriting wealth, most of it based on landed property. Having inherited his income, the landowner could occupy himself in pleasurable pursuits: visiting and entertaining the neighbors; reading in his library; walking and riding in the garden and park; and above all, indulging in field sports. Many landowners spent nearly all their waking hours fishing, shooting, horse racing, and fox hunting. Field sports seemed to celebrate the military virtues of courage and prowess that had once been essential to the feudal nobility.

Landowners spent vast sums on maintaining hunting preserves and keeping sporting horses and dogs. Fox hunting in particular became a well-organized and highly ritualized sport for the Victorian aristocracy and gentry. By custom, the rural districts of Britain were divided into territories (or "countries") hunted by particular groups of landowners. Each hunt country was designated by the pack of foxhounds kept in it: the Belvoir, the Beaufort, the Durham County, and so on. Sometimes one landowner carried the heavy expense of maintaining the hunt servants and pack of hounds, but in many places the hunt was sustained by subscription. In either case, the fox hunters claimed the right of access to all land in the area, as well as protection of the foxes for them alone to kill. In those areas where tenant farmers joined the hunt, the hunt meetings expressed the coherence of country life. Often, however, tenants could only stand by to see their crops trampled by the horses and hounds, in which case the hunt revealed the true inequalities of landed society.

When the landed gentleman was not engaged in field sports, he was apt to be involved in public service. Disinterested service to local society as justice of the peace (JP), overseer of the Poor Law, officer of the yeomanry, patron of the parish church, and supporter of village charities was thought to be the privilege and obligation of the landed proprietors. Until the last decade of the century, the landed gentry kept local government in their own hands throughout the rural districts. As one description of a widely admired gentleman shows, the "manly" virtues of hunting and the selfless virtues of public service formed the ideal of the country landlord:

> His character—personal appearance and habits—impetuosity of temper— generosity of disposition—skill in games and sport—kindness to animals and liberality to his servants—his strong sense of justice—high character as Master of Hounds, and as a daring horseman—testimony of his contemporaries.

This notion of the ideal gentleman was part of a revived aristocratic ideology. Although some landowners abandoned paternalism and adopted political economy following the anxiety-ridden years of the French Revolution, others in the landed orders rehabilitated their belief in a hierarchical society and paternal care for the poor. In the interests of patriarchal order and social coherence, they explicitly criticized the individualistic social ideals of utilitarianism and political economy. As one aristocratic writer put it, Tory principles, "while they maintain the due order and proportion of each separate rank in society, maintain also that protection and support are the right of all." This vision inspired, and was inspired by, a romantic nostalgia for medieval England. It set high store by the Church of England as the conscience of the state, a view best expressed by Coleridge in his *On the Constitution of Church and State* (1830). It also revitalized the chivalric idea of the gentleman. One group of Tory paternalists, including the future prime minister, Benjamin Disraeli, went so far as to articulate a new feudalism. This *Young England* movement of the 1840s not only argued on behalf of a natural alliance between aristocracy and poor, but also tried to revive medieval pageantry, including jousting in full armor!

In early Victorian Britain, the professions were satellites of the aristocracy and gentry. Initially, there were only four recognized professions: military/naval service, the church, law, and medicine. Over time, the number of occupations accepted as professions grew. In each case, the professionals regarded disinterested service rather than personal profit as their social ideal. The older professions, especially the officer corps of the military and the Anglican clergy, were recruited from the younger sons of the landed families. The officer corps thus tended to be arrogant and bold but, at least in the army, not technically proficient. The Anglican clergy closely identified with their landlord patrons. Indeed, the Church of England was regarded as "the Tory party at prayer." The squire and the parson often were the dominant figures in rural society.

Yet the Church of England was changing. Evangelicalism infected High and Low Churchmen alike with a sense of seriousness and emotional commitment. Indeed, the new vitality of both the High and Low Church positions caused considerable tension in the parishes. Both despised the easygoing, liberal latitudinarians, but Low Churchmen wanted to see more evidence of emotional fervor and personal morality, whereas High Churchmen wanted to revive religiosity by returning to traditional rituals, ceremonies, and vestments. Both sides made the ordinary broad-shouldered, fox-hunting squire very uneasy. Most English gentlemen took religion as a matter of social propriety and habit, an institution to be observed but not to be thought deeply about.

The educational institutions of the aristocracy and gentry were shaped by the fact that these social orders still formed a hereditary ruling elite. Elite schools and universities needed to give no training for an occupation, but rather social polish and habits of authority. Most boys from the landed class went to one of the nine famous "public" schools—private boarding schools such as Eton, Harrow, and Winchester. (Public schools for girls sprang up after mid-century.) The school curriculum consisted almost exclusively of lessons in Latin and Greek language and literature—*the classics*. More practical subjects were despised as *utilitarian*, fit only for boys going into trade. Sports such as distance running, football, and cricket were as important as scholarship, for they taught character and self-discipline. Studies were not the highest priority. As Thomas Arnold, the most famous public school headmaster, said, "What we must look for . . . is 1st, religious and moral principles; 2ndly, gentlemanly conduct; 3rdly, intellectual ability."

A university education was not necessary for the sons of the landed elite, but it was often thought to be desirable. Oxford and Cambridge were extremely expensive, and they remained the only English universities until the University of London was founded in 1836. Scotland's four universities were more accessible to young men of modest wealth, but Oxford and Cambridge were by far the most prestigious institutions of higher education in Britain by dint of their rich tradition and their connection with the Church of England. They were partly seminaries and partly advanced finishing schools for boys from landed and professional families. Many of the aristocratic youths who attended Oxford or Cambridge never bothered to sit for examinations or to take a degree. Of the students who did earn the BA, a majority went into the clergy. The teaching faculty of the universities—the college tutors—had to be ordained ministers of the Church of England, and most of them expected to have careers not as professional academics but as parish priests. Consequently, the *Oxbridge atmosphere* reflected the lackadaisical attitude of the faculty and the drunken, fox-hunting extravagances of the wealthiest students.

Daughters of the aristocracy and gentry before the 1850s rarely went away to school and never to a university. They were educated at home by private tutors in such polite subjects as music, sewing, literature, and French, in preparation for the day that they would become wives, mothers, and hostesses in landed households. It was unthinkable for a woman from the landed orders to have a career. At the same time, custom gave aristocratic women considerable personal freedom. Marriage, of course, was assigned to them as their goal in life, but wealthy daughters usually came into marriage with their own money. This was settled on them by their fathers and did not become the property of the husbands. Because having their own money liberated them from complete dependence on their husbands, aristocratic wives had considerable liberty to conduct themselves as they pleased, provided that they observed the rules of public propriety. Moreover, aristocratic women were less likely than their less well-off sisters to have fallen under the sway of evangelical morality. Hence, they often considered themselves free to travel, speak, and behave as they liked, provided only that they avoided scandal.

## THE MIDDLE CLASS

Important as were the aristocracy and gentry, it was the middle class that formed the soul of Victorian Britain. "Never in any country beneath the sun," wrote one middle-class newspaper editor, "was an order of men more estimable and valuable, more praised and praiseworthy, than the middle class of society in England." Self-conscious and aggressive, middle-class men seemed bent on making Britain over in their own image. Middle-class women were every bit as important, for they shaped the homes and families and inculcated the moral virtues central to Victorianism.

The middle class grew as a proportion of the British population, from about 15 percent in 1820 to more than 20 percent in 1850—perhaps one million families, which ranged very widely in wealth. The richest bankers and commercial tycoons made as much as the wealthiest aristocrats, and the biggest industrialists only a little less. Hanging onto the bottom rung of the middle-class ladder were clerks, office workers, and shopkeepers, who earned only £100 to £150 a year. In income, these men and women of the lower middle class were not much better off than skilled artisans. For them, the struggle to maintain middle-class status was unrelenting, the minimum income for a secure middle-class existence being about £300 a year. Yet if there was a huge income gap between the richest and poorest of the middle class, all of the men shared the qualities of working for a living (but not with their hands), of intense class consciousness, and of aspiration for a "respectable" lifestyle.

The middle-class style of life required both a house and servants. Clerks and shopkeepers normally had six-room semidetached houses and a maid and could keep their wives from working outside the home. At £300 a year, the middle-class family could have an eight- to ten-room suburban house and a garden, as well as a second maid and perhaps a cook. Three servants were necessary to relieve the mother and daughters of all work in the house; this was assured at £500 a year. The middle class thus was a servant-keeping class, for servants alone made possible the gentility and propriety of home and family cherished by business and professional people.

The better-off members of the middle class aspired to the wealth and status of the landed gentry. Men who made sufficiently large fortunes typically bought estates and retired from work. Few, however, made it that far up the economic scale. For most men, work remained central to their lives, and for many of them, that work was fraught with anxiety. The cycles of boom and bust that racked the early industrial economy made them feel that disaster lay just beyond the next day's trade figures. Moreover, many industrial and commercial men had everything to lose because most businesses were family firms and because investors were liable for the losses of their firms to the full extent of their personal property. Limited liability companies were not legalized by Parliament until 1862. Given the competitiveness of early capitalism and the desire of middle-class males to rise in society, these business conditions dictated a life of hard work and self-denial. To the early Victorian bourgeois male, life was a battle in which the indecisive, the incompetent, and the unlucky lost out.

Victorian middle-class men and women alike wanted their homes to be a refuge from the harsh economic world. Indeed, they made a cult of the home and family. Where the world of trade and industry was public, competitive, and stressful, the home was to be private, supportive, and restful. Here, in the private sphere, women reigned supreme. Men assigned to their wives the task of ensuring that the household functioned smoothly to aid their daily recuperation from life's struggle. In many cases, wives in less well-off middle-class families contributed significantly to establishing their family fortunes by working in the family business. But as soon as possible women were relieved of gainful employment, and their heavy responsibilities in housework or managing a corps of servants were not seen as work at all. The fact that the husband, in theory, alone supported the family gave him irresistible authority. A revival of the patriarchal-style family was the inevitable result.

The role of women in the Victorian middle class ideally was restricted to the home and family. *Separate spheres*—the public for men and the private for women—were the generally accepted rule. Gainful employment for most middle-class women was out of the question; moreover, in England a married woman's property (including anything she brought into the marriage and any earnings) belonged to her husband. A woman was trapped in marriage even when it failed. Before the Marriage Act of 1857, divorce was impossible except by private act of Parliament. Even after 1857, women had to prove adultery *plus* bigamy, cruelty, desertion, incest, or unnatural sexual offenses to get a divorce. In addition, until the passage of the Custody of Infants Act in 1839, a woman lost access to her children if she divorced. In sexual mores as in marital law, a double standard prevailed: if a man engaged in sex outside marriage, he was thought to have offended respectability, but in an understandable and pardonable way; if a woman did likewise, her offense was beyond comprehension and unforgiveable. A "fallen woman" was ruined forever. Women were to be "undamaged goods" in a marriage; moreover, a woman was supposed to be the perfect guardian of morality—"the angel in the house."

Women were regarded as by nature passionless. As the famous nurse and medical reformer Florence Nightingale, who herself dared to remain unmarried, declared in 1851: "Women don't consider themselves as human beings at all, there is absolutely no God, no country, no duty to them at all, except family." To bear children (the average number per family being six), to rear them in morality, and to keep the home an orderly preserve for the male were the functions for which women were thought to be biologically and emotionally suited. As one preacher said, "Woman's strength lies in her essential weakness. She is at this hour what 'in the beginning' the great Creator designed her to be—namely, Man's help . . . accustomed from the first to ministrations of domestic kindness and the sweetest charities of home."

Such remarks revealed the profound religiosity of middle-class life in Victorian Britain. The evangelical revival of the late eighteenth and early nineteenth centuries reinvigorated Nonconformity and called the middle class to seriousness. Indeed, evangelicalism played a crucial role in shaping the culture that became identified as middle class. The values and outlook

Queen Victoria, Prince Albert, and Their First Five Children, *by Franz Winterhalter (1847). The domestic ideal exemplified.*

of evangelical Nonconformity became those of the Victorian middle class. To be sure, not all middle-class people were Nonconformists; some were Anglicans. Nor were all Nonconformists of the middle class; Nonconformity had a hold on certain segments of the working class. Yet the degree of overlap between the middle class and Nonconformity—Baptists, Congregationalists, Wesleyan Methodists, Quakers, Presbyterians, and Unitarians—was substantial. And Nonconformity was growing: in 1851, about half of the adult population of England and Wales attended church, and almost half of those churchgoers were Nonconformists.

Nonconformity contributed to the sturdy individualism, the moralism, and the reformist drive of the middle class. Most Nonconformist denominations emphasized the right of the individual to read the Scriptures and to establish a personal relationship with God; they also insisted on the right of individual congregations to govern themselves. As evangelicals, most Nonconformists believed that sin and the devil were everywhere and that conformity to a strict moral code was necessary to fight them. As one observer put it, in Nonconformity "pleasure is distrusted as a wile of the devil." Nonconformists frowned on drink, dancing, and the theater, and they promoted Sabbatarianism (the policy of prohibiting trade and public recreation on Sundays). Nonconformists also felt aggrieved at the disabilities they suffered at the hands of the established Church: they had to pay rates to the Church of England; they could not be buried in parish churchyards; they had to be baptized and married in Anglican ceremonies; and until 1828, the Test and Corporation Acts made them second-class citizens. In these grievances they found a substantial agenda for reform.

Education was crucial to middle-class males, both because of their belief in individualism and because of their work in commerce, industry, and, increasingly, the professions. However, Nonconformists were excluded from Oxford and Cambridge, and many middle-class families found the old public schools impractical and expensive. Some middle-class males found the education they needed—English grammar, arithmetic, history, and foreign languages—at reformed *grammar schools*, which were endowed private day schools. Most, however, were educated at various new kinds of private tuition-supported schools that sprang up to meet the demand. Many of these were little more than one-room schools set up by enterprising teachers to give a rudimentary and utilitarian training to lower middle-class boys. Others, the *proprietary schools*, were established in fine buildings, often by subscriptions from the parents. Many of them at the outset taught "modern" subjects, but they tended over time to metamorphose into imitations of the ancient public schools. In turn, many of the public schools such as Rugby opened themselves to middle-class youth. The proprietary and public schools eventually had the effect of inculcating in the sons of well-to-do commercial and industrial families something of the values and attitudes of the landed gentry. They tended to lead boys away from middle-class occupations and into the professions; yet at the same time, these same schools helped pass on some of the middle-class devotion to work and morality to the sons of the landed orders.

It is important not to overestimate the speed at which the expensive private schools diluted the drive and force of the middle class. For one thing, there were few places in such schools; in 1868, fewer than twenty thousand boys were enrolled in all public, grammar, and proprietary schools together. For another, middle-class men had a very firm and resilient set of values and social ideals—an ideology and a sense of masculinity—that they promoted at every turn. These values and ideals were rooted deeply in both the economic role and the religion of the middle class. To begin with, they valued a man by what he achieved rather than by the social stratum he was born into. They set high value on work, especially work of the entrepreneurial sort: active, enterprising, organizing, and directive work. By this measure they found the aristocracy to be idle and parasitic—"double-barreled dilettantes," in Carlyle's memorable phrase. They had a strange love-hate attitude toward the landed orders: they wanted not to destroy the aristocracy and gentry, but to take their places.

Yet middle-class males admired their own ability to get things done and despised the inherited elegance and patronage of the traditional elite. Middle-class people liked to see a constant increase in the outpouring of material goods, and they valued the entrepreneur who was responsible for it. They valued competition rather than patronage as the society's lubricant because they believed that competition maximized production and efficiency. Competition allowed the strongest individuals, businesses, institutions, and even ideas to thrive, while condemning the weak and outmoded to fall by the wayside.

A set of personal virtues followed from these values and defined "manliness." One was duty. The Victorian middle class had a strong sense of personal responsibilities that each person had a duty to fulfill. The main duty, for males at least, was to be as productive as possible and protective of females. Usefulness was a related virtue: the Victorians believed it was wrong to spend capital or energy on things or activities that were not useful to production and progress. Even art ought to be useful, by instructing, uplifting, or invigorating the mind. Thrift naturally was important because by thrift people avoided the waste of God-given talents and resources and maximized production. Similarly, prudence guided people toward the reasoned and cautious calculation of means and ends.

Perhaps the highest of all virtues for men was self-help. Middle-class Victorians idealized the self-made man, the man who independently took responsibility for making something of himself. They assumed that men could rise in life if they only would. Unfortunately, members of the middle class also tended to create a personal myth about themselves, namely that they *had* made themselves, forgetting, like Charles Dickens' famous character Josiah Bounderby, the contributions that other people and good luck made to their success. They assumed that social misery was the result of personal failings such as intemperance, imprudence, and sloth. Thus, their answer to social problems was often simply to exhort the poor to help themselves.

A very powerful political ideology derived from these middle-class values and ideals: *liberalism*. The specific content of liberalism will be examined in chapter 14. Suffice it to say here that liberalism was the great political movement of nineteenth-century Britain and that it was essentially the middle class's way of bringing Britain's social and political institutions into line with middle-class interests and values. Although the Liberal party was not founded until 1859, liberalism was at work from the early years of the century, and it operated within both the Whig and the Tory parties.

Liberals often disagreed over particular policies, but generally they believed in individualism and competition. They supported free enterprise, free trade, and free competition among religious sects. They opposed the privileges of the landed orders, though they devoutly upheld private property itself. They sought to create a free market in labor, not least by restricting or prohibiting trade unions; they also sought to spread education so as to make the individual's decisions free from ignorance and superstition. Most important, liberals wanted to reform the parliamentary system in order to make Parliament representative of the nation's reasoning individuals. Here is where Victorian ideas about gender locked liberals into a major inconsistency: women, they believed, must be excluded from the vote because they were like criminals, lunatics, and children in not being independent, self-responsible, and fully rational individuals. Otherwise, liberals generally favored extension of the franchise and codification of the laws. Individualism, utilitarianism, political economy, and evangelical Nonconformity were the taproots of liberal ideology, each growing in rich middle-class soil.

Even the monarchy conformed to middle-class values in Victorian Britain. By birth and social position, of course, Queen Victoria and her husband (and first cousin) Albert were members of the aristocracy; yet they had what was in many ways a middle-class marriage. Unlike her royal uncles with their myriads of mistresses and illegitimate children, Victoria doted on her duty-bound and serious-minded husband. Theirs was not a dual monarchy—Albert was prince regent, not king—but in the domestic affairs of the royal family, Albert possessed the supreme power. (And with Victoria frequently sidelined by pregnancy, he played an ever more dominant political role.) In an age of continental revolutions, the German-born Albert was well-aware that the position of royalty could be precarious and so he paid close attention to the public image of the royal family. Paintings and lithographs presented the queen and prince as a loving couple, fond but firm parents of an ever-expanding brood of offspring—a middle-class monarchy.

## THE EMERGING WORKING CLASS

The early Victorian laboring population was not nearly as close-knit in experience or outlook as either the landed orders or the middle class. As chapter 14 will show, class consciousness spread within the working population only in the process of political agitation. For this reason, *working classes* is at least as good a term as *working class* to denote the laboring poor down to 1850; even as late as the 1870s, several large occupational groups such as agricultural laborers and domestic servants showed few signs of class identity. Still, it is possible to speak of the working class in early Victorian Britain in the sense of denoting all those who worked with their hands—approximately 75 to 80 percent of the total population. Some of these people made as much as £100 a year, and others less than £50, but all clearly stood below the ceiling that separated them from the middle class and landed folk. They were distinct from the upper classes by income, clothing, education, accent, and personal bearing, and anyone could spot the differences.

The working class comprised three broad categories: skilled artisans, semiskilled workers, and unskilled laborers. The skilled artisans amounted to 10 to 15 percent of all workers. Most artisans were males who still set high store by the male-bonding rituals of their apprenticeship and journeyman training. Many worked in old crafts such as plastering, printing, watchmaking, and cabinetry. Others worked in trades spun off by the new industries: locomotive engineering, machine-tool engineering, and certain special kinds of textile spinning. In all cases, artisans learned their skills through long apprenticeships. They were able to control the quality of their finished products and commanded fairly high wages, perhaps £100 in a good year. Many belonged to more-or-less secret trade unions and despised the "dishonorable" (nonunion) men who degraded their craft. Almost all of the artisans were literate, and they tended to be highly class conscious and political. Together, they formed an *aristocracy of labor* and the core of the self-conscious working class.

The semiskilled workers composed a largely new group interposed between the artisans and laborers. The Industrial Revolution generated a large number of jobs for both men and women in factories and shops that required a middle level of skill at the same time as it destroyed some traditional crafts such as handloom weaving. Coal miners can be included in this category, for although coal mining was an old industry, industrialization expanded it enormously. Mining was a highly differentiated trade, with women and children doing many simple though backbreaking or mind-numbing tasks, and adult males, the hewers above all, doing work that required considerable knowledge as well as courage and stamina. Factory operatives made up the bulk of the semiskilled occupations. Most of them came from the ranks of agricultural labor. They were attracted to the factories by relatively high pay: about 30 shillings a week (£75 a year if fully employed) for seventy-two hours of hard and tedious work, as compared to 20 shillings per sixty-hour week for coal miners. Women were always paid less and generally were relegated to auxiliary tasks. All told, about 40 percent of all workers held semiskilled positions by 1850.

Below the semiskilled workers in status and earnings was the mass of unskilled laborers, about one-half of the entire working class. These were the men, women, and children who did the staggering volume of work that is today done by machines. As Professor J. F. C. Harrison has written,

> A vast amount of wheeling, dragging, hoisting, carrying, lifting, digging, tunneling, draining, trenching, hedging, embanking, blasting, breaking, scouring, sawing, felling, reaping, mowing, picking, sifting, and threshing was done by sheer muscular effort, day in, day out.[1]

Prominent among the unskilled were the *navvies* and agricultural laborers. The navvies did the physical work in building the railroads, cutting across hills, tunneling through mountains, and moving enormous amounts of earth and stone. They earned at best £1 per week as well as the reputation of being the roughest and most unruly of all workers, working, drinking, and fighting in prodigious measure. Agricultural laborers like all the unskilled were nonunionized and unable to protect their wages, and they remained the largest single occupational group even in the 1850s, as well as the worst paid. A male agricultural laborer earned on average ten shillings a week for very long hours of hard work in all weather. Sometimes the farm laborer also had a *tied cottage* provided by the farmer as part of his wage, or sometimes a patch of ground to raise vegetables or a pig. In most cases, the life was without variety, physically harsh, and psychologically stultifying. The agricultural laborer, wrote one journalist, "has grown up, and gone to service; and there he is, as simple, as ignorant, and as laborious a creature as one of the wagon-horses he drives."

Domestic service was another major occupation for the unskilled. Because of the demand for servants generated by the middle class, it was a rapidly growing industry, the second largest occupational group, and by far

---

[1]Harrison, *The Early Victorians, 1832–51*, 35

the largest for women. About 40 percent of all women in Victorian Britain were employed (not counting unpaid labor, which was the lot of most wives and mothers), and a majority of these were domestic servants: scullery girls, housemaids, nursemaids, cooks, and housekeepers. Only about one-tenth of all servants were males. Because of their isolation, their direct subordination to their employers, and their conditions of employment, domestic servants were the least class conscious of workers. Most domestics *lived in*—that is, they lived in the cellars and attics of the homes they worked in. Where a number of servants were employed, a strict hierarchy prevailed, with the housekeeper and butler at the top and the scullery girls and chambermaids standing in awe at the bottom. The work for most was hard and tedious. The domestics tended the fires, lit the lamps, carried the water, cooked the meals, washed the dishes, cleaned the clothes, and emptied the slops (flush toilets not being common until the 1850s) in middle- or upper-class homes. A butler might make as much as £50 a year, a housemaid £10 to £15, and all received bed and board as well. Employer and employee alike regarded domestic service at all but the highest levels as menial. One middle-class advice manual revealed the accepted upper-class attitude toward servants:

> It is better in addressing [servants] to use a higher key of voice, and not to suffer it to fall at the end of a sentence. . . . The perfection in manners in this particular is to indicate by your language that the performance is a favour, and by your tone that it is a matter of course.

Given such a wide variety of occupations and incomes, it is not easy to generalize about the working-class (or working classes') lifestyle in the first half of the nineteenth century. Nevertheless, some aspects of life were common to most workers. First, in the early 1800s, as in all of the past, hard work was the lot of everyone in the working class—men and women alike—except beggars, criminals, and vagrants. Children went to work at age eight or nine and became fully employable as adults at fourteen or fifteen. Everyone worked until illness or death intervened.

Second, almost all working people faced poverty at some point in their lives. Even for the better-off laboring people, much work was seasonal or part-time. Bouts of unemployment were common, and the highest wages did not allow any margin for families to save for illness and old age. Newly married couples could expect hard times when their children were too young to contribute to the family income. At age fifty, all working people could look forward to a time of declining employment and earnings and of increasing privation.

Third, education was hard to come by through the 1860s. Economic need often forced working-class parents to send children to work rather than to school. Working-class educational options were few: some private, fee-supported schools, mostly of questionable quality, set up by individual teachers; a few old charity and endowed schools; a slowly growing number of factory schools set up by philanthropic industrial captains; and above all, Sunday schools (which taught reading). By the 1850s, three-fourths of all children attended Sunday school at some point in their lives—but probably half of all British children attended no school (other than Sunday school), and of those who did, few attended for more than two or three years. Scarcely any attended past age eleven. The haphazard nature of working-class schooling was the product, in part, of upper-class attitudes. Many in the upper classes argued that schooling for working people only contributed to discontent and agitation. One scientist declared in 1807:

> However specious in theory the project might be of giving education to the labouring classes of the poor, it would in effect be prejudicial to their morals and happiness: it would teach them to despise their lot in life, instead of making them good servants to agriculture and other laborious employments to which their rank in society had destined them . . . [and] it would enable them to read seditious pamphlets, vicious books and publications against Christianity.

Slowly, however, this prejudice against working-class schooling began to diminish. Educational reformers included both utilitarians, who promoted the increase of knowledge—the *march of mind*—and evangelicals, who regarded the ability to read the Bible as essential. Both regarded education as a means of making the poor more politically docile, less vice-ridden, and more efficient. Evangelicals had the greatest impact on British working-class education. In 1808, Nonconformists founded the British and Foreign School Society to establish schools for working-class children. Alarmed, evangelicals within the Church of England set up a rival organization, the National Society, three years later. Both societies adopted the *monitorial system*, invented simultaneously by Joseph Lancaster and Andrew Bell. Economical to the extreme, the system used older children to teach the younger ones; hence, one adult teacher might be in charge of over two hundred pupils. Although not the most effective pedagogical system, it did bring schooling to the masses. When, in 1833, the government took its first step toward state provision for public education, it did so by granting the two societies £20,000. By 1850 the societies' grant amount had grown by 1,000 percent. Unfortunately, the rivalry between Anglicans and Nonconformists led to a great deal of sectarian squabbling over education and in many ways limited the state's role in providing and regulating schools.

Under the circumstances, it was remarkable that the literacy rate grew at all; yet it did. The early urban environment was destructive of literacy, just as it was of life expectancy. Nevertheless, the literacy rate by the 1840s probably rose to include two-thirds of all men and one-half of women. Almost all artisans were literate at a fairly high level. Most others who were literate probably could read at only an elementary level; they could sound out a newspaper headline or billboard, or perhaps read a simplified story. Clearly, the British working people were beginning their long march from an oral to a literate culture, but they were as yet not far along the road.

The upper classes in the early nineteenth century tried to take advantage of what literacy there was both by restricting the reading matter available to the working class and by flooding them with cheap literature designed to entertain them and to make them reliable, sober, and moralistic. Generally speaking, the British state did not resort to censorship to control reading materials, though it did prosecute some radicals for blasphemy and sedition. The main instruments of control were a tax of four pence on each newspaper sheet and taxes on printed advertising. These made newspapers much too expensive for working men. William Cobbett got around these heavy *taxes on knowledge* by publishing his *Political Register* as a pamphlet; however, the taxes remained a significant obstacle until they were repealed in 1854–55.

Meanwhile, the upper classes made respectable reading widely available. The Society for the Propagation of Christian Knowledge published tracts, pamphlets, and penny magazines to evangelize the poor. Middle-class businessmen established mechanics institutes in the industrial cities to offer useful knowledge and lessons in self-help to workers. The utilitarians in the 1820s founded the Society for the Diffusion of Useful Knowledge to promote the march of mind. On the whole, such efforts to indoctrinate working people did not succeed, mainly because the upper classes in their writings failed to show a sympathetic understanding of working-class problems. Working-class men and women preferred their own commercialized literature to the cheap moralistic tracts produced for them by the upper classes. As Professor R. K. Webb has written, the poor preferred "to hammer out their own society, their own culture."[2]

---

[2]Webb, *The British Working Class Reader, 1790–1848,* 162.

It is extremely difficult to say how religion fit into this working-class culture. Clearly, the evangelical revival stopped the decline in religious affiliation that was so characteristic of the eighteenth century, and Methodism (particularly Primitive Methodism) won a strong hold on working people, especially the artisanal ranks. The Church of England was unable (or unwilling) to keep up with the growth of the urban working-class population, for it was simply too bound up with the landed social orders. Only the Nonconformist denominations and Roman Catholicism grew faster than the population itself. In 1840, probably 60 percent of all Nonconformists were from the working class, as were nearly all the Catholics, who were by then largely Irish immigrants. But even Nonconformity had little luck in attracting semiskilled or unskilled urban laborers. Nonconformity could express the aspirations of fairly well-off and literate skilled workers; it gave them a measure of community and a legitimate means of rejecting traditional society. Yet it had little appeal for workers of no independence or hope. Of the half of the adult British populace who attended no church at all in 1851, nearly all were of the working class.

The churches' campaign against traditional popular pastimes and for the spread of *rational recreation* no doubt alienated some of these workers. Evangelicals (and middle-class people in general) strove to put down fairs, animal baiting, and cock fighting on the grounds that such activities encouraged immoral and irrational behavior. Their attempts to replace these popular recreations with much more sober and "improving" activities such as cricket, choral groups, and brass bands did not always meet with a warm welcome in working-class communities.

The evangelical war on drink struck most aggressively at the emerging working-class culture. The consumption of alcohol, especially beer, was a principal feature of working-class life, and in the cities the pub and the beerhouse were central institutions of working-class districts. The pubs offered a warm and attractive alternative to cold and dismal working-class homes; moreover, alcohol was "the quickest way out of Manchester." Working-class families frequently spent a third of their incomes on drink. In the 1870s beer consumption alone amounted to thirty-four gallons per person per year. Evangelical temperance reformers campaigned against drink, insisting that it was the main social problem of the day. They had some success in establishing temperance clubs and recruiting working-class teetotalers, and in some places they succeeded in polarizing the populace into *church* and *pub* camps. Pubs, however, remained the centers of working-class leisure, providing relaxation, conviviality, handy meeting rooms, and diversions such as pub sports, gambling, and popular entertainment.

Finally, the working-class style of life included a variety of attempts to preserve and reconstruct *community*—a pattern of face-to-face relations and mutual support among people with similar interests and experiences. One way was for families to maintain their integrity and their connection with kin-groups, even in the move from the country to the city. As village communities were broken down, families sought with limited success to rent housing near each other in town, to find employment for each other, and to lend and borrow in seasons of financial trouble.

Another way was to form trade unions. Trade combinations had originated in the early eighteenth century and proliferated during the Triple Revolution, but only among artisans and only on the local level. Many cotton spinners (again, on the local level), the first factory workers to organize, had formed unions by 1815. Though formally outlawed by the Combination Acts of 1799 and 1800, trade unions continued to spread among skilled workers as they acted to protect their wages and status from technological change and dishonorable labor. Sometimes, as we have seen in chapter 10, union activity alternated with Luddism. The unions' struggle to repeal the Combination Laws and to form national organizations we will explore in chapter 14. Suffice it to say here that unions, though they included a very small proportion of the whole working population and almost always excluded women, did offer an expression and a support for artisans' sense of community.

The *friendly societies* such as the Foresters and the Oddfellows also promoted the artisans' sense of community. These mutual-aid clubs, some of which also had trade union functions, collected weekly dues from the members and in return gave sickness and burial benefits. A workingman typically contributed a few pennies a week to buy insurance against pauperdom. As early as 1803, there were some 9,600 friendly societies with 700,000 members; by 1872, there were more than 32,000 societies with more than 4 million members. True, the friendly societies taught to the working class the bourgeois lessons of prudence and self-help, but they also offered working men and women opportunities for conviviality and belonging through their ceremonies and monthly meetings. This was an important prop to community in the otherwise atomizing urban environment.

### Suggested Reading
Arnstein, Walter L. *Queen Victoria*. New York: Palgrave Macmillan, 2003.
Beckett, J. V. *The Aristocracy in England, 1660–1914*. Oxford: Blackwell, 1986.

Brown, Callum. *Religion and Society in Scotland Since 1707*. Edinburgh: Edinburgh University Press, 1997.

————. *The Death of Christian Britain: Understanding Secularisation 1800-2000*. London: Routledge, 2001.

Brown, Stuart J. *The National Churches of England, Ireland, and Scotland, 1801–1846*. New York: Oxford University Press, 2001.

Burnett, John, ed. *Annals of Labour: Autobiographies of British Working-Class People, 1820–1920*. Bloomington: Indiana University Press, 1974.

Cannadine, David. *Lords and Landlords: The Aristocracy and the Towns, 1770–1967*. Leicester, UK: Leicester University Press, 1980.

————. *The Rise and Fall of Class in Britain*. New York: Columbia University Press, 1999.

Clark, Anna. *The Struggle for the Breeches: Gender and the Making of the British Working Class*. Berkeley: University of California Press, 1995.

Davidoff, Leonore, and Catherine Hall. *Family Fortunes: Men and Women of the English Middle Class, 1780–1850*. Chicago: University of Chicago Press, 1987.

Evans, Eric J. *The Forging of the Modern State: Early Industrial Britain, 1783–1870*, 2nd ed. London: Longman, 1996.

Floud, Roderick, and Donald McCloskey. *The Economic History of Britain Since 1700*. Vol. I, *1700–1860*, 2nd ed. New York: Cambridge University Press, 1994.

Golby, J. M., and A. W. Purdue. *The Civilisation of the Crowd: Popular Culture in England, 1750–1900*. New York: Schocken Books, 1985.

Harrison, J. F. C. *The Early Victorians, 1832–51*. New York: Praeger, 1971.

Himmelfarb, Gertrude *The Idea of Poverty: England in the Early Industrial Age*. New York: Knopf, 1984.

Jones, Gareth Stedman. *Languages of Class: Studies in English Working Class History, 1832–1982*. New York: Cambridge University Press, 1984.

Joyce, Patrick. *Visions of the People: Industrial England and the Question of Class, 1840–1914*. Cambridge: Cambridge University Press, 1990.

Knight, Frances. *The Nineteenth-Century Church and English Society*. Cambridge: University of Cambridge Press, 1998.

Koditschek, Theodore. *Class Formation and Urban-Industrial Society: Bradford, 1750–1850*. Cambridge: Cambridge University Press, 1990.

McLeod, Hugh. *Religion and the Working Class in Nineteenth-Century Britain*. London: Macmillan, 1984.

Perkin, Harold. *The Origins of Modern English Society, 1780–1880*. Toronto: University of Toronto Press, 1969.

Peterson, M. Jeanne. *Family, Love, and Work in the Lives of Victorian Gentlewomen*. Bloomington: Indiana University Press, 1989.

Price, Richard. *Labour in British Society: An Interpretive History*. London: Croom Helm, 1986.

Robb, George. *White-Collar Crime in Modern England: Financial Fraud and Business Morality*. New York: Cambridge University Press, 1992.

Rose, Sonya O. *Limited Livelihoods: Gender and Class in Nineteenth-Century England*. Berkeley: University of California Press, 1992.

Rule, John. *The Labouring Classes In Early Industrial England, 1750–1850*. New York: Longman, 1986.

Thompson, E. P. *The Making of the English Working Class*. London: Victor Gollancz, 1963.

Thompson, F. M. L. *English Landed Society in the Nineteenth Century*. London: Routledge & Kegan Paul, 1963.

Tosh, John. *A Man's Place: Masculinity and the Middle-Class Home in Victorian England*. New Haven, CT: Yale University Press, 1999.

Wahrman, Dror, *Imagining the Middle Class*. Cambridge: Cambridge University Press, 1995.

Webb, R. K. *The British Working Class Reader, 1790–1848*. London: Allen & Unwin, 1955.

# Chapter 14

# Politics and the State, 1815–1850

The structure of British politics and the nature of the state were remade during the first half of the nineteenth century. A wider franchise, a more equal representation of the people, and a more efficient government service were the results. These developments have given to the period labels such as the Age of Improvement and the Age of Progress. Improvements did not, however, come about by the steady unfolding of a progressive consensus. Instead, the process of change was a matter of conflict and compromise among the three social classes into which British society was hardening.

This is not to say that every issue that arose within the world of parliamentary politics can be understood in terms of class analysis, for Parliament remained largely in the hands of the landed elite. But if *politics* is construed broadly to include extra-parliamentary movements, then the idea of class conflict alone can make sense of it. In fact, political conflict helped form class consciousness. Power was at stake: both the middle class and the emerging working class wanted to remake the political structure and formulate the state agenda according to their own interests, whereas the landed class sought to retain its political control. The conflict among the classes brought Britain repeatedly to the brink of chaos, and as late as 1848 it was not clear that the nation would successfully address its social and political problems without revolution.

## THE STRUCTURE OF POLITICS AND THE SCOPE OF THE STATE IN 1815

The oligarchical constitution remained almost intact in 1815. Despite the waves of war and social change that threatened to engulf the country, Parliament remained an exclusive gathering of property owners returned to Westminster by inheritance and a tiny electorate. The House of Lords consisted of titled nobility—approximately three hundred great landlords, and only men of wealth and leisure could afford to sit in the House of Commons: all MPs had to meet a steep property qualification, and most faced the expense of elections and the cost of maintaining themselves in London during the parliamentary *season*. Most MPs were landowners, though very rich businessmen could sometimes "buy" a small borough seat, and talented intellectuals occasionally earned nomination by borough patrons. Defenders of the unreformed constitution saw these features of the political structure as advantages: "It is the very absence of symmetry in our elective franchises which admits of the introduction to this House of classes so various." As one might expect, the cabinets drawn from such a Parliament were predominantly aristocratic.

The electorate for the House of Commons was very small and irrationally defined. Only in the counties, where *forty-shilling freeholders* had the vote, was there any regularity. Because many of these freeholders were in fact tenant farmers, they were subject to the influence of their landlords, and because county electoral contests were rare, the freeholder electorate exercised less independence than one might think. In the boroughs, the electorates varied from all male householders in a few places to owners of a handful of particular properties in others. More than half of the English boroughs had fewer than 300 voters; upward of 250 borough MPs were simply named by great property owners. In all, perhaps 500,000 men in England and Wales had the vote—about 1 in 42 of the total population. An even smaller proportion in Scotland and Ireland could vote. Moreover, given the ancient and obsolete distribution of seats, most of the new industrial towns went without representation, whereas a patch of turf like Old Sarum returned two members.

One important set of changes had occurred: the political influence of the Crown had declined since the 1780s. During the war against the French Revolution, stricter parliamentary controls over government contracts, revenues, appropriations, and accounting had eroded the Crown's ability to buy support during elections. Only the right to distribute honors such as knighthoods and peerages remained unaltered, but there were not enough honors for this to be a politically important privilege. The decline of the power of the Crown entailed a decline in the power of the executive over the House of Commons. Increasingly, cabinets regarded themselves as responsible to Parliament and not to the monarch, but they had little power with which to construct and maintain a majority.

Parliament, therefore, remained an unrepresentative institution. The most significant level of government in the ordinary lives of the people was local, and local government was still in the hands of wealthy landowners and municipal oligarchies. The role of the central government remained confined to external affairs, taxation, and public order despite the onset of urgent, nationwide social problems. The British state was, compared to those in France, Prussia, or Russia, small and passive. As late as the 1820s, there were fewer than thirty thousand government employees, most of whom worked in the tax-collecting departments. The Home Office had a staff of seventeen and the Colonial Office only fourteen. Moreover, these public officials were often incompetent, chosen as they were for their connections rather than their ability.

## POLITICAL REFORM, 1815–1835

This was a structure of politics and government calculated to drive both middle class and working class to distraction. Middle-class men resented their exclusion from local and national government, and they disliked the unsystematic and inefficient character of the legal system, government service, and parliamentary structure. For their part, working-class activists found the government unresponsive to the needs of the common people because it neither protected customary ways of life nor defended standards of living. Both sets of reformers aimed to make the government more responsible to the people. Differing class interests, however, made it difficult for reformers to work together and so diminished their effectiveness.

Reform-minded people in addition faced the huge problem of how to move an unreformed Parliament to reform itself as well as the other institutions of government. A few radicals believed that revolution was the only way; hence, there was an elusive and fragmentary revolutionary impulse that protruded at critical moments right down to 1848. Most reformers, however, including nearly all those from the middle class, refused to countenance violence. For them, persuasion and pressure by a mobilized *public opinion*, expressed mainly by newspapers, petitions, and pressure groups, were the only acceptable tactics.

Not all members of the landed elite stood opposed to any change to the existing order. The call for administrative reform attracted significant support from both Whigs and Tories. Whigs such as Sir Samuel Romilly and Sir James Mackintosh joined Benthamites and Tory humanitarians in working for rationalization of the legal code. They focused on the vast number of crimes punishable by death because they wanted to make the law less savage and more efficient. Tories of the Pittite tradition serving in Lord Liverpool's ministry (1812–27) were open to this type of liberalizing influence. In particular, the Home secretary, Sir Robert Peel (son of a wealthy textile manufacturer), brought to his office a powerful impulse toward high-minded administrative professionalism. Peel (1788–1850) consolidated the criminal code, abolished fees and perquisites for judges, began the reform of prisons, drastically cut the number of criminal offenses, and in 1829 established the London police—the first professional police force in Britain (nicknamed "bobbies" because of Peel's first name).

Administrative reform was one thing, however, and political reform was another. The Tories, including Liverpool, Peel, and the hero of Waterloo—the duke of Wellington—insisted that the British Parliament provided the best government in the world. They believed that Parliament represented all the legitimate interests of the country; that it gave due weight to property owners, who were the most stable and wisest segment of the population; and that political reform would lead to "unmanly" subservience of Parliament to an irresponsible electorate that was bent on the pillaging of property.

Advocacy of political reform from within the elite was left to the Foxite Whigs, a small faction remaining from the large parliamentary party of the 1770s and early 1780s. These Whigs were loyal to the memory of Charles James Fox and to the defense of liberty established, they believed, in 1688. Largely excluded from office since 1783, the Foxite Whigs argued that the Crown (and therefore the executive) exerted undue influence over Parliament. Hence, they sought to reduce government patronage even more, as well as to defend civil liberties. They also favored granting full citizenship for Nonconformists and Catholics, on grounds of religious liberty.

In the first three decades of the nineteenth century, the Foxite Whigs gradually took up the cause of parliamentary reform. As they did so, other Whig factions shifted over to the Tory ranks, leaving the Foxites as custodians of the Whig banner. The Foxite motives were threefold: first, having been out of government for more than thirty years, they came to believe that reform was an issue they could ride into office; second, they realized that reform would strengthen the House of Commons against the executive; and third, they thought that moderate reform could alone head off a dangerous alliance between respectable and radical reformers outside Parliament. They feared revolution as much as the Tories, but as one Whig wrote in 1810, they hoped parliamentary reform would "temper" the extra-parliamentary agitation "till it can be guided in safety to the defense, and not to the destruction of our liberties."

The respectable reformers the Whigs had in mind were those of the middle class. For example, Lord John Russell, a leading Whig, recalled that what had converted him to reform in the 1820s was his recognition that "the middle class, as compared with the corresponding body in the previous century, had risen in wealth, and intelligence and knowledge, and influence." Middle-class people wholeheartedly agreed with this assessment, for it was the view put forward by powerful new provincial newspapers such as the *Manchester Guardian* and the *Leeds Mercury*. "Never in any country beneath the sun [wrote Edward Baines of the *Leeds Mercury*] was an order of men more estimable and valuable, more praised and praiseworthy, than the middle class of society in England." Middle-class Nonconformists thought that they deserved a share of power in local government, and men of property believed that their interests should count in national policy. Middle-class reformers also contended that the long continuation of the war against Napoleon, the Orders in Council (1812), and above all the Corn Law (1815) discriminated against commerce and industry on behalf of the narrow interests of the landlords. Increasingly, middle-class men agreed with Bentham that the individual knew his own interests better than any oligarchy and therefore that a more representative system would ensure that Parliament reflected the views of the people.

Radical reform—that is, universal manhood suffrage—was to most middle-class people out of the question. What they wanted was enfranchisement of responsible and independent males. These could best be chosen by a property qualification. As we have seen, they typically believed that women, like children, were either dependent or irresponsible and consequently not eligible for the vote. But all adult males of substantial property, regardless of their religion, should have the right to vote and to hold office.

The politically active members of the working class, however, tended to favor more extreme proposals harking back to the radicalism of the early 1790s. Leaders of popular radicalism who themselves were not of working-class origins—men like William Cobbett, Sir Francis Burdett, and Major John Cartwright—agitated for the old program of household suffrage (giving the vote to who owned or rented property at a certain value), annual Parliaments, and equal electoral districts. Working men and women typically went further, taking up the cry of universal manhood suffrage, especially when the end of war in 1815 brought severe economic depression. For them, democracy was the prerequisite to protection from the twin evils of depression and industrial exploitation.

The popular reform movement, therefore, was one part of a broad range of working-class responses to hard times. Luddism and agrarian rioting were, as we have seen, widespread in 1811–12 and again in 1816. Trade unions proliferated as artisans organized to protect their standards of living and control over their crafts. Union growth was especially rapid after the Combination Laws were repealed in 1824. There were even attempts to form national unions in the late 1820s and early 1830s. Working people also resorted to petitions to Parliament, addresses to magistrates, and strikes against employers, all of which were ominously widespread between 1810 and 1830. Workers tended to oscillate between one or another of these activities and the parliamentary reform agitation, depending on the immediate circumstances.

Socialist ideas and organizations also began to spread among literate workers between 1815 and 1830. Here the unifying concept was simply that capitalism itself caused the hardships of the working class. Utopian industrialist Robert Owen (1771–1858), for instance, put forward the view that cooperation ought to replace competition, for competition among workers forced wages down and kept consumption unnaturally low. Owen believed that human nature was malleable and that institutional change could nurture cooperative instincts. Thus, he advocated the establishment of utopian cooperative communities. Many Owenites went so far as to advocate ending patriarchal power in marriage and votes for women. Other socialists, such as Thomas Hodgskin, emphasized that labor is the source of all value and therefore that profit is unearned and unjustifiable.

All of these popular responses to economic and social hardship tended to raise and spread class consciousness among working people, as did the oppressive reaction of the authorities. The repeal of the Combination Laws had been expected to reduce trade union activity, but when it did not, the government in 1825 imposed strong sanctions against union activities that could be seen as restraining trade. Moreover, as six agricultural laborers in Dorset (the Tolpuddle martyrs) were to discover in 1833, the government could use old statutes forbidding the taking of oaths in its battle against unionization. The government also waged war against the *unstamped* popular press in the 1830s. Parliament ignored popular petitions and the government broke up mass meetings, sometimes by force. In 1819, for instance, the local magistrates and yeomanry scattered a peaceful gathering of about sixty thousand people in St. Peter's Fields, Manchester. In this infamous Peterloo Massacre, eleven people were killed, and later that same year Parliament passed the Six Acts to reinforce magistrates against public meetings and to strengthen the laws against unstamped publications.

These efforts at repression only increased the number of working people who associated their troubles with the belief that the government was corrupt. This tradition, dating back to the old Tory and country Whig ideology of the early 1700s, was the key to the popular reform movement. Working people who suffered from industrial and demographic change and from downturns in the business cycle concluded that their difficulties arose because the oligarchy was inefficient and extravagant. On this point, middle-class and working-class radicals could agree, at least in certain localities. In Birmingham and Sheffield, for example, small workshops with close relations between masters and working-class people formed the main pattern in manufacturing. There, political cooperation between middle-class and working-class activists was possible. In cotton towns such as Manchester and Leeds, however, where great spinning mills set the pattern for industrial relations, the clash of middle-class and working-class interests made political cooperation impossible.

In any case, pressure on the old constitution was intense by the latter 1820s. The first part of the old system to crumble under the stress was the Anglican monopoly. By 1827, most politicians agreed that the Test and Corporation Acts were of symbolic value only. The Whigs were united in favor of repealing them, and Nonconformist pressure from outside Parliament was very strong. The Tory government (now led by Wellington, who cared little about religion) saw no reason to resist. Parliament in 1828 abolished the acts with little dispute.

Giving full political rights to Roman Catholics was more controversial. Many Protestants equated the admission of Catholics to Parliament and other high office with rejection of the very principles of the Reformation and the settlement of 1688–89. The Whigs favored emancipation of Catholics, but public opinion remained hotly anti-Catholic. In retrospect, it seems clear that, if England, Wales, and Scotland alone had been consulted, then Catholics would not have received emancipation until much later in the century. But, as chapter 15 will show, Ireland was intensely concerned with the issue. Irish Catholics, mobilized by a nationalist leader of unparalleled oratorical power, Daniel O'Connell, fought hard for emancipation. O'Connell, himself a Catholic, won a by-election in 1828 and thereby presented the Wellington government with a stark choice between Catholic emancipation or civil war in Ireland. Wellington and Peel, both of them hard-headed realists, opted for Catholic emancipation, and it was passed in 1829.

Catholic emancipation, so innocuous to the English-speaking world of the twenty-first century, spelled the end of the Tory government, and thus indirectly it made parliamentary reform immediately possible. Ultra-Protestant Tories did not forgive Wellington and Peel for "betraying" Anglican interests and withdrew their support from the Tory government. A general election in 1830, necessitated by the death of King George IV, coincided with news of fresh revolution in France. Discussions of reform intensified. At the same time, another downturn in the economy and a sharp increase in food prices roused public agitation. Finally, in November 1830, the beleaguered Tory government resigned, and a successor was formed by the Whig Lord Grey (1764–1845). This grand Foxite earl had long believed in parliamentary reform, on the grounds that the antiquated constitutional machinery had to be brought into line with new economic and social realities if aristocratic rule, which he cherished, was to be saved.

In the circumstances of 1830–31, Grey believed that the extra-parliamentary reform movement was dangerous and could be pacified only by passage of a substantial measure. He and his allies thought that the number of county members, widely regarded as independent and incorruptible, had to be enlarged; the new towns had to be given representation; pocket boroughs had to be abolished; and a uniform borough franchise had to replace all the existing irregular franchises. By this combination of provisions, the middle class would be co-opted, Parliament strengthened, and landed power ultimately preserved. As Grey put it, the middle class had become the "real and efficient mass of public opinion . . . without whom the power of the gentry is nothing."

The bill proposed in 1831 by Grey's ministry was therefore bolder than most people had expected. It succeeded in attracting the support of middle-class reformers and even some of the popular radicals. Some working-class democrats argued that the reform bill was a cruel disappointment because it offered nothing to working men; however, others saw it as a stepping stone to further reform. This debate within working-class circles was fierce during the spring and summer of 1831, but when the House of Lords rejected the bill in October 1831, radical opinion tended to consolidate behind it. There were spontaneous outbreaks of violence in a number of towns. Even some middle-class radicals, including Benthamites such as James Mill and his friend, the radical tailor Francis Place, seemed to countenance armed rebellion. The threat of revolution was probably exaggerated in aristocratic minds, but it was decisive. Wellington was unable to form an alternative government to Grey's, so King William IV had to promise Grey to create enough pro-reform peers to pass the bill through the upper house. The Lords preferred even reform to dilution of their ranks and therefore gave way. The reform bill became law in June 1832: the Great Reform Act.

To complete the account of constitutional reform, it is necessary to jump ahead to 1835, when the Municipal Corporations Act was passed. This act did at the local level what the Reform Act of 1832 did at the national level: it opened the corridors of power to middle-class men, including above all the Nonconformists. The Municipal Corporations Act (and a similar one for Scotland) substituted a structure of broadly elected town councils for the oligarchical borough corporations. The counties continued to be ruled by appointed officials, mainly drawn from the gentry, but the towns were now in the hands of the business and professional people who swarmed into local office and occupied themselves with making municipal bureaucracies and services more businesslike and efficient. Eventually, their work would have a great effect on the quality of life in the towns.

## THE STRUCTURE OF POLITICS AFTER 1832

The structure of politics established by the Reform Act of 1832 (and by similar separate acts for Scotland and Ireland) changed many political practices, but it also left much of the old system in place. The Irish Reform Act retained a very high property qualification established by the Catholic Emancipation Act in 1829. In England, Wales, and Scotland, however, the Reform Acts made essentially two types of changes. First, they abolished many tiny *rotten* boroughs and redistributed those seats to the more populous constituencies, mainly the industrial towns. In England and Wales, for instance, eighty-six boroughs lost all or half their seats, and forty-two new boroughs were created. Second, the acts imposed a uniform property qualification for the vote in all boroughs: any male occupying a household worth £10 a year. In the counties the 40-shilling freehold franchise was kept, but farmers who held tenancies worth £50 a year were added as a sop to the landowners, who presumably would be able to browbeat them. Altogether about eight hundred thousand men had the vote after 1832—about a 60-percent increase, though still only about one in thirty of the population (or one-seventh of adult males).

The reforms of 1832 therefore did not create a democracy. Women still could not vote. A number of boroughs still had fewer than two hundred voters, and perhaps sixty more boroughs were small enough to be in the pocket of a big proprietor. The landlords still influenced the way that their tenants voted in the counties. Corruption, in the form of bribery or treating voters to lavish food and drink, remained the style in many constituencies. The £10 household franchise was meant to be a rough-and-ready means of including the middle class while excluding the working class, and it accomplished its purpose fairly well. Its precise effect varied from borough to borough because economic conditions and pay rates differed from one place to another, but only in a few places did the working-class voters amount to a majority of the electorate. In most big cities such as Manchester, Birmingham, and Leeds, workers composed no more than 10 to 20 percent of the voters.

In such conditions, deference remained a major factor in determining how a vote was cast. Tenants tended to vote with their landlords, tradesmen with their patrons, and in some cases, industrial workers with their factory owners, especially where the masters adopted paternalist attitudes toward their men. Nor was Parliament flooded with businessmen. The hold of the landed elite was only slowly eroded, and not until the 1880s did the number of middle-class MPs approach a majority. Industrial and commercial men, as we will see, made their weight felt in other ways.

Nevertheless, the structural changes worked by the 1832 reforms were extremely important. By both the terms of the acts and the process by which they were passed, the balance in the constitution was shifted toward the House of Commons, which was now clearly attached to public opinion. In the boroughs, public opinion spoke through the voice of middle-class newspapers, journals, and pressure groups. Further, the decline of the influence of the Crown meant that governments had less ability than before to command a majority in the House of Commons. If organized, a majority could determine who would form the government. Inevitably, then, stronger party groupings emerged in Parliament, and in terms of enabling a ministry to get its work done, the parties took the place of patronage.

The parties were also strengthened outside Parliament as an unintended consequence of the 1832 reforms. The Reform Acts established a system of voter registration for the first time, and the constituency registers became the key to electoral success. Both Whigs and Tories (or Liberals and Conservatives, as they became) found that they had to employ professionals, usually solicitors, to maximize their own registrations and minimize their opponents'. Local party organizations sprang up to defend party electoral interests. In London, two great political clubs were founded to coordinate national electoral activities: the Carlton Club (1832) for the Tories and the

Sir Robert Peel, *by H. W Pickersgill. Peel was Conservative prime minister in 1835 and from 1841 to 1846. The model of public spirit and probity, Peel carried repeal of the Corn Law in 1846.*

Reform Club (1836) for the Whigs and other reformers. The club secretaries pushed local organizations into action and suggested parliamentary candidates to them. Thus, extra-parliamentary party organizations were established for the first time in Britain; although they could not dictate policy to the MPs, who cherished their independence, they formed important bridges between the voters and their representatives.

Meanwhile, the fluid alignments of parliamentary politicians called Tories and Whigs began to coalesce into firmer, more broad-based groupings called Conservatives and Liberals. The new alignments reflected the widespread sense among active politicians that because of the new political structures the policies and institutions of society would be questioned in a direct and forceful way. Catholic emancipation and the reforms of 1832 had unsettled the Tory parliamentary faction, and only the clear ascendancy of Sir Robert Peel pulled conservatively minded people together. Peel taught the Tories that they could live with the reformed constitution. Recognizing the renovative tendencies of the times, Peel committed himself to cautious reform of the central institutions of the state so as to save them. In his famous Tamworth Manifesto of 1834, Peel called for a "careful review of institutions, civil and ecclesiastical" aiming at "the correction of proved abuses and the redress of real grievances." By then, Peel was acknowledged as the leader of a Conservative party. In 1841 he became prime minister after a general election, the first time that the electorate had turned out one government and installed another.

The touchstones of the early Victorian Conservatives were defense of agricultural interests and defense of the Church of England. The Whigs were as firmly rooted in the land as the Tories, but in the 1830s landlords and farmers alike drifted to the Conservative party. They did so because they realized that the Whigs were allied with their enemies—middle-class businessmen and radical anti-aristocrats. Preservation of the Corn Law of 1815 became a Conservative preoccupation. As for the Church of England, most Conservatives opposed reform of the institution itself even if they accepted removal of the civil disabilities of non-churchmen. They feared that the reformed Parliament, now open to Catholics and Nonconformists, would destroy the Church. As W. E. Gladstone, then a brilliant young Conservative orator, declared in 1836, "The doctrine and the system of the Establishment contain and exhibit the truth in its purest and most effective form." Once again it was the pragmatic Peel who in the 1830s dragged the Conservatives, kicking and grumbling all the way, to accept administrative reform of the Church, on grounds that, if they did not reform it, the radicals would.

The evolution of the Liberal party was more complicated. In the 1830s and 1840s, the word *liberal* came to be generally used to refer to an alliance of Whigs, "philosophic radicals" (that is, Benthamites) and other radical reformers, and Daniel O'Connell's Irish faction. There was no one individual around whom they could rally: Grey was too old; his successor, Lord Melbourne (prime minister in 1834 and 1835–41), was a kindly friend and mentor to the young Queen Victoria. but lacked energy and force; and John Russell (prime minister from 1846 to1852) showed fiery eloquence, but proved ineffective both as administrator and as party leader. Nevertheless, the crystallization of the Conservatives around Peel forced the Whigs, radicals, and Irish MPs to compromise their differences. They had to ally in order to maintain power and to move on with the reforms that, to varying degrees, they desired. By the 1840s, ordinary political language referred to this often unhappy alliance of reformers as the Liberal party, although the party was not founded in the formal sense until 1859.

What did the Liberals stand for? It is convenient to start with the radicals because they were the group most eager to take the initiative. The radical group included not only Benthamite intellectuals like the young John Stuart Mill (1806–73), but also militant Nonconformists like Edward Miall

(1809–81). Whether Benthamites or Nonconformists, these middle-class radicals wanted to remake the institutions of state and church to conform to the principles of individualism and competition. Aristocratic influence, they believed, had to go. Hence, they favored further extension of the franchise, the secret ballot, and shorter Parliaments, all of which would make Parliament more directly representative of the constituencies. They wanted to abolish the Corn Law, which, they believed, gave preference to the agricultural interest over industry and commerce. Furthermore, they wanted to restrict the privileges of the Church of England. Many wished to disestablish it altogether, for which purpose they formed in 1844 a pressure group called the Anti-State Church Association (later renamed the Liberation Society). In the meantime, radicals sought to pare away the excessive wealth of the Church, to abolish compulsory church rates (local taxes), to allow Nonconformists to have their own rites for marriage and burials, and to open Oxford and Cambridge to dissenters.

The Whigs displayed a more diffuse range of policies because they were members of a particular group of aristocratic families rather than ideologues. Generally speaking, they regarded 1832 as final in constitutional reform, but they favored alteration of the Church, both to conciliate middle-class Nonconformist opinion and to make the Church less vulnerable to extremists who wished to disestablish it. Because the Whigs only gradually took up the cause of repealing the Corn Law, the Church issue was what most clearly distinguished them from the Tories. In 1832, the Whig government appointed an ecclesiastical commission to investigate the wealth of the Church, the anomalies in clerical salaries, and the long-standing problems of pluralism and nonresidence (clergymen holding more than one position and so frequently not residing in the parish for which they were responsible). In 1833, the Whigs abolished ten bishoprics of the Anglican Church of Ireland, an egregiously top-heavy institution. In 1836, they sponsored legislation that legalized Nonconformist marriages and set up state (rather than church) registration of births, deaths, and marriages.

The Conservatives and Liberals of early Victorian Britain were not class parties in any rigorous sense. Both of them had aristocratic, middle-class, and even to some extent working-class elements. Yet the center of gravity in the social composition of the one differed from that of the other. The Conservatives increasingly spoke for landed Anglican England, whereas the Liberals voiced the outlook of Nonconformist business and commercial men and of Scottish and Irish interests. Such differences did not emerge in connection with every issue, and they would be blurred when Peel accepted repeal of the Corn Law in 1846, but the centrality of religion to the process of class formation in Britain produced a significant degree of class orientation in the two political parties even by mid-century.

## THE CONDITION OF ENGLAND QUESTION AND THE GROWTH OF THE STATE, 1832–1850

Whatever their differences, Conservatives and Liberals were men of property and shared a broad consensus about the framework of the society and the constitution. Thus, on many issues that came before them, MPs did not divide along party lines. Chief among these nonparty issues was the so-called Condition of England Question (although it related to conditions in Wales, Scotland, and Ireland as well). As we saw in the last chapter, the appalling slums of Manchester and other industrial cities bore witness to the massive economic and social problems generated by demographic, industrial, and urban change.

Faced with such problems, members of both parties felt conflicting impulses. Liberals generally believed in laissez-faire, the notion that the market economy was self-regulating and would, if left alone, automatically reach maximum production and full employment—and so enable individuals to take action to improve their own conditions, without any governmental action or interference. Many Liberals, however, were also utilitarians who believed that the government should intervene in society in order to produce the greatest happiness of the greatest number; hence, they admired "scientific" analysis of social problems and expert administration, and recognized that some issues could not be resolved by individual action. Unlike the Liberals, Conservatives tended to remain committed to the paternalist ideal of a communal social order in which the powerful take care of the powerless and so they often opposed laissez-faire. But because they were also devoted to local interests and the rights of property, they mistrusted centralization and feared an active government. Both parties were therefore pulled in both directions: for and against state intervention in society and economy. The political results were contradictory and complex. Different solutions to the condition of England problem reflected different mixes of these fundamental attitudes, as an examination of the new Poor Law, factory reforms, and public health legislation reveals.

The first major social issue that Parliament addressed after 1832 was the Poor Law. The existing Poor Law, which dated back to the Elizabethan period, had become by the 1800s a ramshackle system. Worse yet, it was expensive. In 1831–32, the Poor Law cost £7 million. Yet it did not ensure social peace, as the Swing Riots of 1830 showed. By then, the propertied classes agreed that the Poor Law must be reformed, and the Whigs appointed a royal commission to investigate in 1832.

The Poor Law Commission reported in 1834 and issued a classic monument of middle-class ideology. The commission was dominated by political economists—most notably, Edwin Chadwick (1800–90), the first great civil servant in British history and an embodiment of Benthamite relentlessness, narrowness, and intolerance. It concluded that the Poor Law itself created poverty by teaching the laboring poor to depend on *outdoor relief*—that is, financial assistance given outside the workhouses. As one witness said, "The system of allowances is most mischievous and ruinous, and till it is abandoned the spirit of industry can never be revived." The able-bodied poor should be forced off the relief rolls and those who could not support themselves and their families forced into the workhouse, where conditions should be miserable—"less eligible" than those of the lowest paying job in the locality. Hence, people who really could work would be driven to do so. A central board would set out and implement the new regulations.

The Poor Law was amended along these lines in 1834, with very little opposition. Paradoxically, though enacted on laissez-faire principles, the new Poor Law resulted in the growth of central government. Under the old Poor Law, the initiative had rested with local authorities, but now the secretary to the new Poor Law Board—Chadwick himself—badgered local Poor Law unions incessantly to build workhouses and halt all outdoor relief. Poor Law inspectors, employed by the state, enforced the new law. Yet, as promised, the new system did cut costs: by 1840, Poor Law expenditure was down to £4.6 million a year.

Although middle- and upper-class ratepayers thus had reason to welcome the new Poor Law, workers responded in anger. To them the Poor Law and its *workhouse test* symbolized the heartlessness of the new industrial order and the shattering of communal ties. Moreover, in the industrial North, where large numbers were unemployed during periods of recession, the workhouses simply could not cope, for the new Poor Law had been based on the false theory that the able-bodied could always find work.

Although liberal ideology and the desire to cut costs motivated the new Poor Law, a curious combination of trade union radicalism and paternalist humanitarianism drove forward factory reform legislation. Workers themselves organized in unions such as the Manchester Cotton Spinners, led by John Doherty, and Conservative Evangelical elites such as Richard Oastler and Michael Sadler demanded that the state address the new industrial order. The trade unions wanted a reduction of hours of labor in the factories in order to ease the hardship of factory work and create opportunities for unemployed adult men. The Evangelical reformers were especially moved by child labor in the factories. In 1830, Oastler wrote of "thousands of little children . . . sacrificed at the shrine of avarice, without even the solace of the Negro slave." The general hope of all factory reformers was to restrict the working day of children to ten hours, on the assumption that this would cause adult labor to be restricted as well.

The dispute over the proposed ten-hours policy was heated. Paternalist Conservatives stood for the restriction as opposed to Whigs, Liberals, and the majority of manufacturers, who argued that restricting child labor constituted unwarranted state interference in the marketplace. Sadler lost his seat in 1832, and parliamentary leadership of the factory reform movement passed to the most remarkable Tory Evangelical of the century, Lord Ashley (later earl of Shaftesbury). The Whigs appointed a commission to study factory reform in 1833; it was led by the ubiquitous Chadwick. In his report, Chadwick refuted many of the humanitarian arguments, but admitted that children were not free agents in the labor market and therefore warranted protection. The resulting Factory Act of 1833 prohibited the employment of children under age nine in textile mills and restricted the hours of all those under eighteen. More importantly, the act established a professional inspectorate to supervise compliance with its regulations.

This inspectorate eventually contributed to further reform. The ten-hours movement continued to agitate inside and outside Parliament, but it had little effect until the factory inspectors uncovered weaknesses in the 1833 act. Their expert testimony, effectively marshaled by Lord Ashley, resulted in additional restrictions of child labor in 1844 and finally in a Ten Hours Act for all textile workers in 1847.

Professional expertise also played a crucial role in focusing the power of the state on the great problem of public health in the industrial towns, the third aspect of the Condition of England Question. In this case, many of the experts were doctors who had firsthand experience with the horrors of cholera and typhus in congested urban areas. Physicians such as Sir James Kay (Manchester) and Southwood Smith (London) based their conclusions on statistical rather than biological evidence, but they were right nevertheless: filth and disease were closely related. Meanwhile, work on the Poor Law Board turned Chadwick's attention to public health, and in 1842 he issued a *Sanitary Report* that shocked its readers and became a bestseller. Sheer facts had persuaded him that the unsanitary urban environment caused disease, and disease caused poverty and dependence on the Poor Law. Other royal commissions and parliamentary committees in the 1840s drew the same conclusions.

Yet public health legislation was slow in coming. English localist tradition—the belief in the rights and authority of borough governments—stoutly opposed centralization. Moreover, the institutions that provided water, waste removal, and drainage for the towns were private companies, and they fought effectively to protect their rights and profits. Significant action did not come until 1848, when a breakthrough Public Health Act was passed. It established a central Board of Health (headed, of course, by Chadwick) with some power to compel local authorities to undertake sanitary reform. Chadwick, however, alienated many local officials and was dismissed in 1854; four years later, in an apparent victory for localism (and defeat for public health), the Board of Health was disbanded. But the man who in effect succeeded Chadwick, Sir John Simon, was a much more pragmatic and successful administrator. His privy council medical department prepared the ground for effective government intervention, which came in the latter 1860s.

By the 1850s, then, the scope and size of the British state had grown markedly because of utilitarian calls for rational reform, the moral outrage of evangelical and paternalist humanitarianism, and the development of professional expertise. A new pattern in the legislative process emerged: humanitarian reformers brought an issue before Parliament; a royal commission was appointed to gather facts; a law was passed and professional administrators appointed; and thereafter, the professionals provided irresistible impetus for further reform. By 1870, the number of government employees stood at fifty-four thousand. Experts now regulated in varying degrees the Poor Law, the prisons, the railways, and most textile mills; the central government was beginning to take a hand in cleaning up the cities; and the state had become registrar of births, marriages, and deaths as well as regular census taker.

Not only was the state engaged in activities never dreamed of a century earlier, but also the standard of performance was much higher. Professionalism was making a genuine civil service out of government employees. To advance this process, two businesslike administrators, Sir Charles Trevelyan and Sir Stafford Northcote, issued in 1853 a report calling for a unified civil service based on the principles of appointment by open competitive examination and promotion by merit. This was a bitter pill to swallow for those devoted to aristocratic government, but the scope and complexity of social problems had made the medicine necessary. Civil service exams were introduced in the 1860s, and patronage in most departments ended in 1870. In fact, sons of the aristocracy and gentry continued to monopolize government service, for they had the classical education favored by the examiners. The growth of the British state thus was doubly paradoxical: the state grew during the great era of laissez-faire ideology, and the elite maintained their grip on public office by accepting bourgeois principles of competition and merit.

## CLASS POLITICS: THE ANTI-CORN LAW LEAGUE AND THE CHARTIST MOVEMENT

Class conflict, so evident in the passage of the new Reform Act and the new Poor Law, boiled over ominously in two extra-parliamentary movements: the Anti-Corn Law League, the archetype organization of middle-class interests, and Chartism, the first nationwide working-class movement. The Anti-Corn Law League was founded in Manchester in 1838. It gave voice to the middle-class belief in political economy: the efficiency of the free market and the virtues of free trade. The Corn Law of 1815 had been a key event in the awakening of middle-class consciousness. Businessmen recognized that in its intention of keeping grain prices high, the Corn Law was a blatant attempt by the landlords to protect their own interests at the expense of the rest of the nation. The Corn Law, according to the Anti-Corn Law League, kept food prices high and reduced commercial and industrial profits by forcing employers to pay artificially high wages. Even the introduction of a sliding scale on grain duties did not satisfy the captains of industry and trade. In fact, the Corn Law (now modified) failed to keep grain prices up, but that did not mute the drumfire of criticism coming from the business sector. After 1836, when bad harvests drove food prices up and trade went into a slump, middle-class discontent intensified and then found an organizational outlet in the Anti-Corn Law League.

Richard Cobden and John Bright, the leading figures in the Anti-Corn Law agitation exemplified Victorian middle-class ideals. Cobden (1804–65), an Anglican owner of calico mills in Manchester, was a self-made man. He preached even to the working class "the love of independence, the privilege of self-respect, the disdain of being patronised . . . the desire to accumulate, and the ambition to rise." He believed that state interference in the economy

*Dear bread and cheap bread: a membership card of the National Anti-Corn Law League. The elaborate designs served a propagandist purpose when the cards were displayed on a wall or mantelpiece.*

only promoted privilege and monopoly, which he despised. Further, he reasoned that free trade would strengthen British farming by exposing it to competition, and if adopted around the world, it would lead nations into specialization of production and networks of trade that would spell international peace. Cobden recognized that persuasion alone would not win Parliament over; the League had to bring pressure on every candidate, regardless of party, and work for the defeat of Corn Law defenders. He thus created the first modern pressure group.

Bright (1811–89), a Quaker industrialist from Rochdale, supplemented Cobden's tactical shrewdness with moral passion. He made the campaign against the Corn Law into a moral crusade and became the symbol of the Nonconformist in politics: bluff, moralistic, and righteous. To such people, the Anti-Corn Law struggle involved much more than economics, for it encompassed a blow at the aristocracy and the Anglican church. As one pro-League newspaper declared in 1841: "The value of tithes and teinds on which they [the Anglican clergy] fatten is vastly enhanced, they know, by the aristocratic restrictions on the food of the community."

The Anti-Corn Law League between 1838 and 1846 held countless meetings; sponsored thousands of tracts, pamphlets, and lectures; and presented many motions in the House of Commons. But it never persuaded a majority to vote for repeal. True, it convinced Peel himself, who as prime minister in 1845 remarked to a colleague after hearing Cobden speak, "You must answer this for I cannot." It was famine in Ireland that brought the Corn Law down. Beginning in 1845, the Irish potato crop failed, and the most terrible famine in modern British history settled on Ireland (see chapter 15). Peel believed that he had no choice but to seek repeal of the Corn Law in 1846 in order to allow cheap food to be imported into Ireland. He and his personal following (the "Peelites") joined the Liberals in overturning the Corn Law. Peel gave credit to Cobden, but Cobden himself admitted that, without the crisis in Ireland, the League would not have succeeded.

Repeal of the Corn Law did not have the consequences either side had anticipated. It neither saved the Irish poor nor undercut the power of the landed class. Nevertheless, it was seen as a great victory for middle-class ideas, though once again enacted by a Parliament of landowners. When stable prosperity blessed Britain in the 1850s and 1860s, free trade got the credit. Britons of the governing classes concluded that free trade was the key to economic success. This would be a difficult lesson to unlearn.

Repeal of the Corn Laws also had unintended—and momentous—parliamentary consequences. Fractured by the repeal debate, the Conservative party split in two. The split became permanent when Conservative M P Benjamin Disraeli, who had ferociously attacked Peel in the contentious repeal debate, ascended into the ranks of the Conservative leadership. The Peelites, a group containing some of the most able administrative talents in the Commons, including the future prime minister W. E. Gladstone, could not forgive Disraeli for his treatment of Peel. Peel himself died in 1850 and the Peelites merged with the Whigs in the Liberal party.

Throughout the long campaign to abolish the Corn Law, the Anti-Corn Law Leaguers asserted that, because the middle and working classes had identical interests, the working class should support the League. But the great majority of politically minded working men and women remained suspicious of the League, which they regarded as the rationalization of middle-class interests. Working-class activists cautioned that, if repeal of the Corn Law did result in cheaper food, then employers would only reduce wages. This argument was particularly powerful in the Chartist movement that emerged in the 1830s. Chartists thus sometimes broke up Anti-Corn Law meetings; what they wanted was political empowerment.

Chartism was the largest mass movement in Victorian history, so large and dramatic that at times it seemed to threaten revolution. It had roots in the popular radicalism of the eighteenth century—the tradition of the moral economy of the crowd and the radical belief in democracy and a free Parliament. The Chartist program varied widely by region and by social group, but most Chartists agreed with the working-class radicals of the 1820s that social problems were caused by governmental failings and that political reform would in some unspecified way lead to radical social and economic change. At the same time, most Chartists were backward-looking in their desire to restore lost independence and community. Hence, Chartism always found its warmest support among artisans. Factory workers in some towns became Chartists, but their activity tended to wax and wane as the economy slumped and boomed. The largest number of Chartists, and the most militant, came from the outworkers, artisans such as handloom weavers, framework knitters, and nail makers who were suffering because they could not compete with dishonorable labor and the factories.

The founding of Chartism had two immediate causes: first, the frustration of working-class radicals with the parliamentary reform of 1832, and second, the popular hatred of the new Poor Law of 1834. While their former middle-class allies were taking up repeal of the Corn Law, working-class radicals continued to work for a broader franchise. At the same time, the anti-Poor Law campaign was very widespread in the North of England, especially in the bad years of 1836–37. Working people thought that the new Poor Law was cruel and degrading, because it forced them to seek relief in "Poor Law Bastilles," where they had to wear prison-like uniforms, undergo separation of family members, and work at miserable tasks such as stone breaking and bone grinding. In 1839, representatives of popular radicalism and the anti-Poor Law campaign met in London to consider possible courses of action. They wrote up what they called *the Charter*: a manifesto that contained six key demands, known as *the six points*: universal manhood suffrage, equal electoral districts, no property qualification for MPs, annual elections, payment of MPs, and the secret ballot. All of these but annual Parliaments have since been enacted, but at the time, they were regarded as extremely radical proposals.

One radical proposal that did not appear in the Charter was female suffrage. The first draft drawn up by the London Chartist Association had included a demand for the woman's vote, but the fear that such a proposal "might retard the suffrage of men" ensured that it was dropped. Most Chartists, moreover, had internalized the doctrine of *separate spheres* for men and women; many, in fact, were drawn into radical politics by their uneasiness with the new industrial order, particularly the large-scale employment of women and children in factories and the high rates of unemployment for men. The National Female Charter Association, for example, warned that the "order of nature is being inverted" with "the female driven to the factory to labour for her offspring, and her husband unwillingly idle at home, dependent on female labour." Chartist publications frequently demanded that men be paid higher wages so that women and children could remain at home. "No women's work except in the hearth and schoolroom" was a frequent Chartist battle cry.

Yet women worked very publicly in the Chartist movement. According to one (male) Chartist, "the women were the better men." More than one hundred separate Chartist women's organizations existed. They took a leading role in setting up Chartist day and evening schools for both children and adults, led boycotts of hostile shopkeepers, and organized fundraisers. At Chartist demonstrations and mass rallies, women often assumed their traditional protest role: standing in the front ranks of the protesters, they lobbed jeers, obscenities, and sometimes rocks and mud at the opposing rows of police or soldiers.

Despite such mass participation, Chartism from its very beginnings was divided by personal clashes among its leaders and by strong disagreements over tactics and ultimate objectives. For example, some militants wanted the first Chartist convention to set itself up as an alternative Parliament. Others sought to intimidate Parliament by means of a national strike. Still others hinted broadly at using physical force. The moderates, however, wanted simply to petition Parliament to enact the six points. Most middle-class radicals in the 1839 convention became alarmed at the loose talk of the militants and withdrew. An attempt in 1841–42 to rally middle- and working-class moderates behind a combined program of repeal of the Corn Law and passage of the six points foundered on the rocks of class antagonism. Thereafter, Chartist leaders followed very different paths: some engaged in conspiracy, arming, and drilling; others organized Christian Chartist or temperance and self-help societies. London Chartists were never in phase with those in the industrial North. Moved by old grievances against the local anglicized ruling elite, Welsh Chartists were as much Welsh nationalists as political radicals. Given these divisions, Parliament's determination to reject the Chartist petitions out of hand, and the government's aggressive tactics of spies, informers, and preventive arrests, Chartism faced formidable obstacles.

Chartism went through three phases. In the first (1839–40), the Chartist convention adopted the six points, argued about tactics, presented the first Chartist petition (which Parliament rejected overwhelmingly), and then dissolved. Scattered violence followed. In Yorkshire and Lancashire some Chartists conspired for rebellion, and in Newport (South Wales), Welsh Chartists marched on the town. Twenty-four died when the British army moved in and the conspiracy elsewhere fizzled out. In 1839–40, the government arrested more than five hundred Chartists, and a general strike fell flat. By midsummer of 1840, the first phase was over.

Irish-born demagogue Feargus O'Connor (1794–1855) dominated the second phase of Chartist history (1840–42). A landowner, a romantic, and an enemy of the machine age, O'Connor published in England the greatest Chartist newspaper, *The Northern Star.* He was a spellbinding orator, though often a victim of his own rhetoric. He spoke boldly of revolution, but was temperamentally incapable of planning one, and it is doubtful that he meant what he said. In any case, O'Connor in 1842 gathered a second petition for the six points containing about three million signatures. Parliament abruptly rejected it. T. B. Macaulay, historian and MP, spoke for the great majority of the House of Commons when he declared that universal suffrage "would be fatal to the purposes for which government exists," for it was "utterly incompatible with the existence of civilization." In the industrial North, violence broke out as workers engaged in strikes and, in some places, removed the plugs from steam boilers to stop factory operations. O'Connor dithered in his attitude toward this industrial action, and moderate Chartists and trade unionists exerted themselves against it. Agitation for a time was quieted.

The third phase (1842–48) included both a back-to-the-land scheme and the final Chartist petition. O'Connor dreamed of restoring the people to the land. He established, therefore, a Chartist cooperative to buy land in England and lease it to individual Chartists. Not only would working people return to a kind of yeoman status, but also the oversupply of labor in industry would be reduced. Unfortunately, after some initial success the cooperative soon sank into deep financial trouble. In 1848, when popular revolutions broke out across Europe, O'Connor returned to petitioning and mass demonstrations. A simultaneous rising of the starving tenantry in Ireland would, he hoped, help overawe the government. O'Connor claimed to have gathered five or six million signatures and planned to deliver the petition to Parliament, accompanied by one hundred thousand Chartists.

*The last great Chartist demonstration, 1848. A photograph of the Chartist crowd on Kennington Common, London.*

The government recognized the seriousness of the situation, but did not panic. This time, while the northern provinces were relatively quiet, Chartism caught fire in London. The government summoned 4,000 policemen, 8,000 troops, and 85,000 special constables (the great majority of whom were middle-class men) and consulted the duke of Wellington on tactics. Though some 150,000 Chartists gathered on Kennington Common south of the Thames, O'Connor decided not to defy a government ban on a procession across the river to Parliament. Had the Chartists attempted to march on Westminster, a bloodbath would surely have resulted, and possibly a revolutionary conflict would have begun.

In the end, O'Connor delivered the petition (which had less than two million signatures, including obvious fakes such as "the duke of Wellington," "Robert Peel," and "Victoria Rex") by taxicab. Parliament quickly rejected it. The Irish peasantry did not rise up at the key moment, and during the summer of 1848 the London police mopped up conspiratorial bands of Chartists. Worse yet, a parliamentary investigation found the finances of the land cooperative in chaos. The cooperative was closed, and O'Connor spent the rest of his days in an insane asylum.

Chartism thus failed, whereas the Anti-Corn Law League succeeded. The League was better organized, its single policy less revolutionary, and its social base (the middle class) more powerful than that of Chartism. Nevertheless, Chartism was of great historical significance. It did more than any other popular movement to spread class consciousness among the working people of Britain and to express their antagonism both to the landed proprietors and to the middle class. At the same time, its failure taught British workers that they must operate within the political and economic system for more limited goals. Furthermore, the Chartist episode contributed to the acceptance of the middle class by the landed orders because the two upper classes had stood shoulder to shoulder against the Chartist threat. Lady Palmerston, wife of the Whig statesman, expressed this outcome best: "I am sure," she wrote, "that it is very fortunate that the whole thing has occurred, as it has shown the good spirit of our middle classes."

## Suggested Reading

Belchem, John. *Popular Radicalism in Nineteenth-Century Britain*. New York: St. Martin's Press, 1996.

Bentley, Michael. *Politics Without Democracy, 1815–1914*, 2nd ed. London: Fontana, 1996.

Brock, Michael. *The Great Reform Act*. London: Hutchinson, 1973.

Brundage, Anthony. *The English Poor Laws, 1700–1930*. New York: Palgrave, 2002.

Burns, Arthur, and Joanna Innis, eds. *Rethinking the Age of Reform: Britain 1780–1850*. Cambridge: Cambridge University Press, 2003.

Chase, Malcolm. *Chartism: A New History*. Manchester, UK: Manchester University Press, 2007.

Derry, John W. *Charles, Earl Grey: Aristocratic Reformer*. Oxford: Blackwell, 1992.

Dinwiddy, J. R. *From Luddism to the First Reform Bill*. Oxford: Blackwell, 1986.

Eastwood, David, *Governing Rural England; Tradition and Transformation in Local Government, 1780–1840*. Oxford: Clarendon Press, 1994.

Englander, David. *Poverty and Poor Law Reform in Nineteenth Century Britain, 1834–1914: From Chadwick to Booth*. London: Longman, 1998.

Epstein, James. *The Lion of Freedom: Feargus O'Connor and the Chartist Movement, 1832–1842*. London: Croom Helm, 1982.

Evans, D. Gareth. *A History of Wales, 1815–1906*. Cardiff: University of Wales Press, 1990.

Finer, S. E. *The Life and Times of Sir Edwin Chadwick*. London: Methuen, 1980.

Fraser, W. Hamish, and R. J. Morris, eds. *People and Society in Scotland*. Vol. II, *1830–1914*. Edinburgh: John Donald, 1990.

Frasier, Antonia. *Perilous Question: The Drama of the Great Reform Bill 1832*. London: Weidenfeld and Nicolson, 2013.

Gash, Norman. *Politics in the Age of Peel*. London: Longmans, Green, 1953.

———. *Sir Robert Peel*. London: Longman, 1972.

Gaunt, Richard. *Sir Robert Peel: The Life and Legacy*. London: I. B. Tauris, 2010.

Hilton, Boyd. *A Mad, Bad, and Dangerous People? England, 1783–1846*. Oxford: Oxford University Press, 2006.

Lees, Lynn Hollen. *The Solidarities of Strangers: The English Poor Law and People, 1700–1948*. New York: Cambridge University Press, 1997.

LoPatin, Nancy D. *Popular Unions, Popular Politics, and the Great Reform Act of 1832.* New York: St. Martin's Press, 1999.

McCaffrey, John F. *Scotland in the Nineteenth Century.* New York: St. Martin's Press, 1998.

Palmer, Stanley H. *Police and Protest in England and Ireland, 1780–1850.* New York: Cambridge University Press, 1988.

Parry, Jonathan. *The Rise and Fall of Liberal Government in Victorian Britain.* New Haven, CT: Yale University Press, 1993.

Pickering, Paul, and Alex Tyrell. *The People's Bread: A History of the Anti-Corn Law League.* Leicester, UK: Leicester University Press, 2000.

Porter, Roy. *Disease, Medicine and Society in England, 1550–1860.* Cambridge: Cambridge University Press, 1995.

Roberts, David. *The Social Conscience of the Early Victorians.* Stanford, CA: Stanford University Press, 2002.

——. *Victorian Origins of the British Welfare State.* Hamden, CT: Archon Books, 1969.

Sack, James J. *From Jacobite to Conservative: Reaction and Orthodoxy in Britain. c. 1760–1832.* Cambridge: Cambridge University Press, 1993.

Saville, John. *1848: The British State and the Chartist Movement.* New York: Cambridge University Press, 1987.

Schwarzkopf, Julia. *Women in the Chartist Movement.* New York: St. Martin's Press, 1991.

Smith, E. A. *Lord Grey, 1764–1845.* Oxford: Clarendon Press, 1990.

Thompson, Dorothy. *The Chartists.* New York: Pantheon Books, 1984.

# Chapter 15

# Ireland from the
# Union to the Famine

With the Act of Union in 1800, Britain and Ireland in theory became parts
of a single state. Yet the differences between Britain and Ireland were fundamental, and the United Kingdom of Great Britain and Ireland never really
worked. While England (along with South Wales and Lowland Scotland) was
industrializing and modernizing, Ireland remained a backward agricultural
society. Britain was, however painfully, becoming the wealthiest and most
progressive society in the world, but Ireland stood stagnant, mired in
poverty, agrarian violence, and sectarian strife. It is safe to say that Britain,
the predominant partner, never understood Irish problems the way the Irish
did—never saw Ireland through Irish eyes. What was called the Irish Question thus became an intractable and frustrating set of issues for the British;
what might have been called the British Question became an alternately
maddening and demoralizing brick wall for the Irish. If the new state created in 1800 had worked, the attachment of Ireland to Britain could have
been of enormous benefit to the mass of Irish people, but it did not, and the
consequence was the greatest catastrophe in Irish history.

## THE IRISH QUESTION

The so-called Irish Question of the early nineteenth century had three
parts: political, religious, and economic. The political aspect arose from the
fact that the Act of Union created a situation in which the great majority of
the Irish people were disaffected from their government. The Anglican
Ascendancy and the Ulster Presbyterians, approximately 15 to 20 percent of
the Irish population, thought that the Union was their sole protection, but
most of the rest of the Irish regarded the Union as the source and symbol of
their oppression. As Arthur Wellesley (later the duke of Wellington) said in

1807, "We have no strength here but our army. Ireland, in a view to military operations, must be viewed as an enemy's country." The Act of Union abolished the Irish Parliament and gave Ireland 100 MPs (out of 658) in Parliament at Westminster. Catholics could vote, but could not serve as members of Parliament. From 1801 to 1921, then, all major decisions on Irish policies were made by the British cabinet and Parliament in London, neither of which allowed the Irish much influence.

Likewise, the Catholic majority of the population had little influence on the administrative machinery in Ireland. The lord lieutenant, usually a British nobleman, headed the Irish administration and ruled from Dublin Castle, the symbol of Anglo-Protestant and British governmental power. The main political figure was the chief secretary, a leading British politician who had to defend the government in the House of Commons as well as administer the country on a day-to-day basis. The administrative staff, the legal officers, the magistrates, and the judiciary through whom the lord lieutenant and chief secretary executed policy were all drawn from Irish Protestantism. Protestants also controlled local government.

In the 1820s and 1830s, the scope of government in Ireland expanded to include public works, state education, and a Poor Law. In all of its functions, the Irish executive could depend little on the voluntary services of the aristocracy and gentry; hence, the administration became more centralized than that in England. Because execution of the law was in Protestant hands, the Catholics did not trust the judiciary. In order to see that the law was enforced impartially, British administrators like Peel sometimes adopted measures that would have been unacceptable in England. For instance, they often resorted to *stipendiary magistrates*—magistrates employed by the central administration—instead of local JPs. This tendency toward central governmental control also suited the British attitude toward Ireland, which, despite the Union, held that Ireland was a strange and savage place. As Sir Robert Peel, chief secretary from 1812 to 1818, said, "I believe an honest despotic government would be by far the fittest government for Ireland."

A kind of honest despotism, answerable to the British Parliament, is in fact what prevailed in Ireland. In order to control endemic agrarian violence as well as dangerous political movements, Parliament frequently resorted to *coercion acts*—laws suspending civil liberties for designated periods of time. Rarely was Ireland in the nineteenth century free from coercion. The British army in Ireland consistently numbered between twenty thousand and forty thousand men and was backed by a yeomanry of another thirty-five thousand. Dublin Castle officials used the army to enforce the law and even to collect tithes and carry out evictions of tenants for nonpayment of rent. Ireland thus in theory was part of the United Kingdom; in practice it was an occupied country.

The religious aspect of the Irish Question was clear: the established Church of Ireland, which was Anglican, represented only about 10 percent of the population. Nonconformists (mostly Ulster Presbyterians) composed another 8 to 10 percent; all the rest were Roman Catholics. Further, the Church of Ireland was top-heavy with a huge hierarchy: for eight hundred thousand Anglicans, the Church in 1831 had four archbishops; eighteen bishops; numerous cathedrals, deans, and chapters; and about fourteen hundred parish clergymen. Some Anglican parishes had not a single Protestant resident. This lavish establishment was supported by tithes, which all Irishmen, regardless of religion, had to pay. The Catholics hated the tithe, and in the early 1830s resistance to paying the tithe, backed by agrarian secret societies, spread widely through southern Ireland. The government used large numbers of police and army troops to collect the tithe, and the resulting tithe war caused much bloodshed and ill-feeling.

Meanwhile, the Catholic church in Ireland was getting its own house in order. Having survived the penal laws, the Catholic church turned its attention to the twin problems of the population explosion and evangelical Protestant missionaries. The Catholic hierarchy undertook organizational reform, building of churches and chapels, renewal of discipline, and parochial education. By the 1830s, the church had a much firmer grip on the people. Moreover, that grip was exercised at the parish level by priests trained in the Catholic seminaries at Maynooth, Carlow, and elsewhere in Ireland. Whereas the older generation (who now held the top positions in the Irish hierarchy) had been trained abroad, the younger parish clergy (who had close daily contact with the people) were educated at home. One Protestant observer said that the Irish priests "displayed the bitterest feelings of the partisan and the grossest habits of the peasant." This is a prejudiced view, no doubt, but the Catholic clergyman, who lived in a small world dominated by the Protestant squire, parson, and the tithe collector, did tend to be highly political. To him, Irish patriotism and Catholicism were one and the same.

The economic dimension of the Irish Question was simply that Ireland was very poor. The Irish in the first half of the nineteenth century were caught in a *poverty trap*, in which poverty itself—low incomes, primitive markets, and a low rate of capital formation—defeated every impetus for economic growth. Moreover, the economic obstacles to prosperity were reinforced by seemingly immovable political and social conditions. Politics, society, and economics fed on each other to make a vicious circle of instability, insecurity, and stagnation.

To begin with, there was, as we have seen, little industrialization in Ireland except in Ulster. The Union had envisioned a single free-trade area for the British Isles, but when free trade was actually enacted in 1824, it had severe consequences for the Irish economy. The cotton textile industry centered in Belfast was destroyed by competition from British mills. Belfast was able to switch back to its old staple, linen; however, in the rest of Ireland, British machine-made goods ruined the most important cottage industry, domestic weaving. Given the comparative attractiveness of the burgeoning English and Scottish industrial sector, no one wanted to invest in new industries in Ireland. There was little capital in Ireland, and few English or Scottish investors wanted to transfer their capital into the Emerald Isle. Outside of Ulster, therefore, the great majority of the Irish people became more dependent than ever on agriculture.

Irish farming in the first half of the century was able to increase its production, but it remained inefficient compared to English agriculture, now in the full tide of agricultural revolution. In Ireland, there was a steady shift of land from tillage to pasturage, but not much improvement of farming techniques. The problem once again was lack of investment. In order to improve farming, some part of Irish society had to invest in the reorganization of the land, new crops, fertilizer, scientific breeding, and so on. But no one did. Landless laborers and cottiers (cottagers) were too poor to do so and tenant farmers too insecure of their holdings. Tenants feared that, if they made improvements, their rents would go up. Only in Ulster, where *Ulster custom* prevailed, were tenants entitled to compensation for improvements that they made on their land; not surprisingly, in Ulster tenants were more progressive farmers, and landlord-tenant relations were more cooperative than in Leinster, Munster, and Connacht. Irish landlords had the money to invest, and a few in fact tried to improve their estates, but the results inevitably involved evictions of "excess" tenants and considerable violence. Fearful of the chronic agrarian terrorism that afflicted the countryside, landlords tended to view improvements as a bad bargain.

The great majority of the Irish people still depended on the land for a living. Upwards of two-thirds of all occupied people worked in farming. They labored on the land, but did not own it. In England, the tendency was for landholdings to grow in size, but in Ireland, the rapid increase in the population and the lack of alternative employment put enormous pressure on the land. By subdivision, tenancies became smaller and smaller, as did the plots of land rented by cottiers and wage laborers. A royal commission in 1845 found that to sustain a family of five, a farm in Ireland had to be between six and ten acres, but by the 1840s, 45 percent of all holdings were below five acres, and another 37 percent were between five and fifteen acres.

Meanwhile, competition for holdings and a general decline of agricultural prices pushed rentals (in terms of tenants' purchasing power) up. Arrears of rent were common, as were evictions for nonpayment of rent. To defend themselves from rent increases and eviction, Irish peasants formed secret societies, which used tactics such as cattle mutilation and assassination to intimidate not only landlords, but also tenants who dared bid for a holding from which a family had been evicted. Whiteboys, Whitefeet, Ribbonmen, Rockites, and the like spread widely, especially from the 1820s. Most observers thought that the violence protected the peasantry from predatory landlords, but it also contributed significantly to the vicious circle of poverty and stagnation.

The hard-pressed Irish population became even more dependent on the potato. Generally, the Irish tenants and cottiers produced grain, pigs, and cattle, either on their own holdings or on someone else's, to pay the rent, but they grew potatoes to feed themselves. The poorer the region (mainly in the West), the greater the dependency on the potato. By the 1840s, one-third of all land under tillage was devoted to potatoes, and one-third of the population (nine-tenths in County Mayo) ate little else. Travelers in Ireland even noticed fewer pigs living in the peasants' huts, not because standards of hygiene had gone up, but because fewer cottiers and laborers could afford them. Cash money had little part to play in the life of the ordinary peasant in the western counties; in these rocky lands there was at best a primitive market system and little access to alternative foodstuffs. Localized famine was common wherever the potato crop failed. This was a setting for disaster.

## DANIEL O'CONNELL AND CATHOLIC EMANCIPATION

It would seem obvious that Ireland in the early nineteenth century was ripe for revolution, but in the opening decades of the century, the Irish political scene was quiet. Most Protestants had turned against patriotic politics and looked to the Union as their salvation. The small Catholic middle class had no way to revoke the Act of Union. The demoralized masses were inert, and the horrors of 1798 were fresh in everyone's mind. Thus, when the youthful Robert Emmet, a Protestant lawyer, and the vestiges of the

United Irishmen staged a rising in Dublin in 1803, it was abortive. Emmet's rebellion came to nothing except his own execution and the making of another martyr for the revolutionary strain in Irish nationalism. Independence or autonomy for Ireland was out of the question.

Full civil and political rights for Catholics were another matter. The Younger Pitt, it will be remembered, had hoped to include Catholic emancipation as part of a package with the Union. In the decades after the Union, many English and Scottish Whigs as well as radicals adopted the issue. In Ireland, middle-class and professional Catholics also continued to work for emancipation, partly on principle and partly in the hope that they would benefit directly from public office or the prestige of a seat in Parliament. Divisions within the Irish Catholic leadership, however, weakened the campaign's impact. The divisions had to do with the questions of *safeguards* insisted on by the British as the price of emancipation: first, state control over appointments of Catholic bishops, and second, state payment of the Catholic clergy. Presumably, these safeguards would ensure the loyalty of the Catholic church, and many upper-class English and Irish Catholics were content to accept them. Other Irish Catholics, however, including most priests and some bishops, would not; consequently, the movement was paralyzed.

Then in 1823, Daniel O'Connell transformed the Catholic emancipation movement. One of the great leaders of Irish nationalism in the nineteenth century and enshrined in Irish memory as "The Liberator," O'Connell (1775–1847) was the heir of an old Catholic gentry family of County Kerry. Educated abroad in French Catholic schools, O'Connell read for the bar in London and then became a successful and popular lawyer in Dublin. While studying in London, he became a deist and a Benthamite. The deism he soon abandoned when he returned to Catholicism, but the Benthamism he retained. O'Connell was thus one of a certain European type—a liberal Catholic—but also a paternalist landlord, fluent in Gaelic, as well as a passionate Irish patriot strongly opposed to the Union. His firsthand experience of the French Revolution in 1791–93 and of the Irish rebellion of 1798, however, gave him a permanent abhorrence of revolutionary violence. His reaction to the bloody Wexford rising (see chapter 11) reflected a profound insight: "Good God! What a brute man becomes when ignorant and oppressed! Oh liberty, what horrors are perpetuated in thy name! May every virtuous revolutionary remember the horrors of Wexford."

As a Catholic barrister practicing in the Irish law courts, O'Connell was intensely aware of the civil disabilities suffered by Catholics. Yet he refused to accept emancipation with the safeguards, on grounds that religious liberty should not be won at the price of shackling the church. His goal was to win emancipation without the safeguards; his strategy was to harness a mass popular agitation to a constitutional parliamentary movement. In 1823 he helped found a new Catholic Association and the next year opened it to ordinary tenant farmers by reducing the membership fee to a penny a month. A stroke of genius, this decision enabled the Catholic Association to tap the energy of the tenants and to collect thousands of pounds a year for its political fund. Moreover, it mobilized the parish priests, who were held in great esteem in the Catholic communities and who happily urged their parishioners each Sunday to join the Association.

O'Connell's Catholic Association was the first modern political organization in Britain. Why did it succeed in appealing to the Irish peasantry, who, after all, would not personally benefit from Catholic emancipation? (The franchise remained limited to large property owners.) One reason was that O'Connell had the gifts of uncanny eloquence and a magical voice. He was a born demagogue, who by his forceful denunciations of British rule, acted out the wishes and dreams of his mass audiences. He spoke to the people from within their traditions and appealed to their sense of independence and pride. At the same time, O'Connell made the agitation seem dangerous to the authorities because, although always eschewing revolution, he deliberately referred to the violence that might occur if Catholic emancipation were not granted. In British eyes, there loomed behind O'Connell the shadowy nightmare of popular revolution.

In 1826, the Catholic Association turned to direct electoral pressure. In the counties, approximately eighty-five thousand Catholic tenants had the vote as forty-shilling freeholders. Traditionally, they yielded to intimidation and voted with their landlords. But the Catholic Association and the parish priests were able to persuade the tenants in Waterford and five other constituencies to defy their landlords and vote for parliamentary candidates supporting Catholic emancipation. In 1828, O'Connell himself dared stand for Parliament in County Clare. He won decisively and thereby presented Wellington and Peel, the leaders of the Tory government, with a hard choice: whether to give in to pressure for emancipation or to reject O'Connell's election (and all the others that were sure to follow) and use military force against the rising that almost everyone expected to be the result.

As we saw in chapter 14, Wellington and Peel gave in. They did, however, exact a stiff price: the Catholic Emancipation Act of 1829 allowed Catholics to sit in Parliament and to hold all but a few Crown offices, but it raised the property qualification for voters to possession of freehold land worth at least £10 (a fivefold increase from the previous 40 shillings) and so disfranchised about 80 percent of the Irish electorate. O'Connell struggled against the disfranchisement, but finally agreed to it because both the English Whigs and the upper-class Irish Catholics supported it and undermined his resistance. Otherwise, Catholic emancipation was a great victory for O'Connell, for the act opened all public offices (except an insignificant few) and Parliament to Catholics, and it included no safeguards.

O'Connell took his seat in the House of Commons in 1830 and for some years enjoyed unparalleled popularity—even adulation—in Ireland. Many Irish Protestants gloomily predicted the end of their Ascendancy, fearing that democracy, disestablishment, and confiscation of property would follow; many peasants joyfully expected the same outcome. In the short run both were wrong. Still, O'Connell's triumph in the campaign for Catholic emancipation was of immense significance. For one thing, it taught the Irish people that they could win by demands and agitation what they could not by reason and persuasion. For another, it affirmed the importance of priests in national politics. Most importantly, O'Connell's strategy welded Irish nationalism to Catholicism—an ironic outcome, given that O'Connell, a liberal Catholic devoted to religious toleration, envisaged a nonsectarian Ireland.

## REPEAL AND YOUNG IRELAND

O'Connell had always intended Catholic emancipation to be the first step toward his ultimate objective: repeal of the Act of Union. Neither a republican nor a separatist, he sought a dual monarchy: "I desire no social revolution, no social change," he said. "In short, salutary restoration without revolution, an Irish Parliament, British connection, one King, two legislatures." But he faced total opposition from the British Parliament on this issue. Not only were the Conservatives unalterably opposed to repeal, but so also were O'Connell's former Whig and radical allies. When he first raised the question in Parliament (in 1834), he was defeated by 532 to 39. His support included, besides his own repeal party, only one English MP, who was none other than the future Chartist (and Irish nationalist) Feargus O'Connor.

Given this blanket opposition, O'Connell thought it wise to win from Parliament whatever help he could for the Irish people within the structure of the Union. Though the Whigs were as touchy on law and order in Ireland as the most unbending Tories, at least they included Ireland in their program of parliamentary reform. Hence, the Irish Reform Act of 1832 expanded the electorate, particularly in the boroughs, and gave Ireland five extra seats. In 1833, the Whig government reorganized the Anglican Irish Church, abolishing ten bishoprics and reducing the income of the others. Hoping for additional reforms, O'Connell made an alliance in 1835 with the Whigs—the so-called Lichfield House Compact.

By this agreement, O'Connell and his repealers acted with the Liberal parliamentary alliance and put repeal on the back burner. The alliance, however, was for O'Connell only moderately successful. The Whig government in 1838 tried to solve the problem of Irish tithes, but against ferocious opposition it was able only to convert the tithe into a rent charge in effect collected by the landlords. In 1839, the Whigs imposed on Ireland the dubious gift of a Poor Law system, complete with workhouses. In 1840, a reform of Irish municipal corporations was passed.

The most beneficial aspect of O'Connell's alliance with the Whigs was a change in the tone of the Dublin Castle administration. The key figure in this administrative reform was the Sctosman Thomas Drummond (1797–1840), undersecretary from 1835 to 1840. Determined to enforce the law without the usual prejudice in favor of the Protestants, Drummond opened the Irish judiciary as well as civil service to Catholics, and even evicted from the bench the more bigoted Protestants. He took strong action against secret terrorist societies, but for once also brought pressure on the Protestant Orange Order and so broke its political power. Drummond understood the economic roots of agrarian crime and admonished the landlords that "property has its duties as well as its rights." In sum, Drummond did more than any other British official before 1870 to win the confidence of the Catholic majority.

Drummond, however, died in 1840, and with the Whig government on its last legs, O'Connell decided to renew the campaign for repeal of the Union. There was no prospect of allying with the Conservative leader, known to the Irish as "Orange Peel." In 1840, therefore, O'Connell founded the Loyal National Repeal Association, hoping to win repeal by the same tactics as in 1828–29: parliamentary pressure backed by a massive popular agitation in Ireland.

The moment seemed ripe for repeal, in part because of the inspired journalism of a small number of romantic journalists called Young Ireland. In 1842, three young men devoted to the cultural as well as the political autonomy of Ireland founded *The Nation* newspaper. They were Thomas

*O'Connell Memorial, Dublin. Designed by John Henry Foley, 1882.*
*This massive memorial to Daniel O'Connell bears witness to the Liberator's central role in the history of modern Ireland. The memorial stands at the southern end of one of Dublin's main streets: known as Sackville Street while Ireland was part of the United Kingdom, it was renamed O'Connell Street in 1924 after the formation of the Irish Free State.*

Davis (a Protestant barrister), Charles Gavan Duffy (an Ulster Catholic), and John Blake Dillon (a southern Catholic). Their policy was repeal of the Union, but their ultimate goal was renewal of the Irish identity based on old Irish cultural traditions and a potent mythology of Irish heroes and martyrs. They wanted the Irish to be more than "West Britain." Their national ideal was nonsectarian, and their propaganda was lofty and effective. By 1843, *The Nation* had a readership of more than 250,000.

Backed by *The Nation*, O'Connell designated 1843 as the repeal year. He staged a series of giant open-air gatherings dubbed monster meetings to demonstrate the depth of Irish feeling. More than one hundred thousand people attended some of these monster meetings. O'Connell spoke at the meetings in a crescendo of violent rhetoric. To cautious people in England and Ireland, he seemed to be threatening revolution. In June 1843, for example, he warned his audience that "you may have the alternative to live as slaves or die as freemen." By the autumn of 1843, the political temperature of Ireland was at its peak, and the British, already concerned about Chartism, felt embattled.

The problem for O'Connell was that he was deliberately bluffing and had no alternate plan should the British government simply defy him. And defy him they did. Prime minster Peel and his Conservatives, as well as nearly all the Liberals, simply would not countenance repeal of the Union. In 1834 Peel had declared: "I feel and know that the Repeal must lead to dismemberment of this great empire; must make Great Britain a fourth-rate power of Europe, and Ireland a savage wilderness." What repeal ran up against, then, was British nationalism, the deep British mistrust of Catholicism, and the British certainty that autonomy for Ireland would destroy the empire. Peel said in 1843: "Deprecating as I do all war, above all, civil war, yet there is no alternative which I do not think preferable to the dismemberment of this empire." In October 1843, Peel banned what was to be the biggest monster meeting and summoned troops to enforce that ban. O'Connell, who had always loathed violence and bloodshed, canceled the meeting. Even so, the government arrested him shortly afterward and convicted him of conspiracy. O'Connell was imprisoned for five months and emerged a more cautious and weary man. The repeal agitation was finished.

## THE GREAT FAMINE, 1845–1850

Repeal was in any case soon made irrelevant to the Irish masses. Famine became the reality, and suffering was the everyday experience of millions of

*The Great Famine in Ireland, 1846: starving peasants receiving charity along a roadside.*

Irish men, women, and children. In the autumn of 1845, the Irish potato crop was heavily damaged by a fungus now recognized as *phytophthora infestans*. The blight turned most of the potatoes into a foul mass of putrefying pulp. Dependent as they were on the potato, a large segment of the Irish population suffered grievously through the winter of 1845–46 and then the crop of 1846 failed utterly. The winter of 1846–47 brought widespread starvation and disease. Many peasant families ate their seed potatoes; therefore, although the blight did less damage in 1847, the harvest was too small. In 1848, the potato crop failed totally again and only began to improve in 1849. By 1850, the blight had largely disappeared, but in the meantime famine had made a horror of life in Ireland.

Population statistics reveal the impact of the Great Famine in stark terms. In 1841, the Irish population stood at 8.2 million people, and by its natural rate of increase would have risen to about 9 million in 1851. In actuality, the census of 1851 found only 6.5 million, leaving a gap of about 2.5 million between the expected and the actual population. Of these, about 1.5 million were emigrants; the rest, about 1 million people, were the casualties of the Great Famine. Some died of hunger, but most died of famine-related diseases such as typhus, relapsing fever, and dysentery. These million dead amounted to nearly 20 percent of the Irish population of 1841. For comparison, it should be noted that Ireland lost more people because of the Famine than all of Britain did in any war between 1688 and the present.

Irish suffering during the Famine is incalculable. The poorest elements in the society—laborers and cottiers—suffered most, but the small tenant farmers, particularly in the west, also faced terrible deprivation. None of these classes had any reserves of wealth or possessions with which to buy food. Irish farms, ironically, continued to produce food throughout the famine years, and indeed Irish farmers and merchants continued to export food (grain, cattle, and dairy products) to England, Scotland, and Wales. But the Irish peasants who grew those foodstuffs to pay their rent had nothing left after the rent with which to buy food. Thousands fell into arrears on their rents anyway, and many were evicted. Evicted families crowded the roads and poured into overfull workhouses and hospitals. Reports by careful observers of the misery of the people are numerous and heartbreaking: reports of women and children starving, of bodies too numerous to be buried, of dogs eating corpses. Here is a passage from one letter written by a magistrate to the duke of Wellington:

> I accordingly went on the 15th instant [December 1846] to Skibbereen. . . . I was surprised to find the wretched hamlet apparently deserted. I entered some of the hovels to ascertain the cause, and the scenes which presented themselves were such as no tongue or pen can convey the slightest idea of. In the first, six famished and ghastly skeletons, to all appearances dead, were huddled in a corner on some filthy straw, their sole covering what seemed a ragged horsecloth, their wretched legs hanging about, naked above the knees. I approached with horror, and found by a low moaning they were alive—they were in fever, four children, a woman and what had once been a man.

The suffering of the emigrants was scarcely less. Emigration was an old story in Irish history: approximately 1.75 million emigrated between 1780 and 1845, most of them choking the streets and alleys of Britain's worst industrial slums. Now, most went either directly to North America or to Liverpool, where they found passage to Canada or the United States. In both cases, the crossing was hazardous and miserable. Many of the ships called into the passenger service were inadequate. Some sank; on others the mortality rate ranged from a third to a half. For instance, the Agnes sailed in 1847; of her 427 passengers, only 150 survived. Even when they arrived in the New World, the Irish emigrants faced severe hardships. These rural people were forced practically overnight to become urban dwellers, and at the bottom rank of society to boot. The Anglo-Saxon (and Protestant) American elite hardly welcomed this influx of poor Catholics; "No Irish" signs became a common feature of cities such as Boston and New York. Over time, the

Irish in America learned to protect themselves by building self-sufficiency in their neighborhoods through Catholic parishes, parochial schools, and machine politics. This experience nurtured their Irish identity, and the Irish immigrant communities in America became hotbeds of intensely anti-British Irish nationalism.

Together, a pernicious blend of inability, ignorance, and ideology ensured that the British government's response to the Famine was horribly inadequate. Peel, who was prime minister when the Famine began, largely embraced the liberal ideal of non-activist government, but faced with the emergency in Ireland, he acted energetically. In November 1845, he had his agents in America buy £100,000 of Indian corn (maize) to be sold cheaply to local relief organizations, and he helped set up committees of Irish landlords to collect charitable funds and distribute food. Like most liberals, however, Peel believed that food distribution interfered with the market, harmed private merchants, and threatened to make the hungry dependent on the state. Thus, he also set the Board of Works to construct roads in Ireland as a means of providing employment and, most importantly, he undertook repeal of the Corn Law in 1846. If trade were free, Peel believed, the natural force of competition would ensure the flow of cheap grain into Ireland. As we have seen in the previous chapter, repealing the Corn Law was a costly decision for Peel. It split his party and brought down his government. And, tragically, as far as Ireland was concerned, free trade in grain did not work: the impoverished Irish people could not generate any economic demand for food.

Peel's successor as prime minister was Lord John Russell (1792–1878), scion of one of the grandest Whig families, a hero of 1832, and a strong liberal in his social and economic views. The actual day-to-day execution of British governmental policy in Ireland rested with Sir Charles Trevelyan (1807–86), assistant secretary to the Treasury, a doctrinaire liberal who declared that "the great evil" in Ireland was not famine but "the selfish, perverse, and turbulent character of the people." Trevelyan regarded the Famine as an act of divine providence, the means by which God would remake Ireland along English lines. By forcing Irish peasants off the land, Trevelyan contended, the Famine would also force landowners to modernize Irish agriculture, revitalize the Irish economy, and so transform Irish society.

Two assumptions guided Russell and Trevelyan in their policy making: first, that too much assistance would "demoralize" the hungry Irish—it would rob men of their self-reliance and hence their future ability to take care of themselves and their families—and second, that the market, not government, must determine food prices. Forced by events into intervening in Ireland, Russell and Trevelyan nevertheless struggled incessantly to minimize the government's role. "It must be thoroughly understood," Russell wrote in 1846, "that we cannot feed the people." He did not mean that he intended the Irish poor to starve; his faith in laissez-faire economics, however, made such an outcome inevitable. As one government agent in Ireland wrote Trevelyan, "You cannot answer the cry of want by a quotation from political economy."

Initially, the scale of the Famine in Ireland compelled Russell's government, like Peel's before it, to adopt interventionist policies that contradicted its liberal ideals. It first expanded the public works program that Peel had initiated. By the end of 1846, however, the failure of the program was all too clear. Starving, diseased, emaciated Irish men and women could not perform the physical labor of road building. In early 1847, then, the Whig government took the dramatic step of ordering that soup kitchens be set up all over Ireland to feed the starving. In the months that it took to get the kitchens up and running, thousands and thousands died, but by the summer of 1847, the soup kitchens were feeding three million people a day.

Russell's government did not, however, view the direct feeding of the hungry as a satisfactory policy. Instead, it declared in mid-1847 that "Irish property must pay for Irish poverty"—that taxes paid by the Irish landowning and middle classes must cover the costs of famine relief through the Poor Law. Russell and Trevelyan saw Irish landowners as lazy wastrels who must be taught the lessons of political economy. Optimistic reports about the fall potato harvest, its own nervousness about the detrimental effects of government intervention in the economy, and its determination to shift the burden onto the Irish propertied classes led Russell's government to halt the soup kitchen program in September of 1847. The results were disastrous. The debt-ridden Irish property owners could not pay the necessary taxes and the numbers of the starving overwhelmed Irish workhouses. Diseases such as typhus spread quickly through the overcrowded buildings, which soon became little more than charnel houses. Numbers in the workhouses peaked in 1849, numbers of evictions in 1850. Yet the Russell government held fast to its decision: the Poor Law must be allowed to work. It didn't.

Voluntary charitable efforts by the British were impressive, although inadequate by themselves for the task at hand. Various relief organizations, most notably the British Relief Association, raised funds in England and Ireland for soup kitchens and infirmaries. The Quakers distinguished themselves in this voluntary effort by sending many Friends to Ireland, where they not only set up the first soup kitchens, but also reported back to England about the true state of affairs in Ireland. The established Church of Ireland also did what it could to relieve distress, though some Anglican clergymen demanded conversion as the price of food. The actions of this minority in the Church of Ireland left a legacy of bitterness in the Catholic peasants that lasted long after the Famine was over.

Increased bitterness between the Irish and English was in fact one of the important consequences of the Great Famine. Many Irish concluded that the British had let Irish men, women, and children starve even though Britain was the wealthiest nation on earth, and that the British would never have let a million Englishmen or Scotsmen perish when food was available. (In fact, the potato crop in the western Highlands and islands of Scotland also failed, and Highland crofters suffered as grievously as the Irish poor.) The Irish survivors of the Famine at home and abroad repeatedly expressed their bitterness toward England in violence and bloodshed, as well as in song and verse. Many English, on the other hand, concluded that Irish elites were incompetent and irresponsible and that Irish peasants were a savage, even racially inferior people. The conservative *Quarterly Review* put it this way: ". . . all of the civilization, arts, comfort, wealth that Ireland enjoys she owes exclusively to England . . . all her absurdities, errors, misery she owes herself."

The Great Famine was a watershed in Irish economic and social history. The immediate demographic consequence we have already seen; the Irish population never recovered to its pre-1845 level. Moreover, the Famine began to roll back the subdivision of land. In 1841, 45 percent of all agricultural holdings in Ireland were between one and five acres; in 1851, only 16 percent were. As consolidation of holdings slowly went forward, so also did cereal farming and cattle grazing. Small family farms worked by tenants became the norm; furthermore, the new but profound concern of the tenants with protecting the family farm caused a rise in the average age at marriage and a corresponding decline in the birth rate. Unfortunately, *landlordism* (the predatory attitude of Irish landlords) survived. Many of the old landowners lost their estates to savvy investors and middlemen during the Famine. These new owners, however, proved to be just as devoted as their predecessors to collecting rents without providing agricultural leadership. Here were the roots of rural tension and violence in Ireland for the next fifty years.

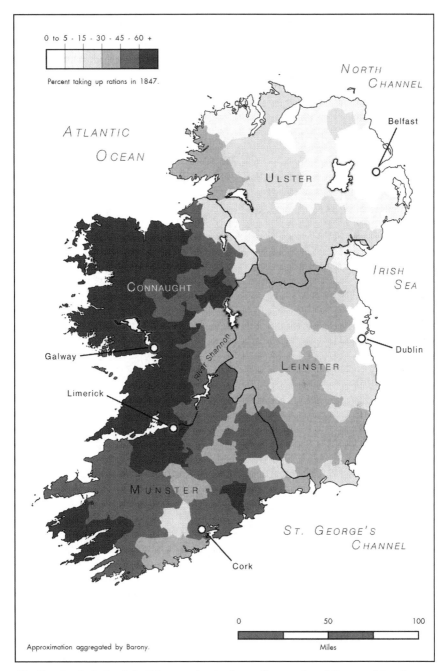

0 to 5 · 15 · 30 · 45 · 60 +

Percent taking up rations in 1847.

*A TLANTIC*

*O CEAN*

*N ORTH*
*C HANNEL*

Belfast

*U*LSTER

*I*RISH
*S EA*

*C*ONNAUGHT

Galway

River Shannon

Dublin

Limerick

*L*EINSTER

*M*UN*S*TER

*ST. G EORGE'S*
*C HANNEL*

Cork

0          50          100

Miles

Approximation aggregated by Barony.

*The Famine in Ireland.* As this map clearly shows, the peoples of Connaught and Munster suffered the most severely during the Famine.

## YOUNG IRELAND AND 1848

Relations between Daniel O'Connell and Young Ireland cracked under the stress of the Famine. The ineffectiveness of the British governmental response pushed *The Nation* toward a more militant stance. One editorial declared: "Better a little blood-letting to show that there is blood, than a patient dragging of chains and pining beneath them slowly for generations leading to the belief that all spirit is fled." O'Connell, however, responded firmly that "the greatest political advantages are not worth one drop of blood." This dispute aggravated disagreements between O'Connell and the Young Irelanders. After the failure of repeal in 1843 and the return of the Whigs to office in 1846, O'Connell thought it best to work with the Whigs in order to get what he could for Ireland. The Young Irelanders, however, preferred to stick defiantly to repeal. By mid-1846, the repeal movement had split wide open. Early in 1847, the Young Irelanders withdrew from the Repeal Association and founded their own organization, the Irish Confederation.

From that moment on, some Young Irelanders slipped hesitantly into a revolutionary posture. O'Connell, by then fatally ill, made one last pathetic appeal to Parliament for help against the Famine and then died on the way to Rome. Young Ireland became more radical. One of the radicalizing influences was James Fintan Lalor, who joined Young Ireland in 1847. He emphasized the rights of the tenants against those of the landlords and urged that "the national movement" temporarily be put aside for a tenant-right agitation. Everyone recognized that in Ireland tenant rights were a socially explosive issue. Another Young Irelander, John Mitchel, took up Lalor's ideas and began to combine them with advocacy of physical force. He wrote, "It is indeed full time that we cease to whine and begin to act . . . Good heavens, to think that we should go down without a struggle."

Despite the advent of such views within the Young Ireland movement, there was no overt action toward violent revolution until early 1848. The outbreak of the European revolutions of 1848, first in France and then throughout much of central Europe, precipitated the Young Ireland conspiracy. Mitchel and some other Young Irelanders seized the moment to call for an Irish republic—a step far beyond repeal of the Union. These Young Irelanders sent a deputation to Paris and established relations with the British Chartists. Once again, as in 1796–98, the British government faced a dangerous combination of British radicals and Irish nationalists.

Unfortunately for them, the Young Irelanders made poor revolutionaries. Government spies penetrated their organization. Young Ireland's leaders failed utterly to coordinate their rising with the Chartists. Mitchel was arrested and convicted of sedition in March of 1848, and in July Parliament suspended habeas corpus in Ireland. Aware that the government would soon arrest them, a few Young Irelanders set out to raise the peasantry of south-central Ireland in revolt. The leader was William Smith O'Brien, a chivalrous Protestant landlord who completely lacked the ruthlessness required of a successful revolutionary. The peasants were much too beaten down by the Famine to respond; they had no arms and no organization, and their priests urged them not to rebel. The *Rising* of 1848 thus ended in a miserable scuffle in a cabbage patch in County Tipperary. The leaders were arrested, convicted, and transported to Australia.

Tragic-comic as it was, the Young Ireland rising of 1848 nevertheless had considerable significance. The Young Irelanders' romantic and nonsectarian brand of nationalism and their refusal to renounce the revolutionary heritage inspired many later nationalists. Their defiant gesture in 1848 helped emphasize to Irish nationalists the notion that revolutionary acts, no matter how hopeless, can be morally elevating. The connection made by Young Ireland between tenant rights and nationalism, like their rejection of English utilitarian and laissez-faire principles, tended to radicalize subsequent Irish nationalist movements. Irish politicians after 1848 turned for a time to conventional parliamentary tactics, but the idealistic and extremist strain typified by Young Ireland did not die out.

## Suggested Reading

Boyce, D. G. *Nineteenth-Century Ireland: The Search for Stability*. Dublin: Gill and Macmillan, 2005.

Crowley, John, William J. Smyth, and Mike Murphy, eds. *Atlas of the Great Irish Famine*. New York: New York University Press, 2012.

Davis, Richard. *The Young Ireland Movement*. Dublin: Gill & Macmillan, 1987.

De Nie, Michael. *The Eternal Paddy: Irish Identity and the British Press, 1798–1882* Madison: University of Wisconsin Press, 2004.

Devine, T. M. *The Great Highland Famine: Hunger, Emigration and the Scottish Highlands in the Nineteenth Century*. Edinburgh: John Donald, 1988.

Donnelly, James S. *Captain Rock: The Irish Agrarian Rebellion of 1821–1824*. Madison: University of Wisconsin Press, 2009.

———. *The Great Irish Potato Famine*. Stroud, UK: Sutton Publishing, 2001.

Foster, Roy. *Modern Ireland, 1600–1972*. London: Allen Lane, 1988.

Gray, Peter. *Famine, Land and Politics: British Government and Irish Society, 1843–1850*. Dublin: Irish Academic Press, 1999.

Hoppen, K. T. *Elections, Politics, and Society in Ireland, 1832–1885*. Oxford: Clarendon Press, 1984.

Kerr, Donal A. *"A Nation of Beggars?" Priest, People, and Parties in Famine Ireland*. Oxford: Clarendon Press, 1994.

Lengel, Edward. *The Irish Through British Eyes: Perceptions of Ireland in the Famine Era*. Westport, CT: Praeger, 2002.

MacDonagh, Oliver. *Ireland: The Union and Its Aftermath*. London: Allen & Unwin, 1977.

———. *The Emancipist: Daniel O'Connell, 1830–47*. New York: St. Martin's Press, 1989.

———. *The Hereditary Bondsman: Daniel O'Connell, 1775–1829*. New York: St. Martin's Press, 1988.

Miller, Kerby A. *Emigrants and Exiles: Ireland and the Irish Exodus to North America*. New York: Oxford University Press, 1985.

Mokyr, Joel. *Why Ireland Starved*. London: Allen & Unwin, 1983.

Morash, Christopher, and Richard Hayes (eds.). *"Fearful Realities": New Perspectives on the Irish Famine*. Dublin: Irish Academic Press, 1996.

Neal, Frank. *Black '47: Britain and the Famine Irish*. New York: St. Martin's Press, 1998.

O'Faolain, Sean. *King of the Beggars: A Life of Daniel O'Connell*. London: T. Nelson & Sons, 1970.

O'Ferrall, Fergus. *Catholic Emancipation: Daniel O'Connell and the Birth of Irish Democracy, 1820–1830*. Dublin: Gill & Macmillan, 1985.

O'Grada, Cormac. *Black '47 and Beyond: The Great Irish Famine in History, Economy and Memory*. Princeton, NJ: Princeton University Press, 1999.

———. *Ireland: A New Economic History*. New York: Clarendon Press, 1994.

Ó Murchadha, Ciárán. *The Great Famine: Ireland's Agony*. London: Bloomsbury, 2011.

O'Tuathaigh, Gearoid. *Ireland Before the Famine, 1798–1848*. Dublin: Gill & Macmillan, 1972.

Palmer, Stanley. *Police and Protest in England and Ireland, 1780–1850*. New York: Cambridge University Press, 1988.

Toibin, Colm and Diarmaid Ferriter. *The Irish Famine: A Documentary*. New York: St. Martin's Press, 2002.

Vaughan, W. E. *Landlords and Tenants in Mid-Victorian Ireland*. Oxford: Clarendon Press, 1994

# Chapter 16

# Mid-Victorian Society and Culture, 1850–1870

The disintegration of Chartism and the collapse of Young Ireland in 1848 marked the end of more than a half-century of social and political turmoil. In Britain there followed a period of relative prosperity and social harmony. Poverty, urban misery, and class divisions did not disappear, but economic conditions improved compared to what had gone before, and social conflict was channeled into workable institutions. An atmosphere of confidence bathed the society. This atmosphere was reinforced by English preeminence within the British Isles and by British preeminence on the seas and in the world markets. The result was what Professor E. L. Burn has called the Age of Equipoise—the two decades of the 1850s and 1860s, when social and cultural forces reached a precarious equilibrium: forces of continuity seemed to balance those of change; forces of conservatism seemed to balance those of progress.

The mid-Victorian years from 1850 to 1870 were the high noon of Victorianism. On the basis of relative security and prosperity, the high culture of Victorianism flourished and blossomed. Later, Modernists of the twentieth century were to react strongly against Victorian culture, and Victorianism still carries negative connotations of bourgeois complacency and hypocrisy. This hostility toward Victorian culture fails to give credit to the Victorians, either for their achievements or for the sincerity of their attempts to deal with difficult problems. In culture, as in society, Victorianism was a balance of dynamic forces—conservative and progressive, believing and doubting, romantic and utilitarian.

## ECONOMIC STABILITY

Prosperity, or at least the illusion of it, was the foundation of the mid-Victorian equipoise. Britain in the 1850s and 1860s was the greatest nation on earth because of its economic power. Britain's head start in commercial and industrial expansion put it for a time far in advance of other countries. In 1850, for example, the British produced about 28 percent of the world's industrial output, including 60 percent of the coal, 50 percent of the iron, 70 percent of the steel, and nearly 50 percent of the cotton textiles. By the 1860s, the British controlled 25 percent of the world's trade, and an even greater percentage of international trade in manufactured goods. Britain had become "the workshop of the world."

Even the agricultural sector of the economy prospered. The repeal of the Corn Law in 1846 did not result in any decline of farm prices or rents. As a result of the Agricultural Revolution, British farming by 1850 was among the most advanced in the world, and in the 1850s and 1860s British farmers adopted even more productive techniques. The consequent highly intensive and capitalized method was called *high farming*. It included the use of steam engines for plowing and harvesting and systematic fertilization to increase crop yields. At mid-century, therefore, the British could still produce about half of the wheat and six-sevenths of the meat they consumed. The mid-Victorian years were a golden age for British agriculture as well as for British industry.

The productive power of the British industrial sector gave Britain an unusual position in the world economy. The British sold manufactured goods abroad and in turn imported vast quantities of primary products (food and raw materials). Foreign trade had always been important to the process of industrialization in Britain, but now it became more so, rising to 25 percent of the gross national product (GNP). Britain sat like a spider at the center of a web of worldwide trade. In the mid-Victorian years, more than one-fourth of all international trade passed through British ports. This fact allowed the British to enjoy very healthy *invisible income*—that is, profits from the transactions of trade itself, such as finance, insurance, brokerage, and shipping, plus capital investment abroad. The British owned perhaps one-third of all the merchant ships in the world, and by the 1870s they were earning £50 million a year as a return on their foreign investments. This invisible income was crucial to the British economy because it made up a substantial deficit between imports and exports. Britain was not only the workshop but also the banker and creditor of the world.

The mid-Victorian decades also brought conditions of stability and growth that contributed to an expansive attitude among businessmen. After a slowing of the rate of growth in the early 1840s, the British enjoyed a fresh bout of economic growth from the early 1850s through the mid-

1860s, mainly due to the rapid construction of railways. Moreover, because of the rapid accumulation of capital, the banks were able to keep interest rates low, which made additional investments in industry relatively cheap. More important yet for the middle-class mood was a mild inflation: the mid-Victorian years saw an increase in prices, not enough to dampen demand but sufficient to bring commercial and industrial men the sense of ever-improving earnings. Prices generally ran ahead of wages paid to working people; hence, businessmen enjoyed improved profit margins. For this reason, British businessmen of the 1850s and 1860s were somewhat less anxiety-ridden and somewhat more openhanded in granting wage increases to their workers than they had been in the first half of the century.

## MUTING OF SOCIAL CONFLICT

The expansive attitude of mid-Victorian commercial and industrial men contributed to a muting of social conflict. Social tensions eased—or were at least channeled into safe outlets—even though trends in the economy led to an increase in inequality. Wages continued to do less well than profits and rents. In 1803, for instance, the richest 2 percent of families in Britain enjoyed one-fifth of the national income; in 1867, the richest 2 percent had two-fifths. True, wages did rise, but not as fast as prices or profits. Moreover, as Victorian firms matured, there were fewer opportunities for working men to go from rags to riches than in the early days of industrial triumph. Nevertheless, this period did see a general movement of working people from lower paid to higher paid jobs, made possible by the broad expansion of the economy and the consequent multiplication of semiskilled, skilled, and clerical positions.

More important than actual social mobility was the myth of social mobility. As we have seen in chapter 13, the middle class preached to the working class the ideas of self-help and the self-made individual. By self-help, the message went, any person could rise in the world. Britain enjoyed, wrote Walter Bagehot, "a system of removable inequalities." In the words of Lord Palmerston,

> We have shown the example of a nation in which every class of society accepts with cheerfulness that lot which Providence has assigned to it, while at the same time each individual of each class is constantly trying to raise himself in the social scale not by injustices and wrong, not by violence and illegality, but by persevering good conduct and by the steady and energetic exertion of moral and intellectual faculties with which the Creator had endowed him.

That a viscount could mouth such bourgeois sentiments is proof conclusive of the triumph of middle-class ideas.

Of particular importance as the propagandist for these middle-class social ideals was Samuel Smiles (1812–1904), a Scottish doctor, journalist, and railway executive who wrote a number of best-sellers in the years between 1850 and 1880: *Self-Help, Thrift, Lives of the Engineers, Character*, and *Duty*. His view was that neither political radicalism nor socialism could help the working class; instead, individual moral reform was required. Smiles preached a simple and clear message: "Thrift is the basis of Self-Help and the foundation of much that is excellent in character." Illustrated by inspirational biographies, this message had a strong impact at a time when, because of the failure of Chartism and the consolidation of the factory system, many British working men and women were inclined to accept their place in the industrial capitalism.

Furthermore, the doctrines of self-help and the self-made individual were part of a package of softened middle-class attitudes and social policies. As chapter 14 showed, by the 1850s evangelicalism and paternalism were merging with utilitarian expertise to produce genuine social improvements such as the factory acts and public health reform. Temperance reform and *rational recreation*, both preached by the middle-class to the working-class, were genuinely meant to help working men and women rise in material well-being and social status. These middle-class virtues in part were supposed to make the working class tame and orderly, but they were also an invitation to join the middle class in respectability. Whereas Hannah More and other upper-class propagandists of the early nineteenth century sought to keep the laboring poor in their proper place, intellectual leaders of the mid-Victorian middle-class stressed the unity rather than the differences between middle-class and working-class folk. They insisted that, given the appropriate education and charitable treatment, individual members of the working class could achieve the independence and morally reliable behavior characteristic of all respectable people. John Stuart Mill, for example, wrote in his great textbook *Principles of Political Economy* (first published in 1848) that working people were advancing "in mental cultivation, and in the virtues dependent upon it."

Respectability and progress thus were key mid-Victorian concepts. They arose from the middle class, but served to encourage class reconciliation. "Respectability" became a cult word in the mid-Victorian years. It implied behavior that displayed acceptance of conventional Christian morality—

independence, orderliness, cleanliness, and propriety. Anyone in any class could become respectable by individual choice. On the one hand, respectability was the means by which a commercial or industrial captain and his wife showed that they were worthy of being called a gentleman and a lady, terms that increasingly connoted a moral quality rather than the old notion of bloodlines; on the other hand, respectability was the means by which working men and women sought to claim an independent place in the social and political order. Hardly anything warmed the heart of Victorian reformers more than the sight of a respectable working-class family—sober, scrubbed, and clothed in their Sunday best, on the way to church or chapel—but such working-class respectability did not translate into working-class acceptance of the social and political status quo.

By *progress* the Victorians meant not only the increase in technology and material production of modern society, but also the perception that ever greater numbers of people were choosing respectable lifestyles. The obvious accomplishments of industry and commerce, and the fortunate turn of Britain away from revolution in favor of reform, led the British into vigorous nationalism by mid-century. Pride in their legal, constitutional, commercial, and industrial institutions led many mid-Victorians into belief in the intrinsic, even biological, excellence of what they called the British (or English) "race." It also led the British to think that progress is automatic, that it is identical to change, and that it is a central theme in human history. Many Victorian historians celebrated progress in English history and thereby created a magnificent and useful, though somewhat inaccurate, myth of the English past. Historian H. T. Buckle (the son of a shipowner) put it best: English history, he said, is "the progress from barbarism to civilization"; indeed, "history is the living scroll of human progress."

Progress was a concept that the better-off members of the working class could share, and many members of the *aristocracy of labor*—the skilled craftspersons—met the middle class halfway along the road to respectability. As one former Chartist said, "It is in the very nature of the intelligent and virtuous to feel self-respect, and the claims of manhood as a man." Now that Chartism and sweeping attempts to form revolutionary national unions had failed, these working men stood ready to accept inequality of wealth, but they insisted on recognition of their equality in moral virtue and mental capacity. Working-class people realized that middle-class propagandists were trying to brainwash them, but they also accepted that capitalism and industry had arrived to stay, and that through temperance, prudence, hard work, and self-education, the top stratum at least of the working class could improve itself. As one working man put it, through working-class organizations such as cooperative societies, workers "become independent, and feel morally as well as socially elevated."

Once Chartism failed, the main institutions of the working class embodied efforts by working people to come to terms with capitalism and industry. First, the *friendly societies*, essentially institutions of collective thrift, that had originated within the ranks of skilled artisans now expanded. In these voluntary associations, workers joined together for the purpose of providing social security, such as unemployment, sickness, and old-age benefits. By 1872, friendly societies enrolled approximately four million members. Second, the cooperative societies evolved from utopian socialist communities into practical voluntary associations for cooperative production and shopkeeping. They were an effective way of securing a place for the traditional concern for community inside a market economy.

Finally, there were *new model trade unions*. These were not revolutionary organizations, but cautious and businesslike craft unions devoted to protecting their members within the industrial system. These unions—the Amalgamated Society of Engineers, the Amalgamated Society of Carpenters and Joiners, and so on—all had relatively high subscription fees because they set unemployment benefits as a high priority. For these reasons, the craft unions of the mid-Victorian years never enrolled more than about 10 percent of adult laborers, nor did they adopt an aggressive strike strategy. Their objective was simply "a fair day's wage for a fair day's work," and they succeeded because they could keep the skills of their members exclusive. Their prudent behavior slowly won not only benefits for the working-class elite, but also the approval of a section of the liberal middle class. Eventually, in the 1870s, the new model trade unions earned from Parliament legal recognition of trade unions and of peaceful methods of pursuing trade disputes.

## THE CRYSTAL PALACE, 1851

The Great Exhibition of 1851 symbolized the prosperity, the faith in progress, and the social reconciliation of mid-Victorian Britain. The brainchild of Queen Victoria's beloved husband, Prince Albert, the Great Exhibition was the first world's fair. A tireless promoter of science and technology as well as head of the thoroughly bourgeois royal family, Albert sought to invite all nations to put on display the material evidence of the advance of

*The Crystal Palace, 1851. The huge but graceful building was constructed from prefabricated iron and glass panels. It symbolized science, technology, and progress to the Victorians.*

civilization and so celebrate humanity's achievements. In fact, however, the Great Exhibition celebrated *British* achievements and boosted British pride, for the exhibits in manufactures, machinery, and fine arts demonstrated Britain's industrial, commercial, and imperial preeminence. Speaking in effect for the nation, Queen Victoria wrote, "I never remember anything before that everyone was so pleased with, as is the case with this Exhibition."

The building that housed the Exhibition was one of the principal reasons for satisfaction. Known appropriately as the Crystal Palace, the exhibition hall was a perfect symbol for the age—a splendid hall over 1,800 feet long and 108 feet high at the peak of its great arched transept and made of prefabricated iron columns, girders, and glass panels. The Crystal Palace was designed by Joseph Paxton, himself a symbolic figure: formerly a gardener employed by the duke of Devonshire, Paxton by 1850 was a self-made engineer and railway director. His design—in effect a giant greenhouse—took less than a year to plan and build, yet it expressed in its beautiful functionalism the industrial miracle of the British economy. It was a cathedral devoted to material progress. (Eventually, the Crystal Palace was moved from Hyde Park to Sydenham, where it remained until fire destroyed it in 1936.)

The Crystal Palace proved to be a meeting ground for Britons of all social classes. Although the upper-class promoters of the Great Exhibition feared at first that members of the working class might cause embarrassing trouble at the Crystal Palace, the working people who came were well-behaved and respectable. Huge numbers came: more than six million tickets were sold in less than a year. Railway companies ran cheap trains for ordinary people to take day-long excursions to the Exhibition. At the Crystal Palace, working-class folk rubbed elbows amicably with the rich. Who would have thought, mused the *Times*, that such events "should have taken place not only without disorder, but also without crime." The events of 1848 seemed to have receded into the distant past.

## HIGH CULTURE OF THE VICTORIAN PERIOD

Victorian writers were a major force behind the mid-Victorian social consensus and the *meliorism* (reformism) of the ruling elite. They typically urged charity and social harmony on their middle-class readers even as they preached bourgeois values to the working class. In the mid-Victorian years, British intellectuals generally reflected the optimism of the period, not blindly or complacently, but with faith that social relations and cultural values could be improved. They were often very critical of particular institutions and attitudes—the churches, the schools, and the judicial system or the greed, the self-interest, and the utilitarianism of the commercial and industrial men—but always with the view that progress and reconciliation were possible. Not surprisingly, mid-Victorian intellectuals expressed a balance between the two great streams of thought that they inherited: the romantic and the utilitarian.

In the Victorian years, intellectuals in Britain were called *men of letters*, a term that indicated a particular kind of writer standing in a special relationship to the public. The men of letters were neither alienated intellectuals nor academic specialists. Instead, the label applied to a wide variety of writers—novelists, poets, social critics, historians, political economists, philosophers, and so on—who were tied directly to the general reading public by the sale of books and articles in a market system. Men of letters thus included writers of fiction, poets and social critics.

The audience for the men of letters exerted great influence on their work. By the early Victorian years, a general reading public buying reading matter in great quantities had replaced patronage as the means by which writers earned their living. The lack of an educational system for the working class and the relatively high price of books and magazines limited this general reading public to the well-off. The middle class was by far the larger of the two upper classes; thus, the middle class dominated the reading public. Middle-class men and women hungered for entertainment, information, social instruction, and moral guidance. As members of a new social order, they lacked the traditional breeding that satisfied such needs among the aristocracy and gentry. They looked instead to formal education and to reading matter of all kinds—newspapers, magazines, books, manuals of etiquette, encyclopedias, and the like. Thus, the middle class created a demand for writing and called into being the men of letters.

The men of letters themselves came overwhelmingly from the middle class. Many young men—and, as we will see, women—found the opportunity to make money as writers irresistibly attractive. As novelist Anthony Trollope wrote, the profession of literature required "no capital, no special education . . . no apprenticeship." Many of the men of letters depended wholly on the sale of their work for their livelihood, and some with great success. Dickens made a fortune on his novels, selling some of them to publishers for as much as £4,000 apiece; Trollope ascended from the ranks of the lower civil service to the status of landed gentlemen by dint of his novels, which he turned out with businesslike routine; and historian T. B. Macaulay made more than £20,000 on the third and fourth volumes alone of his monumental *History of England*. In short, a young man (or woman) of energy but no connections might make a comfortable living as a professional writer, combining in his (or her) work journalism, criticism, and fiction. This success helped keep the men of letters from becoming angry and alienated.

Their influence also worked against alienation. The Victorian men of letters were not prohibited by official censorship (except in regard to blasphemy and libel) from saying what they wanted. Further, the reading public was relatively compact and accessible, and it included nearly all the people who made Britain's political, social, and economic decisions. The men of letters knew that serious works of fiction, history, or social criticism would reach nearly everyone who counted. Moreover, not only the market system, but also bonds of sympathy tied the men of letters to the public. Authors and their reading public understood and trusted each other. Men of letters on the whole tended to share middle-class values: order, progress, work, self-help, and a more or less orthodox Christian morality.

One result of the close bonds between serious Victorian writers and their public was that all agreed on the proper function of intellectuals. The public expected men of letters to be *useful* as entertainers, as instructors, and as moral guides to help their readers through the troublesome times of economic and social change. The Victorians felt strongly the gravity of the new problems they encountered, and they turned not only to the churches, but also to the men of letters for mental and moral help. The public in effect asked the authors to serve as teachers, preachers, and prophets—sages for a secular society. The men of letters for their part accepted this didactic function, even though they were sometimes uncomfortable with narrow utilitarian or moralistic standards for judging intellectual or artistic work. After all, this social utility gave them high status.

## EXEMPLARS: CARLYLE, DICKENS, TENNYSON, AND MILL

We can see examples of the different ways of fulfilling the didactic function adopted by Victorian men of letters by looking at four important writers of the nineteenth century. For Thomas Carlyle (1795–1881), perhaps the prime example of the men of letters, the way was that of the prophet. As he wrote, what England needed was a heroic "Prophet or Poet to teach us." In a long career of rumbling and thundering, Carlyle incessantly warned Britain about what he saw as its abandonment of the spirituality and cultural coherence of medieval society for the materialism and fragmentation of modernity. Carlyle's essays and histories (most notably *The French Revolution, On Heroes and Hero Worship, Sartor Resartus*, and *Past and Present*) arose from an unusual outlook—namely, a volcanic combination of Scottish Calvinism and German Idealist philosophy. Calvinism taught Carlyle that the world's history is the irresistible unfolding of God's will; from Idealism, he learned that the material world is only the clothing for the true spiritual reality. According to Carlyle, Britain's problem was that most people, caught up as they were in a philosophy of utilitarianism and self-interest, failed to see the underlying spiritual nature of reality. Consequently, they confused means and ends, and their society lost its grounding. Yet Carlyle combined such sharp criticism of Victorian culture with an affirmation of core middle-class values. His demand for "heroes" (those who have insight into God's will and who dare to act accordingly) accorded with the middle-class emphasis on responsibility and individual agency; more straightforwardly, his praise for work as the agency of divine purpose echoed the middle-class insistence that the effortless life was not worth living. By the end of his life, Carlyle was known as "the sage of Chelsea," for his message appealed to the religiosity, the seriousness, and the dutifulness of the Victorians.

One of the many men of letters deeply influenced by Carlyle's warnings of a social catastrophe such as the French Revolution was Charles Dickens (1812–70). In a time when novels were the dominant literary form, simultaneously providing entertainment, social observation, and moral instruction, Dickens was the most imaginative of all Victorian writers of fiction. He wrote a series of sprawling best-sellers through which he established an intimate connection to his audience: *Oliver Twist, A Tale of Two Cities, David Copperfield, Hard Times,* and *Little Dorritt,* to name only a few. In these novels, Dickens displayed an ability to be at once a great comic writer and a serious social critic and reformer. His works provided a miraculously rich panorama of portraits taken from industrial capitalist society. He did more than any other person, whether in public office or in intellectual life, to help his fellow Victorians see what was actually all around them—the suffering of the Hungry '40s, the misery of urban life for most of the working class, the harshness of utilitarian philosophy, the blindness and hypocrisy of many middle-class people, and the need for a renewal of simple human charity and sympathy.

The reading public that consumed the fat *three-decker* (three-volume) novels by Dickens and others found in them just the kind of information and guidance that it needed. Fiction was the perfect art form for the Victorian middle class. That same audience tended to be resistant to poetry, at least poetry of all but a certain kind. Victorian readers valued poetry when it was useful to them in some way, especially in stating truths in a poignant manner or in providing moral uplift. Many poets found this situation uncomfortable. As heirs to the romantics, they naturally felt a desire to make art a refuge from the hurly-burly of industrialization, a realm of higher values such as beauty, contemplation, and spirit. Yet Victorian poets were also drawn by the urgency of social and cultural change to keep in touch with the main themes of the times and to speak to the concerns of the broad spectrum of literate people. Thus, most Victorian poets were divided as to their purpose and were profoundly concerned with defining a poetic role for themselves.

No one exemplified these tensions or found solutions more agreeable to the reading public than the greatest of the Victorian poets, Alfred, Lord Tennyson (1809–92), who was appointed poet laureate by Queen Victoria in 1850. Deeply affected by an unstable home life, Tennyson developed a powerful streak of melancholy and found relief only in the discipline of writing verse. He grew up in the heyday of the romantic poets and was drawn to the romantic ideal of the isolated poetic genius. At Cambridge University in the late 1820s, however, fellow members of a secret society of undergraduate intellectuals urged Tennyson to use his poetry for the good of the nation. As his closest friend said, "Poems are good things, but flesh and blood is better." Most of Tennyson's early poetry reflects the rival attractions of poetic isolation and public teaching and takes the dilemma of writing poetry in unpoetic times as a main theme. Tennyson also read modern science, including the emerging evolutionary geology and biology, which threw doubt on conventional religious belief.

These issues came to a crisis for Tennyson in 1833, when his closest undergraduate friend and moral guide died. *In Memoriam* (1850), written by Tennyson over ten years as a verse diary of psychological recovery, raises and resolves fundamental questions: What is the use of poetry in times of great national change? Is there life after death? Can one believe in a benevolent God when the death of individuals and the struggle for survival in nature seem to prove otherwise? To all these questions, Tennyson was able to give ringing affirmative answers, but only after profound struggle. His ability to adopt a positive outlook and to affirm belief in progress attracted his readers. Without intending to, Tennyson spoke for all literate Victorians. He had learned from both science and religion, and in so doing he had forged a balance from the two rival lines of thought in the Victorian period. Such a balance was characteristic of the mid-Victorian decades.

Another great man of letters who learned from both streams of thought was John Stuart Mill (1806–73), by far the preeminent Victorian philosopher and liberal thinker. Mill labeled the two streams of nineteenth-century thought the Benthamite (empiricist, scientific, liberal) and the Coleridgean (romantic, idealist, conservative), and with characteristic fairness, he gave both credit for Victorian progress. The son of James Mill, and a close friend of Jeremy Bentham, J. S. Mill was raised as a complete utilitarian philosopher—"a logic-chopping engine," as Carlyle called him. When Mill was twenty, however, he had a nervous breakdown, which he attributed to the failure of his upbringing in developing his emotions. He turned to the romantic poets and the whole Coleridgean type of thought in order to cultivate his feelings. Thereafter, his utilitarian philosophy and liberal politics showed a flexibility and sensitivity lacking in Bentham's ideas. Mill acknowledged that mental and spiritual pleasures are higher than the physical; his political economy advocated capitalism, but leaned toward socialist values; and his political philosophy tempered democracy with concerns about majority rule. Mill was an individualist, but he interpreted individualism in terms of maximum moral self-development. His major works—*A System of Logic, Principles of Political Economy, On Liberty, Representative Government,* and *Utilitarianism*—stand as a compendium of nineteenth-century liberal and empiricist philosophy.

## WOMEN WRITERS IN THE VICTORIAN PERIOD

One of the most ironic facts about the Victorian "men" of letters is that so many of them were women. Especially in the genre of fiction, women writers emerged in large numbers in the Victorian period; thus, though women novelists probably remained in the minority between 1830 and 1870, writing became one of the main outlets for middle-class female talent and energy. Women did not find that becoming a professional writer was easy: not only did women lack opportunities for education, but also they were severely limited by the image of the "proper lady." Victorians assumed that the Creator designed women for domesticity: they were supposed by nature to be protectors of morality in the home and suppliers of warmth and consolation to children and husbands. The proper lady was never to put herself forward. Yet some middle-class women had to find a way to earn income, either because they were unmarried or because the financial burdens of the family fell on them. Others simply found that they had to express their creative impulses.

Women of talent adopted striking devices to mask or compensate for the "improper" activity of writing for publication. A few, accepting the convention that women's work was work for others, refused to accept any pay. Most went out of their way to celebrate domestic virtues and to parade antifeminist attitudes. Others adopted pseudonyms in order to hide their identity— and to get a fair hearing from the reviewers: Emily Brontë published as Ellis Bell, Charlotte Brontë as Currer Bell, and Marian Evans as George Eliot.

Despite these handicaps, some Victorian women writers achieved a literary and intellectual level at least as great as any of the males. Many literary scholars, for example, regard George Eliot (1819–80) as a writer of unparalleled intellectual power. In novels such as *Adam Bede, The Mill on the Floss,* and above all, *Middlemarch,* she painted the psychological landscape, the egoism, and the moral weaknesses of the Victorians. A thorough rationalist and freethinker, Eliot had given up her evangelical religion but not her moral imperative, which she translated into the simple desire to help her fellow human beings: "Heaven help us! said the old religion; the new one, from its very lack of that faith, will teach us all the more to help one another." For her, as for most Victorian novelists, realism was the necessary style of fiction because only a realistic depiction of society could supply the needed information about social structure and social relations or about new kinds of moral and intellectual problems.

The novels of Elizabeth Gaskell (1810-65) also exemplify this combination of realism with social critique and moral teaching. Gaskell wrote social novels that offered realistic and riveting portrayals of working-class life in industrial England—*Mary Barton*, for example, places the reader in the midst of Chartist-inspired tumult and trade union unrest in the booming northern industrial city of Manchester. Gaskell grew up in the still largely rural southern England but after her marriage lived in Manchester. In perhaps her greatest novel, *North and South*, she drew on her own experience of these two very different cultures as she traced the physical and emotional journey of her heroine, Margaret Hale, from Helstone, a sleepy southern village, to the grimy, growing mill town of Milton (a fictionalized version of Manchester). At first contemptuous of all she sees, Margaret learns to love the vitality of the new industrial order and the possibilities it offers for individual achievement and expression.

## VICTORIAN PAINTING AND ARCHITECTURE

The visual arts of the Victorian period, dominated by the interests of the new industrial and commercial middle class, displayed the same themes of realism (or truth to nature) and moralism. In painting, the two most notable developments after Constable and Turner were *genre* painting and *the Pre-Raphaelite movement*. In genre painting, the impulse to be instructive was dominant: paintings, like narratives, told a story. William Frith (1819–1909), for instance, painted large canvases giving realistic panoramic views of society: on Derby Day, in a train station, or at the post office. With technical skill but cloying sentimentality, Augustus Egg (1816–63) painted little moral lessons, such as the value of female chastity. The Victorian cult of domesticity and the moralistic aesthetics often trapped painters in sentimentality, and this sentimentality undermined the realistic style. For example, Edwin Landseer (1802–73) made technically exact paintings of animals, but gave them human emotions.

Past and Present, Number One, *by Augustus Egg (1858). This moralistic Victorian painting shows an adulterous woman being banished from her home by her husband. Note the impending collapse of the children's house of cards.*

The Pre-Raphaelites—Dante Gabriel Rossetti (1828–82), William Holman Hunt (1827–1910), and John Everett Millais (1829–96)—were self-conscious aesthetes (lovers of beauty) and rebels against the *painting-by-rules* favored by the Royal Academy. Influenced by the critic John Ruskin, they took inspiration from the Middle Ages and rejected what they regarded as the "unnatural" painting from Raphael on. Like Ruskin and other advocates of the Gothic, they believed in truth to nature, and so painted in minute, realistic detail. Yet they also sought to paint in glowing colors like a medieval manuscript and refused to use earth tones. Moreover, although they created an ideal world of medieval myth, beauty, and religiosity—plainly a rejection of industrial Britain—they also accepted the moral and narrative standards desired by the middle class. Their confusion of beauty with religiosity and their rejection of the ordinary world were important steps toward the substitution of art for religion that became characteristic of twentieth-century high culture.

*The Houses of Parliament, by A. W. Pugin and Charles Barry. The most famous example of Victorian Gothic architecture; designed 1836–1837 and built 1840–1860.*

In Victorian architecture, the moralistic and truth to nature impulses were not easily compatible. Because of their burgeoning wealth and expanding population, the Victorians built a huge number of structures of all kinds, but they had trouble developing an original and authentic style. In fact, the Victorians built in two different modes: one, *industrial* building, tended to be purely functional, with relatively straightforward materials and designs; the other, the obviously *architectural* building, tended to be extremely ornate, with lavish decorations drawn from some past historical epoch and endowed with heavy moral overtones.

Industrial building was not thought of as truly architectural in the day, and only later was it recognized as distinguished in its own way. Iron and brick were the cheapest building materials; thus, factories, warehouses, and dockyards were constructed on iron frames and with brick facades. Many of these were elegantly simple. Others, particularly bridges and viaducts, were strikingly innovative, for the Victorian engineers could span distances and carry weights not even the Romans could imagine. Beginning with Abraham Darby's Iron Bridge at Coalbrookdale (1780), industrial engineers built a series of amazing iron structures, including I. K. Brunel's Royal Albert Bridge at Saltash (1859), Robert Stephenson's Britannia Bridge over the Menai Strait (1850), and Sir John Fowler's Forth Bridge (1890). The greatest example of engineering design was, as we have seen, Joseph Paxton's Crystal Palace, which showed that iron pillars and frames could be graceful and beautiful as well as utilitarian.

Buildings that Victorians regarded as properly architectural imitated either the classical or the Gothic style. The best classical examples are the British Museum and the Town Hall in Leeds; the Gothic is exemplified by the Houses of Parliament, the Royal Courts of Justice (London), the Manchester Town Hall, and countless churches everywhere. Gradually, the battle of the styles was won by the Gothic, largely because the Victorians associated it with the coherent Christian culture of England's past. The leading theorists of the Gothic were A. W. Pugin and John Ruskin, both of whom were strong critics of industrial society. Pugin (1812–52), who with Charles Barry rebuilt the Houses of Parliament (1840–60), regarded the Gothic as the Christian style, harking back to an idealized hierarchical and devout society. Ruskin (1819–1900) argued that only a morally great society can produce great art; he found his ideal in the Venice of the Middle Ages. Under his influence, Victorian Gothic began to reflect the Byzantine influence on Venice, with multicolored brickwork and vivid, ornate decorations. In All Saints Church (Margaret Street, London) and Keble College (Oxford), both designed by William Butterfield, this riotous Victorian Gothic reached its peak.

Perhaps the finest of Victorian architectural achievements occurred when the industrial and Gothic styles were joined. One of the best examples of this combination was St. Pancras railway station and hotel. The station is a huge, gracefully arched iron and glass train shed, and the attached hotel is an extreme version of the Gothic, massive but with countless pointed arches, gables, and steeples. Another splendid example is the Oxford University Science Museum (1851), which has a lovely restrained exterior derived directly from Ruskin's Venetian Gothic and an exhilarating interior based on slim iron pillars vaulting up to an iron and glass roof.

## THE RISE OF SCIENCE

The Oxford Science Museum is symbolic of the advent of science in nineteenth-century Britain. If natural science could penetrate the tradition-bound walls of Oxford, it could do anything. Indeed, science by any measure ascended in the 1800s to take a dominant position in the culture. By the late Victorian years, science had not only won a place in the British universities,

*St. Pancras Railway Station and Hotel (1868). This splendid example of Victorian neo-Gothic architecture exemplifies Victorian confidence and exuberance.*

but it had also extended its jurisdiction to almost every area of human understanding, including social behavior and cosmology. In addition, scientists had formed well-organized and aggressive institutions to put forward their claims. Fundamental scientific discoveries—in electricity, in historical geology, in organic chemistry, and in evolutionary biology—proliferated on all sides.

Yet British scientists in the first half of the century liked to complain that science in Britain was declining and that scientists abroad were better supported and thereby enabled to be more productive. Such claims were misleading. True, the prevailing ideology of laissez-faire restricted government support for science, and industry as yet was not so sophisticated as to require research laboratories. In other words, the free market did not by itself provide for either research in pure science or careers for scientists. British scientists without independent income found it very difficult to devote their lives to science. The great English universities, Oxford and Cambridge, devoted as they were to classics, mathematics, and theology, made small provision for science. Even the Royal Society, founded in the seventeenth century, had come under the control of aristocratic amateurs.

Nevertheless, natural science in the early 1800s already played an increasingly important part in British society and culture. Many early industrialists had taken an active interest in science, and they had based some of their technical innovations (most notably, in steam power and iron metallurgy) on scientific discoveries. The Victorian public attributed much of their industrial growth to science. In many industrial cities, scientific institutions, such as "literary and philosophical societies," provided opportunities for business people to participate in the *march of mind* and polite scientific inquiry. Most important, scientific knowledge was regarded as part of the accepted view of the world. Early Victorians normally did not see science as opposed to religion, but as a vital source of knowledge of the will of God. The natural world was another book of revelation, and science was the key to reading it.

The fact that scientists felt left out of landed society, and especially left out of Oxford and Cambridge, gave them an urge to advance the claims of science. Their real position of strength made their claims irresistible. The scientists of the first half of the century felt very strong professional aspirations. In 1831, they had founded the British Association for the Advancement of Science (BAAS), which satisfied some of their professional objectives but not others. Many wanted to win places for themselves and for science at Oxford and Cambridge. This urge put the scientists among the forces seeking to reform the ancient universities. They found allies, first, in the Nonconformists, who wanted to open the universities to non-Anglicans; second, in the utilitarians and other liberals, who wanted to connect the universities with industrial and commercial life; and third, in some of the younger *Oxbridge* tutors, who wanted for themselves careers within the universities as professional teachers and scholars.

Beginning in the 1850s, the reformers broke through the universities' defenses. Parliament appointed Royal Commissions to investigate Oxford and Cambridge and then passed laws opening them to Nonconformists and endorsing "modern" courses of study, including natural science. The tutors won careers as teachers with expertise in their own fields. (In the 1870s, Nonconformists were allowed to take advanced degrees, and tutors were allowed to marry.) Under the influence of science, research became a much more important activity, and the old-style generalist approach to knowledge gave way to specialized study. New disciplines such as history, anthropology, and economics were founded, each of them on the model of science. Provincial universities began to be established in the major industrial cities—the beginnings of the University of Manchester coming first in

1851. By the late nineteenth century, then, natural science (though not industrial technology) had secured a high place for itself in British culture.

## RELIGION, SCIENCE, AND THE CRISIS OF FAITH

The central place of science in Victorian culture may seem to conflict with the Victorians' intense religiosity—but most Victorians did not think so. Throughout the nineteenth century, *natural theology* and the assumption that the scientific study of nature revealed God's workings in the world remained powerful. So, too, did the churches, both Anglican and Nonconformist, in political, social, and cultural life. As historian George Kitson Clark wrote, "Probably in no other century, except the seventeenth and perhaps the twelfth, did the claims of religion occupy so large a part in the nation's life, or did men speaking in the name of religion contrive to exercise so much power."[1]

This era saw Nonconformists throw off their political disabilities and impose much of their culture on the wider Victorian society. The Religious Census of 1851, which found that half of all Victorian churchgoers did not attend the established church, marked Nonconformity's triumph. At the same time, Anglo-Catholicism (also called Tractarianism) revitalized much of the Church of England with elaborate liturgies, a strong respect for the importance of aesthetic beauty in worship, and a reassuring emphasis on authority and tradition. The fervency and vitality of Victorian Christianity fueled the overseas missionary movement, a confident exercise of cultural imperialism by which British Victorians sought to extend their faith and values across the world.

Nevertheless, despite the apparent strength of Victorian Christianity, many Victorians worried deeply about what they perceived as a decline of religion. Two developments provoked much anxiety and soul-searching: the growth of urban, working-class neighborhoods that seem largely *unchurched*, and the crisis of faith among some of the educated sectors of society.

As we have seen, during the eighteenth century, the Church of England failed to maintain contact with the rapidly expanding ranks of the urban laboring poor. This problem intensified in the industrial cities of early Victorian England. Moreover, in those churches that did exist, the practice

---

[1] G. Kitson Clark, *The Making of Victorian England* (New York: Atheneum, 1976), 20.

of renting pews to the well-to-do led many working-class folks to conclude that church membership was simply not for their sort of people. By 1851, then, half the population of England—most of them working class—were not attending church. Of course, the fact that the working class was vastly larger than the middle and upper classes meant that the 50 percent of the population that was attending church included many workers. Indeed, during the Victorian era a greater percentage of the laboring classes attended church than at any time before or since. Nevertheless, the specter of the unchurched masses greatly alarmed middle-class Victorians, who feared a breakdown in social morality. Both the established Churches of England and Scotland and the Nonconformist denominations responded with church-building campaigns and domestic missions in the industrial cities. They failed, however, to bridge the gap between institutional Christianity and working-class culture.

Yet the existence of this gap did not mean that the British working class was anti- or even non-Christian; only a minority of working-class people embraced the politically radical and virulently anti-Christian *free thought movement*. Most workers simply did not equate "Christian" with church member or churchgoer. Instead, they defined Christianity in terms of a thoroughly pragmatic morality. Working-class Christianity was not a matter of belief, but of action, primarily the action of helping out one's neighbor in a time of need. Victorian working-class families tended to view the churches in instrumental terms. They sent their children to Sunday school, looked to the churches for material assistance, and attended religious services, not on Sunday mornings but on occasions that had symbolic (or superstitious) meaning in working-class culture: Watch Night (New Year's Eve), Harvest Festival, or the christening of a child.

The blend of superstition and pragmatism in working-class religiosity caused great anxiety among middle-class religious leaders; even more alarming, however, was the onset of a crisis of faith within the ranks of the upper classes. The primary precipitant of this crisis was an ethical reaction against the harshness of certain Christian teachings. Here evangelicalism was crucial because it heightened the intensity of the individual conscience and the drive for personal morality. In addition, the evangelical emphasis on good works as necessary for saintliness and the growing material capacity of the nation to do real social good created a powerful meliorism, indeed an impulse toward *perfectibilism*—the notion that people and social institutions are capable of perfection. By the 1840s and 1850s many Victorians were finding their meliorist attitude inconsistent with orthodox doctrines of hell and everlasting punishment. Surely, they thought, a loving God could not condemn millions of souls to eternal torment. They also began to reject the orthodox doctrine of atonement, which taught that God's justice demanded death as a punishment for sin, that the sinless Jesus Christ died in the place of sinners, and thus that Jesus's crucifixion served as a blood sacrifice that atoned for the sins of believers. Increasingly, Victorians rejected this theology as barbaric, akin to the sort of "primitive" religious customs that they encountered in places such as India and Africa.

At the same time, historical criticism of the Bible led to doubts about its literal truth. From the late eighteenth century on, German scholars had applied critical methods to the study of the Bible; beginning in the 1830s these methods made their way into Britain. Slowly, this *higher criticism* undermined orthodox belief by arguing that the Christian Scriptures should be understood as the works of real men in historical circumstances. It was necessary, higher critics contended, to separate legend from historical fact and to distinguish between historical assertions and allegorical statements of belief. Such arguments were not only heretical to those who clung to the Bible as God's literal words, but they also threatened to make the Bible understandable only by a committee of academic experts.

Developments in the new science of geology exacerbated this religious crisis by challenging the traditional Christian consensus around Archbishop James Ussher's dating of the earth (according to the Biblical genealogies) at 4004 BC. As early as 1795, James Hutton disputed both the earth's age and the then-common argument that the Biblical account of an all-encompassing flood explained changes observed in the geological record. In his *Theory of the Earth, with Proofs and Illustrations*, Hutton argued that natural causes, still in operation, explained the geological and fossil evidences thus far gathered. The publication of Sir Charles Lyell's *Principles of Geology* (1830–33) and Robert Chambers' *Vestiges of the Natural History of Creation* (1844), both arguing in favor of scientific theories of geological change that relied on natural processes occurring gradually over enormous stretches of time, strengthened the challenge that geology posed to traditional Christianity. The writer John Ruskin wrote movingly in 1851, "If only the Geologists would let me alone, I could do very well, but those dreadful Hammers! I hear the clink of them at the end of every cadence of the Bible verses."

A sense of religious crisis, then, had already enveloped much of educated society well before Charles Darwin (1809–82) published his findings regarding the evolution of species. As a naturalist aboard *HMS Beagle* in the 1830s, Darwin had two convergent experiences: first, he read Lyell's *Principles of Geology*, which persuaded him that the operation of uniform natural laws must explain scientific data; second, he observed the complex distribution of natural life in South America (and particularly in the Galapagos Islands), which showed him that all creatures are specially adapted to their environment. Back in England, Darwin struggled to understand how the uniform working of natural law modified species to fit their environment. Malthus's *Essay on Population* (see chapter 12), which had shown that all living things struggle ceaselessly for limited resources, helped him find his answer.

In 1859 Darwin published his *Origin of Species*, in which he summoned a wide variety of evidence to make three points: (1) species *had* varied—they were not created in immutable forms; (2) each species had evolved from antecedent species and ultimately from one or a few forms; and (3) the mechanisms of change were *variation* and *natural selection*. Variation refers to crucial biological advantages that assist in the struggle for survival (a slightly longer neck or a curved beak) and so provides the means of natural selection, the process by which the "fittest" survive. Then in *The Descent of Man* (1871) Darwin made explicit what was implicit in the *Origin of Species*: humanity followed the same pattern of evolution as did other species.

Darwinism immediately became the subject of heated controversy. The initial reaction of many leaders in the churches was negative. At Oxford in 1860, for example, Bishop Samuel Wilberforce debated Darwinism's chief propagandist, T. H. Huxley, by asking in a supercilious tone whether Huxley claimed descent from monkeys through his grandmother or his grandfather. That kind of reaction enabled Huxley to charge Wilberforce (and by implication, all orthodox Christianity) with *obscurantism*, that is, with deliberately hindering the spread of knowledge and obscuring the facts. The debate made science seem the agent of liberty of thought and progress, and religion the agent of authoritarianism and ignorance.

Within two or three decades after 1859, however, most British theologians and ordinary believers had made their peace with Darwinism. Ironically, a widespread misunderstanding of Darwinism contributed to its acceptance. The Darwinian understanding of nature as a battlefield—"red in tooth and claw," as Tennyson put it—threatened to knock the pillars out from under natural theology by destroying the idea that nature was "providentially designed," that all things were created by a benevolent God according to a divine plan. Yet, because they failed to understand the utter randomness of evolutionary adaptation, most British theologians and religious thinkers—and many scientists and scientific popularizers—argued that the process of natural selection revealed God at work in the world and so that evolutionary theory upheld rather than undermined natural theology.

This domesticated form of Darwinism proved very attractive to middle-class Victorians. It not only brought vast realms of phenomena under the grasp of the human mind, but it also provided scientific authority for many of the things that middle-class Victorians desperately wanted to be true. Natural selection and evolution seemed to justify inequality: the fittest *had* risen to the top. To middle-class Victorians, Darwinism was free enterprise biology. They understood themselves and their society to be the products of an evolutionary process designed to make the strong stronger, the best better, and the moral even more so.

### Suggested Reading

Barringer, Tim. *Reading the Pre-Raphaelites*. New Haven, CT: Yale University Press, 1998.

Bendiner, Kenneth. *An Introduction to Victorian Painting*. New Haven, CT: Yale University Press, 1985.

Bowler, Peter. *The Non-Darwinian Revolution: Reinterpreting a Historical Myth*. Baltimore: Johns Hopkins University Press, 1988.

Burn, W. L. *Age of Equipoise: A Study of the Mid-Victorian Generation*. New York: Norton, 1964.

Cheyne, A. C. *The Transforming of the Kirk: Victorian Scotland's Religious Revolution*. Edinburgh: St. Andrew's Press, 1983.

Clark, Kenneth. *The Gothic Revival*. New York: Harper & Row, 1974.

Collini, Stefan. *Public Moralists: Political Thought and Intellectual Life in Britain, 1850–1930*. New York: Oxford University Press, 1991.

Daunton, Martin, ed. *The Organisation of Knowledge in Victorian Britain*. Oxford: Oxford University Press, 2005.

Flanders, Judith. *Inside the Victorian Home: A Portrait of Domestic Life in Victorian England*. New York: Norton, 2003.

Flint, Kate. *The Victorians and the Visual Imagination*. Cambridge: Cambridge University Press, 2006.

Goldman, Lawrence. *Science, Reform, and Politics in Victorian Britain: The Social Science Association, 1857–1886*. New York: Cambridge University Press, 2002.

Gross, John. *The Rise and Fall of the Man of Letters*. New York: Macmillan, 1969.

Heyck, T. W. *The Transformation of Intellectual Life in Victorian England*. New York: St. Martin's Press, 1982.

Holloway, John. *The Victorian Sage*. New York: Norton, 1965.

Hoppen, K. T. *The Mid-Victorian Generation, 1846–1886*. New York: Oxford University Press, 1997.

Jordan, Robert Furneaux. *Victorian Architecture*. Harmondsworth, UK: Penguin, 1966.

Kirk, Neville. *The Growth of Working-Class Reformism in Mid-Victorian England*. Urbana: University of Illinois Press, 1985.

Larsen, Timothy. *Contested Christianity: The Political and Social Contexts of Victorian Theology*. Waco, TX: Baylor University Press, 2004.

Macleod, Dianne Sachko. *Art and the Victorian Middle Class: Money and the Making of Cultural Identity*. Cambridge: Cambridge University Press, 1996.

Mandler, Peter. *The English National Character*. New Haven, CT: Yale University Press, 2006.

Mason, Michael. *The Making of Victorian Sexuality*. New York: Oxford University Press, 1994.

McLeod, Hugh. *Religion and Society in England, 1850–1914*. Basingstoke, UK: Macmillan, 1996.

Newsome, David. *The Victorian World Picture*. New Brunswick, NJ: Rutgers University Press, 1997.

Otter, Chris. *The Victorian Eye*. Chicago: University of Chicago Press, 2008.

Perkin, Harold. *The Origins of Modern English Society, 1780–1880*. Toronto: University of Toronto Press, 1969.

Perkin, Joan. *Victorian Women*. New York: New York University Press, 1993.

Poovey, Mary. *A History of the Modern Fact: Problems of Knowledge in the Sciences of Wealth and Society*. Chicago: University of Chicago Press, 1998.

———. *Making a Social Body: British Cultural Formation, 1830–1864*. Chicago: University of Chicago Press, 1995.

———. *The Proper Lady and the Woman Writer*. Chicago: University of Chicago Press, 1984.

Robbins, Keith. *Nineteenth-Century Britain: Integration and Diversity*. Oxford: Clarendon Press, 1988.

Rose, Jonathan. *The Intellectual Life of the British Working Classes*. New Haven, CT: Yale University Press, 2001.

Rowell, Geoffrey. *Hell and the Victorians*. Oxford: Clarendon Press, 1974.

Ruse, Michael. *The Darwinian Revolution*. Chicago: University of Chicago Press, 1979.

Showalter, Elaine. *A Literature of Their Own*. Princeton, NJ: Princeton University Press, 1977.

Thompson, F. M. L. *The Rise of Respectable Society: A Social History of Victorian Britain, 1830–1900*. London: Fontana Press, 1988.

Thorne, Susan. *Congregational Missions and the Making of an Imperial Culture in Nineteenth-Century England*. Stanford, CA: Stanford University Press, 1999.

# Chapter 17

# The Overflow of Power: British Empire and Foreign Policy, 1815–1870

Britain dominated the global system of international relations in the first half of the nineteenth century. Its industrial and commercial head start gave the British state preeminence in world-power relationships and made the Empire a key feature of nineteenth-century British power and diplomacy. In the decades after 1815, then, British power overflowed the shores of the British Isles and rippled out in ever larger waves to touch nearly every island and continent on earth.

## BRITISH POWER AND INTERESTS

This is not to say that Britain was the same sort of buccaneering, mercantilist power as it was in the eighteenth century. Even though the British Foreign Office, diplomatic service, and imperial government remained in aristocratic hands, external policy reflected the outlook of the middle class. Peace and free trade were the predominant themes because the British knew that they could usually get their profits without force. It is true that British forces were engaged in a series of little wars almost continuously throughout the first half of Queen Victoria's reign—wars in India, China, Afghanistan, South Africa, Burma, and elsewhere. By British standards, however, these were normally little more than skirmishes; between 1815 and 1854, the British took no part in any major war.

British power was real and enormous, but it was economic, not military. Distrustful as always of a large standing army, Britain cut back on military spending after Waterloo. The army before the 1850s never numbered more than 140,000 regulars, of whom about a quarter were stationed in the

British Isles and another quarter in India. The British spent less than 2 percent of the gross national product on the army—far less than in either the eighteenth or the twentieth century. With an army this small, Britain could not think of major interventions in Europe.

British interests lay in overseas trade rather than European conquest. The British regarded the rest of the world as their market and their warehouse of raw materials. In the 1850s, Europe as a whole produced more than 50 percent of the total manufacturing output of the world. As Professor Bernard Porter has written, Britain "had more factories, consumed more coal and iron and raw cotton, and employed more men and women in manufacturing industry than the rest of Europe put together." About 40 percent of British trade was with the Continent, but the other 60 percent was with the non-European world: North America, Asia (including India), South America, Africa, and Australia, in descending order of importance. Furthermore, as we saw in chapter 13, the British invested an increasing amount of capital abroad each year.

To protect this all-important trade, Britain had to have a navy. The British let the navy dwindle after 1815 and only built it back up in the 1850s and 1860s. Nevertheless, throughout the whole period from 1815 to 1870, no country could challenge British sea power. Indeed, the British navy was generally more powerful than the next three or four largest navies put together. Naval squadrons could be (and were) dispatched to assert British interests in the Atlantic, the Mediterranean, the Indian Ocean, and the Pacific. British ships were active around the world in putting down piracy and slavery and in protecting British merchant shipping. After the adoption of ironclad, steam-powered gunboats in the 1840s, the navy could (and did) inject British powers inland by controlling rivers and coastal waters.

## THE FREE TRADE EMPIRE

The British navy protected the interests of the British Empire, already in the first half of the nineteenth century by far the largest in the world and quite unlike any empire that had ever existed. Decentralized and non-mercantilist, this was an empire built on and around free trade. Recall that, in mercantilist empires, colonies exist to serve the mother country by supplying raw materials and buying its manufactured goods; thus, in such empires the colonies were prohibited from trading with other nations and from competing with the mother country. Because Britain had such an industrial and commercial advantage over the other Western nations in the years before 1870, a mercantilist empire was no longer necessary. The British needed neither to exclude other nations from trading with British colonies nor to establish formal control over all of the territories that its commerce penetrated.

British imperial influence resulted from its industrial and commercial predominance. For this reason, it is useful to think of British overseas power in terms of *informal* as well as *formal* empire. In their informal empire, the British dominated many regions without establishing formal governmental control over them. As we have seen, the British industrial sector of the early nineteenth century established satellite economies all around the world—economies of primary producers that were dependent on Britain. Much of Central and South America, for instance, was part of Britain's informal empire, though the British directly governed only the Miskito Coast (now Belize and part of Nicaragua) and British Guiana (now Guyana). Similarly, the cotton-producing states in the southern United States were tied to Britain, and in a sense New Orleans was as much a part of the Empire as Calcutta or Montreal.

Given their economic advantage, the Victorians preferred to expand their influence without taking formal control whenever they could because it was cheaper. No soldiers or governors or judges were required. Nevertheless, the British possessed an enormous formal empire in 1815, the legacy of the age of mercantilism and of the Napoleonic Wars. This formal empire comprised variegated colonies around the world. India was the biggest, richest, and most important part of the formal Empire; it will be discussed in the next section.

The rest of the colonies formed a curious collection of territories, some having value as settlements for British emigrants, some as trading posts or naval bases, and some having no value at all. The British islands in the West Indies—Jamaica, Barbados, Trinidad, and many others—had once been the richest part of the Empire, but the sugar boom on which they depended faded in the nineteenth century, and their economies received a heavy blow when slavery was abolished in 1833. By mid-century the West Indies were the slums of the Empire. Canada had value as a partner in trade, supplying Britain with furs and timber in return for manufactured goods, but it was more important as a home for thousands of emigrants from the British Isles, especially Scottish clansmen fleeing the Highland Clearances and Irish peasants fleeing poverty and oppression. Australia, claimed in the 1770s by the Royal Navy, was used as a dumping ground for convicts between 1788 and 1840. When transportation of convicts to New South

Wales (the main colony in Australia) ended, more than fifty thousand convicts were working off their sentences there. The Cape Colony in South Africa was acquired in 1815 as a convenient port on the long sea route between Britain and India, and the British had other naval stations in the Indian Ocean for the same purpose. Gibraltar (1713) and Malta (1814) had been won in wars against Spain and France and were kept as naval stations to control the Mediterranean. Altogether, the British Empire in 1815 included about two million square miles and approximately twenty-five million people.

What to do with this huge formal Empire caused much discussion in the early nineteenth century, now that the mercantilist assumptions that had driven its formation no longer held sway. A few "Little Englanders," such as free trader Richard Cobden, regarded the colonies as outdated, useless, and expensive. Cobden and his free-trade allies believed that, if the colonies were simply let go, Britain would retain their trade anyway. But a majority of the British governing elite found them useful. Strategically, the colonies provided ready-made allies for the British; economically, they offered secure harbors and naval stations essential for trade. For Benthamites like Edward Gibbon Wakefield, the colonies served as markets for British goods and as safety valves for Britain's excess population. Indeed, emigration in the early nineteenth century was one of the few constructive social policies that won general consent. In the 1820s, the British government expended £65,000 to aid emigration, and between 1840 and 1873, the government-sponsored Colonial Emigration Committee assisted 6.5 million people to emigrate, most of them to the United States, but many to Canada and Australia.

Mainly, however, the British retained the colonies because they believed it their duty to do so. Because Britain—so the Victorians thought—was the most advanced nation on earth, the British had a responsibility to spread civilization to the less progressive peoples under their control. As one Colonial Secretary put it:

> The authority of the British Crown is at this moment the most powerful instrument, under Providence, of maintaining peace and order in many extensive regions of the earth, and thereby assists in diffusing amongst millions of the human race, the blessings of Christianity and civilization.

Not surprisingly, evangelical missionaries actively worked to spread these blessings. Evangelicals in the Church of England and in the Nonconformist denominations alike established numerous missionary societies, such as the British and Foreign Bible Society (1804), to support the proselytizing effort. The number of British missionaries, most of them evangelicals, grew throughout the nineteenth century; by 1900 there were some ten thousand scattered through the Empire. These remarkably energetic and self-assured folk tended to ignore the virtues and complexities of native cultures, but they nevertheless injected a humanitarian note in the imperial march. Many missionaries became the sole advocates for the welfare of indigenous populations (though not of indigenous cultures), as well as tireless opponents of the slave trade.

The missionary movement helps explain why the formal British Empire expanded quite rapidly during the period from 1815 to 1870, despite the ideological preference for informal control. Missionaries brought with them western assumptions and institutions, which often destabilized traditional societies. Such instability threatened British economic interests and created momentum for political intervention and, frequently, formal political control. The empire thus expanded through a process of *creeping colonialism* that grew out of the British exaltation of free trade. The British did not insist on exclusive rights to trade within their empire or in other parts of the world, but they did believe that any country, sheikdom, or tribe ought to cooperate in the regular rules of free trade and to provide security of person and property for British merchants. When an indigenous government across the sea refused to accept trade on British terms, was unable to provide security for British commercial establishments, or insisted on collecting tribute from British merchants, then the British government was prepared to use force. Merchants, like missionaries, inevitably caused trouble with traditional societies on the imperial frontiers, and this *frontier turbulence* frequently drew the British army and navy into action and the government into exerting formal control. As Lord Palmerston, the plainspoken and patriotic prime minister, said in 1860, "It may be true that in one sense that trade ought not be enforced with cannon balls, but on the other hand trade cannot flourish without security, and that security may often be unattainable without the exhibition of physical force."

One of the most blatant examples of the British use of force to secure adherence to free trade occurred in China. Although the imperial Chinese government restricted western trade to a few coastal ports, the British East India Company developed a lucrative commerce with China by exchanging Indian opium for Chinese tea, which it then exported to the West. Opium addiction, however, constituted an enormous social problem for the Chinese government, which repeatedly attempted to stop the opium traffic. Finally, in 1839 China's rulers declared the sale and distribution of opium to be a capital crime and at the same time attempted to collect tribute from British merchants. Conflict between Chinese officials and British traders followed. In 1840–42, British steam gunboats shattered the Chinese navy and a number of fortresses. This First Opium War forced the Chinese to cede Hong Kong to Britain and to open five port cities to British trade. Shanghai in effect became a British-governed city. A decade later, the Second Opium War (1856–60) forced the Chinese government to grant additional trade rights as well as to cede the Kowloon Peninsula (on the Chinese mainland across from Hong Kong) to Britain. Thus *gunboat diplomacy* forced open China to the West even as it protected the British rights to sell opium to China's addicts.

The expansionist impulses of colonists themselves also contributed to creeping colonialism. Consider the example of Canada. Beginning with several thousand Loyalists from the thirteen colonies in 1783, the population of Canada grew rapidly, reaching 350,000 in 1815 and 4 million in 1870. Led at first by fur traders and then by farmers, the Canadian people expanded into the Great Plains north of the forty-ninth parallel to the Rocky Mountains and claimed the Columbia River basin in the Pacific. These people, almost entirely of British extraction, simply pushed the Native Americans aside.

As the history of Canada shows, *internal expansionism* often involved the mistreatment or even destruction of indigenous peoples. Internal expansionism in Australia, New Zealand, and South Africa followed a similar pattern. In Australia, an increasing number of free immigrants from the British Isles joined the convicts sentenced to transportation. As the New South Wales colony grew, it threw out new shoots in Victoria and Queensland and pushed inland from the southeast coast to develop extensive cattle-grazing ranches. At the same time, Edward Gibbon Wakefield sponsored partially successful colonies in South Australia and Western Australia. As the British population pushed into the interior, they came into conflict with the indigenous Australian Aborigines, a seminomadic, Stone Age people. The Aboriginal population could not resist the firearms and diseases of the settlers, and by 1860 their numbers had been reduced by two-thirds. In New Zealand, traders followed hard on the heels of whaling captains, and in the 1830s, another of Wakefield's projects brought colonists from Britain. These colonists, eager for pasturage for their sheep, fought a series of bloody wars with the indigenous Maoris between 1843 and 1872. By the end of the wars, the Maori population had been reduced by half, and its social structure and land tenure system undermined.

In South Africa, British colonists faced not only indigenous African peoples (Bushmen, Hottentots, and Bantus), but also approximately twenty-five thousand cantankerous Dutch (Boer) farmers who had settled the Cape Colony in the seventeenth century. The Boer farmers regarded themselves as a racially superior people elected by God to dominate the blacks of Africa. They held Hottentots as slaves. The British, who arrived in 1815, sought to control the Cape Colony for strategic reasons, but also sought to protect the Hottentots and control the land-hungry Boers. Reacting against British pressure, the Boers looked for fresh grazing lands to the east and north of the Cape Colony. That expansionism brought them into conflict with the Bantus, who for some time had been migrating south and west, into the path of the Boers. Finally, in 1836, thousands of Boers sought to escape British control and trekked east and north, setting up Boer republics in Natal, the Transvaal, and the Orange Free State. The British had no desire to annex territory, but found the spillover from the incessant frontier wars between Boer and Bantu intolerable. In 1843, Britain annexed Natal and then in 1848 took over the other two Boer colonies. In the 1850s, however, Britain recognized the independence of the Transvaal and Orange Free State: the Boers were, for the time being, too difficult a meal to swallow.

Meanwhile, an important development occurred in colonial government. Most of the colonies were ruled autocratically by Britain as if they were conquered territories. Theoretically under the control of the Colonial Office, these *Crown colonies* were actually run by local British governors. After the American rebellion, however, colonies with large numbers of white settlers were allowed—indeed, encouraged—to rule themselves through representative institutions. Largely because they had learned from their experience with the American colonies that the old adversarial relationship between colonial governors and their legislatures did not work, the British developed over time a new system of *responsible government*. By this system, the local executive became responsible to the colonial legislature and not to the governor, who increasingly played the role of constitutional monarch in his colony.

The initial development of responsible government occurred in Canada. In 1791, to keep the French and British colonists apart, the British created Upper and Lower Canada. Governed as they were by the old autocratic system, neither province succeeded, and in 1837 rebellions broke out in both provinces. The Whig government then sent Lord Durham, a radical aristocrat who believed in responsible government, to Canada to solve the problems. In 1839, Durham submitted an extremely influential report, which called for the union of Upper and Lower Canada (in which the French colonists would be outnumbered) and for the establishment of cabinet government, according to which the colonial executive would be responsible to the colonial legislature. Upper and Lower Canada were joined in 1840, and responsible government was established in 1848.

Responsible government was government as cheap as possible for Britain and thus in many ways represented the free trade empire in its ideal form. Not surprisingly, then, responsible government was extended to other colonies as soon as their British (white) population had grown large enough to fend for itself. The Australian colonies received responsible government in the 1850s, and New Zealand in 1856. Jamaica and the other West Indian colonies never developed responsible government because the white population was so much smaller than the population of ex-slaves; indeed, they reverted back to Crown colony status. In South Africa, the settlers in Cape Colony were finally persuaded in 1872 to accept responsible government, including responsibility for paying for the wars against the Bantus.

## THE JEWEL IN THE CROWN: INDIA

India was the most highly valued part of the Victorian Empire, the jewel in the imperial crown. As the cotton mills of Lancashire began to export textiles to clothe millions of Indian peasants, trade with India became increasingly important to the British economy. India was most valuable, however, because its army made Britain a great power in Asia. The Indian army epitomized the mid-Victorian imperialist ideal: it gave power for very little expenditure. Numbering about two hundred thousand men, including the British officers and a few British regiments, the Indian army was larger than the regular army of Britain, yet it was entirely paid for by Indian taxes. The British administration in India, which remained in the hands of the East India Company until 1858, was largely a tax-collecting institution. It collected the taxes by which the Indian masses paid for their own subjection.

This strange situation had come about as the East India Company flowed into the power vacuum left by the collapse of the old Moghul Empire. By the 1790s, as we saw in chapter 7, the Company ruled Bengal and was one of the half-dozen strongest powers in India. For a time, the Company focused on trade rather than territorial expansion. But beginning in 1798, when Richard Wellesley (the brother of the duke of Wellington) became governor-general, the Company adopted an aggressive policy.

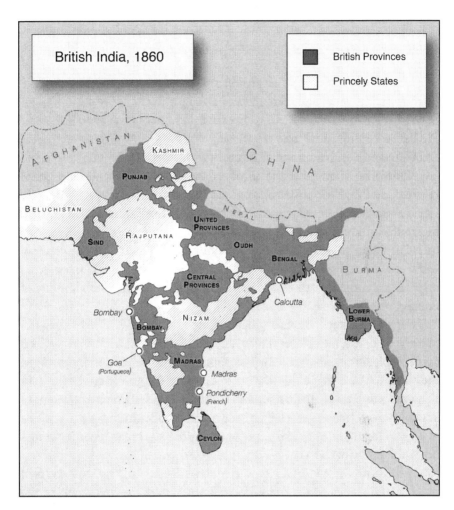

*The British in India, 1860.* As the map shows, Britain did not govern all of India directly. However, the rulers of the princely states knew that, if they wished to retain their wealth and power, they should heed their British "advisors."

Wellesley wanted to stop certain Indian states from allying with the French and to secure the Company's trade and property by imposing political order in the territories surrounding the Company's holdings. Long after the French threat was gone, Wellesley and his successors inexorably extended British rule and influence to reduce turbulence on the Company's frontiers. Some large states in southern India fell first, followed by several of the Maratha states in central India. By 1805, the Company controlled Delhi and the Moghul emperor himself. By 1813, when the Company's charter came up for renewal, it was in fact the paramount political power in India. The

British government recognized the Company's true function by ending its commercial monopoly in India, except for the lucrative opium trade with China.

The final wave of British expansion in India began in 1839. By then, only the Punjab, the Sind, and Afghanistan in the northwest of the subcontinent were truly independent states. The British government was concerned about Russian expansion into the area through Persia and Afghanistan. To preempt Russian designs on India, the British deposed the Afghan rulers and put their own favorite on the throne. The fiercely independent Afghans revolted, and in a furious war from 1839 to 1842 fought the British to a stalemate. In 1845, however, the British annexed the Sind and so controlled the route into Afghanistan. Sir Charles Napier expressed the British role with disarming honesty: "We have no right to seize Sind, but we shall do so, and a very advantageous, useful, humane piece of rascality it will be." During the 1840s, the British also managed to subdue the warlike Sikh state of Punjab (now Pakistan).

Burma was taken in two gulps (1823–26 and 1852). Thereafter, the British annexed a number of Indian states. Whenever an Indian prince died without a legitimate heir, the British could, by the *doctrine of lapse*, annex the state; they did this a number of times under the governor-generalcy of Lord Dalhousie. The British under Dalhousie also claimed the right to annex a state if they regarded it as badly governed. By this privilege of *paramountcy*, the British in 1856 annexed Oudh, the last big independent Muslim state in northern India.

As British power in India grew, so did the British inclination to reform traditional Indian customs and social structure. In the previous century, the Company had been content to leave Indian society and institutions alone; it even prohibited Christian missionaries from working in British India. The British desire to westernize India became irresistible, however, as the moral foundations of Victorianism hardened. Evangelicals saw magnificent opportunities for gaining converts in the subcontinent and lobbied hard to be allowed in. They won entry in 1813. Over the next decades, the increasingly confident British endeavored to remake Indian culture along British lines. Thus, they banned both the Indian custom of *sati* (suttee), whereby a Hindu widow was supposed to burn herself on her husband's funeral pyre, and *thuggee*, a ritual robbery and murder cult.

In addition, the British replaced Delhi with Calcutta as the capital of India, deposed the Moghul emperor, introduced new Westernized civil and criminal law codes, and imposed a British-style land system, complete with

*An imperial scene: blowing sepoy mutineers from the muzzles of cannons. Indian Mutiny, 1857.*

individual ownership and a free market in land. They also set up a new educational system, including university-level education in Western science and literature. This educational system created a new Westernized ruling elite; it also confirmed English as the official language for the country.

The new Western-style elite never won the allegiance of the mass of Indians, and the Indian people deeply resented many of the other reforms. In 1857 a violent reaction changed the tone and texture of British India. This outburst, the Indian Mutiny of 1857–58 (also called the Sepoy or Indian Rebellion), proved to be a traumatic event for the British because it threatened to smash the jewel in the imperial crown, because it shook Victorian self-assurance, and because it unleashed demons of racial hatred that could never be penned up again. The mutiny—regarded by many Indians as the first war of Indian national liberation—began among Indian troops (sepoys) near Delhi. Their British officers issued them cartridges that were greased with beef and pork fat and so insulted the religious sensibilities of both the Hindu sepoys, who regarded cows as sacred, and the Muslims, who thought pigs unclean. The mutineers killed their officers and took Delhi; thereafter, mutinies and civilian rebellions broke out in perhaps one-fifth of India, mostly in the central and northern regions.

The mutiny/rebellion was finally put down, but only after strenuous efforts by the British and loyal Indian troops amid scenes of appalling bloodshed. Mutineers slaughtered all the Europeans they could find, and the British responded with savage counterattacks and brutal retributions. Fortunately for the British, the rebels never had a concerted plan, and most of the sepoys in Bengal remained loyal. The British governor-general was also able to deploy British regular regiments to retake Delhi and the other rebel strongholds. After eighteen months, it was all over, but British India, which lasted until 1947, was never the same.

In the aftermath of the mutiny, the British had to reconsider their role in India. They recognized that the rebellion had been a reaction against British interference with India's traditional customs, institutions, and rulers. After 1858, the British, therefore, became much more conservative in propounding westernizing reforms. Strict controls limited Christian missionary activity and British policy shifted to favor traditional princely rulers and great landowners over the new westernized elite. The British now directed progress toward material development—railways above all, but also irrigation systems, roads, and public works. By 1881, India had almost ten thousand miles of railways and thirty million acres of irrigated land.

The mutiny also pushed the British government to take the rule of India away from the East India Company and put it under the British cabinet and Parliament. The governor-general now became *viceroy*, responsible in theory to a cabinet officer—the secretary of state for India—who was in turn responsible to Parliament. The Indian Civil Service, long a professional service that was exclusively British, now formally became British government employees. The Indian army was also reorganized, with a higher proportion of British troops—roughly 60,000 British soldiers and 120,000 Indians. As the British in India—the Anglo-Indians—increasingly brought wives and families out to India, they became more and more a self-conscious, provincial clique that ruled the 200 million Indians in a spirit of aloof, racially inflected elitism.

## AN IMPERIAL CULTURE?

How much did India, and the expanding empire in general, mean to ordinary British men and women before 1870? Clearly, British politicians and policymakers regarded the Empire as crucial to British prosperity and security. Moreover, as more and more colonial goods such as products of native crafts, foodstuffs not grown in Europe, and raw materials for British manufactures penetrated the British market, they altered day-to-day living and expectations. For example, the modern game of lawn tennis is very much the byproduct of mid-Victorian imperialism. Tennis needs tennis balls, and the British Empire guaranteed ready access to India rubber, a latex produced in the tropics and the core material of the first modern tennis balls. The world's first tennis club opened in Leamington Spa in the south of England in 1874; the Wimbledon Championships began three years later. Golf, too, is linked to empire: The invention of *gutta percha* from a latex drawn from Malayan trees made it possible to produce golf balls cheaply and led to a golfing boom in the second half of the nineteenth century.

But did the use of imperial products translate into imperial *consciousness* and an imperial *culture*? Should the mid-Victorian merchant happily driving his gutta percha golf ball down the fairway be considered an imperialist? And what about that merchant's cook? How aware was she of the many links to empire in her kitchen? How imperialist was her culture? Historians disagree about the extent to which imperial ideas and attitudes permeated British culture, and particularly popular culture, between 1815 and 1870.

It seems clear that, among the middle and upper classes, the definition of *Britishness* had become substantially imperial by this era. By providing access to essential raw materials and markets, the Empire underlay much of middle-class prosperity and opportunity. But perhaps just as importantly, Britain's imperial expansion underlay much of middle-class national pride. It revealed not only Britain's economic but also its moral strength. Imbued with *providentialism*—the belief that God guided human history for the working out of his will in the world—middle-class men and women saw the Empire as a visible sign and consequence of the righteousness of Victorian values. On a more pragmatic level, imperial service offered middle-class families a fast track to higher living standards: In India, for example, a middle-class family could live like the landed elite at home.

The responses and attitudes of ordinary men and women to mid-Victorian Empire remain somewhat opaque. The soldiers and sailors who extended Britain's imperial boundaries came largely from the working classes, but poverty rather than patriotism impelled most of these men into national uniform. Certainly by the mid-nineteenth century Victorians of all classes encountered various goods and expressions of Empire at almost every turn. The quintessential English cup of tea was, as we have seen, steeped in Empire, as was the fight to abolish slavery. Museums and exhibitions, beginning with the Crystal Palace of 1851, increasingly put imperial products on display. The evangelical emphasis on overseas missionary work led to a proliferation of literature about "primitive" peoples and places. Likewise, commercial panoramas, melodramas, music hall productions, and popular publications often turned to the Empire for colorful characters and a splash of exoticism, as well as for stirring narratives of exploration, adventure, and military conquest. Yet the ordinary working Briton's preoccupation with the day-by-day economic struggle, as well as the limits imposed by low levels of literacy, constricted the flow of imperialist culture downward from the ruling classes.

## FOREIGN POLICY UNDER CASTLEREAGH AND CANNING

The other side of Britain's imperial power was the fact that, regarding Europe, Britain was a satiated state. Protected from Europe by the navy's control of the English Channel and the North Sea and preoccupied with economic growth, Britain had no aggressive ambitions on the Continent. British public opinion often expressed sympathy for liberalism and constitutionalism wherever they emerged in Europe, but the British were in no mood to go to war over ideology. The one overriding British interest in Europe was to keep the Continent from being dominated by one power. Such a condition would threaten Britain economically and strategically. Hence, the British, as in the eighteenth century, pursued a balance of power in Europe. The British of the nineteenth century differed from their predecessors, however, in practicing balance of power tactics without committing themselves to alliances. They preferred *splendid isolation*. Technically the policy of avoiding treaties that specified the conditions under which Britain would go to war, splendid isolation also describes British policymakers' preference for the flexibility of independent action, whereby they could shift their influence as the states of Europe grouped and regrouped. Such a strategy, though it seemed to follow no principles, gave consistency to British policy through a succession of governments and foreign secretaries.

British foreign policy in the years between the end of the Napoleonic Wars and the 1830s lay largely in the hands of two men who loathed each other: Robert Stewart, Viscount Castlereagh (foreign secretary from 1812 to 1822) and George Canning (foreign secretary from 1822 to 1827). Serving together in the duke of Portland's government between 1807 and 1809 (Castlereagh as secretary of war, Canning as foreign secretary), the two men disagreed so sharply on the conduct of the war that Canning conspired to have Castlereagh removed from office and Castlereagh responded by challenging Canning to a duel—and shooting him in the thigh. Not surprisingly, this unsavory episode created a permanent rift between these two ambitious politicians.

Personality and background also divided the two men. Both came from Ireland's Protestant Ascendancy, but there the similarities ended. Castlereagh (1769–1822), who grew up in luxury and privilege, was icy and secretive, a poor orator, and wary of public opinion. Viewed as a reactionary, he was not a popular figure. In the poem "The Mask of Anarchy," for example, Shelley depicted Castlereagh tossing human hearts to bloodhounds. In contrast, Canning (1770–1827) could charm crowds with his speeches, had a flair for what we now call public relations, and was seen as a liberal in his approach to foreign affairs. Unlike his rival, Canning grew up in relative poverty: His father, disinherited for marrying a fortuneless woman, died while Canning was still a child and his mother took to the stage to support her young son, a scandalous step in an era when actresses were considered to be jumped-up prostitutes.

Despite these differences in upbringing, personality, and public image, however, both men pursued the same goal: maintaining a balance of power in Europe and thus creating a stable climate for British trade. Castlereagh had hoped to achieve this goal by holding periodic congresses of the great powers (*the Concert of Europe*), but the movement of the other states toward a general commitment to intervene on behalf of autocracy warned him off. Britain, therefore, did not join the reactionary governments of Russia, Prussia, and Austria in the *Holy Alliance* that sought to preserve autocratic regimes across Europe by active intervention.

In 1822 Castlereagh killed himself and Canning became foreign secretary. The new foreign secretary followed the same general policies as his predecessor, but with a flair for public relations that made him seem much more liberal. For example, when French troops intervened in Spain in 1823 to put down the newly installed liberal regime, Canning responded by encouraging the independence of Spain's colonies in America—but less because of an ideological commitment to liberalism than as a way to ensure that France did not gain too much power: "I resolved that, if France had Spain, it should not be 'Spain with the Indies.' I called the New World into existence to redress the balance of the Old." Moreover, with Spain removed and France blocked, Britain was now positioned to dominate Latin American trade.

The interlocked goals of pursuing the European balance of power and protecting British economic interests also shaped Canning's approach to southeastern Europe, where the specter of Russian expansion loomed large. British diplomats and imperial governors feared that Russia might damage British interests in the eastern Mediterranean by controlling the Straits of the Bosporus and the Dardanelles. The British regarded the Ottoman Empire as the dam that blocked the flow of Russian power into the Mediterranean. Making sure that dam remained in place was, therefore, essential. This helps explain why, when Greek patriots revolted in the 1820s against their Ottoman rulers, Canning did not fully support the rebellion.

British sympathy was all for the Greeks; the Romantic hero Lord Byron even fought and died for the cause of Greek independence. Canning, however, feared that Greek independence could lead to the collapse of the Ottoman Empire. He thus sought to win for the Greeks not outright independence, but rather some autonomy under reformed Ottoman rule. His plan failed when the Ottoman government refused British mediation and proved resistant to British bullying—including the destruction of the

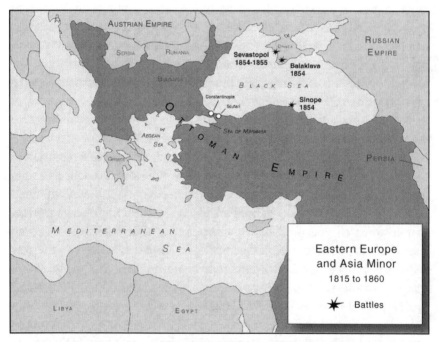

*Eastern Europe and the Ottoman Empire, 1856.* Limiting the spread of Russian power southward and propping up the Ottoman Empire were key goals of British foreign policy throughout much of the nineteenth century.

Ottoman navy by a combined British, French, and Russian fleet at the Battle of Navarino in 1827 (the last major naval engagement fought entirely with sailing ships). In 1830, Greece became independent. The Ottoman Empire did not collapse, but the loss of Greece marked an important step in the slow dwindling of its power.

## FOREIGN POLICY UNDER PALMERSTON

The third great foreign secretary of nineteenth-century Britain was Henry John Temple, Viscount Palmerston (1784–1865), who dominated British foreign affairs for nearly thirty years (foreign secretary 1830–34, 1835–41, and 1846–51; prime minister, 1855–58 and 1859–65). Palmerston shared Canning's talent for appealing to public opinion and outdid him in manipulating the press, but in his diplomatic dealings he was notoriously impatient and abrasive—so abrasive, in fact, that his nickname was "Lord Pumicestone." A roguish aristocrat, Palmerston nevertheless made himself the spokesman of the self-confident and brassy British middle class. Above all, he was a patriot and an opportunist. As a Whig, Palmerston regarded the Reform Act of 1832 as the best possible constitution for Britain and often spoke in favor of liberal regimes abroad: "I consider the constitutional states to be the natural allies of this country. . . . No English ministry will be performing its duty if it is inattentive to their interests." Yet Palmerston in fact was a pragmatist and never sacrificed British strategic or commercial interests for ideology.

Palmerston's diplomatic style and intentions can be seen in the three main foreign areas. First, in 1830, liberal revolutions broke out across Western Europe. Palmerston enthusiastically greeted the French Revolution of 1830 and its new constitutional monarchy. But he resisted the expansion of France's new regime into the Low Countries, where British trade interests were vital. In 1830, the Belgians revolted against the Dutch, to whom they had been joined in 1815. This revolt seemed to open the way for French intervention. Palmerston achieved his goal of keeping the ports of the Low Countries open to British trade by sponsoring Belgian independence, achieved finally in 1839.

Second, in the years from 1839 to 1841, Palmerston came to the support of the Ottoman Empire, even though his action caused a rift with the French. The French backed Mehemet Ali, the ruler of Egypt, when he rebelled against Ottoman control. Like Canning, Palmerston feared that, if the Ottoman Empire collapsed, the Russian Empire would flow into the vacuum. He managed to bring about an agreement with the Austrians and Russians against Mehemet Ali, the defeat of Ali's forces, and the bombardment of Beirut. In 1841, Palmerston got all the interested powers (including the Turks and Russians) to sign the Convention of the Straits, which declared that the straits between the Black Sea and the Mediterranean would be closed to foreign warships as long as the Ottoman Empire was at peace. Hence, he blocked Russian naval influence in the eastern Mediterranean and protected British economic and military interests.

Finally, during the European revolutions of 1848, Palmerston publicly approved of the liberal-nationalist revolutionaries, but did little to support them. His policy seemed anti-Austrian, especially when he encouraged the Italian independence and unification movement. Actually, however, Palmerston wanted to maintain the balance of power under the new conditions, and that goal required the continued existence of a strong Austria. Palmerston simply believed that the Austrian Empire would be stronger without the recalcitrant Italian provinces. Thus, he accepted Austrian suppression of the revolt in Hungary, even though he publicly criticized its brutality. Palmerston was independent and vocal—these qualities got him dismissed from office in 1851—but he was a pragmatic agent of British interests all the same.

## THE CRIMEAN WAR

Several key concerns of the British converged in the 1850s to lead Britain into its only European war between 1815 and 1914. The British concern for the security of India and for the route to India through the Mediterranean and the Middle East had committed them to the defense of the Ottoman Empire, chronically the "sick man of Europe." At the same time, the traditional British concern about the balance of power in Europe made the British statesmen and public opinion alike highly suspicious of the Russian Empire, which seemed potentially the dominant power on the Continent. The British believed, as we have seen, that the Ottoman Empire stood as a bulwark against Russian expansion into both eastern Europe and Asia Minor. Unfortunately for the British, the Ottoman Empire was a tottering dinosaur, whose weakness was a constant temptation to the Russians and an anxiety to the British. By the 1850s, the menace to Turkey by the Russian bear was rousing the British lion to fight.

In this awakening of British belligerence, another Victorian theme had strong influence: British self-confidence. By the 1850s, Britain's prosperity and progress had bred a pride in British "civilization" that swelled easily into bumptious nationalism. Palmerston had given voice to this attitude in 1850, when, in defense of a British citizen in Athens, he declared that, "as the Roman in days of old had held himself free from indignity when he could say *civis Romanus sum* [I am a Roman citizen], so also a British subject, in whatever land he may be, shall feel confident that the watchful eye and the strong arm of England will protect him against injustice and wrong." This arrogant British pride by the 1850s was directed at the Russian Empire, for in the eyes of the liberal Victorian middle class the tsarist state stood as the very symbol of oppression and reaction.

The tsarist regime in fact had brought some of British Russophobia on itself. The Russian army of eight hundred thousand men was much larger than any other in nineteenth-century Europe. Tsar Alexander I (r. 1777–1825) had dreamed up the reactionary Holy Alliance of 1815, and Tsar Nicholas I (r. 1825–55) was an aggressive autocrat. His armies had put down with great brutality the revolutions of 1848 in Poland and Hungary. Moreover, although the Russians did not seek to destroy Turkey, they were certainly pleased to pick up some pieces as it destroyed itself. By 1853, Nicholas I believed the time had come to carve up the Ottoman Empire. In that year, the Russians claimed the status of protectors of Christians living in the Ottoman Empire and then occupied two of its Danubian provinces. In October 1853, the Turks went to war with Russia.

The British government dithered during the events leading to the Russo-Turkish war and then stumbled into hostilities on the side of the Turks. The government, headed by Lord Aberdeen, could not face down popular enthusiasm for war, nor could it force the Turks to give in to Russian demands. As Aberdeen frequently and pathetically noted, "We are drifting helplessly to war." After reaching an alliance with the French, who had their own grievances with the Russian Empire, as well as a need for a dose of *la gloire*, Britain went to war in March of 1854.

The ineptitude of British diplomacy leading up to the war was exceeded by the incompetence of their war effort. The Crimean War was a throwback to eighteenth-century wars of maneuver: the British did not mean to conquer Russia or overthrow the tsarist regime, but to punish the Russians enough to exact concessions from them. The specific target in the Crimea was the Russian naval base on the Black Sea, Sebastapol, to which the British and French laid siege. The besieging armies were themselves pressured by the massive, if ill-armed and ill-trained, Russian forces that descended on them from the north.

Furthermore, the British army was still operating on aristocratic lines left over from the Napoleonic wars. During the long peace after 1815, the army had ossified. Its logistical arm proved incapable of supplying the initial expeditionary force of thirty thousand men some four thousand miles from Britain. Many supply ships were destroyed by a storm in the fall of 1854, leaving the British troops to suffer horribly from a lack of food, warm clothing, and dry shelter in the winter of 1854–55. Thousands died of cholera and dysentery, medical care being backward and haphazard at best. The army bureaucracy was so impenetrable that it took a superhuman effort by Florence Nightingale, the self-appointed autocrat of nursing, to improve the army hospital at Scutari (across the Bosporus Strait from Constantinople).

To make matters worse, the military leadership was spectacularly inept. The commander of the expeditionary army, Lord Raglan, had fought at Waterloo but had never commanded troops in the field. A staff officer to the core, Raglan issued orders in terms of requests and habitually spoke of the enemy as "the French." His ranking officers held their commissions by purchase rather than by merit. Two of them, Lord Cardigan (commander of the Light Brigade of cavalry) and Lord Lucan (commander of the Heavy Brigade) were brothers-in-law who had long engaged in a personal feud and who now distinguished themselves as arrogant nitwits. Their aristocratic stupidity resulted in the most glorious event of the war, the magnificent but futile Charge of the Light Brigade directly into the Russian artillery at Balaclava. Lord Cardigan survived the charge, but his brigade was destroyed.

The incompetence of the war effort roused a frenzy of frustrated nationalism at home. The leading newspapers were vehemently anti-Russian and pro-Turk. The *Times*'s correspondent in Crimea, W. H. Russell, sent home by telegraph (a first in the history of war) vivid reports of the army's bungling. Radical politicians blamed aristocratic government for the inefficiency of the war effort; obviously, they thought, Britain's businessmen could run the war better. Pacifist radicals like John Bright and Richard Cobden were scorned by public opinion, whereas war-hawk radicals like J. A. Roebuck became wildly popular. Palmerston emerged as the people's choice to reinvigorate the war effort, which public opinion demanded of the Aberdeen government. In 1855, Roebuck carried in the House of Commons a motion calling for an inquiry into the conduct of the war. The cabinet resigned, and Palmerston formed a government.

Palmerston displayed his usual energy and decisiveness, but in fact the Franco-British forces had already turned the corner in the Crimea. The logistical and medical branches in the Crimea became effective and supplies

*Roger Fenton,* The Shadow of the Valley of Death (1854). *Sent to photograph the Crimean War for the* Illustrated London News, *Roger Fenton was one of the first war photographers. This image of cannonballs on a road after a battle was widely associated with the ill-fated Charge of the Light Brigade, although in fact it shows a smaller valley several miles to the southwest. In an earlier Fenton photograph of the same scene, no cannonballs litter the roadway; some historians conclude that Fenton altered the scene to enhance the emotional impact of the image.*

flowed ashore. At home the War Office was reorganized. The Russian army showed the effects of its own antiquated systems of supply, training, and weaponry. Sebastapol fell in September 1855, bringing an end to the fighting. The Treaty of Paris (1856) gave the British what the diplomats (if not the public) had sought: a Russian guarantee of Turkish independence, autonomy for the Danubian provinces (later to become Rumania), an end to Russian claims to be protectors of Christians under Ottoman rule, and neutralization of the Black Sea. These results meant that the Eastern Question—the interlocking problems of Ottoman decline and Russian expansion—was put on the back burner for twenty years.

    The Crimean War also had important results for the British military. The experience of the war forced the British public to accept a larger standing army, whose numbers now rose to about 225,000 men. This army gradually began to mirror Victorian social values. The reform of the military services begun during the war continued. Ability and merit slowly replaced connection and wealth as the means for advancement in the army and finally, in 1871, the purchase system itself was abolished. Merit, not birth, would determine military rank. In the navy, the main changes were technological, as armored ships, breech-loading cannons, and steam power replaced the old wood-and-sail fleets in the 1860s.

Perhaps the most important result of the Crimean War was the damage it wrought to British prestige and influence in Europe. Britain thus played no significant role in the great dramas of Italian and German reunification, which redrew the map of Europe in the 1850s and 1860s. In the case of Italy, the British were torn between sympathy for Italian nationalism, the commitment to keep the Austrian Empire strong as part of the balance of power, and the belief that Austria would be better off without its troublesome holdings in Italy. In the case of Germany, the British were caught unaware, for in focusing on Austria, they failed to notice the effectiveness of Bismarck's campaign to unify Germany around the steel core of Prussian power. The British stood by in their splendid isolation when Prussia defeated Austria in 1866 and France in 1870–71, and a new and powerful united Germany was born.

By 1870, then, the British stood in a paradox: Tremendously prosperous at home and economically powerful abroad, Britain formally and informally had a gigantic empire, but was standoffish and ineffectual on the Continent. It may be that these apparently contradictory facts were actually mutually reinforcing. In any case, the policy of splendid isolation, which had enabled Britain to play the role of independent makeweight in the balance scales of European power, now was beginning to look less splendid and more isolated. British confidence, so characteristic of the mid-Victorian decades, became more dependent on possession and expansion of the Empire. The question for the decades to come would be whether the Empire would continue to be, or seem to be, a source of strength, or whether it would become a source of foreign rivalry and a drain on British resources.

### Suggested Reading

Bayly, C. A. *Indian Society and the Making of the British Empire*. Cambridge: Cambridge University Press, 1988.

Bew, John. *Castlereagh: From Enlightenment to Tyranny*. London: Quercus, 2011.

Bourne, Kenneth. *The Foreign Policy of Victorian England, 1830–1902*. Oxford: Clarendon Press, 1970.

Bridge, F. R., and R. Bullen. *The Great Powers and the European States System, 1815–1914*. London: Longman, 1980.

Brown, David. *Palmerston: A Biography*. New Haven, CT: Yale University Press, 2011.

———. *Palmerston and the Politics of Foreign Policy, 1846–55*. Manchester, UK: Manchester University Press, 2002.

Dalrymple, William. *The Last Mughal: The Fall of a Dynasty, 1857*. London: Bloomsbury, 2006.

Farwell, Byron. *Queen Victoria's Little Wars*. London: Allen Lane, 1973.

Fieldhouse, D. K. *The Colonial Empires: A Comparative Survey From the Eighteenth Century*. London: Weidenfeld & Nicolson, 1986.

Figes, Orlando. *The Crimean War: A History*. New York: Metropolitan Books, 2011.

Fisher, Michael. *Counterflows to Colonialism: Indian Travellers and Settlers in Britain, 1600–1857*. New Delhi: Permanent Black, 2005.

Hall, Catherine. *Civilising Subjects: Metropole and Colony in the English Imagination, 1830–1867*. Chicago: University of Chicago Press, 2002.

Halstead, John P. *The Second British Empire: Trade, Philanthropy, and Good Government, 1820–1890*. Westport, CT: Greenwood Press, 1983.

Headrick, Daniel R. *The Tools of Empire: Technology and European Imperialism in the Nineteenth Century*. New York: Oxford University Press, 1981.

Hibbert, Christopher. *The Great Mutiny: India, 1857*. London: Allen Lane, 1978.

Hunt, Giles. *The Duel: Castlereagh, Canning and Deadly Cabinet Rivalry*. London: I. B. Tauris, 2008.

Hyam, Ronald, *Britain's Imperial Century, 1815–1914*, 3rd ed. London: Palgrave Macmillan, 2002.

Kennedy, Paul. *The Rise and Fall of British Naval Mastery*. London: Allen Lane, 1976.

Parsons, Timothy. *The British Imperial Century, 1815–1914: A World History Perspective*. London: Rowman and Littlefield, 1999.

Pati, Biswamoy. *The 1857 Rebellion*. Oxford: Oxford University Press, 2007.

Porter, Andrew, ed. *Oxford History of the British Empire: The Nineteenth Century*. Oxford: Oxford University Press, 1999.

Porter, Bernard. *Britain, Europe and the World, 1850–1982*. London: Allen & Unwin, 1983.

———. *The Absent-Minded Imperialists: What the British Really Thought About Empire*. London: Oxford University Press, 2005.

———. *The Lion's Share: A History of British Imperialism, 1850–2011*, 5th ed. London: Longman, 2012.

Royle, Trevor. *Crimea: The Great Crimean War, 1854–1856*. London: Palgrave Macmillan, 2004.

Woodham-Smith, Cecil. *Florence Nightingale, 1810–1910*. New York: McGraw-Hill, 1951.

———. *The Reason Why*. New York: McGraw-Hill, 1954.

Part **IV**

# The Decline of Victorian Britain

# 1870–1914

# Chapter 18

# Upheaval in Economy and Society, 1870–1914

In the years between 1870 and 1914, the foundations of Victorian culture were seriously eroded so that the whole structure was toppled by the First World War. Although the late-Victorian period (1870–1901) gave way to the Edwardian period (1901–14), which took its name from Victoria's eldest son and successor, Edward Vll, long-run trends tied the whole together. These were the years when Britain's economy began to descend from the heights of world preeminence, when social change again intensified class antago-nism, when Victorian confidence turned to uncertainty and anxiety, and when intellectual rebellion began to create modernism from the scattered pieces of the Victorian mind. No one factor caused the changes in late-Victorian and Edwardian Britain, but just as industrial and agricultural change altered the face of Britain in the years from 1760 to 1840, so eco-nomic and social difficulties in the period from 1870 to 1914 helped mold a new social and cultural order.

Between 1870 and 1914, British economic growth began to falter, and foreign rivals started to catch up and even in some areas pull ahead. The mood of expansive confidence characteristic of the upper classes in the mid-Victorian period slowly evaporated and was replaced by one of anxiety and concern. The relative social peace of the 1850s and 1860s consequently degenerated into class conflict. To be sure, Britain remained a great eco-nomic power in 1914. Many a British businessman could sit down every morning to his breakfast and newspaper with pride in his company's profits and his country's successes. Many others, however, could hardly bring themselves to read the morning's paper, for fear of finding news of declining profits; of a strike in a vital industry; of a heated political stalemate; or worse yet, of another trade in which German producers now outpaced the British.

## AGRICULTURAL DEPRESSION IN ENGLAND AND WALES

For British landowners and tenant farmers, the late-Victorian period was a time of serious economic crisis and significant structural change. Cereal (mainly wheat) farming sharply declined in the Midlands and South of England—long the grain belt of the nation and the seat of the landed elite's political and social prestige. Two developments caused this decline: first, a series of exceptionally cold and wet winters in the latter 1870s, and second, the collapse of grain prices in Britain. The former cause was short term and its impact eventually disappeared, but the price collapse had effects that lasted through the 1930s.

What happened was that cheap foreign wheat flooded the British market from the 1870s on. Vast plains were brought under the plow in the United States, Canada, Argentina, and Australia after the 1860s. Railways and steamships made exportation of wheat from these newly productive areas very cheap. By the 1880s, in economic terms, Chicago was as close to London as a Midlands estate. Because the Corn Laws had been repealed in 1846, there was nothing to discourage wheat imports. Such imports doubled between 1870 and 1890, and the prices that British cereal farmers earned for their crops fell drastically; by 1900, the price of wheat in Britain had fallen by 50 percent. Livestock farmers fared better, but from the 1880s, refrigerated ships made it possible to export to Britain beef from Argentina and lamb from New Zealand. By 1900, more than one-third of the meat consumed in Britain came from abroad.

As prices for cereals fell, the traditional tenant farmers of the Midlands and southern counties were hard pressed. Some farmers diversified, others scrimped on maintenance of fields and farm buildings, and some received rent abatements from their landlords. Many tenants, however, could not survive the crisis. By 1900, numerous tenancies stood vacant. Approximately 340,000 agricultural laborers left rural life for urban occupations or overseas.

The landlords themselves now found it hard to sustain their luxurious style of life. Many discovered that their incomes were cut in half as rent-rolls declined, yet their cost of living remained high. Late-Victorian landlords typically sought outside income by investing in business and industry; by 1890 any self-respecting bank or railway could boast of several titled nobles on its board of directors. At the same time, many landlords retrenched by cutting back on household staff, by closing a house in town or in the country, or by entertaining less lavishly. In 1870, for example, the earl of Verulam's family drank 590 bottles of sherry and 250 of brandy, but in 1880, they consumed a mere 298 of sherry and 75 of brandy!

In Wales, the agricultural depression worsened landlord-tenant rela-tionships that were already significantly more hostile than those in Eng-land. The ownership of land in nineteenth-century Wales was heavily con-centrated: In the 1870s, about 570 families owned 60 percent of the land; very little tilled land was owned by the people who occupied and farmed it. Until the 1880s, a few great landed families—the Wynns, the Vaughns, the Butes, and others—dominated Welsh society and politics. Highly anglicized in taste and interests, as well as Anglican in religion, these aristocratic and gentry families stood apart from their solidly Nonconformist tenants and farm laborers. As agricultural depression worked severe hardship on these tenants, anti-landlord sentiment became an enduring theme in Welsh pop-ular politics and culture.

## LAND WARS IN IRELAND AND THE SCOTTISH HIGHLANDS

As in Wales, the agricultural depression exacerbated longstanding land-lord-tenant hostilities in Ireland and the Scottish Highlands, but in these regions, rural unrest proved strong enough to force the British government to enact significant land reform legislation. We will take the case of Ireland first.

The sharp drop in agricultural prices hit Irish tenant farmers particu-larly hard because of the inflexibility of Irish rental agreements: farmers found they could not pay rent at the rates arranged in more prosperous times, but many landlords, mortgaged to the hilt, refused to consider rent reduction or abatement. Several years of potato crop failures in the late 1870s worsened the situation, as did a cholera epidemic that devastated Irish poultry flocks. As the number of evictions rose, so, too did hunger and food shortages. By 1879, whispers of famine could be heard throughout the western regions of Ireland.

But Ireland had changed since the Great Famine of the 1840s as a result of four significant developments. First, the post-Famine reduction in small-holdings meant there were far fewer households living on the edge of star-vation. Second, many families could count on assistance from sons and daughters who had emigrated to the United States, Australia, and England. Third (and rather ironically), the state school system, established by the British government in 1831 to make of each student "a happy English child," had by 1879 produced a generation of literate tenant farmers, far bet-ter equipped than their fathers and grandfathers to mobilize for relief. Finally and perhaps most importantly, the memory of the Great Famine scarred the Irish psyche and motivated Irish men and women to act.

The result was the Irish Land War of the late 1870s and 1880s. Led by the Land League, which was established in 1879 and at its height claimed 200,000 members, Irish tenants began a series of rent strikes and met evictions with violence. Angry tenants maimed cattle, destroyed property, and attacked landlords and their men. They also shunned the landlords' agents or other tenants who took over farms from evicted families—a move of devastating effectiveness in close-knit rural communities. (The application of this treatment to one estate manager, Captain Boycott, gave the term *boycott* to the English language.) The British government responded in 1881, with a Land Act. It gave Irish tenants the *Three F's*: fixity of tenure, fair rents (set by a court), and free sale by tenants of their improvements. In effect, the act made tenants co-owners of their holdings with the traditional estate owners. As we will see later in chapter 20, even such radical legislation did not transform most Irish men and women into happy British subjects, but it did constitute a significant break with the liberal ideal of the sanctity of private property.

The Irish Land War helped inspire one in the Highlands of Scotland as well. We saw in chapter 6 that Highland landlords had long preferred sheep over people on their lands. Many Scottish landlords did not want any tenants at all. They sought to turn their estates into pasturage or game preserves for deer and grouse. A series of trespass and game laws transformed much of the Highlands into vast shooting parks for the wealthy. To shoot game, even on his own land, a farmer had to possess over one hundred acres. The luckiest of the poor lived by raising sheep and eating potatoes. The unlucky, especially in the western Highlands and islands, were under constant threat of eviction. Isolated from their English-speaking landlords by their Gaelic tongue, the peasantry of the western Highlands and islands—known as *crofters* (from their tiny land holdings called crofts)—scraped out an existence next to vast sheep runs and deer preserves.

The agricultural depression thus worsened an already volatile situation, with landlords demanding higher rents from tenants whose food supplies were dwindling. Inspired by the Land War in Ireland, crofters began to refuse to pay rent or to obey eviction notices. In April 1882, three hundred men and women on the Isle of Skye battled a police force sent to arrest the leaders of a rent strike; this Battle of Braes marked the beginnings of open violence in the Crofters' War.

Over the next few years, rent strikes and violence spread across the Highlands. Proclaiming that "the People are mightier than a Lord," the Highland Land League demanded not only lower rents, but also security from eviction and grazing rights. The British government found itself in the position of having to send gunboats and marines to try to restore order. Then, in the general election of 1885, the Highland Land League fielded a Crofters' party that won five parliamentary seats. Faced with this political challenge, the Liberal government in 1886 passed the Crofters' Holdings Act. By granting crofters security of tenure, this legislation freed the Scottish Highlanders from the threat of eviction. It also removed rent-setting power from the landlords and gave it to a new Crofters' Commission, which tended to reduce rents. Yet the act did nothing about the crofters' central grievances: their marginalization on poor land, their lack of grazing rights, and the conflict between their interests and the game and trespass laws. Unrest in the Highlands therefore continued and poverty remained the central fact of crofters' lives.

## RELATIVE INDUSTRIAL DECLINE

Although crisis characterized late-Victorian agriculture, the record of Britain's industrial sector in this era is more mixed. Many businessmen thought that the economy had taken a radical turn for the worse, and their concern inspired the government to appoint a Royal Commission on the Depression in Trade and Industry, which reported in 1886. There was, in fact, no depression of the sort that was to come in 1929: no reversal of growth, no mass unemployment, and no collapse of the industrial sector. The British economy continued to grow throughout the last quarter of the nineteenth century, and it continued to produce significant advances in the material standard of living.

Yet there were serious economic difficulties, especially compared to the mid-Victorian years. Two simple facts are very revealing: first, overall economic growth from 1870 to 1900 averaged about 2 percent a year, as opposed to almost 3 percent a year for the first three-quarters of the century; second, in 1900, both the United States and Germany produced more iron and steel than Britain did. In general, from the 1870s on, British industrial production grew more slowly than that of two giant foreign rivals, Germany and the United States. Thus, as shown in Table 18.1, Britain's share of world manufacturing output gradually shrank.

For the first time since industrialization began, Britain had economic rivals. All around the world, British businessmen met competition in the sale of manufactured goods. They did not find it pleasant or think it fair. Both Germany and the United States protected their industries by tariffs,

**Table 18.1: Relative Shares of World Manufacturing Output**

|               | 1860 | 1880 | 1900 |
| ------------- | ---- | ---- | ---- |
| Britain       | 19.9 | 22.9 | 18.5 |
| Germany       | 4.9  | 8.5  | 13.2 |
| United States | 7.2  | 14.7 | 23.6 |

Source: Paul Kennedy, *The Rise and Fall of the Great Powers* (New York: Random House, 1987), 149.

but British industry labored under free trade. By the 1880s, some British businessmen had come to think that Britain ought to adopt protective tariffs in order to create conditions of *fair trade*, but the mystique of free trade remained influential, and most commercial men realized that Britain needed free trade in order to have the widest markets possible. In any case, resentment toward Germany grew. In 1896, for instance, E. E. Williams published a book entitled *Made in Germany* in which he claimed that competition from the Germans in Britain and abroad had become "a deliberate and deadly rivalry."

In addition, many British manufacturers found the prices of their products falling and their profit margins squeezed. Prices for manufactured goods fell by about 25 percent in the late-Victorian years. The price decline meant that for *employed* workers, the era of the depression was actually a time of increasing living standards, but unemployment and underemployment rose sharply. At the same time, the lower level of profits denied British industry part of its traditional source of investments—plowed back from the industry itself.

Most of the problems were concentrated in heavy industry. The old staples of the Industrial Revolution—cotton textiles, iron, and, to a lesser extent, coal—now faced widespread competition from newly industrializing countries, all of which adopted the most up-to-date technologies, whereas the British lagged behind in technical innovation. Of the older industries, only in shipbuilding did the British increase their lead. The British also failed to keep pace in the very important new electrical and chemical industries. The industrial use of steam and gas was deeply entrenched in Britain; thus, the new electric power industries that grew rapidly in Germany and the United States met strong resistance in Britain. In industrial chemicals as in electricity, British scientists made many of the fundamental discoveries, but industrialists of other nations made the practical applications. German industry, for instance, made great advances in the production of aniline or synthetic dyes, which were first discovered in Britain.

Where the British excelled in the late-Victorian years was in light indus-tries and domestic retailing. New light industries such as sewing machines, armaments, and above all, bicycles were founded on the solid base of the mechanical craft skills of the Midlands. The bicycle industry of Coventry was, moreover, the first British industry to adopt American mass production methods. In retail sales, new entrepreneurs brought about major changes by establishing retail chains that sold standardized items in the high streets of every village and town: Boots the Chemist (drug stores), Sainsbury (gro-ceries), and Thomas Lipton (groceries). W. H. Smith established bookstalls in every railway station, selling cheap reading matter to travelers and com-muters, and commercially oriented publishers established mass circulation newspapers in the cities.

How can the relatively poor performance of British industry in the late nineteenth century be explained? How did the most prosperous and indus-trially advanced economy begin to falter and fall behind? Part of the expla-nation must simply be that, as other nations began to industrialize, they would by definition break Britain's monopoly in industrial production and inevitably take some share of the world's markets. But the central fact is that British industry was handicapped by its great head start. British industry by the 1870s and 1880s produced huge income for the nation as a whole, and this could have been transformed into capital investment that would have kept British industry ahead. But as the economy matured, British society unconsciously opted for consumer pleasures over capital investment—as seems the fate of most industrial societies—and the British also habitually invested huge sums of money abroad. Because Britain, with its relatively older technology and expanding service sector, did not produce returns on investment to match those in newly industrializing areas, the British exported capital throughout the nineteenth century and at a greater rate after 1870 than before: assets abroad exceeded £1 billion in 1875 and £2 bil-lion in 1900. And of course the British commitment to laissez-faire policies meant that governments would not consider policies that might have kept that capital at home.

The British head start in industrialization also created psychological and structural disadvantages. While foreign entrepreneurs aggressively pur-sued innovations in order to catch up, British industrialists found it hard to break with old habits in management, sales, and industrial relations. They tended to look to the past as the model for success. Similarly, British capi-talists were reluctant to discard the factories and machines that they and their workers knew well; hence, they tended to squeeze profits from existing technology by incremental changes rather than by undertaking wholesale recapitalization. British entrepreneurs were slow to adopt new forms of industrial organization such as cartels and trusts that were emerging in Germany and the United States. Although British business did gradually shift from individually owned firms and partnerships to public and private companies, the ordinary firm was much smaller than those in Germany or America. British firms *did* grow in size, and this slowly brought about a split between ownership and management, but British commerce and industry remained comparatively splintered. In the British coal industry, for instance, there were still nearly sixteen hundred coal companies in 1913.

The traditionalism of British industry and the burden of past habits affected the late-Victorian economy in another way: they retarded the deliberate application of science to industry, which was the wave of the future. Theoretical or *pure* science in Britain was second to none. But the British lagged behind Germany and the United States in both the industrial application of science and the scientific training of the work force at every level. German and American factories regularly had research laboratories by the late nineteenth century, but British industry rarely did. The British preferred the more informal methods of training and development that had served so well in the past. Victorian Britain had no state school system until 1870 and relatively few secondary schools. British higher education remained open only to the few and concentrated on the liberal arts and sciences, while despising technology and engineering. With a population roughly 70 percent that of Germany, Britain in 1913 had only 9,000 university students, whereas Germany had nearly 60,000; Britain graduated only 350 students in all fields of science and mathematics, whereas Germany graduated 3,000 in engineering alone.

The attitudes that limited the educational system in Britain arose in part from a commitment to laissez-faire, but also from certain cultural assumptions inherited from the past. The landed gentleman remained the ideal for most British businessmen. Many British capitalists yearned to emulate the landed orders—to make a fortune, buy an estate, and retire to a gracious life untainted by trade. British cultural elites tended to regard self-interest and profit, like industry and cities, as distinctly inferior to public service and country life. The public schools (that is, exclusive private boarding schools), in which an increasing proportion of middle-class boys were educated, inculcated the values of the leisured landowner and the amateur public servant. British literary culture from the Romantic period on taught the superiority of the preindustrial world and the life of the mind. By the late-Victorian period, the hard edge of many industrial families had been worn down, and what the British middle class gained in culture, it lost in drive and entrepreneurship.

## THE EDWARDIAN FALSE DAWN

As the nineteenth century gave way to the twentieth, the British economy did seem to recover and prices once again began to climb. This recovery was in many ways, however, a false dawn. The main economic themes that had emerged in the late-Victorian years remained in place. The principal factor in the apparent prosperity before 1914 was a recovery of prices. Overall, the prices of food and manufactured goods increased between 20 and 25 percent from 1900 to 1914. As usual, this increase cut different ways in different social classes: manufacturers, financiers, commercial men, and their families enjoyed higher incomes again, whereas the working class, whose wages did not go up as fast, found their consuming power stagnant. This they found a bitter pill after the improvement in real wages of the 1880s and 1890s.

Meanwhile, many long-term trends remained unfavorable for the economy. Economic growth slowed between 1900 and 1914 and by some calculations stopped altogether. Productivity (production per capita) slowed, and Britain's share of the world's manufacturing output fell to slightly less than Germany's and less than half that of the United States. Capital was formed at a lower rate than at any time in the nineteenth century and at a rate much lower than in Germany or the United States. The British in the Edwardian period had a more favorable balance of payments than in the late-Victorian years, but that positive balance was much more dependent on *invisible income*—from shipping, the sale of financial services, and earnings from investment—and on the sale abroad of capital goods, such as coal, steam engines, and industrial machinery. In consequence, the British economy grew ever more vulnerable to disturbances in both the pattern and volume of world trade and to the industrialization of previously underdeveloped regions in the British spheres of influence.

It is, however, important to keep these gradual changes in perspective. Britain in 1914 was one of the three great global economic powers. It was the third largest industrial producer on earth, with South Wales alone producing one-third of the world's coal exports. The British enjoyed the second highest (behind the United States) per capita income. Britain remained the greatest trading and financial nation in the world, as well as the leading power in shipping, international banking and finance, and overseas trading services.

## SOCIAL CHANGE: THE CLASS SYSTEM

Social change in the late nineteenth and early twentieth centuries was as profound as in any period of similar length in the British past. Britain remained a class society, but the class system itself underwent three important alterations: (1) the merger of the landed elite and the upper middle class into the *plutocracy*, (2) the expansion of the lower middle class, and (3) the solidification of working-class culture in the context of heightened class tensions.

The first of these changes—the formation of a plutocracy, or class that ruled by means of its wealth—resulted from economic troubles among the aristocracy and gentry. As men in the landed orders sought to bolster their incomes by investing in business and industry and by lending their names to commercial enterprises, they blurred the line that had long divided the landed class from the upper levels of the middle class. At the same time, the agricultural depression made landowning less viable. By 1914, the upper class was no longer *landed* but simply *propertied*. Elite status no longer depended on owning a landed estate.

The accelerated expansion of the professions also contributed to the formation of the new propertied elite. Often drawing their recruits from the middle class but functioning in close relationship to the gentry, British professionals stood almost as a separate class. To enter a profession and gain professional status, one needed not land or economic capital, but rather intellectual capital, or expertise. The professionals thus mediated between the landed and the middle classes, transmitting both values and personnel from one to the other. The professions had grown throughout the nineteenth century, but the increasing complexity of industrial society expanded their numbers rapidly. By 1914, the professional ranks included not only military officers, clergymen, doctors, and lawyers, but also university scholars, artists, architects, surveyors, engineers, and accountants.

Meanwhile, in the years between 1870 and 1914, a second change was occurring within the class society: the emergence of the lower middle class or *petty (petit) bourgeoisie* as an important and largely conservative social

81 Banbury Road, Oxford. *A typical home of the substantial middle class in late-Victorian Britain. Note the Gothic influence.*

force. In the first half of the nineteenth century, artisans, shopkeepers, and small business owners often marched in the front ranks of radical and democratic movements; by the late-Victorian era, however, these groups had largely embraced middle-class liberal values, particularly the liberal faith in individualism and its concurrent suspicion of activist government. The late-Victorian decades also saw this traditional petty bourgeoisie widen to include a new social grouping: *black-coated* (later called *white-collar*) *workers*. These bank tellers, sales clerks, shop assistants, travelling salesmen, and the like not only tended to earn less money and have little more education than skilled factory workers or coal miners, but they also spent their working day taking orders and doing as they were told. They did not, however, think of themselves as working class. Because they did not perform manual labor, because they went to work in a frock coat and bowler hat, they could, and most adamantly did, claim middle-class status. Struggling to abide by middle-class standards of gentility (without the support of a middle-class level of income), they sought desperately to maintain their social distance from the proletariat—a matter of "keeping up with the Joneses and keeping away from the Smiths," as one historian has put it.[1] As epitomized by the bank clerk, Mr. Pooter, in George Grossmith's *Diary of a Nobody* (1892), the lower middle class rejected the collectivist ethos of the working class and instead championed individual advancement and a retreat into private family life.

The third important change in terms of the class structure was the solidification of urban working-class culture. In the years between 1870 and 1814, British working people, whose experiences were now predominately industrial and urban, settled into a distinct pattern of life—to use one historian's phrase, "a life apart."[2] The working class of the late nineteenth and early twentieth centuries made up 75 percent of the British population (as opposed to 5 percent for the plutocracy and 20 percent for the middle class). By the early 1900s, the great majority of workers were employed in trade and industry; less than 10 percent were now working in agriculture. A majority of the employed working class were males, but nearly 10 percent of working-class women also held jobs outside their homes, most as domestic servants. Except for the domestics, few of these people had much to do with the upper classes; the face-to-face contacts of the preindustrial world were almost entirely gone, and suburbanization had completed the geographical segregation of the classes. At the same time, the divisions within the working class grew less sharp: the long-standing wage differential between skilled and less-skilled workers tended to diminish as the progress of both management techniques and technological development in mass industry worked toward de-skilling of the artisanal elite.

Work, which began at 6:00 a.m. and lasted until 5:30 p.m., dominated the lives of working-class people, even though the industrial worker rarely regarded it as fulfilling. British workers maintained a clear distinction between work and leisure time. They spent their weekday evenings after work in the pub, and they spent Saturday afternoons (which an increasing number had free) in relaxing over tea and newspapers such as *Tit-Bits*, the *Daily Mail*, and *Answers*. Sundays they rarely dedicated to church or chapel, but to sleeping in and visiting with friends. Few had paid holidays; thus, most working men and women spent their holidays at home or on day excursions to the country or the seashore.

---

[1]Peter Bailey, "White Collars, Gray Lives: The Lower Middle Class Revisited," *Journal of British Studies*, 38 (1999), 275.
[2]Meacham, *A Life Apart: The English Working Class, 1890–1914* (1977).

Besides work, three other institutions became crucial to urban working-class culture after 1870: the music hall, professional football (soccer), and fish and chips. Music halls, which were lowbrow variety theaters for the masses, offered bright lights, music, comedy, and drink. Their performers, the pop stars of the day, were themselves drawn from the working class and relied on songs and jokes drawn directly from working-class experience. Football (soccer), a medieval village sport, was revived in the 1860s by upper-class men who wished to involve working men in a vigorous and "wholesome" recreation. But in the 1880s, working men began to form their own football clubs, which quickly became professional as competition among them intensified. These clubs—Manchester United, Sheffield United, West Ham, and so on—provided focal points for local pride, rituals of communality, and diversions from dismal living conditions. As for fish and chips (a great British contribution to human civilization), British workers had consumed little seafood until the late nineteenth century, when rapid transportation and refrigeration made fresh fish available in all the big cities. By 1914, fish and chips had become a staple in the working-class diet.

In creating these institutions, the British working class was developing its own life apart from that of the plutocracy and middle class. The boundary between working-class and middle-class status, never easily penetrated, became more impermeable than ever before, especially for working-class males. Working people in growing numbers during the late-Victorian and Edwardian years rejected the moralistic preachings of their social superiors, preferring to go their own way.

Churchgoing was therefore not central to English working-class culture, although many workers—particularly those in the ranks of the higher skilled and better paid—continued to find not only solace and meaning, but also the opportunity to gain organizational and leadership experience in the chapels of Nonconformity. Most members of the working class espoused an informal form of Christian belief (what one historian has labeled "diffusive Christianity"[3]), which emphasized neighborliness and charity over adherence to specific doctrines, trusted that God would reward good behavior in the afterlife, and insisted that it was not necessary to go to church to be a good Christian. Most working-class parents, however, did continue to send their children to Sunday school and regarded religious lessons as an essential part of the regular school curriculum. Moreover, throughout urban

---

[3]Jeffrey Cox, *The English Churches in a Secular Society: Lambeth, 1830-1930* (New York: Oxford University Press, 1982), p. 92.

*Late-Victorian urban poverty: Saltney Street, Liverpool. This photo shows the common pump and open drain in a cramped street in working-class Liverpool.*

Britain, both church and chapel retained their traditional role as sources of material assistance in times of trouble.

And such times could be very frequent indeed. The severe poverty suffered by many working-class people was amply demonstrated by sociological research. In the mid-1880s, Charles Booth, a wealthy manufacturer, began a massive survey published in 1889–1902 as the *Life and Labour of the People in London*. Booth intended to disprove socialist claims about the dire poverty among working people, but he found the opposite of what he expected. Defining the poverty line stringently—as the amount above which a family was barely able to maintain "decent independent life"—Booth discovered that about 30 percent of London's population lived at or below the line. In 1901, social investigator Seebohm Rowntree and others realized what working people knew firsthand: that all of the working class, except the skilled artisans (who were about 10 percent of the total) lived on the edge of the abyss of poverty and would fall into it if they lost employment or fell ill. Both joblessness and underemployment posed serious problems for the working class—so serious that the word *unemployment* was invented in the 1880s. During the late-Victorian years, the decline of prices brought substantial improvement in real wages for *employed* working men and women—perhaps as much as a 40-percent improvement—but price increases rolled back some of this gain after 1900. The average wage for a working man was no more than £60 or £70 a year, as opposed to £200 a year for the middle class and £1,000 a year for the upper class.

The grinding poverty of many in the working class had dire effects on their health and way of life. Most men and women worked fifty-four hours a week or more, when they could get work. For this labor, they lived on forty-five shillings a week per family, spending over half on an unvarying diet—bread (thirty-three pounds a week per family), potatoes (in the North, porridge), butter, sugar, a dozen eggs, and some meat. As the chief wage earners, men were given the choicest food; children got what was left. Boys and girls regularly went to work at eight or nine years of age even after compulsory education (legislated in 1880) brought them into school for part of the day. A large percentage of children suffered from rickets, open sores, and other diseases related to malnutrition. When the Boer War (1899–1902) brought thousands of volunteers to the army, two of every three from the working class were rejected as physically unfit. Working-class youths at age thirteen were on average two or three inches shorter and fifteen pounds lighter than upper-class children of the same age.

One important change in these years would eventually provide ambitious and talented working-class children with the means to escape the prison of poverty. In 1870, the Forster Education Act established a state elementary school system for England and Wales (similar legislation was passed for Scotland in 1872). In 1880, additional legislation made schooling compulsory for children under eleven years old, and in 1902, another major act doubled the number of secondary schools. In the long term, the effects of the new school system would be revolutionary: before 1870, the rate of illiteracy among men was 33 percent and among women 50 percent; by 1900, illiteracy had been abolished. Abolition of illiteracy radically increased the ability of working men and women to construct their own ideology and policies appropriate to a working-class point of view.

But the results of universal literacy did not come suddenly, and by 1914 they had only begun to work. Late nineteenth-century schools often were badly overcrowded and poorly taught. Their lessons were not meant to help boys and girls to improve their social status, but to prepare them for the station into which they were born. Patriotism, imperialism, and respect for their social superiors were the main themes. Moreover, many working-class families were suspicious of the new schools—as they were of most governmental intervention in their lives—and besides, they needed their children to work. Working-class families generally took their children out of school as soon as possible. In 1906–07, for example, only 35 percent of fourteen-year-olds were still in school, and only 18 percent of sixteen-year-olds. Consequently, the level of literacy that the schools inculcated was low: before 1914, a majority of the working class still could not comprehend a text containing any but simple ideas and one-syllable words.

Few working men or women, then, held an elaborate political or economic ideology. Experience taught them that tomorrow would be much like today. As one working man wrote, "One can dream and hope, and if by chance God gives such a one imagination, it is more of a curse than a blessing." Yet the late-Victorian and Edwardian working people did have a strong class consciousness, expressed in terms of *them* and *us*. The ups and downs of life lived on the brink of destitution typically made working people "cheeky" and wise in their own way—inclined to let things roll off their backs, not to take themselves too seriously, and above all not to accept that *them* were better than *us*.

## SOCIAL CHANGE: GENDER ROLES AND RELATIONS

Gender roles and relations also altered in the late-Victorian period, although in quite different ways for working- and middle-class women. In working-class families, at least in the ranks of the respectable working class, improved living standards (relative to those earlier in the nineteenth century) meant that, increasingly, the working-class mother stayed at home with her children. In some ways, then, the middle-class ideal of *separate spheres*—the man in the public sphere of the work world and the woman in the private sphere of the home—became a possibility for many working-class families in these decades. Yet middle-class ideas of private domestic space remained inaccessible to most workers. Neighbors lived cheek-by-jowl in the densely crowded cities. Neighborhoods functioned as inner-city villages, where everyone knew each other and neighbors felt obliged to help each other out, if only because existence for everyone was precarious at best.

In these working-class neighborhood networks of support, women played a central role. A matriarchy composed of the married women of the neighborhood carefully observed social status and public behavior. No one escaped their oversight. Neighbors who violated the accepted standards of respectability would soon find their public status falling. Every urban neighborhood contained its own social hierarchy: an elite of skilled workers (provided they observed the codes of respectable behavior), unskilled workers, and the down-and-out of the streets.

Women also played a vital role in holding families together. The woman's skills in household management played an important role in assuring the survival of her family. As an observer wrote, "When the mother dies the family goes to pieces." One of Charles Booth's investigators reported:

If she be a tidy woman, decently versed in the rare arts of cooking and sewing, the family life is independent, even comfortable, and the children may follow in the father's footsteps or rise to better things. If she be a gossip and a bungler—worse still, a drunkard—the family sink to the lowest level of the East London street; and the children are probably added to the number of those who gain their livelihood by irregular work and by irregular means.

The working-class wife and mother thus served as the treasurer of the family's meager resources—planning, scrimping, saving, shopping, and pawning household items at the end of the week in order to stretch the meager family income—as well as guardian of the family's respectability. A family that pawned good shoes and clothes earned high status and respectability, whereas pawning rugs, pots and pans, and bed clothes revealed low wages or imprudent living.

Ironically, the same period that saw working-class women claiming domesticity also witnessed middle-class women moving into the public spheres of education and employment. A key factor here was the spreading practice of family limitation. This major social change was tied directly to late-Victorian economic pressures on the middle class. During the mid-Victorian decades, middle-class couples had on average about six children during the span of marriage. The dynamism of the economy meant that they could keep up their high level of consumption, employ the proper number of servants, and provide for their children (including the appropriate education), even with such large families. Once the economic difficulties of the late-Victorian years began to beset middle-class families, however, couples began to recognize the expense of children, especially because the increasing complexity of society required more years of education and professional training. The average age at marriage already was high—not far below thirty years of age for men; thus, there was little opportunity to delay it further. Birth control proved to be the answer. The techniques and devices—coitus interruptus, condoms, diaphragms, and the "safe" period or rhythm method—had long been known (although most physicians believed that a woman was least fertile at the midpoint of her menstrual cycle, the time when she is, in fact, most likely to conceive). Only in the later Victorian decades, however, did middle-class couples have the economic incentive to limit the number of children in their families. Working-class couples had no such incentive. Working-class children entered the labor force at a much earlier age than did their middle-class counterparts and so posed less of an economic drag on working-class living standards. Workers, therefore, did not begin to limit the size of their families until after 1900.

The demographic results of the adoption of birth control are clear. The average number of children in each family in Britain (discounting Ireland) fell from about six in 1870 to a little over three in the early twentieth century. By the 1920s, it had fallen to just over two per marriage. The population growth that had exploded upward in the eighteenth century began to slow down, *even though the mortality rate was falling*. The growth of the population, which had reached 17 percent per decade in the 1810s and held at 11 percent per decade in the 1850s and 1860s, declined to about 10 percent per decade in the early 1900s. By the 1920s, the British population was barely growing at all.

This demographic shift began with the late-Victorian middle class and had important consequences for late-Victorian middle-class women. The reduction of the number of children served as a liberation from some of the burdens of childbearing and child care and therefore as a release for activities outside the home. One result was an increase in the number of middle-class women involved in philanthropy and other good causes such as temperance reform and social work in the slums. Well-to-do married women still found paid employment socially unacceptable, but voluntary social work gave them an alternative outlet for their energy and talent; it was an extension outside the home of the traditional female role of moral care. By such philanthropic activity, thousands of middle-class women gained valuable experience and expertise in public life.

At the same time, as middle-class males put off marriage or emigrated, the number of unmarried women grew. The goal for respectable women was still marriage, but the number of unmarried women had risen markedly between 1851 and 1871: in the 1870s, almost one of every three British women between twenty-four and thirty-five was unmarried. As a result, the number of middle-class women who went to work outside the home increased sharply. Not only were more middle-class women (almost all of them single) seeking work, but also the economy was producing more jobs suitable for respectable women. No longer was the middle-class girl in need of income restricted to becoming a governess; the more service-oriented economy opened positions for nurses, teachers, clerks, shop assistants, and secretaries.

## THE WOMEN'S MOVEMENT

All of these changes made powerful contributions to the emergence of the women's movement. This first wave of feminism was not by any means a single, organized campaign. Some feminists, such as Sophia Jex-Blake (1840–1912) and Elizabeth Garrett Anderson (1836–1917), worked to break the male monopoly over the medical profession. They succeeded: Jex-Blake opened even the medical schools to women in the 1880s, despite Queen Victoria's vehement disapproval. Others, such as Emily Davies (1830–1921), sought to establish women's colleges even within the staunch male preserves, Oxford and Cambridge. They founded colleges for women in both of the ancient universities, despite fears on the part of some males that academic standards would be lowered and male undergraduates would be distracted from their work. (Women were not allowed to take degrees from Oxford until 1921 and from Cambridge until 1948.) Josephine Butler (1828–1906) and others attacked the notorious Victorian double standard in sexual morality by campaigning to have the Contagious Diseases Act abolished. This act, passed in the 1860s, enabled police in army and navy towns to force prostitutes to submit to medical inspection for venereal disease. After a long campaign, in which Butler called on men to practice the same chastity they preached to women, Parliament repealed the act in 1886.

Another element in the women's movement worked to reform the legal position of women in marriage. Irish writer Frances Power Cobbe (1822–1904) agitated successfully in the 1860s and 1870s for magistrates to impose more severe sentences on wife beaters. Women gradually won some custody rights over their children in divorce cases. By a series of laws culminating in 1882, married women were allowed to retain their property. Divorce, however, was not granted to women on the same grounds as men until 1923; until then, they still had to prove something in addition to adultery to win a divorce.

Finally, there was a campaign to win the national suffage. Given the importance of Parliament in British life, the women's movement inevitably focused much of its energy on gaining the right to vote. Beginning with J. S. Mill's famous essay *The Subjection of Women* (1869), a slowly growing

Going Shopping. *This Edwardian era postcard shows a genteel suffragette setting off to shatter shop windows with a hammer hidden in her handwarmer. Both the pro- and anti-women's suffrage campaigns used postcards and posters to communicate their messages.*

number of men and women argued that women were as capable as men of that reasoned behavior required by the suffrage. Led by Lydia Becker (1827–90) and Millicent Fawcett (1847–1929), *suffragists* campaigned for women's votes ("on the same terms as men") by means of persuasion: reasoned appeals, lobbying, petitions, and political pressure. This essentially middle-class movement met staunch resistance from people—female as well as male—who believed that the vote would spoil the innocent purity of women, that it would ruin marital harmony, or that the justifiable claims of women were being met without it. Most women, like most men, continued to think that the proper sphere for women was the home and that the proper woman's role should be, as one wife wrote, that of "a quite unillustrious, more or less hampered, dependent wife and mother."

In the early twentieth century, the militant *suffragettes*, a highly visible minority in the feminist movement, cast off the relatively sedate tactics of the suffragists. The central figures in this new phase of the feminist movement were Mrs. Emmeline Pankhurst (1858–1928) and her two daughters,

Christabel and Sylvia. Mrs. Pankhurst, wife of a radical Manchester lawyer, founded the Women's Social and Political Union (WSPU) in 1903. Within two years of its founding, the WSPU turned toward militant action: disruption of political meetings; demonstrations; political marches; and, from 1912, window smashing, arson, and even physical assault. In 1913, a suffragette threw herself under the hooves of the king's horse on Derby Day and was killed. The suffragette movement directly challenged the political and cultural status quo. By taking to the streets, these women attacked the assumption that a woman's proper place was in the home and that the proper place for politics was in Parliament. Even more fundamentally, by opting for violence rather than reasoned debate, they rejected the liberal faith in the rational individual. The sight of respectable middle-class wives and mothers smashing windows and assaulting politicians accelerated the erosion of Victorian certainties.

## Suggested Reading

Alford, B. W. E. *Britain in the World Economy Since 1880*. New York: Longman, 1996.

Banks, J. A., and Olive Banks. *Feminism and Family Planning*. New York: Schocken, 1964.

Booth, Alan. *The British Economy in the Twentieth Century*. New York: Palgrave, 2001.

Bourke, Joanna. *Working Class Cultures in Britain, 1890–1960: Gender, Class and Ethnicity*. London: Routledge, 1993.

Brown, Callum. *The Death of Christian Britain: Understanding Secularisation, 1800–2000*. London: Routledge, 2009.

Caine, Barbara. *English Feminism, 1780–1980*. New York: Oxford University Press, 1997.

Cannadine, David. *The Decline and Fall of the British Aristocracy*. New Haven, CT: Yale University Press, 1990.

Crossick, Geoffrey, and Heinz-Gerhard Haupt. *The Petite Bourgeoisie in Europe, 1780–1914: Enterprise, Family, and Independence*. New York: Routledge, 1995.

Floud, Roderick, and Donald McCloskey, eds. *The Economic History of Britain Since 1700*. Vol. 2, *1860 to the 1970's*. New York: Cambridge University Press, 1981.

Gourvish, T. R., and Alan O'Day, eds. *Later Victorian Britain, 1867–1900*. New York: St. Martin's Press, 1988.

Harris, José. *Private Lives, Public Spirit: A Social History of Britain, 1870–1914*. New York: Oxford University Press, 1993.

Holton, Sandra Stanley. *Suffrage Days: Stories from the Women's Suffrage Movement*. New York: Routledge, 1996.

Kidd, Alan J., and David Nicholls, eds. *Gender, Civic Culture, and Consumerism: Middle-Class Identity in Britain, 1800–1914*. Manchester, UK: Manchester University Press, 1999.

Kent, Susan Kingsley. *Sex and Suffrage in Britain, 1860–1914*. New York: Routledge, 1990.

Kirk, Neville. *Change, Continuity and Class: Labour in British Society, 1850–1920*. Manchester, UK: Manchester University Press, 1998.

Landes, David. *The Unbound Prometheus*. Cambridge: Cambridge University Press, 1969.

Levine, Phillippa. *Victorian Feminism, 1850–1900*. Tallahassee: Florida State University Press, 1989.

Mayhall, Laura E. Nym. *The Militant Suffrage Movement: Citizenship and Resistance in Britain, 1860–1930*. Oxford: Oxford University Press, 2003.

McKibbin, Ross. *The Ideologies of Class: Social Relations in Britain, 1880–1950*. New York: Oxford University Press, 1990.

Meacham, Standish. *A Life Apart: The English Working Class, 1890–1914*. Cambridge, MA: Harvard University Press, 1977.

Pollard, Sidney. *Britain's Prime and Britain's Decline: The British Economy, 1870–1914*. London: Edward Arnold, 1989.

Prochaska, F. K. *Women and Philanthropy in Nineteenth Century England*. New York: Oxford University Press, 1980.

Purvis, June. *Emmeline Pankhurst: A Biography*. London: Routledge, 2002.

Roberts, Elizabeth. *A Woman's Place: An Oral History of Working-Class Women, 1890–1940*. Oxford: Basil Blackwell, 1984.

Roberts, Robert. *The Classic Slum*. Manchester, UK: Manchester University Press, 1972.

Rose, Jonathan. *The Intellectual Life of the British Working Classes*. New Haven, CT: Yale University Press, 2001.

Rubenstein, W. D. *Capitalism, Culture, and Decline in Britain, 1750–1990*. New York: Routledge, Chapman & Hall, 1993.

Saul, S. B. *The Myth of the Great Depression, 1873–96*. London: Macmillan, 1976.

Searle, G. R. *A New England? Peace and War 1886–1918*. Oxford: Oxford University Press, 2005.

Thompson, F. M. L. *English Landed Society in the Nineteenth Century*. London: Routledge and Kegan Paul, 1963.

———. *Gentrification and English Culture, 1780–1980*. New York: Oxford University Press, 2001.

Thompson, Paul. *The Edwardians*. London: Weidenfeld & Nicolson, 1975.

Walkowitz, Judith, *City of Dreadful Delight: Narratives of Sexual Danger in Late-Victorian London*. Chicago: University of Chicago Press, 1992.

Williams, Sarah. *Religious Belief and Popular Culture in Southwark c.1880–1939*. New York: Oxford University Press, 1999.

# Chapter 19

# Crisis of Confidence, 1870–1914

The economic and social changes of the late-Victorian and Edwardian years contributed to a crisis of confidence as the difficulties of the economy, the "discovery" of chronic poverty, and the alteration of the social structure threw many Victorian ideas into doubt. To many men and women in the educated classes, especially younger people, Victorian ideas and values no longer seemed satisfying. Consequently, in cultural life, the years between 1870 and 1914 in Britain were filled with exploration and speculation as people searched for new ordering principles. An explosion of *isms*—not only feminism but also scientific naturalism, New Liberalism, socialism, and aestheticism—bore witness to the cultural ferment of this troubled and exciting period.

## SCIENTIFIC NATURALISM

One of the most influential intellectual efforts to find a new ordering principle for both an understanding of the natural world and a guide for behavior was *scientific naturalism*, the British variety of a cult of science that emerged in most of the Western world in the late nineteenth and early twentieth centuries. As the influence of Christianity diminished, science, which was as yet seen as incapable of doing any harm, seemed to many thinkers to be the best alternative. One English writer said in 1878, "In the struggle of life with the facts of existence, Science is the bringer of aid; in the struggle of the soul with the mystery of existence, Science is the bringer of light." Many scientists in the late-Victorian period, including Herbert Spencer, T. H. Huxley, and Francis Galton, aggressively asserted the claims of science as a new religion and of scientists as a new priesthood.

British scientific naturalists intended to create nothing less than a science-based culture. Their doctrine comprised four basic points. First, they held that the universe, or nature, is a mechanism, and therefore all events have material causes, in the sense of being mechanically determined like the movement of cogs in a machine. Thought and ideas cannot cause the natural world to move and interact; all causes are material. Second, they believed that evolution describes the working of this machine. Third, as Huxley said, there is "but one kind of knowledge and but one method of acquiring it": empirical science, which should be extended to all realms of thought, including ethics and social behavior. Finally, they contended that, because it is not possible to have any knowledge of the supernatural, the correct outlook is agnosticism: not the claim that God and the supernatural do not exist, but simply that one cannot have any valid knowledge about them at all. Ethics and morals must be derived from the facts of the natural world, not from the unknowable.

Perhaps the greatest—certainly the most prolific and famous—scientific naturalist was Herbert Spencer (1820–1902). It is hard to overestimate the influence of Spencer in late-Victorian Britain (and America, where he was even more influential). In the 1890s, a letter was delivered to him addressed: "Herbt. Spencer, England, and if the postman doesn't know where he lives, why, he ought to." Widely regarded as a prodigious genius, Spencer tried to create a comprehensive philosophy by universalizing science. He was trained as a civil engineer, and his philosophy always reflected that no-nonsense background. Impenetrably self-confident, Spencer acquired his fundamental ideas early and never swerved from them: (1) that evolution, operating through the "survival of the fittest" (a phrase he invented), explains change in nature, human life, and society; (2) that evolution moves from "simple homogeneity" to "complex heterogeneity"—that is, there is in society as in nature a continuous specialization of function; and (3) that every event is caused, but "every cause produces more than one effect."

Spencer drew from these evolutionary views a strong defense of laissez-faire economics and an anti-interventionist attitude toward government policy. He believed that because it is impossible to predict the effects of economic or social legislation, governments should try to do as little as possible. Furthermore, Spencer believed that social welfare policies only prevent people from adapting to their environment, which they must do to survive. Spencer saw society in biological terms: "I have contended that policies, legislative and other, while hindering the survival of the fittest, further the propagation of the unfit [and] work grave mischiefs." He thought that social progress was inevitable if people were left alone because the natural evolution of society is toward more complex specialization and interdependence.

*Herbert Spencer. The most famous evolutionary philosopher in late-Victorian Britain and one of the most influential thinkers in the Western world at the time.*

Such views became the stock-in-trade of defenders of capitalism and opponents of governmental social reform after 1870.

Spencer's application of evolutionary theory to social policy places him among the most prominent scientific naturalists of the late-Victorian and Edwardian years, the *Social Darwinists*. In fact, Spencer's view of evolution was not exactly that of Darwin, for Spencer believed in the inheritance of acquired characteristics, and Darwin did not. Social Darwinists applied Darwinian theory to society as a whole. Some Social Darwinists advocated domestic social reform to make society stronger and more "efficient." But many Social Darwinists opposed measures of social reform on the same grounds as did Spencer. They thought it wrong to interfere with what Spencer called the "progressive" forces of nature: "There is no greater curse to posterity than that of bequeathing to them an increasing population of imbeciles and idlers and criminals." These Social Darwinists believed that private charity was adequate for all reasonable relief of poverty and that state intervention would block the natural struggle of life and prevent the beneficial weeding out of the weak. To interfere with this process would be harmful to the "British race" and to the world. Alfred Marshall (1842–1924), the leading economist of the late 1800s, wrote:

> . . . if the lower classes of Englishmen multiply more rapidly than those which are morally and physically superior, not only will the population of England deteriorate, but also that part of the population of America and Australia which descends from Englishmen will be less intelligent than it otherwise would be.

Such views obviously were racist—a common failing of Social Darwinism—and also led logically to *eugenics*, the idea of deliberately improving the genetic pool of the population. The leading British eugenicist was Francis Galton (1822–1911), a Social Darwinist, social scientist, and statistician. Galton argued that accepting evolution as the key to progress meant that natural selection should be assisted in doing its work. "Eugenics," he said, "cooperates with the workings of Nature by securing that humanity shall be represented by the fittest races. What Nature does blindly, slowly, and ruthlessly, man may do so providently, quickly, and kindly." Society should not attempt to cut the high mortality rate of the poor by social legislation, but it should promote the marriage and fertility of "the fit" by measures such as creating a register, for interbreeding purposes, of the best families. Other eugenicists later advocated policies to discourage marriage and reproduction among the criminal, disabled, or chronically ill segments of the population.

Social Darwinism enjoyed its heyday in the 1880s and 1890s in Britain, and it retained a wide popularity in more or less diluted form among the middle class through the first half of the twentieth century. The well-to-do found Social Darwinism a satisfying explanation of why they were at the top of the heap and the poor were at the bottom. But in the years between 1900 and 1914, British academic philosophers abruptly took the whole theory of scientific naturalism in a new direction. The rejection of Social Darwinism as a basis for ethics was first articulated by two young philosophers at Cambridge University, G. E. Moore (1873–1958) and Bertrand Russell (1872–1970). By means of highly technical logical analysis, Moore and Russell showed that the logical base of Social Darwinism—indeed, of utilitarianism and all other previous ethical systems—was vague and indefensible.

Yet Moore and Russell clearly stood in the broad tradition of British empiricism and the scientific approach to knowledge. Moore, an analytical philosopher of ethics, set as his goal the foundation of "any ethics that can claim to be scientific." Russell, a mathematical logician of scintillating genius and acerbic wit, wanted to make philosophy consistent with modern science and indeed to reshape philosophy according to the latest scientific and mathematical discoveries. In a large number of popular lectures and books, most notably *Why I Am Not a Christian*, Russell carried on in the tradition of T. H. Huxley in attacking what he regarded as the hypocrisy, cruelty, and irrationalism of Christianity. Throughout the twentieth century in Britain, this has been the position of a broad stream of progressive (often left-wing), scientifically oriented intellectuals, the heirs of David Hume and the Enlightenment.

## NEW LIBERALISM

The search for a new ordering principle for society also produced a new direction for liberalism—the *New Liberal* movement. Between 1870 and 1914, the New Liberals, a group of intellectuals, most of whom were professional writers and journalists rather than businessmen, modified Victorian liberalism by calling for greater concern with society as a whole and for a more positive role for the state. Often referred to as *collectivists* in their own day, the New Liberals never captured the rank and file of the Liberal party; nevertheless, they were extremely influential in creating both the philosophy and the reality of the British welfare state.

Like their Victorian Liberal predecessors, the New Liberals were individualists, but they had very different ideas concerning how the good of the individual was to be promoted. Earlier British Liberals, as we saw in chapter 13, believed in the rationality and perfectibility of individuals, in constitutional liberty and representative government, and in the self-regulation of the free-market economy. They thought that the natural action of economic and social forces, if unimpeded by either privilege or the state, would maximize freedom and prosperity. But the "discovery" of chronic poverty by social investigators such as Booth and Rowntree and by social activists such as the Reverend Andrew Mearns (author of a best-selling pamphlet in 1883, *The Bitter Cry of Outcast London*) proved that the economic and social systems had not, in fact, worked for all. Confronted with these social realities, New Liberals insisted that the state would have to intervene in society to correct the shortcomings of capitalism.

The contrast between liberalism and New Liberalism can be seen clearly in the works of J. A. Hobson (1858–1940), a prolific writer on social subjects and a heretical economist. Hobson dared to take on Adam Smith by arguing that the economic system did not regulate itself automatically. In fact, the unequal distribution of incomes allowed the rich to save too much and therefore to depress consumption, and under-consumption caused periodic depression and chronic unemployment. In *Imperialism: A Study* (1902), Hobson applied his theory of malfunctioning capitalism to imperialism to show that the motives for empire were not as noble as they professed to be. While impoverishing the masses, Hobson contended, unregulated capitalism generates huge capital surpluses for an elite, who must then find somewhere to invest these surpluses. Imperialism, then, is the inevitable result of capitalism.

From 1880 to 1914, the New Liberals generated a substantial body of reform proposals, including old age pensions, unemployment insurance, health insurance, and a minimum wage, based on the philosophy of *positive freedom*. This philosophy held that the historic role of liberalism—the abolition of obstacles to individual liberty of action—was over, and that the time had come for constructive action by the state to create an environment in which all individuals had *freedom to act*, not just *freedom from arbitrary authority*. Thus, the New Liberals shifted the focus of liberalism from the autonomous individual to the person as part of a whole society, and they conceived of the state as society's agency for producing democracy and equality. As one New Liberal wrote: "'New Liberalism' differed from the old in that it envisaged more clearly the need for important economic reform, aiming to give a positive significance to the 'equality' which figured in the democratic triad of liberty, equality, and fraternity."

New Liberal philosophy stemmed from three intellectual sources. One was the thought of John Stuart Mill, the great mid-Victorian liberal. During his lifetime Mill had shifted the emphasis of liberalism from material to moral self-development of the individual. From the 1860s on, British liberal thinkers concerned themselves with establishing the conditions in which individuals had maximum opportunity for moral improvement. It was a short step for his successors to conclude that the state should actively create conditions in which people, even the working class, could exercise genuine freedom of moral choice: conditions that would be free of poverty, misery, disease, ignorance, and economic servitude.

The second intellectual source of New Liberalism was evolutionary thought. Whereas evolution taught some thinkers such as Spencer that survival of the fittest required laissez-faire policies, it taught others that society is an organism, with the well-being of any individual depending on the well-being of the others. By this view, the direction of social evolution is toward cooperation, not competition, and cooperation can be assisted by the rational use of state power. According to the leading New Liberal intellectual, J. T. Hobhouse (1864–1929), human evolution involved progress toward intellectual and moral improvement; therefore, the state could (and should) intervene rationally in society to create the environment that in turn shapes the development of individuals.

The third source of New Liberal thought was *philosophical idealism*, particularly the ideas of T. H. Green (1836–82). Green was an Oxford philosopher and a teacher who possessed great personal magnetism. Like many of the other idealist philosophers of his generation, Green was the son of an Evangelical clergyman; he found, however, that modern science and scholarship made adherence to orthodox Christianity impossible. For Green, an idealist philosophy drawing on the German thinkers Kant and Hegel provided a rational substitute for religion. As he put it, his interest in philosophy was wholly religious, in the sense that it is "the reasoned intellectual expression of the effort to get to God." Green's philosophy, like that of all the British idealists, was highly technical and ridden with Germanic jargon, yet it became the dominant style of philosophy in the British universities in the late-Victorian years.

The idealists sought to see all things—nature, the universe, experience—as a whole and to show how the mind itself plays a role in constituting what we perceive as reality. In this regard, it was antiscientific, for scientists liked to investigate nature one piece at a time and to regard each bit as existing independently of the human mind. Moore and Russell after 1900 led a ferocious attack on idealism on behalf of scientific naturalism, but in the meantime, idealism had become the most influential mode of philosophy in late-Victorian Britain. To Green, God was the infinite and eternal unifying feature of the world, expressed in people as generous and altruistic morality. People express their "best selves" and find unity with God by high-minded, socially oriented behavior. In other words, people reach their highest ethical potential only in society and only in sacrifice of their own interests for others. Thus, for Green, and for his many disciples among the New Liberals, individualism was related not to the pursuit of self-interest but to self-sacrifice.

Green inspired a generation of Oxford students and gave them a motive for social action. Many of the New Liberals had lost their religion and were seeking a substitute. As members of the elite, many of them felt a sense of guilt in the wake of revelations of poverty and class divisions. This combination of class-inspired guilt and New Liberal idealism helped shape the university settlement movement. Middle- and upper-class university students and graduates lived in settlement houses in urban slums. Living and working among the poor, they sought to close the gap between working and upper classes through both personal connections and educational programs.

## SOCIALISM

Among the various efforts to find a new ordering principle, the one that most upset conventional middle-class businessmen was socialism. Socialism may be generally defined as any ideology that holds cooperation rather than competition as the organizing principle of society; hence, socialism focuses on the social as opposed to the individual aspect of human nature. In the late-Victorian and Edwardian years, many people, most of them from the middle class, began to think that socialism offered a better analysis of poverty as well as more idealistic values than capitalism.

In the mid-Victorian era, socialism took shape as a romantic protest against the atomizing impact of industrialization. Romantic socialism had both Christian and aesthetic impulses. Christian Socialists such as F. D. Maurice (1805–72) urged individual and social reforms aimed at reconciling class interests and building up a Christian commonwealth in which God's love, incarnate in Christ, served as the model for social relations. At the same time, cultural critic John Ruskin reworked Thomas Carlyle's vehement critique of industrial capitalism into a call for a new kind of social order based on an idealized vision of medieval society and the desire to restore the respect for craftsmanship and for the craftsman that he thought had been lost in the modern world.

Karl Marx (1818–83) offered a brand of socialism that was very different from Ruskin's romantic medievalism. Marx set out a "scientific" analysis of classical political economy and of British society under capitalism. Marx, of course, was German, but he worked as an exile in London from 1849 until his death. In his mature work, *Das Kapital* (*Capital*), first published in German in 1867, Marx combined German philosophy, French socialist theory, and British political economy. He regarded capitalism, of which Britain was the most advanced example, as a system that necessarily exploited its workers. The key, he thought, is that the value of any object is equal to the labor that went into its production, yet a worker in capitalist industry produces objects worth much more than is needed to give him or her subsistence. An oversupply of laborers ("the reserve army of labor") keeps wages at a subsistence level. The difference between the value of what the worker produces and what he or she is paid is profit, and the capitalist takes all of it for his own purposes. Marx believed that, when capitalism reached maturity, it would cause its own collapse. As capitalists exploited their workers more and more ruthlessly, the workers would spontaneously rebel and establish a socialist state.

*Speaker's Corner in Hyde Park, 1892. The artist's animal-like depiction of the socialist speaker conveys the political message of this sketch.*

The failure of British workers to revolt in the 1850s and 1860s frustrated Marx. He regarded the union movement as the product of *false consciousness*—that is, workers misunderstood the real structure of capitalism and their own real interests and thus tried by unionizing to secure a place within the system, rather than seeking to overthrow that system. British working men and women, however, remained largely unpersuaded by Marx's arguments, although by the 1880s, the troubles in the British economy gave Marxism some credibility. *Capital* was not published in English until 1887; thus, British radicals knew of Marx's ideas only through pamphlets or summaries published by people other than Marx himself. Nevertheless, as collectivists of all sorts, including socialists, began to multiply and organize clubs and societies in the 1880s, Marxist ideas formed one of the traditions upon which they drew.

H. M. Hyndman (1842–1921) was one of the British socialists most heavily influenced by Marx. A businessman and utilitarian, Hyndman read a French translation of *Capital* in 1880. At about the same time, he began organizing the Social Democratic Federation, a club that included both middle-class and working-class radicals. In his book, *England for All*, Hyndman borrowed extensively from Marx (and, much to Marx's annoyance, without acknowledgment). But in certain ways Hyndman's views differed from those of Marx. In particular, Hyndman tended to think that significant change could occur through gradual state and local social reforms, whereas Marx preferred not to cooperate with existing institutions.

In any case, Hyndman had a domineering personality, and this caused a break with one of the most influential British socialists, William Morris (1834–96). Morris founded a rival organization, the Socialist League—but he was far from just a political organizer. He was, in fact, a multitalented genius—poet, painter, designer, architect, social critic, and founder of the British arts and crafts movement. Guided by Ruskin's aesthetic critique of industrial capitalism, Morris followed a path from High Church Anglicanism to socialism. Like Ruskin, Morris was a romantic medievalist, an admirer of the Gothic style, the coherent medieval culture, and the craftsmanship of the medieval guilds. He wanted above all to create a society in which the ordinary worker took joy in producing genuinely useful and beautiful objects. He wrote:

> Apart from the desire to produce beautiful things, the leading passion of my life has been and is hatred of modern civilization. . . . The struggle of mankind for many ages had produced nothing but this sordid, aimless, ugly, confusion.

*William Morris's bed in his home at Kelmscott Manor. This splendidly crafted piece of furniture shows how medievalism, socialism, and aestheticism came together in the arts-and-crafts movement inspired by Morris.*

Morris grafted Marxism onto this aesthetic vision. He believed that Marx explained what Ruskin had observed: that modern industry turned the craftsman into a cog in the industrial machine. He thought a profound revolution in both social relations and individual values was needed, and to this end he devoted himself, not to politics or trade union organization, but to raising the consciousness of both the middle class and the working class by writing and speaking. In *News from Nowhere* (1891) Morris presented an anarchistic utopia: a society in which all political, economic, and social regulations had disappeared and the individual was free to create spontaneously. Such aesthetic views were too impractical to attract more than a small following, but in a more general way they became very influential in a romantic and idealistic stream of British socialism. Morris's ideas have repeatedly emerged in Christian, guild, and anarchist types of socialism in Britain.

*Fabianism,* the dominant form of British socialism in the years between 1880 and 1914, could not have been more different from Morris's vision. Fabian socialism was utilitarian, practical, and gradualist, and it was committed to social efficiency and rule by experts in social science. The essence of Fabian doctrine was that social institutions, not the whole culture or human nature itself, needed reform. Parliament and local government provided the means to reform; thus, revolution was neither necessary nor desirable. Most Fabians were middle-class intellectuals, most of whom had close friends and associates among the New Liberals. Fabianism grew out of an organization characteristic of late-Victorian Britain—the Fellowship of the New Life, a society of young men and women of deep ethical concerns, looking for a new principle to live by. The founders of the Fabian Society in 1884 were the more practical members of this group. Over time, they developed from their ethical interests a distinctive socialist outlook and program.

Sidney Webb (1859–1947) and Beatrice Webb (1858–1943) became the most influential of all the Fabians. Husband and wife, as well as partners in economic and social research, the Webbs had a high regard for bureaucrats and expertise (Sidney was a civil servant and Beatrice a professional social scientist). As Beatrice was later to say, she and Sidney were "benevolent, bourgeois, and bureaucratic." They were also people of unflagging industry, a formidable if rather strange pair.

Sidney Webb rooted Fabian economics in the British tradition of political economy. He accepted the economic value of individual self-interest: "It is the business of the community not to lead into temptation this healthy natural feeling but so to develop social institutions that individual egoism is necessarily directed to promote the well-being of all." The key to implementing this idea, Webb insisted, was to extend the idea of *rent*, as it had been set out in classical political economy, to other forms of property. Ever since the early 1800s, British political economists such as David Ricardo and J. S. Mill had argued that rent in modern society goes up because of the growth of the population and the economic development of the community, not because of the landowner's efforts. The community is justified, therefore, in taxing this "unearned increment" of rent to its full value, and in turning it to the use of the community. Webb extended this theory to capital and "special skills," for he believed that these forms of property were also socially created wealth and eligible for state expropriation for the good of all.

The Fabians' admiration of the expert and the state, their practicality, and their interest in social efficiency gave them an influence across the political spectrum. In the 1880s and 1890s, the Fabians sought to accomplish their goals through the Liberal party. But the Webbs' concern for national efficiency and their belief in the superiority of progressive nations such as Britain made them enthusiasts of empire. Such views linked them to imperialists among the Conservative party as well as some Liberals. It was, however, the new Labour party, formed in 1906, that most clearly embraced the gradualist, administrative, democratic, and reformist tendencies of Fabianism.

Throughout the late-Victorian and Edwardian years, socialism in all its permutations remained largely a movement of middle-class intellectuals. As Robert Roberts recalled from his boyhood in the slum of Salford, near Manchester: "Before 1914 the great majority of the working class were ignorant of Socialist doctrine in any form." Nevertheless, socialism did begin to penetrate small circles in the working class in the 1880s. By 1900, there were perhaps thirty thousand socialists in Britain. After 1900, *syndicalism* (a revolutionary ideology that sought to use militant industrial action to bring about a more egalitarian society) won a foothold in some of the biggest unions, most notably the coal miners. Most working-class socialists, however, were not doctrinaire but idealistic, deriving their ideals of equality and community from the works of cultural critics such as Carlyle and Ruskin. They wanted greater control over and participation in industrial decisions, a reinvigoration of craftsmanship and community life, and the restoration of independence and dignity to workers. Such views were expressed by the socialist most widely read by British working people, Robert Blatchford, whose paper, the *Clarion*, sold forty thousand copies a week in 1894.

## AESTHETICISM

New Liberalism and socialism were obviously directed toward political and social action, and as we have seen, scientific naturalism had political implications. But the other main *ism* of the years between 1870 and 1914 was a very different kind of movement: aestheticism. There were many varieties of aesthetes in late-Victorian and Edwardian Britain—cultural critics, bohemian poets, urbane dandies, and ardent modernists—but all of them rejected conventional Victorian attitudes in favor of art, beauty, and intellect, each to be exercised for its own sake. Out of this anti-utilitarian and anti-moralistic revolt was born *modernism*, the dominant theme in twentieth-century British (and European) high culture. An umbrella term, modernism embraces a huge variety of artistic and literary movements, but at its core is a rebellion against Victorian standards and values.

Before modernism, however, came aestheticism. British aesthetes were part of a long native tradition of opposition to industrial society and its dominant middle class. From the time of the Romantic poets through Carlyle and Dickens, many British writers had tried to speak as prophets to the general reading public, warning of the disastrous cultural consequences of industrialization, self-interest, and greed. In the 1860s and 1870s, however, writers began to turn away from the public, to write for each other, and to preserve a refuge for art. They consequently adopted the doctrine of "art for art's sake."

How can this turn in the romantic tradition be explained? Part of the answer can be found in the receding tide of religion, which left many British intellectuals stranded on the shoals of doubt and disbelief; for them, art became yet another substitute for religion. Additionally, the characteristic late-Victorian loss of confidence created an unease that the aesthetes shared, as well as a disillusionment that they felt on realizing the failure of earlier writers such as Carlyle and Dickens to effect a social transformation. Finally, there was a sense among serious writers that they were losing control over their audience. In the earlier Victorian period, writers knew that their readership was relatively compact, middle-class, and influential, and they instinctively understood this audience. But with the spread of state schools, a new, massive, semiliterate, working-class audience came into existence.

Journalists and hack writers given to sensationalism could reach this audience, but serious writers felt bewildered and threatened by it. They lost confidence in themselves as prophets and increasingly sought to write only for each other.

The seeds of this aesthetic tendency began to germinate in the ideas of Matthew Arnold (1822–88) in the 1860s. An influential literary critic, Arnold was also a profound social observer. He believed that the Victorian age, with its materialism, its devotion to self-interest, its class conflict, and its political battles, was a supremely unpoetic age. Modern life seemed to him diseased, "with its sick hurry, its divided aims/Its heads o'ertaxed, its palsied hearts." By the latter 1860s, Arnold believed that class conflict, in which the middle class (or Philistines, as he labeled them) was dominant, was creating a kind of spiritual anarchy. He argued that, because Christianity no longer could supply the necessary coherence, culture must be the antidote to anarchy. He defined *culture* in a highly intellectualized way: the pursuit of perfection by the study of the best that has been thought and said in the world.

Arnold still held on to the hope for social revitalization, but many of his disciples in the late-Victorian years found it impossible to sustain that hope. Many felt so alienated from the values of bourgeois society that they could not engage in socially constructive writing. In reaction, they idealized a life spent in the rarified atmosphere of art, spirit, and intellect. They aggressively rejected the notion that society had any claims on their art. They insisted that all art—painting, writing, and music—ought to be judged by standards peculiar to itself. Art was for art's sake only.

The twin themes of aestheticism—that one's life itself should be a work of art and that art is independent of social usefulness—appeared in much late-Victorian literature, but were expressed most clearly in the life and work of Walter Pater (1839–94), an Oxford tutor, literary critic, and novelist. Pater insisted that art is to be judged by its own standards of perfection and that the goal of life "is not action, but contemplation—being as distinct from doing—a certain disposition of mind." One should seek always to burn with a "hard, gem-like flame" of aesthetic ecstacy. For such aesthetes, art had become the new religion.

In the 1890s, this doctrine spawned a small circle of artists who took it to the extreme—the *decadents*, as they came to be called. One of the most famous of these glitterati was the Irish novelist and playwright Oscar Wilde (1854–1900). Wilde and his fellow decadents loved to shock the bourgeoisie of London with their clever and ironic turn of phrase, their praise of exotic (and erotic) beauty, their exploration of the pleasures of evil, and their dandified dress and manners. Wilde confronted Victorian values with decadent epigrams in the preface to his novel, *The Picture of Dorian Gray*:

The artist is the creator of beautiful things . . .
They are the elect to whom beautiful things mean
  only Beauty.
There is no such thing as a moral or immoral book.
Books are well written, or badly written. That
  is all . . .
All art is quite useless.

Decadence was a dead end, but aesthetic ideas about life and art helped shape the outlook of the most famous literary and intellectual circle of Edwardian Britain, the Bloomsbury Group (named after the area in London in which many of them lived between 1905 and 1925). Most of the male members of the Bloomsbury Group (Leonard Woolf, Lytton Strachey, E. M. Forster, and J. M. Keynes) were students at Cambridge around the turn of the century, and most had been members of a secret undergraduate society called the Apostles. The dominant figure of the Apostles was the unworldly but personally charismatic young philosopher G. E. Moore (1873–1958). He taught his students and friends to adopt a refreshingly rigorous analytical style of thought and to accept the elitist view that the two highest values were states of mind: the contemplation of beautiful objects and the enjoyment of personal friendships. The Apostles believed that these doctrines liberated them from the restrictions and oppressions of Victorian convention. As they moved to Bloomsbury from Cambridge and rounded out the group with two sisters, Virginia and Vanessa Stephen (who married Leonard Woolf and Clive Bell, respectively), they made Moore's philosophy into a creed: "We repudiated entirely," Keynes wrote, "customary morals, conventions, and traditional wisdom."

The aesthetic theory of the Bloomsbury Group was a foundation stone of modernism in Britain. Because, in their view, contemplation of beautiful objects was a complex and learned activity, in practice it was suitable only for an artistic elite. The "Bloomsberries" were snobs, and by the same token, they thought that art was the only refining activity in life, apart from cultivation of the most exquisite personal relationships. They tended to think that all political and social policy should be directed to the creation and support of art. They thought that ultimately art would recivilize society, but not by direct social action. Works of art, they believed, are not the servants or the mirrors of society; their role is not social instruction or propaganda. A true work of art is autonomous: a painting is not a photograph, a biography is not a slavish chronology, nor is a novel a realistic description or a moral

*Bloomsbury: Bertrand Russell, John Maynard Keynes, and Lytton Strachey in 1915. These three intellectuals were among the members of the Bloomsbury Group, which dominated British high culture in the early years of the twentieth century.*

lesson. Art calls for an emotion of its own ("the aesthetic emotion"), which arises from the relations among the formal elements of the work—the lines, volumes, colors, images, and symbols. Bloomsbury theory thus added *formalism*, an important ingredient of modernism, to aesthetic values.

The aesthetic belief in the special role of the artist or intellectual revived the romantic belief in symbolism. *Symbolists* believed that by symbols alone can truths about the unseen or supernatural world be communicated. Symbolism connects the works of two of the most important English Edwardian novelists, who were in other ways about as different as two writers can be: E. M. Forster and D. H. Lawrence. The upper-middle-class Forster (1879–1970) was a Cambridge graduate, a writer of mild temperament, and an unforceful Liberal with a refined sensibility. In *Howards End* (1910), Forster used a country house to symbolize England itself; the inheritance of the house, like that of the country itself, is contested by the pushy business class and the sensitive intellectuals.

D. H. Lawrence (1885–1930) was one of the first English working-class novelists. The son of a coal miner, he had to break through the constrictions imposed by the industrial and class systems, as well as the oppressive affection of his mother. His social and psychological vision gave Lawrence a unique perspective on society, personality, and sexuality that informed a series of novels of astonishing energy and originality, including *Sons and Lovers* (1913), *Women in Love* (1920), and *Lady Chatterley's Lover* (1928). Lawrence's hostility to Victorian moral, social, and literary convention revealed modernism in full force.

## Suggested Reading

Beckson, Karl E. *London in the 1890s: A Cultural History*. New York: Norton, 1992.

Bevir, Mark. *The Making of British Socialism*. Princeton, NJ: Princeton University Press, 2011.

Bowler, Peter J. *Reconciling Science and Religion: The Debate in Early Twentieth-Century Britain*. Chicago: University of Chicago Press, 2001.

Calloway, Stephen, ed. *The Cult of Beauty*. London: V&A Publishing, 2011.

Collini, Stefan. *Liberalism and Sociology: T. L. Hobhouse and Political Argument in England, 1880–1914*. Cambridge: Cambridge University Press, 1979.

Crook, D. P. *Benjamin Kidd: Portrait of a Social Darwinist*. Cambridge: Cambridge University Press, 1984.

Francis, Mark. *Herbert Spencer and the Invention of Modern Life*. Ithaca, NY: Cornell University Press, 2007.

Freeden, Michael. *The New Liberalism: An Ideology of Social Reform*. Oxford: Clarendon Press, 1978.

Hall, Lesley. *Sex, Gender and Social Change in Britain Since 1880*, 2nd ed. Basingstoke, UK: Palgrave Macmillan, 2012.

Harrison, Royden J. *The Life and Times of Sidney and Beatrice Webb, 1858–1905: The Formative Years*. Basingstoke, UK: Palgrave Macmillan, 2001.

Heyck, T. W. *The Transformation of Intellectual Life in Victorian England*. New York: St. Martin's Press, 1982.

Hough, Graham. *The Last Romantics*. London: Duckworth, 1949.

Hynes, Samuel. *The Edwardian Turn of Mind*. Princeton, NJ: Princeton University Press, 1968.

Johnson, Dale. *The Changing Shape of English Nonconformity, 1825–1925*. New York: Oxford University Press, 1999.

Koven, Seth. *Slumming: Sexual and Social Politics in Victorian London*. Princeton, NJ: Princeton University Press, 2004.

Lineham, Thomas. *Modernism and British Socialism*. London: Palgrave Macmillan, 2012.

MacKenzie, Norman, and Jeanne MacKenzie. *The Fabians*. New York: Simon & Schuster, 1977.

McBriar, A. M. *Fabian Socialism and English Politics, 1884–1918*. Cambridge: Cambridge University Press, 1962.

Perkin, Harold. *The Rise of Professional Society: England Since 1880*. London: Routledge, 1989.

Pierson, Stanley. *British Socialists: The Journey from Fantasy to Politics*. Cambridge, MA: Harvard University Press, 1979.

Prettejohn, Elizabeth. *Art for Art's Sake: Aestheticism in Victorian Painting*. New Haven, CT: Yale University Press, 2007.

Richter, Melvin. *The Politics of Conscience: T. H. Green and His Age*. Cambridge: Cambridge University Press, 1964.

Searle, G. R. *The Quest for National Efficiency*. Berkeley: University of California Press, 1971.

Soloway, Richard. *Birth Control and the Population Question in England, 1877–1930*. Chapel Hill: University of North Carolina Press, 1982.

Thompson, E. P. *William Morris*. New York: Pantheon Books, 1977.

Trentmann, Frank. *Free Trade Nation: Commerce, Consumption, and Civil Society in Modern Britain*. Oxford: Oxford University Press, 2009.

Turner, Frank Miller. *Between Science and Religion*. New Haven, CT: Yale University Press, 1974.

Walkowitz, Judith. *Nights Out: Life in Cosmopolitan London*. New Haven, CT: Yale University Press, 2012.

Waters, Chris. *British Socialists and the Politics of Popular Culture, 1884–1914*. Stanford, CA: Stanford University Press, 1990.

# Chapter 20

# Revival on the Celtic Fringe

The English were quick to assume that what was good for England was good for the rest of Britain. England was by far the biggest and strongest segment of Great Britain, having in 1911 approximately 75 percent of all the people of the British Isles. The English habitually said "England" when they meant "Britain," and on the basis of prejudice rather than science, they asserted that the "Anglo-Saxon race," from which English men and women allegedly descended, was far superior to the "Celtic race" of Wales, Scotland, and Ireland. In the late-Victorian years, Wales, Scotland, and Ireland came to be known in England as "the Celtic fringe"—a perfect verbal symbol of their marginal status in the minds of the English. In reaction, political and cultural leaders in each of the three Celtic countries asserted their own national identities and sponsored national cultural revivals. These revivals were largely independent of each other; each national revival took a different form and achieved a different expression of national identity. There was revival *on* the Celtic fringe, not revival *of* the Celtic fringe. Viewed together, however, these revivals composed an important force in British political and cultural history; they helped create the political and cultural contexts in which millions of inhabitants of the British Isles have identified themselves.

## WALES: COAL, NONCONFORMITY, AND LINGUISTIC NATIONALISM

In Wales, cultural revival was inseparably tied with two important themes: the rapid growth of the coal industry and the dominance of Nonconformist Christianity. In the second half of the nineteenth century, coal became the great Welsh industry, with the famous coal mines of the Rhondda valleys opening in 1851. By 1913, more than 250,000 men worked in the Welsh coalfields.

The middle-class entrepreneurs of the Welsh coal industry were largely Welsh-born and Nonconformist in religion. Thus, they shared the language and the religion of their workers, who were mostly Welsh-speaking and

South Wales coal miners. *The densely populated mining valleys of South Wales in the late nineteenth and early twentieth centuries were a notable feature of the British industrial landscape and home to Welsh nonconformity and radicalism.*

almost entirely Nonconformist. Until the twentieth century, when class conflict overcame these bonds, the Welsh middle and working classes shared common ground and ranged themselves against the anglicized and Anglican traditional elite. The Welsh industrial enclave, concentrated so densely in South Wales, was therefore thoroughly Welsh in culture to the end of the nineteenth century.

Yet English influence grew relentlessly. English, after all, was the language of the government, the courts, education, the professions, and high-level commerce. As the coal owners grew richer and more established, then, they, too, became more English. At the same time, the work force also underwent a certain degree of anglicization. Scottish and English migrants poured into South Wales, while Welsh coal miners came to understand that they had the same problems as English workers and found their strongest support among English and Scottish trade unionists. Class identity in this sense functioned as a strong pan-British integrative force. By the early 1900s, Welsh miners were holding their meetings in English. Industrialization, which in its early stages helped preserve the Welsh language and culture, in the long run corroded Welshness.

In the last half of the nineteenth century, however, there was still a high correlation between Welsh-speaking areas and Nonconformist areas: to be Welsh was to be Nonconformist. As we saw in chapter 12, evangelicalism took Wales by storm; the Welsh became people of the chapel rather than the church. By the late nineteenth century, almost 90 percent of the Welsh were Nonconformists, and many of them belonged to the more puritanical sects: Baptists, Congregationalists, and Calvinistic Methodists. The Church of England (the established church in Wales) had made little attempt to reach out to the people at large: the first Welsh-speaking bishop in more than a century was appointed only in 1870. As one Welsh Anglican said: "Churchmen in Wales were comprised almost exclusively of the richer portions of society . . . so that they had in Wales a church kept up for the rich man at the expense of the poor majority."

Welsh popular culture revolved around Nonconformity. Chapel vestries dominated their communities, offering chapel members social opportunities, adult education, Sunday schools, and above all choirs to sing in. Nonconformists imposed their Sabbatarianism on Wales, making the Welsh Sunday peculiarly bleak even by Victorian standards. But Nonconformist ministers also were the heart and soul of the literary celebrations of Welsh culture, the annual *eisteddfoddau*, both national and local; they were in a sense the new bards, evangelical style.

Participation in the British Liberal party helped keep Welsh Nonconformist radicalism from becoming a separatist movement. Welsh Nonconformists found allies in the Liberal party because the Liberals generally supported the cause of Nonconformists against the privileges of the established church and the claims of the middle class against the landlords. The Welsh Nonconformists did not want independence for Wales, for they believed that the Welsh economy was far too dependent on England's to survive alone. But in the 1880s and 1890s, some militant young Welsh politicians including Tom Ellis and David Lloyd George earned great influence in the Liberal party and won commitment of the party not only to disestablishment of the Anglican church in Wales, but also to Home Rule (a degree of regional autonomy) for Wales.

At the same time, a cultural nationalist movement took root in Wales. It was not separatist, for even Welsh cultural nationalists were comfortable with two patriotisms—British and Welsh. Almost all of the Welsh nationalists of the years between 1880 and 1914 identified themselves as British as well as Welsh. Their *British* identity pertained to matters external to the British state, whereas their *Welsh* identity concerned things internal to the British Isles. Welsh cultural nationalists such as Owen Morgan Edwards (1858–1920) took pride in the British monarchy and Empire, but they also emphasized Welsh distinctiveness, glorified the allegedly virtuous and independent Welsh peasant, and reveled in the Welsh language. As a schoolboy, Morgan was frequently required to wear the *Welsh Not*, a board that was tied around the child's neck to discourage him from speaking Welsh. Clearly the punishment did not work, for Morgan grew up to become a passionate advocate for the Welsh language.

Cultural nationalists such as Morgan worked to collect and revive Welsh literature, to celebrate the Welsh past, and to save the Welsh language. They urged establishment of a Welsh national museum, library, and university, all of which had been accomplished by 1914. Briefly, in 1894–96, a Young Wales (Cymru Fydd) movement attempted to fuse cultural and political nationalism, but interest in Welsh independence was too slight for it to thrive. What Welsh cultural nationalism did achieve was to spread an enduring sense of the Welsh past and of the differentness of Welsh culture. For the time being, that was enough.

## SCOTLAND: NATIONAL IDENTITY AND THE GAELIC REVIVAL

Next to the national revivals in Wales on the one hand and Ireland on the other, the revival in late-Victorian Scotland seems a pale creation. But that is in part because the Scots brought into the period a strong sense of historical identity, one that needed cultivation rather than revival. As a result of centuries of independent existence, followed by the negotiated Union of 1707, the Scots had retained their own established (Presbyterian) church, system of laws and courts, and educational structure. The Romantic movement had revived a sense (admittedly somewhat bogus when it came to kilts and tartans) of historic distinctiveness. Even Lowland Scots came to celebrate Scottish heroes such as Robert Bruce, William Wallace, Mary Queen of Scots, and Bonnie Prince Charlie.

Unlike that in Wales, Scottish cultural identity did not focus on language. The Gaelic language was dying out, as traditional Scottish (that is, Highland) society dwindled rapidly. Gaelic was not taught in the state schools, and cultivation of Gaelic language and literature remained an academic pastime. But as in Wales, political separatism won few adherents. As one statesman said, "No Scotsman, except a handful of Celtic enthusiasts in the Highlands, wants a separate parliament for Scotland."

There was in Scotland, however, a growing sense that Scottish rights within the United Kingdom needed vindication. Following the Irish example (discussed later in this chapter), many Scottish Liberals committed themselves to Scottish Home Rule in 1886. In 1900, some militant Liberals founded the Young Scots Society. The feeling in Scotland that Scottish rights would be protected only if Scotland enjoyed greater regional autonomy produced four Scottish Home Rule bills between 1886 and 1914. None was passed, but in 1885 the British government created the position of secretary of state for Scotland, with supervision over a number of Scottish administrative boards, many of them already in existence. The British also granted fairer distribution of governmental expenditures, and a Scottish Grand Committee, made up of the Scottish members of Parliament (MPs) only, was given limited control over purely Scottish legislation. Thus, a limited degree of *devolution* was established in recognition of the strong Scottish sense of distinctiveness.

At the same time, a Scottish cultural revival reinforced this sense of distinctiveness. The artists, writers, and thinkers of this Gaelic Revival were not backward-looking; instead, they looked to Scottish mythologies and history for inspiration in shaping Scotland's future. City planner Patrick Geddes

The Charles Rennie Mackintosh dining room at the Hunterian Gallery in Glasgow. *Like William Morris, Charles Rennie Mackintosh refused to accept any distinction between art and craft, and sought to use design to make life more beautiful.*

(1854–1932), for example, pioneered the concept of *region* in architecture and design. He urged planners and architects to look to the locality and to the culture of the people who actually would live in their plans and designs. Similarly, architect and artist Charles Rennie Mackintosh (1868–1928) used Celtic motifs and influences to design clean-flowing modernist furniture, jewelry, and buildings.

## IRELAND: FROM THE DEVOTIONAL REVOLUTION TO THE HOME RULE MOVEMENT, 1850–1890

Celtic cultural nationalism blossomed most vigorously in Ireland, but here it intertwined with various outcroppings of political nationalism. Increasingly in Ireland, Britishness and Irishness stood as opposing identities.

One important factor in shaping Irish national identity was the mid-nineteenth century *devotional revolution*—a revitalization and Romanizing of Catholic worship. Led by Archbishop Paul Cullen (1803–78), the Irish Catholic hierarchy built new churches and convents, raised the standards of the parish clergy, and multiplied and regularized religious services. Cullen looked to Rome for guidance and spread practices that were popular in the Vatican: novenas, the rosary, and so on. The Irish Catholic laity became one of the most devout Catholic populations in the world. Ireland produced a surplus of priests and nuns, many of whom carried Irish Catholicism to the English-speaking world. Strongly conservative, Cullen opposed militant Irish nationalism. Nevertheless, his policies tightened the bond between Irish Catholicism and Irish nationalism; "faith and fatherland" was his ideal—that is, to be a patriot was to be a Catholic.

In the decades after the Famine and the collapse of Young Ireland (see chapter 15), Irish political nationalism swung between two poles: one was constitutional and devoted to parliamentary action, and the other embraced revolutionary violence. In the 1850s, some Irish MPs founded the Independent Irish party, hoping to defend the rights of Irish Catholics and to win some security for Irish tenants. Able to claim no more than a small minority in the British Parliament, it soon fell apart. By the end of the 1850s, constitutional politics had reached a dead end.

The nationalist pendulum now swung to a new revolutionary society— the Irish Republican Brotherhood (IRB), or Fenians (so-called because of the legendary warrior band, the *Fianna*). The IRB sought the overthrow of British rule by force and the establishment of an independent and nonsectarian Irish republic. Operating as an underground terrorist organization, it was quickly penetrated by British agents. In 1865, British authorities shut down the Fenian newspaper and arrested many IRB leaders. In 1866, about six hundred American Fenians "invaded" Canada but were easily forced back across the border. Finally, in 1867 the remaining IRB leaders in Ireland defiantly staged a rebellion before they could be arrested. It was quickly suppressed. After 1867, Irish nationalism swung back to the constitutional path, but the IRB continued to carry out attacks, such as bombing Scotland Yard in 1883, and to build up a network of support among Irish-American emigrés who had carried their memories of the Famine and their hatred of the British across the Atlantic.

The constitutional effort that overshadowed the IRB was the Home Rule movement, founded by Isaac Butt (1813–79), a Conservative Irish barrister who believed that revolution in Ireland would surely occur if the legitimate grievances of the Irish people were not settled. His solution was neither independence nor repeal of the Union, but Home Rule: Ireland would have its own Parliament for Irish affairs, yet would be subordinate to the Parliament at Westminster. In the general election of 1874, the new Home Rule party, founded only four years before, won 59 of the 105 Irish seats in the House of Commons. Butt did his best to persuade the British Parliament to accept Irish Home Rule, but he did not succeed. To the British, Home Rule, no matter how restricted the powers of an Irish Parliament might have been, was simply a plan to turn over Ireland and its Protestant population to papists and to split the Empire at its core.

Home Rule party members soon grew impatient with Butt's politics of persuasion. They advocated the tactics of confrontation—specifically, to obstruct the proceedings of Parliament. If Britain, they said, would not let Irishmen rule Ireland, then the Irish would not let Parliament rule Britain. Between 1877 and 1880, one of the advocates of the confrontational approach—the more forceful and militant nationalist, Charles Stewart Parnell—supplanted Butt as leader of the Home Rule movement.

Parnell (1846–91) was, along with Daniel O'Connell, one of the two towering figures in nineteenth-century Irish nationalism. A Protestant landlord and a man of icy demeanor, Parnell achieved an iron discipline over the Home Rule party and an almost magical hold on the imagination of the Irish people. The secrets of his success were his personal charisma, his supreme self-confidence, his passionate dislike of England, and his political ruthlessness. By refusing to bend to English will and yet staying just inside the boundaries of the law, Parnell managed to bind together the constitutional and the revolutionary wings of Irish nationalism. He simultaneously won

*Charles Stewart Parnell, the charismatic and tough-minded leader of the Irish Home Rule movement.*

control over the Home Rule parliamentary party and the organized force of militant tenants in Ireland, the Land League, as well as the support of the IRB. The Parnellite Home Rule movement became a constitutional (if aggressive) parliamentary force backed up by agrarian agitation and violence at home.

In 1881, William E. Gladstone's Liberal government responded to the unrest in the Irish countryside with a Land Act that addressed many tenant grievances and effectively made tenants co-owners of their farms. At the same time, however, the Liberal government also passed a *coercion act* (one of over a hundred such acts passed by British governments between 1801 and 1920) that denied Irish activists the right to trial by jury. And in 1882, when Parnell declared that the Land Act did not go far enough and encouraged further agrarian agitation, Gladstone used the coercion act to arrest Parnell and confine him in Kilmainham Gaol outside Dublin.

Imprisoning Parnell proved a huge mistake. It simply added "martyr" to his long list of nationalist credentials and encouraged further unrest across Ireland. Later that year, Parnell and Gladstone reached an agreement according to which the Irish leader would be released and the Irish tenants would receive additional relief, in return for Parnell's support of the Land Act. Called the Kilmainham Treaty, this agreement highlighted Parnell's political clout.

This clout became even more apparent in 1885, when Parnell returned to his confrontational politics in hopes of forcing one British party or the other to grant Home Rule. In that year's general election, he instructed Irish voters living in Britain to vote Conservative, his aim being to bring about a deadlock in the House of Commons, to which the Home Rule party would hold the key. As luck would have it, the election results *did* hand him the balance of power: neither party would be able to form and sustain a government without the support of the eighty-six Home Rulers. Parnell would be able to turn out of office one cabinet after another. Appalled by this fundamental threat to the British constitution, Gladstone concluded that the Liberal party must back Irish Home Rule.

As we will see in chapter 21, this commitment to Home Rule was the most dramatic event in late-Victorian politics. It forced through a realignment of Britain's political parties, but it did not achieve Home Rule. Twice, in 1886 and in 1893, a Liberal government introduced Home Rule bills, at great electoral cost to the Liberal party, and twice they were defeated. By the time the second Home Rule bill was rejected, however, the Liberal-Home Rule alliance had collapsed and Parnell was dead.

The fall of Parnell became a tragedy of mythic proportions in Irish popular culture. As the so-called Uncrowned King of Ireland, Parnell seemed invincible. Then, in 1889, his long-term affair with Kitty O'Shea, wife of a member of the Home Rule party, was revealed. Parnell's adultery was intolerable to both the British Nonconformists, who made up the backbone of the Liberal party, and to the Irish Catholic bishops, who exerted a great deal of political influence in Ireland. The Catholic clergy hounded Parnell, and the Liberals demanded that the Home Rule party depose him. After a bitter fight, the party majority did the Liberals' bidding. Parnell, however, refused to step down and so split the movement he had helped create. His health destroyed, Parnell died in 1891 and so took his place in the pantheon of Irish national martyr-heroes.

## IRELAND: LITERARY RENAISSANCE AND CULTURAL NATIONALISM, 1890–1914

With the Irish Home Rule party bitterly divided, British politicians were able to put Home Rule on the back burner. Instead, the Conservative governments of 1886–92 and 1895–1905 decided to "kill Home Rule with kindness." The key to their Irish policy was land purchase: by a series of laws culminating in Wyndham's Act of 1903, the British government loaned money to Irish tenants on very favorable terms so that the tenants could buy their holdings from the landlords. Wyndham's Act also gave the landlords bonuses to sell out. By 1920, the old problem of landlordism in Ireland had been eliminated.

By the early twentieth century, however, the Irish desire for some kind of national autonomy was so wide and deep that it could not be killed with kindness by this or any British government. There had taken root in late-Victorian Ireland a *cultural* nationalism that could not be satisfied with material progress. One aspect of this cultural revival was *Celticism*, a pro-Celtic reaction against the Anglo-Saxonism prevalent in late-Victorian England. Celtic history, fairy tales, and folklore were told and retold to recall the supposed excellence of ancient Celtic society and to celebrate legendary heroes such as Cuchulain and Finn MacCuchail. Historian Standish O'Grady's *History of Ireland* (published in 1878–80) opened up to the Irish imagination the lost realms of Celtic culture and literature. O'Grady portrayed the Irish peasants as racially pure, morally virtuous, politically democratic, and instinctively heroic—all in sharp contrast to the stolid and unimaginative *Sassennachs* (the English).

The organization that popularized the values of the Celtic revival was the Gaelic Athletic Association (GAA). Established in 1884 by Michael Cusack (1847–1906), an Irish-speaking teacher of civil service candidates, the GAA aimed to replace English games such as cricket and soccer with Irish games such as hurling and Gaelic football. By attracting young men into Irish-style (and often extremely rough) games, the GAA developed a fierce local and national pride and anti-English attitude. Inevitably, these emotions had political consequences: support for the more aggressive varieties of nationalism. In 1891, for instance, two thousand GAA hurlers marched in Parnell's funeral as an expression of approval of his final defiance of the English. The IRB quickly infiltrated the ranks of the GAA and recruited widely within it.

The intellectual and scholarly aspects of the Irish Celtic revival found expression in a host of antiquarian, literary, and folklore societies. The most important of these was the Gaelic League, established in 1893. Its leading figures were Eoin MacNeill (an Ulster Catholic) and Douglas Hyde (a southern Irish Protestant). Their objectives were to preserve the Irish language, to extend its use among the people again, and to cultivate a new literature in Ireland. The term *Irish-Ireland* summed up their philosophy. Hyde gave voice to it in a famous lecture called "The Necessity of de-Anglicizing Ireland." He argued that Irish men and women were stuck in a "half-way house" between Irish and English culture: they hated the English, but imitated them. Only if the Irish deliberately cultivated Irish literature, customs, games, names, and above all language would they be able to sustain a distinctive Irish national identity. By 1910 the Gaelic League had made significant progress on the cultural front. Although by then the Irish language was spoken by only about 12 to 13 percent of the Irish people, Irish was being taught for the first time in Ireland's state schools, and Irish was now required for entry into the new Irish National University (established in 1908).

It is somewhat ironic, then, that the great literary revival that blossomed in Ireland between 1880 and 1914 was not in Irish, but in English. The movement revolved around a close-knit band of writers who turned to Celtic history and culture for inspiration. Because most of these writers were members of the Anglo-Irish elite, many scholars regard the Irish literary renaissance as a product of *post-colonialism*: a profound attempt by the colonists to come to terms with the culture of the colonized. Whatever the explanation, their conscious objective was to create, as Professor F. S. L. Lyons wrote, "a modern Irish literature in English."

All of the leading figures in the Irish literary revival struggled with the opposing claims of nationalism and artistic creativity. Playwright J. M. Synge (1871–1909), for example, sought to render the rhythms and patterns of the Irish language into English and so to preserve the unique beauty of Irishness. But in his two most well-known works, *In the Shadow of the Glen* (1903) and *The Playboy of the Western World* (1907), Synge also portrayed the Irish peasants as they really were, warts and all. Advocates of Irish-Ireland and Catholic nationalists alike found the reality unacceptable, for they idealized the peasantry. As one Irish-Irelander declared, "All of us know that Irish women are the most virtuous in the world;" he refused to let Synge, or the newly founded Abbey Theatre, say otherwise.

The tension between nation and art was also pronounced in the career of the poet W. B. Yeats (1865–1939). A believer in magic and the occult and in the reality of a supernatural world, Yeats was drawn both to the premodern outlook of Irish folklore and to modernist symbolism. He was a political as well as cultural nationalist, with connections to the IRB; his play *Cathleen ni Houlihan* (1902) led one playgoer to wonder whether such patriotic plays should be produced "unless one was prepared for people to go out and shoot and be shot." But Irish nationalism, which demanded the artist's total commitment, proved too restrictive of Yeats's creativity. The nationalists' criticism of Synge's plays repelled Yeats, who thereafter tended to adopt an aristocratic disdain for the common, "vulgar" features of Irish culture.

James Joyce (1882–1941), one of the most innovative of modernist writers, reacted even more strongly against conventional Irish life. Joyce left Ireland for the Continent in 1904 and never returned. He also abandoned Catholicism and took up literature as his vocation. He believed Irish culture—or at least Dublin culture—to be paralyzed and paralyzing: priestridden, whiskey-soaked, intellectually degraded, and politically hypocritical. Yet he set all his important work in Ireland, including the highly experimental novel *Ulysses* (1922). In it, as in all his mature work, Joyce managed to combine symbolism with realism and mimicry with experiment in the use of language. In the process he painted an indelible portrait of the culture of the Irish nation.

## IRELAND: NEW EXPRESSIONS OF POLITICAL NATIONALISM, 1890-1914

The Irish cultural revival proved to be inseparable from politics. The strong sense of Irish nationality reinforced political ideas of national self-reliance, and these ideas led to political organization. First, in 1900 the Home Rule party, so disastrously divided after Parnell's fall, re-united under the leadership of John Redmond (1856–1918). Over the next decade, the party once again emerged as a powerful parliamentary force and the demand for Home Rule again dominated Irish political nationalism.

The Home Rule party, however, now had a new rival. Beginning in 1898, self-reliance was expressed as an ideology under the banner of *Sinn Fein* (ourselves alone) by journalist and intellectual Arthur Griffith (1872–1922). Griffith wanted not only to establish an independent Irish literature, history, and language, but also to free Ireland from economic and political dependence on England. He proposed policies of economic self-sufficiency and political separation for Ireland, and by any means possible: "Lest there might be a doubt in any mind, we will say that we accept the nationalism of '98, '48 and '67 as the true nationalism and Grattan's cry 'Live Ireland—perish the Empire!' as the watch-word of patriotism." This attitude put Sinn Fein, formally established as a political party in 1905, squarely in the extremist tradition of Irish nationalism, as opposed to the more moderate constitutionalism of the Home Rulers.

At about the same time, the urban working class of Dublin began to organize along militant nationalist lines. The central figures were James Larkin (1876–1947) and James Connolly (1868–1916), two syndicalist union organizers who set up the Irish Transport Workers Union (TWU). By violent agitation and strikes, the Dublin workers won a number of concessions from their employers, but in 1913 they lost an extended and bitter conflict with the United Tramway Company of Dublin. The main British union council, the Trades Union Congress, which had its own battles to fight and which was leery of the syndicalism, failed to give sustained support to the Irish TWU. In reaction, the Irish workers became more nationalist than socialist in their outlook. In that heated atmosphere of both increasing class conflict and nationalist militancy, Connolly formed a small force to defend the union men against the police: the Irish Citizen Army. In 1914, the "Army" committed itself to a radical socialist and nationalist principle: "The ownership of Ireland, moral and material, is vested in the people of Ireland."

This was revolutionary talk. Against the whole militant nationalist movement there stood by 1914 an equally militant loyalist sentiment: *Unionism*. Partly in reaction to Gaelic cultural nationalism and partly in response to Belfast's burgeoning industrial economy, Protestants in Ulster developed a strong Unionist identity that saw itself as an outlying fortress defending the British Crown and the Protestant Church in a backward and hostile land. They thus regarded as sacrosanct the Act of Union that created the United Kingdom of Great Britain and Ireland in 1801. Unionism took deepest root in the substantial number of Scottish Protestants first planted in Ulster in the seventeenth century. Though Protestants constituted the majority in six of Ulster's nine counties (and about half the Ulster population as a whole), these Scotch-Irish were well aware that they accounted for only 20 percent of the Irish people. The Protestant *Orange Order* became the heart and soul of Ulster Unionist resistance to Home Rule. When the first Home Rule bill was proposed in 1886, the Orange Order declared that the old struggle between Catholics and Protestants for control over Ireland had been revived. To Orangemen, Home Rule meant "Rome Rule."

With Home Rule back on the parliamentary agenda in the early 1900s, Unionism grew stronger. James Craig (an Ulsterman) and Sir Edward Carson (a southern Irish Unionist) organized the Ulster Unionist Council to arouse opposition to Home Rule. Even in the 1880s, many Unionists had openly spoken of resisting Home Rule by force of arms. In 1886, English Conservative Lord Randolph Churchill (father of Winston Churchill) declared, "Ulster will fight and Ulster will be right." By 1912, at least the first half of that declaration seemed prophetic. That year almost half a million Ulster Protestants signed a Solemn League and Covenant to use any and all means to defeat the creation of a Home Rule Parliament in Ireland; many of those who signed did so in their own blood. In 1913, with Home Rule due to be implemented the next year, the Ulster Unionist Council recruited a

An Ulster Unionist demonstration. *In the middle is the Unionist leader, Sir Edward Carson. The Ulster Protestant Unionists were implacably opposed to Home Rule for Ireland and would have opposed its implementation by force if necessary.*

paramilitary force of one hundred thousand men—the Ulster Volunteer Force—to defend the Union with Britain, even if it meant armed rebellion against the very British state to which they were pledging their loyalty.

In reaction, Home Rule advocates, led by Gaelic League founder Eoin MacNeill, formed their own military force. These Irish Volunteers grew from 10,000 men to 180,000 by September 1914, and like the GAA, were rapidly infiltrated by the IRB. Civil war in Ireland seemed inevitable. This impending disaster was a severe challenge to the British state and political system, which already were facing major crises at home and abroad.

### Suggested Reading

Bew, Paul. *Enigma: A New Life of Charles Stewart Parnell*. Dublin: Gill & Macmillan, 2011.

———. *Ideology and the Ulster Question: Ulster Unionism and Irish Nationalism, 1912–1916*. Oxford: Oxford University Press, 1994.

Brown, Malcolm. *The Politics of Irish Literature from Thomas Davis to W. B. Yeats*. London: Allen & Unwin, 1972.

Brown, Stewart J. *Thomas Chalmers and the Godly Commonwealth in Scotland*. Oxford: Oxford University Press, 1982.

Carruthers, Annette. *The Arts and Crafts Movement in Scotland: A History*. London: Paul Mellon Centre for Studies in British Art, 2013.

Checkland, Sidney, and Olive Checkland. *Industry and Ethos: Scotland, 1832–1914*. London: Edward Arnold, 1984.

Curtis, L. P., Jr. *Anglo-Saxons and Celts*. Bridgeport, CT: Conference on British Studies at the University of Bridgeport, 1968.

Davies, E. T. *Religion and Society in the Nineteenth Century (A New History of Wales)*. Llandybie, UK: C. Davies, 1981.

Donaldson, Gordon. *Scotland: The Shaping of a Nation*. Newton Abbot, UK: David & Charles, 1974.

Dunleavy, Janet, and Gareth Dunleavy. *Douglas Hyde: A Maker of Modern Ireland*. Berkeley: University of California Press, 1991.

Edwards, Owen Dudley. *Celtic Nationalism*. London: Routledge & Kegan Paul, 1968.

Foster, Roy. W. B. *Yeats: A Life*, 2 vols. Oxford: Oxford University Press, 1997, 2003.

Hechter, Michael. *Internal Colonialism*. London: Routledge & Kegan Paul, 1975.

Howarth, Herbert. *The Irish Writers: Literature and Nationalism, 1880–1940*. London: Rockliff, 1958.

Jones, Gareth E. *Modern Wales*. Cambridge: Cambridge University Press, 1984.

Kee, Robert. *The Green Flag*. New York: Delacorte Press, 1972.

———. *The Laurel and the Ivy: The Story of Charles Stewart Parnell and Irish Nationalism*. London: Hamish Hamilton, 1993.

Kiberd, Declan. *Inventing Ireland*. London: Jonathan Cape, 1995.

Lee, Joseph. *The Modernization of Irish Society, 1848–1918*. Dublin: Gill & Macmillan, 1973.

Lyons, F. S. L. *Charles Stewart Parnell*. New York: Oxford University Press, 1977.

———. *Culture and Anarchy in Ireland, 1890–1939*. Oxford: Oxford University Press, 1979.

———. *Ireland Since the Famine*. London: Weidenfeld & Nicholson, 1971.

Morgan, Kenneth O. *Rebirth of a Nation: Wales, 1880–1890*. New York: Oxford University Press, 1981.

Morgan, Prys, and David Thomas. *Wales: The Shaping of a Nation*. Newton Abbot, UK: David & Charles, 1984.

O'Grada, Cormac. *Ireland: A New Economic History, 1780–1939*. New York: Oxford University Press, 1994.

Robbins, Keith. *Nineteenth-Century Britain: Integration and Diversity*. Oxford: Clarendon Press, 1988.

Smout, T. C. *A Century of the Scottish People, 1830–1950*. London: Collins, 1986.

Turner, Michael. *After the Famine: Irish Agriculture, 1850–1914*. Cambridge: Cambridge University Press, 1996.

Vaughan, W. E., ed. *Ireland Under the Union II: 1870–1921*. New York: Oxford University Press, 1996.

———. *Landlords and Tenants in Mid-Victorian Ireland*. Oxford: Oxford University Press, 1994.

Williams, Gwyn. *When Was Wales?* London: Black Raven Press, 1985.

# Chapter 21

# Politics and the State, 1867–1914

By 1914, the mid-Victorian political balance and sense of consensus had frayed to the breaking point. Relative economic decline, demands for a radically expanded electorate, class antagonism, the women's movement, and Irish Home Rule each challenged the British state in the late-Victorian and Edwardian periods—and sometimes all at once. The record of response was mixed: British politicians and statesmen responded to some of these issues effectively, but on others they moved ineffectively or not at all. The process of coping with the challenges of the period altered the political system in ways that no one in the 1860s could have anticipated: extra-parliamentary parties grew in importance, Ireland caused a realignment of parties, and the working class claimed direct representation in Parliament.

## THE REFORM ACT OF 1867

The British political system of the 1850s and 1860s was not, and was not supposed to be, democratic. It was intended to represent stable, responsible individuals who had a stake in society—educated and propertied men. The Reform Act of 1832 had given the vote to about 800,000 men in England and Wales. By the 1860s, inflation, prosperity, and population growth had increased the number of electors to about 1 million in England and Wales and over 1.3 million in the United Kingdom as a whole—one in twenty-four of the population.

When the Great Reform Act passed in 1832, many parliamentary leaders, Whig and Tory alike, insisted that it constituted the final revision of the political structure. Desire for further parliamentary reform, however, had never died away. It had been kept alive by ex-Chartists and by middle-class radicals who hoped that an additional dose of reform would destroy the aristocracy's grip on political power. Liberal MP John Bright, a Quaker, whom Tennyson had called the "broad-brimmed hawker of holy things," argued that parliamentary reform would purify the state by checking the self-interest and irresponsibility of the aristocracy: "The class which has hitherto ruled this country has failed miserably. . . . If a class has failed, let us try the nation!"

Although most of the governing elite rejected this attack against the aristocracy, they came around to the idea of parliamentary reform as prosperity and social peace worked their magic. Even the prominent Whig Lord John Russell, known as "Finality Jack" in 1832, came to accept the argument that progress in the economy and education had created more "responsible" men among the populace, and that by the logic of 1832, responsible men were entitled to the vote. William E. Gladstone (1809–98), a rising force in the Liberal party, agreed. He believed that the Lancashire cotton workers had displayed their moral fitness for the vote when they supported the fight against slavery even as the American Civil War disrupted the supply of raw cotton to British mills and created mass unemployment in northern textile towns. In 1864, Gladstone declared that "every man who is not presumably incapacitated by some consideration of personal fitness or of political danger is morally entitled to come within the pale of the constitution." Such arguments, however, meant little as long as the immensely popular and powerful Lord Palmerston was alive: this popular politician opposed extension of the franchise beyond the limits set in 1832. But once Palmerston died in 1865, the forces of reform were unleashed.

Reformers in the Parliament of the 1860s were not moved by fear of revolution (as many had been in 1830–32), but by the relative social peace of the time. Working-class reformers reinforced this spirit of accommodation by moderating their own claims. The main working-class reform organization, the Reform League, spoke for the comparatively well-off and respectable skilled workers, the same people who had successfully founded the moderate craft unions of the mid-Victorian years. The League sought limited extension of the franchise rather than universal suffrage, and advocated it not as a right but as a privilege that had been earned. Working-class reformers cooperated readily with radical intellectuals and with provincial Nonconformists such as Bright on the objective of breaking the power of the landowners. As one radical journalist, John Morley, declared, the issue was between "brains and numbers on the one side and wealth, vested interest, rank and possessions on the other."

The growing consensus favoring parliamentary reform set into operation the dynamics of party rivalry in the House of Commons. Because a reform act by the mid-1860s seemed inevitable, Liberal and Conservative leaders alike wanted to be able to take credit for it and tailor it for party advantage. The Liberal government of Lord John Russell (with Gladstone as

leader of the House of Commons) introduced a moderate reform bill in
1866. A small number of the more cautious members of the Liberal party
defected to the opposition, and the Conservatives, led by Benjamin Disraeli
(1804–81), opposed the bill in order to be able to seize the initiative themselves. This combination defeated the bill, and the Liberal cabinet resigned
from office. Outside the House, popular demonstrations in favor of reform
erupted, including one that broke down railings in Hyde Park, but there was
nothing like the dangerous popular movement of 1831.

The Conservative government that took office needed little pressure to
sponsor its own reform bill. Although a minority of Conservatives believed
that any extension of the franchise would create an inferior electorate, most
thought that because parliamentary reform could not be avoided, the Conservatives should take charge and pass a safe measure. Disraeli, the Conservative leader in the House of Commons, believed that the Conservatives
could survive in a more democratic future, but not if they condemned themselves to a role of sullen opposition to popular measures. He also needed a
victory to consolidate his own leadership of the Conservative party, and he
desperately desired the delightful experience of beating his rival Gladstone.
Disraeli's objective, therefore, was to pass whatever reform bill he could. The
details he cared little about; parliamentary victory was what counted.

Disraeli's brilliant management of his reform bill of 1867 steered the
fine line between his own party, which opposed any extreme measure, and
the radical wing of the Liberals, which would have defeated any moderate
bill. His strategy was to introduce a moderate bill and then to accept radical
amendments while taking care to defeat those presented by Gladstone. One
by one, Disraeli accepted amendments that stripped away reservations, leaving an act that gave the vote to all urban householders. The Second Reform
Act passed finally in August 1867. It was Disraeli's triumph; on returning
home after victory in the wee hours of the morning, he found his wife had
prepared for him a meat pie from the elegant shop Fortnum and Mason and
a bottle of champagne. "Why, my dear," he said, "you are more like a mis-
tress than a wife."

## THE IMPACT OF THE 1867 REFORM ACT

The Reform Act of 1867, and the accompanying redistribution of seats,
did not usher in democracy or even universal manhood suffrage, but it did
make for very substantial changes—"a leap in the dark," as one Conservative
described it. The act expanded the electorate from 1.3 to 2.5 million, so that

one in twelve of the population (or one of three adult males) had the vote. Skilled workers now for the first time formed the majority of borough voters. The well-to-do, however, were protected by *plural voting*, for the act provided that a man could vote in every constituency in which he met the property qualification. Some wealthy property owners might cast as many as ten votes. (An amendment proposed by J. S. Mill to give votes to women was rejected.)

Further changes followed the Second Reform Act. In 1872, the secret ballot was introduced, followed by the Corrupt Practices Act of 1883. This legislation, along with the sheer size of most constituencies, brought about the gradual end of the traditional expenditure of vast sums of money to bribe voters. Then in 1884 and 1885, the dynamics of party rivalry produced further measures of reform and redistribution. The Third Reform Act (1884) extended the householder franchise from the boroughs to the counties, increasing the electorate to 5.7 million, or one in every six of the population. The Redistribution Act of 1885 met Conservative concerns by dividing the country generally into single-member constituencies of approximately equal size, an arrangement that preserved safe seats for the Tories. From 1884 to 1918, then, a householder franchise for males only, but not yet universal manhood suffrage, prevailed in Britain. In the 1880s, for the first time, the middle class outnumbered the traditional landed elite in Parliament.

In the wake of the 1867 Reform Act and the subsequent reforms, three developments helped create a new political structure. First, party discipline within the House of Commons grew tighter as politicians responded to the public's rising expectation of parliamentary legislation. Cabinets found they needed to control business in the Commons more tightly and to marshal their parliamentary forces more efficiently. During the years between 1867 and 1900, the frequency of pure party votes grew rapidly. The day of the old-fashioned independent MP was over.

Second, political parties became a much more important part of local culture. The increase in the urban electorate prodded both parties to contest all constituencies in general elections. Moreover, the two parties found that they had to organize aggressively in each borough in order to win their share of the two or three seats. Full-time professional party agents in each constituency now became the keys to electoral success. Local party organizations sprang up. Supported by both politicians and party agents, these constituency associations engaged in recreational as well as electoral activities; thus, in late-Victorian Britain, party politics in the form of picnics, football teams, and brass bands became an important part of popular culture.

Finally, as a result of the challenge presented by the massively enlarged electorate, extra-parliamentary party "machines" were established. In the Conservative party the impetus came from the top down. As early as 1867, Tory politicos founded a federation of Conservative constituency organizations—the National Union of Conservative and Constitutional Associations. In addition, parliamentary leaders established the Conservative Central Office to function as the party headquarters. This central bureaucracy controlled the National Union and also the Primrose League, a highly effective network of political clubs for party volunteer workers, including a large number of women. Together with the Conservatives' superior wealth, these organizations served as useful electoral instruments. Hence, the Conservatives were able to appeal to the respectable middle class as well as to the landowners, and even to win consistently some 30 percent of working-class voters.

On the Liberal side, the party organization grew from the bottom up. Middle-class Nonconformist grievances had produced a number of national, voluntary, single-issue organizations patterned on the old Anti-Corn Law League: the United Kingdom Alliance (temperance), the Peace Society (pacifism), the Liberation Society (disestablishment of the Church of England), and the National Education League (free, nonsectarian state education), among others. These Nonconformist societies, with their main strength in the Midlands and North of England and in Scotland and Wales, were united by their common antipathy to Anglican landlords and by their underlying aim of turning Britain into a middle-class, moral society. Their members were attracted naturally to the parliamentary Liberal party, which had maintained the traditions of parliamentary reform, civil liberties, free trade, and religious freedom. They also felt an instinctive admiration for the intensely religious and moralistic Liberal leader, Gladstone. Provincial middle-class Nonconformity, therefore, attached itself to the Liberal party.

In Wales in particular, Nonconformist religion and Liberal politics came together in a potent blend. Almost 90 percent of the Welsh population was Nonconformist, and both popular and political culture in Wales revolved around the chapel. Once male urban householders received the vote in 1867, Welsh radical Nonconformity powered a political steamroller. Allied with the British Liberal party, Welsh radicals won twenty-nine of thirty-two Welsh parliamentary seats in 1880, and at least that many in every election until 1922. Welsh Nonconformity formed one of the big battalions in the late-Victorian and Edwardian Liberal army.

In Scottish politics as in Welsh, liberalism and the British Liberal party exerted overwhelming dominance in the second half of the century, and again religion played a crucial role. In the early decades of the nineteenth century, evangelicals within the established (Presbyterian) Church of Scotland had fought the moderate ruling body over a number of issues, most notably patronage. (The evangelical Presbyterians insisted that each congregation could call its own minister, whereas the moderates supported the right of patrons to appoint the ministers.) Finally, in 1843, the evangelicals split off to form the Free Church, taking about 40 percent of the clergy with them. The Disruption, as this event became known, shook up Scottish life and gave a boost to Scottish liberalism. The Free Church spread rapidly and Free Churchmen increasingly called for the disestablishment of the Church of Scotland. The demand for disestablishment aligned naturally with the Liberal party's reformist agenda, as did middle-class Scots' predictable opposition to the overmighty Scottish landlords.

## GLADSTONE AND DISRAELI

Late-Victorian Britain was highly politicized, and everyone, whether in the Celtic countries or in England, seemed to be a partisan. In one of the delightfully satirical operettas that he wrote with Arthur Sullivan, W. S. Gilbert claimed

That every boy and every gal
   That's born into the world alive,
Is either a little Liberal
   Or else a little Conservative!

Daily newspapers such as the *Times*, the *Daily Telegraph*, and the *Daily News* of London, as well as the *Manchester Guardian*, the *Leeds Mercury*, and the *Sheffield Independent*, gave full coverage to political news and quoted parliamentary speeches at length. This politicization of literate Britain was a sign not only of the rise of parties, but also of the classic duel between the two great party leaders of the period, Benjamin Disraeli and W. E. Gladstone. Masters of parliamentary debate, these two giants of the House of Commons were enabled by the expanded electorate, the rise of the political press, and the shrinking of Britain by the railways to become *national* party symbols.

The two titans could hardly have been more different: it was as if a playful deity had designed each of them to challenge and irritate the other. Gladstone was the model of Victorian religiosity and rectitude, a man who regarded his career in politics as God's calling. In contrast, the flamboyant and witty Dis-

*The Great Rivalry:* Car-
toon from Punch *in 1872
depicting Disraeli (front)
and Gladstone as two
opposing lions making
speeches in Lancashire.*

THE LANCASHIRE LIONS.

" SO HAVE I HEARD ON INKY JEWELL'S SHORE,
*ANOTHER LION* GIVE A LOUDER ROAR,
AND THE FIRST LION THOUGHT THE LAST A BORE."
*Bombastes Furioso.*

raeli regarded politics as a great game. When he became prime minister in
1868, he proclaimed, "I have climbed to the top of the greasy pole." The two
men loathed each other. Disraeli described Gladstone as a "maniac" who was
driven by an "extraordinary mixture of envy, vindictiveness, hypocrisy and
superstition," whereas Gladstone believed that under Disraeli's leadership the
Conservative party had lost all purpose and principle.

The son of a wealthy Liverpool businessman, Gladstone combined traits
of both Liverpool and Oxford: unparalleled mastery of government finance,
a commitment to individual liberty, and a profound (if somewhat eccentric)
devotion to the classics and theology. Under the surface, he was a man of
prodigious energy and passion, so torn by self-doubt that he sometimes
whipped himself for having experienced temptations of the flesh. Blessed
with a strong and beautiful speaking voice, he excelled in both parliamentary debate and platform oratory. He also had a strong sense of personal destiny, which prompted one critic to say that, although he did not object to
Gladstone's always having an ace up his sleeve, he *did* object to Gladstone's
belief that God had put it there!

Gladstone's career was a long march from High Church Toryism to ardent Liberalism. His first speech in the House of Commons (1833) was a defense of his father's slave-holding interests in the West Indies. In the 1830s and 1840s, he distinguished himself by his advocacy of the privileges of the established Church of England. But his severe sense of duty and public service aligned him with Sir Robert Peel, and he never forgave Disraeli for his attacks on Peel in 1846. With the other Peelites, Gladstone drifted into the Liberal party. His liberalism flowered in his advocacy of financial retrenchment, which he saw as limiting the power of the state, and in his emotional sympathy for oppressed nationalities abroad. To him, Britain should always act as a moral force for good in the world. His moralistic approach to politics attracted the Nonconformists of England, Wales, and Scotland, to whom he became a heroic figure. Over time, Gladstone became convinced that the ordinary people had a greater capacity for virtuous public behavior than the landed elite, who, he believed, looked out only for their own self-interest.

Although Disraeli outmaneuvered him in 1867, Gladstone and the Liberals won the first general election (1868) held after passage of the Second Reform Act. Gladstone became prime minister for the first of four times (1868–74, 1880–85, 1886, and 1892–94). His first ministry was by far the most successful, for it rode the crest of a united party to act on many long-standing Liberal concerns. Its many legislative victories included two important measures meant to address Irish grievances: disestablishment of the Anglican Church of Ireland (1869) and a land act (1870) aimed at giving Irish tenants a degree of security of tenure. These measures did not resolve what was becoming known as the Irish Question, but the Gladstone government was more successful in other areas. It rationalized the legal system, abolished purchase of commissions in the army, introduced competitive civil service exams, ended religious tests at Oxford and Cambridge, gave trade unions legal recognition for the first time, and established (by W. E. Forster's Education Act of 1870) the first state school system in England.

This was nineteenth-century Liberalism at its best, but each of these acts seemed to alienate one segment of Liberal support. In particular, Forster's Education Act infuriated many Nonconformists because it incorporated existing Anglican schools in the new state system. Moreover, some of the more cautious Whigs and upper-middle-class men grew concerned about the government's activism, and they began a slow drift of propertied people away from Liberalism that was to go on for nearly fifty years. Thus, the Liberals lost the general election of 1874, and Gladstone resigned from the leadership and announced his retirement from public life.

Gladstone's archrival now held the top position in the British parliament. The son of a Jewish man of letters, and himself an incurable romantic, Disraeli was the most improbable success story in Victorian political history. Though he was baptized as an Anglican at age thirteen, Disraeli was always proud of his Jewish heritage and was a courageous advocate of admitting Jews to Parliament (finally granted in 1858). This position was unpopular with the Conservative party, and besides, Disraeli was not a member of the landed elite whom he sought to lead. Furthermore, Disraeli was much too flamboyant, too melodramatic, and too openly ambitious to be attractive to Conservatives. They never really liked him, yet he had talents they could not do without after the Peelite split: he was devastating in parliamentary debate, a master of political opportunism, and a magician of public gestures and symbols.

Disraeli had first made his reputation as a novelist, and some historians see in these novels his political agenda. In *Coningsby* (1844), for example, Disraeli asserted that there is a natural alliance between aristocracy and people, and thus that the Tories were England's natural, and best, rulers. This theme he pushed even more effectively in *Sybil* (1845), which contends that England had become two nations, the Rich and the Poor, and that political leaders had a duty to bridge this gap. Some historians argue, then, that in these novels we find Disraeli's hopes for a "Tory Democracy" and that in the Second Reform Act and in the social reforms passed by his government of 1874–80 we see its implementation.

Other historians have found little evidence for this view. They point out that Disraeli ran on a platform in 1874 of giving people relief from "incessant and harassing legislation." He had no interest in legislative details and made little effort to lead his cabinet even by stating general principles. To be sure, his government was very successful in passing a number of pieces of social legislation, including legalization of picketing by trade unions (1875), extensions of the Factory Acts, a law to prevent adulteration of food and drugs, and permissive acts allowing towns to build working-class housing (1875) and to improve public health by cleaning up slum areas (1875). Most of these acts, however, were due to the hard work of a middle-class Conservative cabinet member, R. A. Cross, who complained that he got little help from Disraeli.

Yet historians agree that Disraeli helped his party, which might otherwise have faded along with the landed interest, survive in the new democratic age. He showed the Conservatives how to win and how to appeal to new working-class voters. He also made it a comfortable refuge for commercial and industrial men who, anxious about property, government interference, and public order, gradually drifted away from the Liberals and into the ranks of the Conservatives.

Disraeli's renovation of the Conservative party did not, however, translate into electoral victory in 1880. The Liberals, once again led by Gladstone, returned to power. What brought Gladstone out of retirement was a massive public outcry against Disraeli's pragmatic policy of supporting the Ottoman Empire, despite Turkish massacres of thousands of Christians in the Ottoman province of Bulgaria. This *Bulgarian Atrocities* episode of 1876 not only vaulted Gladstone back from retirement, but it also epitomized the differences between Disraeli's pragmatism and Gladstone's principles. In Disraeli's view, Britain's national interest in propping up the ramshackle Ottoman regime and so blocking any Russian expansion into the Mediterranean region took precedence over any moral obligation to protect Bulgarian Christians. He even joked about the atrocities, saying that reports of torture could not be true because the Turks "seldom, I believe, resort to torture, but generally terminate their connexion with culprits in a more expeditious manner." Outraged at what he saw as Disraeli's lack of principle and at his refusal to use British power for moral purposes, Gladstone weighed in with a powerful pamphlet entitled *Bulgarian Horrors and the Question of the East*, in which he called for British intervention as a matter of honor. Inspired by Gladstone's moral message, Nonconformists across the North of England held hundreds of protest meetings.

Disraeli, however, refused to act: "Our duty at this critical moment is to maintain the Empire of England." It was only after Russia intervened, defeated the Ottoman forces, and drew up a treaty (1878) seeming to threaten British interests that Disraeli responded—and then he did so with vigor. He sent a fleet to guard Constantinople, called out the army reserves, and had Cyprus occupied. Finding an ally in Austria-Hungary, which also was concerned about Russian intrusion into the Balkans, Disraeli helped bring about the Congress of Berlin, a meeting of the European powers to revise the Russo-Turkish treaty. Disraeli returned from the Congress claiming "peace with honour": Russia was forced to give up much of its winnings, and Britain won possession of Cyprus and retained its dominance in the eastern Mediterranean.

In 1880, however, the Liberals won the general election; Gladstone's moral leadership during the Bulgarian campaign assured him the post of prime minister in the new government. This second government (1880–85) was not nearly as productive as Gladstone's first. Plagued throughout by intractable problems in Ireland and in the Empire, the government was able to carry little of the Liberal program except the Third Reform Act (1884). The government did not respond at all to Britain's long-term economic difficulties, for the Liberals were too committed to the existing economic system even to consider a change. The government's major achievement was the Irish Land Act of 1881, a measure that sought to quell Irish unrest by resolving tenant grievances. As we saw in chapter 20, however, this legislation did not pacify the Home Rule movement. As we will see below, continued upheaval in Ireland led Gladstone to embrace the cause of Irish Home Rule, but not even the "Grand Old Man" of British politics, as he was known, was able to resolve the long-standing Irish Question.

## HOME RULE AND BRITISH POLITICS

In the 1880s and 1890s, Irish issues continually intruded into British politics. Though British politicians wanted to get on with "British" issues, Ireland seemed to take up most of their time. Irish issues such as land reform raised the collective British blood pressure, while the frequent resort to coercion acts taxed the British liberal conscience. For Gladstone, Ireland became almost an obsession. As early as 1868, when Gladstone learned that the queen would ask him to form a government, he responded, "My mission is to pacify Ireland." He tried mightily, but Gladstone's mission failed and his efforts to resolve the Irish Question split the Liberal party.

The main issue was, of course, Home Rule: the demand for a separate Irish Parliament to deal with Irish issues. For most Britons, Irish Home Rule represented the thin edge of the wedge that would lead to the disintegration of the British Empire. But as we saw in the last chapter, by the 1880s, Charles Stewart Parnell and the Irish Home Rule party had succeeded in forcing the issue onto the political agenda by perfecting the techniques of obstructing the business of the House of Commons. Then came the general election of 1885, which gave the Home Rule party the balance of power: eighty-six Home Ruler MPs could turn out of office any government formed by either party. Gladstone, who was by then seventy-six years old and widely expected to retire, concluded that this constitutional predicament was intolerable and that Home Rule must be enacted. He realized that in governing Ireland the only alternative to granting Home Rule was to enact more coercive acts, and he found this both morally and politically unacceptable. He also believed that only the burdens of self-rule could teach responsibility to the Irish. The Grand Old Man, therefore, decided not to retire until the Irish Question was settled.

This extraordinary decision won Gladstone the support of the Home Rulers, and he came back into office early in 1886 committed to try a Home Rule bill. The bill that he introduced convulsed British politics. It would have removed Irish representatives from the British Parliament and set up a subordinate Irish Parliament in Dublin to deal with strictly Irish matters. Gladstone argued that a measure of local autonomy for Ireland would secure the Empire at its core. Opponents of the bill—including all of the Conservatives, most of the Whigs, and a few radical Liberals—contended that Home Rule would turn Ireland over to people who were little better than criminals and who would persecute the Irish Protestant minority, despoil Irish property, and then separate Ireland completely from Britain. Home Rule thus would damage the Empire at its base.

After two months of impassioned debate, Gladstone's Home Rule bill was defeated in the House of Commons by thirty votes. More than ninety Liberals, including almost all the remaining Whigs, not only voted against the bill but also left the party. In the subsequent general election of 1886, the Conservatives and the newly formed Liberal Unionist party formed a political alliance and inflicted a major election defeat on Gladstone's Liberals and the Irish Home Rulers.

Home Rule thus contributed to a realignment of the British parties. The Liberal Unionists merged into the Conservative party, which now stood unambiguously as the party of the propertied. In turn, the Liberal party became more radical. Nonconformist and radical issues such as church disestablishment in Wales and Scotland, the end of plural voting, and elective parish councils were now promoted to the official Liberal party platform. The Liberal commitment to Irish Home Rule, however, overshadowed this radical program—and Home Rule was never very popular with the English electorate. Gladstone introduced his second Home Rule bill in 1893, and after a tedious repetition of all the arguments that had been heard for eight years, the bill passed the House of Commons, only to be summarily thrown out by the House of Lords. As the Liberal government dithered between campaigning to reform the power of the Lords and trying to pass other items of their program, their support dwindled. Gladstone resigned (for good this time) in 1894 and the Liberal lost heavily in the general election the following year. For the next ten years, the Conservatives held power and the Liberals drifted, divided. For some, Irish Home Rule remained a moral

*Liberal leader William E. Gladstone being kicked up in the air over Irish Home Rule by an unusual combination of opponents. From left to right: John Bright, Joseph Chamberlain, Randolph Churchill, Lord Salisbury, and Stafford Northcote.*

crusade; to others, it was an electoral millstone around their necks. To many New Liberals, the focus on Home Rule prevented the party from attending to a growing threat from the left: the desire among militant laboring men and socialists for an independent labor party.

## NEW UNIONISM AND THE RISE OF LABOUR

After the Reform Act of 1867, the Liberals could count on winning two-thirds of the greatly expanded working-class vote. The Liberals always regarded themselves as a party that spoke for both the middle class and the working class. The allegiance of trade union members to the Liberal party was especially strong, for these organized skilled workers regarded middle-class Nonconformists, who composed the backbone of the Liberal party, as their allies in the struggle against the Anglican landed elite. The Trades Union Congress (TUC), formed in 1868 by the mid-Victorian craft unions, was closely tied to the radical left of the Liberal coalition. In 1874, two trade unionists (both of them coal miners) won election to Parliament as Liberals. Working men thus had reason to hope, not only that the Liberals would act on their behalf, but also that over time the Liberal party might evolve into a radical, working-class party.

Such an evolution did *not* occur; instead, by 1914 an independent Labour party had set up shop as a rival to the Liberals in claiming working-class votes. Why did this happen? One key factor was the response of middle-class employers to *New Unionism*. In the 1880s, British trade unionism took a radical turn. New Unionism involved both the organization of semiskilled and unskilled workers in industries not organized before and the adoption of much more aggressive tactics by all unions, old and new. In 1889, for example, socialist Tom Mann (1856–1941) helped the dockers, who had always been casual (that is, hourly) laborers, organize and strike for higher wages and more regular work. After a bitter and well-publicized struggle with their employees, the dockers won. Union membership more than doubled, reaching two million in 1901. This and other successes, however, provoked a strong reaction from employers, who throughout the 1890s used various tactics to weaken the unions' legal position.

Many working-class leaders concluded that the only way to defend New Unionism against the employers' counterattack was to represent working-class parliamentary constituencies themselves. In theory, the Liberals could have agreed, but in practice, the wealthy commercial and industrial men who had founded and financed the Liberal associations could not abide this prospect. Few of them liked the eight-hour day, almost none of them accepted socialism, and most of them had their defenses raised by the heated class antagonism of the day. Perhaps it was inevitable, given the revived class consciousness of the period—the strong sense of *them versus us*—that the working class demanded independent working-class MPs.

The career of James Keir Hardie (1856–1915) illustrates growing working-class disaffection from the Liberals. Hardie was a Scottish coal miner, a romantic soul who in the 1880s converted to an ethical, non-Marxist brand of socialism. Like many miners in the 1880s, Hardie became an advocate of the eight-hour workday as a way of expanding employment and improving working conditions for miners. The refusal of one TUC official who sat as a Liberal MP to accept the eight-hour day earned a blast from Hardie in 1887. The next year, Hardie's local Liberal association turned down his request to stand as a Liberal candidate in a parliamentary by-election (special election) in Mid-Lanarkshire. He ran instead as an independent candidate. Although defeated soundly, Hardie continued to lobby for establishment of independent labor representation at annual meetings of the TUC, and in 1892 he won a parliamentary seat from the East End of London. He was the first independent working-class MP and showed his affiliation by wearing a working man's cloth cap when he took his place.

The first effort by Hardie and other working-class leaders to establish an independent party for labor came in 1893. In the North of England, hard times in coal-mining and cotton mill towns had spawned many labor clubs and working-class socialist societies. Representatives of these organizations, plus the Social Democratic Federation, the Fabian Society, and a few trade unions, met in Bradford in January 1893. They formed the Independent Labour party (ILP), which vowed to "secure the collective ownership of the means of production, distribution, and exchange." The ILP attracted a number of men and women passionately devoted to ethical socialism, people who were to serve for many years as the conscience of the British left, yet the ILP was too idealistic and its leaders too individualistic ever to become a mass party. The foundation of an effective party for labor would depend on the trade unions.

Despite their traditional attachment to the Liberals, many trade unions began to move toward foundation of a workers' party in the latter 1890s because of the employers' offensive against the New Unionism. Legal action and lockouts by employers against trade unions gradually persuaded union leaders that the Liberals, many of whose MPs were the very employers that they faced, would give the unions little satisfaction. In 1900, representatives of trade unions, the ILP, and a number of small socialist societies set up the Labour Representation Committee (the LRC), which eventually became the Labour party. Its founding resolution said nothing about socialism and little about policy: the LRC's task was simply to promote in Parliament the interests of labor.

The LRC did not automatically claim the allegiance of all trade unionists, still less the support of all working-class voters. Many of the biggest unions, including the coal miners, refused to affiliate. In the election of 1900, only two LRC candidates won seats in the House of Commons. The turning point came in 1901 with the famous—or, from the workers' point of view, the infamous—Taff Vale decision. After a strike on the Taff Vale railway in South Wales, the company sued the union, and the House of Lords ruled in favor of the company that unions were liable for damages in a strike. This decision made strikes impossible, and convinced many trade unionists that an independent working-class voice in Parliament was an immediate necessity. More than 120 unions now joined the 41 that had already affiliated with the LRC, and the party's electoral fund grew rapidly.

The potential electoral clout of the LRC concerned the Liberal party leadership. The Liberals did not wish to split working-class votes with the LRC and so give up seats to the Conservatives. Liberal leaders consequently struck an electoral bargain with the LRC in 1903: where possible, Liberal and LRC candidates would avoid contesting the same constituencies; in return, Labour MPs would support a future Liberal government. This *Lib-Lab pact* allowed the LRC to win twenty-nine seats in the general election of 1906. Shortly after the election, the LRC members of Parliament elected their own whips and took the name of the Labour party.

The Labour party did not, however, embark on any steady rise to power. Labour MPs decisively influenced only one piece of legislation, the Trades Disputes Act (1906), which reversed the Taff Vale decision, gave the unions legal immunity from suit by employers, and thereby sanctioned strikes and picketing. The Liberal party seemed to hold the initiative and Labour representatives to serve only as the tail on the Liberal dog. In the country at large, however, two crucial developments were taking place: first, the number of union affiliations with the Labour party was growing along with union militancy; second, at the local level, the Lib-Lab electoral pact was breaking down. Both trends promised big trouble for the Liberals, and at just the time when wealthy property owners were shifting from the Liberal to the Conservative party.

## THE TRIUMPH OF NEW LIBERALISM, 1906–1910

The Conservative party ruled Britain almost continuously from 1886 to 1905. Popular concern about Britain's international standing and the threat of socialism worked to the benefit of the Conservatives, who were the party of Empire and private property. In the early years of the twentieth century, however, the Conservatives divided over an intensely emotional issue—tariff reform. In 1903, the colonial secretary Joseph Chamberlain (1836–1914) declared himself in favor of a tariff duty on imports. Chamberlain, a radical

*Joseph Chamberlain speaking in favor of tariff reform. The former leader of the radical wing of the Liberal party became a key figure in early twentieth-century conservatism. Here he argues that a tariff would not raise the cost of food significantly.*

leader who led the Liberal Unionists out of the Liberal party, was a dominant figure in British politics, and free trade held almost sacrosanct status in Britain; Chamberlain's declaration, then, was stunning. He proposed to give preferential treatment to the colonies on their farm exports to Britain and so to tie the Empire more closely together, as well as to use tariffs on manufactured goods to both protect British industry and finance social reforms. Chamberlain's tariff reform constituted a bold and comprehensive strategy, but many Conservatives were devout free traders and tariffs on farm imports were especially unpopular because they would raise the price of food.

The Liberal party rode the unpopularity of tariffs (their slogan promoted the "big loaf" of cheap food versus the Tories' "little loaf") back into power. The general election of 1906 was in fact a Liberal landslide, with the

Liberals, Labour, and Home Rulers winning a majority of 355 over the Conservatives and Liberal Unionists.

The election of 1906 marked a particular triumph for New Liberalism. The New Liberal luminaries in the new administration included H. H. Asquith (1852–1928), who served as chancellor of the exchequer from 1906 to 1908 and then as prime minister; David Lloyd George (1863–1945), a Welsh radical and energetic opportunist who became chancellor of the exchequer under Asquith; and Winston Churchill (1874–1965), who had come over to the Liberals because of the tariff issue. Together, these New Liberals enacted a remarkable series of social reforms, including, in 1906, an act to permit local authorities (local governments) to provide school meals for poor children, the establishment of old age pensions in 1908 to remove the stigma of pauperism from the growing number of workers who lived to old age, and the creation of labor exchanges in 1909 to improve the mobility of labor and so tackle the problem of unemployment. In 1909 the Liberals also passed the Trade Boards Act, setting up boards to fix wages in the so-called sweated industries such as tailoring and lace making. The capstone of the New Liberal legislation came in 1911 with the National Insurance Act of 1911, which provided protection against workers' sickness and unemployment in certain major industries. Both the unemployment and sickness benefits were built on the insurance principle: workers contributed from their pay while employed and received benefits while unemployed or ill. Employers and the state also made contributions.

The body of social legislation passed by the Liberals between 1906 and 1911 reflected a New Liberal consensus that the state should ameliorate the worst symptoms of poverty and inequality, but did little to attack the roots of the problem—unemployment, falling real wages, and the inability of workers in some industries to make a living wage. The Lloyd George budget of 1909, however, was truly radical. As chancellor of the exchequer, Lloyd George in 1909 boldly designed a budget aimed not only at financing New Liberal social programs, but also at forcing the landed elite to pay for what he regarded as unearned privileges. His budget of 1909 thus raised death duties (inheritance taxes on estates), increased the rate of graduation on income taxes, added a *supertax* on incomes over £5,000, and—most controversial of all—put taxes on land values. The tax rates of the Lloyd George budget by later standards were not high, but the People's Budget, as the Liberals called it, clearly endorsed the radical principle of transfer payments—that is, the wealthy paid taxes that were transferred to the poor through social programs.

Lloyd George's budget caused a major uproar and led to a constitutional crisis. The budget passed in the House of Commons, but the Conservatives, who labeled it as socialistic, used their huge permanent majority in the House of Lords to defeat it. The Lords' veto raised a serious constitutional issue: could the House of Lords, which was not responsible to the electorate, refuse to fund the elected government? "That way," Asquith warned, "revolution lies." In December 1909 the Liberal majority in the Commons resolved that the rejection of the budget by the Lords was "a breach of the Constitution and a usurpation of the rights of the Commons" and called a general election for January 1910. Although their majority was sharply reduced, the Liberals won that election; the Lords accepted the verdict of the electorate and passed the budget. The Liberals, however, were now determined to curtail the power of the House of Lords.

## THE TRIALS OF LIBERALISM, 1910–1914

The start of the second decade of the twentieth century thus ushered in an especially turbulent time in British politics. In addition to its fight with the Lords, the Liberal government faced off against militant suffragettes, trade union unrest, an increasingly truculent Conservative party, and nationalist and Unionist violence in Ireland. The consensus of the mid-Victorian years seemed to be collapsing and the effectiveness of Parliament weakening. One historian, George Dangerfield, labeled the period as "the strange death of liberal England"—not the death of the Liberal party, but the end of a political culture in which Liberalism could flourish.

The battle over Lloyd George's People's Budget convinced many Liberals that the time had come to embark on further parliamentary reform, this time aimed at the House of Lords. In April 1910, therefore, Asquith introduced a reform that would end the Lords' authority over budgets and restrict their power over other bills to a two-year delay. The Parliament Bill readily passed in the Commons. Asquith knew that the Lords would now reject it, entailing yet another general election. He prevailed on the new king, George V, to promise to create enough Liberal peers to pass the bill if the Liberals won the election—which they did. The Asquith government proceeded with the Parliament Bill and the lords now faced the prospect of seeing their august chamber swamped with middle-class men.

The resistance of many Conservative Lords, and of Conservatives in general, now reached a fever pitch. "Ditchers"—Lords who would resist curtailment of their power to the last ditch—tussled with "hedgers"—those who would reluctantly accept some reforms in order to keep the social status of the peerage undiluted. The Liberals pressed on resolutely and the hedgers prevailed. The bill reforming the Lords' power passed into law in August 1911.

Asquith's Liberal government, however, had little time or space to celebrate the victory as they faced the expanding suffragette challenge (see chapter 18). Enraged by parliamentary inaction on women's suffrage, suffragettes turned to disrupting the public appearances of Liberal politicians, as well as defacing property and assaulting cabinet ministers. The Liberal government responded by arresting suffragettes and, when the women went on hunger strike, by subjecting them to ghastly force-feeding. All of this pressure seems to have stiffened Asquith's resolve against granting votes for women on the grounds that violence must not be rewarded.

Yet Asquith was more accommodating to the trade unionists, who were raising the heat in the nation at the same time. In 1910, for example, a violent strike in the South Wales' coal fields required the government to dispatch troops to the area, and in the summer of 1911, a dockers' strike caused outbreaks of violence in London. Later that same summer, railwaymen went on strike; troops were required to keep order in London, and several union members were killed. Keir Hardie declared: "The men who have been shot down have been murdered by the Government in the interests of the capitalist system." The Liberal government, however, did not simply send in the soldiers; increasingly both the public and the politicians expected governments to mediate between employees and trade unionists. Already in 1908, strikes in coal mining had led to legislation limiting the miners' workday to eight hours. When, early in 1912, the coal miners went on strike for a minimum wage, the Asquith cabinet rushed through emergency legislation to grant it. The Liberals also sponsored other legal changes aimed at pacifying the unions. In 1911 the Liberal government passed legislation allowing for the payment of MPs (a big help to the Labour party) and giving trade unions the right to contribute funds to the Labour party (provided only that union members be allowed to "contract out," that is, to refuse that portion of their dues that went into the political fund).

Nevertheless, labor unrest continued to escalate. The rise in prices and the corresponding decline in the real wages, plus the militancy of the trade unions and the stubbornness of most employers, generated more and more violence. Nearly forty-one million workdays were lost to strikes in 1912. And the situation promised to worsen: in 1913–14, the miners, railwaymen, and dockers took up a proposal to form a Triple Alliance of mutual support in industrial disputes.

Soldiers in Liverpool. *In 1911, the Liberal government deployed troops to put down industrial unrest in this key port city.*

As if the obstreperous behavior of the Lords, suffragettes, and trade unionists was not enough, the Liberals now faced unreasonable and unconstitutional behavior by the Conservatives and Ulster Unionists over Irish Home Rule. The issue of Home Rule had always been lurking behind the controversy over the reform of the House of Lords. The Conservatives knew that if the power of the upper House was limited, then Home Rule could be enacted; it was, after all, the Lords' veto that had killed Home Rule in 1893. The Home Rule party reunited in 1900 and helped bring the Liberals into office in 1906. After the general elections of 1910, the very survival of the Liberal government depended on Home Rulers' votes in the House of Commons. As expected, then, Asquith introduced the third Home Rule bill in April 1912, and this time it would pass into law because the reformed Lords could only delay it for two years.

The seemingly sure prospect of Irish Home Rule drove Ulster Unionists to extremes of opposition. They prepared to resist Home Rule by all means necessary. Andrew Bonar Law (1858–1923), a Canadian of Scotch-Irish ancestry who had succeeded Balfour as leader of the Conservative party, fully supported the Unionists in their belligerence. "I can imagine," Bonar Law declared, "no length of resistance to which Ulster can go in which I should not be prepared to support them." This was to hint at civil war, for which the Ulstermen were preparing. In early 1913, the Ulster leadership set to arming and drilling the Ulster Volunteer Force to fight against the implementation of Home Rule. Irish nationalists responded by forming their own paramilitary force, the Irish Volunteers.

By the end of 1913, Ireland was well on the way to civil war. Asquith faced the real possibility of having to use British troops to force Home Rule on the most fanatically loyalist part of the Irish population, the Ulster Unionists. And the army itself was not reliable. In 1914, officers at the Curragh military post in Ireland resigned rather than prepare to march against Ulster. Asquith felt he had no choice but to recognize the power of Ulster's claim. He suggested an amendment allowing Ulster counties with Protestant majorities to opt out of Home Rule for six years. He was unable, however, to bring the Home Rulers and the Unionists to agreement.

In any event, external events soon overwhelmed all such political maneuvering: Britain was enveloped by war in Europe. Home Rule passed into law, but it was suspended for the duration of the war. For the time being, divisive issues had to take second place to urgent matters requiring national unity; Ireland, labor unrest, women's suffrage, and Conservative obstruction all receded into the background. The First World War thus saved Britain from bloody civil conflict, but at a price too horrible to contemplate.

### Suggested Reading

Adelman, Paul. *The Decline of the Liberal Party, 1910–31*. London: Longman, 1995.

Aldous, Richard. *The Lion and the Unicorn: Gladstone vs. Disraeli*. New York: Norton, 2007.

Barrow, Logie, and Ian Bullock. *Democratic Ideas and the British Labour Movement, 1880–1914*. Cambridge: Cambridge University Press, 1996.

Bew, Paul. *Ideology and the Ulster Questions: Ulster Unionism and Irish Nationalism, 1912–1916*. Oxford: Oxford University Press, 1994.

Brooks, David. *The Age of Upheaval: Edwardian Politics, 1899–1914*. Manchester, UK: Manchester University Press, 1995.

Coetzee, Franz. *For Party or Country: Nationalism and the Dilemmas of Popular Conservatism in Edwardian England*. New York: Oxford University Press, 1990.

Cowling, Maurice. *1867: Disraeli, Gladstone and Revolution*. Cambridge: Cambridge University Press, 1967.

Daly, Mary, and K. Theodore Hoppen, eds. *Gladstone: Ireland and Beyond*. Dublin: Four Courts Press, 2011.

Dangerfield, George. *The Strange Death of Liberal England*. New York: Smith & Haas, 1935.

Gilbert, Bentley. *David Lloyd George: A Political Life: The Architect of Change, 1863–1912*. Columbus: Ohio State University Press, 1987.

Grigg, John. *Lloyd George: The People's Champion, 1902–11*. London: Methuen, 1978.

Hall, Catherine, Keith McClelland, and Jane Rendall. *Defining the Victorian Nation: Class, Race, Gender and the British Reform Act of 1867*. Cambridge: Cambridge University Press, 2000.

Hawkins, Angus. *British Party Politics, 1852–1886*. New York: St. Martin's Press, 1998.

Heyck, Thomas William. *The Dimensions of British Radicalism: The Case of Ireland, 1874–1895*. Urbana: University of Illinois Press, 1974.

Jenkins, Roy. *Gladstone: A Biography*. New York: Random House, 1997.

Langley, Helen, ed. *Benjamin Disraeli: Scenes from an Extraordinary Life*. Oxford: Bodleian Library, 2005.

Lawrence, Jon. *Speaking for the People: Party, Language, and Popular Politics in England, 1867–1914*. Cambridge: Cambridge University Press, 1998.

Laybourn, Keith. *The Rise of Labour: The British Labour Party, 1890–1979*. London: Edward Arnold, 1990.

Leonard, Dick. *The Great Rivalry: Gladstone and Disraeli*. London: I. B. Tauris, 2013.

Marsh, Peter T. *Joseph Chamberlain: Entrepreneur in Politics*. New Haven, CT: Yale University Press, 1994.

Matthew, H. C. G. *Gladstone, 1875–1898*. Oxford: Oxford University Press, 1995.

O'Kell, Robert. *Disraeli: The Romance of Politics*. Toronto: University of Toronto Press, 2013.

Pelling, Henry. *Popular Politics and Society in Late Victorian Britain*. London: Macmillan, 1979.

Powell, David. *The Edwardian Crisis, 1901–1914*. New York: St. Martin's Press, 1996.

Pugh, Martin. *Speak for Britain!: A New History of the Labour Party*. London: Bodley Head, 2010.

Searle, G. R. *A New England? Peace and War, 1886–1918*. Oxford: Oxford University Press, 2004.

———. *The Liberal Party: Triumph and Disintegration, 1886–1929*. New York: St. Martin's Press, 1992.

Shannon, Richard. *The Age of Disraeli, 1868–1881: The Rise of Tory Democracy*. New York: Longmans, 1992.

Shelden, Michael. *Young Titan: The Making of Winston Churchill*. New York: Simon and Schuster, 2013.

Smith, Paul. *Disraeli: A Brief Life*. Cambridge: Cambridge University Press, 1996.

Tanner, Duncan. *Political Change and the Labour Party 1900–1918*. Cambridge: Cambridge University Press, 1990.

Thorpe, Andrew. *A History of the British Labour Party*, 2nd ed. London: Palgrave Macmillan, 2001.

# Chapter 22

# The British Empire and the Coming of War, 1870–1914

The years from 1870 to 1914 are rightly known as the Age of Imperialism. During that half-century, European domination of the world reached its highest point as the states of Western Europe (and later the United States and Japan) expanded their imperial holdings around the globe, carving up Africa, seizing Pacific islands, and establishing claims in Asia. By any measure, Britain was the leading power in that imperial thrust. The British began the late-Victorian period with the biggest empire by far and then expanded fastest. The British Empire stood in 1914 as the largest empire the world had ever known and as an inspiration—and source of envy—to the other Western nations.

Yet the same years from 1870 to 1914 also witnessed the beginning of the end of the *Pax Britannica,* for real British power eroded relative both to the power of other nations and to Britain's ability to fulfill its global commitments. In the early twentieth century, Britain consciously withdrew from its role as the world's policeman, at least in certain areas. Likewise, the erosion of British power ended Britain's *splendid isolation.* These trends— imperial expansion and erosion of power—though apparently contradictory, were in fact opposite sides of the same coin. Together, they explain how Britain drifted into a war in 1914 that was nearly to end Britain's status as a great power.

## THE IMPERIALIST IDEA

In the years between 1870 and 1914 the British Empire expanded at a breathtaking rate. Areas that had been part of the *informal empire* (see chapter 17) came under formal rule and new areas were annexed. In 1871, the Empire included 235 million people and almost 8 million square miles;

in 1900, it encompassed 400 million people and 12 million square miles—almost one-fourth of the earth's land surface. Yet just as important as expansion itself in designating these years as the Age of Imperialism was the elaboration of an imperialist ideology. Through most of the nineteenth century the British had increased their imperial holdings, but had lacked a positive rationale for empire. As one statesman said, the colonies seemed to have been acquired "in a fit of absence of mind." But from the 1870s, new foreign rivalries and economic pressure caused the British not only to expand aggressively, but also to formulate imperialism as an idea.

British imperialism was a strange compound of confidence and anxiety. The more confident element arose from long-standing pride in British achievements overseas and above all in British governing institutions. People of all parties shared this feeling. As an editorial in the *Times* (1867) put it, "We are all proud of our empire, and we regard our Colonies and dependencies as the various members of such a family as earth never yet saw." This pride was consistent with the view of the so-called Little Englanders, exemplified by William Gladstone, that as the colonies of white settlement grew to maturity they would drop like ripe fruit off the imperial tree. Increasingly in the late nineteenth century, however, the Little Englanders' outlook came to be rivaled by the imperialists' notion that the colonies should be bound more closely to Britain. In 1872, Benjamin Disraeli, in a famous speech at the Crystal Palace, committed the Conservatives to protection of the nation's institutions and preservation of the Empire. From that point on imperial consolidation came to be associated with the Conservative party, though there were Liberal imperialists who believed in it as well.

Pride in the Empire included a sense of trusteeship that all members of the governing elite could share. The British regarded themselves as the new Romans, especially talented in the techniques of government and bringing material progress to backward peoples. Justifiably proud of their parliamentary system, they believed that they had much to offer the world. Around the Empire, declared the colonial secretary in 1878, "we have races struggling to emerge into civilization, to whom emancipation from servitude is but the foretaste of the far higher law of liberty and progress to which they may yet attain." The British governing class was confident in Britain's ability to carry out this mission of noble trusteeship. Joseph Chamberlain, perhaps the most eminent imperialist politician, put it bluntly in 1895: "I believe that the British race is the greatest of the governing races that the world has ever seen."

The more anxious and defensive side of imperialism arose from the perception that Britain was locked in a global economic and political rivalry with other states. According to the *Pall Mall Gazette* in 1885:

> In times past . . . we did what we pleased, where we pleased, and as we pleased. All that has changed. . . . At every turn we are confronted with the gunboats, the sea lairs, or the colonies of jealous and eager rivals.

Imperialists believed that "pegging our claims" around the world would enable Britain to stay ahead of these rivals. In addition, they argued that British national interests demanded self-sufficiency through empire: securing of imperial possessions as markets and investment opportunities for British goods and capital, and cultivation of colonies that would assist Britain in global rivalries, including war.

Christianity also played an important role in the imperialist idea. Many Britons equated the forward march of the Union Jack with the Christianization, and thereby, they believed, the spiritual salvation of the world. The late-Victorian era was in many ways the high noon of the British missionary movement, with older missionary societies expanding and new organizations proliferating. The Anglican Church Missionary Society, for example, grew from 250 to 1000 missionaries between 1880 and 1900. Throughout the nineteenth century, missionaries had served as the vanguard of an expansionist British culture, although at the same time often acting as sharp critics of imperialist abuses. Britain's missionaries aimed to Christianize rather than anglicize the world, and many of them sought desperately to respect the cultural integrity of the societies they entered. But in their conversionist efforts, missionaries wielded what historian Jeffrey Cox has described as the "three great battering rams": education, women's outreach to women, and Western medicine.[1] These battering rams could not help but smash through indigenous customs and contribute to the advance of British cultural institutions and values.

Social Darwinism contributed even more to the imperialist idea. For Social Darwinists, the struggle for empire mirrored the wider struggle among races for supremacy and even survival: "The truth is," one imperialist wrote in 1896, "that what we call national rivalry is to all intents and purposes part of the universal scheme that makes Nature 'red in tooth and claw.'" Many Social Darwinists believed that the British had to achieve greater *social efficiency* to survive in international competition. Social

---

[1]Cox, *The British Missionary Enterprise Since 1700*, 217.

Darwinists shared a widespread concern about the potential degeneration of what they called "the British race"; thus, oddly enough, many imperialists were also social reformers. Some Social Darwinists such as mathematician Karl Pearson (1857–1936) put their hope in eugenics; others, such as the sociologist Benjamin Kidd (1858–1916), argued for reforms including improved education and nutrition to produce stronger and healthier potential soldiers. Likewise, they hoped to inculcate through sports and paramilitary organizations habits of order and discipline. The cult of school sports, the Boy Scouts (founded in 1908), and the spread of numerous cadet brigades were all results of the quest for social efficiency and thereby national supremacy. As the Social Darwinists put it, the struggle was racial:

> The facts are patent. Feeble races are being wiped off the earth, and the few, great incipient species arm themselves against each other. England, as the greatest of these—greatest in race-pride—has avoided for centuries the only dangerous kind of war. Now, with the whole earth occupied and the movements of expansion continuing, she will have to fight to the death against successive rivals.

As this passage shows, the racist quality of imperialist thought was ambiguous: imperialists tended to be both anxious about the quality of the so-called British race and confident of Britain's racial superiority. One Fabian socialist said, "If we are breeding the people badly, neither the most perfect constitution nor the most skillful diplomacy will save us from shipwreck." Yet at the same time imperialists believed that the British or "Anglo-Saxon race" (note the exclusion of the Celtic peoples) was naturally superior to black, brown, and yellow races (not to mention Slavic, Mediterranean, and Celtic peoples), and that this justified rule by the British. Indeed, they thought, the "colored" races were childlike and incapable of ruling themselves, whereas the British stood at the top of the evolutionary mountain. The *Daily Mail* caught this racial pride in exclaiming about the white troops in the Jubilee parade of 1897: "every man such a splendid specimen and testimony to the Greatness of the British race . . . the sun never looked down until yesterday on the embodiment of so much energy and power."

Racial pride and the sense of Britain's unique governing ability enabled British imperialists to think of imperialism as a duty rather than as a naked expression of economic and political power. Psychologically this was very important. All over Britain, upper middle-class and professional families sent their sons out to the Empire in the spirit of sacrificing self-interest to a noble burden. This helps explain why British administrators in fact set such a high standard of fairness and incorruptibility, if not cultural sensitivity. Rudyard Kipling evoked the spirit of duty perfectly in his "White Man's Burden" (1899):

Take up the White Man's Burden–
Send forth the best ye breed–
Go bind your sons to exile
To serve your captives' need.
Take up the White Man's Burden—
And reap his old reward:
The blame of those ye better,
The hate of those ye guard.

Racial pride, noble sacrifice, religious faith, global struggle, heroic adventures, faraway exotic places—all constituted a heady brew that affected popular emotions more than did New Liberalism or socialism. In addition, imperialists had an instinctive sense of public relations. They used the new state schools to inculcate imperial pride: every child learned to recognize the pink or red areas on the map as *ours*, while history textbooks glorified the exploits of soldiers, sea captains, and explorers. Mass-circulation newspapers celebrated jingoism, and cheap literature for children linked imperialism with patriotism. *The Boy's Own Paper* and dozens of other magazines played on related themes of athleticism, militarism, violence, and empire. The most famous writer for the youth market, G. A. Henty, thrilled a generation of boys with his eighty-two novels, many of which purveyed an imperial ideology and celebrated the superior vigor, initiative, decency, and pluck of the British race. The monarchy itself became identified with empire: in 1876, Parliament granted Queen Victoria the title empress of India, and in 1887 and 1897 the queen's jubilees treated the London masses to spectacular parades of British and imperial troops. Just how far working people accepted the ideas behind imperialism is subject to debate, but it seems clear that imperial patriotism was an important counterbalance to class hostilities.

## GREAT POWER RIVALRIES AND IMPERIAL EXPANSION

Intensified great power rivalries fueled the accelerated imperialist drive after 1870. In these years, the international environment became much more difficult and dangerous for Britain than it had been for half a century. In Europe, the formation of united nation-states in Italy and Germany in 1870–71 upset the balance of power and created new competitors for Britain. Although hampered by economic backwardness in its southern region and by imperfect national cohesion, Italy began to industrialize and by 1913 supported significant naval and military forces. The much more

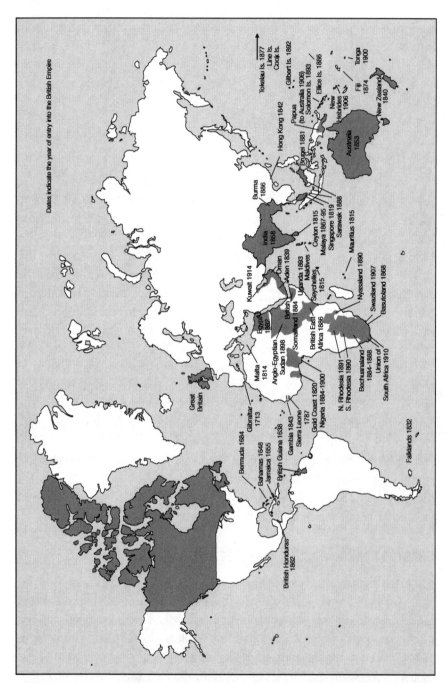

*The British Empire in 1914.* As the twentieth century dawned, many Britons regarded the sprawling empire as a sign of Britain's global strength; more accurately, however, the expansion of formal political control over many regions resulted from Britain's increasing vulnerability to international economic competition.

potent Germany industrialized at a very rapid rate after 1870, especially in coal, iron, steel, electricity, and industrial chemicals. Drawing on a rapidly growing population of 49 million in 1890 (compared to 37.4 million for Britain) and on the Prussian military tradition, Germany was bound to play a central role, not only in European but in world affairs. By the mid-1880s, Germany began to acquire colonies in Africa and the Pacific and to expand German influence in the Middle East. The German government became aggressively imperialistic, believing that the superiority of German culture warranted imperial rule and the struggle for survival among the great powers demanded it.

Overseas, the emergence of Japan and the United States as world powers radically altered the international order. Japan, which for centuries had been an isolated and feudalistic country, modernized by strong state leadership after 1868. Consciously imitating the Western nations, Japan borrowed techniques from both the British navy and the German army. By 1895, Japan had become a major power in the Pacific. Its development, however, was dwarfed by that of the United States, which experienced unprecedented demographic, agricultural, and industrial growth after the end of the Civil War in 1865. Occupied through the 1880s with the task of conquering a continent, the United States began to assert itself overseas only toward the end of the 1890s. Even after the Spanish-American War, the United States preferred to act independently and to remain outside European entanglements. But by 1900, many Europeans, including British statesmen, believed that in the future giant states like the belatedly but rapidly industrializing Russia and the United States might dominate the world.

Unnerved by these great power rivalries, the British turned to empire. From the 1870s on, Britain gained a remarkable number and variety of colonies. These included Zanzibar (1870), Fiji Islands (1874), the Transvaal (1877, 1900), Cyprus (1878), Bechuanaland (South Africa, 1884), Somalia (East Africa, 1884), Kenya (1885), New Hebrides (South Pacific, 1887), Rhodesia (1888–89), Uganda (1889), Sudan (1898), and Tonga (South Pacific, 1900). Many of these were acquired during the so-called scramble for Africa in the mid-1880s. The European states codified the partition of Africa at a congress in Berlin in 1884–85, when they declared that any European state could acquire a piece of Africa simply by occupying it and notifying the other powers.

Despite the public popularity of imperialism, many of the leading British statesmen of the period were reluctant imperialists. British officials knew that annexation of territory was expensive. They much preferred informal to

*Imperial rivalry: the European powers and the United States show their envy over British imperial possessions.*

formal control, and when forced to annex a piece of land, they preferred protectorates and spheres of influence to direct rule, wherever possible. Gladstone and much of his Liberal party were positively hostile to imperial expansion; Gladstone devoted his famous Midlothian electoral campaigns of 1879 and 1880 to a crusade against Disraeli's "forward policy." But neither Gladstone nor any other respectable politician opposed the Empire itself, and everyone agreed that the government had to protect what Britain already owned and even to secure, by force if necessary, British interests around the world. Thus, for example, Britain added Egypt to its empire on Gladstone's watch. After an Egyptian army revolt in 1881, worries about the security of the Suez Canal (Britain's main route to India since its construction in 1869) led Gladstone to order British troops to occupy Egypt. In fact, between 1880 and 1885, the Liberals expanded the Empire at the rate of 87,000 square miles a year—a far faster pace than the Conservatives recorded between 1874 and 1880.

At the same time, the Empire was profitable for the officials who ran it—approximately 6,000 people—and provided employment for the 120,000 troops who patrolled it. It was rightly observed that the Empire was a source of employment—"a vast system of outdoor relief" (that is, welfare)—for the landed class. Increasingly, families of the civilian and military rulers of the Empire formed a self-conscious element within the British ruling elite, with influence at home as well as overseas. Many investors and businessmen also profited from the Empire, most notably those involved in financing and developing colonial agriculture, mining, and public utilities. Their imperial profits went largely to investors from the upper class, while the British public at large had to pay the taxes that supported Britain's administration and defense of the colonies. Because even the white settlement colonies such as Canada, Australia, and New Zealand were reluctant to share these costs, Britain's expenditures amounted to a subsidy paid to the colonials by the British taxpayers. In this sense, we can say that the British colonies exploited the mother country! The dominions (as the white settlement colonies were increasingly called) refused to contribute to Britain's military forces or to bind themselves in advance to support British foreign policy. It soon became apparent that the ties of empire between Britain and the self-governing colonies would be limited, as Lord Salisbury said, to "mutual good will, sympathy, and affection." India alone functioned as an ideal imperial possession (from the British point of view): not only did India take an increasing portion of British exports, but also Indian taxpayers were required to pay for their own government and defense, and for an Indian army that was used to expand British imperial might elsewhere.

The rapid colonial expansion of the European powers brought them into conflict with each other. Britain faced competition with Germany in the Pacific, China, Southwest Africa, West Africa, and East Africa. In each case, German intrusion into the colonial scramble threatened some prior arrangements favoring British interests. In general, the British reacted by staking out their own claims and then reaching agreements with Germany by which each recognized the spheres of influence of the other. The most important example of this process occurred in East Africa, where the British thought that German imperialism threatened the headwaters of the Nile River—and therefore Egypt. To prevent that eventuality, the British claimed Uganda in 1888–89, and in 1890 they traded to Germany the small North Sea island of Heligoland in return for German recognition of British control of Uganda.

British colonial conflict with the French seemed as or even more dangerous than rivalry with Germany. The French dreamed of establishing a North African empire across a broad belt of territory running east and west from the Sahara to the Red Sea. They were also angry about Britain's occupation of Egypt in 1882. For Britain, control of Egypt required control of the

Nile south of Egypt; thus, British and French interests clashed in the vast territory of the Sudan.

The British already had a major emotional investment in the Sudan. In the early 1880s, the Sudan was subordinate to Egypt, but the revolt of a puritanical Muslim sect led by Mohammed Ahmed ("The Mahdi") had ended effective Egyptian rule of the area. In 1884, Gladstone recognized the collapse of Egyptian control in the Sudan and sent a British general, Charles "Chinese" Gordon, to withdraw the last Egyptian forces from that desert wilderness. Alas, Gordon was a religious fanatic and a megalomaniac as well. He disobeyed his orders to withdraw, found himself besieged in Khartoum, and was slaughtered along with his garrison by the Mahdi in 1885. Gladstone came under fierce criticism by an outraged British public, but his government completed the withdrawal anyway—one of the few instances of a British decision to give up territory during the age of imperialism.

But then, in the 1890s, the French sent an expedition under Captain Jean Marchand to occupy the Sudan. This roused the British lion to fresh action. Policy making lay in the hands of Robert Cecil, third marquess of Salisbury (1830–1903), who succeeded Gladstone as prime minister in 1886 and dominated British external policy almost continuously until his retirement in 1902. To counter the French advance in the Sudan, Salisbury's government in 1898 dispatched a much larger force led by Sir Herbert Kitchener southward from Egypt. Along the way, Kitchener's army took revenge on the Sudanese dervishes for Gordon's death, killing eleven thousand of them at Omdurman in less than five hours. According to Winston Churchill, who took part in the battle, it was "the most signal triumph ever gained by the arms of science over barbarians." Moving on up the Nile, Kitchener arrived at Fashoda a few days after Marchand. In Paris and London, tensions were high; war loomed as a distinct possibility. Forced to withdraw, the French nursed their bitterness against Britain for half a decade.

## THE SOUTH AFRICAN WAR, 1899–1902

The most serious colonial conflict Britain faced, however, was not with any European state, but with the white settlers of Dutch descent in South Africa—the Boers or Afrikaners. This conflict resulted in Britain's biggest war between the Crimean War and the First World War, and it revealed Britain's isolation and weakness. In this regard, as in the moral and political conflict it provoked at home, the Boer War was for Britain what Vietnam was later to be for the United States.

The conflict between Briton and Boer arose from different ideas of which white population should dominate southern Africa. The two peoples also differed in their views of the native African peoples: the British held a more paternalistic view and believed in theory at least that the black African could be civilized, whereas the Boers believed that the Africans were an irretrievably inferior race. Racial views, however, did not prove to be the cause of war. The issue ultimately at stake was who would rule in the area. In 1837–38, Afrikaner farmers had trekked northward out of the Cape Colony to escape British rule. They established two republics, the Orange Free State and the Transvaal, that were effectively independent of British control.

As British imperial ambitions heated up, they were increasingly inclined to impose British rule over the whole area. In 1877, an official of Disraeli's government annexed the Transvaal and got away with it, partly because the Transvaalers were concerned about the well-organized Zulu military power that lay to their east. But when the British army defeated the Zulus in the Anglo-Zulu War of 1879, it also eliminated the Transvaalers' need for the British. The Transvaalers revolted and dealt the redcoats a nasty defeat at Majuba Hill in 1881. Gladstone lived up to his moral opposition to the use of force for imperial expansion by giving independence to the Transvaal. But the settlement was left ambiguous, for the British still claimed *suzerainty*— an undefined degree of power—over all of southern Africa.

The discovery of gold in the Transvaal in 1886 threw this shaky settlement between Britons and Boers into turmoil. The gold mines quickly turned the Transvaal into a prosperous state. By the 1890s, the Transvaal was buying modern weapons from abroad, mainly from Germany. These developments meant that one day the Transvaal instead of the Cape Colony might dominate southern Africa. This prospect horrified British imperialists such as Cecil Rhodes (1853–1902). A self-made millionaire, Rhodes indulged in fantastic dreams of British colonial dominion over all of Africa, much of the Middle East, the Pacific islands, and commercial settlements on the coasts of China and Japan. He even imagined that the United States could be recovered for the British Empire. To Rhodes, Britain had to have a huge empire to ensure employment for Britain's "surplus" population. "If you want to avoid civil war," he said, "you must become imperialists." Among Rhodes's dreams was a British railway running through British territories from the Cape to Cairo.

For Rhodes and for many imperialists including the colonial secretary Joseph Chamberlain and the British high commissioner in South Africa, Lord Alfred Milner, the Orange Free State and the Transvaal stood as major

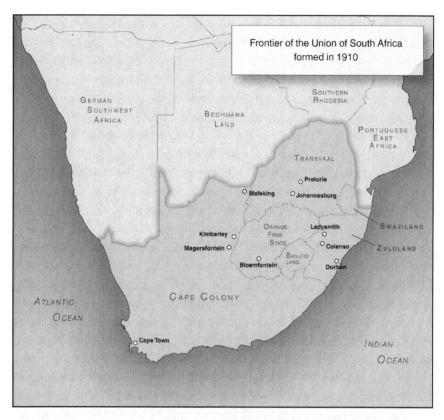

*Southern Africa at the End of the Nineteenth Century.* Although defeated by the British in the South African War of 1899–1902, the Afrikaners (or Boers) became a dominant political force in the Union of South Africa, which joined the formerly Afrikaner states of the Transvaal and the Orange Free State with the Cape Colony.

obstacles on the road to Britain's glorious imperial destiny. They sought to spark a war that would enable Britain to remove these obstacles once and for all. After years of rising tensions, British imperialists got the war they wanted in 1899. The South African War (1899–1902), however, did not proceed the way they expected: the Boer army of less than fifty thousand sharpshooters put up a spirited fight against the British army of some four hundred thousand men.

The war passed through three phases. In the first (October 1899 to January 1900), the Boers inflicted several embarrassing defeats on stupidly commanded British forces, and they laid siege to Kimberley, Mafeking, and Ladysmith. In the second phase (the rest of 1900), the British, now effectively led by Field Marshall Lord Roberts and General Kitchener, defeated

*Boer riflemen at the siege of Mafeking during the Boer War. Such troops punctured the pride of the vaunted British army.*

the Boer army and relieved the three besieged towns. By December 1900, the British thought the end of the war was in sight. In reality, it was only entering the third phase (1901–02), in which the Boers resorted to hit-and-run guerrilla tactics. The British had no luck in cornering the Boer commandos and resorted to systematic sweeps through Boer territory to deny the support of the populace. British troops burned hundreds of farms and herded the population into concentration camps, in which about twenty-five thousand Afrikaners and at least fourteen thousand black Africans died of disease and malnutrition. Finally, the war closed with the Peace of Vereeniging in 1902, by which the Boers recognized British sovereignty, and the British promised eventually to restore self-government to the Boers. (The British promise was fulfilled in 1907, when the Orange Free State and the Transvaal recovered their autonomy within the British Empire. In 1910 the two Boer states joined the Cape Colony and Natal to form the Union of South Africa, a self-governing dominion.)

Both abroad and at home the South African War, called the Boer War at the time, did Britain's reputation little good. The spectacle of Britain's inability to put down the little army of Afrikaner citizen-soldiers damaged Britain's image of invincibility in the minds of European statesmen. In Britain, the war divided the Liberal party (and much of the British public). The pro-Boers, including the anti-imperialist section of the Liberal party led by the Gladstonian John Morley and the Welsh radical David Lloyd George, inveighed against the immorality of the whole affair, whereas the Liberal imperialists backed the war effort without flinching. The Conservative government won a big victory over the Liberals in the "khaki election" of 1900 when the war was going well, but in the long run the Boer War further eroded British confidence.

## BRITAIN AND EUROPE: FROM ISOLATION TO ALLIANCE

The South African War brought to a head a number of concerns that had been growing since the 1870s about Britain's relative weakness in world affairs. The unification of Italy and especially Germany, and the disintegration of the Ottoman Empire in Europe, had destroyed the balance of power. From the 1870s on, each great power pursued its own interests and security vis-à-vis all the others through an intricate and shifting system of alliances, from which Britain sought to remain aloof. But by the end of the South African War, British policy makers began to feel strongly that as an isolated power they could no longer defend vital interests and therefore that alliances with other powers were needed.

At the core of the alliance system were two sources of conflict: the hostility between France and Germany (a result of Germany's annexation of the French provinces of Alsace and Lorraine in 1871) and the rivalry of Russia and Austria-Hungary for influence in the Balkans. The latter rivalry was made possible by the fact that the Ottoman Empire was such a decrepit empire that it could not control its Balkan provinces. As for the former problem, to protect Germany from French revenge, German chancellor Otto von Bismarck sought to isolate the French by building alliances against them. In 1879 he formulated the Dual Alliance with Austria-Hungary, to which Italy was soon added (the Triple Alliance of 1882).

The French all this time stewed in their bitterness against Germany. Although no longer the dominant nation on the Continent, France was still a great power. The French went to great lengths to field a huge conscript army—over half a million men before 1900. The French economy was modernizing at a moderate pace, and in the 1880s and 1890s France acquired an empire in North and West Africa and in Indochina. But an empire was no substitute for power in Europe; consequently, the French persisted in their effort to find an ally against Germany. Finally, in the 1894 they succeeded in reaching an understanding (*entente*) with Russia. The entente of 1894 quickly developed into a military alliance.

For Great Britain, the Franco-Russian entente represented a combination of their two rivals of longest standing—a serious situation for a nation that was growing uneasy over imperial rivalries and relative economic decline. With a population four times as large as Britain's, Russia had a standing army in 1900 of more than a million men. The tsar's government was driving forward Russian industrialization and pushing to expand Russian influence in the Balkans, to control the straits at Constantinople between the Black Sea and the Mediterranean, and to extend Russian power into Persia and Afghanistan. Such Russian pressures made for incessant clashes, not only with the Ottoman Empire and Austria-Hungary in eastern Europe, but also with Britain in the Middle East.

The British remained capable of supporting huge military forces, but with an economy devoted to industry and overseas commerce, they preferred to stay with their tried-and-true principles: free trade, overseas investment, low taxes, no conscription, a small army, and a naval force second to none. In the 1870s, the British army stood at about 200,000 men (130,000 at home and the rest in India)—a force smaller than that of Germany, France, or Russia. The Indian army, officered by the British, added another 200,000 men; it was this army that sustained British power in southern Asia and the Middle East.

The British navy, in contrast, was by far the most powerful in the world. Determined to protect the Empire and far-flung trade, Britain regularly increased budgetary outlays on its navy. In the 1870s, the Royal Navy was larger than the navies of the *next three* powers (France, Russia, and the United States) combined. In their quest to maintain naval supremacy, however, the British faced two serious problems. First, naval technology (iron and steel armored ships, steam power, screw propellers, and breech-loading naval guns) advanced rapidly, making old ships obsolete and raising the costs of new construction; second, other industrializing powers opted to build modern navies of their own. The French built up their navy in the early 1880s, resulting in a significant "naval scare" in Britain. The British naval budget increased by more than 50 percent between 1882 and 1897, and yet, relative to the rest of the world, British naval strength decreased.

As we have seen, Britain's imperial and foreign policy during this era lay in with Lord Salisbury. A sagacious pessimist and a pragmatic statesman, he realized that Britain's power relative to that of other nations was beginning to deteriorate. Convinced that Britain's continued greatness depended on expansion of the Empire, Salisbury favored inactivity in Europe: as he said in 1887, "Whatever happens will be for the worse and therefore it is in our interest that as little should happen as possible." Concerned about the growth of the French and Russian navies, Salisbury's government in 1889 adopted the *two-power standard*: Britain's navy would always be larger than those of the next two powers combined. Otherwise, Salisbury avoided broad permanent alliances.

The South African War, however, called into question Salisbury's isolationist policies and heightened concerns about Britain's international standing. In this new and more uncertain era, Conservatives and Liberals alike sought to enhance Britain's military power. With Salisbury's nephew, Arthur Balfour, now prime minister, the Conservative government in 1904 established a general staff for the British army. In subsequent years, the Liberal secretary for war, R. B. Haldane, reorganized the army. He provided that six fully equipped divisions could be sent to Europe on short notice, backed the regular army with three hundred thousand well-trained territorial reservists, and promoted an Officer Training Corps in universities and public schools.

At the same time, British policy makers recognized that the time had come to cut back on some commitments abroad. The tremendous growth of American power, for instance, meant that it was impossible for the British to contemplate a war in North America or to continue their dominant role in the waters of the Western Hemisphere. Hence, the British from the 1890s forward were inclined to settle their differences with the United States largely on American terms. Britain recognized the validity of the Monroe Doctrine and in 1901 conceded to the Americans the right to build and control a canal across the Isthmus of Panama. Within a few years, Britain had withdrawn most of its warships from American waters and left the defense of British interests there to the United States Navy.

Britain's treaty with Japan in 1902 was even more dramatic. Along with Britain and Russia, Japan had become one of the great powers in the Far East. The Franco-Russian entente of 1894 threatened British naval strength in the Pacific, for the combined French and Russian fleets would outnumber Britain's by a wide margin. If the British allied with Japan, they would win security in Asian waters and at the same time be enabled to strengthen the home fleet. In 1902, therefore, Britain and Japan pledged mutual aid should either be attacked by more than one power in Asia. By this treaty, the British gave up their cherished policy of isolation, which no longer seemed so splendid, and set terms in advance under which they would go to war.

At the same time, British policy makers began to effect a quiet diplomatic revolution. They recognized that a colonial agreement with France would greatly enhance British security. The outbreak of war between Japan and Russia in 1904 hurried Britain and France into agreement because neither wanted to be drawn into a Pacific conflict. In April 1904, Britain signed an entente with France. The entente specifically covered only colonial issues—the British, for example, recognized French control over Morocco while the French did the same with British control over Egypt—but it opened the way for broader cooperation between these two ancient enemies.

Because France was already allied with Russia, the door was now open for completion of a triangle of agreements among Britain, France, and Russia. Thus, after protracted discussions, Britain and Russia in 1907 reached a settlement of colonial disputes: Britain won Russian recognition of Afghanistan as a British sphere of influence; Russia won Britain's agreement not to annex Afghanistan outright; and the two powers divided Persia into zones of influence, Russian in the north and British in the south. By separate agreements, the British admitted that they would not resist eventual Russian control of Constantinople and the straits, and the Russians recognized British control in the Persian Gulf. This settlement with another old rival completed Britain's diplomatic revolution: in place of isolation, the British had now involved themselves in the European treaty system.

## THE DRIFT INTO WAR, 1905–1914

Although the ententes between Britain, France, and Russia technically concerned colonial matters, the British statesmen who negotiated them had their eyes on Germany the whole time. The rise of Anglo-German antagonism was one of the key themes, perhaps an unavoidable one, in European history between 1890 and 1914. It explains how Britain's participation in the European treaty system, instead of keeping the British out of a general European war, eventually drew them into one.

The Anglo-German antagonism originated in the development of German rivalry to British supremacy in the world. As early as the 1870s, members of the British ruling elite were expressing concern about the power of the German state, the superiority of the German educational system, and the growth of the German industrial economy. Literary fantasies of German invasion of Britain became popular reading in Britain: *The Invasion of Dorking* (1871), *The Riddle of the Sands* (1903), and *The Invasion of 1910* (1906) to name a few. In the early 1900s this hostility toward Germany became entrenched among the permanent officials of the Foreign Office—most notably Eyre Crowe (1864–1925), the senior clerk, who was troubled by what he saw as the consistently anti-British stance of the German government. By 1907, Crowe's view that Britain must reassert its rights and power against Germany's policy of expansion was dominant in the policy-making circle of the British state.

The most important source of British antagonism toward Germany was the rapid growth of the German navy. British power rested ultimately in the Royal Navy, and competition on the high seas appeared to threaten Britain's most vital interest. Beginning in 1898, the Germans began building up their navy with the obvious intent of catching up with Britain. Kaiser Wilhelm II and his chief naval planner, Admiral von Tirpitz, decided that a great navy was necessary for Germany to claim its rightful "place in the sun." Successive expansive German naval building programs inevitably threatened British maritime superiority, and Tirpitz aggravated the situation by concentrating a so-called risk fleet in the North Sea—a fleet that the British could not take the risk of failing to cover with its own fleet, and therefore a means of diverting British ships from other oceans. The British might have reached an alliance with Germany on condition that Germany cut back on naval construction. As late as 1912, R. B. Haldane appealed to the Germans on these terms. But the German emperor was adamant: Germany would have a big navy because all great nations do.

The British, however, would not and could not be outbuilt in ships by the Germans. The British, after all, did not have to maintain a large standing army as did the Germans, and thus they could devote their defense spending largely to the navy. As Lord Esher, government official and military reformer, said in 1912: "Whatever the cost may be, it is cheaper than a conscript army and an entangling alliance." The British steadily improved and increased the British fleet, adopting the dominant design of the day—the all-big-gun *Dreadnought* class of battleship—in 1906 and building twenty of them (against Germany's thirteen) by 1914.

At the same time that naval rivalry worsened relations between Britain and Germany, so also did German international behavior. After the British and French made their *entente cordiale* in 1904, the Germans hoped to break it down by diplomatic pressure. In 1905, Kaiser Wilhelm visited Morocco and demanded that the entente's Moroccan provisions be abandoned. But instead of crumpling British support for France, the Moroccan crisis strengthened it. At an international conference at Algeciras in 1906, the British stood by the French, and at the same time the two governments began to hold secret military staff talks that would eventually transform the nature of the entente. A second Moroccan crisis in 1911, caused by Germany's dispatch of a gunboat to Agadir in Morocco, had the same effect of driving Britain and France closer together.

*British naval power at its peak:* The Channel Squadron, *by E. de Martineau (1912).*

The secret Anglo-French staff talks continued from 1905 to 1914. They were officially authorized by Sir Edward Grey (1862–1933), foreign secretary from 1905 to 1914. A Liberal Imperialist but not an ideologue, Grey appeared to be a simple aristocratic fisherman and birdwatcher, but underneath his Northumberland country gentleman's appearance, he was a clever and secretive diplomatist who grew ever more suspicious of Germany. He regarded the German naval buildup as proof of Germany's anti-British intent: "If the German Navy ever became superior to ours, the German Army can conquer this country. There is no corresponding risk of this kind to Germany: for however superior our fleet was, no naval victory would bring us nearer to Berlin."

Grey did not tell the cabinet of the secret staff talks until 1911 (although both of the prime ministers he served under knew of them), and even then he insisted that the discussions did *not* amount to a formal alliance with France. He did, however, believe that the entente cordiale and the staff talks represented a moral commitment. Grey came to think that the defense of France was the defense of Britain because a Europe subservient to Germany would be intolerable. Yet he also believed—no doubt fooling himself on this point—that, because Britain had not signed a formal military and political alliance with France (or with Russia), it still retained freedom of action and could play the role of an honest broker. As events would finally teach Grey, he could not have it both ways.

The danger of dividing Europe into a pair of antagonistic alliances was that these systems were intricate mechanisms: once one part was set in motion, the other cogs and wheels would have to grind as well. Further, the increase in armaments in all the states had created an atmosphere of fear and suspicion, not least in Britain and Germany. The alliance system and the armaments race together made all of the powers to varying degrees dependent on the advice of military and naval officers and on their tactical plans and timetables. The very internal dynamics of this system moved irresistibly toward war.

War between Austria-Hungary and Russia over some Balkan issue might have flared up on a number of occasions. In October 1912, for instance, four Balkan states long at odds with the Ottoman Empire—Serbia, Bulgaria, Greece, and Montenegro—formed an alliance, went to war with the Turks, and prepared to split up the winnings. Austria-Hungary and Russia felt they had to intervene, and the other great powers were barely able to enforce a settlement, which soon fell apart in a second Balkan war in 1913. That neither of these two wars resulted in a general conflict between the two alliances was due largely to the restraint exercised by Germany on Austria and by Britain on Russia. Unfortunately, such restraint was seen within each alliance as weakening that alliance and therefore as something that must not be tried again.

When, therefore, a Serbian nationalist assassinated the Austrian heir apparent, Archduke Franz Ferdinand, in Sarajevo (Bosnia) on June 28, 1914, the necessary restraint was missing. Three weeks later, in a move cal-

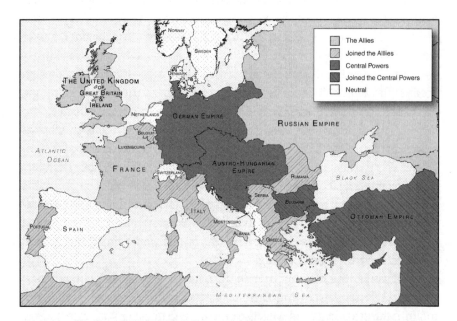

*Europe on the Eve of World War I.* Concerned about Germany's growing economic and naval might, the British abandoned their long tradition of "splendid isolation" from Continental affairs and entered into a series of agreements with the Russians and French in the years before World War I.

culated to end the Serbian problem once and for all, Austria issued to Serbia an ultimatum that would have limited Serbian independence. Already, the German government had resolved to back the Austrians. When the Russians began to mobilize their forces, various national war plans were set in motion. Germany declared war on Russia on August 1. Because the German war plan—originally designed by Count Alfred von Schlieffen in 1905—specified that Germany must attack France through Belgium before turning on the much slower, more cumbersome Russian army, the Germans invaded Belgium on August 3.

The Austrian ultimatum to Serbia thus caused a Balkan war, and the alliance system turned it into a Continental war. What was Britain to do? The rapid march of events after June 28 caught the British politicians and public alike by surprise, for their attention was riveted on the converging crises of domestic politics: labor unrest, Irish Home Rule, and Ulster resistance. Once the cabinet began to focus on unfolding events in Europe, it was deeply divided as to whether Britain should intervene in the war. But when Germany invaded Belgium, almost the entirety of the cabinet united quickly in favor of intervention. The same feeling of sympathy for "little Belgium" also persuaded Parliament and public opinion that Britain must fight. Thus, Britain entered the war with a high degree of unity: on August 4, crowds in Whitehall and Downing Street sang "God Save the King" as the time expired for a German reply to the British ultimatum. In subsequent days most politicians and newspapers pledged enthusiastic support of the war effort. Indeed, the outbreak of war to many Britons seemed a relief from the mounting strain of domestic conflict.

The German invasion of Belgium, therefore, was decisive for British opinion—but Grey and Prime Minister H. H. Asquith did not need the Belgian issue to persuade themselves that Britain must intervene. They had come to believe that a German victory on the Continent would be disastrous to British interests. As Grey told the cabinet, not only honor, but also "substantial obligations of policy" required it to back the French. Thus, it was not the German invasion of Belgium that in his view ultimately required Britain's entry into the war, but Grey used that invasion effectively for his own purpose at the moment of crisis. If Asquith and Grey had known how terrible the war would be, and how destructive to British strength, they might have kept Britain out. But no European statesman anticipated how long and costly the war would be; none realized that it would change the world permanently or that it would substantially alter Britain's place in that world.

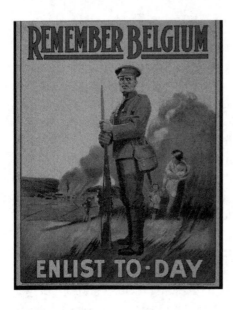

Remember Belgium—Enlist to-day
*(Parliamentary Recruiting Committee
poster, 1915). The German invasion of
Belgium provided a popular rationale
for British entry into World War I.*

## Suggested Reading

Beaven, Brad. *Visions of Empire: Patriotism, Popular Culture and the City, 1870–1939.*
Manchester, UK: Manchester University Press, 2012.

Bentley, Michael. *Lord Salisbury's World: Conservative Environments in Late-Victorian
Britain.* Cambridge: Cambridge University Press, 2001.

Bourne, Kenneth. *The Foreign Policy of Victorian England, 1830–1902.* Oxford:
Clarendon Press, 1970.

Brown, Judith M., and W. Roger Louis, eds. *The Twentieth Century.* Vol. 4, *The Oxford
History of the British Empire,* ed. W. Roger Louis. Oxford: Oxford University
Press, 1999.

Buettner, Elizabeth. *Empire Families: Britons and Late-Imperial India.* Oxford: Oxford
University Press, 2004.

Clark, Christopher. *The Sleepwalkers: How Europe Went to War in 1914.* New York:
Harper, 2013.

Cox, Jeffrey. *Imperial Fault Lines: Christianity and Colonial Power in India, 1818–
1940.* Stanford, CA: Stanford University Press, 2002.

Darwin, John. *Unfinished Empire: The Global Expansion of Britain.* London:
Bloomsbury Press, 2013.

Friedberg, Aaron L. *The Weary Titan: Britain and the Experience of Relative Decline,
1895–1905.* Princeton, NJ: Princeton University Press, 1988.

Gilmour, David. *The Ruling Caste: Imperial Lives in the Victorian Raj.* London: John
Murray, 2006.

Headrick, Daniel. *The Tools of Empire: Technology and European Imperialism in the
Nineteenth Century.* New York: Oxford University Press, 1981.

Huttenback, Robert A., and Lance E. Davis. *Mammon and the Pursuit of Empire*. Cambridge: Cambridge University Press, 1986.

Hyam, Ronald. *Britain's Imperial Century, 1815–1914*, 3rd ed. London: Palgrave Macmillan, 2002.

Kennedy, Paul M. *The Rise of the Anglo-German Antagonism, 1860–1014*. London: Allen & Unwin, 1980.

Krebs, Paula. *Gender, Race, and the Writing of Empire: Public Discourse and the Boer War*. Cambridge: Cambridge University Press, 1999.

Lewis, David L. *The Race to Fashoda: European Colonialism and African Resistance in the Scramble for Africa*. London: Weidenfeld Nicolson, 1987.

Lowe, C. J. *The Reluctant Imperialists: British Foreign Policy, 1878–1902*, 2 vols. London: Routledge & Kegan Paul, 1967.

MacDonald, Robert H. *The Language of Empire: Myths and Metaphors of Popular Imperialism, 1880–1918*. Manchester, UK: Manchester University Press, 1994.

Mackenzie, John M. *Imperialism and Popular Culture*. Manchester, UK: Manchester University Press, 1986.

———. *Propaganda and Empire*. Manchester, UK: Manchester University Press, 1984.

Marder, A. J. *From the Dreadnought to Scapa Flow: The Royal Navy in the Fisher Era, 1904–1919*, 5 vols. London: Oxford University Press, 1961–1970.

Nasson, Bill. *The South African War*. London: Hodder Arnold, 1999.

Parkinson, Roger. *The Late Victorian Navy: The Pre-Dreadnought Era and the Origins of the First World War*. Woodbridge, UK: Boydell Press, 2008.

Parsons, Timothy. *The British Imperial Century, 1815–1914: A World History Perspective*. London: Rowman and Littlefield, 1999.

Porter, Bernard. *Britain, Europe and the World, 1850–1982*. London: Allen & Unwin, 1983.

———. *The Absent-Minded Imperialists: Empire, Society, and Culture in Britain*. New York: Oxford University Press, 2006.

———. *The Lion's Share: A History of British Imperialism, 1850–2011*, 5th rev. ed., London: Longman, 2012.

Roberts, Andrew. *Salisbury; Victorian Titan*. London: Weidenfeld and Nicolson, 2000.

Roberts, Brian, *Cecil Rhodes: Flawed Colossus*. London: Hamish Hamilton, 1987.

Rotberg, Robert I. *The Founder: Cecil Rhodes and the Pursuit of Power*. Oxford: Oxford University Press, 1988.

Spiers, E. M. *Haldane: An Army Reformer*. Edinburgh: Edinburgh University Press, 1981.

Steiner, Zara. *Britain and the Origins of the First World War*, 2nd ed. London: Palgrave Macmillan, 2003.

Thompson, Andrew. *The Empire Strikes Back? The Impact of Imperialism on Britain from the Mid-Nineteenth Century*. London: Longman, 2005.

Thornton, A. P. *The Imperial Idea and Its Enemies*. London: Macmillan, 1959.

Wilson, Keith M. *The Policy of the Entente: Essays on the Determinants of British Foreign Policy, 1904–1914*. Cambridge: Cambridge University Press, 1985.

# Appendix A

# Kings and Queens of Great Britain, 1685–1914

| Monarch | House | Reign |
|---|---|---|
| James II<br>(of England and James VII of Scotland) | Stuart | 1685–88 |
| William III and Mary II | Stuart | William: 1688–1702;<br>Mary: 1688–94 |
| Anne I (of the United Kingdom) | Stuart | 1702–14 |
| George I | Hanover | 1714–27 |
| George II | Hanover | 1727–60 |
| George III | Hanover | 1760–1820 |
| George IV | Hanover | 1820–30 |
| William IV | Hanover | 1830–37 |
| Victoria I | Hanover | 1837–1901 |
| Edward VII | Windsor | 1901–10 |
| George V | Windsor | 1910–36 |

# Appendix B
# Chief Cabinet Ministers, 1721–1914

The modern party system is not regarded as having come into existence until the late eighteenth century. Hence, party affiliations in this list are given from William Pitt the Younger (1783). Before that time, all of the king's ministers were of the Whig persuasion.

| Minster | Post* | Dates | Party |
|---|---|---|---|
| Sir Robert Walpole | First Lord of the Treasury | 1721–42 | |
| John Carteret | Secretary of State, Northern Department | 1742–44 | |
| Henry Pelham | First Lord of the Treasury | 1744–54 | |
| Duke of Newcastle | First Lord of the Treasury | 1754–56 | |
| William Pitt (the Elder) | Secretary of State, Southern Department | 1756–57 | |
| Duke of Newcastle | First Lord of the Treasury | 1757–61 | |
| William Pitt (the Elder) | Secretary of State, Southern Department | | |
| Duke of Newcastle | First Lord of the Treasury | 1761–62 | |
| Earl of Bute | Secretary of State, Northern Department | | |
| Earl of Bute | First Lord of the Treasury | 1762–63 | |
| George Grenville | First Lord of the Treasury | 1763–65 | |
| Marquess of Rockingham | First Lord of the Treasury | 1765–66 | |
| William Pitt (the Elder), Earl of Chatham | Lord Privy Seal | 1766–68 | |
| Duke of Grafton | First Lord of the Treasury | 1767–70 | |
| Lord North | First Lord of the Treasury | 1770–82 | |

| Minster | Post* | Dates | Party |
|---|---|---|---|
| Marquess of Rockingham | First Lord of the Treasury | 1782 | |
| Charles James Fox | Secretary of State for Foreign Affairs | | |
| Earl of Shelburne | First Lord of the Treasury | 1782–83 | |
| William Pitt (the Younger) | Chancellor of the Exchequer | | |
| Charles James Fox | Secretary of State for Foreign Affairs | 1783 | |
| Lord North | Secretary of State for Home Affairs | | |
| William Pitt (the Younger) | Prime Minister and First Lord of the Treasury | 1783–1801 | Tory |
| Henry Addington | Prime Minister and First Lord of the Treasury | 1801–04 | Tory |
| William Pitt (the Younger) | Prime Minister and First Lord of the Treasury | 1804–06 | Tory |
| Lord Grenville | Prime Minister and First Lord of the Treasury | 1806–07 | Whig |
| Charles James Fox | Foreign Secretary | | |
| Duke of Portland | Prime Minister and First Lord of the Treasury | 1807–09 | Tory |
| Spencer Perceval | Prime Minister and First Lord of the Treasury | 1809–12 | Tory |
| Earl of Liverpool | Prime Minister and First Lord of the Treasury | 1812–27 | Tory |
| Viscount Castlereagh | Foreign Secretary | | |
| George Canning | Prime Minister | 1827 | Tory |
| Viscount Goderich | Prime Minister | 1827 | Tory |
| Duke of Wellington | Prime Minister | 1828–30 | Tory |
| Sir Robert Peel | Home Secretary | | |
| Earl Grey | Prime Minister | 1830–34 | Whig |
| Lord Brougham | Lord Chancellor | | |
| Viscount Melbourne | Prime Minister | 1834 | Whig |
| Sir Robert Peel | Prime Minister | 1834–35 | Conservative |
| Viscount Melbourne | Prime Minister | 1835–41 | Whig |

| Minster | Post* | Dates | Party |
|---------|-------|-------|-------|
| Viscount Palmerston | Foreign Secretary | | |
| Sir Robert Peel | Prime Minister | 1841–46 | Conservative |
| Lord John Russell | Prime Minister | 1846–52 | Whig |
| Viscount Palmerston | Foreign Secretary | | |
| Earl of Derby | Prime Minister | 1852 | Conservative |
| Benjamin Disraeli | Chancellor of the Exchequer | | |
| Earl of Aberdeen | Prime Minister | 1852–55 | Peelite/Whig |
| William E. Gladstone | Chancellor of the Exchequer | | |
| Viscount Palmerston | Prime Minister | 1855–58 | Whig |
| Earl of Derby | Prime Minister | 1858–59 | Conservative |
| Benjamin Disraeli | Chancellor of the Exchequer | | |
| Viscount Palmerston | Prime Minister | 1859–65 | Liberal |
| William E. Gladstone | Chancellor of the Exchequer | | |
| Lord John Russell | Prime Minister | 1865–66 | Liberal |
| William E. Gladstone | Chancellor of the Exchequer | | |
| Earl of Derby | Prime Minister | 1866–68 | Conservative |
| Benjamin Disraeli | Chancellor of the Exchequer | | |
| William E. Gladstone | Prime Minister | 1868–74 | Liberal |
| Benjamin Disraeli | Prime Minister | 1874–80 | Conservative |
| William E. Gladstone | Prime Minister | 1880–85 | Liberal |
| Joseph Chamberlain | President of the Board of Trade | | |
| Marquess of Salisbury | Prime Minister and Foreign Secretary | 1885–86 | Conservative |
| William E. Gladstone | Prime Minister | 1886 | Liberal |
| Marquess of Salisbury | Prime Minister | 1886–92 | Conservative (Unionist) |
| William E. Gladstone | Prime Minister | 1892–94 | Liberal |
| Earl of Rosebery | Foreign Secretary | | |
| Earl of Rosebery | Prime Minister | 1894–95 | Liberal |
| Sir William V. Harcourt | Chancellor of the Exchequer | | |
| Marquess of Salisbury | Prime Minister | 1895–1902 | Conservative |
| A. J. Balfour | First Lord of the Treasury | | |
| Joseph Chamberlain | Colonial Secretary | | |
| A. J. Balfour | Prime Minister | 1902–05 | Conservative |

| Minster | Post* | Dates | Party |
|---------|-------|-------|-------|
| Joseph Chamberlain | Colonial Secretary | | |
| Sir Henry Campbell-Bannerman | Prime Minister | 1905–08 | Liberal |
| H. H. Asquith | Chancellor of the Exchequer | | |
| H. H. Asquith | Prime Minister | 1908–15 | Liberal |
| David Lord George | Chancellor of the Exchequer | | |
| Sir Edward Grey | Foreign Secretary | | |
| Winston Churchill | President of the Board of Trade and later First Lord of the Admiralty | | |

*The title prime minister was used occasionally in the early eighteenth century, and one can argue plausibly that Sir Robert Walpole (1721–42) was the first prime minister. However, some historians contend that the first of the genuine prime ministers, with complete control over choice of ministers for this cabinet, was William Pitt the Younger (1783–1801). By the early nineteenth century, the title of prime minister was in common use.

# Index

# Credits

English Heritage Images. Page 393, An Imperial Scene of the Indian Mutiny, 1857: Mansell/ TimePix. Page 403, *The Shadow of the Valley of Death*. Page 14, 81, Banbury Road, Oxford: National Building Record; Library of Congress. Page 422, Late Victorian Urban Poverty: City of Liverpool, Engineer's Department. Page 428, Suffragette postcard-Going Shopping: Michael Nicholson/Corbis. Page 433, Herbert Spencer: Bettmann/Corbis. Page 439, Speaker's Corner, Hyde Park, 1892: Illustrated London News/Mary Evans Picture Library. Page 440, William Morris's bed at Kelmscott Manor: A. F. Kersting. Page 446, Three members of the Bloomsbury Group, 1915: Dr. Milo Keynes. Page 450, South Wales coal miners: National Museum of Wales. Page 453, Charles Rennie Mackintosh dining room: Maurice Rougemont/Getty Images. Page 456, Charles Stewart Parnell: Mansell/TimePix. Page 462, Ulster Unionist demonstration: Hulton Archive/Getty Images. Page 471, Punch cartoon-The Great Rivalry: Punch Cartoons. Page 477, Gladstone being kicked up in air over Irish Home Rule-cartoon: Mansell/TimePix. Page 481, Joseph Chamberlain speaking in favor of tariff reform: Mansell/TimePix. Page 485, British soldiers in Liverpool, 1911: People's History Museum, Manchester. Page 496, Imperial Rivalry-cartoon: *Puck*, February 19, 1896. Page 501, Bower riflemen at Seige of Mafeking: Hulton Archive/Getty Images. Page 507, The Channel Squadron, National Maritime Museum. Page 510, Remember Belgium-poster: Library of Congress.